ANCIENT GREECE

A HANDBOOK

LESLEY ADKINS & ROY A. ADKINS

SUTTON PUBLISHING

This book is dedicated to
Ralph Jackson.

First published in 1997 by Facts on File Inc.

This edition first published in 1998 by Sutton Publishing Limited
Phoenix Mill · Thrupp · Stroud · Gloucestershire GL5 2BU

A catalogue record for this book is available from the British Library

ISBN 0 7509 1973 6

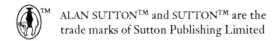
Typeset in 9/11pt Janson.
Printed in Great Britain by
WBC Limited, Bridgend, Mid-Glamorgan.

CONTENTS

"The isles of Greece, the isles of Greece!

Where burning Sappho loved and sung,

Where grew the arts of war and peace,

Where Delos rose, and Phoebus sprung!

Eternal summer gilds them yet,

But all, except their sun, is set."

—Byron, *Don Juan*

———————————————————

ACKNOWLEDGMENTS ⎯⎯⎯⎯⎯⎯⎯⎯⎯⎯

We would like to thank Stephen Minnitt and Robert Boulton (Somerset County Museums Service) for help in obtaining photographs, and the staff of Jessops in Taunton, Somerset, for advice on photographic problems. We would also like to express our thanks to the libraries of the University of Bristol and the Society of Antiquaries of London, and to the Joint Library of the Hellenic and Roman Societies. We are of course indebted to all the authors of the published sources that we have consulted. Finally, we would like to thank our editors, Hilary Poole, Elizabeth Oakes, and Jeffrey Golick, for their work and patience.

INTRODUCTION

The Greek period lasted for three millennia, from the beginning of the Minoan civilization in Bronze Age Greece (around 3000 BC) until the Romans took control of the last of the Greek territories (around 30 BC). During this time the cultures of the Minoans and the Mycenaeans developed and disappeared, and Greece passed through an anarchic Dark Age to emerge as a collection of city-states and colonies that were fleetingly merged into the Empire of Alexander the Great. The breakup of his Empire into smaller Hellenistic states achieved a kind of equilibrium that, in some areas, continued well into the Roman period.

The Roman conquest stripped Greece of its heritage. Works of art were removed, and skilled artisans and trained professionals served the Roman Empire, leaving Greece a backwater for the next 2,000 years. Paradoxically, this dispersion of culture undoubtedly led to the high achievements in Greek art, architecture and philosophical thought having an enormous and lasting influence on the development of Western culture.

The aim of this book is to present information relating to Greek history from the Minoan period to the Roman conquest. The chapters are organized thematically rather than chronologically, in order to give readers easier access to particular topics. By consulting the extensive index, the book can also be used as a dictionary. All too often, archaeological and historical evidence are used in isolation from each other. We have therefore tried to select the most important aspects of both disciplines. No attempt has been made to separate historical from archaeological elements in the text, and so there are no specific chapters devoted solely to archaeological evidence or artifacts.

Often a particular topic can be viewed in more than one way, so it may be covered in more than one section. For example, pottery can be considered as a container, as part of a manufacturing process, or as a work of art. Where this occurs, repetition of information has been kept to a minimum. The reader should make full use of the index to find all references to a particular subject and also the meanings of particular words. Inevitably, there is room to do no more than summarize the various topics, but we have tried to provide further references for readers wishing to know more about any subject. In addition to technical, historical and archaeological terms, we have also tried to give the meaning of those Greek words and phrases more commonly encountered in other works on the subject.

Place-names are usually in English, except where convention prefers the Greek (transliterated) or where no English equivalent exists. Where the names of modern countries are used, only the names of properly defined territories at the time of writing have been used. Standard U.S. measurements are given, with metric equivalents in parentheses. Precise dates are given wherever possible, but at times only approximate dates are known. A date written as c. 360 BC means approximately (circa) 360 BC. One written as c. 360–c. 250 BC means approximately 360 BC to approximately 250 BC. Written as c. 360–250 BC, it means approximately 360 BC to precisely 250 BC; and 360–250 BC means precisely 360 BC to precisely 250 BC.

Transliteration of Names and Words

The transliteration of Greek names and words from the Greek alphabet is a problematic area, because people invariably have preferences. Many words are more familar today in a Latinized or Anglicized form, while others are more familiar in their original Greek form. Furthermore, there were differences in names even amongst the Greeks. The least familiar method of presenting names and words is direct transliteration, such as Aiskhylos, Kleon, Lysandros, Perikles, Epeiros, Mykenai. The Romans transliterated words by using *c* for kappa,

ch for chi, *ae* for alpha iota, *oe* for omicron iota, *u* for omicron upsilon, *y* for upsilon, *-us* for an *-os* ending, and *-der* for a *-dros* ending.

Generally, the Roman spelling is followed in this book. Consequently, Aiskhylos becomes Aeschylus, Kleon becomes Cleon, Lysandros becomes Lysander, Perikles becomes Pericles, Epeiros becomes Epirus and Mykenai becomes Mycenae. The Greek transliterated version is given in italics, usually with *kh* rather than *ch* and *k* not *c*. So for archon, the ancient Greek version will be presented as *arkhon*. The Greek upsilon can be transliterated as *y* or *u*.

No attempt is made in this book to differentiate between the long and short vowels *e* and *o* (eta and epsilon, and omega and omicron). In some cases the modern Greek words or the Anglicized forms are used, such as "Athens," "Lesbos" and "Cos." What has been chosen in this book is the term that is likely to be most familiar to the reader. There is no agreement between scholars on how Greek terms should be presented to a modern audience.

1

CIVILIZATIONS, CITY-STATES AND EMPIRES

BRIEF HISTORY

Greece was never a single nation but was a series of states, often in conflict. The Greek world existed until 30 BC, when Ptolemaic Egypt (the last major Hellenistic kingdom) came under Roman rule. Early Greek history (particularly 8th century BC and earlier), before the advent of alphabetic writing, is dependent solely on archaeological evidence, with limited credence given to mythological accounts. Later Greek history, based increasingly on written accounts, is more certain. Most dates before 600 BC are approximate, while dates after this period can still be subject to problems and dispute. Further details on historical events are given in chapter 2 (biographies of prominent people) and in chapter 4 (on geography).

Minoan and Mycenaean Civilizations

This period is the Bronze Age, 3300–1050 BC.

DATING METHODS

Earliest farming settlements in mainland Greece and Crete date from the 7th to 4th millennium BC (the Neolithic Period and Copper Age, fig. 1.1). The Bronze Age began around 3300 BC, characterized by the use of copper alloy or bronze for tools and weapons. Since the early 20th century, the Aegean Bronze Age has tended to be divided into three chronological periods, a tripartite system that was originally intended to mirror the Old, Middle and New Kingdoms of Egypt. The Aegean also tends to be divided into three geographical regions for this period: mainland, Cyclades and Crete. The dating continuously undergoes revision, and the phases (often referred to in abbreviated form) are no longer distinct. Relative chronology is based mainly on pottery styles, and it is not often possible to use absolute dates, even with the availability of some radiocarbon dates.

CRETE

In Crete the Bronze Age begins with the Minoan culture, named after the legendary king Minos. The earliest phase is the Prepalatial Period, to about

Fig. 1.1   Early settlement of the late Neolithic period and Early Bronze Age at Khirokitia in Cyprus.

2200 or 2000 BC. It is divided into Early Minoan I (EMI), Early Minoan II (EMII) and Early Minoan III (EMIII); the latter is a transitional phase over-lapping with Middle Minoan IA (MMIA).

The next period (c. 2200 or 2000–c. 1700 or 1600 BC) is the First Palace Period (or Old Palace Period), equating approximately to Middle Minoan IB (MMIB), Middle Minoan IIA (MMIIA), Middle Minoan IIB (MMIIB) and Middle Minoan IIIA (MMIIIA). Vast palaces were built across Crete during the First Palace Period. The end of the first palaces c. 1700 BC may have been due to a severe earthquake (or series of earthquakes) or to warfare and conquest, with Knossos emerging as the leading center.

The next phase (c. 1700 or 1600–c. 1500 BC) is the Second Palace Period, equating approximately to Middle Minoan IIIB (MMIIIB), Late Minoan IA (LMIA) and Late Minoan IB (LMIB). During the Second Palace Period the palaces were promptly rebuilt, including at Knossos, Mallia, Phaistos and Zakros. A system of writing known as Linear A was also developed (fig. 7.1). In this period Minoan in-fluence (though probably not settlement) is appar-ent elsewhere in the Aegean, including the mainland. The eruption of the Thera volcano (which brought about the legend of the lost city of Atlantis) was once thought to have marked the end of the Second Palace Period, causing the destruc-tion of the palaces on Crete c. 1500 BC. This date is no longer accepted, and the eruption is generally believed to have occurred before the end of Late Minoan IA and Late Helladic I (around 1630/20 BC) (fig. 1.2). Indeed, the eruption may not have had such devastating consequences as was once thought. Instead, the palaces and other settlements on Crete could have continued for over 100 years, only then being destroyed by devastating fires or severe decline and prolonged abandonment. Internal conflict is the most likely explanation; an invasion by mainland Mycenaeans is no longer an accepted view, even though they apparently invaded Crete shortly after this period of decline.

The Third Palace Period (c. 1500–c. 1200 BC) equates approximately to Late Minoan II (LMII) and part of Late Minoan III (LMIIIA1, LMIIIA2, LMIIIB). In the Third (and last) Palace Period on Crete, Knossos was powerful, exerting influence over a wide area of the Aegean. It is debatable whether the Mycenaeans ever controlled Crete. Linear B (fig. 7.1) was adopted, and the last palace at Knossos was destroyed by fire, preserving the

Fig. 1.2 The eruption of the volcano at Thera took place around 1630/1620 BC, destroying the settlement of Akrotiri.

Linear B archives (written on clay tablets). This may have occurred c. 1400 BC along with the de-struction of other Cretan palaces, or it may have been at the end of LMIIIA2 (late 14th century BC) or even as late as 1200 BC.

The Postpalatial Period, from c. 1200 to c. 1050 BC, is approximately equivalent to Late Minoan IIIC (LMIIIC). Previously occupied sites did con-tinue in use, but they were fewer in number, with apparent depopulation.

CYCLADES

In the Cyclades Islands there are various dating schemes, the simplest termed "Cycladic": Early Cycladic I (ECI), Early Cycladic II (ECII) and Early Cycladic III (ECIII) are all equivalent to the Prepalatial Period. The Middle Cycladic (MC) is partly equivalent to the First Palace Period, with the later part equivalent to the Second Palace Period. Late Cycladic I (LCI) and Late Cycladic II (LCII) are also equivalent to the Second Palace Period. Late Cycladic III (LCIII) is equivalent to the Third Palace and Postpalatial Periods.

MAINLAND

On the mainland various dating schemes exist for the Bronze Age, the most common being termed "Helladic" and usually divided into three: c. 3300–c. 2100 BC is Early Helladic, c. 2100–c. 1550 BC is Middle Helladic and c. 1550–c. 1050 BC is Late Helladic or Mycenaean. The Prepalatial Period comprises Early Helladic I (EHI), Early Helladic II (EHII) and Early Helladic III (EHIII). The First Palace Period comprises the early part of Middle Helladic (MH). The Second Palace Period comprises the later part of Middle Helladic, as well as Late Helladic I (LHI) and Late Helladic IIA (LHIIA). Possibly because of Minoan influence and trade, a ruling class became established at Mycenae and elsewhere on the mainland, represented by much wealth and rich burials, and probably by the first palaces on the mainland.

On the mainland the Third Palace Period comprises the Late Helladic IIB (LHIIB) and Late Helladic III (LHIIIA1, LHIIIA2, LHIIIB1 and LHIIIB2), while the Postpalatial Period is Late Helladic IIIC (LHIIIC). The Third Palace Period was the main Mycenaean period, with the mainland becoming more important than Crete. Several palaces (such as Tiryns, Mycenae, Pylos and Thebes) and many new settlements were established (fig. 1.3). The 14th and 13th centuries BC especially were the Heroic Age of the poets, when legends and oral traditions were mixed with some element of truth. During this time many of the palaces were protected by massive fortifications (fig. 1.4), probably in preparation for sieges. The threat may have been from afar or from neighboring states.

From about 1250 BC a breakdown of settled conditions began in the eastern Mediterranean, Egypt and Asia Minor, and c. 1220 BC level VIIa of

Fig. 1.3   The Late Bronze Age site at Mycenae, Greece, situated on the nearer hill.

Fig. 1.4   Cyclopean masonry outside the Lion Gate at Mycenae, dating to the late 13th century BC. These fortification walls were about 20 ft (6.09 m) thick.

Troy was destroyed (fig. 1.5). This was a time of great insecurity, and in c. 1200 BC there was widespread destruction and/or abandonment of many major Mycenaean sites and palaces. Like Crete, some sites did continue to be inhabited for several decades, but they were far fewer in number. Following the final collapse of Mycenaean culture, the Dorians (Indo-Europeans from the Danube area) invaded much of mainland Greece from approximately 1200 to 1000 BC. It is no longer accepted that their invasion caused the major collapse of Mycenaean civilization.

Dark Age

The Dark Age, a period about which little is known from the archaeological record, is equivalent to the end of the Bronze Age and the Iron Age (c. 1050–c. 750 BC). By almost 1000 BC the Dorians had settled much of the Peloponnese, Crete and southwest Asia Minor and its nearby islands. From 1050 to 950 BC the Ionian Greeks and other Greeks migrated from the mainland to the Aegean Islands and

Asia Minor's west coast. Most inhabitants of mainland Greece (except Arcadia) in the Classical Age called themselves Dorian Greeks. Despite the term "Dark Age," some settlements were evidently quite prosperous at this time. There also seems to have been a division into separate political organizations, which become clearer in the ensuing Archaic Age. The term "Geometric" is usually applied to the period 875–750 BC when describing pottery.

Archaic Age

This period is c. 750–479 BC, when the Persian invasions ended. The cities of Chalcis and Eretria in Euboea emerged as the leading settlements in Greece. From 800 BC the Greeks began to travel far afield and colonized many parts of Europe and Asia Minor, mostly by sea. Chalcis and Eretria were responsible for the earliest colonies, and in 733 BC Corinth followed with colonies at Corcyra and Syracuse. The Lelantine War between Chalcis and Eretria for the fertile Lelantine Plain broke out around 730 BC and developed into a conflict involv-

Fig. 1.5   Troy in western Asia Minor was destroyed c. 1220 BC. This view is of the earlier Troy VI East Gate of c. 1500 BC and the sloping city walls.

ing many Greek states, leading to the disintegration of Euboea's power.

From about 730 BC Corinth emerged as the most advanced city in Greece. Other important cities included Corinth's neighbors Sicyon and Megara, as well as Aegina, Samos, Miletus, Athens and Sparta. From the mid-7th century BC there were revolts to overthrow some aristocratic city governments. In Corinth around 657 BC, Cypselus became the first tyrant to overthrow an aristocratic government. Similar revolts followed in Megara and Sicyon, and an attempted revolt by Cylon in Athens failed in 632 BC. Although tyrannies seem to have been widespread in the 7th and 6th centuries BC, Sparta's hereditary kingship and unique system of rule endured. Thought to have been established by Lycurgus in the early 7th century BC, Sparta's system resembled one in Crete and had probably developed from earliest times.

In the years following 625 BC Sparta and then Athens dominated mainland Greece. Many tyrannies were overthrown (such as at Corinth) and were replaced by oligarchic governments or democracies. Economic problems in Athens were addressed by Solon, the archon in 594/593 BC, who refused the role of tyrant. Nevertheless, Peisistratus became tyrant of Athens from c. 560 BC, succeeded by his sons Hipparchus and Hippias, the former subsequently assassinated and the latter forced into exile. Cleisthenes then undertook reform at Athens, and by the end of the 6th century BC Athens became very powerful and came into conflict with Sparta. By now Sparta was head of an alliance (the Peloponnesian League, but known then as "the Lacedaemonians and their allies"), which included all states of the Peloponnese except Argos.

By the 6th century BC Greek settlements existed in Asia Minor, northern Africa, Egypt and the Mediterranean basin. Some colonies were established for political purposes and for trade. Many were agricultural settlements, owing to overpopulation and a shortage of suitable fertile land on mainland Greece. Athens did not participate in colonization, as it had sufficient agricultural land,

and Sparta had only one colony (Taras), until Heraclea Trachinia in the mid-5th century BC.

In 546 BC the Persians under Cyrus the Great conquered Lydia and came into contact with the Ionian Greek cities of Asia Minor. Conflict with Persia dominated the late Archaic Age (until 479 BC). In 513 BC Darius invaded Thrace and Scythia. Persia came to control Thrace as far as Macedonia, as well as Asia Minor, the Middle East, Egypt, and northern Africa as far as Cyrene (beyond which was the Phoenician colony of Carthage, a threat to Greek Sicily and southern Italy). In 499 BC the Ionian Greeks revolted against Persian control. Sparta refused to help, but Athens and Eretria sent assistance. The Persians crushed the revolt and destroyed Miletus (494 BC). In 492 BC the Persians under Mardonius took Thasos and campaigned in Thrace. In 490 BC Darius again attempted to invade Greece, probably to punish Athens and Eretria, but was defeated by Athens at the battle of Marathon (fig. 2.4), with the loss of 6,000 Persian troops but only 200 Greeks.

The Persians did not invade again for another 10 years, this time under Xerxes. In Athens, Themistocles became an influential leader and prepared for another Persian invasion by building new warships and fortifying Piraeus (fig. 3.17). Thirty-one Greek states attended a conference at Sparta in 481 BC and one at the Isthmus of Corinth in spring 480 BC, forming an alliance known as the Hellenic League and led by Sparta to combat the Persians. Also in 480 BC the Persians invaded Greece for a second time and defeated the Greeks at Thermopylae (fig. 2.3) and Artemisium (Euboea). They moved through central Greece, and were supported by Thebes. Athens was next taken by the Persians, but the Persians were finally defeated at the naval battle of Salamis (fig. 1.6). Possibly on the same day in 480 BC, Sicilian forces under Theron and Gelon at the battle of Himera (north coast of Sicily) defeated the Carthaginians under Hamilcar.

Xerxes sailed to Asia Minor to prevent a revolt there, and his general, Mardonius, moved north to Thessaly for the winter. In 479 BC a combined Greek force defeated the Persians under Mardonius at the battle of Plataea (fig. 1.7) and then moved to Thebes, where the town was besieged and its leaders executed for supporting the Persians. In Ionia the Greeks revolted against the Persians. The Hellenic League now incorporated island states such as Chios, Lesbos and Samos. The Greeks

Fig. 1.6 Silver tetradrachm of Athens of c. 450 BC, obverse side with Athena wearing a helmet. The palmette with olive leaves on her helmet and the waning moon on the coin reverse (fig. 5.6) may commemorate the battle of Salamis and the defeat of the Persians in 480 BC. These motifs were added as signs of victory from about 479 BC.   Courtesy of Somerset County Museums Service.

sailed to Asia Minor and defeated the Persians at Mycale (near Samos). Sestus (base of the Persians) was then attacked and destroyed by Xanthippus (479/478 BC).

Classical Age

DELIAN LEAGUE

The 5th and 4th centuries BC are regarded as the Classical Age of Greece, from the end of the Persian invasions to the accession of Alexander the Great (479–336 BC). In 478 BC Pausanias was sent with an allied fleet to recapture Byzantium from the Persians, but was recalled by Sparta. From 478 BC Athens rose to power, particularly under Pericles, and replaced Sparta as leader of the Greeks. Sparta's displeasure when Athens began to rebuild its walls lessened after Themistocles was ostracized (c. 471 BC) and Cimon became powerful. Athens became

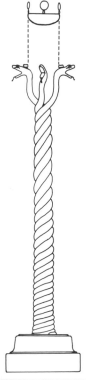

Fig. 1.7A After the Persians were defeated at the battle of Plataea (479 BC), a serpent column made from booty was set up at Delphi, comprising a stone pedestal, three intertwined snakes and a gold tripod.

leader of a group of allies called the Delian League, set up to fight against the Persians. The Delian League, also known today as the "Confederacy of Delos," was known in the 5th century BC as "The Athenians and their allies." Developed from the Hellenic League, its treasury and meeting place were at Delos. Some states contributed money and others contributed ships. Until 461 BC the Delian League forces were led by Cimon who was pro-Spartan. The Delian League undertook various activities against Persia and also for and against its own members, including besieging and capturing Eion (476 BC), clearing Scyrus of pirates (475–473 BC) and subjugating a revolt at Naxos (469 BC).

Although the battle of the Eurymedon (in southern Asia Minor) in c. 467 BC removed the Persian threat, Athens continued the Delian League. Revolts by member states were suppressed, including one by Thasos in 465 BC. Sparta offered to help Thasos, but was prevented by a devastating earthquake and a revolt by the helots of Messenia. Cimon, whose offer to send Sparta assistance from Athens was rejected, was ostracized in 461 BC (fig. 1.15). From that date the Delian

Fig. 1.7B The pedestal of the serpent column.

League was gradually converted into an Athenian Empire. Athens adopted a greater imperialist strategy, using the Delian League to pursue its own interests, which attracted opposition from Sparta and Corinth. From c. 460 to 446 BC the First Peloponnesian War was fought between Athens and the Peloponnesian League (involving mainly Corinth). The Delian League treasury was moved to Athens in 454 BC. With the influence of Cimon, a five-year truce was signed between Athens and Sparta c. 451 BC.

Cimon renewed attacks on Persian-held territory, and the Persians were finally defeated at the battle of Salamis off Cyprus in 449 BC. A peace treaty (called the Peace of Callias) between Athens and Persia was negotiated in 449/448 BC. In the treaty, Athens agreed not to attack Persian territory, and the Greeks of Asia Minor were to be autonomous. From 450 to 446 BC Athens undertook colonization in the form of cleruchies, including Thurii in southern Italy and Amphipolis in the northern Aegean. In 446 BC Sparta invaded Attica but then withdrew. The First Peloponnesian War was settled the same year, and peace between Athens and Sparta lasted 15 years.

At this point there was little justification for the prolonged existence of the Delian League, but Athens forced the allies to continue paying tribute. From 445 BC Athens and Sparta drifted toward war. In 435 BC Corinth and Corcyra fought over Epidamnus. Athens intervened, but the 30-year peace treaty between Athens and Sparta held. In 432 BC, Potidaea (a colony of Corinth) revolted from the Delian League. The Peloponnesians and Athenians sent forces; the Athenians were victorious and then besieged Potidaea. Sparta subsequently declared war in 431 BC.

SECOND (OR GREAT) PELOPONNESIAN WAR

The first part of the war (431–421 BC) was the Archidamian War (after Archidamus II). Attica was invaded annually by the Peloponnesians, but its population was concentrated at Athens and Piraeus within the defensive walls. When plague broke out in Athens, leading to the death of Pericles, Cleon became the dominant leader. After Brasidas and Cleon were killed in 422 BC, Athens and Sparta wanted peace, and a 50-year truce (Peace of Nicias) was signed in 421 BC.

When Sparta's allies refused to ratify the treaty, Athens, Argos, Mantinea and Elis formed an alliance. Corinth and Megara formed a new alliance with Sparta. The Spartan alliance was victorious at the battle of Mantinea (418 BC). Sparta and Argos then agreed on an alliance, and then Alcibiades played an important part during the Peloponnesian War (until the battle of Notium in 406 BC). In 416 BC Athens conquered the independent island of Melos, and in 415 BC sent a huge expedition to Sicily to help Segesta against Selinus (an ally of Syracuse) and to cut off supplies to the Peloponnese. Before the expedition embarked, nearly all the stone herms at Athens were mutilated, which caused an outrage and resulted in accusations against Alcibiades. In 414 BC the Athenians attempted to besiege Syracuse; reinforcements were sent under Demosthenes, but Athens suffered disastrous defeats in 413 BC.

Meanwhile Sparta established a fortified base at Decelea, north of Athens, which controlled routes to Boeotia and Attica. This base facilitated invasions into Attica, which severely affected Athenian trade, mining and agriculture. The final phase of the Peloponnesian War (to 404 BC) is therefore called the Decelean War; it was fought almost entirely at sea in the eastern Aegean. In 412 BC Sparta signed the Treaty of Miletus with Persia, surrendering to Darius II the Greek communities in Asia Minor in return for support in its war against Athens. Consequently, Athens made Samos its naval base. An oligarchic revolution in 411 BC overthrew the democracy in Athens. The soldiers and sailors at Samos declared themselves the true government of Athens, and full democracy was restored in 410 BC.

Athens gained several naval victories against Sparta in 411 BC, and the Spartan fleet was destroyed. Sparta sued for peace, but was rejected by Athens. Persia assisted Sparta financially in building a new naval fleet, and consequently Lysander of Sparta defeated the Athenians at the naval battle of Notium (near Ephesus). Athens then defeated Sparta at the naval battle of Arginusae, but executed its own victorious generals for failing to pick up survivors. Athens was finally defeated at the naval battle of Aegospotami (405 BC) and was then besieged at Piraeus. In 404 BC Athens surrendered to Sparta and had to suffer the loss of its navy, destruction of the Long Walls, loss of foreign territories, and an alliance with Sparta. An oligarchy of Thirty

Tyrants was established, who acted ruthlessly against the democrats. The democrats seized Piraeus (403 BC), and civil war ensued, with the subsequent restoration of full democracy. However, the political power of Athens was lost.

CORINTHIAN WAR

About this time in Sicily (405 BC), Dionysius I became tyrant of Syracuse with Spartan help, which caused disquiet in Corinth. Despite the cessation of the Peloponnesian War, interstate conflict continued in the Greek world, with the rise in power of

Fig. 1.8   Grave stele of a young man portrayed as a victorious warrior on horseback lunging at a fallen enemy. The sculpture is carved in high relief, and the spear and reins were added in bronze. An inscription identifies this as the warrior Dexileos who died at the age of 20, fighting the Corinthians in the Corinthian War in 394 BC. Kerameikos Cemetery, Athens.

lesser states such as Thebes. In 400 BC Sparta assisted the Persian Cyrus against his brother Artaxerxes II. The Greek cities of Asia Minor called on Sparta to assist them against Persia. Agesilaus II went to their aid, but his campaign was cut short by the Corinthian War (395–386 BC), in which Athens, Argos, Thebes and Corinth (backed by Persia) fought against Sparta (fig. 1.8). In 394 BC Sparta won land battles, but was defeated at sea in the battle of Cnidus by a Persian fleet under the Athenian admiral Conon. In 393 BC the Long Walls of Athens were rebuilt (fig. 3.17), and some territory was recovered. In 390–389 BC Athens made alliances with Thasos, Samothrace and many cities of Asia Minor. Persia then joined Sparta to defeat Athens in a naval battle in the Hellespont. In 386 BC the Corinthian War was terminated; the King's Peace was signed at Sardis by the Persian king Artaxerxes II and the Greek states. The peace was to be enforced by Sparta, with any dangerous alliances broken up. All states were to be autonomous, Persia was to keep Asia Minor and Cyprus, Thebes was to give up leadership of the Boeotian Confederacy, and Athens had to abandon plans to regain its Empire.

RISE OF THEBES

In 382 BC Sparta seized the citadel of Thebes (Cadmea), and in 379 BC destroyed the Chalcidic Confederacy (a group of settlements in Chalcidice centered on Olynthus) for infringing on the King's Peace. Athens established the Second Athenian League (or Confederacy) in 378 BC against this Spartan aggression. The new league defeated Sparta in a naval battle off Naxos in 376 BC. In 371 BC another treaty known as the Peace of Callias was signed by all Greek states except Thebes; in the same year Thebes defeated Sparta (which had invaded Boeotia) at the battle of Leuctra, which ended Spartan military domination and the Peloponnesian League. In 370/369 BC Thebes extended its influence over Thessaly and intervened in the Peloponnese, reestablishing Messenia as an independent state, which deprived Sparta of its helots and its economic base. An alliance of states was set up against Sparta (Arcadian Confederacy), with a new capital at Megalopolis. Thebes was also active in the north and in the Aegean. The power of Thebes collapsed in 362 BC at the battle of Mantinea, which was fought against the Spartans,

Fig. 1.9   Philip II was assassinated in 336 BC by Pausanias in the theater at Aegae at the celebration of his daughter Cleopatra's marriage to King Alexander of Epirus. He was buried in a tomb nearby.

Athenians and Mantineans, when the Theban leader Epaminondas was killed.

RISE OF MACEDONIA

In 359 BC Philip II became king of Macedonia, which had been weakened by dynastic struggles. Macedonia subsequently became the dominant power in the Greek world. In order to facilitate access to the sea and to gain control of the gold mines of Mount Pangaeus, Philip II repeatedly came into conflict with Athens (including the capture of Amphipolis in 357 BC and Methone in 354 BC). Athens embarked on the Social War (357–355 BC) against allies of the Second Athenian League who had revolted, while Sparta attempted in vain to recover Messenia. Philip II took advantage of the situation. He gained the support of the Chalcidic Confederacy by capturing Potidaea and handing it over to Olynthus (356 BC). He intervened in the Third Sacred War against Phocis (355–346 BC), and in 349–348 BC he attacked the Chalcidice promontory, destroying Olynthus and enslaving its inhabitants, with little opposition from Athens.

In 346 BC Athens and Philip II made peace (Peace of Philocrates), although Philip crushed the Phocians later that year. He besieged Perinthus and Byzantium (340–339 BC), which had revolted from the Macedonian alliance, but failed to take either. In 339 BC he took part in the Fourth Sacred War, and in 338 BC inflicted a devastating defeat on Thebes and Athens at the battle of Chaeronea. He then summoned a congress of Greek states at Corinth, with another in 337 BC, in which he put forward his military plans to attack Persia. His assassination in 336 BC (fig. 1.9) led to the accession of Alexander the Great.

Hellenistic Period

The term "Hellenistic" describes the period from the accession of Alexander the Great in 336 BC to the final conquest of the Greek world by Rome in 30 BC—a period of about 300 years. During this time city-states declined, but there was a huge expansion in Greek territory as far as Afghanistan, with the establishment of numerous monarchies, the founding of many Greek cities, and a shift of the cultural center to Alexandria in Egypt. On his accession Alexander acted against the tribes of the lower Danube and suppressed a revolt in Greece, in which he destroyed Thebes, killing and enslaving its inhabitants (335 BC). Alexander next pursued Philip II's plan to invade the Persian Empire; within 12 years he had conquered as far as the steppes of Russia, Afghanistan and the Punjab (fig. 2.2), all of which became part of the Hellenistic world. For his campaigns, see pp. 43. All Hellenistic rulers throughout his empire came to use the title "king."

AGE OF THE SUCCESSORS (DIADOCHI)

After Alexander's death there was a struggle among his former generals (the Successors, *diadokhoi*) to retain control of Alexander's empire (323–301 BC), initially by the regent Perdiccas. From 321 BC. Ptolemy I had established Egypt as a separate kingdom. Greek states including Athens tried to revolt against Macedonia, but were defeated by Antipater in the Lamian War (323–322 BC), and Athens was occupied by the Macedonians. In 320 BC Perdiccas died, and Antigonus I tried to gain control of the Empire. The other generals—Cassander, Lysimachus, Ptolemy I and Seleucus I—formed alliances against Antigonus I and his son Demetrius I Poliorcetes. By 306 BC Alexander's family had been eliminated, and the Successors claimed the title of king in their own areas (fig. 1.10). Demetrius I

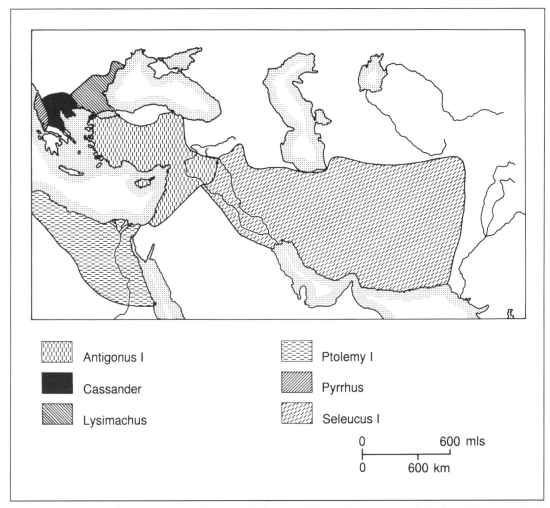

Antigonus I

Cassander

Lysimachus

Ptolemy I

Pyrrhus

Seleucus I

0   600 mls

0   600 km

Fig. 1.10   *Territory of the Successors of Alexander the Great in 303 BC. Other areas (mainland and Crete) remained independent.*

Poliorcetes and Antigonus I were defeated at the battle of Ipsus in 301 BC, so destroying any chance of holding together Alexander's empire.

FORMATION OF HELLENISTIC KINGDOMS

Demetrius I Poliorcetes became king of Macedonia in 294 BC, but was defeated and captured in 285 BC by Seleucus I when trying to regain Asian territories. Lysimachus and Pyrrhus of Epirus took over Macedonia (288 BC), but Lysimachus was defeated and killed in 281 BC by Seleucus I. Pyrrhus was pushed back to Epirus and then intervened in Sicily and southern Italy against Rome. By about 275 BC three main Hellenistic kingdoms had emerged—Macedonia, Egypt and the Seleucid Empire. The Ptolemies held not only Egypt, but also Cyrene, Coele-Syria, Cyprus, the Aegean Islands and parts of Asia Minor. The Antigonids held Macedonia and dominated parts of Greece. The Seleucids occupied the largest kingdom, holding northern Syria, parts of Asia Minor and Persia, and Babylonia. The 3rd century BC saw conflicts between these kingdoms and the emergence of a new Greek kingdom when the Attalids (centered at Pergamum) established independence from the Seleucids.

From 334 to 264 BC Rome gradually expanded its control of Italy, and from 264 BC it began expansion into Sicily, Corsica and Sardinia. Rome then became involved in the First Punic War, a result of Carthaginian expansion in Spain. From 220 to 167 BC Rome brought much of the Mediterranean area under its control. Sicily became a Roman province in 211 BC, and other areas followed.

GREECE AND MACEDONIA

In 268 BC the Chremonidean War started, in which Athens and Sparta (supported by Ptolemy II) unsuccessfully revolted against Antigonus II of Macedonia. Athens was taken by the Macedonians (262 BC). In 251 BC Aratus freed Sicyon and united it with the Achaean Confederacy against Macedonia. In 249 BC Alexander of Corinth revolted against Antigonus II, declaring Corinth independent. In 243 BC Aratus of Sicyon freed Corinth from the Macedonians (who had regained control there), but in 222 BC he joined with Antigonus III to defeat Cleomenes III of Sparta at the battle of Sellasia.

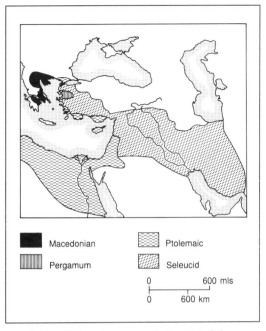

Fig. 1.11   Hellenistic empires of c. 240 BC. Other Greek kingdoms (mainland and Crete) remained independent.

In 221 BC Philip V became king of Macedonia (see p. 71 for his campaigns). He became involved in two Macedonian wars against Rome (in 215–205 and 200–197 BC). He was defeated at the battle of Cynoscephalae in Thessaly in 197 BC, and harsh penalties were imposed. Perseus became king of Macedonia in 179 BC and fought the Third Macedonian War against the Romans (171–168 BC), in which he was defeated. Macedonia was then divided into four republics by Rome (167 BC), and it became a Roman province in 148 BC after the defeat of the pretender Andriscus. In 146 BC the actions of the Achaean Confederacy led to Corinth being sacked by Rome and the rest of Greece becoming part of the Roman province of Macedonia. In the First Mithridatic War against Rome, Mithridates VI of Pontus liberated much of Greece, which led to the Roman general Sulla besieging and sacking Athens (86 BC).

SELEUCID SYRIA

The Ptolemies and Seleucids fought six Syrian wars, mainly in the 3rd century BC, over possession of Coele-Syria. Civil war was also waged between Seleucus II and his younger brother Antiochus Hierax. In the east the empire started to disintegrate, and Bactria became an independent Greek kingdom c. 240 BC (fig. 1.11). In 223 BC Antiochus III became Seleucid king (see p. 46 for his campaigns). He attempted to conquer Syria and Palestine but was defeated at the battle of Raphia by Ptolemy IV in 217 BC. Antiochus emulated Alexander the Great in his expedition as far as India and on his return, he and Philip V of Macedonia attacked Ptolemy V in the Fifth Syrian War (202–195 BC), with the Seleucid Empire finally gaining Coele-Syria. Antiochus invaded Greece and was consequently attacked by the Romans and defeated in 189 BC at Magnesia ad Sipylum. In the Peace of Apamea, Antiochus had to give up much of Asia Minor, and the Seleucid Empire was no longer a Mediterranean power.

Antiochus IV became king in 175 BC, and the Sixth Syrian War against Egypt took place (170–168 BC), followed by a revolt of the Jews under Judas Maccabaeus (from 167 BC). Numerous dynastic struggles and civil wars followed, and in 64 BC Pompey made Syria a Roman province at the end of the Third Mithridatic War.

PTOLEMAIC EGYPT

Six Syrian wars were fought against the Seleucids, and c. 202 BC Ptolemy lost Coele-Syria (fig. 1.12). The Ptolemies suffered from dynastic struggles from the time of Ptolemy VI (170 BC). In 96 BC Cyrene was bequeathed to Rome by Ptolemy Apion; it was made a Roman province in 74 BC, with Crete becoming part of the province in 67 BC. In 59 BC Ptolemy XII ceded Cyprus to Rome. Cleopatra VII formed an alliance with the Roman Mark Antony, which ended in her suicide in 30 BC. Egypt, which had been bequeathed to Rome in 87 BC, became the Roman province of Aegyptus in 30 BC.

OTHER TERRITORIES

In 133 BC Attalus of Pergamum bequeathed his kingdom to Rome, and it became the Roman province of Asia in 129 BC (fig. 1.13). Mithridates VI of Pontus occupied much of Greece and Asia Minor and fought three Mithridatic wars against Rome (88–63 BC). When he committed suicide his kingdom became part of the new Roman province of Bithynia et Pontus (Bithynia had been bequeathed to Rome in 74 BC by Nicomedes IV). Commagene, the last minor Hellenistic kingdom, did not become part of the Roman province of Syria until AD 72.

TABLE OF EVENTS

All dates are BC, unless otherwise stated. Most dates before 600 BC are approximate, and no attempt has been made in this list to prefix dates with c. (circa), as most are subject to some sort of dispute or discussion.

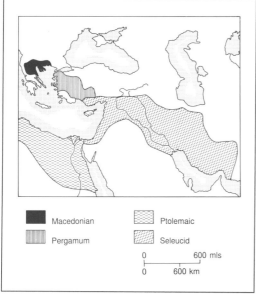

Fig. 1.12   *The Hellenistic world c. 185 BC. Other Greek territory remained independent.*

7000–3300	Neolithic and Copper Age.

Bronze Age (3300–1050 BC)

3300–2200	Prepalatial Period.
2200–1700	First Palace Period: first palaces on Crete.
1700–1500	Second Palace Period: second palaces on Crete.
1630/1620	Eruption of Thera volcano.
1550	Shaft graves at Mycenae.

1525	Eruption of Thera volcano (date no longer widely accepted—see 1630).
1500–1200	Third Palace Period: final palaces on Crete; Mycenaean palaces on mainland.
1220	Troy VIIa (possibly Priam's city) destroyed, possibly the historical event behind the Trojan War legend.
1200–1050	Widespread destruction of Mycenaean sites. Postpalatial Period.
1200–1000	Invasion of Dorian Greeks into mainland Greece.
1184/1183	Traditional date of Greek writers for destruction of Troy.

Dark Age (Bronze Age to Iron Age, 1050–750 BC)

1050–950	Migrations of Ionians and other Greeks from the mainland to Asia Minor's west coast and the Aegean islands.
950	Beginnings of widespread use of iron in Greece.
875–750	Geometric Age.

Archaic Age (750–479 BC)

800	Euboean cities of Chalcis and Eretria became the leading settlements in Greece. Colonization began. Euboeans established a trading post at Al Mina (north Syria) (by early 8th century).
776	First Olympiad: traditional start of Greek history and Archaic Age.
775	Euboeans established a trading settlement at Ischia (early 8th century).
753	Traditional date for founding of Rome.
734	Foundation of Naxos, first colony in Sicily.
733	Colonies were established at Corcyra and Syracuse by Corinth.
730–680	Lelantine War between Chalcis and Eretria, the first recorded interstate conflict in Greece.
730–710	First Messenian War: Spartans conquered Messenia in southwest Peloponnese.

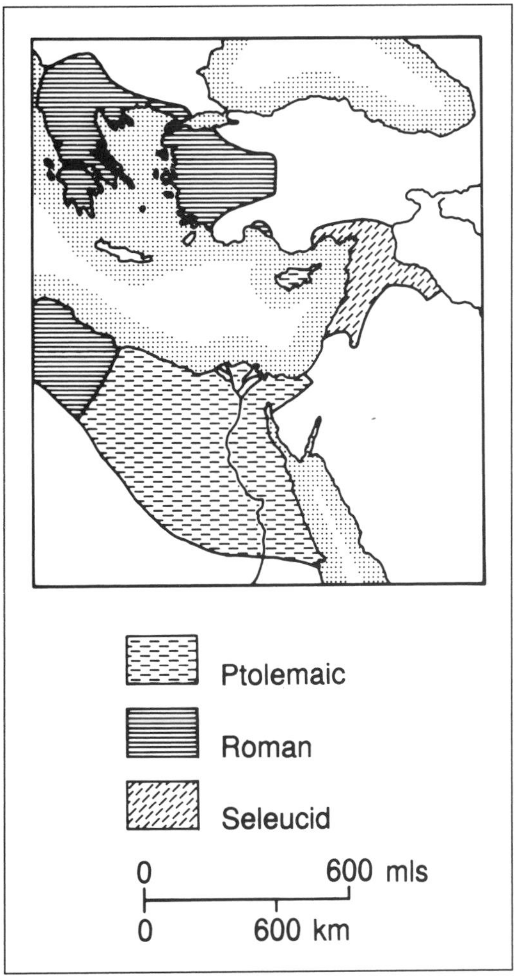

Legend:
- Ptolemaic
- Roman
- Seleucid

0 ——— 600 mls
0 ——— 600 km

Fig. 1.13 Hellenistic territory c. 90 BC. Much of Asia Minor consisted of independent kingdoms, while many areas were coming under Roman control.

730	Corinth emerged as the most advanced city in Greece.
720	Colony of Sybaris (south Italy) was founded. Colonization of Chalcidice (north Greece) by Chalcis. Greeks began to move into the Hellespont area.
706	Traditional date for founding of Taras by Sparta.
685	Gyges became king of Lydia.
683	Athenian archon list began.

680	Thasos was colonized by Greeks from Paros.
669	Sparta was defeated by Argos at the battle of Hysiae.
657	Cypselus became tyrant at Corinth (to 627).
650	Second Messenian War.
	Zaleucus of Locri produced the first Greek law code.
640	Theagenes became tyrant at Megara (to 620).
632	Attempted tyranny at Athens by Cylon.
630	Foundation of Cyrene (north Africa).
625	Periander became tyrant of Corinth (to 585).
	Thrasybulus became tyrant of Miletus (to 600).
620	Draco's first written law code at Athens.

Dates become more accurate:

600	Smyrna was destroyed by Alyattes.
	Foundation of Massilia by Phocaea.
595	Cleisthenes became tyrant of Sicyon (to 570).
594/593	Solon was appointed archon at Athens and undertook reforms.
590	Pittacus became tyrant at Mytilene (to 580).
	First Sacred War for control of Delphi.
590–560	Tegean War between Sparta and Tegea.
585	End of tyranny at Corinth.
580	Acragas was founded.
569–525	Reign of Amasis in Egypt.
566	Reorganization of Panathenaic festival at Athens.
560	First tyranny of Peisistratus began at Athens.
	Tegean War between Sparta and Tegea ended in an alliance.
559	Cyrus founded the Persian Empire.
556	Peisistratus was forced to leave Athens by his political opponents.
556/555	Chilon was ephor at Sparta.

550	Second tyranny of Peisistratus, which resulted in his exile the same year.
546	Sparta defeated Argos at the battle of the champions.
	Battle of Pallene.
	Third tyranny of Peisistratus began at Athens.
546–540	Conquest of Lydia and of Ionian Greeks by the Persians.
540	Polycrates became tyrant of Samos (to 523).
535	Greeks were defeated in the naval battle of Alalia (off Corsica) by a Carthaginian and Etruscan fleet, halting Greek expansion in the western Mediterranean.
527	Death of Peisistratus.
	Hippias became tyrant at Athens.
525/524	Cleisthenes was archon at Athens.
523	Polycrates was killed.
521	Darius I became king of Persia.
520	Cleomenes I became king of Sparta (to 488).
519	Alliance of Athens and Plataea against Thebes.
514	Harmodius and Aristogiton assassinated Hipparchus at Athens.
513	Darius crossed the Bosphorus with his army to march to Thrace and Scythia.
512	Darius conquered Thrace (but not Scythia).
510	The tyrant Hippias was expelled from Athens; Cleisthenes returned.
509	Traditional date for foundation of Roman Republic.
508/507	Reforms of Cleisthenes at Athens.
506	Spartans, Chalcidians and Boeotians invaded Attica.
	Spartans withdrew from Attica.
	Athens defeated the Chalcidians and Boeotians.
499–494	Ionian Greek revolt against the Persians.
498	Athenians and Eretrians helped Ionian Greeks to destroy Sardis.
	Athenians were defeated near Ephesus by the Persian army.
	Hippocrates became tyrant of Gela.

497	Cyprus joined the Ionian revolt but was besieged and subdued by the Persians.		The tyrant Terillus was expelled from Himera.
496	Revolt in Caria against the Persians.	482	Aristides was ostracized.
495	Alexander I became king of Macedonia.	481–480	Conference of Greek states at Sparta and then at the Isthmus of Corinth formed the Hellenic League (allies against the Persians) under Spartan leadership.
494	Defeat by Persians of Ionian fleet at the battle of Lade (near Miletus). Destruction of Miletus, when its people were sold into slavery. End of Ionian revolt. Anaxilas became tyrant of Rhegium. Spartans defeated Argos at the battle of Sepeia.	480	The second Persian invasion of mainland Greece, now under Xerxes. Naval battle of Artemisium against the Persian navy (Greek loss). Spartans were defeated by Persians at the battle of Thermopylae, with the death of Leonidas. Evacuation of Athens was ordered. Greek navy defeated Persians in the battle of Salamis, and Xerxes withdrew to Asia Minor. Carthaginians were defeated by Theron and Gelon at the battle of Himera.
493	Histiaeus was killed. Miltiades fled to Athens from Thrace. Miltiades was prosecuted.		
493/492	Themistocles was archon at Athens. Fortification of a naval base and harbor at Piraeus was begun.		
492	Persians conquered the islands of Chios, Lesbos and Tenedos. Under Mardonius, the Persians took Thrace and Thasos.	479	Attica and Athens were sacked by the Persians under Mardonius. Revolt in Asia Minor against the Persians. The Persian army was defeated by an alliance of Greek states under Pausanias at the battle of Plataea; Mardonius the Persian general was killed. Thebes was punished for supporting the Persians by the execution of its leaders. Greeks destroyed the Persian army and navy at the battle of Mycale, near Samos.
491	Gelon became tyrant of Gela. Demaratus (king of Sparta) was deposed.		
490	First Persian invasion of mainland Greece (to punish Eretria and Athens). Destruction of Eretria by Persians. Persian army was defeated by Greeks, led by Athenians, at the battle of Marathon.		
489	Siege of Paros.		
489/488	Aristides was archon at Athens.		
488	Suicide of Cleomenes I of Sparta. Theron became tyrant of Acragas (to 472).		
487	Archons were selected by lot at Athens.	**Classical Age**	
487–482	Ostracisms at Athens.	479/478	Xanthippus captured and destroyed Sestus.
486	Xerxes became king of Persia.	478	Byzantium was captured from the Persians by Pausanias. Sparta recalled Pausanias. Foundation of Delian League, an alliance of Greek states under Athenian leadership against the Persians. Rebuilding and refortification of Athens began.
485	Gelon became tyrant of Syracuse.		
484/483	Xanthippus was ostracized from Athens.		
483	Themistocles persuaded Athens to create a navy from the revenue of the Laurium silver mines.		

CIVILIZATIONS, CITY-STATES AND EMPIRES

	Death of Gelon, tyrant of Syracuse. Hieron I became tyrant of Syracuse.	458	Athens besieged Aegina. Corinthians were defeated by Athenians at Megara.
476	Naval campaigns of Cimon began (to 473). Pausanias was driven from Byzantium by Cimon. Eion, on the Strymon River, was besieged and recaptured from the Persians.	457	Athenians and allies were defeated by the Peloponnesians at the battle of Tanagra. Athenians invaded Boeotia and defeated the Boeotians at the battle of Oenophyta.
475–473	Scyrus Island was cleared of pirates.	456	Aegina surrendered to Athens.
474	Hieron I defeated the Etruscan fleet at the battle of Cumae.	454	Failure of Athenian expedition to Egypt. Treasury of the Delian League was moved to Athens from Delos.
472	Hieron I overthrew the tyranny at Acragas. Carystus (in southern Euboea) was forced to join the Delian League.	451	Five-year peace treaty was signed between Athens and Sparta. Thirty-year peace treaty was agreed upon between Sparta and Argos.
471	Themistocles was ostracized from Athens.		Pericles' law on citizenship. Ducetius captured Aetna on Sicily.
469	Revolt of Naxos from the Delian League was defeated.	450	Cimon campaigned against Persia in Cyprus, where he died. Ducetius was defeated in Sicily.
467	Cimon won the battle of the Eurymedon, destroying the Persian navy and removing the Persian threat.	449	Persians were defeated at Salamis (Cyprus).
467/466	Death of Hieron I; tyranny ended at Syracuse.	449/448	Peace of Callias was possibly negotiated by Callias between Athens and Persia (recognizing mutual spheres of influence).
465–463	Revolt of Thasos from the Delian League: it was besieged by Cimon.		
465/464	Assassination of Xerxes; Artaxerxes I succeeded as king of Persia. Violent earthquake at Sparta killed more than 20,000 people.	447	Loss by Athens of Boeotia at the battle of Coronea.
464	Revolt of Spartan helots began.	447–432	Major program of public works on Athens' Acropolis.
464–455	Third Messenian War.	446	Revolt of Euboea was suppressed by Pericles. Sparta invaded Attica.
463	Cimon was prosecuted by Pericles (but acquitted).	446/445	Thirty-year peace between Athens and Sparta (ended in 431).
462/461	Radical democratic reforms were introduced at Athens under Ephialtes and Pericles.	443	Athens founded a colony at Thurii (southern Italy). Thucydides (son of Melesias) was ostracized.
461	Cimon was ostracized. Ephialtes was murdered.		
461–429	Supremacy of Pericles.	440–439	Revolt of Samos was suppressed by Athens after a siege. Byzantium revolted against Athens.
460–446	First Peloponnesian War.		
460/459–454	A revolt against the Persians in the satrapy of Egypt was supported by Athens, which sent ships from Cyprus.	436	Athens founded Amphipolis.
		435	War between Corinth and Corcyra over Epidamnus.
458–456	Building of Long Walls from Athens to Piraeus.	433(?)	Athenian alliance with Corcyra.
		432–430	Siege of Potidaea.

HANDBOOK TO LIFE IN ANCIENT GREECE

432	Megarian Decree.
431–404	Second Peloponnesian War between Athens and Sparta.
431–421	Archidamian War (the first part of the Second Peloponnesian War, named after King Archidamus of Sparta).
430	Invasion of Attica by Sparta. Plague broke out at Athens. Surrender of Potidaea.
429	Death of Pericles from plague. Sitalces invaded Macedonia and Chalcidice.
429–427	Plataea was besieged by Spartans and Thebans.
428/427	Revolt of Lesbos was led by Mytilene against Athens.
427	Capture of Mytilene by Athenians and execution of ringleaders. Capture and destruction of Plataea in Boeotia by Spartans. First expedition of Athenians to Sicily. Civil war in Corcyra.
425	Capture of Pylos and adjacent island of Sphacteria by Athenians. One hundred twenty Spartan citizen hoplites were taken as prisoners by Cleon to Athens.
424	Spartans under Brasidas marched to Thrace at the request of Thrace and Macedonia. Boeotians defeated Athenians at battle of Delium. (Winter) The historian Thucydides was exiled from Athens.
424/423	Brasidas took the Athenian cities of Amphipolis and Torone.
423	Armistice was signed between Athens and Sparta (lasted one year).
422	Brasidas and Cleon were killed in the battle of Amphipolis, which the Athenians lost.
421	Peace of Nicias (50-year truce) signed between Athens and Sparta, but ended in 420.
418	Spartan defeat of Athenian/Argive alliance at the battle of Mantinea. Alliance between Sparta and Argos.

417/415	Hyberbolus was ostracized.
416	Athenians conquered the island of Melos, enslaving its population.
415	Mutilation of the herms (stone busts), for which Alcibiades was blamed. Athenian expedition to Sicily (to 413). Alcibiades went into exile.
414	Athens began to besiege Syracuse. Lamachus died at Syracuse.
413	Sparta established a permanent fort at Decelea in Attica. Final phase of Peloponnesian War (Decelean War) started, fought almost entirely at sea (to 404). Archelaus became king of Macedonia. Athens suffered a naval defeat by the Syracusans, and a defeat on land at the battle of Assinarus River (40,000 men lost).
412	Treaty of Miletus between Persia and Sparta, which surrendered Ionia to Persia in return for Persian support against Athens.
411	Oligarchic revolution at Athens, which established the Council of Four Hundred. Council of Five Thousand replaced the Four Hundred. Athenian naval victories over Sparta at the battles of Cynossema and Abydus. Hyperbolus was murdered.
410	Athens' naval victory under Alcibiades over the Spartans and Syracusans at the battle of Cyzicus. Full democracy was restored at Athens.
409	Carthaginian invasion of Sicily.
409/408	Hannibal besieged Himera.
408	Alcibiades returned to Athens from exile and was elected commander-in-chief of the fleet.
406	Athenian naval defeat by Lysander at the battle of Notium. Athenian victory over Spartan fleet at the battle of Arginusae. Lycophron became tyrant of Pherae.

CIVILIZATIONS, CITY-STATES AND EMPIRES

	Hannibal sacked Acragas.
405	Annihilation of Athenian fleet at the battle of Aegospotami by Lysander; over 3,000 Athenians were executed.
	Athens was besieged by Sparta with the blockading of Piraeus.
	Dionysius I became tyrant of Syracuse.
404	(Spring) Surrender of Athens to Sparta, with the destruction of its fortifications, loss of all foreign territories, surrender of the navy, and acceptance of Spartan leadership.
	Pro-Spartan oligarchy of Thirty Tyrants imposed at Athens under Critias.
404/403	Democratic exiles under Thrasybulus seized Phyle.
403	Thrasybulus seized Piraeus.
	Fall of Thirty Tyrants and restoration of democracy at Athens.
402/400	Agis II invaded Elis.
401	Expedition (*anabasis*) of Cyrus the Younger to take the Persian throne from his brother Artaxerxes II; battle of Cunaxa, with the defeat and death of Cyrus.
400–387	War of Sparta against Persia.
399	General amnesty at Athens allowed exiles to return.
	Agesilaus II became king of Sparta.
398–392	War between Carthage and Dionysius I of Syracuse.
396–395	Campaigns of Agesilaus against the Persians in Asia Minor.
395–386	Corinthian War: Corinth, Boeotia, Argos and Athens backed by Persia against Sparta.
395	Lysander was killed at the siege of Haliartus.
394	Sparta and allies won the battle of Nemea against Athens, Corinth, Boeotia, Argos and others.
	Athenians and Boeotians were defeated by Sparta under Agesilaus II at the battle of Coronea.
	The Persian fleet under the Athenian Conon defeated the Spartan navy at the battle of Cnidus.

393	Athens rebuilt its Long Walls, and Piraeus was refortified.
390	Gauls sacked Rome.
390/389	Athens made an alliance with Thasos, Samothrace and many cities of Asia Minor.
387	Spartans and Persians defeated the Athenian fleet in the Hellespont.
386	King's Peace (also known as Peace of Antalcidas or Common Peace) was signed at Sardis.
386–385	City of Mantinea was destroyed by Spartans.
385	Jason became tyrant of Pherae.
383–375?	War between Dionysius I and Carthage.
382	Spartan troops seized the citadel at Thebes (Cadmea).
379	Spartans forced Olynthus to surrender and dissolved the Chalcidic Confederacy for infringing the King's Peace.
379–378	Thebans regained their city from Spartan control.
378	Foundation of Second Athenian League.
377/376	Mausolus became satrap of Caria (to 353/352).
376	Spartans were defeated at sea off Naxos by the Second Athenian League.
	(Winter) Dionysius I was defeated by Carthage at the battle of Cronium.
375	Battle of Tegyra.
	Renewal of the King's Peace.
373	Plataea was attacked and destroyed by Thebes.
371	(Early) Peace of Callias (one of many examples of a treaty of Common Peace) was signed at Sparta by all Greek states except Thebes.
	(July/August) Spartans under Cleombrotus were defeated by Thebans under Epaminondas at the battle of Leuctra, ending Spartan leadership in Greece.
370/369	(Winter) First Theban invasion of Peloponnese, including Laconia. Messenia was liberated and became an independent state.

	Formation of Arcadian Confederacy.	356–346	(Summer) Phocis seized Delphi and provoked the Third Sacred War (Phocis against Thebes, Locris and Thessaly).
369	Second invasion of the Peloponnese by Thebes under Epaminondas.		
	Alexander became tyrant of Pherae.	354	Philip II took Methone (and lost an eye).
368	Foundation of Megalopolis as the capital of the Arcadian Confederacy.		Thessalian League appealed to Philip II for help against the tyrants of Pherae.
367	Death of Dionysius I.		(Autumn) Phocis was defeated at the battle of Neon.
	Dionysius II became tyrant of Syracuse.		Dion was murdered.
366	Dion was expelled from Syracuse.	353	Philip II was defeated twice.
366	Satraps' Revolt from Persian domination (to 360).	352	Victory by Philip II at the battle of Crocus Field.
	Thebes seized Oropus.		Philip II was prevented from marching south at Thermopylae by Phocian troops and allies.
365	Common Peace (possibly).		
	Athens captured Samos from the Persians.	351	Demosthenes' *First Philippic* oration advocated an anti-Macedonian policy.
364	Thebes destroyed Orchomenus.		
	Battle of Cynoscephalae, in which Pelopidas died.	351/350	Philip II campaigned against Illyria and Epirus.
362	Thebes under Epaminondas defeated a force of Spartans, Athenians and Mantineans at the battle of Mantinea. Epaminondas was killed, marking the end of Theban supremacy.	349–348	Philip II campaigned in Chalcidice.
		348	Philip II attacked and destroyed Olynthus, enslaving the inhabitants.
362/361	Treaty of common peace amongst Greek cities, except Sparta.	346	Philip II and Athens made peace (Peace of Philocrates).
361	Expedition by Agesilaus against Persians.		Philip II crushed the Phocians.
	Callistratus was executed.	346/345	Aeschines was prosecuted by Demosthenes.
361/360	Archidamus III became king of Sparta.	345	Philip II campaigned against Illyria.
360	Death of Agesilaus.	344	Timoleon went to assist Syracuse against Dionysius II and the Carthaginians.
359	Philip II succeeded Perdiccas III as king of Macedonia.		
358	Philip II defeated the Paeonians.	344–343	Timoleon liberated Syracuse from Dionysius II.
357	Philip II captured Amphipolis.		
	Outbreak of war between Athens and Macedonia.	342	Philip II campaigned in Thrace and removed its king.
357–355	Social War between Athens and important allies who had revolted from the Second Athenian League.	341/339	(June) Timoleon defeated the Carthaginians at the battle of Crimisus River in Sicily.
356	Dion controlled Syracuse (to 354).	340	Siege of Perinthus by Philip II.
	Battle of Embata, which the Athenian navy lost to Chios.		Siege of Byzantium by Philip II (to 339).
	Birth of Alexander the Great.		(Late) Athens declared war on Philip II.
	(Spring) Siege of Potidaea by Philip II.	339	Fourth Sacred War of Philip II.

338	(2 August) Philip II defeated Athens and Thebes at the battle of Chaeronea. First congress of Corinth. Archidamus III was killed at the battle of Manduria, Italy.
337	(Spring) Second congress of Corinth agreed on a Common Peace. (Summer) Corinthian League of Greek states (Hellenic League) was established by Philip II and agreed on war against Persia to avenge the wrongs of Xerxes.
336	Assassination of Philip II. Proposal by Ctesiphon that Demosthenes should be crowned for his services.

Hellenistic Period

336	Accession of Alexander III (the Great). Accession of Darius III of Persia.
335	Alexander destroyed Thebes, killing and enslaving its population.
334	Alexander crossed into Asia, defeating Darius III at the battle of Granicus River (near the Hellespont); he then conquered Asia Minor.
333	(November) Defeat of Darius III by Alexander at the battle of Issus. Antigonus I was appointed satrap of Persia.
332	Alexander besieged and took Tyre and Gaza. (December) Alexander entered Egypt.
331	(6 April) Foundation of Alexandria in Egypt. Alexander visited the oracle of Zeus Ammon at Siwa. (November) Alexander defeated Darius III at the battle of Gaugamela (or Arbela). Alexander took Mesopotamia and entered Babylon and Persepolis. Antipater defeated Agis III at the battle of Megalopolis.
331/330	Alexander I of Epirus was defeated at the battle of Pandosia.

330	Destruction of Persepolis by Alexander's forces. Darius III was murdered in Bactria. (October) Plot against Alexander the Great was suppressed. Ctesiphon was prosecuted by Aeschines.
330–328	Alexander conquered Bactria and Sogdiana.
328/327	Cleitus was murdered by Alexander.
327	Marriage of Alexander and Roxane. Conspiracy of the pages (a plot to murder Alexander). Alexander began the India Expedition.
326	Alexander crossed the Indus, won the battle of Hydaspes (Jhelum) River and conquered the Punjab. At the Hyphasis River, Alexander's army refused to proceed further. Alexander and his army sailed down the Indus to the Indian Ocean.
325	Alexander returned through Baluchistan, with his army suffering great loss of life in the waterless deserts.
324	Alexander returned to Susa. Exiles' Decree issued by Alexander to repatriate exiles to their cities. Macedonian army mutiny at Opis on Tigris River.
323	(10 June) Death of Alexander the Great at Babylon, age 32. Demosthenes retired to Aegina. Perdiccas became regent of Alexander the Great's empire.
323–322	Athens and other Greek states revolted against Macedonia (Lamian or Hellenic War).
322	(August) Battle of Crannon (Macedonian victory over the allied Greek states). Athens was occupied by Macedonians, and an oligarchy was established. Death of Demosthenes.
320	Death of Perdiccas.

319–316	Conference at Triparadeisus. Polyperchon was driven from Macedonia and much of Greece by Cassander.	303	Treaty concluded between Seleucus I and the Indian king Sandracottus.
319–301	Antigonus I attempted to reunite and rule the entire empire of Alexander the Great.	301	Battle of Ipsus: Antigonus I was killed and the power of Demetrius Poliorcetes was destroyed.
319	Death of Antipater. Ptolemy I seized Palestine and Coele-Syria.	297	Death of Cassander, ruler of Macedonia. Pyrrhus became king of Epirus (to 272).
317	Philip III Arrhidaeus was murdered by Olympias.	295	(Spring) Athens was starved into surrender by Demetrius I Poliorcetes.
317/316	Agathocles became tyrant of Syracuse.	294	(Autumn) Demetrius Poliorcetes became king of Macedonia.
315	(Spring) Olympias, mother of Alexander, was executed by Cassander. Seleucus I fled to Ptolemy I.	288	Lysimachus and Pyrrhus gained Macedonia from Demetrius I Poliorcetes.
315–311	Coalition of satraps fought against Antigonus I.	285	Pyrrhus was pushed back to Epirus by Lysimachus. Demetrius Poliorcetes surrendered to Seleucus I and died in 283.
312	(Late) Ptolemy I defeated Demetrius Poliorcetes at the battle of Gaza. Seleucus I recaptured Babylon.	283/282	Ptolemy I Soter died; Ptolemy II Philadelphus succeeded (to 246).
311	Alexander IV and Roxane were executed. Peace treaty among the Successors recognized the division among Antigonus (Asia), Cassander (Macedonia/ Greece), Lysimachus (Thrace), and Ptolemy (Egypt), although omitting the eastern satrapies of Seleucus I.	281	Battle of Corupedium: Lysimachus of Thrace was defeated and killed by Seleucus I. Seleucus I was assassinated and succeeded by his son Antiochus I. Foundation of the Achaean Confederacy.
310–306	War between Agathocles and Carthage: invasion of Africa.	280–275	Campaigns of Pyrrhus of Epirus against Rome in south Italy and Sicily.
309/308	Areus I became king of Sparta.	280	Pyrrhus won the battle of Heraclea against Rome.
307	Demetrius I Poliorcetes freed Athens from Cassander.	279	Pyrrhus won the battle of Asculum against Rome. Gauls invaded Macedonia and Greece as far as Delphi.
307–304	Four Years' War (Athens against Cassander).	277	Antigonus II Gonatas defeated the Gauls near Lysimachia.
306	Naval victory by Demetrius I Poliorcetes over Ptolemy I at Salamis. Peace between Agathocles and the Carthaginians.	276	Antigonus II Gonatas became king of Macedonia, founding the Antigonid dynasty.
306–304	Antigonus, Ptolemy and Seleucus I proclaimed themselves kings.	276/275	Ptolemy II married his sister Arsinoë II.
		275	Pyrrhus was beaten by the Romans at the battle of Beneventum.
305–304	Siege of Rhodes by Demetrius I Poliorcetes, "The Besieger."	274/273–271	First Syrian War between Ptolemy II and Antiochus I Soter.

CIVILIZATIONS, CITY-STATES AND EMPIRES

272	Surrender of Tarentum to Rome. Death of Pyrrhus of Epirus.	240	Former Seleucid province of Bactria became independent.
270	Hieron II became king at Syracuse (to 215).	239	Demetrius II succeeded Antigonus II Gonatas as king of Macedonia.
268–263/262	Chremonidean War: Ptolemy II unsuccessfully supported Athens and Sparta against Antigonus II of Macedonia.	239–238	Demetrian War between Macedonia and the Achaean and Aetolian Confederacies.
265	Mamertines were defeated by Hieron II at the battle of Longanus River.	239–236	War of the Brothers (Seleucus II against Antiochus Hierax).
264	Roman army entered Sicily to help the Mamertines against Carthage. Romans seized Messana. Beginning of the First Punic War.	238	Emergence of Parthia.
		235	Cleomenes III became king of Sparta (to 222). Megalopolis joined the Achaean Confederacy.
263	Eumenes I succeeded Philetaerus as ruler of Pergamum. Hieron II of Syracuse became an ally of Rome.	229	Antigonus III Doson succeeded Demetrius II.
262	Antiochus I was defeated near Sardis. Antigonus II Gonatas took Athens.	228	Antigonus III Doson defeated the Aetolians and Thessalians.
261	Antiochus II succeeded Antiochus I as Seleucid king.	228/227	Major earthquake at Rhodes, which destroyed the Colossus.
260–253	Second Syrian War between Ptolemy II and Antiochus II.	227	Spartan victory at the battles of Mount Lycaeus and Ladocea.
251	Aratus recovered Sicyon, uniting it with the Achaean Confederacy against Macedonia.	227/226	Cleomenes III reformed the Spartan constitution.
		226	Death of Antiochus Hierax. Seleucus III succeeded Seleucus II.
249	Revolt of Alexander of Corinth against Antigonus II Gonatas on the death of Craterus the Younger.	225–224	Antigonus III Doson occupied Acrocorinth.
		224	Antigonus III Doson founded a Hellenic League of allies.
246	Ptolemy III succeeded Ptolemy II as king of Egypt. Seleucus II succeeded Antiochus II as Seleucid king.	223	Antiochus III succeeded Seleucus III as Seleucid king. Cleomenes II sacked Megalopolis.
246–241	Third Syrian (Laodicean) War, between Ptolemy III and Seleucus II.	222	(July) Battle of Sellasia near Sparta: defeat of the Spartans under Cleomenes III by the Achaeans and Antigonus III.
244–241	Agis IV became king at Sparta and attempted reforms.	221	Philip V succeeded Antigonus III Doson. Ptolemy IV succeeded Ptolemy III as king of Egypt. Antiochus III invaded Palestine.
243	Aratus of Sicyon and the Achaeans captured Corinth from the Macedonians. Lydiadas became tyrant of Megalopolis.	220–217	Social War: Philip V and his allies against Aetolia.
		220	Revolt of Achaeus.
242	Leonidas II was deposed as king by Agis IV.	220/219	Prusias I campaigned against Byzantium.
241	Attalus I became ruler of Pergamum. Agis IV was executed.	219–217	Fourth Syrian War between Ptolemy IV and Antiochus III.
		218	Prusias I defeated the Galatians.
		217	Battle of Naupactus.

Peace of Naupactus.

Ptolemy IV defeated Antiochus III at the battle of Raphia.

215	Philip V of Macedonia formed an alliance with Hannibal of Carthage.
215–205	First Macedonian War between Rome and Philip V.
214	Philip V lost his navy off Illyria.
213	Death of Aratus of Sicyon.
	Romans besieged Syracuse.
212–205	Antiochus III campaigned in the east (his *anabasis*) as far as India, emulating Alexander the Great.
211	Roman alliance with the Aetolian Confederacy against Philip V.
	Romans captured Syracuse, and Sicily became a Roman province.
209	Attalus I of Pergamum allied with Rome against Philip V.
207–187/186	Revolt of Upper Egypt.
205	(Summer) Peace of Phoenice between Rome and Philip V, which ended First Macedonian War.
204	Ptolemy V succeeded Ptolemy IV in Egypt.
202	Philip V and Antiochus III made an alliance against Egypt.
202–195	Fifth Syrian War, between Antiochus III and Ptolemy V.
201	Philip V was defeated in a naval battle off Chios.
200	Second Macedonian War between Rome and Philip V (to 197).
	Ptolemy V was defeated at the battle of Panion.
197	Defeat of Philip V by the Romans at the battle of Cynoscephalae.
	Eumenes II succeeded Attalus I.
196	(Summer) Roman general Flamininus proclaimed the liberation of the Greeks at the Isthmian Games.
194	Roman forces left Greece.
192	Antiochus III invaded Greece.
192–188	Syrian War between Antiochus III and Rome.
189	Battle of Magnesia ad Sipylum (Roman victory).
188	Peace of Apamea.
187	Death of Antiochus III.
183	Hannibal committed suicide.
180	Ptolemy VI succeeded Ptolemy V.
179	Philip V died and was succeeded by Perseus.
	Perseus renewed an alliance with Rome.
175	Antiochus IV Epiphanes succeeded Seleucus IV as king.
171–168	Third Macedonian War against the Romans.
170–168	Sixth Syrian War, between Egypt and Antiochus IV.
170	Ptolemy VIII became king of Egypt.
169	Antiochus IV raided the temple of Jerusalem.
168	Perseus was defeated by Rome at the battle of Pydna, ending the kingdom of Macedonia.
167	Rome divided Macedonia into four republics.
	Rome declared Delos a free port.
	Antiochus IV raided the temple of Jerusalem for a second time.
	Revolt of Jews led by Judas Maccabaeus began.
163	Antiochus V succeeded Antiochus IV.
162	Demetrius I became Seleucid king.
161/160	Judas Maccabaeus was killed in battle.
160	Orophernes seized the throne of Cappadocia.
159	Attalus II succeeded Eumenes II.
157	Ariarathes V was restored to the Seleucid throne.
156–154	War between Prusias II and Attalus II.
155	Ptolemy VIII threatened to bequeath Cyrene to Rome.
150	Polybius and other Achaean hostages held since the battle of Pydna were freed.
	Demetrius I killed in battle by Alexander Balas.
148	Macedonia became a Roman province.
146	Achaean War: Corinth was destroyed by Rome.
	Achaean Confederacy was dissolved.

CIVILIZATIONS, CITY-STATES AND EMPIRES

	Rest of Greece became part of the Roman province.
145	Alexander Balas was killed by Demetrius II Nicator.
	Death of Ptolemy VI.
144	(August) Ptolemy VII was murdered by Ptolemy VIII.
142	Diodotus Tryphon usurped the Seleucid throne.
139	Demetrius II Nicator was captured by the Parthians, and Antiochus VII became Seleucid king.
138	Attalus III succeeded Attalus II.
	Antiochus VII defeated and killed the usurper Diodotus Tryphon.
133	Attalus III of Pergamum bequeathed his kingdom to Rome on his death.
132	Revolt by Cleopatra II against Ptolemy VIII.
129	Antiochus VII died fighting the Parthians.
	The kingdom of Pergamum became the Roman province of Asia.
125	Demetrius II was killed by Alexander II Zabinas.
	Antiochus VIII became Seleucid king.
123	Antiochus VIII deposed Alexander II Zabinas.
116	Death of Ptolemy VIII.
114	Antiochus IX became Seleucid king.
114/113	Civil war began between Antiochus VIII and Antiochus IX.
101	Ptolemy X murdered his mother Cleopatra III.
96	Cyrene was bequeathed to Rome by Ptolemy Apion.
	Death of Antiochus VIII.
95	Antiochus IX died.
88–84	First Mithridatic War (Mithridates VI against Rome).
87	Death of Ptolemy X. Egypt was bequeathed to Rome.
86	Sulla besieged and destroyed Athens.
83–82	Second Mithridatic War.
81	Death of Ptolemy IX.
80	Accession of Ptolemy XII as king of Egypt.

74–63	Third Mithridatic War.
74	Nicomedes IV bequeathed Bithynia to Rome.
	Cyrene became a Roman province.
67	Crete was incorporated in the Roman province of Cyrene.
64	Pompey made Syria a Roman province.
63	Mithridates VI committed suicide, ending the Third Mithridatic War.
59	Ptolemy XII ceded Cyprus to Rome.
51	Ptolemy XII was succeeded by Ptolemy XIII and Cleopatra VII.
48	Cleopatra VII was expelled from Alexandria.
	Alexandrian War against Julius Caesar (to 47).
	(28 September) Pompey was murdered by ministers of Ptolemy XIII.
47	Death of Ptolemy XIII, defeated by Julius Caesar.
44	Death of Ptolemy XIV.
31	Battle of Actium.
30	Death of Mark Antony and Cleopatra VII. Egypt became a Roman province.

POPULATION

Citizens

In the Greek world men, not women, were citizens. In Homer's time citizens were apparently male heads of households with many dependents, mainly women, other relatives and slaves. From archaic times the polis consisted of male citizens, as well as a large population of women, slaves, dependent lower classes and foreign residents. Most Greek states divided their citizens into hereditary tribes (*phylai*, sing. *phyle*). Dorian cities usually had three tribes and Ionian cities four, some with identical names. Many citizens also belonged to brotherhoods or clans known as phratries (*phratriai*, sing. *phratria*), or *patrai* in some states. Citizenship normally passed through the father only, but Athens (followed by other states) legislated that it should be through both parents.

ATHENS

Every citizen belonged to a phratry (*phratria*), which controlled his religious and social life, though not his political life. A phratry usually consisted of one or more *genes* (sing. *genos*—family or clan). The *genos* was comprised of one or more families (usually aristocratic) who claimed descent from a common ancestor. Its members were *gennetai*, and they had exclusive rights to certain priesthoods of important city cults.

Citizens were also divided into four traditional Ionian tribes (*phylai*), in which membership was hereditary: Geleontes, Aegicoreis, Argadeis and Hopletes. Each of these four tribes was composed of three *trittyes* (thirds)—a total of 12 *trittyes*.

In the early 6th century BC Solon divided the male citizens into four property classes, reflecting the system of eligibility for military service, but assessing them in terms of agricultural produce. The richest were the *pentakosiomedimnoi* (500-bushel men), then the *hippeis* (equivalent to the cavalry) and the *zeugitai* (equivalent to hoplites); the remaining citizens were the *thetes*. The nine archons and state treasurers came from the highest two classes, not from the aristocratic Eupatridae as previously. Minor magistracies and membership in the boule could be held by the *zeugitai*, while the *thetes* were eligible only for membership in the Assembly and jury service, and could not hold magistracies.

Cleisthenes undertook far-reaching political reform in the late 6th century BC, breaking the power of the aristocratic families. He changed the division of Attica from the four Ionian tribes into 10 new artificial *phylai* named after local traditional heroes (Erechtheis, Aigeis, Pandionis, Leontis, Akamantis, Oineis, Kekropis, Hippothontis, Aiantis and Antiochis). The old tribes were retained for religious purposes. Each new tribe (*phyle*) was composed of three units called *trittyes*, making a total of 30 new *trittyes*. A *trittys* itself was a group of demes (*demoi*) selected from three geographical regions of Attica: the coast, the city (Athens, Piraeus, Phalerum and part of the plain of Athens) and the inland. No *phyle* therefore had a continuous territory or local interest.

There were 139 or 140 demes (later about 170), but no specific number of demes per *trittys*, as the demes could vary in size. The word *demos* (pl. *demoi*) generally denoted a village, but under Cleisthenes it became an artificial political division. In Athens a deme probably constituted a ward of the city, but elsewhere in Attica a deme contained one or more centers of population—a town, village or sanctuary. Each citizen was enrolled in one deme. Membership in a deme was hereditary and did not reflect actual domicile. Every Athenian citizen subsequently cited his deme as part of his name. Under Cleisthenes' reforms, many freedmen and metics were enrolled as citizens, and *zeugitai* became eligible for election as *strategoi*. See also chapter 4 for Cleisthenes' reforms.

In 451 BC a law restricted citizenship to Athenian parentage on both sides, and in the early 4th century BC marriage to a noncitizen (a foreigner) became illegal. *Atimia* was the loss of civic rights, either temporarily or permanently, as punishment for an offense: the citizen was stripped of political rights and could not speak in a law court.

SPARTA

From early on, male Spartan children underwent a harsh system of education (*agoge*) and lived communally from the age of seven (see chapter 3). At the age of 20, they were eligible for election to *syssita*; these were men's clubs that formed the basis of Spartan social and military life. They could live in their own home but had to eat communally in the *syssita*. These male citizens were the warrior or hoplite class, regarded as *homoioi* (literally, equals). Some citizens were excluded, such as those who had failed their military training or were defeated in war. Citizens of Sparta were called Spartiates (*Spartiatai*), also classified as Lacedaemonians, along with the *perioikoi*. Each adult citizen was given an allotment of land (*kleros*) to be worked by helots, so that he could devote himself to public and military service. Particularly with the liberation of Messenia, many Spartan citizens became so poor that they were reduced to the status of *hypomeiones* (inferiors). There were also free noncitizens (*neodamodeis* and *mothakes*), such as those who had lost their citizenship and helots who had been freed for good military service.

A citizen had no rights in other cities, and so formal friendship (*xenia*) was made between the cities. Local citizens were appointed as *proxenoi* to look after the interests of citizens from states with which they had formal ties.

Women

Women were not regarded as citizens and had no political rights. They were legally under the care of their male relatives and played virtually no part in the political and social system, except for a religious function. Their role was primarily in the home, and at times even confined to their own quarters. In Sparta the family itself was devalued, and here women had far more rights and greater freedom than elsewhere. They were able to own land, which was illegal at Athens, and some aristocratic women exercised influence in politics, although only in a major way from the Hellenistic period. Women of the royal family in Macedonia could have immense power, and marriages were often arranged for military or political reasons. See also chapter 10.

Slaves

Imported slaves were common in many states. In Attica, where slaves may have been as numerous as free inhabitants, they served as a substitute for wage labor. Many free inhabitants owned at least one slave, with rich citizens owning large numbers. They could be freed and given the same status as metics. Other states such as Macedonia had no slaves. For slaves, see also chapter 10.

Serfs

In many states serfdom was common. In Attica serfs were called *hektemoroi* (sixth-part men), because they worked the land at a rent of one-sixth of their produce. They were not technically slaves but were semiservile peasants or serfs, possibly bound to landowners by debt. If they failed to pay their debts, serfs could be sold into slavery. Solon reformed their status by the *seisakhtheia* (shaking off the burdens), which canceled their debts. In Thessaly the land was owned by very few people who controlled many serfs called *penestai*.

Helots

Sparta conquered and colonized neighboring Messenia in the later 8th century BC. The land was shared out equally in *kleroi* amongst the Spartiates and was worked by the defeated Messenian population. Messenian helots (*heilotes*) spoke Greek and were serfs, not slaves owned by individual people. They were bound to the land and possibly had to surrender half their produce to their masters. They could be manumitted only by the state. They also provided lightly armed soldiers (also called helots) for the army. Every year the Spartan citizens formally declared war on the helots. In 464 BC a serious revolt of the helots began that lasted to 455 BC. In 369 BC the Messenian helots were liberated, depriving the Spartan citizens of their *kleroi* and the use of the helots. There was a similar system of helots in other areas such as Crete, where they may have been slaves.

Perioikoi

When city-states conquered neighboring territory, the inhabitants could be regarded as perioeci (*perioikoi*, dwellers round about)—free inhabitants but not citizens. This occurred in places such as Crete, Elis, Thessaly and Sparta. The *perioikoi* of the semiautonomous towns and villages around Sparta were classified as Lacedaemonians, along with the Spartiates. They provided troops for the Spartan army but did not undertake the same training as the Spartiates. They also conducted various trade and craft businesses since Spartiates were prohibited from such work by their devotion to military matters. Perioeci seem to have regarded their status as privileged.

Metics

In city-states about one-third of free inhabitants could be noncitizens, including those foreign residents who had acquired the status of metics (*metoikoi*, sing. *metoikos*). A large and often prosperous metic population resided at Athens. Though they enjoyed full civil rights, metics had no political rights and were not able to own land or houses in Attica or to legally marry citizens. They were obliged to pay an annual poll tax (*metoikion*) and to pay property tax (*eisphora*) at a slightly higher rate than citizens. They undertook the normal duties of citizenship, such as naval and military service and liturgies, but had little chance of becoming full citizens. Most metics at Athens engaged in commercial and industrial activities, based largely at Piraeus. Some metics were physicians, philosophers, sophists, orators and poets.

Numbers

Population estimates are beset with difficulties, and most information is for Athens where various kinds of citizen lists were maintained. In the 5th century BC there were about 45,000 adult male citizens in Athens, and about 30,000 in the 4th century BC. Other contemporary cities probably had about half this number or less. In Sparta the ratio between Spartan citizens and helots may have been one to seven, and the ratio between citizens and perioeci seems to have been equal. When land was divided amongst the Spartiates (possibly by Lycurgus or later), there were apparently 9,000 lots (*kleroi*), indicating 9,000 citizens. At the end of the Persian Wars (479 BC), there were about 8,000 full Spartan citizens. The number dropped dramatically in the following decades, probably through continuous warfare and the earthquake around 465/464 BC. By the battle of Leuctra (371 BC), the number of male citizens at Sparta seems to have been around 1,500, though 400 more died in that battle. By the end of the Hellenistic period, the free population of Alexandria was 300,000, but it is unclear if women and children were included in this figure.

GOVERNMENT

Many city-states had a king, council and assembly, although over time the type of government changed.

Types of Government

MONARCHY

The earliest type of known government is monarchy (*basileia*), rule by kings, often with a council of advisers surrounding the king. It dates to the Dark Age and earlier, but in many places may have been more an aristocracy than a hereditary monarchy. Evidence for a hereditary kingship exists for some states, such as Corinth, Messenia, Sparta and Sicyon, but the monarchy virtually disappeared in the 8th century BC, evolving into an aristocracy.

At Sparta a hereditary dyarchy (rule by two kings) survived. It may have originated from two separate communities that had combined by agreement. There was often friction between the two kings, especially over succession. The kings commanded the army (not the navy) in war, although occasionally the Spartans chose other commanders. They also held certain judicial powers and enjoyed some privileges, though there were no palaces, and they were expected to eat communally with the other Spartiates.

Macedonia also had a hereditary monarchy, dating from c. 650 BC, with Perdiccas I being the first recorded Temenid king from Argos in the Peloponnese. The Macedonian kings were also the military leaders. There is no evidence for a Council of Elders, but instead the king had various advisers: *hetairoi* (Companions), *philoi* (Friends) and *hegemones* (Commanders). The *hetairoi*, who were probably aristocrats, served as advisers, performed important military functions, and rode in the elite cavalry (Companion Cavalry). The sons of leading Companions became Royal Pages (*basilikoi paides*). Numerous monarchies were established throughout Alexander the Great's Empire in the late 4th century BC, including the Ptolemies in Egypt and the Seleucids in Asia.

SATRAPY

Persian provincial governors were called satraps, in effect vassal kings. Alexander the Great preserved this system of government by satraps in his newly conquered territories. Satraps were responsible for collecting tribute, as under the former Persian system, although in larger satrapies separate officials were in charge of taxation. In Egypt he placed a nomarch in charge of civil administration.

ARISTOCRACY

"The rule of the best," originally the nobles, seems to have been the prevalent method of rule in the Dark Age and earlier. In the poleis the aristocrats replaced the monarchy, if one had existed. They formed the knights or cavalry (*hippeis*), owned most of the land and ruled the city-states through a council. After the 8th century BC, they lost their power due to changing military tactics—strength and superiority in war no longer lay with them, but with the hoplite soldiers. New sources of wealth also enabled more people to acquire the same status as the old aristocracy, who instead became the oligarchy. The overthrow of the aristocracy usually led to the establishment of a tyranny.

TYRANNY

A common form of monarchical government in the 7th and 6th centuries BC was rule by tyrants ("Age of the Tyrants"). The word *tyrannos* is non-Indo-European, probably of eastern origin and meaning "king." The tyrants were often wealthy and ambitious leaders, who seized power unconstitutionally, usually by overthrowing oppressive aristocratic governments. With the wealth of a city at their disposal, many tyrants were patrons of the arts and of festivals. Rule by tyrants occurred in many of the major city-states, particularly near the Isthmus of Corinth, including Corinth, Megara, Sicyon, Athens, Mytilene, Miletus and Samos. Tyrants included Cypselus, Periander, Polycrates, Cleisthenes, Peisistratus and Pheidon. The last tyrants of this period were Theron, Gelon and Hieron in Sicily. Thessaly, Boeotia and Sparta never had tyrannies, and Athens avoided one until the mid-6th century BC. From the 5th century BC, the concept of tyranny implied a reign of terror and the worst form of government, and tyrannies usually fell to oligarchies. The later tyrants in Asia Minor and Sicily were military dictators and forerunners of a new age of monarchy.

An *aisymnetes* (pl. *aisymnetai*) was a type of tyrant or dictator, such as Pittacus of Mytilene, elected for life or a specified period by a city-state in a time of crisis. Magistrates in some city-states were also called *aisymnetai*.

OLIGARCHY

The "rule of the few" developed from the old aristocracies, with wealth not birth as the deciding factor. Particularly when tyrannies were overthrown, political power was still with a minority of wealthy people. Although many full citizens were present in an oligarchy, they still did not have full political rights (such as voting). The oligarchic system was a common form of constitution, although it could differ from state to state. The political power of the oligarchs was usually vested in a council, such as the Areopagus.

The number of oligarchs could be limited to a fixed total. In 411 BC the Four Hundred was an extremist revolutionary oligarchic council established to rule Athens and overthrow the democrats. When the council of the Four Hundred was overthrown, an oligarchic council of Five Thousand was instituted (the franchise being extended to 5,000 citizens). In 410 BC full democracy was restored. At the end of the Peloponnesian War (404 BC), the oligarchs again controlled Athens. Thirty oligarchs were elected to draw up a new constitution, but they seized power and set up a new council under their control. A reign of terror ensued under these "Thirty Tyrants," but they were deposed by moderate oligarchs in 403 BC. Full democracy was restored later that year.

DEMOCRACY

Demokratia (rule of the people) started with Solon in Athens. Democracy at Athens meant that every full citizen had the right to be a juror, vote in the Assembly and be elected to any state office. The word "democracy" had not been invented by the time of Cleisthenes (late 6th century BC). *Eunomia* (good order) was replaced with the word *isonomia*, meaning "equal order" or political equality. This was the first word to indicate democracy. In the time of Pericles, the word *demokratia* replaced the word *isonomia* to describe the political status of Athens, incorporating ideas of law, freedom and equality. There was no word for politician, but in 4th-century Athens they were referred to as "orators and generals." In a democracy the people in the assembly made the decisions, which were proposed and carried out by magistrates and the council. The people also acted as jurors in law courts.

Prehistoric Government

The earliest known political system in the Greek world was centered on the palaces of Crete and later the mainland. Operating independently, each palace center seems to have controlled the surrounding countryside. Clay tablets reveal that the palaces were centers for the reception and storage of produce, and that they probably housed a major official. Linear B texts from Mycenaean palace sites show that the *wanax* was the most important figure in the state (possibly the king), followed by a *lawagetas*. The palaces, however, were not necessarily the headquarters of a ruler, and the earliest form of government may not always have been a monarchy. The term *basileus* (pl. *basileis*) found in later texts may mean a hereditary aristocrat rather than a king. In Homer the top of society consisted of elite warriors called heroes, who were chieftains (*basileis*) of one or more villages.

Poleis

In the Archaic and Classical periods the Greek world was divided into a number of sometimes very small self-governing independent states called in Greek *poleis* (sing. *polis*, city), which increased in number due to colonization. A polis consisted of a city surrounded by countryside. The population lived in the countryside and in the city. The political system (or politics) was actually the membership, organization and function of a polis undertaken only by male citizens, and the government of the polis was concentrated entirely in the city. After the conquests of Alexander the Great in the late 4th century BC, the poleis lost much of their autonomy.

The governments of the hundreds of city-states were not standardized. They usually started with monarchy (or aristocracy), then tyranny, and then democracy or oligarchy. Usually each polis had a council, assembly and magistrates, with a public gathering place (agora). In tribal areas of Greece, the *ethnos* (tribe) was the main form of social organization, rather than the polis. See also chapter 4 for poleis and chapter 6 for towns in general.

Athens

The government of Athens originally consisted of a king, a council of advisers and probably an assembly. The king was replaced by archons, and the council (Areopagus) was later joined by a second council (known as the *boule*). In Attica, Cleisthenes undertook extensive political reform in the late 6th century BC, breaking the power of the aristocratic families. Each deme formed the local administrative unit, with a local government and responsibility for

maintaining citizen lists; its chief official was the *demarkhos*. Cleisthenes also created (or reformed) the boule, and subordinated its role and that of the Areopagus to that of the *ekklesia* (Assembly). The government of Athens in the 5th and 4th centuries BC had much influence on other city-states and is most well known. See also chapter 4 for Cleisthenes' reforms.

Sparta

Sparta became a warrior state, with two kings, five annually elected ephors, a council of elders (*gerousia*) and an assembly of the citizens (*apella*). The inhabitants had three types of recognized status—citizens of Sparta (Spartiates), *perioikoi* (noncitizens from surrounding villages) and helots from Messenia.

Boeotia

From about the 6th century BC a federal system existed in Boeotia, but this Boeotian Confederacy was disbanded after it had sided with the Persians in the early 5th century BC. In 447 BC Boeotia reconstituted the federal oligarchic constitution amongst its various cities. It was the first type of federal government. There were 11 poleis, some incorporating smaller settlements. Each possessed a local boule (council), which varied in size according to the size of population. The boule was split into four, so that only one-quarter of the councillors sat at any one time. For the federal government there were also 11 wards (which did not equate exactly with the poleis; for example, Thebes comprised four wards). Each ward supplied one magistrate (*boiotarkhos*), as well as 60 councillors for the federal Council of 660. The Council met on the Cadmea of Thebes. When Thebes was destroyed the federal system was again reconstituted but largely for religious purposes.

Councils, Assemblies and Magistrates

COUNCIL

The boule was originally a council of nobles advising the king. In an aristocracy and oligarchy it was the most powerful body, but it was subordinate to the assembly in a democracy. The councillors were *bouleutai*.

In Athens the boule was originally the council known as the Areopagus, but it was replaced by a second boule in the 6th century BC (possibly by Solon, but reformed by Cleisthenes at the end of the century). This new boule at first consisted of 400 male citizens (Council of Four Hundred), 100 from each of the four traditional tribes. From the time of Cleisthenes it consisted of 500 male citizens over 30 years old (Council of Five Hundred), 50 from each of the 10 new tribes (*phylai*). They were appointed annually by the demes of Athens and Attica in proportion to the deme population size (between 1 and 22 per deme). They could not serve more than twice in their lifetime. After the early 4th century BC, the number of councillors varied, and by the 4th century AD there were 300. The boule was originally elected and unpaid, but from c. 450 BC the councillors were chosen by lot and were paid subsistence rates. They were paid from c. 411 BC, at a rate of five obols a day in the late 4th century BC.

During one-tenth of the year the 50 representatives from each of the 10 tribes served as a group of presidents (*prytaneis*) or an executive committee of the boule. This period of time was known as a prytany (*prytaneia*)—anything between 34 and 39 days in length. Each day one person out of the 50 was chosen by lot to be president (*epistates*) of any meetings of the boule and also chairman of the Assembly. The boule met daily except on festivals and unlucky days. During the oligarchic revolution at Athens (411–404 BC), the boule was replaced by oligarchic councils, but was subsequently restored and continued into the Roman period. From the late 4th century BC *proedroi* (chairmen) instead of *prytaneis* presided over the boule.

The council prepared all proposals (*probouleumata*) for the Assembly and implemented decisions of the Assembly (which were delegated to boards of officials). It also received embassies and undertook the everyday affairs of the state, such as controlling public finance and administering public buildings. It was responsible for certain religious cults and sacrifices and had some judicial functions. The bouleuterion was the council chamber, where the boule normally met (fig. 1.14). A meeting and feasting hall for the *prytaneis* was next to the new bouleuterion at Athens (built 5th century BC), called the tholos (rotunda) because of its circular shape.

AREOPAGUS

The council of aristocratic advisers that originally advised the king in Athens was known simply as the council (*boule*). It came to be known as the Areopagus, as it sometimes met on the *Areios pagos* (hill of Ares), just west of the Acropolis (fig. 4.7). As the monarchy declined the Areopagus became more powerful, and by the 7th century BC it was the main body of government and was responsible for murder trials. It was composed entirely of ex-archons, who were Eupatridae (*Eupatridai*), the aristocracy of Athens. The Eupatridae may have been a hereditary ruling class, although it could just refer to "nobles." The Areopagus had a membership of about 200–300 citizens.

In the late 6th century BC Solon reformed the constitution, and any wealthy person could be an archon. After a year of office, these people joined the Areopagus, so that the power of the Eupatridae was gradually broken. Solon may also have created the second council (boule), which was reformed by Cleisthenes. The Areopagus remained a powerful body until the Persian Wars, but its powers were restricted by Ephialtes in 462 BC, after which it retained jurisdiction only in homicide and administration of sacred property. The Areopagus still existed in the 4th century AD, with a membership of 31 chosen by the Roman proconsul.

GEROUSIA

The *gerousia*, a council of elders (*gerontes*), was the only council at Sparta. Its 30 members included two kings and 28 *gerontes* who had to be over 60 years of age and from certain aristocratic families. These elders were elected for life in a similar way to ephors, although later the office was annual. Little is known of the precise functions of the *gerousia*, although it did try cases involving the kings, exile, death or *atimia* (loss of civic rights), and it probably prepared proposals for the assembly (*apella*) and could veto decisions of the *apella*. City councils in Hellenistic towns of Asia Minor were also called *gerousiai*.

ASSEMBLY

The assembly was called an ecclesia (*ekklesia*). It was the ultimate ruling body in most Greek poleis. In some states it was called a *halia*, *haliaia*, *agora* or *apella*. An assembly was open to all male citizens of a polis, although membership could be subject to qualifications such as age and wealth. Most assemblies met in the agora, where they considered and decided upon foreign policy, military and financial issues, and legislation.

The Assembly of Athens changed its character with the development toward democracy, and it became the main political body there. All adult male citizens over 18 years of age were entitled to attend, speak and vote. Attendance was normally over 5,000 in the 5th century BC. It usually met on the Pnyx, which was a low hill west of the Acropolis (fig. 4.7). This could hold about 6,000—not the entire male citizen population. From c. 403 BC the Pnyx was remodeled and could house about 6,500. There is no evidence for seats. From the late 4th century BC, the Assembly met in the theater of Dionysus, which had seats. Meetings also took place in the agora if a ballot was required. Voting was usually by a show of hands, or by pebbles (*psephoi*) as ballots.

Meetings of the Assembly were summoned by the boule. By the 4th century BC there were four regular meetings in each prytany (40 per year), with extra meetings if necessary. Payment for attendance was introduced after 400 BC. Initially one obol per meeting, the fee reached six obols by 327 BC, with nine obols for the main meeting in each prytany.

The Assembly considered business that had been prepared by the boule, and no decree (*psephisma*) or law (*nomos*) could be passed without prior deliberation (*probouleusis*) before the boule. The agenda for each meeting was partly dictated by law, with several routine issues coming up regularly, such as food supply, defense of the state and religious matters. It had the right to depose magistrates and generals. From the 4th century BC, laws and decrees were separated. Laws were revised by *nomothetai* (lawgivers), while the Assembly could only issue decrees (*psephismata*) that were in accordance with the established law. Indictments were made for proposing decrees contrary to law (*graphe paranomon*).

Leading figures became dominant in the Assembly and could wield much influence, such as Pericles who was elected *strategos* for many successive years. The death of Pericles led to the rise of demagogues, who were usually wealthy and aristocratic, but who introduced a populist style of oratory.

At Sparta and elsewhere there was a festival of Apollo called *Apellai*. At Sparta people from the

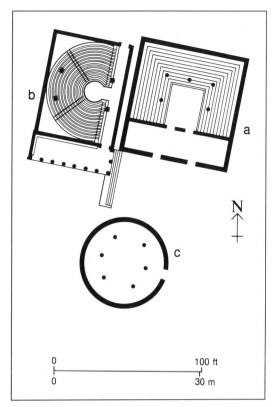

Fig. 1.14 Simplified plan of: a. old bouleuterion (subsequently became the metroon); b. new bouleuterion; and c. tholos, situated on the west side of the agora at Athens.

surrounding countryside gathered for this monthly festival, after which an assembly of Spartiates was held, now termed the *apella*. From the 5th century BC the meetings were presided over by one of the ephors. The *apella* could not initiate proposals, but decided on proposals from the *gerousia*. It could elect ephors and members of the *gerousia*; appoint military commanders; decide on disputed royal successions, peace, war and treaties; and approve the emancipation of helots. It also had to approve any proposed changes in the law. The members of the *apella* did not include all the Spartan citizens, as there were also birth and wealth qualifications.

Voting

The assembly at Sparta (the *apella*) usually voted by shouting or acclamation (*boa*), and very rarely by division. The most common method of voting in city-states (such as in the Athenian Assembly) was by a show of hands (*kheirotonia*), which was estimated; pebbles (*psephoi*) were used if a secret ballot was required. Sortition or lot (*klerosis*) was a method of choosing magistrates in many democratic city-states; it was introduced for choosing archons at Athens in 487/486 BC.

Ostracism

This was a method of banishing prominent citizens for 10 years from Attica without confiscation of property or loss of political rights. The people voted whether an ostracism (*ostrakophoria*) should be held. It took place without debate in the agora under the supervision of the archons and the boule. A citizen wrote the name of the person he wished to banish on a potsherd (*ostrakon*, fig. 1.15). It seems that if more than 6,000 ostraka were cast, the man with the largest vote

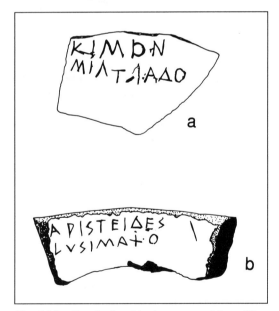

Fig. 1.15 Ostraka found in the agora at Athens. The names inscribed on potsherds are a. Kimon (Cimon), son of Miltiades, ostracized in 461 BC; b. Aristeides (Aristides), son of Lysimachus, ostracized in 482 BC.

was banished within 10 days for 10 years. Alternatively, banishment may have occurred only if at least 6,000 ostraka had been cast against one man.

Ostracism may have been introduced by Cleisthenes in 508/507 BC, although it was not used until 487 BC, and only sparingly from 482 BC. Those ostracized include Hipparchus (a relative of the tyrant Hippias) in 487 BC, Megacles (486 BC), Xanthippus (484 BC), Aristides (482 BC), Themistocles (c. 470 BC), Cimon (461 BC) and Thucydides (443 BC). The last person to be ostracized was Hyperbolus (c. 416 BC), after which the system fell into disuse, as *graphe paranomon* was a more effective way of attacking politicians.

Over 7,000 ostraka have been found in excavations in the agora and Kerameikos, some with names of unknown politicians. Ostracism also took place in Argos, Megara and Miletus, while at Syracuse there was a method called petalism, because names were written on olive leaves (*petala*).

Magistrates

Magistrates were usually elected annually and were not eligible for reelection; instead they often became life members of the city-state's council. In a democracy magistrates had no real political power, only an executive role, and were obliged to carry out decrees of the people. There could be hundreds of different magistrates and officials in a city-state, many serving on boards of three, five, 10 or more men. Many officials such as finance officers were elected and received no pay, but lower officials received salaries. Candidates for office in Athens were subject to prior scrutiny (*dokimasia*) to ensure eligibility, and on leaving office they were subject to review (*euthyna*) by the accountants (*logistai*).

In the Hellenistic period, magistrates were paid professionals; the highest posts were held by Greeks and the lower posts by natives. A hierarchical, bureaucractic system existed, especially in Egypt.

ARCHONS

Archons (*arkhontes*, rulers) were holders of the highest magistracies in city-states in central

Greece, including Athens, and they had wide executive and judicial duties. When Athens ceased to be a monarchy (possibly 11th century BC), the religious, military and judicial duties of the king were shared among three archons: the *arkhon basileus* (king archon), *arkhon eponymos* (eponymous archon) and the *polemarkhos* (polemarch). The archon basileus assumed the king's duties, was responsible for some religious ceremonies and presided over the Areopagus. The polemarch's original function was to command the army, but this power was lost to the *strategoi* after 487 BC, when archons were appointed by lot. Instead, the polemarch assumed certain religious functions and legal duties concerning non-Athenian citizens. The name of the eponymous archon was used to date the year. Until 487 BC he was the principal magistrate and nominal head of state. His legal duties were extensive, and he was also responsible for the Panathenaea and Dionysia festivals.

Archons in Athens may have originally been elected for life from the aristocracy, but there is evidence to suggest that their terms were eventually reduced to 10 years, and then to one year from 682 BC. Later, the post of archon could be held only once. All ex-archons became members of the Areopagus for life. The number of archons was increased, with the addition of six junior archons called *thesmothetai*, who were originally judicial officials. Archons were originally elected from the Eupatridae, but from the time of Solon the magistracy was open to other wealthy citizens. This system failed, and political factions (*hetairiai*) developed in different parts of Attica, with the formation of the Pedieis (plainsmen), Paraloi (coastmen) and later the Hyperakrioi or Diakrioi (hillmen). Eventually, this led to the tyranny of Peisistratus, which lasted until the late 6th century BC.

From 487 BC archons were chosen annually by lot since they were no longer politically important. Their number was increased to 10, with the addition of a secretary of the *thesmothetai*, possibly as part of the reforms of Cleisthenes. Archon lists began to be published from 683 BC, although there is doubt about the accuracy of dates before 594/593 BC. *Anarkhia* was the term given to a year when no archon was elected because of conflict. In Macedonia a deputy was appointed as ruler (*arkhon*) when the king went abroad to campaign.

STRATEGOI

From 501/500 BC a board of 10 generals (*strategoi*, sing. *strategos*) was elected by the Assembly from each of the new tribes at Athens, which must have reduced the power of the polemarch. Originally, *strategoi* were probably a board of military advisers, but from 487 BC they replaced the polemarch as military commanders. *Strategoi* also acquired importance as political leaders, particularly in the Assembly. They also seem to have been able to attend meetings of the boule. They were elected annually and could be reelected immediately. From the 4th century BC they were apparently professional soldiers who took little part in politics. In the Hellenistic period *strategoi* were officials with extensive military and political power in the Aetolian and Achaean Confederacies. In Egypt a *strategos* was the governor of a district (*nomos*), assisted by many officials.

EPHORS

Ephor (pl. *ephoroi*) was the name given to a magistrate in several Dorian states, particularly Sparta. Ephors may have originally been servants of the king. By at least the late 5th century BC, there was a board of five ephors at Sparta, elected annually by the *apella*. They were not eligible for reelection. The senior ephor gave his name to the year. Ephors traditionally controlled the conduct of the two kings, settled disputes between them and even prosecuted them before the *gerousia*. On campaigns a king was accompanied by two ephors. They presided over the *gerousia* and *apella*, and negotiated foreign treaties and received foreign envoys. In the 5th and 4th centuries BC they undertook much everyday state business. The office survived to at least AD 200.

BOEOTARCH

From 447 BC Boeotia reconstituted its federal type of government. There were 11 wards, each of which supplied one magistrate (*boiotarkhos*, leader of the Boeotians). These boeotarchs served as executive magistrates and as military commanders.

TAGOS

The *tagos* was the chief magistrate of Thessaly, a civil and military leader. At times the *tageia* (office of *tagos*) was left vacant, and it ceased to exist when a new Thessalian Confederacy was formed c. 369 BC. After this time the chief magistrate was an archon.

LAW

Lawmaking

Law and justice were essential elements of the polis, and each city made its own laws, many of which were probably similar. Most information about law derives from Classical Athens, although generally evidence is lacking.

The most common word for law in the 5th century BC was *nomos*, while *eunomia* meant law and order. In the Archaic Age, law was removed from the control of the aristocrats by the establishment of written law codes, which magistrates had to follow. Previously, laws were unwritten. These law codes were made by one lawgiver (*nomothetes*, pl. *nomothetai*), although later laws were made by the whole community. Lawgivers, some of whom were legendary, included Zaleucus, Charondas, Draco and Solon. Solon (eponymous archon at Athens in 594/593 BC) apparently rewrote all Draco's laws and established a complete code of laws that served as the basis of the Athenian legal system for at least 300 years. It covered all areas of the law (civil, criminal and religious) and was revised at the end of the 5th century BC.

Written laws were often inscribed on stone. Crete seems to have been the earliest place to have had unwritten laws and then to codify them in writing. The earliest surviving written law is from Drerus in Crete (late 7th century BC). Many colonies also had written law codes at an early date. The *axones* (axles) were vertically revolving shafts on which Draco and Solon's laws were written in Athens. They were originally wooden and were square or triangular in cross-section. They were on permanent display in the Prytaneum. Similar *axones* seem to have been used elsewhere. Athens ap-

pointed a commission of *nomothetai* in 410 BC to comprehensively revise its laws; the work was interrupted by the oligarchic revolution but was completed in 400/399 BC. The laws were inscribed on stone walls set up in the Stoa Basileos (office of the archon basileus). These new laws lasted until the overthrow of democracy by the Macedonians (322 BC).

The Athenian Assembly passed decrees that sometimes had the effect of laws. After 403/402 BC, laws and decrees were kept distinct, and revision of laws was undertaken by *nomothetai*. From the 4th century BC, if a decree contrary to established law was proposed in the Assembly, the proposer could be indicted on the charge of *graphe paranomon* (accusation of contravening the law). The proposed decree was suspended until the case was heard in court. *Graphe paranomon* was first recorded in 415 BC and was used frequently in the 4th century BC in place of ostracism.

Sparta never had a written law code. However, the earliest surviving political constitution known as the Rhetra or Great Rhetra (7th century BC) is from Sparta. It may have been the work of the lawgiver Lycurgus, and was allegedly brought back from Delphi as an oracle concerning the *gerousia*.

In Athens orators (*rhetores*) were not officeholders, but anyone who proposed decrees in the Assembly or boule, proposed laws before the *nomothetai* or supported action in the law courts. Professional orators such as Demosthenes were in effect politicians, who debated public cases before the law courts.

Law Courts

Jurisdiction is best documented at Athens, where it was performed by a variety of courts, councils and officials. Punishments were usually fines, exile, loss of civic rights or death. Imprisonment was rarely used, except for those awaiting trial or execution.

Originally, cases were tried by one or more archons (including the *thesmothetai*). The Areopagus tried cases of murder, arson and wounding. *Ephetai* tried cases of unintentional killing and killing of noncitizens; they consisted of a board of 51 citizens over the age of 50, and served under the presidency of the archon basileus. One advance in the administration of justice was Solon's introduction of a right of appeal against the decision of a magistrate.

Appeals were heard by a court of appeal known as the *heliaia*, which may have originally been the Assembly. This appeal court probably evolved into a jury court.

Trial by juries (instead of by magistrates) was instituted in the 5th century BC, with different size juries for different cases (anything from 200 to 1,000 or more jurors). By the 4th century BC odd numbers of jurors were used to avoid a tie in voting. Payment for jury service was introduced by Pericles to encourage volunteers for jury service; originally this was probably two obols a day, and before 425 BC it was increased to three. Almost all jurisdiction was taken over by these jury courts, which were known as dicasteries (*dikasteria*, sing. *dikasterion*). Magistrates could impose fines up to a certain limit, beyond which the case had to be tried before a jury. Archons and other magistrates had the responsibilty to act as chairmen of the courts in specific cases, but not to act as judges. For example, *strategoi* were involved in military cases, the polemarch in cases involving noncitizens, the archon basileus in religious cases and the *thesmothetai* in general cases. Many minor magistrates were involved in specific matters such as the markets. The *heliaia* was now the law court of the *thesmothetai*, not a court of appeal. The Areopagus conducted investigations leading to trials in the dicasteries, and the boule took over the role of the Areopagus in investigating illegal behavior of magistrates.

For most offenses in Athens there was no public prosecutor. Solon introduced two classes of action: a private case brought by the aggrieved person, often called a *dike* (case), and a public case brought by an individual on behalf of the entire community. The latter was often called *graphe*, as it probably once had to be put in writing to the *thesmothetai*. There was some abuse of the system, and it was often manipulated by political rivals and orators. Some public cases brought great financial reward to the accuser (prosecutor). Compensation could also be paid to the accuser in private cases. To encourage citizens to bring public prosecutions, financial reward was given if the case was successful. Penalties were also imposed if an accuser dropped a case after starting it, or if it failed to win one-fifth of the jurors' votes. These penalties discouraged misuse of the proceedings, particularly by sycophants (*sykophantai*) who frequently brought prosecutions for reasons such as personal reward, especially in the 5th century BC.

In murder cases the nearest male relative had to bring a prosecution. Before the main trial of a private case, an objection could be heard that the prosecution was inadmissible as it was contrary to the law. This procedure was known as *paragraphe* and was introduced c. 400 BC. Many private cases were subject to arbitration (*diaita*) prior to the jury trial. An official system of arbitration was introduced in 399 BC, using citizens over 60 years of age as arbitrators (*diaitetai*). If either litigant did not agree with the verdict of the arbitrators, the case could still go to jury trial.

In a trial the accuser and accused had the same amount of time to speak, measured by a water clock (*klepsydra*). Lawyers were not allowed to speak on their behalf, although a professional speechwriter could be employed. The accuser spoke first, then the accused. Witnesses could be called in the allotted time (not women, children or slaves). Written evidence of slaves was admissible if they had been tortured. The jury voted immediately without discussion or summing up. They voted by placing pebbles or shells (later bronze disks) in urns to indicate conviction or acquittal. In some cases they could also vote on the type of penalty.

READING

See also reading for chapters 2 and 4.

History

GENERAL

Biers 1992: dating and chronology; Buck 1979: history of Boeotia; Burl and Meiggs 1975; Cook 1969: on chronology; Fine 1983; Green 1973: useful illustrated summary; Hammond 1989b: history of Macedonia; Hammond and Scullard (eds.) 1970 passim; Sealey 1976: 700–338 BC, with much discussion on dating.

PREHISTORIC AND DARK AGE

Barber 1987: Bronze Age Cyclades; Dickinson 1994, 9–22, 295–309: chronology of Aegean prehistory; Drews 1993: end of Bronze Age; Finley 1981: Bronze Age; Foxhall and Davies (eds.) 1984: Trojan War; Hardy et al. (eds.) 1990: numerous papers on the volcanic eruption at Thera; Hardy and Renfrew (eds.) 1990: numerous papers on the various methods of dating Thera; James 1991: reassessment of the chronology of the Dark Age; Manning 1995: detailed analysis of Early Bronze Age chronology with immense bibliography; Popham 1994: collapse of Aegean civilization; Taylour 1983: Mycenaeans; Wardle 1994: Minoan and Mycenaean Crete and Greece; Warren and Hankey 1989: Bronze Age chronology, with extensive bibliography; Whittle 1994, 136–149: Neolithic.

ARCHAIC AND CLASSICAL

Andrewes 1956: on tyrants; Balcer 1995: major source on Persian conquests; Cartledge 1987: Spartan history 404–362 BC, with extensive bibliography; Crossland 1988: early migrations; Finley 1981: Bronze Age; Forrest 1988: Archaic Age; Grant 1987: 1000–494 BC; Green 1970a: Athenian Sicilian expedition; Green 1970b: 480–479 BC; Hamilton 1979: Corinthian War of 395 BC; Hooker 1980: Sparta; Hornblower 1983: 479–323 BC; Hornblower 1988: Classical period; Hornblower and Greenstock (eds.) 1984: Athenian Empire; Jeffery 1976: major source on Archaic Age; Krentz 1982: The thirty tyrants at Athens; Lazenby 1993: Persian Wars 490–479 BC; Smith 1990: Persian War and Ten Thousand; Wilson 1979: campaign at Pylos 425 BC.

HELLENISTIC

Borza 1990: very useful overview of Macedonia from prehistory to Alexander, with extensive bibliography; Bosworth 1988; Buckler 1989: Philip II, 362–346 BC; Grant 1990: Hellenistic period; Green 1990: substantial work on the Hellenistic period, with many references; Hammond 1991: Macedonia; Heckel 1992: Macedonian Empire; McShane 1964: Attalid Empire; Price 1988: Hellenistic period.

Population

Burstein 1988: class structure; Hammond and Scullard (eds.) 1970, 861–863: population numbers; Jeffery 1976: includes discussion of population in archaic city-states; Sallares 1991, 50–107: population size; Stanton 1994: demes and *trittyes*; Wiedemann 1988: slaves and serfs.

For women, see bibliography for chapter 10.

Government

Brenne 1994: ostracism; Cartledge 1987: includes government of Sparta; Grant 1988: monarchies and federalism; Jeffery 1976: includes discussion of types of government in Archaic Age; Hammond 1989b: includes discussion on government of Macedonia; Hammond and Scullard (eds.) 1970 passim: government types and officials; Murray 1988: forms of government; Perlman 1988: interstate relations; Samuel 1988, 195–241: Athenian archon and Spartan ephor lists; Sealey 1976: includes discussion on government of various states; Stanton 1990: sourcebook; Starr 1988: administration of states; Whitehead 1986: government of Attic demes.

Law

Bauman 1990: political trials; Cartledge et al. (eds.) 1990: various aspects of Athenian law; Gagarin 1986; Garner 1987: various aspects of Athenian law; Harrison 1968: family and property law of Athens; Harrison 1971: procedure in Athenian law; Jeffery 1976: includes discussion on lawmakers and constitutions; MacDowell 1978: law in Classical Athens; MacDowell 1986: Spartan law; MacDowell 1988; Sealey 1990: women and the law.

2

RULERS AND
LEADERS

BIOGRAPHIES

Until the late 8th century BC, it is difficult to be certain about the authenticity of people in Greek history. Some legends are based on fact, but others are mythological, fictional accounts. Before this period many of the legendary figures are Greek heroes such as Odysseus, who are mythological creations with some possible basis in truth.

Following are the main characters of Greek history, listed under the name by which they are most commonly known, followed by the transliteration of their original Greek name in italics (even where spelled the same).

ACHAEUS (*Akhaios*): Died 213 BC. He was a supporter of Seleucus II against Antiochus Hierax. In 223 BC he accompanied Seleucus III on an expedition to regain Seleucid territory lost to Attalus of Pergamum, but Seleucus III was murdered. Achaeus subsequently supported Antiochus III (successor of Attalus) as king, who appointed him governor of Seleucid Asia. In 220 BC Achaeus revolted and proclaimed himself king of Phrygia. In 216 BC Antiochus blockaded him in Sardis, and in 213 BC Achaeus was caught trying to escape and was executed.

AESCHINES (*Aiskhines*): Lived c. 390–c. 322 BC. Born in Athens, he became an orator and great rival of Demosthenes. Only three of his speeches survive. Faced with Macedonian expansion by Philip II, Aeschines was sent in 346 (possibly 348) BC by Eubulus to Arcadia to propose a Common Peace amongst Greek states, so that no state would ask the Macedonians for military support. When this failed, Aeschines and Demosthenes were sent to make peace with Philip II, which was agreed upon in 346 BC (Peace of Philocrates). Along with an associate Timarchus, Demosthenes prosecuted Aeschines in 346/345 BC for accepting bribes from Philip II. Aeschines retaliated with *Against Timarchus*, a speech in which he invoked a law forbidding those guilty of misconduct from addressing the Assembly. In 343 BC Demosthenes continued his prosecution of Aeschines (as if Aeschines had been solely responsible for negotiating the Peace); Aeschines responded with a speech of the same name (*On the False Embassy*) and was acquitted.

In 339 BC Aeschines was one of the Athenian representatives on the Amphictyonic Council, where he provoked Philip II to start the Fourth Sacred War. Aeschines was sent as part of the embassy to negotiate with Philip II after the battle of Chaeronea in 338 BC. In 336 BC Ctesiphon proposed that Demosthenes should be crowned for his services to Athens, and in 330 BC Aeschines prosecuted Ctesiphon for making an unconstitutional proposal (*Against Ctesiphon*), denouncing Demosthenes' policies. Demosthenes replied with *On the Crown* and won decisively. Aeschines retired to Rhodes, where he taught rhetoric until his death.

AGATHOCLES (*Agathokles*): Lived 361–289 BC. Tyrant and king of Syracuse 317/316–289 BC. Born at Thermae Himerae, he migrated to Syracuse with his father. He was involved as a mercenary in wars against Acragas and conquered the Bruttii tribe of southern Italy, but was exiled by the ruling oligarchy of Syracuse. He overthrew them in 317 BC and ruled as tyrant of Syracuse. He captured most of eastern Sicily, but the Carthaginians intervened and blockaded Syracuse. Agathocles escaped to Africa and attacked Carthage (310 BC). The Carthaginians agreed to a peace in 306 BC and Agathocles adopted the title of king in 305/304 BC. He later intervened in southern Italy and even occupied Corcyra c. 300/299 BC. He arranged marriage alliances with Pyrrhus and Ptolemy I. Just before his death (possibly by poisoning) he allegedly "restored Syracusan freedom."

AGESILAUS II (*Agesilaos*): Lived c. 444–360 BC. Eurypontid Spartan king from 399 BC. Son of Archidamus II and half brother of Agis II. He became king largely through the influence of the general Lysander. He campaigned against the Persians in Asia Minor in 396–395 BC, but this campaign was cut short by the Corinthian War. He won an unproductive victory at the battle of Coronea in 394 BC against the Athenians and Boeotians (related in Xenophon's *Hellenica*) and then fought elsewhere in Greece. His continued hostility to Thebes led to the battle of Leuctra in 371 BC which Sparta lost, thus ending its leadership of Greece. Hopes of financial gain led him to conduct an expedition against Persia in 361 BC, and he died at Cyrene on the homeward voyage during the winter of 361/360 or 360/359 BC.

AGIADS (*Agiadai*): This senior royal house at Sparta with ceremonial precedence over the Eurypontid house was named after the legendary Dorian king Agis. Its kings included Cleomenes I and II, Leonidas and Pausanias.

AGIS II (*Agis*): Eurypontid king of Sparta from 427/426 to 400/399 BC, this son and successor of Archidamus II commanded Peloponnesian forces in the Archidamian War in 426 and 425 BC. He campaigned against Argos and other enemies of Sparta in 418 BC, gaining victory at the battle of Mantinea and reestablishing Sparta's control over the Peloponnese. He made Decelea a permanent base in 413 BC at the start of the Decelean War, and collaborated with Lysander in blockading Athens in 405–404 BC. In 402/400 BC Agis II invaded Elis.

AGIS III (*Agis*): Eurypontid king of Sparta from 338 to 331/330 BC. Son of Archidamus III. During Alexander the Great's campaigns in Asia, he organized an army against Macedonian domination, using mercenaries from survivors of the battle of Issus and Persian money and gifts. His revolt was not widely supported, especially by Athens and Megalopolis. When besieging Megalopolis, Antipater's army attacked Agis III, who was killed (late 331 or early 330 BC).

AGIS IV (*Agis*): Lived 262–241 BC. Son of Eudamidas II, he was Eurypontid king of Sparta from 244 BC. He became king in a period of financial crisis, and his controversial methods of combating the crisis met with opposition. In 242 BC he deposed his co-king Leonidas II and the ephors. While Agis IV was absent helping Aratus of Sicyon against the Aetolians in the same year, Leonidas returned and seized power. Agis IV was executed.

AGYRRIUS or AGYRRHIUS (*Agyrrhios*): Floruit 403–389 BC. An Athenian democratic politician, particularly associated with public finance and business. In addition to restoring the *theorika*, he introduced and later increased payment for attendance at the Assembly. He spent several years in prison as a state debtor after charges of embezzlement.

ALCIBIADES (*Alkibiades*): Lived c. 450–404 BC. An Athenian politican from a noble family and later a military leader. His unscrupulous personal ambi-

tion caused the Athenians to disregard him at periods when his leadership was crucial. When his father Cleinias died at the battle of Coronea, Alcibiades was raised by his guardian Pericles and became a friend of Socrates. He was involved in the siege of Potidaea (432–430 BC) and the battle of Delium (424 BC). In 420 BC he was elected *strategos* and arranged an alliance between Athens and Elis, Mantinea and Argos (Peloponnesian states opposed to Sparta) that led to the collapse of the Peace of Nicias. This alliance was defeated by Agis II at the battle of Mantinea (418 BC). In 417 BC Hyperbolus tried to ostracize Alcibiades, but was himself ostracized.

In 416 (or 424) BC Alcibiades entered seven chariots for the Olympic Games, winning first, second and fourth places. Also in 416 BC, he supported an expedition to Sicily to assist Segesta against its rival Selinus. He was appointed to command the expedition with Nicias and Lamachus, but was recalled on an accusation of mutilation of the herms and other profanations at Athens. He escaped ship at Thurii and took refuge with the Spartans, providing them with military advice. In his absence he was condemned to death, and his property was confiscated. In 412 BC he accompanied a Spartan fleet to Ionia, but fled to Tissaphernes, the Persian satrap. The Athenian fleet at Samos appointed Alcibiades general, and he destroyed the Spartan fleet in 410 BC at the battle of Cyzicus. In 408 BC he returned to Athens and was elected *strategos* in 407 BC, but was later held responsible for the defeat of the Athenian fleet at Notium in 406 BC. In the summer of 406 BC he retreated to the Thracian Chersonesus. In 405 BC his advice before the battle of Aegospotami was ignored, and Athens was utterly defeated. In 404 BC Alcibiades fled to Phrygia where he was murdered, possibly through the influence of the Thirty Tyrants and Lysander.

ALCIDAS (*Alkidas*): A Spartan who was admiral in the early part of the Peloponnesian War. Due to his hesitation, he arrived too late to assist the revolt of the Mytilenean aristocrats against Athens in 427 BC, and in 426 BC he lost a naval battle against the Athenian and Corcyran fleets. He was sent to found the colony Heraclea Trachinia in 426 BC.

ALCMAEONIDAE or ALCMAEONIDS (*Alkmaionidai*): One of the leading Athenian aristocratic families prominent in politics. One

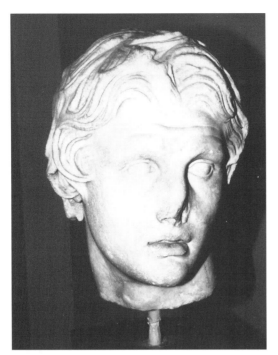

Fig. 2.1   Head of Alexander the Great.

early member, Megacles, was responsible for successfully besieging Cylon on the Acropolis c. 630 BC, but received a hereditary curse for the sacrilege, which was frequently invoked against the family in political disputes at Athens. His son Alcmaeon (*Alkmaion*) won the family and Athens' first victory at the Olympic Games in 592 BC. Alcmaeon commanded the Athenian forces in the First Sacred War (c. 590 BC). His son Megacles married the daughter of Cleisthenes (tyrant of Sicyon). As a leading rival of Peisistratus, Megacles spent some time in exile. His son Cleisthenes reformed the Athenian constitution, but was in turn exiled by the tyrant Hippias, returning in 510 BC. After c. 500 BC the family suffered decline, partly because of its pro-Persian tendencies. Pericles' mother was an Alcmaeonid, as was the mother of Alcibiades.

ALEUADAE (*Aleuadai*):   One of the leading aristocratic families of Thessaly whose leader Thorax supported Persia in 480 BC. After 404 BC the Aleuadae opposed the tyrants of Pherae and invited intervention from Macedonia. Philip II annexed Thessaly and divided it into tetrarchies in 342 BC.

ALEXANDER I or ALEXANDER OF EPIRUS (*Alexandros*):   King of Molossia in Epirus 342–330 BC. He was made king by his brother-in-law Philip II, in order to safeguard control of Epirus. Philip II was murdered at Alexander I's marriage celebrations to Cleopatra (Alexander the Great's sister). Alexander I made Epirus an important power united to Macedonia. From 334 BC he conquered much of southern Italy at the instigation of Tarentum, but was defeated at the battle of Pandosia (331/330 BC) and was murdered.

ALEXANDER I PHILHELLENE (*Alexandros*): King of Macedonia c. 495–452 BC. In 492 BC he submitted to Persia and served with the Persian forces under Xerxes in their invasion of Greece. At the same time he apparently assisted the Greeks and was admitted as a Hellene to the games at Olympia. He was the first king of Macedonia to enter Greek politics, and he attempted to hellenize his court. He invited Pindar and Bacchylides to his court and competed at Greek festivals. He took over Thracian territory, whose mines produced silver for the first Macedonian coinage. Cimon's conquest of the island of Thasos in 463 BC prevented Alexander's further expansion into Thrace.

ALEXANDER II (*Alexandros*):   King of Macedonia 370–368 BC. He intervened in Thessaly at the request of the Aleuadae, but a rebellion forced him to return to Macedonia. Pelopidas made an alliance with him, but shortly afterward Alexander was murdered.

ALEXANDER II (*Alexandros*):   King of Molossia in Epirus 272–c. 240 BC. Son of Pyrrhus of Epirus. In the Chremonidean War (c. 268–263/262 BC), Epirus was an ally of Athens against Macedonia. Alexander II invaded Macedonia when Antigonus II Gonatas was besieging Athens. Alexander was driven from Epirus (about 259 BC) but was restored by the Aetolians. He then conquered Arcarnania, sharing it with the Aetolians. On his death the Aetolians invaded his half of Arcarnania.

ALEXANDER III THE GREAT (*Alexandros*): Lived 356–323 BC. King of Macedonia 336–323 BC and of Persia 330–323 BC. Son of Philip II and Olympias of Epirus. One of his tutors (from 342 BC) was Aristotle. In 338 BC Alexander (fig. 2.1) led the Macedonian cavalry at the battle of Chaeronea, in which Athens and Thebes were defeated. When his father was murdered Alexander succeeded without opposition, but murdered Philip's baby son by his latest wife Cleopatra-Eurydice and later ordered the murder of his uncle Attalus. Alexander initially secured his position in Greece, including his northern borders. In 335 BC, false reports of his death led to revolts by some Greek states, especially Thebes, which Alexander ruthlessly suppressed, destroying Thebes. He left his general Antipater in control of the Greek states and proceeded in 334 BC to undertake his father's mission to attack Persia in punishment for the wrongs inflicted on Greece during the Persian Wars (fig. 2.2). He crossed into Asia with a force of about 43,000 men and 50 warships. At the battle of the Granicus River (near the Hellespont)

in 334 BC, he defeated Darius III and proceeded to liberate cities of Asia Minor such as Sardis, Ephesus, Miletus and Halicarnassus. He continued through Asia Minor and in November 333 BC he defeated Darius III at the battle of Issus. He refused Darius' favorable terms for peace, intending to conquer the entire Persian Empire.

The next year (332 BC) Alexander continued through Phoenicia, Palestine and Egypt, besieging and taking Tyre, so that Persia ceased to be a Mediterranean power. Early in 331 BC (April 6) he founded Alexandria on the Nile delta and visited the desert oracle of Zeus Ammon at Siwa. He left Egypt for Babylonia, and in November 331 BC he defeated the Persian army at the battle of Gaugamela east of the Tigris River. He then occu-

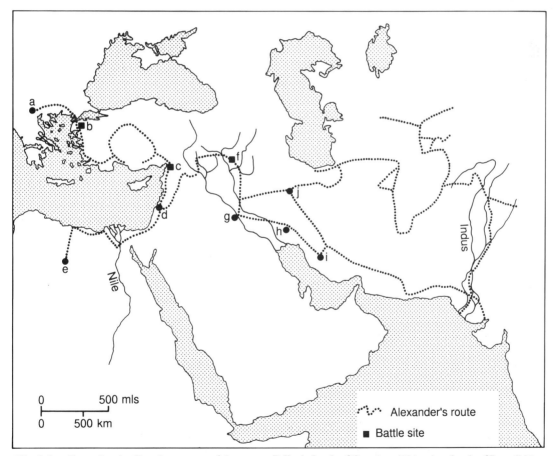

Fig. 2.2 Alexander the Great's conquests of the east: a. Pella; b. battle of Granicus (334 BC); c. battle of Issus (333 BC); d. siege of Tyre (332 BC); e. oracle at Siwa (331 BC); f. battle of Gaugamela (331 BC); g. Babylon; h. Susa; i. Persepolis; j. Ecbatana.

pied the Persian capitals of Babylon, Susa, Persepolis and Ecbatana, possibly not intending to destroy Persepolis (early 330 BC), which was the ritual center of Persia. Soon after, Darius III was murdered by Bessus (satrap of Bactria), and Alexander became ruler of Persia, even adopting Persian dress. He treated further resistance as rebellion.

From 330 to 327 BC Alexander pursued Bessus, subduing huge areas of Hyrcania, Aria, Drangiana, Bactria and Sogdiana, and crossing the Hindu Kush. In Sogdiana he eventually captured and killed Bessus. During this period, he suppressed a conspiracy against him (October 330 BC), murdered Cleitus (328/327 BC), which he bitterly regretted, and founded eight cities, all called Alexandria. In 328 BC he reached the farthest northeast boundary of the Persian empire (Jaxartes River—*Syr Darya*), where he founded Alexandria Eschate (the farthest). Early in 327 BC he captured and immediately married Roxane, daughter of a Bactrian aristocrat. Also in 327 BC there was apparently another plot to murder him (conspiracy of the pages), involving Callisthenes, the expedition's historian, who was imprisoned and executed.

In summer 327 BC Alexander began his Indian Expedition; he crossed the Indus in 326 BC and fought his last great battle at the Hydaspes (Jhelum) River against Porus, king of the Paurava. Alexander's horse Bucephalas died there. He advanced through the rest of the Punjab to the Hyphasis (Beas) River, where his army refused to proceed to the Ganges. It returned to the Hydaspes, and a huge fleet was constructed to transport the army down the Indus to subdue the people of southwest India. Here Alexander was nearly killed besieging Multan. In 325 BC he reached the Indus delta where he left the fleet with half the army, choosing a route through the waterless deserts of Baluchistan, with the rest of his army suffering great loss of life.

Alexander reached Susa in 324 BC and found misgovernment and disloyalty among his subordinates. He ruthlessly purged them, but there was imminent warfare in Greece. He forced his officers into marriages with Persian women, and his enrollment of Persians into the army caused a mutiny at Opis in 324 BC. He executed the ringleaders. It is possible that in 324 BC he requested the Greek cities to treat him like a god, and he may have believed in his own divinity. In autumn 324 BC his closest companion Hephaestion died, and Alexander later returned to Babylon. Here he fell ill and died on 10 June, 323 BC, possibly by poison or fever. He was buried at Alexandria, and his coffin was seen by the Roman emperor Augustus three centuries later.

Alexander extended the Greek language and customs across the eastern world, and the center of the Greek world in Hellenistic times shifted to Alexandria in Egypt. The main historical source for his campaigns is the *Anabasis* by Arrian, who drew on contemporary sources.

ALEXANDER IV (*Alexandros*): The posthumous son of Alexander the Great and Roxane; king of Macedonia 323–c. 311 BC, he became joint king with Philip III Arrhidaeus. Alexander was captured by Cassander in 316 BC and murdered in 311 BC or soon after, marking the end of the Argead dynasty.

ALEXANDER BALAS (*Alexandros*): Pretender to the Seleucid throne 150–145 BC after he defeated and killed Demetrius I Soter. He was supported by Attalus II of Pergamum, Rome and Egypt. In 150/149 BC he married Cleopatra Thea, daughter of Ptolemy VI. Ptolemy VI switched his support to Demetrius II Nicator (son of Demetrius I), who defeated and killed Alexander Balas in a battle in 145 BC, marking the beginning of the disintegration of the Seleucid Empire.

ALEXANDER OF CORINTH (*Alexandros*): Lived c. 290–c. 245 BC. Son of Craterus the Younger, succeeding him as *strategos* of Corinth and Euboea. He declared himself independent from Antigonus II Gonatas in 249 BC, calling himself king. He became an ally of the Achaean Confederacy.

ALEXANDER OF PHERAE (*Alexandros*): Tyrant of Pherae in Thessaly 369–358 BC. Nephew and successor of Jason. Most cities of Thessaly opposed Alexander, refusing to recognize him as *tagos*. He became allied with Athens to prevent Theban expansion, but was defeated by the Theban general Pelopidas at the battle of Cynoscephalae in 364 BC. A further defeat forced him to become a Theban ally. He was assassinated by his wife's brothers.

ALYATTES (*Aleuttes*): Fourth king of Lydia c. 610–560 BC and founder of the Lydian Empire. He continued his predecessor's efforts to conquer Greek Ionia, including Smyrna, which he destroyed in 600 BC, but eventually made peace with Miletus.

He sent offerings to Delphi. He was buried in a huge round-barrow tomb.

AMASIS (*Amasis*):   Egyptian pharaoh c. 569–c. 525 BC. His long reign was noted for its peace and prosperity. He encouraged the Greeks to settle at Naucratis and became an ally of several Greek states, including Lydia and Samos. Just after his death, Egypt was invaded by Persians.

AMYNANDER (*Amynandros*):   King of Athamania (between Macedonia and Aetolia) c. 210–c. 189 BC. He tried to mediate between Philip V and Aetolia in 209 BC. An ally of Rome in the Second Macedonian War, he became involved in the struggle between Greece and Rome. In 192–191 BC he became an ally of Antiochus III and of the Aetolians against Rome and Philip. He was driven from his kingdom by Philip but recovered it through Aetolian help in 189 BC and probably died soon afterward.

AMYNTAS (*Amyntas*):   A dynastic name in the Macedonian royal house, the most famous being Amyntas III, king of Macedonia c. 393 to 370/369 BC. He consolidated his kingdom, especially through diplomacy, and died a natural death. He was father of Philip II.

ANACHARSIS (*Anakharsis*):   A 6th-century BC Scythian prince who traveled to Greece. He was executed in Scythia for attempting to introduce the cult of Cybele. He allegedly despised all Greeks except the Spartans and was said to have been a guest of Solon at Athens and one of the Seven Sages.

ANAXILAS (*Anaxilaos*):   Tyrant of Rhegium from 494 BC, when he seized power, to 476 BC. He tried to control Zancle on the Sicilian side of the straits, but the people colluded with Hippocrates of Gela. Anaxilas expelled them and resettled Zancle with Messenians (and changed its name to Messana). In 480 BC he supported the Carthaginian invasion of Sicily, but the Carthaginians were defeated at the battle of Himera by Gelon. He made his peace with Hieron I, whom his daughter married.

ANDOCIDES (*Andokides*):   Lived c. 440–c. 390 BC. An early Attic orator from a wealthy family. He confessed to involvement in the mutilation of the herms in 415 BC and in profaning the Eleusinian Mysteries. He lost his civic rights and left Athens to trade as a merchant. He tried unsuccessfully to return to Athens in 411 and 410 BC, but returned with his civic rights restored under the general amnesty of 399 BC. He was one of the envoys sent to Sparta in 391 BC to try to negotiate peace in the Corinthian War. The terms were rejected by Athens, and Andocides went into exile. Three of his speeches survive: *On his Return*, *On the Mysteries* and *On the Peace*.

ANDRISCUS (*Andriskos*):   An adventurer from Adramyttium, he was a pretender to the Macedonian throne c. 153–148 BC, claiming to be Philip, son of Perseus and Laodice. The Seleucid king Demetrius I (brother of Laodice) handed Andriscus over to Rome, but Andriscus escaped and invaded Macedonia. He was eventually defeated by the Romans and executed.

ANDROTION (*Androtion*):   Lived c. 410–340 BC. An Athenian politician, he was a pupil of Isocrates and opposed Demosthenes and Eubulus' view of an alliance with Persia against Macedonia. He was sent on an embassy to King Mausolus of Caria during the Social War (357–355 BC), and in 355/354 BC he served on a committee to prepare war against Persia. He was accused in 354–353 BC of an unconstitutional proposal and was exiled to Megara where he wrote a history of Attica (*Atthis*) down to 343 BC in eight books.

ANTALCIDAS (*Antalkidas*):   Floruit 393/392 to c. 361 BC. He was a Spartan diplomat and general. He tried to end the war between Greece and Persia in 393/392 BC by surrendering the Greek cities to Persia. He negotiated further with Artaxerxes II in 388/387 BC. Sparta's enemies accepted this King's Peace (or Peace of Antalcidas) after Antalcidas blockaded the Hellespont, abandoning the Greek cities of Asia Minor to Persia. In c. 373 BC he was in Persia again, but his mission of c. 361 BC failed, and he committed suicide.

ANTIGONUS I ONE-EYED (*Antigonos Monophthalmos*):   Lived c. 382/381–301 BC. From a noble Macedonian family, he was a general of Alexander the Great, who appointed him satrap of Persia in 333 BC. In 320 BC Perdiccas was murdered, and Antigonus was appointed Macedonian *strategos* in Asia at the conference of Triparadeisus.

In 319 BC Antipater died, and until 301 BC Antigonus attempted to retake and rule the entire empire of Alexander the Great. In 315–311 BC a coalition of satraps fought against Antigonus, which left him ruler of a reduced area of Asia (fig. 1.10). Peace between the Successors in 311 BC lasted only a year. In 306 BC he proclaimed himself and his son Demetrius Poliorcetes as kings, as did other satraps in 305–304 BC. Antigonus was finally defeated and killed at the battle of Ipsus.

ANTIGONUS II GONATAS (*Antigonos Gonatas*): Lived c. 320–239 BC. King of Macedonia 277–239 BC. He was possibly called Gonatas because he was born at Gonnus, Thessaly. Son of Demetrius I Poliorcetes and grandson of Antigonus I. He was in charge of Demetrius' Greek possessions and assumed the title of king on Demetrius' death in 283 BC. In 277 BC Antigonus II gained control of Macedonia, after defeating around 20,000 invading Gauls near Lysimachia in the Chersonese. He became king, establishing the Antigonid dynasty. He reestablished Macedonia as a nation, to be ruled by his descendants. He was a philosopher, and many poets, philosophers and historians gathered at his court at Pella.

In 272 BC he joined Sparta to destroy Pyrrhus of Epirus who had invaded the Peloponnese. He reestablished his power as far as Corinth. Athens, Sparta and other states, supported by Ptolemy II, began the Chremonidean War against Antigonus (c. 268–263/262 BC). Athens fell to Antigonus in 262 BC, and he imposed a puppet government. He entered into renewed war (Second Syrian War) against Ptolemy II in 260–253 BC, entrusting Corinth to his half brother Craterus the Younger, who died c. 255 BC. Alexander of Corinth (son of Craterus) declared himself independent. Antigonus regained Corinth, but it was taken in 243 BC by Aratus of Sicyon, who united it with the anti-Macedonian Achaean Confederacy. Antigonus then supported the Aetolian Confederacy, which was a threat to the Achaean Confederacy, but the Aetolians concluded peace with the Achaeans in 241/240 BC.

ANTIGONUS III DOSON (*Antigonos*): The meaning of *Doson* is uncertain. Lived c. 263–221 BC, regent and king of Macedonia 229–221 BC, son of Demetrius the Fair. He became guardian to Philip V and married his widowed mother Queen Phthia-Chryseis. He defeated the Dardani (an

Illyrian tribe that had killed Demetrius II) in 229 BC, and in 228 BC he defeated the Aetolians and Thessalians, thereby recovering most of Thessaly. In 227 BC he mounted an expedition to Caria, probably directed against Ptolemy III, and reestablished Macedonian influence in eastern Greece and the Aegean. In 227/226 BC the Achaean Confederacy gained the support of Antigonus Doson against Sparta and Aetolia, in return for Acrocorinth. In 225–224 BC Antigonus Doson occupied Acrocorinth with a Macedonian garrison. In the winter of 224 BC he founded a league of allies (Hellenic League), and in the battle of Sellasia in 222 BC he crushed Cleomenes III (king of Sparta), who fled to Egypt. Antigonus Doson returned to Macedonia to expel the invading Illyrians and died in 221 BC, having burst a blood vessel in battle.

ANTIOCHUS I SOTER (*Antiokhos*, Savior): Lived 324–261 BC. Son of Seleucus I and Apama. He married his father's wife Stratonice in 294/293 BC and became Seleucid king in 281 BC, renouncing further campaigns in the west. Instead, he formed an alliance with Antigonus II Gonatas of Macedonia. During his reign Antiochus I concentrated on holding his eastern kingdom together, but lost territory in Asia Minor (partly in the First Syrian War against Ptolemy II), and many of his eastern satrapies seceded. After Alexander the Great, he was the greatest founder of cities. His greatest victory was the defeat of the invading Galatians c. 270 BC (Elephant Victory), after which he acquired the title *Soter*.

ANTIOCHUS II THEOS (*Antiokhos*, God): Lived c. 287–246 BC. Seleucid king from 261 BC. Younger son of Antiochus I Soter (his elder brother Seleucus may have been executed). In the Second Syrian War of 260–253 BC (in alliance with Macedonia) against Ptolemy II, he recovered territory lost by Antiochus I. He married Laodice I and c. 253 BC Berenice Syra (daughter of Ptolemy II). There was a bitter accession dispute on his death, with his eldest son Seleucus II becoming king.

ANTIOCHUS III THE GREAT (*Antiokhos*): Lived c. 242–187 BC. Younger son of Seleucus II, he became Seleucid king on the death of his elder brother Seleucus III in 223 BC. Antiochus suppressed revolts by his eastern governors and then undertook the recovery and expansion of Seleucid territories that had been lost by his predecessors. He attempted to conquer Syria and Palestine (in the Fourth Syrian War, 219–217 BC), but was defeated in 217 BC by Ptolemy IV at the battle of Raphia. He campaigned in the east (his *anabasis*) 212–206 BC: he acquired Armenia (212 BC), regained Parthia and Bactria (as vassal kingdoms) and reached India, emulating Alexander the Great. He returned to Antioch via Arabia in 205/204 BC, and adopted the title "Great" (*megas*). In alliance in 202 BC with Philip V of Macedonia to divide up Egypt's territory, he conquered Coele-Syria 202–195 BC (Fifth Syrian War), and crossed to Europe to recover Thrace. The Romans were alarmed, and despite lengthy negotiations, Antiochus III decided to reject offers of peace and invaded Greece in 192 BC. He was defeated by the Romans in the battle of Magnesia ad Sipylum in 189 BC. With the Peace of Apamea (188 BC), the Seleucid kingdom ceased to be a Mediterranean power. Antiochus returned to his eastern possessions and was murdered while robbing a temple.

ANTIOCHUS IV EPIPHANES (*Antiokhos*, God Made Manifest): Lived c. 215–164 BC. He was the third son of Antiochus III and was a hostage at Rome after the battle of Magnesia ad Sipylum (189 BC). He became Seleucid king in 175 BC. He invaded Egypt three times (170–168 BC, Sixth Syrian War) but was ordered to retreat by Rome. He attempted to hellenize the Jews, but instead his persecutions provoked Jewish nationalism, and a serious revolt erupted in 167 BC under Judas Maccabaeus. Also as a process of hellenization, Antiochus IV founded several eastern cities. He is reputed to have suffered from eccentricity or madness. He died of an illness at Tabae in Persis.

ANTIOCHUS V EUPATOR (*Antiokhos*, born of a noble father): Lived c. 173–162 BC. Son of Antiochus IV, he ruled through a regent for less than two years, and was executed in Antioch when his cousin Demetrius I Soter claimed the throne.

ANTIOCHUS VI EPIPHANES DIONYSUS (*Antiokhos*, God Made Manifest): Lived c. 148–138 BC. Son of Alexander Balas and Cleopatra Thea (daughter of Ptolemy VI). He was put forward as a candidate for the Seleucid throne in the revolt at Antioch against Demetrius II Nicator, but

was deposed (142 BC) and subsequently killed by the general Diodotus Tryphon.

ANTIOCHUS VII SIDETES EUERGETES (*Antiokhos*; called *Sidetes* because he had lived at Side, and *Euergetes* for benefactor): Lived c. 159–129 BC. Second son of Demetrius I Soter. He became Seleucid king in 139 BC when his brother Demetrius II Nicator was captured in Parthia. In 138 BC he married Cleopatra Thea. He defeated and killed the usurper Diodotus Tryphon at Antioch (late 138 BC), and reconquered Palestine (135–134 BC), but was eventually defeated and killed by the Parthians, losing the Seleucid territories in the east.

ANTIOCHUS VIII GRYPUS PHILOMETOR (*Antiokhos*; *grypos* means hook-nose, *Philometor* is "mother-loving"): Son of Demetrius II and Cleopatra Thea. Seleucid king 125–96 BC. He reclaimed the throne from the usurper Alexander II Zabinas in 123 BC (Zabinas ruled 128–123 BC), but faced a serious revolt from his half brother Antiochus IX from 114/113 BC, which lasted several years. He was assassinated by a minister.

ANTIOCHUS IX CYZICENUS PHILOPATOR (*Antiokhos*, father-loving; also called *Cyzicenus* because he had lived at Cyzicus): Died 95 BC. Seleucid king 114–95 BC. Son of Antiochus VII Sidetes and Cleopatra Thea. From 114/113 BC he revolted against his half brother Antiochus VIII Grypus and captured coastal territories. His attempt to gain sole power after the assassination of his half brother was stopped by Antiochus Grypus' five sons, and he was killed by Seleucus I.

ANTIOCHUS HIERAX (*Antiokhos*, the Hawk): Lived c. 263–226 BC. Second son of Antiochus II and Laodice I. During the Third Syrian War (246–241 BC) he became joint ruler with his brother Seleucus II, and ruled Asia Minor. He refused to renounce his powers and prevented Seleucus II from regaining Asia Minor (War of the Brothers, 239–236 BC). He allied himself with traditional enemies of the Seleucids—Pontus, Bithynia and the Galatians (Gauls). This alliance brought him into conflict with Attalus I of Pergamum (230–228 BC), who drove him from Asia Minor. He was murdered in Thrace.

ANTIPATER (*Antipatros*): Lived 397–319 BC. Macedonian general of Philip II, then of Alexander the Great. He suppressed the revolt of Agis III and was left in charge of Macedonia when Alexander campaigned in the east. Antipater suppressed the revolt of Athens and its allies (Lamian War, 323–322 BC), with Athens surrendering after the battle of Crannon. His death led to the disintegration of Alexander the Great's empire.

ANTIPATER ETESIAS (*Antipatros*): King of Macedonia for 45 days in 279 BC, his rule coinciding with the Etesian Winds after which he is named. He was grandson of Antipater and nephew of Cassander. He was killed or expelled by Antigonus II Gonatas.

ANTIPHON (*Antiphon*): Lived c. 480–411 BC. An Attic orator, whose speeches are the earliest surviving. He composed speeches for others to deliver and seldom spoke in public himself. In 411 BC he was responsible for the oligarchic revolution in Athens and for establishing the Four Hundred. When overthrown, he was tried and condemned to death, after delivering a brilliant speech in his defense. Three speeches for murder trials survive: *The Murder of Herodes*, *On the Choreutes* and *Against a Stepmother*. Also surviving are the *Tetralogies*, three sets of rhetorical exercises for murder trials. He is unlikely to have been the sophist known as Antiphon.

ANYTUS (*Anytos*): Lived 5th–4th centuries BC. Athenian naval commander who failed to hold Pylos from the Spartans in 409 BC. In 403 BC he helped overthrow the Thirty Tyrants and served as *strategos*. In 399 BC he was one of three accusers of Socrates.

APOLLONIUS: Finance minister (*dioeketes*) of Egypt (for Ptolemy II and III) for 20 years from 262 BC. His secretary was Zenon. Apollonius owned a large estate at Philadelphia in the Fayum, a merchant fleet and business interests in Egypt and the Levant.

ARATUS OF SICYON (*Aratos*): Lived 271–213 BC. Military leader and statesman. He was son of the deposed Sicyonian Cleinias and was brought up in exile in Argos. He regained Sicyon in 251 BC, uniting it with the Achaean Confederacy for defense against Macedonia. He took Corinth from the Macedonians in 243 BC, and supported the Achaean Confederacy against Macedonia. When defeated by Cleomenes III of Sparta c. 233 BC, however, he opened negotiations with Macedonia. He fought the Social War against Aetolia with Philip V (220–217 BC), but resisted Philip V's anti-Roman policy.

ARCESILAUS I (*Arkesilaos or Arkesilas*): Lived c. 591?–c. 575? BC. Second king of the Battiads who ruled the colony of Cyrene in north Africa.

ARCESILAUS II THE CRUEL (*Arkesilaos or Arkesilas*): Fourth king of the Battiads who ruled Cyrene after 570 BC. He quarreled with his brothers, who seceded and founded Barca. He was defeated by the Libyans and murdered by his brother Learchus.

ARCESILAUS III (*Arkesilaos or Arkesilas*): Sixth king of the Battiads who ruled Cyrene before 525 BC until after 522 BC. He refused to accept a monarchy stripped of its powers and tried to establish a demagogic tyranny. He went into exile, but later returned and conquered Cyrene. He was eventually assassinated at Barca.

ARCESILAUS IV (*Arkesilaos* or *Arkesilas*): Eighth king of the Battiads who ruled Cyrene from before 462 BC to c. 440? BC. He won a victory in the chariot races at the Pythian Games (462 BC), an event celebrated by Pindar. He was overthrown by a democratic revolution in 440 BC, which ended his dynasty.

ARCHELAUS (*Arkhelaos*): King of Macedonia 413–399 BC. An illegitimate son of Perdiccas II, he murdered contenders for the throne. He increased Macedonia's military strength, moved his capital from Aegae to Pella, adopted the Persian coin standard and invited Greek artists and poets to his court. He reconquered Pydna and parts of Thessaly.

ARCHIDAMUS II (*Arkhidamos*): Eurypontid king of Sparta 476/469 to 427/426 BC. He succeeded his grandfather Leotychidas II. He saved Sparta from a helot attack following the great earthquake of 465/464 BC and participated in the Third Messenian War (464–455 BC). His attempts to dissuade Sparta from a Peloponnesian war failed, and he invaded Attica in 431, 430 and 428 BC and besieged Plataea (429–427 BC). His children were Agis II, Agesilaus and Cynisca.

ARCHIDAMUS III (*Arkhidamos*): Eurypontid king of Sparta 361/360–338 BC. Son of Agesilaus II. He brought back the Spartan army after the defeat at the battle of Leuctra (371 BC). He fought against Arcadia (367 and 364 BC) and against Epaminondas in his invasion of Sparta (362 BC). He supported Phocis in the Third Sacred War (355–346 BC) and undertook expeditions to Crete and to Italy (to defend Tarentum), but was killed there at the battle of Manduria.

AREUS I (*Areus*): Lived c. 312–265 BC. Agiad king of Sparta 309/308–265 BC. He succeeded his grandfather Cleomenes II as king, and unsuccessfully invaded Aetolia in 280/279 BC. In 273/272 BC he was recalled from fighting in Crete to drive Pyrrhus of Epirus from Sparta. He then embarked (c. 268 BC) on the Chremonidean War with Athens and Ptolemy II against Macedonia. He was killed by Antigonus II Gonatas at the battle of Corinth. He was the first Spartan king to glorify his achievements on coins and inscriptions and to maintain an elaborate court.

ARIARAMNES (*Ariaramnes*): Lived 280?–230? BC. Eldest son of Ariarathes II of Cappadocia. He made his son Ariarathes III his co-ruler from c. 250 BC. By about 255 BC he had probably declared Cappadocia independent from the Seleucid kings.

ARIARATHES I (*Ariarathes*): Lived c. 404–322 BC. Satrap of Cappadocia (including Pontus). He claimed descent from Cyrus the Great. He was captured and killed by Perdiccas and Eumenes after Alexander the Great's death.

ARIARATHES II (*Ariarathes*): King of Cappadocia c. 301–c. 280 BC. He escaped to Armenia in 322 BC, but recovered Cappadocia (although not Pontus) after 301 BC, remaining subject to the Seleucid kings.

ARIARATHES III (*Ariarathes*): King of Cappadocia (partly with his father Ariaramnes) c. 250–220 BC. He married Stratonice, sister of Seleucus II. He supported Antiochus Hierax against Seleucus II.

ARIARATHES IV EUSEBES (*Ariarathes*, Pious): King of Cappadocia 220–163 BC. Son of Ariarathes III. He married Antiochis (daughter of Antiochus III) and helped Antiochus III against Rome at the battle of Magnesia ad Sipylum (189 BC). His daughter Stratonice married Eumenes II, king of Pergamum. Cappadocia became an ally of Pergamum and of Rome against Pharnaces I of Pontus.

ARIARATHES V EUSEBES PHILOPATOR (*Ariarathes*, Pious, Father-Loving): King of Cappadocia 163–130 BC and son of Ariarathes IV. He studied philosophy at Athens and promoted Hellenism in his kingdom. He refused to marry the sister of Demetrius I Soter, who later aided Orophernes (a supposed elder brother of Ariarathes IV) to seize the throne (160 BC). Ariarathes recovered his kingdom with the help of Attalus II of Pergamum (c. 157 BC) and sacked Priene because the temple of Athena (fig. 9.14) refused to give him Orophernes' treasure. Ariarathes assisted Rome with men and ships in 131 BC in the war against Aristonicus and was himself killed in this war. His son was given much of Lycaonia as reward.

ARISTAGORAS (*Aristagoras*): Died 497 BC. Ruler of Miletus when his father-in-law Histiaeus (tyrant of Miletus) was absent at the Persian court of Darius I. Aristagoras instigated the Ionian Revolt against Persia in 499 BC. He was defeated by the Persians and went to Myrcinus in Thrace, where he was killed in battle against the Thracians.

ARISTEUS or ARISTEAS (*Aristeus* or *Aristeas*): Died 430 BC. Son of Adeimantus, Corinthian commander at the battle of Salamis in 480 BC. Aristeus commanded Corinthian volunteers who went to support Potidaea when it revolted from Athens (432 BC), but managed to escape from the besieged city. He was sent by the Peloponnesian League in 430 BC on an embassy to Persia, but was captured in Thrace and given to the Athenians for execution.

ARISTIDES (*Aristeides*): Died c. 467 BC. Athenian statesman. He was *strategos* at the battle of Marathon (490 BC) and was rich enough to be archon in 489/488 BC. He was ostracized in 482 BC (fig. 1.15) after rivalry with Themistocles, but returned in 480 BC. He was a military leader at the battles of Salamis (480 BC) and Plataea (479 BC). He fixed the tribute to be paid by each member of the Delian League. He died a poor man.

ARISTODEMUS OF MESSENIA (*Aristodemos*): A traditional hero of Messenia in the First Messenian War against Sparta (late 8th century BC). He became king c. 710 BC. In despair at losing the war, he killed himself on the grave of his daughter, who had apparently been sacrificed to ensure the war's success.

ARISTOGITON (*Aristogeiton*): Died 514 BC. With his lover Harmodius (*Harmodios*), they plotted to kill the tyrant Hippias and his brother Hipparchus (*Hipparkhos*) at the Panathenaic procession in 514 BC. They killed only Hipparchus and were arrested and executed. Although Hippias' tyranny continued until 510 BC, Aristogiton and Harmodius were later honored as tyrannicides, as if Hipparchus had been the tyrant.

ARISTOMENES (*Aristomenes*): 7th-century-BC Messenian war hero. His resistance to Sparta led to the Second Messenian War c. 650 BC. He was eventually defeated by the treachery of the Arcadians and lived in exile in Rhodes.

ARISTONICUS (*Aristonikos*): Died 128 BC. Possibly an illegitimate son of Eumenes II. After the death of Attalus III (133 BC), when Pergamum passed to Rome, Aristonicus led a revolt, particularly amongst slaves and non-Greeks. He was captured and executed by the Romans.

ARISTOPHON (*Aristophon*): Lived c. 435–c. 335 BC. Athenian politician of apparently some importance, who was unsuccessfully prosecuted 75 times under *graphe paranomon*. He opposed Callistratus over the relationship with Thebes. Aristophon successfully prosecuted Timotheus for his part in the Social War (357–355 BC) and opposed the abandonment of Amphipolis by Athens under the Peace of Philocrates (346 BC).

ARSACES I (*Arsakes*): First king of Parthia and founder of the Arsacid dynasty (c. 247 BC to before 209 BC). He rebelled against the Bactrian satrap of Antiochus I during the war between Antiochus Hierax and Seleucus II. His descendants and successors (about 37) bore his name as a title.

ARSACIDS: Royal dynasty of Parthia c. 247 BC–AD 230; founded by Arsaces I.

ARSINOË I (*Arsinoë*): Born c. 300 BC. Daughter of Lysimachus of Thrace and Nicaea, she married Ptolemy II and became queen of Egypt c. 289/288 BC (divorced c. 281 BC). Her three children were Ptolemy III, Berenice (wife of Antiochus I) and Lysimachus. She was accused of treason but was acquitted.

ARSINOË II PHILADELPHUS (*Arsinoë*, she who loves her brother): Lived c. 316–270 BC. Daughter of Ptolemy I and Berenice I. She married Lysimachus of Thrace (c. 299 BC) and fled to Macedonia after the defeat of Lysimachus at the battle of Corupedium (281 BC). She married her half brother Ptolemy Ceraunus who murdered two of her children (280 BC). She fled to Egypt and married her brother Ptolemy II (276/275 BC), becoming queen of Egypt. Her influence on Egyptian affairs was great, and by 272 BC she and her brother were deified as Theoi Adelphoi. She was worshiped as a goddess after her death.

ARSINOË III PHILOPATOR (*Arsinoë*, Father-Loving): Lived c. 235–c. 204 BC. Daughter of Ptolemy III and Berenice II. She married her brother Ptolemy IV in 217 BC, becoming queen of Egypt. Disgusted at her brother's excesses, she was sent away from court. On or before his death in 204 BC, she was murdered.

ARTEMISIA I (*Artemisia*): Lived early 5th century BC. Princess of Caria who ruled as regent over Halicarnassus, Cos, Nisyrus and Calyndria. Herodotus recorded that she accompanied Xerxes' invasion of Greece in 480 BC and showed great bravery at the battle of Salamis.

ARTEMISIA II (*Artemisia*): Sister and wife of Mausolus of Caria. She succeeded him as ruler of Caria in 353/352 BC, and in his memory she began the construction of the Mausoleum. She instituted a literary competition in which the most famous rhetoricians participated.

ASPASIA (*Aspasia*): Mistress of Pericles who lived with him from the 440s BC to his death (429 BC). She was from Miletus. After the death by plague of his two sons by his wife, their son Pericles was legitimized. Aspasia associated with Socrates and was attacked for unduly influencing Pericles.

ATOSSA (*Atossa*): Queen of Persia, late 6th–early 5th centuries BC. Daughter of Cyrus the Great, she married her brother Cambyses (524 BC) and later married Darius I. She was mother of Xerxes and a major character in Aeschylus' *Persians*.

ATTALIDS Dynasty of rulers of Pergamum founded by the general Philetaerus after the division of Alexander the Great's empire. He was succeeded by his nephew Eumenes I, then Attalus I, Eumenes II, Attalus II and Attalus III who died in 133 BC, bequeathing his kingdom to Rome.

ATTALUS I SOTER (*Attalos*): Lived 269–197 BC, ruler of Pergamum from 241 BC. He also received the title *Soter* (Savior) and probably "king" for his victory over the Galatians (Gauls) before 230 BC (possibly 237 BC), which was commemorated by the dying Gaul triumphal monument at Pergamum. Attalus I won control over much of Seleucid Asia Minor by attacking Antiochus Hierax (230–228 BC), but lost this territory to Achaeus in his revolt against Antiochus III. He supported his allies (including Rome) against Philip V of Macedonia in the First and Second Macedonian Wars. His wife was Apollonis of Cyzicus, by whom he had four sons.

ATTALUS II PHILADELPHUS (*Attalos*): Lived 220–138 BC. King of Pergamum 159–138 BC. Son of Attalus I. He was given the title Philadelphus (loving his brother) for loyal service to his older brother Eumenes II. Attalus II married Stratonice (widow of Eumenes II) and supported Rome's policies. He restored Ariarathes V to the Seleucid throne (c. 157 BC) and supported the pretender Alexander Balas.

ATTALUS III PHILOMETOR EUERGETES (*Attalos*, Mother Loving, Benefactor): Lived c. 170–133 BC. Son of Eumenes II. King of Pergamum 138–133 BC. He bequeathed his kingdom to Rome.

BATTUS (*Battos*): Leader of a colonizing expedition from Thera to Libya c. 630 BC on advice from the Delphic oracle. Cyrene was founded, and Battus became its first king.

BERENICE I (*Berenike*): Lived c. 340–c. 275 BC. Queen of Egypt. A widow of Philippus, a Mace-donian, whose children were Megas (king of Cyrene), Antigone (who married Pyrrhus of Epirus) and other daughters. She went to Egypt with Eurydice who married Ptolemy I. With or without divorce, Ptolemy then married Berenice I, and their children were Ptolemy II Philadelphus and Arsinoë II. After her death, Berenice I was deified and worshiped with Ptolemy II as Theoi Soteres (Savior Gods).

BERENICE II EUERGETIS (*Berenike*, Benefactor): Queen of Egypt 246–221 BC. Daughter of King Magas of Cyrene and Apama (daughter of Antiochus I). Although betrothed to Ptolemy III, she was forced by her mother to marry the Macedonian prince Demetrius the Fair. She had him killed and married Ptolemy III in 246 BC. When Ptolemy went to Egypt to support his sister Berenice Syra, Berenice II dedicated a lock of her hair for his safe return. Her children included Ptolemy IV and Arsinoë III. She ruled jointly with Ptolemy IV on the death of Ptolemy III, but was murdered, probably by the ministers Agathocles and Sosibius.

BERENICE SYRA (*Berenike*, the Syrian): Lived c. 280–c. 246 BC. Seleucid queen c. 253–c. 246 BC. She was a daughter of Ptolemy II and Arsinoë I. She married Antiochus II c. 253 BC (who divorced Laodice). On Antiochus' death (246 BC), the sons of both queens were declared king. Ptolemy III went to support his sister Berenice, but she and her son were murdered before he arrived. The ensuing war of revenge was the Third Syrian (or Laodicean) War (246–241 BC).

BRASIDAS (*Brasidas*): Died 422 BC. A Spartan general of the Archidamian War. In 431 BC he saved the town of Methone from an Athenian attack, and participated in the battle at Pylos in 425 BC. From 424 BC he campaigned in Thrace, capturing cities under Athenian domination, including Amphipolis and Torone. The Athenians under Cleon recovered Torone, but both leaders were killed in battle outside Amphipolis.

CALLIAS (*Kallias*): Lived 5th century BC. Athenian politician, the son of Hipponicus, from one of Athens' richest families. He apparently won the chariot race at Olympia three times. By the 4th century BC, it was believed that he had negotiated the Peace of Callias (449/448 BC) between Athens and Persia. His grandson Callias was also an Athenian politician and negotiated peace with Sparta three times, the third time in 371 BC (also known as the Peace of Callias).

CALLICRATES OF LEONTIUM (*Kallikrates*): Floruit 182–149/148 BC. A pro-Roman Achaean statesman, opposing the views held by Lycortas (father of Polybius). He was *strategos* of the Achaean Confederacy in 179/178 BC.

CALLICRATIDAS (*Kallikratides*): Died 406 BC. A Spartan admiral who succeeded Lysander in 406 BC; he blockaded the Athenian fleet under Conon in the harbor of Mytilene, and then attacked a relief Athenian fleet but was defeated and drowned in the battle of Arginusae.

CALLIMACHUS OF APHIDNA (*Kallimakhos*): Died 490 BC. Athenian general and polemarch in 490 BC. He was commander-in-chief of the Greek forces at the battle of Marathon, where he died. He was commemorated in a painting in Athens' Stoa Poikile.

CALLISTRATUS (*Kallistratos*): Floruit 392/391–361 BC. An Athenian politican and orator. In 391 BC he prosecuted the ambassadors who proposed peace with Sparta. In 378 BC he was elected *strategos* when the Second Athenian League (Athens and Thebes against Sparta) was founded, and organized its finances. However, the rise of Thebes led him to advocate peace with Sparta. In 366 BC Thebes seized Oropus, and Callistratus was prosecuted, successfully defending himself in a speech that inspired Demosthenes. A further prosecution forced Callistratus into exile, and he was executed on his return in 361 BC.

CASSANDER (*Kassandros*): Lived c. 355–297 BC. Eldest son of Antipater (general of Alexander the Great) and allegedly responsible for Alexander's murder. Before his death in 319 BC, Antipater appointed Polyperchon as *strategos* in Europe. In 319–316 BC Cassander drove Polyperchon from Macedonia and much of Greece, replacing him as *strategos*. Cassander was responsible for the deaths of Alexander the Great's mother Olympias (315 BC), his son Alexander IV and his wife Roxane (both 311 BC). From 305 BC Cassander declared himself king

of Macedonia. He formed a coalition in 301 BC with Ptolemy I, Lysimachus and Seleucus I, against Antigonus I, defeating and killing him in the battle of Ipsus. He founded two cities, Cassendrea and Thessalonica, the latter named after his wife Thessalonice, daughter of Philip II. He also rebuilt Thebes, which had been destroyed by Alexander the Great.

CHARONDAS (*Kharondas*): Sixth-century-BC lawgiver of his native Catana in Sicily and other western Greek cities. His laws were apparently detailed, but it is unknown if he established a new constitution.

CHILON (*Khilon*): Spartan ephor c. 556/555 BC, famous for his wisdom (regarded as one of the Seven Sages of Greece). He possibly increased the powers of the ephors and was worshipped as a hero at Sparta.

CIMON (*Kimon*): Lived c. 510 BC.–c. 450 BC. Athenian statesman and soldier. Son of Miltiades and father of Lacedaemonius. He was frequently *strategos* from 478 BC and naval commander in nearly all Delian League operations from 476 to 463 BC. Circa 476 BC he expelled Pausanias from Byzantium and recaptured Eion on the Strymon River from the Persians. He conquered and colonized the island of Scyrus c. 475 BC, clearing it of pirates and bringing back to Athens the bones of the hero Theseus. Circa 467 BC he destroyed the Persian fleet at the battle of Eurymedon, and after a two-year siege (465–463 BC) he conquered Thasos, which had revolted from the Delian League.

In 463 BC Cimon was unsuccessfully prosecuted by Pericles for receiving bribes from Alexander I not to invade Macedonia. In 462 BC he persuaded the Athenians to allow him to assist Sparta in a war against the helots. The Spartans turned away his forces, and Cimon was ostracized in 461 BC (fig. 1.15). He was recalled after about five years in exile and negotiated a five-year peace treaty with Sparta (c. 451 BC). He then commanded a final expedition against the Persians to recapture Cyprus, but died while besieging Citium.

CLEISTHENES (*Kleisthenes*): Lived c. 565–c. 500 BC. Athenian statesman, son of Megacles (of the Alcmaeonid family) and Agariste (daughter of Cleisthenes of Sicyon). He was generally considered the creator of Athenian democracy. He was archon under Hippias in 525/524 BC but was later exiled. After Hippias was expelled in 510 BC, Cleisthenes returned to Athens and proposed major democratic reforms. His opponent Isagoras appealed to Cleomenes I of Sparta who invoked the hereditary curse of the Alcmaeonids, forcing Cleisthenes and his supporters to withdraw in 508 BC. They subsequently returned with popular support, carrying out the political reforms. Cleisthenes replaced the four traditional Ionian tribes with a system based on 10 tribes, *trittyes* and demes (see chapter 1). He also created (or reformed) the boule, and possibly introduced ostracism. He was buried in a public tomb in the Kerameikos Cemetery at Athens.

CLEISTHENES OF SICYON (*Kleisthenes*): Tyrant of the ruling house of Orthagoras c. 595–570 BC. Cleisthenes was anti-Dorian and anti-Argive and joined the First Sacred War c. 590 BC in order to free Delphi from the control of Crisa. He also fought a war against Argos. His daughter Agariste married Alcmaeon.

CLEITUS or BLACK CLEITUS (*Kleitos*): Lived c. 380–328/327 BC. A Macedonian general, who saved Alexander the Great's life at the battle of the Granicus River (334 BC). He was killed by Alexander in a drunken quarrel at Maracanda; his death was later bitterly regretted by Alexander.

CLEITUS or WHITE CLEITUS (*Kleitos*): Died 318 BC. A Macedonian general under Alexander the Great. He later defeated the Athenian fleet off the island of Amorgos (322 BC), so ending the Lamian War. He received the satrapy of Lydia (321 BC), but was expelled by Antigonus I (319 BC). He became Polyperchon's admiral, but failed to prevent Antigonus I from crossing the Bosphorus into Europe. He was killed in Thrace soon after.

CLEOMENES I (*Kleomenes*): Son of Anaxandridas II, and Agiad king of Sparta c. 520–488 BC. He expelled the tyrant Hippias from Athens in 510 BC and unsuccessfully supported Isagoras against Cleisthenes in 508 BC. Because of the obstruction of his fellow-king Demaratus, he failed to take control of Attica and reinstate Isagoras and Hippias. Demaratus prevented him from punishing Aegina for favouring Persia, and he consequently had Demaratus deposed in 491 BC with a forged Delphic

oracle on a charge of illegitimacy. This plot was exposed, and Cleomenes eventually committed suicide.

CLEOMENES III (*Kleomenes*): Lived 265/260–219 BC. Agiad king of Sparta 235–222 BC. He was son of Leonidas II (king of Sparta 254–235 BC) and married the widow of his predecessor Agis IV. He undertook successful wars against the Achaean Confederacy, and in 227–226 BC he carried out reforms to Sparta's constitution, such as canceling debts, abolishing the ephorate, redistributing land, and enrolling new citizens from perioeci and metics. In July 222 BC he was defeated by the Achaeans under Aratus of Sicyon at the battle of Sellasia and fled to his patron Ptolemy III Euergetes in Egypt. Imprisoned by Ptolemy's successor, he later committed suicide.

CLEON (*Kleon*): Died 422 BC. An Athenian politician toward whom ancient writers were hostile. He attacked Pericles in speeches in 431 and 430 BC. After Pericles died in 429 BC, Cleon became the most influential Athenian politician. In 427 BC he proposed that all men of Mytilene should be executed after its revolt. He opposed peace with Sparta after Athenian victory at Pylos and Sphacteria in 425 BC, in which he was involved with his general Demosthenes. He raised the pay of jurors from two to three obols, and in 423 BC he proposed the destruction of Scione and execution of its citizens (carried out 421 BC). In 422 BC he was elected *strategos* and led an expedition to Thrace where he was defeated by Brasidas outside Amphipolis, and both men were killed.

CLEOPATRA I (*Kleopatra*): Lived c. 215–176 BC. Daughter of Antiochus III and Laodice. In 193 BC she married Ptolemy V, and after his death (180 BC) ruled as regent for her son Ptolemy VI.

CLEOPATRA II (*Kleopatra*): Lived c. 185/180–116/115 BC. Queen of Egypt c. 175/174–116/115 BC. Daughter of Ptolemy V and Cleopatra I. She married her brother Ptolemy VI c. 175/174 BC and later ruled jointly with him and their brother Ptolemy VIII during the Sixth Syrian War (170–168 BC) against Antiochus IV. Her children were Cleopatra Thea (who married three Seleucid kings), Ptolemy VII and Cleopatra III. She later married Ptolemy VIII (144 BC), who in turn also married her daughter Cleopatra III (142 BC). Cleopatra II revolted against Ptolemy VIII in 132 BC and declared her son Ptolemy Memphites king and herself queen. Her son was murdered, and she offered the Egyptian throne to Demetrius II (Ptolemy VIII and Cleopatra III having fled to Cyprus). She then fled to Demetrius II Nicator who was murdered in 125 BC. The two queens and Ptolemy VIII were reconciled in 124 BC.

CLEOPATRA III (*Kleopatra*): Queen of Egypt 142–101 BC. Daughter of Ptolemy VI and Cleopatra II. She married Ptolemy VIII in 142 BC. On his death (116 BC), she became involved in the struggle for power between her two sons Ptolemy IX and Ptolemy X. The latter may have murdered her. She also had three daughters: Cleopatra IV, Cleopatra Tryphaena and Cleopatra Selene.

CLEOPATRA VII (*Kleopatra*): Lived 69–30 BC. Daughter of Ptolemy XII. She was ruler with Ptolemy XIII from 51 BC, expelled in 48 BC, but reinstated by Julius Caesar, by whom she allegedly had a son (47 BC). She joined in a political alliance with Mark Antony, and followed him in committing suicide (10 August, 30 BC).

CLEOPHON (*Kleophon*): Died c. 404 BC. Athenian politician and lyre maker. After the restoration of democracy in 410 BC, he became a leader of the people (demagogue). He was in charge of Athens' finances from 410 to 406 BC, and introduced a dole (*diobelia*) of two obols for poor citizens. He prevented Athens from making peace with Sparta in 410 and 405 BC, and was prosecuted and condemned to death by the oligarchs in 404 BC.

CONON (*Konon*): Lived c. 444–392 BC. An Athenian of noble birth, he was *strategos* in 414/413 BC, commanding the Athenian naval fleet at Naupactus. In 407–405 BC he commanded fleets in the Aegean and Hellespont. At the battle of Aegospotami (405 BC) he was the only Athenian general to escape the Spartans, finding refuge with Evagoras in Cyprus. He revived Persian sea power and commanded the Persian fleet provided by Pharnabazus at the battle of Cnidus (394 BC), destroying the Spartan navy. Conon returned to Athens and completed the rebuilding of the Long Walls.

CRATERUS (*Krateros*): Lived c. 370–321 BC. A Macedonian general of Alexander the Great, he commanded units at the battles of Granicus (334 BC), Issus (333 BC) and Gaugamela (331 BC). He held independent command in Bactria and Sogdiana (329–328 BC) and at the battle of Hydaspes River in India (326 BC). In 324 BC, he led home the Macedonian veterans and replaced Antipater as *strategos* in Europe. Following Alexander's death he was defeated and killed by Eumenes of Cardia near the Hellespont.

CRATERUS THE YOUNGER (*Krateros*): Lived 321–c. 255 BC. Son of Craterus and Phila (daughter of Antipater). Circa 280 BC he was appointed by his half brother Antigonus II Gonatas as *strategos* over Corinth and Euboea. Areus I of Sparta was killed by him in 265 BC at Corinth on his way to relieve Athens in the Chremonidean War. He may have written a commentary on a collection of Athenian decrees. He was succeeded by his son Alexander of Corinth.

CRITIAS (*Kritias*): Lived c. 460–403 BC. He was from an aristocratic family and was implicated (but released) in the mutilation of the herms. He proposed the recall of Alcibiades, and was apparently later exiled. On the surrender of Athens to Sparta in 404 BC, Critias returned and became leader of the Thirty Tyrants (the pro-Spartan oligarchy). He was portrayed as an unscrupulous leader, and was killed fighting against Thrasybulus in spring 403 BC. He had literary interests and was the author of elegiac poems and tragedies.

CROESUS (*Kroisos*): Last king of Lydia, c. 560–c. 546 BC. He subdued the Greek cities on the Asia Minor coast, but was favorable to the Greeks. Allegedly very wealthy, he made rich offerings at Greek shrines, particularly Delphi. With the rise of Persia, he attacked Cyrus the Great after an ambiguous response from the Delphic oracle ("If you cross the Halys, you will destroy a great nation"). Cyrus defeated Croesus and captured his capital Sardis. Various legends grew up about him being saved from execution.

CYLON (*Kylon*): Seventh-century-BC Athenian aristocrat who won an Olympic victory (possibly 640 BC). He plotted to become tyrant of Athens with the aid of his father-in-law Theagenes, tyrant of Megara. Cylon seized the Acropolis (possibly 632 BC), but was besieged by the archon Megacles the Alcmaeonid. Cylon escaped but his followers were impiously taken from sanctuary at an altar of Athena and executed. As a result, the Alcmaeonids incurred a hereditary curse, often invoked in political disputes at Athens.

CYPSELUS (*Kypselos*): Tyrant of Corinth c. 657–627 BC. He escaped death by the Bacchiads (a dynasty that had ruled Corinth since the 8th century BC) when born by being hidden in a chest (*kypsele*). He overthrew the Bacchiad dynasty and was a popular ruler. His son was Periander.

CYRUS THE GREAT (*Kyros*, Persian *Kurash*): The first king of Persia, 559–529 BC. When attacked by Croesus, he defeated him, and Lydia and the Ionian Greek states became part of the Persian Empire. He became king of a vast empire and was regarded as a model ruler by the Greeks. He probably died in battle, and his tomb is at Pasargadae.

CYRUS II THE YOUNGER (*Kyros*): Lived c. 423–401 BC. Second son of Darius II. As satrap of Lydia he became friendly with Lysander, ensuring Spartan victory over Athens in the Peloponnesian War. When his elder brother Artaxerxes II succeeded his father as king, Cyrus was accused of treason. Released from prison, he returned to Asia Minor and amassed a large force of Greek mercenaries including Xenophon. In 401 BC he set out with an expedition (anabasis) of 20,000 men, but was defeated and killed by Artaxerxes at the battle of Cunaxa (near Babylon). The expedition and the retreating army (March of the Ten Thousand) were described in Xenophon's *Anabasis*.

DARIUS I (*Dareios*, Persian *Darayavaush*): King of Persia 521–486 BC. He was of the Achaemenid family and came to the throne by overthrowing a usurper who was impersonating a brother of Cambyses (king of Persia, 530–522 BC). By 519 BC he had restored order in the Persian Empire, and created 20 satrapies (provinces governed by satraps), a system retained by later rulers. From 513 to 512 BC he campaigned against Thrace and the Scythians, and in 499–494 BC he suppressed a revolt of the Ionian Greek cities. He sent an army to Greece to punish its interference, but this army was

conquered at Marathon (490 BC), and Darius died before he could mount another expedition.

DARIUS III (*Dareios*): Lived c. 380–330 BC. King of Persia 336–330 BC. A great-nephew of Artaxerxes II, he was defeated by Alexander the Great at Granicus (334 BC), Issus (333 BC) and Gaugamela (331 BC). He fled eastward but was hunted down; his own followers murdered him as Alexander approached.

DEMADES (*Demades*): Lived c. 380–319 BC. An Athenian politician and orator, he arranged a peace agreement between Athens and Macedonia after the battle of Chaeronea (338 BC). He led a pro-Macedonian group at Athens, and was subsequently exiled. After Macedonian victory at the battle of Crannon in 322 BC, he was recalled in order to make peace with Antipater, resulting in the deaths of Hyperides and Demosthenes. He was himself executed by Cassander after the death of Antipater.

DEMARATUS (*Demaratos* or *Damaratos*): Eurypontid king of Sparta c. 515–491 BC. He obstructed his fellow-king Cleomenes I, ultimately intervening over Aegina. Cleomenes therefore had him deposed on a false charge of illegitimacy using an oracle from Delphi. Demaratus fled to Darius I and later accompanied Xerxes on his invasion of Greece (480 BC). He was granted land in Mysia as a reward, where he died many years later.

DEMETRIUS THE FAIR (*Demetrios ho Kalos*): Lived c. 286–c. 248 BC. Son of Demetrius I Poliorcetes and Ptolemais (daughter of Ptolemy I) and father of Antigonus Doson. He gained Cyrene from Ptolemy II but was murdered soon after. His nickname was due to his appearance.

DEMETRIUS OF PHALERUM (*Demetrios*): Lived c. 350–c. 283 BC. Athenian philosopher, orator, politician and probably *strategos* for several years from 325/324 BC. He was pro-Macedonian and was condemned to death in 318 BC. However, he was made governor of Athens by Cassander (317 BC), and held power for 10 years. He fled to Boeotia when Demetrius I Poliorcetes liberated Athens (307 BC), and was later librarian in Alexandria (297 BC). Under Ptolemy II Philadelphus, he was exiled to Upper Egypt where he died.

DEMETRIUS OF PHAROS (*Demetrios*): Died 214 BC. He betrayed Corcyra to Rome (229 BC) and was rewarded with the rule of a kingdom centered on Pharos in northwest Illyria. He broke his treaty with Rome and was expelled when Rome invaded Illyria (219 BC). He escaped to his ally Philip V of Macedonia and incited his anti-Roman policy. He was killed in an expedition against Messene.

DEMETRIUS I OF BACTRIA (*Demetrios*): King of Bactria c. 200–185 BC, son of Euthydemus I. He annexed Arachosia and Drangiana and apparently extended his empire as far east as Pataliputra (Patna) in India, intending to imitate Alexander the Great's achievements. According to numismatic evidence, there may have been a Euthydemus II (perhaps a son or brother of Demetrius I), and the Euthydemids may have been challenged by Antimachus Theos. Demetrius I (or possibly a Demetrius II) may have been the Demetrius known in classical sources as "King of India" and who issued bilingual Indo-Greek coins.

DEMETRIUS I POLIORCETES (*Demetrios*, the Besieger): Lived 336–283 BC. He was a son of Antigonus I and king of Macedonia 294–288 BC. He undertook many campaigns in order to reunite Alexander the Great's empire and was defeated by Ptolemy I at Gaza (312 BC). In 307 BC he was sent by Antigonus to liberate Athens from Cassander. He gained Cyprus by a naval victory over Ptolemy I at Salamis (306 BC). He unsuccessfully besieged Rhodes in 305–304 BC, for which he gained his nickname. He revived the League of Corinth and was regarded as the leader of Greece against Cassander. He and his father were defeated at Ipsus (301 BC), and Antigonus' empire in Asia was destroyed. Demetrius was proclaimed king by the Macedonian army (294 BC), and intended to recover the empire in Asia, but instead lost Macedonia to Lysimachus and Pyrrhus (288 BC). He fled with a small force to Asia Minor in 286 BC, but surrendered to Seleucus I in 285 BC and died two years later.

DEMETRIUS I SOTER OF SYRIA (*Demetrios*, Savior): Lived 187–150 BC, Seleucid king 162–150 BC. The elder son of Seleucus IV, he was sent as a hostage to Rome, while his uncle (Antiochus IV) and cousin (Antiochus V) gained the throne. In 162 BC Demetrius escaped from Rome and regained the throne from Antiochus V. He became an unpopular ruler and died in battle against the usurper Alexander Balas.

DEMETRIUS II (*Demetrios*): Lived c. 276–229 BC. King of Macedonia 239–229 BC. Son of Antigonus II Gonatas and Phila. He married Stratonice II (his mother's half sister) c. 253 BC, divorcing her in 239 BC. After becoming king, he married Phthia-Chryseis, daughter of Alexander I of Epirus. From 239 to 238 BC he was engaged in the Demetrian War against the Aetolian and Achaean Confederacies. Demetrius was killed fighting the Illyrian Dardani tribe on his northern border.

DEMETRIUS II NICATOR THEOS PHILADELPHUS (DEMETRIUS II OF SYRIA) (*Demetrios*, Conqueror, God, Loving his Brother): Lived c. 161–125 BC. Eldest son of Demetrius I Soter. Seleucid king 145–139 BC and 129–125 BC. He gained the throne after defeating the pretender Alexander Balas and married Cleopatra Thea, daughter of Ptolemy VI (previously wife of Alexander Balas), all in 145 BC. He was captured by the Parthians in 139 BC and was held for 10 years. He regained the throne from his younger brother Antiochus VII Sidetes, but was later murdered.

DEMOCHARES (*Demokhares*): Lived c. 360–275 BC. An Athenian orator and democratic politician, he defended Athens during the Four Years' War against Cassander (307–304 BC). He was exiled c. 303 BC, returning c. 286/285 BC. He saved Eleusis from an attack by Antigonus II Gonatas and secured Athens' finances with financial aid from Macedonia's enemies. He obtained a decree honoring Demosthenes, his uncle, who had held anti-Macedonian views. On retirement, he devoted himself to speeches and a history of Athens.

DEMOSTHENES (*Demosthenes*): Died 413 BC. An Athenian general prominent in the Peloponnesian War. In 425 BC (along with Cleon) he captured a force of Spartan hoplites on Sphacteria. After an unsuccessful campaign in 424 BC, he was given no major command until 413 BC, when he went to relieve Nicias at Syracuse. He urged withdrawal, but eventually the Athenians were defeated at sea. Demosthenes surrendered and was executed.

DEMOSTHENES (*Demosthenes*): Lived 384–322 BC. An Athenian orator, he was regarded by his contemporaries as the greatest of the Attic orators. He became a speechwriter (*logographos*), and was noted for his orations advocating resistance to Philip II of Macedonia. The *First Philippic* was delivered in 351 BC; there followed the three *Olynthiacs* (349 BC), *On the Peace* (346 BC), *Second Philippic* (344 BC), *On the False Embassy* (343 BC), *On the Chersonese* (341 BC), *Third Philippic* (341 BC) and *Fourth Philippic* (341 BC). In 339 BC Demosthenes arranged an alliance with Thebes against Philip II to prevent him invading Attica, but the alliance lost against Philip at the battle of Chaeronea (August 338 BC). Demosthenes was present at the battle and later delivered the funeral oration. Despite the loss of the battle, his supporter Ctesiphon proposed that Demosthenes should be honored at the City Dionysia with a golden crown in recognition of his services. Aeschines prosecuted Ctesiphon for this proposal in 330 BC. In his speech *Against Ctesiphon*, Aeschines outlined Demosthenes' policies, blaming him for Athens' misfortunes. Demosthenes' defense (*On the Crown*) won decisively. Demosthenes was later accused of receiving bribes and retired to Aegina (323 BC). Following the death of Alexander the Great, he returned to Athens in triumph. After Macedonian victory at the battle of Crannon (322 BC), Demades sentenced Demosthenes to death, but he committed suicide by poison.

DERCYLLIDAS (*Derkyllidas*): Floruit 411–389 BC. A Spartan general. In 411 BC he took Abydus and Lampsacus from Athens, and in 339 BC he concluded a treaty with Tissaphernes. He campaigned against the Persian satrap Pharnabazus in Asia Minor, but was replaced by King Agesilaus II. From 394 BC Dercyllidas was responsible for Spartan interests in the Hellespont.

DIOCLES (*Diokles*): Died after 408 BC. Democratic leader of Syracuse who altered its constitution in line with Athenian democratic principles. In 409/408 BC he led the army against Hannibal, who was besieging Himera. He was sent into exile by supporters of his opponent Hermocrates. After his death he received hero-worship.

DION (*Dion*): Lived c. 408–354 BC. Brother-in-law and son-in-law of Dionysius I. Under Plato's influence he tried to make Dionysius II a philosopher-king, but was expelled from Syracuse c. 366 BC and went to live in Athens, where he was closely associated with the Academy. In 357 BC he led an expedition to Sicily, finally liberating Syracuse and the citadel of Ortygia. He had his lieutenant Heracleides murdered (355 BC). Attempting to govern on Platonic principles (but in effect a tyranny), he was himself murdered by his follower Callippus.

DIONYSIUS I (*Dionysios*): Lived c. 430–367 BC. Tyrant of Syracuse 405–367 BC. In 405 BC he persuaded the assembly to elect him the leading *strategos* (*strategos autokrator*) and give him a bodyguard. As sole ruler, he gained control of much of Sicily and converted Ortygia into a private citadel. In 398 BC he started a new war with Carthage, with Sicily eventually divided between Carthage (in the west) and Syracuse. From 388 BC Dionysius campaigned in Magna Graecia, gaining control over much of that territory. From 383 BC he again fought Carthage, but was heavily defeated at the battle of Cronium (winter 376 BC) and was forced to cede some territory. He began a third war in 368 BC but died the following year.

DIONYSIUS II (*Dionysios*): Tyrant of Syracuse 367–343/342 BC. Eldest son of Dionysius I. He made immediate peace with Carthage and welcomed philosophers to his court. When Dionysius II was in Italy, Dion seized Syracuse and the citadel of Ortygia (355 BC). Dionysius II held Rhegium until c. 351 BC and Locri Epizephyrii until 347/346 BC. He regained Syracuse in 346 BC, but was blockaded at Ortygia and surrendered to Timoleon in 343 BC. He lived in exile at Corinth for many years.

DORIEUS (*Dorieus*): Died after 510 BC. Half brother of King Cleomenes I. When his claim for the throne was rejected, he and his supporters left Sparta to colonize north Africa. Expelled by the Carthaginians, they founded a settlement in west Sicily, but were later killed by the Carthaginians.

DRACO (*Drakon*): Circa 620 BC. An Athenian lawgiver who apparently gave Athens its first written laws. He may also have established a constitution based on the franchise of hoplites. Though he probably made laws only for particular crimes, the penalties were very severe (draconian), and Solon

Fig. 2.3 The pass of Thermopylae, where the Spartan king Leonidas was killed while defending the pass against the Persians in 480 BC.

later repealed all his laws except for the ones addressing homicide.

DUCETIUS (*Douketios*): Died 440 BC. A hellenized leader in eastern Sicily, he formed the native Sicel communities into a league. Between 459 and 451 BC, he founded new Sicel cities and established Menaenum as his hilltop capital. Later he moved down from the hill to Palice. In 451 BC he captured Aetna and came into conflict with Acragas and Syracuse. He was defeated in 450 BC and exiled to Corinth by the Syracusans, but returned five years later to found a new city at Caleacte with the approval of Syracuse.

EPAMINONDAS (*Epameinondas*): Died 362 BC. A Theban general and politician. At peace negotiations in 371 BC, Epaminondas wanted peace to be ratified in the name of all Boeotia, but this was refused and he withdrew. An army was therefore sent by Sparta to invade Boeotia, but was decisively de-

feated at the battle of Leuctra (371 BC). This victory of the Thebans under Epaminondas brought Spartan military supremacy to an end. The following year (370/369 BC) he invaded the Peloponnese to assist Arcadia against Sparta and also liberated Messenia and founded Messene. Further invasions of the Peloponnese took place under him in 369 and 366 BC. When war broke out again in Arcadia, he won an indecisive victory at Mantinea (362 BC), but died of his wounds, which ended Theban supremacy.

EPHIALTES (*Ephialtes*): Died 461 BC. Athenian statesman who replaced Themistocles as the leading democratic politican in opposition to Cimon. He prosecuted several members of the Areopagus and tried to prevent assistance to Sparta during its war against the helots in 462 BC. With the help of Pericles in 462/461 BC, he proposed laws reducing the powers of the Areopagus. He was murdered in 461 BC and buried in the Kerameikos at Athens.

EPHIALTES OF TRACHIS (*Ephialtes*): In 480 BC he allegedly showed Xerxes the path by which the Persians outflanked Leonidas at Thermopylae (fig. 2.3).

EPITADEUS (*Epitadeios*): A Spartan ephor who introduced laws after 404 BC allowing transfer of property.

ERATOSTHENES OF ATHENS (*Eratosthenes*): Lived late 5th century BC. He was an oligarch in 411 BC and became one of the Thirty Tyrants. After their fall (403 BC), he was prosecuted for murder by the orator Lysias, but was acquitted.

EUBULUS (*Euboulos*): Lived c. 405–c. 335 BC. A major Athenian politican, especially in the 340s BC, whose career is poorly documented. As a theoric magistrate, he assumed control of Athenian finances; his fiscal policies allowed increased revenue to be spent on public works and shipbuilding rather than non-essential military operations. He advocated a Common Peace of Greek states against Philip II of Macedonia. After the battle of Chaeronea (338 BC), no more is heard of Eubulus, and by 330 BC he had died.

EUMENES I (*Eumenes*): Ruler (never king) of Pergamum 263–241 BC, and nephew of Philetaerus. He was originally subordinate to Antiochus I whom he defeated near Sardis in 262 BC with the help of Ptolemy II. Eumenes greatly extended his frontiers, and bought immunity for Pergamum from marauding Gauls.

EUMENES II SOTER (*Eumenes*, Savior): King of Pergamum 197–159 BC. Eldest son of Attalus I, he continued his father's policies of cooperation with Rome, particularly against Antiochus III. Through the goodwill of Rome he acquired much new territory. He incited the Third Macedonian War (171–168 BC) between Rome and Macedonia, but was suspected by the Romans of negotiating secretly with Perseus of Macedonia. His brother Attalus II succeeded him.

EUMENES OF CARDIA (*Eumenes*): Lived c. 362–316/315 BC. He was secretary to Philip II of Macedonia and Alexander the Great; on Alexander's death (323 BC), he was appointed satrap of Cappadocia. In the wars of the Successors he sup-ported Perdiccas as rightful heir. After Perdiccas was killed (321/320 BC), Eumenes was besieged for a year by Antigonus I. When the seige finally lifted, he continued the war against Antigonus I on behalf of the regent Polyperchon. His own troops betrayed him, and he was executed.

EURYBIADES (*Eurybiades*): The first recorded Spartan admiral of the Peloponnesian League. In 480 BC he commanded its combined Greek fleet against Xerxes' Persian navy at the battles of Artemisium (Persian victory) and Salamis (Greek victory).

EURYPONTIDS (*Eurypontidai*): The junior royal house at Sparta.

EUTHYDEMUS I (*Euthudemos*): King of Bactria c. 227–200/190 BC, after seizing the throne from Diodotus II. In 208 BC he was attacked and besieged by Antiochus III. Euthydemus agreed to provide the Seleucid army with supplies, while Antiochus recognized him as the rightful ruler. Large numbers of his coins have been found.

EVAGORAS (*Euagoras*): Lived c. 435–374/373 BC. King of Salamis in Cyprus from 411 BC. Through close relations with Athens, he strengthened Hellenism in Cyprus. His court received many Athenian exiles, including Conon in 405 BC. Evagoras clashed with Persia, resulting in his defeat in the naval battle of Citium in 381 BC, when he had to sue for peace after 10 years of fighting. He was assassinated in a private quarrel.

GELON (*Gelon*): Lived c. 540–478 BC. Tyrant of Gela (and later Syracuse) 491–478 BC. He was cavalry commander under the tyrant Hippocrates and guardian to his sons. On Hippocrates' death in 491 BC, Gelon seized power. In 485 BC he captured Syracuse and transferred his power there, leaving his brother Hieron in charge at Gela. Syracuse became the leading Hellenic power at that time. With Theron (tyrant of Acragas), he defeated a huge Carthaginian expedition under Hamilcar at the battle of Himera in 480 BC, apparently the same day as the Greeks defeated the Persians at Salamis.

GYGES (*Gyges*): King of Lydia c. 685–687 BC. He seized the Lydian throne and founded the Mermnadae dynasty, of which Croesus was the last member. He began the conquest of the Greek cities of the Ionian coast and sent rich offerings to Delphi. Archilochus called him "tyrant," the first recorded use of the term in Greek.

GYLIPPUS (*Gylippos*): Late-5th-century-BC Spartan general. Sent in 414 BC to help Syracuse, which was besieged by Athens. He destroyed the Athenian fleet and army in 413 BC. In 404 BC he was accused of embezzlement and went into exile (or committed suicide).

HAMILCAR (*Amilkas*; Punic *Abd-Melkart*): Died 480 BC. A Carthaginian general who invaded Sicily to expel Theron of Acragas from Himera. His invasion was possibly intended to coincide with that of Xerxes in Greece. His army was destroyed at the battle of Himera by Theron and Gelon (480 BC), and he was killed.

HARPALUS (*Harpalos*): Lived c. 355–323 BC. A Macedonian noble and close friend of Alexander the Great, he was an unreliable paymaster of Alexander's Persian expedition. In 333 BC he fled to Greece, but was reinstated by Alexander in 331 BC. During Alexander's absence in India (327–325 BC), Harpalus was entrusted with the treasury at Babylon, but led an extravagant, possibly treasonable, life-style. On Alexander's return, he fled to Athens (324 BC) with money and soldiers. He bribed various politicians there, including Demosthenes. He was imprisoned and his money stored on the Acropolis, but he escaped to Crete, where he was killed by Thibron, one of his officers. Half his money was found to be missing, and Demosthenes' career was ended.

HEGESIPPUS (*Hegesippos*, nicknamed *Krobulos*— topknot—because of his hairstyle): Lived c. 390– c. 325 BC. An Athenian politician and contemporary of Demosthenes, he was extremely opposed to Philip II of Macedonia, including his offer to renegotiate the Peace of Philocrates. His speech *On Halonnesus* (once thought to be a speech of Demosthenes) demonstrates his opposition. He was still alive after the battle of Chaeronea (338 BC).

HEPHAESTION (*Hephaistion*): Lived c. 356– 324 BC. A Macedonian noble and general, and Alexander the Great's closest companion. Alexander awarded him the revived Persian position of chili-

arch. He died suddenly of fever, and Alexander may never have recovered from grief.

HERMIAS (*Hermeias*): Died 341 BC. He was a tyrant of Atarneus in Asia Minor from c. 355 BC. Once a student of the Academy, he encouraged philosophers at his court, including Aristotle who married his niece. At Aristotle's instigation, he negotiated with Philip II of Macedonia. He was consequently arrested by Mentor of Rhodes (a mercenary leader) and taken to Artaxerxes III, who executed him.

HERMOCRATES (*Hermokrates*): Died 407 BC. A Syracusan leader who urged all Sicilian Greeks to resist Athenian interference. In 415 BC he was one of the generals who opposed the Athenian expedition. In 412 BC he was commander of a Syracusan fleet sent to help Sparta; he lost all his ships at the battle of Cyzicus (410 BC) and was banished from Syracuse. In 408 BC he returned to Sicily to fight the Carthaginians; the following year he attempted to take Syracuse but was killed. His daughter married Dionysius I.

HIERON I (*Hieron*): Tyrant of Syracuse 478– 467/466 BC. He was originally appointed ruler of Gela by his brother Gelon. On Gelon's death, Hieron became tyrant of Syracuse as well, despite the claims of his brother Polyzelus. In Sicily he destroyed Catana and refounded it as Aetna with 10,000 new settlers (475 BC). In Italy he prevented Anaxilas of Rhegium from attacking Locri Epixephyrii and acted against Croton (477 BC); in 474 BC he won a decisive naval battle over the Etruscans at Cumae and founded a colony at Pithecusae. In 472 BC he overthrew the tyranny at Acragas. His court was frequented by poets and philosphers, including Aeschylus, Simonides and Epicharmus. Several victories by his chariots in the Olympic and Pythian Games were celebrated in odes by Pindar and Bacchylides.

HIERON II (*Hieron*): Lived c. 306–215 BC. King of Syracuse c. 270–215 BC. He was a lieutenant of Pyrrhus of Epirus, then became *strategos* in Syracuse. He was hailed as king c. 270 BC and reigned for 54 years, during which time Syracuse experienced peace and prosperity. He was defeated by the Mamertines (mercenaries settled by Agathocles in Syracuse), but defeated them at the battle of the

Longanus River c. 265 BC. In 264 BC Hieron unsuccessfully resisted the Roman seizure of Messana for the Mamertines. He concluded an alliance with the Romans in 263 BC for the remainder of his reign, assisting them throughout their Punic Wars with Carthage. He also maintained ties with the rest of the Greek world.

HIPPIAS (*Hippias*): Tyrant of Athens 527–510 BC, who succeeded his father Peisistratus. He was originally a benign ruler who reduced taxation and allowed members of leading families to hold the eponymous archonship. He became increasingly unpopular, and his brother Hipparchus was assassinated in 514 BC. In 510 BC Hippias was forced by the Spartans into exile at Sigeum. He later went to the court of Darius I and accompanied the Persian expedition of 490 BC. He was at the battle of Marathon, but no record of him exists after this.

HIPPOCRATES OF GELA (*Hippokrates*): Tyrant of Gela 498–491 BC. He succeeded his brother Cleander (assassinated 498 BC) and conquered most of eastern Sicily, including Naxus, Leontini and Zancle. He failed to gain Syracuse and died the following year.

HISTIAEUS (*Histiaios*): Died 493 BC. Tyrant of Miletus. He assisted Darius I in his campaign against Scythia (513–512 BC) by guarding the bridge of boats across the Danube. He was rewarded with Myrcinus in Thrace. He later went to Susa (the Persian capital), while his son-in-law Aristagoras ruled Miletus. Both were probably responsible for inciting the Ionian Revolt in 499 BC; Darius allowed Histiaeus to return to Ionia to quell the uprising, but he was unsuccessful and retreated to Byzantium where he became a pirate. In 494 or 493 BC he was captured and executed by the Persian satrap Artaphernes.

HYPERBOLUS (*Hyperbolos*): Died 411 BC. An Athenian demagogue during the Peloponnesian War, he was *strategos* in 425/424 BC and represented Athens at the Amphictyonic Council at Delphi in 422 BC. He became important as leader of the people after Cleon's death (422 BC). He opposed the Peace of Nicias (421 BC), and in 418 BC he proposed the revival of ostracism, expecting to remove Nicias or Alcibiades. Instead, he was himself ostracized (417 or 415 BC). He went to Samos and was murdered by oligarchs.

HYPERIDES (*Hypereides*): Lived 390–322 BC. He was a professional speechwriter and later a public prosecutor who was constantly hostile to Macedonia. He supported Demosthenes, and in 343 BC he successfully prosecuted Philocrates for corruption in the peace negotiations with Philip II (343 BC). After the battle of Chaeronea, he suggested extreme measures and was prosecuted by Demades for illegality. Hyperides was one of the prosecutors of Demosthenes in the Harpalus affair (324 BC). Hyperides was largely responsible for the Lamian War (323–322 BC). After the battle of Crannon, Antipater demanded his surrender, and Hyperides was executed.

IPHICRATES (*Iphikrates*): Floruit 390–355 BC. An Athenian general who led a company of peltasts that destroyed a Spartan hoplite battalion near Corinth in 390 BC. He was responsible for establishing the importance of the peltasts. He was active in the Corinthian War (395–386 BC), and after 387/386 BC he served as a mercenary commander for Cotys of Thrace and married his daughter. He was also sent by Athens to fight for Persia against Egypt. Back in Athens (373 BC), he was sent to help Corcyra against a Spartan invasion. In 367–364 BC he unsuccessfully attempted to recover Amphipolis and afterward returned to Thrace. In 356 BC he commanded the Athenian fleet along with Timotheus at the battle of Embata against Chios. The battle was lost, and he was prosecuted but acquitted.

JASON (*Iason*): Tyrant of Pherae in Thessaly c. 385–370 BC. He took control of all Thessaly, winning Pharsalus, the last important city, in 374 BC. He mediated between Thebes and Sparta after the battle of Leuctra (371 BC). In 370 BC he caused alarm by announcing his plans to lead his entire Thessalian army to the Pythian Games at Delphi. His purpose is not certain, but he was assassinated beforehand and was succeeded by his nephew Alexander.

LAMACHUS (*Lamakhos*): Died 414 BC. An Athenian general who was *strategos* c. 435 BC, and so well known by 425 BC that he was caricatured by Aristophanes in the *Acharnians*. Along with Alcibiades and Nicias, he was appointed in 415 BC to lead the expedition to Sicily, but was killed in a skirmish.

LAODICE I (*Laodike*): Seleucid queen 261–c. 253 BC. She married Antiochus II and had two sons

(Seleucus II and Antiochus Hierax) and two daughters. Antiochus II married Berenice Syra (daughter of Ptolemy II) in 252 BC and favored their son (born 251 BC) as heir-apparent. On the death of Antiochus II (246 BC), a war of succession ensued (Third Syrian War or Laodicean War) to 241 BC. Laodice's supporters murdered Berenice and her son, allowing her son Seleucus II to succeed as king.

LEONIDAS (*Leonidas*): Agiad king of Sparta 488–480 BC. He succeeded his stepbrother Cleomenes I, having married his daughter Gorgo. While Spartans were celebrating the Carnea, he marched to Thermopylae as commander of an allied Greek army of about 6,000 or 7,000 men, occupying the pass to stop the Persians invading central Greece (fig. 2.3). Ephialtes showed the Persians under Xerxes a mountain path around the pass. Leonidas dismissed his allies in the army, but he himself remained and was killed along with 300 Spartans. A hero cult was later established at Sparta.

LEONNATUS (*Leonnatos*): Lived c. 358–322 BC. Macedonian general and satrap. In 332 BC he became personal bodyguard to Alexander the Great. After 328 BC he was a general, with distinguished service in India and during the return to the west. After Alexander's death (323 BC), he became satrap of Hellespontine Phrygia and guardian of Alexander IV. He assisted Antipater in the Lamian War (323–322 BC), but was defeated and killed in Thessaly.

LEOSTHENES (*Leosthenes*): Died 323/322 BC. An Athenian general, he became leader at Taenarum (south Laconia) of 8,000 mercenaries disbanded from Alexander's army. These troops were commanded by him in a Greek army against the Macedonians in the Lamian War (323–322 BC). The Greeks were initially successful, but Leosthenes was killed when besieging Antipater at Lamia.

LYCOPHRON (*Lykophron*): Tyrant of Pherae c. 406–390 BC, about whom little is known. He tried to control all Thessaly and defeated Larissa and other cities on 3 September, 404 BC. However, he was still at war in 395 BC, and his success cannot be determined. Jason may have been his son.

LYCURGUS (*Lykourgos*): Lived c. 390–c. 325/324 BC. A prominent Athenian statesman and ora-

tor, a member of the Eteobutadae clan. He controlled Athens' finances from the battle of Chaeronea (338 BC) until 326 BC, increasing the revenue. He undertook an extensive building program at Athens, and the navy was substantially enlarged at this time. He supported Demosthenes' policy of opposing Macedonia, and in 335 BC his supporters refused to surrender him when Alexander the Great demanded the arrest of those hostile to Macedonia. Only one speech survives, *Against Leocrates*. He was responsible for erecting statues of Aeschylus, Sophocles and Euripides and for an official edition of their works. Much evidence for Lycurgus comes from Plutarch's *Lives of the Ten Orators*.

LYCURGUS OF SPARTA (*Lykourgos*): Possibly 7th century BC or earlier. The legendary founder of Spartan political reforms and its social system (*agoge*), including education and military training. It is possible that the social and political institutions were a gradual development from earliest times, and that Lycurgus as a single legislator never existed.

LYDIADAS (*Lydiadas*): Died 227 BC. Tyrant of Megalopolis c. 243–235 BC. In 251 BC he was a commander of the Achaean Confederacy against Sparta, and later declared himself tyrant to protect his city. He abdicated in 235 BC, and Megalopolis joined the Achaean Confederacy. Lydiadas was appointed *strategos* of the Confederacy several times. Cleomenes III moved against Megalopolis, and Lydiadas was killed at the battle of Ladocea, when he disobeyed orders with a cavalry charge against the Spartans in order to save Megalopolis.

LYSANDER (*Lysandros*): Died 395 BC. A Spartan leader who claimed descent from the Heraclidae. He was appointed naval commander of the Spartan fleet for 408/407 BC. He won the friendship and support of Darius II and defeated the Athenian fleet with Persian support at the battle of Notium in 406 BC. In 405 BC he destroyed the Athenian fleet at Aegospotami and blockaded Piraeus until Athens surrendered in spring 404 BC. Lysander then installed a pro-Spartan oligarchy (Thirty Tyrants). His policies of governing cities formerly allied to Athens provoked opposition from the Spartan government, and his policies were reversed. Lysander tried to change the Spartan constitution to allow for an elected monarchy. He secured the kingship for Agesilaus II (399 BC), but then found himself isolated. At the start of the Corinthian War, he invaded Boeotia but was killed at the siege of Haliartus.

LYSIMACHUS (*Lysimakhos*): Lived c. 360–281 BC. A member of Alexander the Great's Bodyguard and one of his Successors. After Alexander's death (323 BC), he governed Thrace and northwest Asia Minor. From 315 to 311 BC, he joined Cassander and Ptolemy I against Antigonus I. In 309 BC he founded Lysimachia as his new capital. In 306 BC he proclaimed himself king of Thrace. In 301 BC he joined Cassander, Ptolemy I and Seleucus I in defeating Antigonus I and Demetrius I Poliorcetes at the battle of Ipsus. As a reward he was granted northern and central Asia Minor. Circa 299 BC he married Arsinoë II (daughter of Ptolemy I), divorcing his wife Amastris. He was taken prisoner for a short period in 292 BC by tribes north of the Danube in Thrace. In 288 BC he took eastern Macedonia from Demetrius I Poliorcetes, and in 285 BC he won western Macedonia and Thessaly from Pyrrhus, becoming the strongest of the Successors. His former ally Seleucus I defeated and killed him at the battle of Corupedium, and his kingdom was broken up.

MARDONIUS (*Mardonios*; Persian *Mardunija*): Died 479 BC. A Persian general, nephew and son-in-law of Darius I. He took control in Ionia after the Ionian Revolt, replacing the tyrants with democratic governments. He subsequently took Thrace and Thasos (492 BC). According to Herodotus, he was responsible for Xerxes' plans to invade Greece. After the battle of Salamis (480 BC), Mardonius was left in charge of Persian forces. He was defeated and killed at the battle of Plataea.

MAUSOLUS (*Mausolos*): Died 353/352 BC. Satrap of Caria (southwest Asia Minor) 377/376–353/352 BC, he ruled virtually independently of Persia. He extended his rule over the Greek coastal cities in Ionia and over Lycia and moved his capital from Mylasa to Halicarnassus. He caused Rhodes, Cos and Chios to revolt from the Second Athenian League, resulting in the Social War (357–355 BC). Rhodes and Cos became part of his kingdom. On his death, he was succeeded by his widow and sister Artemisia II. His tomb, the Mausoleum, was one of the Seven Wonders of the World.

MEGACLES (*Megakles*): Sixth-century-BC Athenian statesman of the Alcmaeonid family, son of Alcmaeon and father of Cleisthenes and Hippocrates. He married Agariste (daughter of Cleisthenes of Sicyon), possibly in 575 BC. He became leader of a political faction known as the Paraloi (coastmen), opposing Lycurgus and Peisistratus. When the latter became tyrant (c. 560 BC), Megacles and Lycurgus had him expelled. Megacles became reconciled with Peisistratus c. 550 BC and married his daughter, although the reconciliation and marriage subsequently failed.

MILTIADES (*Miltiades*): Lived c. 550–489 BC. An Athenian general, he was the son of Cimon and from the Philaidae family. He was sent to the Thracian Chersonese c. 524 BC to rule the native people as king. He married Hegesipyle, daughter of a Thracian king, and their son was Cimon. Miltiades participated in the invasion of Scythia by Darius I (513–512 BC), but he supported the Ionian Revolt against Persia. When that failed he fled to Athens (493 BC), where he was prosecuted and acquitted of a charge of tyranny in Thrace. He led the army at the battle of Marathon (490 BC), where he won a decisive victory over the Persians (fig. 2.4). In 489 BC he unsuccessfully led the Athenian fleet in a siege of the island of Paros and was wounded. He was prosecuted by Xanthippus and condemned to death. He died of his injuries.

MITHRIDATES II (*Mithridates*): King of Pontus c. 250–c. 185 BC. He possibly died c. 220 BC, with his son Mithridates III reigning until c. 185 BC. He married Laodice, sister of Seleucus II, but supported Antiochus Hierax in his fight against Seleucus II. He gave gifts to Rhodes after the great earthquake of 228/227 BC, which virtually destroyed the city including the Colossus.

MITHRIDATES VI EUPATOR DIONYSUS (*Mithridates*, Born of a Noble Father): Lived c. 132–63 BC. King of Pontus 120–63 BC and son of Mithridates V Euergetes. He was an enemy of Rome and a permanent threat to Rome's client kingdoms in Asia Minor. He shared the throne with his brother, but in 112 BC he killed his brother, imprisoned (and later murdered) his mother, married his sister Laodice and became sole ruler of Pontus. He attempted to expand his kingdom, and was involved in three Mithridatic Wars with Rome, from 88 to 63 BC. In the First Mithridatic War (88–85 BC) he was welcomed by the Greeks as a liberator and occupied much of the Greek mainland, islands and Asia Minor. This led to the siege and capture of Athens by the Roman general Sulla in 86 BC. Mithridates was defeated by the Romans at the battles of Chaeronea and Orchomenus (86/85 BC), and negotiated a peace treaty in 85 BC, which allowed him to retain Pontus. In the Second Mithridatic War (83–82 BC) he again made peace with Sulla, but renewed hostilities in 74 BC (Third Mithridatic War), when he invaded Bithynia. He committed suicide after his son Pharnaces revolted against him.

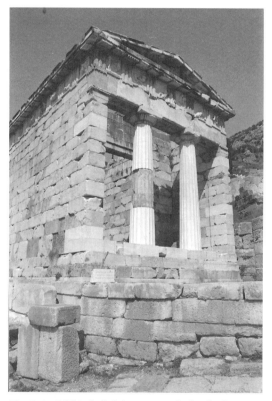

Fig. 2.4 Miltiades led the army at the battle of Marathon (490 BC), where he won a decisive victory over the Persians. The Doric Athenian Treasury at Delphi was possibly dedicated after the battle. It resembled a miniature temple, with a porch with two columns in antis *and a very short cella.*

MYRONIDES (*Myronides*): An Athenian general in 458 BC, when he defeated the Corinthians at Megara with an army of "the oldest and the youngest," and again in 457 BC, when he defeated the Boeotians at the battle of Oenophyta. It is unlikely he was the Myronides who was sent to Sparta with Cimon and Xanthippus (480 BC) and who served as general at the battle of Plataea (479 BC).

NABIS (*Nabis*): Eurypontid king of Sparta 207–192 BC. He was regent to the king Pelops (a minor), and on the latter's death (which Nabis may have caused) he declared himself king. He continued the reforms started by Cleomenes III. In 204–203 BC he raided Megalopolis and in 201 BC attacked Messene. In the Second Macedonian War (200–197 BC) he supported Macedonia against Rome. Although Nabis was allowed to remain in power, he had to give up Argos and the Laconian ports. Nabis attempted to regain his losses, but was quelled by the Roman generals Flamininus and Philopoemon. When Aetolian troops assassinated Nabis, Sparta lost its independence and was incorporated in the Achaean Confederacy.

NICANOR OF STAGIRA (*Nikanor*): Lived c. 360–317 BC. A Macedonian ambassador and general. He was a pupil (possibly with Alexander the Great) of Aristotle, and later married Aristotle's daughter. He may have commanded Alexander's fleet (334 BC), and in 324 BC he was sent to Greece with Alexander's decree ordering repatriation of most Greek exiles. In 319 BC he was Cassander's garrison commander at Piraeus, and in 318 BC commanded Cassander's fleet in the Bosphorus. He was executed by Cassander for treason.

NICIAS (*Nikias*): Lived c. 470–413 BC. An Athenian general and politician, he was often elected *strategos* and led several military expeditions. He was known for his immense wealth and owned hundreds of slaves who worked the silver mines at Laurium. He became a principal opponent of Cleon, advocating peace with Sparta. In 423 BC he was primarily responsible for a year's truce, and in 421 BC he concluded the eponymous Peace of Nicias, a 50-year peace agreement between Athens and Sparta. He subsequently opposed Alcibiades' schemes to intervene in the Peloponnese and Sicily, but was nevertheless appointed one of the generals of the Sicilian expedition with Alcibiades and

Lamachus. Alcibiades was recalled, and Lamachus was killed, leaving Nicias in sole charge. Due to an eclipse of the moon, which was considered a bad omen, he failed to withdraw in time. The Athenian fleet was destroyed and the troops defeated on land at the Assinarus River (413 BC). Nicias was captured and executed.

NICOMEDES I (*Nikomedes*): King of Bithynia c. 279–c. 250 BC. He allied himself with Heraclea Pontica and the cities of the Northern League against the Seleucids. He invited the Gauls to cross the Bosphorus and settle in Phrygia. Nicomedes founded a capital at Nicomedia c. 260 BC. He pursued hellenizing policies and coined Greek money.

NICOMEDES II EPIPHANES (*Nikomedes*, God Made Manifest): King of Bithynia 149–c. 127 BC. He was sent by his father Prusias II as an envoy to Rome to release Prusias from his war indemnity. However, he failed to support his father and joined Attalus II of Pergamum to seize the throne. Nicomedes subsequently assisted Rome against Aristonicus in 133–129 BC and was rewarded with territory in Greater Phrygia.

OLYMPIAS (*Olympias*; also known as Polyxena, Myrtale and Stratonice): Died 315 BC. Daughter of Neoptolemus of Molossia (in Epirus) and mother of Alexander the Great and Cleopatra. She married Philip II of Macedonia in 357 BC. In 331 BC she withdrew to Epirus, which she ruled for many years. After Alexander's death (323 BC), she tried to win support against Antipater. On his death (319 BC), she joined with Polyperchon against Cassander. She invaded Macedonia in 317 BC, which resulted in Philip III Arrhidaeus' murder and his wife Eurydice's forced suicide. Olympias then made her grandson Alexander IV king. Cassander invaded Macedonia and starved Olympias into surrender at Pydna, where she was executed.

OLYMPIODORUS (*Olympiodoros*): Floruit c. 307–280 BC. Athenian leader who was often *strategos*. In 306 BC his alliance with Aetolia enabled Cassander's attack on Athens to fail. After Athens was starved into surrender to Demetrius I Poliorcetes (spring 295 BC), Olympiodorus was archon from 294 to 292 BC. He led a revolt in Athens in 287 BC and successfully attacked the Macedonian garrison on the Hill of the Muses. With Demo-

chares he saved Eleusis from an attack by Antigonus Gonatas. He may also have freed Piraeus from the Macedonians.

ONOMARCHUS (*Onomarkhos*): Died 352 BC. He was a general of Phocis in the Third Sacred War (355–346 BC), and was elected *strategos autokrator* after the Phocian defeat at the battle of Neon (354 BC). He used temple funds from Delphi to bribe Thessaly and to hire mercenaries. He defeated the Boeotians and Locrians and refounded Orchomenus in Boeotia. He also forced Philip II of Macedonia to leave Thessaly (353 BC). When Philip again invaded Thessaly, Onomarchus was defeated and killed by him at the battle of the Crocus Field.

OPHELLAS (*Ophellas*): Died 309/308 BC. An officer under Alexander the Great, he was sent by Ptolemy I in 322 BC to subdue Cyrene, where he became governor and acquired a fairly independent status. In 310/309 BC he made an alliance with Agathocles who had crossed the Libyan Sea with numerous Athenians and colonists, intending to attack Carthage. Ophellas lost many men in the march through the desert; he brought troops and chariots to Agathocles, but was murdered by him.

PARMENION (*Parmenion*): Lived c. 400–330 BC. A Macedonian noble and Philip II's finest general. He later accompanied Alexander the Great to Asia and was second-in-command at the battles of Granicus (334 BC), Issus (333 BC) and Gaugamela (331 BC). In 331/330 BC he was left to guard the Persian royal treasure at Ecbatana when Alexander moved east. Alexander had Parmenion murdered when his son Philotas was tried and executed for treason.

PATROCLES (*Patrokles*): Lived c. 330–c. 275 BC. A Greek commander (*strategos*) under Seleucus I and Antiochus I. In 312 BC he was commander at Babylon and assisted Seleucus I against Demetrius I Poliorcetes. Subsequently, he probably governed the Caspian and Bactrian areas near India. In 285 BC he undertook a naval exploration of the Caspian Sea. The geographical information collated by him was contained in his book the *Periplous* (*Circumnavigation*).

PAUSANIAS (*Pausanias*): Died c. 467/466 BC. A Spartan regent 480–c. 467 BC, he was a member of

Fig. 2.5 Part of the Serpent Column commemorating the battle of Plataea (479 BC). The name of the victorious general Pausanias was erased and replaced by the names of the people of the 31 participating Greek cities.

the Agiad royal family and son of King Cleombrotus. When his uncle Leonidas died at Thermopylae (480 BC), he became a regent for his cousin Pleistarchus. Pausanias commanded the victorious Greek land forces at the battle of Plataea (479 BC). At Delphi he dedicated a bronze serpent column bearing his name, which the Spartans erased and replaced by the names of the 31 Greek states that had fought in the battle (figs. 1.7, 2.5). In 478 BC he recaptured Byzantium from the Persians, but was recalled and accused of treasonable negotiations with Xerxes. He was acquitted and returned to rule Byzantium, but the Athenian Cimon expelled him c. 476 BC. When in exile at Colonae he was ordered to return to Sparta, where he was accused of treason. He was acquitted but was then suspected of instigating a rebellion amongst the helots. He took refuge in a sanctuary of Athena, where he starved to death.

PAUSANIAS (*Pausanias*):   Agiad king of Sparta 409–395 BC and grandson of the regent Pausanias. He first ruled as a minor (445–426 BC), when his father Pleistoanax was temporarily deposed. Pausanias persuaded the ephors to put him in charge of the forces at Athens, replacing Lysander (403 BC). He was responsible for withdrawing Spartan support from the Thirty Tyrants, resulting in the restoration of democracy at Athens (403 BC). In 395 BC he arranged to meet up with Lysander near Haliartus in an invasion of Boeotia; he failed to make contact, and Lysander was killed. Pausanias was sentenced to death and fled into exile at Tegea.

PEISANDER (*Peisandros*):   Floruit 430–411 BC. An Athenian politician who took a leading role in the investigation of the mutilation of the herms (415 BC). In 411 BC he supported the pro-Spartan oligarchic revolution, proposing the new council of the Four Hundred. He fled to the Spartans at Decelea when the oligarchs were overthrown (410 BC) and was condemned for treason in his absence.

PEISISTRATIDS (*Peisistratidai*):   The family of Peisistratus (tyrant of Athens c. 560–527 BC) whose two sons Hippias and Hipparchus continued the tyranny.

PEISISTRATUS or PISISTRATUS (*Peisistratos*): Lived c. 600–527 BC. Tyrant of Athens c. 560–527 BC, he distinguished himself as a polemarch in a war against Megara (c. 565 BC), with the capture of

Nisaea (port of Megara). In a period of unrest he became a leader of a third political party, Hyperakrioi (the poorer hillmen). When he was granted a bodyguard by the Athenian people after an alleged attack, he seized the Acropolis and declared himself tyrant. In 556/555 BC he was expelled by the other two parties (plainsmen and coastmen), but returned briefly c. 550 BC due to a reconciliation with Megacles, an Alcmaeonid, who was leader of the coastmen and wanted a powerful alliance against the plainsmen. The alliance with Megacles and the marriage to his daughter failed, and Peisistratus went into exile for a longer period the same year, building up influence in the Aegean and accumulating money. He returned with a mercenary army, landing at Marathon and winning a battle at Pallene (546 BC). He became tyrant until his death and continued many of the reforms of Solon. He granted poor farmers loans, introduced a tithe on all produce and placated many of the nobles. He carried out many public building works and was a patron of the arts and literature. He gave support to the Panathenaea and City Dionysia festivals and the worship of Demeter at Eleusis. Peisistratus also pursued a skillful foreign policy. He was considered to be a just and humane ruler. His sons Hippias and Hipparchus continued his policies.

PELOPIDAS (*Pelopidas*):   Lived c. 410–364 BC. A Theban general who overthrew the oligarchy at Thebes in the winter of 379/378 BC, recovered the citadel from the Spartans and restored democracy. In 378 BC he was boeotarch. He won great fame in the war against Sparta with his leadership of the Sacred Band, especially at the battles of Tegyra (375 BC) and Leuctra (371 BC), when the Spartans were driven out of central Greece. In winter 370/369 BC he accompanied Epaminondas in his first invasion of the Peloponnese. Later he campaigned against Alexander of Pherae (in Thessaly) and Macedonia, both northern enemies of Thebes. He was captured by Alexander in 368 BC but was rescued by Epaminondas. In 364 BC he defeated Alexander at the battle of Cynoscephalae, but was himself killed.

PERDICCAS (*Perdikkas*):   Died 320 BC. A Macedonian general and regent. Son of Orontes, a Macedonian chieftain, he accompanied Alexander the Great to Asia as taxiarch. In 330 BC he was promoted to the Bodyguard, and in 324 BC he became his second-in-command. After Alexander's death (323 BC), he was effectively regent of Alexander's empire, which was resented by Antipater, Craterus, Antigonus I and Ptolemy I. Perdiccas invaded Egypt to eliminate Ptolemy, but was assassinated by his own officers.

PERDICCAS II (*Perdikkas*):   King of Macedonia c. 450/440–413 BC and son of Alexander I Philhellene. In the 440s and 430s he fought a series of civil wars against his brothers Alcetas and Philip, the latter supported by Athens. When Athens founded Amphipolis in 436 BC, Perdiccas supported the revolt of Potidaea and the Chalcidians (432 BC), but made his peace with Athens in 431 BC (arranged by the Thracian king Sitalces). In 429 BC he halted an invasion by Sitalces, and a marriage alliance was contracted. He effected alliances with the Spartan general in 425 BC against Athens, with Athens in 422 BC, with Sparta and Argos in 417 BC, and with Athens in 415 BC.

PERIANDER (*Periandros*):   Tyrant of Corinth c. 625–c. 585 BC, he was the son and successor of Cypselus and one of the most famous of early tyrants, although allegedly the most cruel; he was said to have murdered his wife. Corinth enjoyed fame and wealth under his rule, and he appeared in some lists of the Seven Sages of Greece. He probably built the *diolkos* across the Isthmus of Corinth. He undertook much public building at Corinth and also supported the arts. He founded colonies in northwest and northeast Greece, including Potidaea. His sons all predeceased him, and he was succeeded by his nephew Psammetichus.

PERICLES (*Perikles*):   Lived c. 495–429 BC. An Athenian statesman who supported democracy (fig. 2.6), he was an Alcmaeonid, the son of Xanthippus. Pericles was leader of Athens at the peak of its power in the 440s and 430s BC, an era called the "Periclean Age." In 472 BC he was choregos when Aeschylus' *Persians* was produced. In 463 BC he prosecuted Cimon for receiving bribes from Alexander I Philhellene not to invade Macedonia (the feud with the Cimonids being hereditary). In 462/461 BC he joined Ephialtes in reducing the powers of the Areopagus. He became the most prominent leader after Cimon's ostracism and Ephialtes' murder (both 461 BC), and the Delian League (an alliance formed against the Persians) was gradually transformed into an Athenian Empire under his leadership.

Not much is known of him in the 450s BC, but he did propose the recall of Cimon (450 BC) and possibly initiated the construction of the Long Walls (458–456 BC). In 454/453 BC he was *strategos*, campaigning in the Corinthian Gulf against Sicyon and Oeniadae. In 451 BC he introduced a law restricting citizenship to those whose parents were both Athenian. After 451 BC he was elected *strategos* 15 times in succession. He led a campaign to restore Delphi to the Phocians (c. 448 BC). In 448–447 BC he proposed a congress of all Greek states to consider universal peace and the rebuilding of temples destroyed by the Persians, but it was opposed by Sparta. He was building commissioner for the Parthenon (begun 447 BC), the Propylaea and other important buildings of this period (fig. 2.7). In 446 BC he harshly suppressed a revolt in Euboea, and in winter 446/445 BC he gained Sparta's recognition of the Athenian Empire with the so-called Thirty Years' Peace. Pericles planted many cleruchies to strengthen the Athenian Empire, particularly in the Hellespont, and he established an important colony at Thurii c. 443 BC to spread Athenian influence in Italy. In 443 BC his most bitter enemy Thucydides (son of Melesias) was ostracized, leaving Pericles with no effective opponent and enabling him to be elected *strategos* annually until his death. After a nine months' siege (440–439 BC), he suppressed Samos, which had revolted from the Athenian Empire. He founded a colony at Amphipolis in 436 BC and led an expedition to establish Athenian influence in the Black Sea area.

When the Peloponnesian War broke out in 431 BC, Pericles was responsible for the entire Athenian strategy. When Attica was invaded and plague broke out in Athens in 430 BC, he was removed from office, tried for embezzlement and fined, but shortly afterward (probably spring 429 BC) he was again elected *strategos*. However, he died soon after of plague. His younger son Pericles was illegitimate (son of his mistress Aspasia), but was granted citizenship out of respect for his father since his other sons by his wife had died of plague. This son was put to death after the battle of Arginusae in 406 BC.

Fig. 2.6 Bust of Pericles, probably a 3rd- or 2nd-century-BC copy from an original, lifesize naked warrior statue by Cresilas.

PERSEUS (*Perseus*): Lived c. 213/212–166 BC. King of Macedonia 179–168 BC and the elder son of Philip V, he fought against the Romans (199 BC) and Aetolians (189 BC). He plotted against his pro-Roman brother Demetrius, who was murdered by Philip V in 180 BC. In 179 BC Perseus renewed an old alliance with Rome and extended Macedonian influence and prestige. He married Laodice, daughter of Seleucus IV, and gave his half sister Apama in marriage to Prusias II of Bithynia. In 174 BC he visited the oracle at Delphi with his army. Rome

Fig. 2.7   Pericles was building commissioner for the Parthenon at Athens, which was begun in 447 BC. This is the east end of the temple.

thought that Perseus was about to declare war, a fear encouraged by Eumenes II of Pergamum who went to Rome to complain of Perseus. On his return, Eumenes was nearly killed near Delphi, blamed by Eumenes on Perseus, which precipitated the Third Macedonian War (171–168 BC). Perseus was initially successful, but was finally defeated by the Roman general Aemilius Paullus with troops from Pergamum at the battle of Pydna (168 BC). Perseus was taken to Rome to appear in Paullus' triumph and died two years later.

PEUCESTAS (*Peukestas*):   Lived c. 360 to after 317/316 BC. A Macedonian general and satrap, he saved Alexander the Great's life in the Indian expedition (325 BC) and was subsequently promoted to the Bodyguard and to satrap of Persis (325–324 BC). He adopted Iranian dress and learned Persian. In 323 BC he assembled 20,000 troops for the Macedonian army. After Alexander's death (323 BC) he retained Persis. He supported Eumenes of Cardia in his war against Antigonus I, but deserted

him at Gabiene (317/316 BC). Antigonus spared his life, but Peucestas was removed from his satrapy and disappeared from history.

PHALARIS (*Phalaris*):   Tyrant of Acragas soon after the city's foundation (c. 580 BC). He was renowned for his cruelty, allegedly roasting his enemies alive in a hollow bronze bull. He was replaced by an oligarchy.

PHARNABAZUS (*Pharnabazos*):   Persian commander, and hereditary satrap of Phrygia c. 413–370 BC, he was a rival of the Lydian satrap Tissaphernes. He initially supported Sparta against Athens in the Peloponnesian War, but in 408 BC encouraged the Athenians to undertake negotiations with Darius II, which broke down when Cyrus the Younger arrived in Ionia in 408 BC. Cyrus' defeat in 401 BC led to a war between Pharnabazus and Sparta from 400 BC. The Spartans were defeated at the battle of Cnidus by a Persian fleet under the Athenian Conon (394 BC). Pharnabazus was recalled to the Persian court at Susa and married a daughter of Artaxerxes II. He was sent in 385–383 BC and again in 374 BC to reconquer Egypt with the aid of the Athenian mercenary commander Iphicrates. He failed on both occasions and died soon after.

PHARNACES I (*Pharnakes*):   King of Pontus c. 185–c. 156 BC. He went to war with most of the other kingdoms in Asia Minor when extending his own territory. He seized Sinope (c. 183 BC) and invaded Cappadocia. The Romans were unable to prevent his aggression, and numerous rulers formed alliances against him. In 179 BC he was forced to surrender most of his gains. He kept Sinope as his capital and founded Pharnaceia farther east.

PHAYLLUS (*Phaullos*):   Died 351 BC. A general of Phocis in the Third Sacred War (355–346 BC), he succeeded his brother Onomarchus after he was killed at the battle of the Crocus Field (352 BC). With assistance from Sparta, Athens and Achaea, Phayllus occupied Thermopylae, preventing Philip II of Macedonia from marching farther south (352 BC). Philip withdrew, and Phayllus waged war against Thebes, but died of illness shortly thereafter.

PHEIDIPPIDES or PHILIPPIDES (*Pheidippides or Philippides*):   An Athenian courier sent in 490 BC before the battle of Marathon to request the help of the Spartan army. He undertook the 125-mile (200-km) journey in two days, and had a vision of Pan on his return journey. The modern marathon race is based on a legend that he ran from Athens to Marathon to join in the battle, then ran back to Athens with the words "Greetings, we win!" and dropped dead.

PHEIDON (*Pheidon*):   King of Argos, possibly early 7th century BC. Facts about him, including his dates, are uncertain. He was a Heraclid, allegedly descended from the original Dorian conqueror Temenus. He may have made himself tyrant and was probably a successful military leader. He is known for standardizing weights and measures, for seizing the running of the Olympian games from Elis and for extending Argive domination over the northeast Peloponnese. He may have been responsible for the defeat of the invading Spartans at the battle of Hysiae (669 BC) and for introducing coins.

PHILAIDS or PHILAIDAE (*Philaidai*):   One of the most distinguished Athenian families who claimed descent from Ajax. They included Cypselus (archon early 6th century BC), Miltiades (son of Cypselus), Cimon, Miltiades (son of Cimon) and Cimon (son of Miltiades).

PHILETAERUS (*Philhetairos*):   Lived c. 343–263 BC. Founder of the Attalid dynasty at Pergamum. He was descended from a Macedonian father Attalus and a Paphlagonian mother. He was an officer of Antigonus I, but deserted him for Lysimachus in 302 BC. He was put in charge of Pergamum, where Lysimachus stored a large treasure. In 282 BC he deserted to Seleucus I. Lysimachus died at the battle of Corupedium (281 BC) and Seleucus I was assassinated soon after. Philetaerus was left as a fairly independent ruler of Pergamum under the Seleucids, and may have extended his territory. He defended Pergamum against Galatian invaders of Asia Minor (278–276 BC). On his death he was succeeded by his nephew (and adopted son) Eumenes I.

PHILIP II (*Philippos*):   Lived 383/382–336 BC. King of Macedonia 359–336 BC. Youngest son of Amyntas (king of Macedonia c. 393–370/369 BC) and Eurydice. As a boy he was sent as a hostage to Thebes, where he learned much from the general Epaminondas. He married seven wives (polygamy was considered desirable), and his third wife was Olympias (a Molossian princess from Epirus); their son Alexander the Great was born in 356 BC. He married Cleopatra (Eurydice) in 337 BC, provoking ill-feeling between himself and Olympias and Alexander. Philip succeeded to the throne after his brother Perdiccas III was killed in battle. He reorganized the Macedonian army and defeated the Paeonians (early 358 BC) and then the Illyrians. In 357 BC he captured the strategically important Amphipolis. From spring 356 BC he besieged Potidaea, which was given to Olynthus, and colonized Crenides, changing its name to Philippi. In 354 BC he besieged and captured Methone (where he lost an eye from a catapult bolt), razing it to the ground.

In 354 BC the Thessalian League asked Philip for assistance against the tyrants of Pherae in central Thessaly. He and the Thessalian allies were defeated twice in 353 BC (the only defeats of his career), once by Onomarchus who drove Philip from Thessaly. In 352 BC he returned to Thessaly and defeated and killed Onomarchus at the battle of the Crocus Field near Pagasae (port of Pherae). He suppressed the tyranny at Pherae and became archon of the Thessalian League, bringing Thessaly under Macedonian control. He marched toward Thermopylae, but the defense of Thermopylae by the Phocians and allies prevented him from marching farther south. From 351 to 350 BC he acted against the Illyrians and Epirus and gradually enlarged his fleet, which came to harass Athens' trade and territory. In 349–348 BC he attacked and annexed Chalcidice, and instigated a revolt in Euboea against Athens. In 349 BC he also attacked Olynthus, which fell in 348 BC, despite Athenian assistance; it was razed to the ground and its inhabitants sold into slavery.

Philip's threat to invade Phocis led Athens to make peace with him (Peace of Philocrates) in 346 BC, with the agreement that Athens and Macedonia would retain the territories currently held. Phocis was not mentioned in the treaty. Athens retained the Thracian Chersonese, but lost Amphipolis and was not able to include Phocis. In 346 BC Philip marched south, took Thermopylae and crushed the Phocians, replacing Phocis on the Amphictyonic Council. Philip presided over the Pythian Games that year. In 345 BC he campaigned against Illyria, and in 344 and 342 BC against Thessaly. In 343/342 BC he intervened in Epirus, installing his brother-in-law Alexander as king of Epirus. He campaigned in Thrace, making it a tribute-paying province of Macedonia in 342 BC and removing its king. He founded several cities there, including Philippopolis (Plovdiv). This action threatened Athenian interests in the Thracian Chersonese, and Demosthenes delivered his *Third Philippic* against Philip (341 BC), urging military action. Philip's attack in 340 BC on Perinthus and Byzantium, which had both revolted from the Macedonian alliance, precipitated Athens' declaration of war (340 BC). He withdrew from the siege of Byzantium into Thrace (340/339 BC) to campaign against the Scythians, returning in the summer of 339 BC. The Amphictyonic Council invited Philip in late 339 BC to lead the Fourth Sacred War against the Locrians of Amphissa for sacrilege. Philip marched south around November 339 BC and took Elatea in Phocis. Demosthenes arranged an alliance between Athens and Thebes to prevent Philip from invading Attica. Philip defeated this alliance at the battle of Chaeronea on 2 August, 338 BC, with his son Alexander the Great leading the cavalry (fig. 2.8).

Philip did not impose pro-Macedonian rule in the newly conquered cities, except in Thebes, which had to give up Oropus and accept a Macedonian garrison. A congress was held at Corinth in 337 BC, where the Greeks established a Common Peace. The League of Corinth was also established, a body that Philip intended to use for military support to attack Persia. Philip was appointed *strategos autokrator*, and arrangements were made for an invasion, but Philip was assassinated by Pausanias at the celebration of his daughter Cleopatra's marriage to King Alexander of Epirus (fig. 1.9). This was possibly a plot of his deposed wife Olympias to secure the succession for her son Alexander the Great. Philip was buried in a tomb at Aegae (Vergina).

PHILIP III ARRHIDAEUS (*Philippos Arrhidaios*): Lived c. 358–317 BC. Son of Philip II and Philinna of Larissa, he became joint king of Macedonia with Alexander IV from 323 BC, until he was captured and murdered by Olympias. He was apparently mentally disabled.

PHILIP V (*Philippos*): Lived 238–179 BC. King of Macedonia 221–179 BC. Son of Demetrius II and Phthia-Chryseis, he was adopted by Antigonus II Doson who ruled as a regent. Philip's actions were largely reponsible for bringing Greece under Roman domination. As a boy he visited Aratus of Sicyon to learn about the Greeks and the Achaean Confederacy. He acquired renown in the so-called Social War of 220–217 BC, acting with the Hellenic League against Aetolia, Sparta and Elis. He was incited by Demetrius of Pharos to attack Roman fleets off Illyria in 216 BC, when Rome was involved in the Second Punic War. In 215 BC Philip V made an alliance with Hannibal, ending any possibility of friendship with Rome. The First Macedonian War ensued (215–205 BC) but was inconclusive. Philip began to attack Messene in 215 BC, and from 213 to 212 BC he continued to harass the cities of Illyria and build up the navy he had lost off Illyria in 214 BC. Rome and Aetolia attacked Philip sporadically from 212/211 to 208 BC, assisted by Attalus I of Pergamum from 209 BC. In 207 BC, Philip sacked Thermum and forced terms upon Aetolia in the following year. The First Macedonian War ended inconclusively with the Peace of Phoenice (205 BC).

In 202 BC Philip V made an alliance with Antiochus III against Egypt, but in 201 BC his fleet suffered great losses in the defeat off Chios by Attalus I and the Rhodians. This provoked the Second Macedonian War between Philip and Rome (200–197 BC). He was finally defeated by Quintus Flamininus at the battle of Cynoscephalae in Thessaly in 197 BC. Harsh penalties were imposed, his rule was confined to Macedonia, and his son Demetrius was taken as hostage to Rome. Philip then collaborated with Rome against Nabis of Sparta (195 BC) and against Aetolia and Antiochus III (192–189 BC). His tribute was therefore remitted by the Romans and his son Demetrius was returned to Macedonia. After 185 BC he campaigned in the Balkans, and in 184 BC he sent Demetrius back to Rome to argue his case. He murdered his pro-Roman son Demetrius in favor of Perseus, then died of sickness (allegedly remorse) at Amphipolis.

PHILOCRATES (*Philokrates*): Floruit 340s BC. An Athenian politician who first proposed peace negotiations with Philip II after his destruction of Olynthus (348 BC). Philocrates was accused by a *graphe paranomon*, but Demosthenes successfully defended him in court (347–346 BC). Philocrates undertook an embassy to Macedonia with Demosthenes and Aeschines in 346 BC to seek peace, and on the return he secured a peace agreement and alliance with Philip, later called the Peace (or Decree) of Philocrates. Before this peace was ratified Philip II had advanced farther into central Greece. Philocrates served on other embassies to Philip, but in 343 BC he was prosecuted for corruption in the peace negotiations and was condemned to death in his absence.

PHILOMELUS (*Philomelos*): Died 354 BC. A Phocian commander in the Third Sacred War (355–346 BC). At the threat of war Philomelus was

Fig. 2.8   The Philippeum at Olympia, a circular building erected by Philip II as a votive offering after his defeat of the Greeks at the battle of Chaeronea in 338 BC. It was finished c. 335 BC to house the statues of the Macedonian royal family. Eighteen Ionic columns stood around the exterior.

elected *strategos autokrator* of Phocis. He seized Delphi with the help of mercenaries (summer 356 BC), gaining control of the sanctuary and defeating the Locrians. He then defeated the Thebans in the winter of 356/355 BC, and made an alliance with Sparta and Athens. In the autumn of 355 BC the Amphictyony declared a Sacred War, and he used sacred funds to hire 10,000 mercenaries. He was eventually defeated late in the autumn of 354 BC at the battle of Neon against the Locrians and Thebans. He committed suicide and was succeeded by his brother Onomarchus.

PHILOPOEMEN (*Philopoimen*): Lived 252–182 BC. An Achaean statesman and soldier from Megalopolis in Arcadia, he was educated by the philosophers Demophanes and Ecdelus. Plutarch described him as "the last of the Greeks." He fought in the unsuccessful defense of Megalopolis (223 BC), which was sacked by Cleomenes III of Sparta. In July 222 BC he was a cavalry commander in the battle of Sellasia (near Sparta), with the Spartans under Cleomenes III being defeated by Antigonus III Doson and the Achaeans. Afterward, Philopoemen went to Crete for 10 years as a mercenary soldier. He returned in 211 BC and was elected hipparch of the Achaean Confederacy in 210/209 BC and general of the Confederacy eight times. He reorganized the cavalry and infantry, and defeated the Spartans on several occasions. In 183 BC he took part in an expedition against Messene, which had revolted from the Achaean Confederacy. He was ambushed and captured by the Messenians and may have been poisoned in prison.

PHILOTAS (*Philotas*): Lived c. 360–330 BC. A Macedonian noble and son of Parmenion, he was the commander of Alexander the Great's Companion Cavalry. He was executed for treason by Alexander, apparently because he had failed to forward information regarding a plot against Alexander.

PHOCION (*Phokion*): Lived 402/401–319/318 BC. An Athenian general and politician, he was elected general (*strategos*) 45 times from 371 to 319/318 BC, and participated in several campaigns, notably in Euboea (spring 348 and 341 BC), in the defense of Megara (343 BC) and in Byzantium (339 BC). He was a skilled orator and became important from the 340s BC. He advocated peace with Macedonia, supporting Eubulus, Aeschines and

Demades against Demosthenes and Hyperides. When Athens was defeated at the battle of Chaeronea (338 BC), he helped Demades to arrange a peace agreement with Macedonia. After Alexander the Great's death (323 BC), he tried to prevent Athens from joining other Greek states in the Lamian War against Macedonia (323–322 BC). In 319 BC Nicanor was commander at Piraeus, and in 318 BC Phocion was put to death on a charge of treason, apparently for complicity with Nicanor.

PHORMION or PHORMIO (*Phormion*): Fifth-century-BC Athenian naval commander, who undertook campaigns c. 439 BC. From 430 BC he blockaded the Gulf of Corinth with his fleet from Naupactus, and the following summer he won two naval victories over the Peloponnesians. On returning to Athens (428 BC) he was accused of embezzlement, and may have died soon after.

PHRYNICHUS (*Phrynikhos*): Died 411 BC. An Athenian politician. In 412/411 BC he opposed the recall of Alcibiades and became one of the extreme oligarchs at the time of the revolution of the Four Hundred (411 BC). He went to Sparta to negotiate peace, but on his return he was assassinated in the agora.

PITTACUS (*Pittakos*): Lived c. 650–c. 570 BC. A statesman from Mytilene (Lesbos), regarded as one of the Seven Sages after his death. He led the Mytileneans in a war against Athens for Sigeum at the mouth of the Hellespont (on which Periander of Corinth subsequently arbitrated). Pittacus became *aisymnetes* (dictator) for 10 years to restore order (c. 590–c. 580 BC). He reformed various laws, including doubling the penalty for all offenses committed when drunk. He banished the nobles who opposed him, including Alcaeus and Sappho. He retired and died 10 years later. Little is known of his life.

POLYCRATES (*Polykrates*): Tyrant of Samos c. 540–c. 523 BC, he established a powerful navy and annexed several neighboring islands in the eastern Aegean. He was a patron of the arts and initiated many public works, most notably the harbor, temple of Hera, and a tunnel that brought water to his capital. Alliances were made with Egypt and Cyrene, but later Polycrates sent Samians to help Cambyses of Persia against Amasis of Egypt. When they returned, they tried unsuccessfully to overthrow

Polycrates with Spartan help. Apparently envious of his success and wealth, the Persian satrap Oroetes pretended to plot against Darius I; he lured Polycrates to Magnesia ad Maeandrum and executed him.

POLYPERCHON (*Polyperkhon*): Lived c. 380–c. 303 BC. A Macedonian general who was taxiarch after 333 BC, serving in Alexander the Great's campaigns in Asia. He was sent back to Europe as Craterus' second-in-command in 324 BC, and was commander in the Lamian War (323–322 BC). The regent Antipater appointed him as his successor in Europe in 319 BC, but Cassander (son of Antipater) at once formed a coalition of generals against him and called on the help of Olympias. Polyperchon was driven from Macedonia and eventually lost his bases in the Peloponnese, with Cassander replacing him as *strategos*.

PORUS (*Poros*): Died 317 BC. An Indian king who was defeated by Alexander the Great in 326 BC at the Hydaspes (Jhelum) River. He impressed Alexander so much that he was allowed to retain his kingdom between the Hydaspes and Acesines (Chenab) Rivers and was later given extra land. He was murdered by the Macedonian satrap Eudamus.

PRUSIAS I CHOLUS (*Prusias*): King of Bithynia c. 230/228–c. 185/182 BC, he increased the territory of Bithynia to its greatest size. In 220/219 BC he campaigned against Byzantium, and in 218 BC he defeated invading Gauls (Galatians). In the First Macedonian War (215–205 BC), he took land from Attalus I of Pergamum. He supplied Philip V with ships, and in 202 BC was rewarded with the ports of Cius and Myrleia (renaming them Prusias and Apamea). In the Syrian War against Antiochus III (192–188 BC) he remained neutral after advice from the Roman Scipios. However, when he was ordered to return land to Eumenes II of Pergamum as part of the Peace of Apamea (188 BC), war broke out (186–184 BC). Prusias was defeated, and Hannibal (a refugee at his court) committed suicide (183 BC).

PRUSIAS II CYNEGUS (*Prusias*): King of Bithynia c. 182–149 BC (fig. 2.9). He was son of Prusias I and husband of Apama, daughter of Philip V. Prusias joined Eumenes II of Pergamum against Pharnaces I of Pontus (183–179 BC). War later broke out between Prusias and Attalus II of Pergamum (156–154 BC), and he had to pay a heavy indemnity when defeated. In order to release himself from this indemnity, he sent his son (Nicomedes II) to Rome as an envoy. However, in 149 BC Attalus supported Nicomedes II in seizing the throne. Attalus and Nicomedes invaded Bithynia, and Prusias was murdered in the temple of Zeus in Nicomedia.

PTOLEMIES (*Ptolemaioi*): A Macedonian Greek dynasty founded by Ptolemy I. It ruled Egypt from 323 BC to the Roman conquest in 30 BC.

PTOLEMY I SOTER (*Ptolemaios*, Savior): Lived c. 367/366–283/282 BC. Macedonian king of Egypt and founder of the Ptolemaic dynasty. A friend of Alexander the Great, he was exiled c. 337 BC, but was recalled after Philip II's murder (336 BC). In 330 BC he was appointed Companion to Alexander (*hetairos*) and fought with distinction in Alexander's campaigns. In 324 BC he married Artacama (granddaughter of Pharnabazus), divorced her after Alexander's death (323 BC), married Eurydice (daughter of Antipater) and then (possibly without divorce) Berenice I.

In the late summer of 323 BC Ptolemy I became satrap of Egypt. In 319 BC he seized Palestine and Coele-Syria, losing them again to Eumenes of Cardia. He fought against Antigonus I and Demetrius I Poliorcetes intermittently from 315 to 301 BC. In 312 BC he defeated Demetrius Poliorcetes at Gaza, and in 311 BC there was peace amongst the Successors, with a recognition of territory. In 310–309 BC Ptolemy installed his brother Menelaus as governor of Cyprus and also occupied Cos. He intervened in Greek affairs 309–308 BC, and in 306 BC was defeated at Salamis (off Cyprus) by Demetrius I Poliorcetes. Ptolemy consequently lost all his Aegean possessions. In 305/304 BC he declared himself king. From c. 301 to 286/285 BC he retook Palestine, Coele-Syria, Cyprus and other territories in the Aegean and Asia Minor.

Ptolemy wrote a firsthand account of Alexander the Great, which was used as Arrian's main source. He established the military and administrative organization of Ptolemaic Egypt and his empire. He founded the cult of Sarapis and established the museum and library at Alexandria.

PTOLEMY II PHILADELPHUS (*Ptolemaios*, Loving his Sister): Lived 308–246 BC. King of

Fig. 2.9 a) and b)   The pedestal at Delphi, built to support the equestrian statue of Prusias II of Bithynia. It dates to c. 180 BC.

Egypt 283/282–246 BC and son of Ptolemy I and Berenice I, born at Cos. He married Arsinoë I (daughter of Lysimachus) c. 289/288 BC. In 285 BC he was joint ruler with his father, and became king in 283/282 BC. He divorced Arsinoë I c. 281 BC, and c. 276/275 BC he married his sister Arsinoë II and made her joint ruler. The marriage caused a scandal among the Greeks, although brother-sister marriage was normal among Egyptian pharaohs. In the First Syrian War against Antiochus I (c. 274/273–271 BC) he invaded parts of Syria and Asia Minor, winning a victory in 271 BC. Ptolemy established the Ptolemaic ruler-cult, deifying himself and Arsinoë II in 272/271 BC. He later adopted her title and cult-title Philadelphus.

Ptolemy suffered losses in the Chremonidean War, supporting Athens and Sparta against Macedonia (286–263/262 BC). In the Second Syrian

War against Antiochus II (260–253 BC), Ptolemy lost large areas of Asia Minor and concluded the war with a marriage between Antiochus II and his daughter Berenice Syra. Ptolemy II (with his advisers) greatly hellenized Egypt. He established much of the strict Ptolemaic financial administration and founded many Greek settlements, especially around Lake Moeris. He built the Pharos and greatly extended the museum and library at Alexandria. He also built a canal from the Red Sea to the Nile. Alexandria, his capital, became the cultural and intellectual center of the Greek world.

PTOLEMY III EUERGETES (*Ptolemaios*, the Benefactor):   Born between 288 and 280 BC, died 222/221 BC. King of Egypt 246–221 BC, he was the son of Ptolemy II and Arsinoë I. He married Berenice II (daughter of King Magas of Cyrene) in

246 BC and united Cyrene with Egypt. In the Third Syrian War (246–241 BC), he invaded large areas of the Seleucid Empire in Syria and Asia Minor. He returned to Egypt due to a revolt, and there was peace in Egypt for the rest of his reign. Ptolemaic expansion subsequently ceased, although he intervened in Greece. In 243 BC he was elected *strategos* of the Achaean Confederacy, after supporting Aratus of Sicyon against Macedonia. He later transferred his support to Cleomenes III of Sparta, but did not assist him at the battle of Sellasia in 222 BC, possibly fearful of war between Macedonia and Egypt.

PTOLEMY IV PHILOPATOR (*Ptolemaios*, Father-Loving): Lived c. 244–204 BC. King of Egypt 221–204 BC. Son of Ptolemy III and Berenice II. In 217 BC he married his sister Arsinoë III. He was more interested in intellectual pursuits than public affairs, which were in the control of his ministers Sosibius and Agathocles. Antiochus III invaded Palestine in 221 BC and again in 219–217 BC (Fourth Syrian War), which ended with victory for Ptolemy IV at the battle of Raphia in 217 BC. Severe internal riots by the native Egyptians took place, and from 207 BC the Thebaid (Upper Egypt) was ruled by Nubian kings. Ptolemy continued to neglect public affairs and was instead devoted to the cult of Dionysus.

PTOLEMY V EPIPHANES (*Ptolemais*, God Made Manifest): Lived 210–180 BC. Joint ruler from 210 BC and king of Egypt 204–180 BC, although in the control of his ministers Sosibius and Agathocles. He was son of Ptolemy IV and Arsinoë III. After his accession, there were serious revolts in Egypt for two decades. Philip V of Macedonia and Antiochus III planned to divide up Egypt, and from 203 BC Ptolemy lost most of the territories in Asia Minor, the Aegean and Palestine. His troops were finally defeated by Antiochus in 200 BC at Panion (near the headwaters of the Jordan River). He made peace with Antiochus III and in 193 BC married Antiochus' daughter Cleopatra I. In 187/186 BC his commander Hippalus reconquered the Thebaid (Upper Egypt), and in 184/183 BC the revolts in Lower Egypt were finally quelled.

PTOLEMY VI PHILOMETOR (*Ptolemais*, Mother-Loving): Lived 186 or 184/183–145 BC. King of Egypt 180–145 BC. Son of Ptolemy V and Cleopatra I. He was joint ruler with his mother from 180 BC until her death in 176 BC. In 175/174 BC he married his sister Cleopatra II. The Sixth Syrian War broke out against Antiochus IV (170–168 BC). Meanwhile, Ptolemy formed a joint rule with his brother Ptolemy VIII and with Cleopatra II (170–163 BC). There was constant disagreement between the two brothers. From 163 BC they agreed on a partition, with Ptolemy VI sole ruler of Egypt, while Ptolemy VIII ruled in Cyrene. In 155 BC Ptolemy VIII threatened to bequeath his kingdom of Cyrene to Rome, and so Ptolemy VI installed his son Ptolemy VII as governor in Cyprus to forestall any invasion by Ptolemy VIII. His daughter Cleopatra Thea was married to Alexander Balas (150/149 BC). Ptolemy VI switched his support to Demetrius II Nicator and was acclaimed Seleucid king jointly with Demetrius II, but was killed in battle against Alexander Balas.

PTOLEMY VII NEOS PHILOPATOR (*Ptolemaios*, New Father-Loving): Lived c. 162/161–144 BC. Son of Ptolemy VI and Cleopatra II. Joint ruler in Egypt in 145 BC with Ptolemy VI, then sole ruler from Ptolemy VI's death (145 BC) until the arrival of Ptolemy VIII in Egypt, when he was murdered in August 144 BC.

PTOLEMY VIII EUERGETES II (*Ptolemaios*, Benefactor; he was also called *Physkon*, pot-belly): king of Egypt 170–116 BC. He was joint ruler with his brother Ptolemy VI in 170–163 BC, then king of Cyrene only, until his brother's death (145 BC). He unsuccessfully tried to recapture Cyprus. Ptolemy IX tried to have Ptolemy VIII assassinated (156/155 BC), and Ptolemy VIII threatened to bequeath Cyrene to Rome if he died childless. Ptolemy VIII returned to Egypt, murdered Ptolemy VII and married his sister Cleopatra II in 144 BC. He then expelled from Alexandria the intellectuals and Jews who were against him, and in 142 BC he seduced and married Cleopatra III (daughter of his brother and of his sister/wife Cleopatra II) without divorcing Cleopatra II. Cleopatra II successfully led a revolt against him in 132 BC and declared her son Ptolemy Memphites king and herself queen. Ptolemy VIII fled to Cyprus, and Ptolemy Memphites was murdered. In 127/126 BC Ptolemy VIII reconquered Alexandria and ruled with the two queens from 124 BC. He bequeathed his power to Cleopatra III and her children.

PTOLEMY IX SOTER II (LATHYRUS)
(*Ptolemaios*, Savior; his nickname *Lathyros* means Chick-pea, the Greek equivalent of Cicero): Lived c. 141–81 BC. King of Egypt 116–81 BC and eldest son of Ptolemy VIII and Cleopatra III. He was a priest of Alexander the Great from 135/134 BC. He later became governor of Cyprus and married his sister Cleopatra IV. In 116 BC he was joint ruler with Cleopatra III, while his younger brother Ptolemy X was sent to govern Cyprus. He divorced Cleopatra IV and married another sister, Cleopatra Selene, who eventually divorced him. In 110 and 108 BC he was forced to accept his brother Ptolemy X as joint ruler. There was constant strife between them, and in 107 BC Ptolemy IX fled from Alexandria to Syria and then to Cyprus. He was involved in conflicts with Antiochus VIII and Antiochus IX. Cyprus and Egypt remained separate states until 88 BC, when Ptolemy IX returned from Cyprus to defeat Ptolemy X and reunite the kingdom. He ruled with his daughter Cleopatra Berenice until his death.

PTOLEMY X ALEXANDER I (*Ptolemaios Alexandros*): Lived c. 140–87 BC. King of Egypt 116–88 BC (intermittently). He was sent to Cyprus as governor in 116 BC to replace his older brother Ptolemy IX. There was constant strife between the two brothers, and in 107 BC Ptolemy IX fled from Alexandria, and Ptolemy X returned as joint ruler with Cleopatra III. He was involved in conflict with Antiochus VIII and Antiochus IX. In 101 BC he allegedly murdered his mother Cleopatra III and married his brother's daughter Cleopatra Berenice a few days later. Ptolemy IX returned from Cyprus in 88 BC, and Ptolemy X was expelled from Egypt (spring 87 BC). He willed his kingdom to Rome and was killed in a naval battle off Cyprus soon after.

PTOLEMY XI ALEXANDER II (*Ptolemaios*): Lived c. 100/99–80 BC. King of Egypt 80 BC, son of Ptolemy X and a first wife. The Roman general Sulla made Ptolemy XI joint ruler with his stepmother Cleopatra Berenice in 80 BC. He married her and murdered her 19 days later, then was killed by the people of Alexandria. He was the last legitimate male descendant of the Ptolemies.

PTOLEMY XII THEOS PHILOPATOR PHILADELPHUS NEOS DIONYSOS (AULETES) (*Ptolemaios*, God, Father-Loving, Loving his sister, New; he was actually known as *Auletes*, piper or flute player. His name "Ptolemy XII" was not used.): Born between 116 and 108 BC. Died 51 BC. King of Egypt 80–51 BC. Illegitimate son of Ptolemy IX and a mistress. In 80/79 BC he married his full sister Cleopatra V Tryphaena. He developed amicable relations with Rome and was fully recognized by Julius Caesar in 59 BC. He was consequently deposed by the Alexandrians in 59/58 BC and ceded Cyprus to Rome. He was restored by Aulus Gabinius (Roman governor of Syria) in 55 BC. His children included Ptolemy XIII, Ptolemy XIV and Cleopatra VII.

PTOLEMY XIII (*Ptolemaios*): Lived 63–47 BC. King of Egypt 51–47 BC, and son of Ptolemy XII. There was conflict between him and his sister Cleopatra VII from 51 BC (she was expelled in 48 BC). Julius Caesar forced him to rule with Cleopatra VII after the murder of Pompey by his ministers (28 September, 48 BC). He declared war on Julius Caesar (Alexandrian War) and was defeated and drowned in the Nile.

PYRRHUS (*Pyrrhos*): Lived 319–272 BC. Molossian king of Epirus and second cousin of Alexander the Great. He reigned as a minor from 307 to 303 BC, when he was exiled. He fled to Demetrius I Poliorcetes and served at the battle of Ipsus (301 BC). Demetrius Poliorcetes sent him as hostage to Ptolemy I in 299/298 BC, where he married Antigone, daughter of Berenice I. In 297 BC he regained the throne at Epirus with the aid of Ptolemy I. On the death of Antigone, he married Lanassa, daughter of Agathocles, and later the daughter of a Dardanian chief with whom he made an alliance.

Pyrrhus aimed to restore Alexander the Great's empire. After a successful war with Lysimachus against Demetrius Poliorcetes (288 BC), he was the most powerful ruler in Greece, in control of Thessaly and western Macedonia. In 285 BC he was pushed back to Epirus by Lysimachus. From 280 to 275 BC Pyrrhus fought against Rome on behalf of the Greeks in Italy and Sicily. Although he was ultimately victorious in battles in 280 (Heraclea) and 279 BC (Asculum), his losses were so great he had to move his forces to Sicily in 277 BC—thus the term "Pyrrhic victory" for an empty or meaningless win. He almost succeeded in ousting the Carthaginians (then allies of Rome) but returned to Italy. He was beaten by the Romans in 275 BC at the battle of Beneventum (then called Maleventum) and so returned to Epirus. In 274 BC he again invaded Macedonia. He recovered most of Thessaly and Macedonia from Antigonus II Gonatas, but in 272 BC turned to invade the Peloponnese. Antigonus meanwhile regained most of Macedonia, and Pyrrhus was killed in an attempt to seize Argos.

ROXANE (*Rhoxane*): Died 311 BC. She was a Bactrian captive who married Alexander the Great in 327 BC. After his death (323 BC), she was said to have murdered his other wife Barsine (Stateira). In 320 BC Roxane returned to Macedonia with her son Alexander IV, but on Antipater's death (319 BC) they fled to Olympias in Epirus. Returning to Epirus they were taken by Cassander (316 BC) and executed in 311 BC.

SANDRACOTTUS (*Sandrakottos*, Sanskrit *Chandragupta*): Indian king c. 321–297 BC who founded the Mauryan Empire in northern India. He resisted an invasion of the Punjab by Seleucus I and was in conflict with him from 308 BC. In 303 BC Seleucus ceded him the satrapies of Gandhara, Arachosia and eastern Gedrosia (the Punjab) in return for a marriage alliance and a gift of 500 war elephants. Sandracottus was in control of much of the Indo-Pakistani subcontinent by 305 BC.

SELEUCIDS: Dynasty founded by Seleucus I that ruled much of Syria and Asia after the death of Alexander the Great (323 BC). The Seleucid Era dates from 7 October, 312 BC on the Macedonian calendar and 3 April, 311 BC on the Babylonian calendar. The rulers included Seleucus I–III and Antiochus I–III.

SELEUCUS I NICATOR (*Seleukos*, Conqueror): Lived c. 358–281 BC. Founder of the Seleucid dynasty, he was one of Alexander the Great's Macedonian Companions. In the Indian campaign against King Porus (326 BC) he commanded the Bodyguard. After Alexander died, Perdiccas made him chiliarch. He married the Persian Apama in 324 BC. In 320 BC he was one of the officers responsible for Perdiccas' murder. He was appointed satrap of Babylonia (321 BC) and supported Antigonus I against Eumenes of Cardia. Seleucus I, fearful of his life, fled from Antigonus I to Ptolemy I in

Egypt (spring 315 BC). With Ptolemy I in late 312 BC, he defeated Demetrius I Poliorcetes (who was trying to invade Ptolemy's territory) at Gaza and then recaptured his kingdom in the east, including Babylon.

In the peace among the Successors of 311 BC, Seleucus was confirmed as the ruler of territories east of the Euphrates. He then attempted to regain eastern territories of Alexander's empire, including Bactria. He proclaimed himself king in 305/304 BC (as did the other Macedonian rulers). He ceded the Punjab to the Mauryan king Sandracottus and received 500 war elephants in 303 BC. He and his war elephants joined Cassander and Lysimachus to defeat his chief rival Antigonus I at the battle of Ipsus (301 BC). With access to the Mediterranean via Syria and Cilicia, Syria became the center of the Seleucid Empire, with a new capital at Antioch (founded 300 BC). He subsequently campaigned against Demetrius I Poliorcetes. In 299/298 BC he married Demetrius' daughter Stratonice (but gave her to his son Antiochus I in 294/293 BC), while keeping Apama. He ruled jointly with his son Antiochus I from 292 BC. He captured Demetrius I Poliorcetes in 285 BC and imprisoned him at Apamea. He acquired the rest of Asia Minor by defeating and killing Lysimachus at the battle of Corupedium in 281 BC. He then invaded Europe in an attempt to take Macedonia, but was assassinated near Lysimachia by Ptolemy Ceraunus, a son of Ptolemy I.

SELEUCUS II CALLINICUS (*Seleukos*, the Triumphant): Lived c. 265–226 BC. Seleucid king 246–226 BC and eldest son of Antiochus II and Laodice I. He was beset with various problems and spent his entire reign on campaign. His stepmother Berenice Syra claimed the throne for her infant son, so her brother Ptolemy III invaded Syria (Third Syrian War, 246–241 BC). Berenice and her son were murdered, and Ptolemy III advanced as far as Bactria, but had to withdraw to Egypt. Seleucus II regained his eastern territories, although Bactria became independent. Seleucus II made his younger brother Antiochus Hierax joint ruler in order to conclude the Third Syrian War against Ptolemy (241 BC). Conflict arose between the two brothers, so the empire was split between them, with Hierax in Asia Minor. After the latter's death in 226 BC, Seleucus II regained sole control of his empire, but large parts of Asia Minor were now controlled by Pergamum. He died in an accident.

SELEUCUS III SOTER (*Seleukos*, Savior): Lived c. 245–223 BC. Seleucid king 226–223 BC and son of Seleucus II. He was murdered on a campaign against Attalus I of Pergamum to regain former Seleucid territory. Seleucus was succeeded by his younger brother Antiochus III.

SITALCES (*Sitalkes*): Died 424 BC. King of the Odrysian Empire in Thrace. He established a powerful state in alliance with Athens, extending from the Danube to the Aegean. He invaded Chalcidice and Macedonia in 429 BC in support of the pretender Amyntas, but returned to his own country soon after with little accomplished. He died in a disastrous expedition against the Triballi, a tribe of the lower Danube.

SOLON (*Solon*): Lived c. 640–after 561 BC. An Athenian statesman, lawgiver and poet. He was archon in 594/593 BC, after having given good advice for winning Salamis in the war against Megara. There were serious problems in Athens at this time, and Solon undertook economic reforms, in particular to help poor farmers who were often reduced to serfdom. He canceled all debts for which land or liberty was the security (a reform known as *seisakhtheia*, "shaking off the burdens" [of the poor]) and prohibited future borrowing on the security of a person. He received some criticism for not redistributing land. He may have introduced other reforms such as a native Attic coinage, a system of weights and measures, prohibition of export of all crops except olives, and granting of citizenship to immigrant craftsmen. He introduced a more humane law code, repealing the laws of Draco (except those which dealt with homicide). He also undertook a major reform of the constitution, making wealth, not birth, the factor in eligibility for political office, thus breaking the power of the Eupatrids. He divided citizens into four property classes, each one eligible for different offices. He reformed the Areopagus and established a second council, the boule of 400 members. After his reforms Solon spent 10 years traveling overseas, including to Egypt and Cyprus, returning to Athens to find it on the brink of tyranny, as Peisistratus had just been granted a bodyguard. Solon wrote elegiac and iambic poetry to explain and justify his political reforms, a major source for later Greek historians.

SPARTOCIDS (*Spartokidai*): A dynasty that ruled in the Milesian colony Panticapaeum in the Cimmerian Bosphorus from 438/437 BC (when a hellenized Thracian Spartocus seized power) until c. 110 BC. It established control over much of the Crimea and Taman Peninsula. Although on the periphery of the Greek sphere of influence, the colony became the largest exporter of grain to Greece, particularly to Athens, and acquired a great deal of wealth. The kingdom became part of the empire of Mithridates VI of Pontus.

TAXILES (*Taxiles*): Floruit 320s BC. An Indian king, whose personal name was Omphis or Mophis. He ruled the country between the Indus and Hydaspes (Jhelum) Rivers, with his capital at Taxila. He welcomed Alexander the Great and fought with him against his neighbor and old enemy Porus. He became subject to the Macedonian satrap Philippus and then ruled independently. By 312 BC his kingdom was part of the empire of Sandracottus.

THEAGENES (*Theagenes*): Tyrant of Megara c. 640–620 BC. He became tyrant after slaughtering the cattle of the rich in a dispute over land. He probably supported his son-in-law Cylon's attempt to become tyrant at Athens. He was later banished from Megara.

THEMISTOCLES (*Themistokles*): Lived c. 528/524–462/459 BC. An Athenian democratic leader of the Lycomidae tribe. He was elected eponymous archon in 493 BC and started the development of the port of Piraeus. In 490 BC he was elected *strategos* of his tribe. After the death of Miltiades (489 BC), attempts were made to ostracize Themistocles, and one-third of surviving ostraka from the 480s BC bear his name. Instead, he managed to ostracize his rivals. In 483 BC he persuaded the Athenians to increase their naval fleet by using the surplus revenue from the silver mines at Laurium. The city was therefore prepared for the Persian invasion under Xerxes. Themistocles took a prominent role in this war, and as *strategos* he commanded the Athenian fleet. He was responsible for the victory at the battle of Salamis (480 BC) and received numerous honors in Sparta. He stayed in Sparta as Athenian envoy in 479 BC, after power had passed to his rivals. Themistocles was ostracized c. 471 BC and went to Argos. Circa 468 BC Sparta claimed that Themistocles and Pausanias were plotting with Persia. In his absence Themistocles was condemned to death, but escaped to Asia. He was given many honors by the Persian king Artaxerxes I after 465 BC and was made governor of Magnesia ad Maeandrum, where he died of sickness or possibly suicide. He was buried outside the walls of Piraeus.

THEOPOMPUS (*Theopompos*): Eurypontid king of Sparta c. 720–675 BC and leader in the First Messenian War (c. 730–710 BC). He may have instituted the ephorate or given it further powers.

THERAMENES (*Theramenes*): Died 404 BC. A moderate Athenian politician and orator, whom Critias called Cothurnus (theatrical boot that fitted either foot). He was one of the leaders of the oligarchic revolution in 411 BC, which resulted in the council of the Four Hundred. He was then responsible for the overthrow of the Four Hundred and establishment of the Five Thousand. When full democracy was restored in 410 BC, he was serving as *strategos* in the Aegean. In 406 BC he was a trierarch at the battle of Arginusae. He failed to pick up survivors, but blamed the generals who were subsequently executed. After the Athenian fleet was totally destroyed at the battle of Aegospotami (405 BC), Theramenes led the peace negotiations with Lysander of Sparta, delaying for three months and causing starvation in Athens. In March 404 BC Lysander appointed him one of the Thirty Tyrants to rule Athens on behalf of Sparta. However, his moderate stance conflicted with the more extreme members, and Critias had him tried and executed.

THERON (*Theron*): Tyrant of Acragas 488–472 BC. He married his daughter Demarete to Gelon, tyrant of Syracuse, becoming his firm ally. In 483 BC he expelled the tyrant Terillus from Himera and installed his son Thrasydaeus as ruler. Terillus appealed for help to the Carthaginian Hamilcar, but the Carthaginian invasion was defeated by Theron and Gelon at the battle of Himera (480 BC). After Gelon's death Theron supported Polysalus (younger brother of Hieron I), but a compromise was reached with the help of the poet Simonides. Theron was succeeded by his son Thrasydaeus. Theron was a supporter of the arts (Pindar was present at his court), and made Acragas a beautiful Greek city.

THRASYBULUS (*Thrasyboulos*): Died 388 BC. An Athenian general. In 411 BC he was leader of the democratic opposition that had been formed by the navy at Samos against the Four Hundred. He was elected *strategos* and was responsible for the recall of Alcibiades. Also in 411 BC he won naval victories over the Spartans at Cynossema and Abydus. In 410 BC he helped Alcibiades at the naval victory against Sparta at Cyzicus. He was trierarch at the battle of Arginusae in 406 BC. Under the Thirty Tyrants he was banished and went to Thebes, where he organized a democratic resistance that seized Phyle in 404/403 BC and Piraeus in 403 BC. After the fall of the Thirty Tyrants (403 BC) he was a prominent leader of the restored democracy at Athens. He led an expedition to recover Thasos, Samothrace, the Chersonese, Chalcedon and Byzantium (389 BC), but was killed at Aspendus on a plundering expedition.

THRASYBULUS OF MILETUS (*Thrasyboulos*): Tyrant of Miletus c. 625–600 BC, best known, according to Herodotus, for the advice he gave to the Corinthian tyrant Periander.

THRASYLLUS (*Thrasyllos*): Died 406 BC. An Athenian democratic leader. He was one of those who organized democratic support in the navy at Samos. He was elected *strategos* and participated in the naval victories at Cynossema and Abydus in 411 BC. When democracy was restored in 410 BC, he returned to Athens. After Alcibiades' fall (406 BC) he was reelected *strategos*, but was one of six generals executed following the battle of Arginusae, after being blamed by Theramenes.

THUCYDIDES (*Thoukydides*): Born c. 500 BC. An Athenian politician and opponent of Pericles, he was the son of Melesias and the brother-in-law of Cimon. He was influential in Athens and in Greece. He succeeded Cimon in leading the wealthy, aristocratic, oligarchic faction. In 443 BC he was ostracized, but returned the same year. He was prosecuted in his old age, and was dead by 420 BC.

TIMOLEON (*Timoleon*): Died c. 334 BC. A Corinthian who liberated Syracuse. Circa 365 BC he conspired to kill his brother Timophanes who tried to make himself tyrant of Corinth. In 344 BC he was sent by Corinth with a small force of mercenaries to assist Syracuse, which had appealed to its mother city for help against the tyrant Dionysius II and the

Carthaginians. Timoleon was a capable general and expelled Dionysius II (343 BC). The Carthaginians sent a large force to Sicily in 341 (or 339) BC, and Timoleon defeated them in June as they were crossing the Crimisus River. He eventually made peace with Carthage, restored peace to Sicily and installed a moderate oligarchic government at Syracuse. Circa 338 BC he retired from public life and remained in Syracuse until his death.

TIMOTHEUS (*Timotheos*): Died 354 BC. An Athenian general, son of Conon and a pupil of Isocrates. In 378 BC he was elected *strategos* when the Second Athenian League was formed. In a naval expedition in 376–375 BC, he gained many allies in northwest Greece, including Corcyra. When peace was concluded with Sparta, Timotheus was recalled from Corcyra, but he broke the peace almost immediately. Sparta acted against Corcyra, and Timotheus was recalled but could not raise sufficient funds. In November 373 BC he was tried but acquitted on a charge of financial maladministration. However, he left Athens to serve Persia as a mercenary against Egypt. He returned to power on the fall of Callistratus (366 BC), advocating an imperialist policy. He captured Samos from the Persians after a 10-month siege (365 BC) and extended Athenian territory in the Thracian Chersonese and Chalcidice, but repeatedly failed to take Amphipolis. He failed to cooperate in an attack on Chios at the battle of Embata in 356 BC, and was fined the huge sum of 100 talents, causing him to leave Athens.

TISSAPHERNES (*Tissaphernes*): Died 395 BC. A Persian satrap of the southern coastal provinces of Asia Minor from 413 BC. After the intervention of Alcibiades in 412 BC, he intermittently supported Sparta in the Peloponnesian War against Athens. In 408 BC he was confined to ruling Caria, and Cyrus the Younger began a pro-Spartan policy. At the battle of Cunaxa (401 BC), the cavalry of Tissaphernes played a key role in the victory of Artaxerxes II over Cyrus, and Tissaphernes was restored to the coastal provinces. When Sparta began war with Persia in 400 BC, he was crushingly defeated by King Agesilaus II near Sardis (spring 395 BC), and Artaxerxes II ordered his execution.

XANTHIPPUS (*Xanthippos*): Early-5th-century-BC Athenian leader and father of Pericles. In 489 BC he successfully prosecuted Miltiades. In 484/483 BC Xanthippus was ostracized on suspicion of supporting the Persians. He was recalled in 480 BC before the invasion of Xerxes, and was elected one of the *strategoi* for 479 BC. He commanded the Athenian fleet which destroyed the Persian navy at the battle of Mycale (479 BC). Xanthippus then led the fleet to the Chersonese and captured Sestus (winter 479/478 BC), so that the grain supply from the Black Sea could be safeguarded.

XERXES (*Xerxes*, Persian *Khshayarshan*): King of Persia 486–465 BC, after succeeding his father Darius I. By 485 BC he had suppressed an Egyptian revolt and another in Babylon in 482 BC. On the advice of Mardonius he planned to invade Greece to punish the Greeks for their part in the Ionian Revolt. He set out in the spring of 480 BC and achieved initial success. He won a naval victory at Artemisium and a land battle at Thermopylae. He also destroyed Athens, but his navy was crushed at Salamis. Xerxes was forced to retreat, leaving Mardonius in command, who was then defeated at the battle of Plataea in 479 BC (fig. 2.5). Xerxes was assassinated in 465/464 BC.

ZALEUCUS (*Zaleukos*): Lived c. 650 BC. A lawgiver who apparently produced for Locri the first Greek law code. It was subsequently adopted by other Greek cities in Italy and Sicily, although his laws were notoriously severe.

LISTS OF RULERS

Dates BC

Kings of Persia

Darius I	521–486
Xerxes	486–465/464
Artaxerxes I	465/464–423
Darius II	423–404
Artaxerxes II	404–358
Artaxerxes III	358–338
Arses	338–336
Darius III	336–330
Alexander the Great	330–323

Sparta

AGIAD KINGS

(Not all dates are known)
Eurysthenes
Agis I
Echestratus
Leobotas
Doryssus
Agesilaus I

Archelaus	c. 785–760
Teleclus	c. 760–740
Alcamenes	c. 740–700
Polydorus	c. 700–665
Eurycrates	c. 665–640
Anaxander	c. 640–615
Eurycratidas	c. 615–590
Leon	c. 590–560
Anaxandridas II	c. 560–520
Cleomenes I	c. 520–488
Leonidas I	488–480
Pausanias (regent)	480–c. 467
Pleistarchus	480–459
Pleistoanax	459–409
Pausanias	409–395
Agesipolis I	395–380
Cleombrotus I	380–371
Agesipolis II	371–370
Cleomenes II	370–309/308
Areus I	309/308–265
Acrotatus	265–262
Areus II	262–254
Leonidas II	254–235
Cleomenes III	235–222
Agesipolis III	219–215

EURYPONTID KINGS

(Not all dates are known)
Procles
Eurypon
Prytanis
Polydectes
Eunomus

Charilaus	c. 775–770
Nicander	c. 750–720
Theopompus	c. 720–675
Anaxandridas I	c. 675–660
Archidamus I	c. 660–645

Anaxilaus	c. 645–625
Leotychidas	c. 625–600
Hippocratidas	c. 600–575
Agasicles	c. 575–550
Ariston	c. 550–515
Demaratus	c. 515–491
Leotychidas II	491–469
Archidamus II	476 or 469–427/426
Agis II	427/426–400/399
Agesilaus II	399–c. 360
Archidamus III	361/360–338
Agis III	338–331/330
Eudamidas I	331–c. 305
Archidamus IV	c. 305–275
Eudamidas II	c. 275–244
Agis IV	244–241
Eudamidas III	241–c. 228
Archidamus V	228–227
Eucleidas	227–221
Lycurgus	219–c. 212
Pelops	c. 212–207
Nabis	207–192

Kings/Rulers of Macedonia

Amyntas I	late 6th century
Alexander I	c. 495–c. 450/440
Perdiccas II	c. 450/440–413
Archelaus	413–399
Orestes	399–396
Aeropus	396–393
Amyntas II	393–392
Pausanias	393–392
Amyntas III	c. 393–370/369
Alexander II	370–368
Ptolemaeus	369/368–365
Perdiccas III	365–359
Philip II	359–336
Alexander the Great	336–323
Phiip III Arrhidaeus	323–317
Alexander IV	323–c. 311
Perdiccas (regent)	323–320
Antigonus I	319–301
Cassander	305–297
Demetrius I Poliorcetes	294–288
Lysimachus	288–281
Pyrrhus	288–285
Ptolemy Ceraunus	281–280
Antipater Etesias	279

ANTIGONID DYNASTY

Antigonus II	277–239
Demetrius II	239–229
Antigonus III	229–221
Philip V	221–179
Perseus	179–168
End of Macedonian kingdom	

Seleucid Kings

Seleucus I	305/304–281 (ruler from 311)
Antiochus I	281–261 (joint ruler from 292)
Antiochus II	261–246
Seleucus II	246–226
Seleucus III	226–223
Antiochus III	223–187
Seleucus IV	187–175
Antiochus IV	175–164
Antiochus V	163–162
Demetrius I Soter	162–150
Alexander Balas (usurper)	150–145
Demetrius II Nicator	145–139
Antiochus VI	145–142
Diodotus Tryphon (usurper)	142–138
Antiochus VII	139–129
Demetrius II Nicator	129–125
Alexander II Zabinas (usurper)	128–123
Cleopatra Thea	126–125
Seleucus V	126/125
Antiochus VIII	125–96
Antiochus IX	114–95
Seleucus VI	96–95
Demetrius III	95–88
Antiochus X	95–83
Antiochus XI	94
Philip I Philadelphus	94–83
Antiochus XII	87–84
Tigranes I of Armenia	83–69
Antiochus XIII	69–64

Attalids of Pergamum

Philetaerus	282–263
Eumenes I	263–241

Attalus I	241–197
Eumenes II	197–159
Attalus II	159–138
Attalus III	138–133

The Ptolemies

Ptolemy I	305/304–283/282
Ptolemy II	283/282–246 (joint ruler from 285)
Ptolemy III	246–221
Ptolemy IV	221–204 (joint ruler with Berenice II in 221)
Ptolemy V	204–180 (joint ruler from 210)
Cleopatra I	180–176
Ptolemy VI	180–145
Ptolemy VI, Ptolemy VIII and Cleopatra II	170–163
Ptolemy VII	145–144
Ptolemy VIII	145–116
Cleopatra III (with Ptolemy IX)	116–107
Cleopatra III (with Ptolemy X)	107–101
Ptolemy X	101–88
Ptolemy IX	88–81
Ptolemy XI (with Cleopatra Berenice)	80
Ptolemy XII	80–59/58, 55–51
Ptolemy XIII	51–47
Cleopatra VII (with Ptolemy XIII)	51–47
Cleopatra VII (with Ptolemy XIV)	47–44
Cleopatra VII (with Ptolemy XV)	44–30

Kings of Pontus

Mithridates I	302–266
Ariobarzanes	266–c. 250
Mithridates II	c. 250–c. 220/c. 185
Mithridates III	c. 220–c. 185
Pharnaces I	c. 185–c. 156

Mithridates IV	c. 156–c. 150
Mithridates V	c. 150–120
Mithridates VI	120–63
Pharnaces II	63–47

Kings of Cappadocia

Ariarathes III	c. 250–220
Ariarathes IV	220–163
Ariarathes V	163–130
Ariarathes VI	c. 130–c. 116
Ariarathes VII	c. 116–c. 101
Ariarathes IX	c. 101–87/86
Ariarathes VIII	c. 96

Kings of Bithynia

Nicomedes I	c. 279–c. 250
Ziaelas	c. 250–before 227
Prusias I	c. 230/228–c.185/182
Prusias II	c. 182–149
Nicomedes II	149–c. 127
Nicomedes III	c. 127–c. 94
Nicomedes IV	c. 94–74

READING

See also reading for chapter 2.

Biographies

Allen 1981: Attalus I, Eumenes I, Philetaerus; Balcer 1995: includes sections on Darius and Xerxes; Billows 1990: Antigonus I One-Eyed; Bowder (ed.) 1982: biographies of many figures; Buckler 1989: Philip II (in 362–346 BC); Bury and Meiggs 1975: history up to the Hellenistic period; Cartledge 1987: Agesilaus II; Caven 1990: Dionysius I (major source); Ellis 1989: Alcibiades; Ellis 1994: Ptolemy I; Errington 1969: Philopoemen; Garaoufalias 1979: Pyrrhus; Grainger 1990: Seleucus I Nicator; Grant 1987: includes profiles of Solon, Peisistratus and Cleisthenes; Grant 1989: profiles of several figures, with detailed bibliography; Green 1970a: Gylippus; Green 1990: a substantial book with information on figures from Alexander the Great's death to the Roman period; Green 1991: Alexander the Great; Hammond 1983: Alexander the Great; Hammond 1989: Alexander the Great (major source); Hammond 1991: includes details on many figures in Macedonia's history; Hammond 1994: Philip II (major source); Hammond and Scullard (eds.) 1970: biographies of many figures; Hansen 1947: Attalids (Attalus I, II and III; Aristonicus; Eumenes I and II; Philetaerus); Heckel 1992: numerous characters associated with Alexander the Great; Hornblower 1982: Mausolus; Krentz 1982, 69–88: Thrasybulus; Lane Fox 1973: Alexander the Great; Lund 1992: Lysimachus; McGing 1986: Mithridates VI Eupator; O'Brien 1992: Alexander the Great; Roisman 1993: Demosthenes (the general); Sanders 1987: Dionysius I; Smith 1990: Xerxes; Tarn 1913: Antigonus II Gonatas; Tritle 1988: Phocion; Walbank 1933: Aratus of Sicyon; Walbank 1940: Philip V; Warner 1972: chapter on Pericles.

Lists of Rulers

Bickerman 1980; Hammond and Scullard (eds.) 1970 passim.

3

MILITARY
AFFAIRS

ARMIES

Because the Greek world was divided into numerous tribes, kingdoms and city-states from prehistory to the Roman period, there was never a single overall army. Most evidence on the organization of armies relates to Sparta, to a lesser extent to Athens, and to the later army of Macedonia. Very little is known about armies of other states, and most evidence is derived from noncontemporary authors.

Prehistoric and Archaic

The earliest evidence for Greek warfare comes from Homer's *Iliad* and *Odyssey*. These epic poems were probably composed in the 8th century BC, but they reflect a much earlier Mycenaean phase. Most military information comes from the *Iliad*, since it deals with the siege of Troy, rather than the *Odyssey*, which deals with Odysseus' travels through a world largely at peace. As they are epic poems, they cannot be treated as reliable and accurate historical documents. However, a great deal of information can be extracted and combined with the available archaeological evidence for the Mycenaean period.

Little is known about how the earliest Greek armies were organized, but it is likely that they were led by a state's ruler, usually a king or chieftain. Such armies were generally small, and there was probably little need for an elaborate chain of command. The only distinction usually made is between the champions or heroes (the more skilled warriors with better weapons and armor) and the general mass of soldiers. The Homeric poems give a few clues to how armies were organized. The *Iliad* shows the besieging Greek army composed of allied forces under individual commanders, led by a commander-in-chief, Agamemnon. He appears to hold his position more through honor and prestige than through a recognized jurisdiction over the other commanders. In the poem a general assembly is held to discuss certain military decisions. Agamemnon, despite his position, must put forward arguments to support his views. He is portrayed as being similar to a feudal king with subordinate lords, over whom he holds sway but not absolute power. This situation contrasts with the command structure of the besieged Trojans, most of whom had Greek names and were probably of Greek extraction. The Trojan forces were commanded by King Priam and his sons, working as a team and holding the allegiance of a substantial area around Troy, extending into Europe and Asia Minor. This was effectively an empire ruled by the dynasty of King Priam, in contrast to the temporary command of Agamemnon, which was apparently only for the duration of the war.

There is no direct continuity between the armies portrayed in Homer and later armies. The next glimpse of Greek military organization comes from the historian Herodotus who, in the 5th century BC, wrote about the Persian wars that took place just before his birth and in his youth. The information from Herodotus can be supplemented from other authors, including Thucydides and Aeschylus. Sources from the Roman period include the writers Polybius (2nd century BC), and Diodorus Siculus and Asclepiodotus (both 1st century BC).

Sparta

KINGS AND HOPLITES

The city-state of Sparta was organized on a military basis. It was governed by two kings and five ephors, but in time of war one king was given supreme power as army commander. All freeborn male Spartan citizens over 20 years of age were liable for military service. They spent their lives as soldiers, other professions being forbidden. The best of them were taken into the army and became fully trained hoplites. They were organized into five companies called lochoi (*lokhoi*; sing. *lokhos*), which reflected the five Spartan tribes. Further troops were drawn from the towns that surrounded Sparta and were under its dominance. Originally the two kings had the right to make war upon whatever state they chose. They personally led the army in battle, each protected by a bodyguard of 300 hoplites (the *hippeis*, a name meaning "horsemen," possibly implying this was originally a cavalry unit). The kings had unlimited power of life and death while in the field. Sometime before the Persian wars (early 5th century BC), the laws of Sparta were changed so that the people chose one king to lead the army, and he was responsible to the people for how the campaign was conducted.

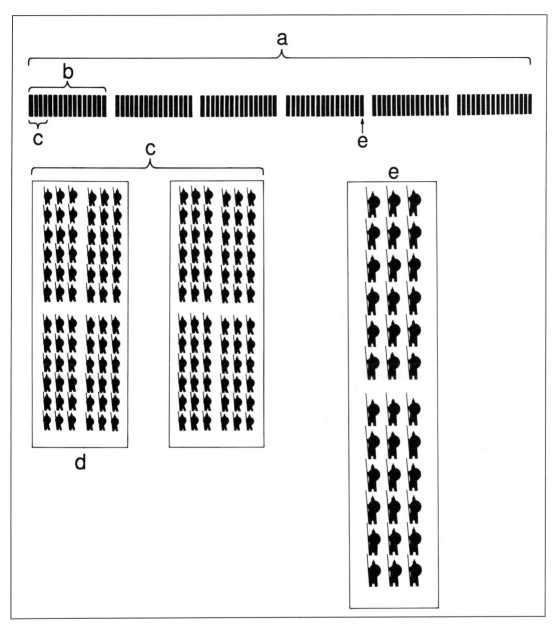

Fig. 3.1   Spartan army of 5th century BC: a. The army consisted of six regiments or morae; b. a mora; c. a lochos (4 lochoi = 1 mora); d. a pentekostys (2 pentekostyes = 1 lochos); e. an enomotia, the smallest unit of the army (2 enomotiai = 1 pentekostys).

EARLY ARMY

The phalanx describes a military formation used from the 4th century BC, although some clues suggest that it developed before then. Because the

Spartan army in the 4th century BC had units called *pentekostyes* (sing. *pentekostys*—literally fifties) of 72 men, it has been suggested that there was an earlier unit of 50 men, possibly as early as the late 8th century BC. It is thought that the early form of lochos consisted of two units called *pentekostyes*. A *pentekostys* consisted of two *enomotiai* (sing. *enomotia*). Each *enomotia* had 23 hoplites, as well as a rearguard officer called an *ouragos* (pl. *ouragoi*) or tergiductor and a commanding officer or enomotarch (*enomotarkhes*). The lochos was commanded by a lochagos (*lokhagos*) who fought at the front of the extreme right-hand file; the left half of the lochos was commanded by a *pentekonter* fighting at the front of the right-hand file of the left *pentekostys*. This formation would give 50 men in each *pentekostys* and 100 men in each lochos, in comparison with 72 men and 144 men in later Spartan formations.

5TH-CENTURY-BC ARMY

At the very end of the 5th century BC, there is detailed information about the Spartan army from two contemporary authors, Thucydides and Xenophon. Thucydides was writing some years earlier than Xenophon, but had difficulty obtaining information about the Spartan army. Xenophon, however, had firsthand knowledge. Where conflicts of evidence exist between the two sources, Xenophon is generally accepted as more accurate.

The Spartan army was at this time still commanded by the king. It was divided into six regiments known as morae (*morai*, sing. *mora*), each of 576 men (fig. 3.1). Each mora was commanded by a polemarch (*polemarkhos*) and consisted of four lochoi. Each lochos (now 144 men) was the standard unit of the phalanx and was commanded by a lochagos. A lochos was divided into two *pentekostyes*. Each *pentekostys* (now 72 men) was commanded by a *pentekonter* and was divided into two *enomotiai*. The *enomotia* was the smallest unit of the army and was commanded by an enomotarch. The *enomotia* was composed of three files of 12 men or six half-files of six men. There were also rearguard officers called *ouragoi*, who could have been an integral part of the unit, forming the rear rank of each *enomotia*. In phalanx formation, the other officers would fight at the front of the right-hand file of the unit that they commanded.

The King's Bodyguard (*hippeis*) served in the first mora. It consisted of 300 specially selected hoplites who were regarded as the best in the army. They were chosen by three hippagretae (*hippagretai*)—men chosen annually by the ephors specifically for selecting hoplites to serve in the *hippeis*. In addition each mora had an attached unit of cavalry, also called a mora. These cavalry units,

each about 60 strong, began to be used only near the end of the 5th century BC, during the Peloponnesian War.

When on the march, the Spartan army was led by the cavalry with the sciritae (*skiritai*) forming a screen in front of the column to provide advance warning. The sciritae were originally perioeci from the town of Scirus. They were foot soldiers serving as lightly armed scouts and outpost guards.

Athens

Originally the armies of Athens were led by the king, but this function was taken over by the polemarch (*polemarkhos*), who was one of the archons. From around the early 7th century BC, the polemarch held office for one year and was elected to office by the council of archons, although his birth and wealth were taken into account in his appointment.

In the early 5th century BC, Cleisthenes introduced a number of constitutional reforms, including dividing Attica into 10 new tribes of citizens. Each tribe was required to supply an infantry regiment to the army known as a *taxis* (pl. *taxeis*), each of which was commanded by a taxiarch (*taxiarkhos*). The *taxeis* were each divided into lochoi. A board of 10 generals (*strategoi*, sing. *strategos*), one from each tribe, was elected by the Assembly. The generals were elected annually, but there was no limit on the number of times they could be reelected. Usually only three *strategoi* went on campaign with the army. The polemarch still led the army in battle, but the importance of his role was greatly diminished. All citizens between the ages of 17 and 59 were liable for military service, and during the 5th century BC this provided about 30,000 hoplites. About half this number were used in campaigns, while the other half (veterans and those under 19 years old) were garrison troops. The hoplites had to supply their own equipment, but a soldier whose father had been killed in battle was provided with arms at public expense.

Other City-States

Much less information is available for the other city-states. Although the organization of other armies was probably subject to local peculiarities, they seem to have followed the system used by Athens, with citizens divided into tribes, each of which supplied military forces to the army. The citizens of Megara, for example, were divided into five tribes, each of which appointed a general and provided a military contingent for the army. These five generals initially shared military power with the king, but later on the monarchy seems to have disappeared.

Similarly, a Thessalian Confederacy was formed in Thessaly around the end of the 7th century BC, and eventually each land allotment or estate was required to supply 40 cavalry and 80 infantry to the federal army of the confederacy. Since war between city-states was endemic, it is likely that any development in military organization by one state was quickly copied by others, just as developments in weapons, armor and tactics appear to have spread rapidly. The phalanx formation was probably adopted, with local variations, by all warring city-states.

Macedonia

PHILIP II

The final developments in Greek warfare came from the Macedonians. In 359 BC Philip II became king of Macedonia, but even before this the Macedonian cavalry, called "the Companions" (*hetairoi*), was probably the best in Greece. It was drawn from the Macedonian aristocracy and probably originated as a mounted bodyguard for the king. In contrast the Macedonian infantry consisted of ill-trained and badly organized peasants. Philip reformed the army, imposing a severe code of training and discipline.

The heavy infantry was reformed into a phalanx, probably based on that of the Theban army. Philip appears to have adopted the Greek model of a file of eight men as the depth of the phalanx, but he used units of two, rather than three, files of eight men. These units of 16 men were called *dekades* (sing. *dekas*, literally "a company of 10"), implying that before Philip's reforms, the files were 10 men deep rather than eight. From later information about Alexander the Great's army, it appears that each *dekas* was commanded by a dekadarch (*dekadarkhos* or *dekadarkhes*) who fought in the front rank. Behind him was a man on double pay and then a "10-stater" man, also probably officers.

Philip called his newly formed phalanx the "Foot Companions" (*pezetairoi*) in recognition of their improved status. The phalanx was possibly divided into 12 *taxeis*, each raised from a specific area of Macedonia. There is little information about the smaller units within each *taxis*, but it has been suggested that the organization of the Macedonian army was similar to that of Alexander's Successors. Each *taxis* would therefore have been divided into six *syntagmata* (sing. *syntagma*), with each *syntagma* possibly divided into four tetrarchies.

It is uncertain exactly how the soldiers of the Macedonian phalanx were armed in Philip's time. They were equipped with a long and heavy two-handed spear (a *sarissa*) and may sometimes have used javelins. They probably wore a helmet, cuirass and greaves and carried a round shield, although there are indications that the amount and type of armor varied according to their position in the phalanx. It is possible that soldiers in the front ranks had the heaviest armor, while those at the rear wore little or none, although the rearguard officers (*ouragoi*) were probably heavily armored. There is evidence that weapons and equipment were supplied free to the soldiers and that they were fined for any losses. As Philip II captured more territory, he increased his army by adding new units, such as Paeonian and Thessalian cavalry, so that the proportion of Macedonian soldiers gradually decreased.

ALEXANDER THE GREAT

No work of contemporary authors has survived to provide information about the army of Alexander (died 323 BC). The main work is by Arrian who wrote in the 2nd century AD, more than 400 years after Alexander's death. Other sources include Polybius (2nd century BC) and Diodorus Siculus (1st century BC). These writers were able to use earlier sources of information, but their accuracy cannot always be trusted. In Alexander's time, there seem to have been 12 *taxeis*, with each *taxis* being about 1,500 strong. Alexander left six *taxeis* in Macedonia and took six to invade Persia. This invasion force seems to have initially comprised 12,000 Macedonian infantry, 7,000 infantry drawn from allied states, 7,000 infantry from the frontiers of Macedonia, and 1,000 archers and *agrianes* (javelin throwers from the mountains on the northern frontier of Macedonia), 1,800 Macedonian cavalry,

1,800 Thessalian cavalry, 600 Greek cavalry, and 900 Thracian and Paeonian scouts.

Alexander's Macedonian infantry consisted of 9,000 Foot Companions and 3,000 hypaspists (lighter infantry). The hypaspists were organized into 1,000-strong chiliarchies commanded by chiliarchs. The first chiliarchy was the King's Bodyguard, called the *agema*. The Macedonian cavalry of 1,800 men (the Companions or Companion Cavalry) was divided into eight units called *ilai* (sing. *ile*), and each *ile* was commanded by an ilarch (*ilarkhes*). The first *ile* (royal *ile*) was larger than the rest and was usually commanded by Alexander. It is thought that the *ilai* were 210 strong, with the royal *ile* 300 strong. It is known that the *ilai* fought in a wedge formation in battle, and these numbers do provide wedge formations of a suitable size. The Companion Cavalry was armed with long spears (*sarissai*).

The 1,800-strong Thessalian cavalry was also divided into *ilai*, but of different strengths than the Companion Cavalry. Little else is known about this cavalry, except that its battle formation was diamond shaped. According to Asclepiodotus (writing in the 1st century BC), the 600 Greek cavalry may have been divided into five *ilai* of 128 men, with each *ile* deployed in a square formation 16 men wide and 8 deep (each horse needing a space twice as long as it was wide). The Greek and Thessalian cavalries were armed with spears, and the Thracian and Paeonian cavalries (used for skirmishing and scouting) were armed with javelins.

As Alexander's campaign progressed, he drafted Oriental horsemen into his cavalry. Eventually he was forced to reorganize the cavalry to cope with this. The royal *ile* was retained, but the other five *ilai* were reorganized into hipparchies (*hipparkhiai*, sing. *hipparkhia*), each with an *ile* of the Companions. The hipparchy became the standard unit of Macedonian cavalry.

HELLENISTIC

Most information about the later Macedonian army comes from Polybius and Asclepiodotus (the latter writing when Hellenistic warfare had virtually ended). Asclepiodotus described what was probably an idealized or theoretical phalanx of 16,384 men (a phalanx as large as 16,000 is recorded only at the battle of Pydna in 168 BC). His description may be based on the late Egyptian or Syrian phalanx, not the Macedonian one. The phalanx he described consisted of 64 *syntagmata*, each commanded by a syntagmatarch (*syntagmatarkhes*). These *syntagmata* consisted of 16 files of 16 men (totaling 256), as well as an *ouragos* (rearguard officer), *hyperetes* (adjutant), *stratokeryx* (herald), *semaiophoros* (signaler) and *salpinktes* (trumpeter). The front-rank men (*protostatai*) of the *syntagma* were all officers. Each file (lochos) was led by a lochagos, and every dilochia or pair of files (*dilokhia*) was led by a dilochites (*dilokhites*). Every pair of dilochiai (four files) was called a tetrarchy and was led by a tetrarch (*tetrarkhes*). Each pair of tetrarchies made up a *taxis*, commanded by a taxiarch (*taxiarkhos*). The *syntagma* had two *taxeis*: the right-hand one commanded by the syntagmatarch and the left-hand one by the taxiarch.

Each file (lochos) was led by an officer at the front and also had a hemilochites (*hemilokhites*) who was leader of a half-file known as a *hemilokhia*. There were also two enomotarchs (*enomotarkhai*: quarter-file leaders) and an *ouragos* (rearguard officer). The remaining individual ranks in each file were alternately called *protostatai* (sing. *protostates*: front rank) and *epistatai* (sing. *epistates*: rear rank). Each file of 16 men therefore comprised an officer in the front rank, followed in turn by an *epistates*, a *protostates*, another *epistates*, an enomotarch, an *epistates*, a *protostates*, another *epistates* (the rear-rank officer of the half-file), a hemilochites, an *epistates*, a *protostates*, an *epistates*, an enomotarch, an *epistates*, a *protostates* and an *ouragos*.

Asclepiodotus also described the organization of *syntagmata* into larger units. However, this description is thought to be a hypothetical system devised by him to explain terms he did not fully understand, and he may have fabricated some terms. In his system, two *syntagmata* formed a pentakosiarchy, commanded by a pentakosiarch (*pentakosiarkhes*), and two pentakosiarchies formed a merarchy of 2,048 men, commanded by a merarch (*merarkhes*). Two merarchies made up a phalangarchy commanded by a phalangarch (*phalangarkhes*), who was originally a *strategos*. Two phalangarchies formed a *keras* (pl. *kerata*) commanded by a kerarch, and two *kerata* formed a phalanx commanded by a *strategos*.

The *syntagma* is not mentioned by Polybius, who refers to a unit called a *speira* (pl. *speirai*). It is thought that the *syntagma* was a Hellenistic army unit used outside Europe, and that the *speira* was the unit of Hellenistic armies within Europe. The *speira* may have been very similar to the *syntagma*, since it was divided into four tetrarchies, each consisting of four lochoi. The taxiarch and dilochites mentioned by Asclepiodotus are not referred to, and so it is uncertain whether these formed part of the *speira*. Four *speirai* made up a battalion, which may have been called a chiliarchy, and four battalions made up a *strategia* commanded by a *strategos*. Three other officers are known (*grammateus, arkhiuperetes* and *hyperetes*). They may have been the administrative officers of the *speira*, the battalion and the *strategia* respectively, forming an administrative hierarchy, although their precise function is unclear.

Descriptions of the organization of the later Macedonian army are problematic because the units cannot easily be combined into the two wings of a phalanx totaling approximately 10,000 men, which appears to have been the usual size of a phalanx at that time. A possible solution is that each wing of the phalanx was a 5,000-strong *strategia*, made up of five not four battalions.

In addition to the phalanx, the later Macedonian army had hypaspists, peltasts, archers and slingers, which do not always appear to have functioned as in Alexander the Great's army. In later armies, hypaspists seem to have been staff officers selected for special duties and members of the King's Bodyguard (*agema*). The later peltasts apparently changed completely and took over many functions of the earlier hypaspists. The most noticeable change in the later armies, though, is the change in emphasis from cavalry to infantry. In Alexander's army, which had to be highly mobile to meet specific needs, the ratio of cavalry to infantry was about 1 to 6, but in later Macedonian armies it was about 1 to 20. This probably reflects Alexander's exceptional use of cavalry, rather than a long-term trend away from cavalry and toward infantry. Other armies in Alexander's time had much smaller ratios of cavalry to infantry.

SOLDIERS

Hoplites

Hoplites were heavily armored infantry that eventually became the regular troops employed by city-states. Citizens who could not maintain horses but had sufficient wealth to equip themselves were required to serve as hoplites. A hoplite was protected by a breastplate, helmet, greaves and a heavy shield called a *hoplon*, from which the name hoplite was derived. A hoplite was armed with a sword and long thrusting spear (fig. 3.2). This set of equipment was very expensive (probably comparable to the cost of a modern automobile), and varied in price according to factors such as quality and style. Hoplites fought in a phalanx in close formation (fig. 3.4).

Phalangites

After Philip II reformed the infantry into "Foot Companions," the Macedonian phalanx consisted of heavy infantry armed differently from the usual Greek hoplite. They are therefore usually referred to as phalangites (soldiers of the phalanx). Their main weapon was the *sarissa* (a name also used for a cavalry spear). At times they were armed with other weapons, such as swords and javelins. The phalangites seem to have worn a cuirass, helmet and greaves, and they carried a round shield. Evidence suggests that the amount of body armor worn varied with the soldier's position in the phalanx. The phalangites in the front ranks apparently had more and better-quality armor than those in the ranks behind, with the rear ranks wearing little or no armor.

Hypaspists

These Macedonian infantry were less heavily armed than the phalangites. The hypaspists (literally, shield-bearers) are not mentioned before the time of Alexander the Great, but were probably developed into proper infantry by Philip II. They were probably lightly armored hoplites, carrying a spear and shield. They usually fought alongside the Foot Companions, between the phalanx and cavalry, probably to protect the flanks of the phalanx. In later Hellenistic armies, such as that of Philip V, the name hypaspist seems to refer to a body of staff officers reserved for special duties and to the King's Bodyguard (*agema*).

Fig. 3.2   Hoplite soldiers with Argive shields and long spears, wearing Corinthian helmets and greaves.

Peltasts

These lightly armed infantry soldiers were named for their lightweight, wickerwork, peltate shield. Originally, peltasts were Thracian tribesmen, fighting in their native dress, which included a patterned cloak, high boots and a Phrygian cap of fox skin with flaps to cover the ears. The name "peltast" came to be used for any similar, lightly armed infantry. The main weapons of the peltast were javelins. Because they were lightly armed, peltasts could avoid the charge of the heavily armored hoplites. Their tactics were to run in, throw their javelins and escape before the hoplites could reach them. Later changes to their equipment, attributed to Iphicrates, included increasing by half the length of their javelins and almost doubling the size of their swords, so that they could act as regular troops and not just skirmishers. The role of peltasts apparently declined after the rise of the Macedonian armies.

Helots

The territory ruled by Sparta was divided into state-owned farms run by helots (serfs) who greatly outnumbered Spartan citizens (Spartiates). As the need grew in the 5th century BC for lightly armed troops to support the hoplites, helots were increasingly used as skirmishers with the Spartan army. A combined army of Spartiates and helots is referred to as Lacedaemonian. On campaign each Spartiate was accompanied by a helot who carried his baggage.

Archers

Archers were used in Greek warfare from earliest times, and archery is mentioned quite often in Homer's *Iliad*. Archery seems to have played a crucial role in the Trojan War, but Homer implies that archers had a lower status than spearmen. Leaders like Teucer and Odysseus were proficient with the bow, but they also fought with other weapons. However, there is some evidence of groups of specialist archers even at this early date.

Later Greek armies concentrated on soldiers of the phalanx (fig. 3.4), and archery seems to have been neglected, except in Crete. Contingents of archers in Greek armies were therefore often mercenaries, usually Scythians or Cretans. Athens employed Scythian and Cretan archers as early as the 6th century BC. Scythian archers were often portrayed in contemporary Attic vase paintings, frequently shooting from a kneeling position. They wore a distinctive long-pointed cap or hat, loose tunic, and trousers; slung from their belt was a bow case, which also contained their arrows. The Scythians protected the hoplites, and in the 5th century BC Scythian archers who had been bought as public slaves for Athens served as a police force in the city.

Nevertheless, the importance of archery was not fully appreciated until the latter part of the Peloponnesian War, and archers were not always used effectively. In part, this may have been because Greek archers pinched the bowstring between thumb and forefinger, a weak grip that did not allow them to use the most powerful bows. The Scythians used the first three fingers of the hand curled around the bowstring (the "Mediterranean loose," still used today) and so could draw the more powerful Scythian bows (fig. 3.13). Hellenistic armies made greater use of archers, but unlike the Parthian armies, the Greeks never used archers as a main element of their forces. Archers were generally armed with only a bow and arrows and did not wear armor. They were almost always foot soldiers; mounted archers were rarely used by the Greeks until the time of Alexander the Great. See also bows p. 108.

Slingers

A simple weapon like the sling was probably used from earliest times. Rare finds of baked clay sling bullets show that the sling was used in the Mycenaean period. Slingers were an important contingent within armies, particularly from the 5th century BC. They were recruited from Crete and from some peoples of northern Greece, but the most famous slingers came from Rhodes and usually served as mercenaries. Rhodian slingers could achieve a range of over 1,140 ft (347 m), a greater range than the bow, and their sling shot could penetrate unprotected flesh from a distance of 300 ft (91 m). Slingers were generally armed with only their sling and a bag of stones, although some carried small shields and wore wide-brimmed hats to protect their eyes from the sun's glare.

Macedonian armies had contingents of slingers. Around 170 BC they developed a short arrow or bolt called a cestrosphendone (*kestros*), which could be fired from a sling. Another late Macedonian invention was a sling mounted on a long pole, which ordinary soldiers, rather than specialist slingers, used to throw large stones. See also slings p. 108.

Elite Units

Several Greek armies had an elite unit of selected warriors. The Theban army had a unit of 300 soldiers called the Sacred Band (*Hieros Lokhos*), which

apparently originated at an early period as 150 charioteers and their drivers. According to Greek tradition (but later denied by Xenophon), the unit was composed of pairs of homosexual lovers. The Sacred Band is first mentioned by name as taking part in the battle of Delium in 424 BC, by which time it was a unit of hoplites. It was probably the unit described as the "300 first and best Thebans" who died at the battle of Plataea (479 BC). These hoplites were probably organized into 12 *enomotiai* of 25 men, and they were the shock troops largely responsible for Theban military successes.

The Spartans also had an elite force of 300 hoplites called the *hippeis* who acted as the royal bodyguard (see p. 86). In Arrian's account of the life of Alexander the Great, there is mention of a unit called the *argyraspides* (Silver Shields). Diodorus Siculus mentions the Silver Shields as an elite unit accompanying Eumenes of Cardia after Alexander's death, but nothing else is known about the unit in Alexander's army.

Auxiliaries

The phalanx of heavily armed hoplites (fig. 3.4) was a massive improvement on the preceeding haphazard battle formations. It was adopted by all Greek states, but in time its weaknesses became apparent. It was of no use for fighting on hills, mountains or rough ground, and was useless against cavalry or lightly armed troops using guerrilla tactics. To cope with these problems, other types of soldiers (auxiliaries) were employed. Athens used Scythian and Cretan archers as early as the 6th century BC, but a need for lightly armed troops was apparently accepted only after the Persian Wars. Light cavalry and light infantry were used in any numbers only during the Peloponnesian War in the second half of the 5th century BC. Peltasts became the most common and most successful form of light infantry, and archers and slingers were also employed. Lightly armed troops were always regarded as inferior to the hoplites. The light infantry's main purpose was to protect the phalanx of hoplites from the enemy's lightly armed troops, and so they were usually stationed on the wings or behind the phalanx. In 390 BC a force of highly trained peltasts led by Iphicrates defeated a Spartan *mora* at the battle of Lechaeum, which completely changed the Greek attitude to lightly armed troops.

Mercenaries

Records from Egypt show that Greeks were serving as mercenaries as early as the 7th–6th centuries BC. Initially such mercenaries found employment outside Greece, often with the Persians, but during the Peloponnesian War between Athens and Sparta (5th century BC), both sides employed mercenaries. Mercenaries were usually used as reinforcements and sometimes on garrison duties, but not in the phalanx. Mercenaries were also employed to provide specialist troops, such as archers from Crete or slingers from Rhodes. At the end of the Peloponnesian War, large numbers of mercenaries who had known no other life were left unemployed. Consequently mercenaries were commonly employed within Greece and beyond.

Chariots and Cavalry

CHARIOTS

Chariots were used from the Mycenaean period, for hunting and ceremonial purposes, as well as warfare (fig. 3.3). Surviving texts from Knossos list more than 400 chariots associated with the palace, which were probably used for military purposes. The landscape of Greece is generally too rugged for chariots, but they do appear to have been used for warfare until at least the beginning of the Dark Age. Chariots could be used effectively only on

Fig. 3.3 Stele from a 16th-century-BC shaft grave at Mycenae. The shallow relief carving shows a warrior mounted in a light chariot drawn apparently by a single horse. Neither he nor his opponent appears to be wearing any armor.

smooth terrain, because uneven ground could cause breakage of the pole that yoked the horses to the chariot body, allowing the horses to bolt and leaving the occupants stranded.

In Homer's *Iliad* warriors are portrayed as riding to battle in chariots driven by other warriors or by specialist drivers. The warriors then fought on foot, and the chariots were held at a short distance, ready for retreat if necessary. There appears to have been little in the way of formal tactics for fighting from chariots. Their main purpose was to deliver a body of warriors swiftly to the point where they fought and to get them away again if they were unsuccessful. The *Iliad* does give some instances of warriors fighting from chariots with spears and bows and arrows. However, chariots were not generally used as fighting platforms and were not used in attempts to charge and break enemy formations.

By the end of the Dark Age, chariots no longer seem to have been used for warfare. Although still portrayed in paintings on pottery, they appear to have been used for ceremonies or possibly races. War chariots were obsolete by about 700 BC, and by the time of the Persian Wars they were used by the Greeks only for sport.

CAVALRY

The military role of chariots was replaced by horses, probably because an improved horse bit was developed, allowing better control of horses. At first horses appear to have been used in the same way as chariots, largely as transport for infantry. Some wealthier citizens rode to war on horses, then dismounted to fight as hoplites. However, very little cavalry is apparent in early Greek armies, probably due to the expense of buying and keeping horses. Greek city-states seem to have relied on Boeotia and Thessaly to provide cavalry contingents. When Boeotia and Thessaly fell to the Persians in the Persian Wars, the other states appear to have fought without cavalry.

Cavalry (*hippeis*) first appears to have been used seriously in the later 5th century BC during the Peloponnesian War. Even then it was only lightly armed, usually with javelins, and was used for skirmishing and protection of the infantry. From the 5th century BC, Athens, Sparta and most other city-states had their own cavalry, but this was often supplemented with auxiliary cavalry from other states, such as Thessaly. Their own cavalry was often formed by the wealthier citizens who served as "knights," probably because of the enhanced social status that this type of service afforded. In some states, such as Eretria, the ruling oligarchy was actually called the *hippeis*. In Sparta wealthier citizens paid for cavalry horses but did not serve in person. Cavalry does not seem to have been used effectively until the Theban campaigns led by Epaminondas in the early 4th century BC. It was still a relatively minor part of Greek armies until the rise of Macedonia in the second half of the 4th century BC.

Macedonia's significant cavalry force during the 5th century BC occasionally supplied contingents to fight in the Peloponnesian War. At this stage the cavalry may have been lightly armed, but at least some wore armor. When Philip II gained power he reformed the army, including the cavalry. His cavalry was drawn from the aristocracy and called "The Companions" (*hetairoi*), implying that it may have originated as a royal mounted bodyguard. It formed a unit of heavy cavalry that could break up opposing infantry units. The Companion cavalry wore armor and carried the long spears known as *sarissai* (or *sarisai*). The cavalry was probably also armed with a slashing sword for close combat.

Xenophon recommended a number of items of armor to be worn by a cavalryman and his horse, although it is doubtful if all the items were used by many cavalrymen. Most cavalrymen probably wore a cuirass, helmet and high boots, and possibly thigh guards and protection for the left arm (a piece of armor that seems to have fallen from fashion soon after Xenophon's death). Little evidence exists for the horse armor listed by Xenophon, such as chest, side and belly armor, although chamfrons (face guards) were used.

Even before the death of Philip II (339 BC), the Macedonian army was swelled by contingents of soldiers from conquered territories, which continued with Alexander's campaigns. The Macedonian cavalry (the Companions) appears to have continued with little change. However, elite detachments were drawn from the Companions, such as the royal squadron of cavalry (first *ile*), which formed its spearhead. The Companions remained the elite corps of Alexander's cavalry, but units were added of lightly armed Thessalian and Macedonian scouts (*prodromoi*), contingents of cavalry from Greek city-states, Persian mounted archers and increasing numbers of Oriental cavalry.

ELEPHANTS

In his campaigns Alexander the Great encountered armies using war elephants. He was impressed by their performance and brought 200 with him on his return from India. Subsequent Greek armies often included a contingent of elephants, which were used almost exclusively against cavalry because horses do not like their smell. The size and appearance of a force of war elephants could also have a demoralizing effect on an opposing army. Occasionally the strength of elephants was useful in siege warfare for such tasks as pulling down palisades. Initially Indian elephants were used, but later a slightly smaller species of forest elephant from North Africa was used as well. The Indian elephants were sometimes fitted with tops or towers from which soldiers could fight.

TRAINING

Sparta

There is little evidence for military training before the Classical period, with most information coming from Sparta and Athens. In the Classical period, Sparta, Crete and possibly some other states had a totalitarian and militaristic approach to education. The Spartan education system (*agoge*) was wholly concerned with maintaining the military strength of the state. From the age of seven years children were entirely under the state's control. They lived away from their parents, in barracks. Boys' education concentrated on making them good soldiers. Their hair was cut short, and they were divided into classes, forming units in which they trained, ate and lived together.

Boys were taught by a mature and experienced citizen, and academic education was minimal; emphasis was placed on discipline and exercise. They went barefoot and generally naked, and food was simple and scarce. This was to encourage them to steal so that, as soldiers, they could endure food shortages and forage successfully. If caught stealing, they were punished for being unsuccessful, not for stealing. At the age of 12 years, the discipline became much harsher, with constant work and exercise. They had only one tunic for winter and summer. Bravery was the highest virtue, and cowardice the worst crime. Fighting was encouraged, but not anger. Fights were supposed to break up immediately when ordered by a citizen. At 20 years of age, men were liable for military service.

Writing about the Spartan army of the late 5th century BC, Xenophon maintained that there was no need to train soldiers to use weapons because the arm actions needed to handle spear and shield developed naturally. Natural ability was doubtless enhanced by practice in mock battles. Paintings on pottery suggest that a simple range of maneuvers with spear and shield was common, possibly the result of training. Soldiers needed to march in order and maneuver as a body in the phalanx (fig. 3.4) because the success of the phalanx was due largely to the discipline of the hoplites. Most training appears to have consisted of perfecting various maneuvers required in battle.

Athens

In Athens an ephebic college was founded by c. 335 BC to give formal military training to 18-year-old men. An *ephebos* (pl. *epheboi*) was a youth between the ages of 15 and 20, but the term came to refer to those being trained for military service. There is no evidence for an organized training institution before this time, although 18-year-old men had always been liable for military service. The *kosmetes* was in charge of the college; he was elected, as were his assistants (*sophronistai*). There were 10 (later 12) *sophronistai*, one from each tribe of Athens, under the general jurisdiction of the *strategoi* (generals). There were also six appointed teachers: two physical training instructors, an archery instructor, catapult instructor, javelin instructor and an instructor on the use of heavy armor. The first year of training consisted of exercises and guard duty, at the end of which the *epheboi* were granted a shield and spear by the state. In the second year they were employed in the countryside and on frontier patrols, after which they became full citizens.

After 305 BC the training ceased to be compulsory, and by 282 BC training lasted for only one year. The trainees were paid a daily allowance of four obols, although this was stopped when training

was no longer compulsory. The ephebic college subsequently became an elite institution for the wealthy. By the end of the 2nd century BC, it had lost most of its military emphasis and provided a more general education.

Macedonia

There is little information about training of Macedonian troops. When Philip II became king of Macedonia in 359 BC, the Macedonian cavalry ("the Companions") was probably the best in Greece, but the infantry was ill trained and badly organized. Philip reformed the army, imposing a severe code of training and discipline. Wheeled transport was banned, and only one servant to carry equipment was allowed for every 10 soldiers. Soldiers had to carry 30 days' rations when starting out on campaign, and Philip trained them by regular marches with full equipment and baggage. The number of servants allowed to the cavalry was also restricted, so that the number of camp followers and the size of the baggage train were minimized. The heavy infantry was reformed into a phalanx, probably based on that of the Theban army, and would have been trained in all the necessary maneuvers to take advantage of the new type of spear (*sarissa*) with which they were equipped. Philip called his newly formed phalanx the Foot Companions.

BATTLE TACTICS

Homeric Warfare

The earliest evidence for Greek tactics comes from Homer's *Iliad*. This gives the impression of a disorganized mêlée, with warriors from each side fighting individual duels. This is probably an unbalanced picture of early Greek warfare, caused by the poet's concentration on the parts played by the champions and heroes. The poem compares the battle line of the Myrmidons (Achilles' elite warriors) to a carefully built wall, the warriors standing with shield touching shield in a solid line. This is likely to have been the position before a battle, with armies drawn up in opposing lines and meeting in this simple formation. The battle probably broke up into a mêlée only after one side had given way, followed by individual duels and single combat. Before and during the battle, missiles such as arrows, stones and javelins rained down on both sides. After one side had broken and fled, chariots would be used for pursuit and escape.

Phalanx

Although the term "phalanx" is found in Homer (probably to signify a group of soldiers fighting together), the term is usually applied more precisely to a military formation used from the 4th century BC. It may have originated at an earlier date in Sparta, possibly as early as the 8th century BC (see p. 87). A more disciplined system of fighting was introduced, possibly in the 8th century BC. Instead of a few long ranks (the previous battle formation), the soldiers were drawn up in many short files. These files were often, but not always, eight ranks deep. Each phalanx was composed of these files of men, with each file being a unit. When one man fell, the soldier behind took his place.

While the phalanx could withstand attacks from cavalry and lightly armed skirmishers, it was too slow and clumsy to be effective against them. Adding cavalry and lightly armed troops to the hoplites of the phalanx gave it a measure of flexibility and also some protection for its flanks. The lightly armed skirmishers could harass the opposing phalanx or protect the flanks of their own phalanx, while the cavalry harassed the enemy. However, the outcome of the battle still depended on the phalanx itself. Usually both sides had cavalry and lightly armed skirmishers, so the advantage of such troops was reduced.

In 390 BC the Athenian Iphicrates routed a Spartan mora of hoplites with a force of lightly armed troops at the battle of Lechaeum, something that was thought virtually impossible. Lightly armed troops had already proved a serious threat in the battle of Sphacteria (425 BC), and after the success of Iphicrates, lightly armed troops played an increasingly important role.

The phalanx battle formation developed parallel with improvements in weapons and armor. Before

the rise of Macedonia, soldiers of the phalanx were hoplites (heavily armored infantry), who originally carried javelins, a sword and shield, but they were later armed with a long thrusting spear instead of javelins, which enabled them to keep a tighter formation in the phalanx. Soldiers in the phalanx of Macedonian armies were of different types and were not always as heavily armed as earlier hoplites. The term "phalangite," meaning a "soldier of the phalanx," is sometimes used when referring to the later Macedonian armies, where the phalanx consisted of more than one type of soldier. See also the various tactics using the phalanx (below).

Hoplites

The heavily armed hoplites fought in a phalanx in close formation, and their tactics were relatively simple. The two main tactics of the hoplite phalanx were to break through or push over the line of the opposing phalanx, or to outflank it. Phalanxes of two opposing armies were drawn up facing each other, four or more ranks deep. The shields of each front rank overlapped to form a defensive wall, and the thrusting spears were held above the shoulder in an overarm grip, so that spears of several ranks could project over the wall of shields (fig. 3.4). Even with their shields hoplites were very vulnerable to attack if they were not in phalanx formation. To prevent outflanking maneuvers, armies that were seriously outnumbered would try to form up for battle in a place where their flanks were protected by natural obstacles, such as in a pass.

The whole success of a battle depended on the outcome of the initial clash of the two phalanxes. As the opposing phalanxes approached, they would break into a run just before impact, but keep in formation. The opposing shield and spear walls would crash into each other. Each phalanx tried to push forward and break up the enemy phalanx formation. As one soldier fell, the one behind took his place. The struggle continued until one side broke and fled. While the phalanx was locked together in combat, casualties were few because there was little room for effective use of spears. When one side broke, the fleeing hoplites usually discarded their shields and were then vulnerable to faster, lighter-armed troops, as well as

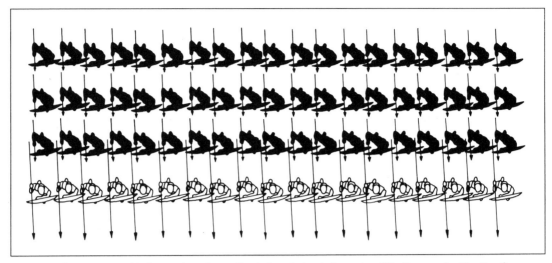

Fig. 3.4 *Diagrammatic bird's-eye view of part of a phalanx in battle formation. The front rank of hoplites forms a wall of shields; the ranks behind stand ready with their shields and spears to reinforce the front rank.*

to pursuing hoplites. Casualties were much higher.

The Theban Tactic

In the 4th century BC there was an important development in hoplite tactics. At the battle of Leuctra (371 BC), the Thebans, led by Epaminondas and Pelopidas, used a different formation of the phalanx and defeated the Spartans. Instead of the front line of the phalanx being straight, the Theban front line was deliberately slanted forward on the left wing. This meant that the left wing, which was 50 ranks deep, impacted with the Spartan right wing, only 12 ranks deep, before other parts of the front line of the phalanx were engaged. The rest of the Spartan line was engaged by light troops and cavalry. The formation overwhelmed the Spartan right wing, traditionally the strongest part of the phalanx with the best troops. The Spartan attempt to reinforce their right wing was stopped by a charge from the Theban Sacred Band, and the Spartan army broke up into disarray. This was the first use of an echelon attack by a Greek army, and Epaminondas used the same tactics successfully at the battle of Mantinea in 362 BC.

Macedonian Tactics

With the reforms of the Macedonian army made by Philip II came improved battle tactics. The phalanx was uniformly deepened to between 16 and 20 ranks. The enemy phalanx would first be attacked by a charge from the cavalry, usually situated on the Macedonian right wing. The cavalry would attempt to crash through the enemy phalanx in a wedge formation in order to swing around and attack from the rear, while the Macedonian phalanx engaged it from the front. The Macedonian phalanx might attack with a straight front line, but usually it was deployed obliquely with the right flank leading. In the battles of Alexander the Great, the initial attack was always from the right wing led by Alexander himself at the head of the Companion Cavalry. Other contingents of cavalry covered the left wing.

Hellenistic Tactics

After Alexander the Great tactics were further elaborated, making use of all available tactical elements: attacking in echelon formation, skirmishing, screening heavily armed troops with lightly armed troops and using heavy cavalry to break the enemy line. A new development was the use of elephants.

They were usually interspersed among units of lightly armed troops, often as part of the frontal screen, in order to disrupt the enemy cavalry. The phalanx was no longer the most important element in the army and was seldom used as the main thrust of the attack, a role now performed by heavy cavalry. Tactics had developed to the point that an army's different elements had to act as a team to gain success.

WEAPONS AND EQUIPMENT

Evidence of weapons and equipment comes mainly from representations on painted pottery, sculpture, models of clay or bronze, and remains of the actual artifacts. Relatively little is known of the use of weapons and equipment before the middle of the 2nd millennium BC, since such evidence comes largely from archaeological finds of the weapons or portrayals of weapons.

Armor

SHIELDS

Before the Mycenaean period, little evidence exists for shields. In the Mycenaean period the most common type appears to have been the figure-of-eight shield (fig. 3.5a). It is depicted in frescoes and other representations and is described by Homer. It had a vertical curved piece of wood, fastened to a horizontal curved piece of wood to form a cross-shaped frame with bowed arms. The figure-of-eight covering built over this frame was made of several layers of toughened bull's hide, then glued and stitched over a wickerwork layer. The rim of the shield was leather, and the horizontal bowed frame was reinforced with a wooden piece that also served as a grip. Homer also described a shield "like a tower." This probably refers to a semi-cylindrical shield with a curved convex top like the one portrayed on an inlaid dagger found at Mycenae. Or it may refer to a shield without the curved top, as

portrayed in some frescoes. In either case, this shield was probably also constructed of leather stretched over a wooden frame.

Both types of Mycenaean shield were full-length body shields and appear to have had shoulder straps for support, so that both hands could wield a spear. The "tower" shield is much less common than the figure-of-eight in early portrayals of warriors. Small round shields appear to have been introduced later in the Mycenaean period, and representations of warriors show that a variety of other shield shapes were also used, such as elliptical and round shields with a segment cut from the bottom edge.

A shield developed from the figure-of-eight shape and a round shield with a central hand grip were both in use through the Dark Age. Bronze shield bosses that probably belonged to a type of round shield have been found. In the early 8th century BC there were two main types of shield. The Dipylon type (named after a cemetery at Athens where representations of it were found) was oval in shape, with a scallop cut from each side. This shield was very similar to the Mycenaean figure-of-eight shield and was probably a direct descendant (fig. 3.5b). The other type of shield was round with a central hand grip. Two late examples of this type, dating to the early 7th century BC, have been found at Delphi. They were made of beaten bronze, had central hand grips, and one had a pronounced central boss. These two Delphi shields were probably obsolete by the early 7th century, since the Argive shield had been developed in the preceding century.

The Argive shield (*hoplon*, for which the hoplites were named) probably developed from an earlier type, as it was also a round shield, but it was much more convex and had a reinforced rim (figs. 3.2, 3.5c). Instead of a central hand grip, Argive shields had an arm band running vertically down the center and a hand grip near the rim, so that the shield could be supported by passing the forearm through the arm band and clasping the hand grip. These shields are shown in vase paintings from the mid-7th century BC. Remains of these shields show that they varied from 31.5 in (0.8 m) to 39 in (1 m) in diameter. They were usually made of wood with an outer facing of bronze or ox hide and a bronze rim. The back of the shield had a thin leather lining and bronze fittings. Because the shield's wooden core was only about 0.2 in (5 mm) thick in the center, a bronze reinforcing plate was often mounted on the back of the shield to provide added protection for the forearm.

Sometimes a leather curtain was hung from the bottom of the shield to protect the legs from missiles. The Argive shield continued to be used by hoplites well into the 4th century BC.

With the increasing use of lightly armed troops against hoplites in the 4th century BC, hoplite shields were sometimes made smaller and lighter. The Macedonian phalangite shield was also smaller and did not have the pronounced rim of the Argive shield. The phalangite shield was of wood faced with bronze, usually with an embossed design. It had an arm band and hand grip as on an Argive shield, but it also had a strap that passed around the neck. Experiments have shown that the shield could be supported and controlled using the arm band and neck strap, leaving both hands free to hold the *sarissa*, which was longer than a hoplite spear and required both hands to support it.

Lightly armed troops, such as peltasts, had lighter shields made of wickerwork, sometimes covered with goat or sheep skin or hide. Shields of Thracian peltasts were known as *peltai* (sing. *pelte*). Originally crescent (pelta) shaped, circular or oval pelta shields became much more common. The peltasts were named after their shields.

BODY ARMOR

The earliest known suit of European armor was found in a tomb at Dendra, near Mycenae, and dates to shortly after 1400 BC. It is plate armor, consisting of a bronze cuirass with a skirt of three articulated bronze plates in front and three behind. A separate neck piece and hinged shoulder plates completed the protection for the torso (fig. 3.6). While not as cumbersome as it appears, it would have required heavy internal padding and would have prevented the soldier standing up once he had fallen. A composite helmet with bronze cheekpieces protected the head. Remains of a pair of greaves and a single arm guard were also found with the armor. A few other pieces of bronze armor from this period are known, but it is unlikely that bronze armor was commonly used. Most armor at this time was probably leather, perhaps reinforced with bronze plates. Breastplates and greaves are mentioned by Homer, but apart from the Dendra armor, no examples of a Greek cuirass survive from earlier than the 8th century BC.

An 8th-century bronze bell cuirass (so called because of its shape) was found in a grave in Argos. It is composed of front and back plates, which have simple decoration reflecting the anatomy of the upper torso (fig. 3.7a). The two plates are held together by a series of catches along the sides and on the shoulders. A semicircular bronze plate (*mitra*) suspended from a belt could be used with this type of cuirass to protect the abdomen. The bell cuirass declined in popularity during the second half of the 6th century BC. It was replaced by the linen cuirass,

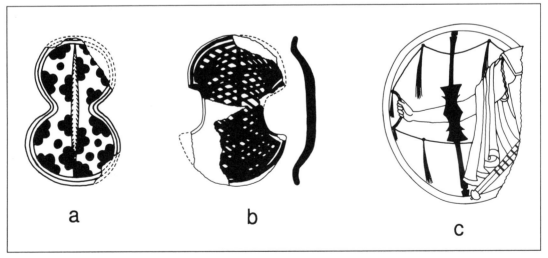

Fig. 3.5   *a. Mycenaean figure-of-eight shield (portrayed on a fresco at Mycenae); b. 8th-century-BC Dipylon shield (front and cross-section of a damaged model); c. back of an Argive shield showing the hand grip and the arm band (from a vase painting).*

although the bronze cuirass continued to be used and evolved into the muscled cuirass.

There were two types of muscled cuirass: a short version, which finished at the waist, and a longer version, which covered the abdomen. The muscled cuirass was molded to reflect the muscles of the torso. It consisted of front and back plates, usually joined with catches at the sides and sometimes at the shoulders (fig. 3.7b). In the 4th century BC the longer version of the muscled cuirass was adapted for cavalry use. The muscled cuirass continued in use until the end of the Roman period.

Linen cuirasses (figs. 3.7c, 3.7d) are thought to have been used since the Mycenaean period and are mentioned in Homer's *Iliad*, but they became standard armor for hoplites only in the late 6th century BC. The linen cuirass was made by gluing together many layers of linen to form a stiff vest about 2 in (5 mm) thick. It was wrapped around the body and tied together on the left-hand side, with another piece protecting the shoulders. Below the waist the cuirass was cut into vertical strips to allow movement. A second layer cut into similar strips (*pteryges*) was glued inside the first layer to cover the gaps. Linen cuirasses were cheaper and lighter than bronze cuirasses, although they were often reinforced by scales or plates. This type of armor remained in use until the introduction of mail armor in the 3rd century BC. An iron cuirass discovered in the tomb of Philip II at Vergina is of the same general design as a linen cuirass.

Cuirasses of bronze and linen continued to be used into the Hellenistic period, but a much greater variation is shown in contemporary sculptures and paintings. Quilted linen cuirasses were also introduced. Linen cuirasses are shown covered with scales or overlapping rectangular plates (lamellar plates). In the 2nd century BC Polybius mentions that wealthier Romans wore mail armor, and it was probably also used by some Greeks at this time.

LEG AND ARM GUARDS

Examples of greaves (full-length protection for the lower legs) are known from the early 14th century BC. Late Mycenaean artistic representations often show warriors apparently wearing greaves. A few bronze greaves of this date are known, and they are also mentioned in Homer's *Iliad*. However, greaves appear to have come into general use only in the 7th century BC. The early types covered the leg

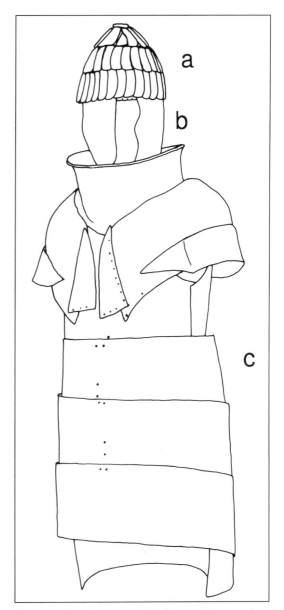

Fig. 3.6   Dendra armor and helmet: a. helmet made of pieces of boar's tusk; b. bronze cheekpieces; c. bronze plate armor.

from the ankle to just below the knee, but later examples were lengthened to cover the knee as well (fig. 3.2). The 7th- and 6th-century-BC types were often highly decorated, but later greaves were molded to reflect the leg muscles in the same way that muscled cuirasses were decorated. Greaves

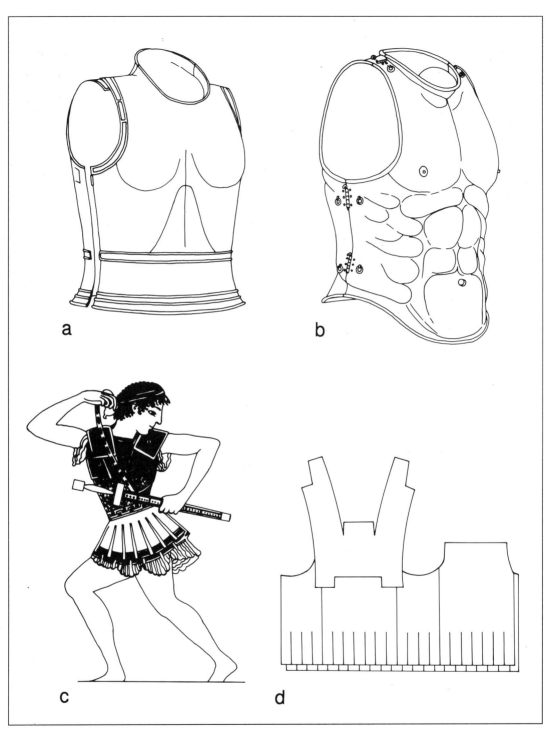

Fig. 3.7   Types of cuirasses: a. bronze bell cuirass; b. bronze muscled cuirass; c. hoplite with a sword in a sheath and wearing a linen cuirass (from a vase painting); d. diagram of the construction of a linen cuirass.

were usually pulled open and clipped onto the legs, but examples from Italy have attachment rings for straps to hold them in place.

Thigh guards are portrayed in contemporary art, but only one example has been found (at Olympia). Ankle guards, which covered both heel and ankle, were much more common, and they were tied on. There are also a few examples of foot guards, which were fitted to sandals to protect the toes and the part of the foot not protected by greaves and ankle guards.

All these bronze guards were lined with leather or fabric. Before the mid-6th century BC the lining was rolled over the edge of the guard and stitched through holes in the bronze. This method of fixing the lining was also used on Mycenaean greaves and limb guards, giving possible evidence of continuity in armor construction through the Dark Age. All limb guards, except for greaves, went out of fashion at the end of the 6th century BC, and even the use of greaves was less popular after this date.

HELMETS

A conical helmet made from pieces of boar's tusk on a base of leather strips, together with bronze cheek-pieces, was found with the bronze armor from a tomb at Dendra, near Mycenae (fig. 3.6a). The helmet dates to just after 1400 BC. The same type of helmet appears in Mycenaean representations of warriors. Later pottery paintings show warriors wearing horned helmets and helmets with a spiky outline, perhaps representing hedgehog pelts. A helmet of the type found at Dendra is also described in Homer's *Iliad*, but the bronze helmets Homer mentions were probably worn mainly by the elite warriors. Ordinary soldiers probably wore leather helmets.

Later helmets show a pattern of development that appears to have evolved from two prototypes, the Kegelhelm and the primitive Corinthian helmet. There is much confusion and controversy over the naming of various types of helmets. Terms such as Attic and Illyrian, still used to identify helmet styles, can erroneously imply specific geographical origins.

The Kegelhelm (a German name meaning a "cone-shaped helmet" or "skittle-shaped helmet") is the earliest type of Iron Age helmet found in Greece (fig. 3.8a). Dating to the 8th century BC, it appears to have gone out of use by the 7th century BC. Two types developed from the Kegelhelm: the Insular and Illyrian. The Insular dates to the 7th century BC and is known from a fragmentary exam-

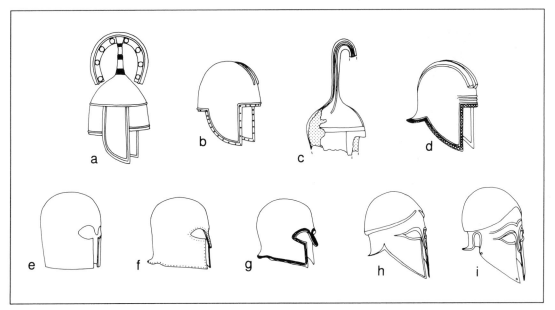

Fig. 3.8   Types of helmets: a. Kegelhelm; b. Illyrian; c. Insular, with crestholder (damaged); d. one-piece Illyrian; e. Corinthian (8th century BC); f. Corinthian (7th century BC); g. Myros type of Corinthian helmet; h. Corinthian (5th century BC); i. Chalcidian.

ple and many miniature models, all from Crete (fig. 3.8c). The Insular and Illyrian types were made in two halves that were riveted together, but the Illyrian, which also dates to the 7th century BC, was being made in one piece by the first half of the 6th century BC (figs. 3.8b, 3.8d). Variations of the Illyrian remained in use into the 5th century BC.

The Corinthian helmet was the most successful Greek helmet, undergoing a number of changes over a period of several centuries (figs. 3.8e–h). It covered the head, leaving only the eyes, nose and mouth clear. The primitive Corinthian helmet dates to the 8th century BC. The 7th-century versions of this helmet developed an indentation on the bottom edge, separating the neckline from the jawline. This feature is also found on early-6th-century-BC helmets, such as the Myros, apparently a very popular helmet as many examples have been found, including one with the name *Myros*. The cheekpieces of the Corinthian helmet were very flexible, so that the helmet could be pulled down over the head and still fit closely to the face. This also allowed the helmet to be pushed back on top of the head (where the grip of the cheekpieces held it in place), leaving the face and ears free when the soldier was not fighting (fig. 3.9). Variations of the Corinthian helmet were used in Greece until the early 5th century BC, but the type continued in Italy, with very evolved forms surviving to the 1st century AD.

Both Illyrian and Corinthian helmets completely covered the ears, making hearing impossible. To

Fig. 3.9   The goddess Athena Chalinitis wearing a Corinthian helmet with a leather neck guard. The helmet is pushed back on the top of her head. This silver stater from Leucas (a colony of Corinth) dates to c. 360 BC, when Leucas issued coins of purely Corinthian type. Courtesy of Somerset County Museums Service.

alleviate this problem, the Chalcidian type of helmet was developed (fig. 3.8i). This helmet is depicted in vase paintings from the early 6th century BC and is characterized by a cutaway area around the ears that allowed the wearer to hear properly.

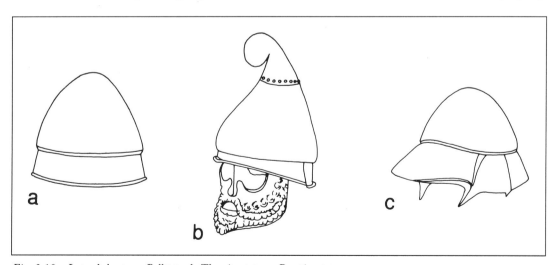

Fig. 3.10   Later helmets: a. Bell type; b. Thracian type; c. Boeotian type.

Cheekpieces on Chalcidian helmets were either fixed or hinged. One variation of the helmet lacked a nose guard; this latter helmet is often called the Attic type and is known from Italy, with no examples from Greece.

The Thracian type of helmet (fig. 3.10b) developed independently of the Corinthian and Illyrian and was in use from the 5th century BC. Thracian and Chalcidian helmets continued to be popular in the 4th century BC, when they were often more decorated. A simple bell-type cap was also popular at this time (fig. 3.10a). The Boeotian type of helmet (fig. 3.10c), with only vestigial cheekpieces, provided good all-around vision. It was used by the Macedonian Companion Cavalry. In the Hellenistic period the Thracian type of helmet continued to be popular. However, there was now a much greater diversity of helmet styles, all more or less loosely based on previous helmet types, and often with the addition of new decorative features.

All bronze helmets were lined or worn over caps to provide padding that reduced the force of blows to the head. Early helmet linings were held in place by being rolled over the helmet's edges and stitched through holes in the metal, but later linings were glued in place.

Spears

Bronze spearheads with a partial socket (sometimes called a "shoeslot") were used in the First Palace Period. Spearheads with very long sockets into which the spear shaft fitted appear to have been introduced in the Second Palace Period. These spearheads were generally very long, ranging from 11.8 in (0.3 m) to 23.6 in (0.6 m). They were used on thrusting spears, although some smaller spearheads may also have been used on javelins. In the Third Palace Period "one-piece" spearheads were used; they were about the same length as the long-socket type, but the one-piece spearhead incorporated the socket completely within the blade. Some were decorated and were obviously prestige weapons. Spearheads in use toward the end of the Third Palace Period were shorter, seldom over 9.8 in (0.25 m) in length, and with a definite socket. The trend toward smaller spearheads appears to have continued, resulting in a short, leaf-shaped spearhead. Both long and short spearheads were in use in the Postpalatial Period.

Homer refers to spears in the *Iliad*. Throwing spears (javelins) were usual, but some were obviously thrusting spears, such as Hector's, which was supposed to be 11 cubits long (about 18 ft, 5.5 m). According to Homer, spear shafts were made of ash wood.

In a Dark Age grave at Vergina, an iron spearhead and an iron spike on the butt of the shaft were found in situ, showing that the spear was about 7.5 ft (2.3 m) long. This is consistent with the estimated size of spears later portrayed in vase paintings, which appear to be between 6.6 ft (2 m) and 9.9 ft (3 m) long. Spears shown in vase paintings are leaf shaped, and many socketed iron spearheads of this type have been found. These spears sometimes had a socketed iron or bronze spike on the butt of the shaft; the use of socketed bronze spear butts had begun during the Mycenaean period. If the spearhead was broken off, the shaft and the spear butt could be used instead, and armor has been found that was apparently pierced by spear butts.

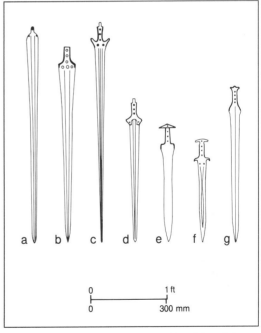

Fig. 3.11 Bronze Age bronze swords: a. Type A; b. Type B; c. Type C; d. Type D; e. Type F (short sword or dagger); f. Type G; g. European Type II.

The part of the shaft where the spear was held was bound with leather thonging to provide a secure grip. These thrusting spears were the main weapon of the hoplite, and changed little for several centuries. In phalanx formation the spear was held in one hand in an overarm grip (fig. 3.4).

Throwing spears (javelins) were used by the lightly armed troops, such as peltasts, who supported the phalanx of hoplites. These spears were shorter and lighter, with smaller spearheads. A thong was often fixed to the spear shaft and twisted around it, and the loop at the end of the thong was held around the thrower's fingers. When the spear was thrown, the thong provided extra leverage and also caused the spear to spin in flight, giving it greater accuracy.

After the reforms of Philip II the phalangites of the Macedonian phalanx were armed with a long two-handed spear called a *sarissa*. Ancient sources disagree about its size. According to Theophrastus the longest *sarissa* was 12 cubits (c. 18 ft, 5.4 m)

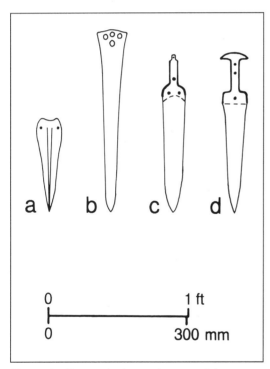

Fig. 3.12   Bronze Age bronze daggers and short swords: a. Prepalatial Minoan Period dagger; b. Second Palace Period large dagger; c. Type E; d. Type F short swords or daggers of the Third Palace Period.

long, but Polybius said they were 14 cubits (c. 21 ft, 6.3 m) long and originally 16 cubits (c. 24 ft, 7.2 m). The shaft of the *sarissa* was made of cornel wood (from the cornelian cherry tree). It may have been made in two pieces and joined with an iron sleeve. Such a sleeve has been found with the iron head and butt of a *sarissa* at Vergina. The name *sarissa* was also used for the smaller spears used by the Macedonian Companion Cavalry.

Swords

Swords always seem to have taken second place after spears (fig. 3.11). Bronze swords were used by the end of the First Palace Period. They had a long tapering bronze blade with a strengthening midrib and are usually classified as Type A swords. The sword hilt was joined to the blade by a short tang and a few rivets, which could not have provided a particularly strong joint. By the Second Palace Period these swords were a main part of a soldier's armament, and blades over 35.4 in (0.9 m) have been found, although the usual length was probably less than 27.5 in (0.7 m).

A Type B sword was developed, which had a larger, flanged tang and a broader base to the blade, providing a better method of joining it to the hilt. A fully developed Type B sword has not been found in Second Palace Period contexts on Crete itself, but was probably developed by mainland Mycenaean bronzesmiths.

In the Third Palace Period several types of swords were in use that are generally classified as Types C, D and G. The Type C sword had projections at the base of the blade to protect the hand, while the Type D sword was shorter and had shoulders at the base to protect the hand. The Type G sword was even shorter, but also had projections to protect the hand and a blade less tapered than previous swords.

Toward the end of the Third Palace Period, Types E and F short swords (or daggers) were in use, and at the very end of the period the European Type II sword (Naue Type II) was introduced. This was a longer sword that had a blade with parallel edges and a flanged hilt. It became the predominant sword type in the Postpalatial Period. Some Type II swords have hilts with ivory hilt plates and decorative gold bands. The Type II sword was in use at the very end of the Mycenaean period, and similar iron swords dated to the Dark Age show that the same style of sword continued, but was made of iron instead of bronze. A slashing weapon, it slowly evolved into a slightly shorter leaf-shaped slashing sword with a blade about 23.6 in (0.6 m) long. This became the normal hoplite sword, used only for fighting at close quarters or if the hoplite's spear broke (fig. 3.7c).

In the 6th and 5th centuries BC, a sword with a curved iron, single-edge blade (*kopis*) gradually appeared as an alternative to the hoplite sword. Early versions of this sword were slashing weapons, with blades about 25.5 in (0.65 m) long. They later evolved into shorter cut-and-thrust swords with blades about 17.7 in (0.45 m) long that were popular in Macedonia.

Daggers

Early bronze daggers are known from the Prepalatial Minoan Period. They were short, usually under 7.9 in (0.2 m) long, and may have been all-purpose knives as much as weapons. Hilts were attached by riveting them to the base of the blade; reriveted blades show that this was not always a strong method of attachment. The blades were strengthened by a central midrib. By the First Palace Period longer blades around 13.8 in (0.35 m) were in use, and by the Second Palace Period large daggers were being produced. It is often very difficult to distinguish a short sword from a long dagger (fig. 3.12). Toward the end of the Third Palace Period, short daggers (or swords) known as Types E and F were in use. As a weapon the dagger appears to have been totally eclipsed by the sword.

Daggers continued in use through the Dark Age and succeeding periods. After the Dark Age (if not before), they may have been regarded more as all-purpose knives than as weapons. Short swords or daggers were carried particularly by lightly armed troops such as slingers and archers, who would otherwise be unarmed when they had fired all their missiles.

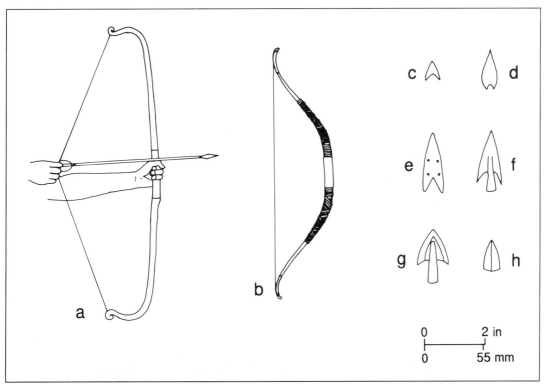

Fig. 3.13 Bows and arrowheads: a. simple one-piece Cretan stave bow (from a vase painting); b. Scythian composite bow; c. Middle Helladic stone arrowhead; d. Late Helladic stone arrowhead; e. LHIII arrowhead; f. LHIII socketed bronze arrowhead; g. and h. 5th-century-BC socketed bronze arrowheads.

Fig. 3.14 Lead sling shot with an inscription dexa *(take that).*

Bows

Although bows were used throughout the Bronze Age, no examples from Greece have been found. Arrowheads were at first made from stone such as chert and obsidian, as in the preceding Neolithic period, but were later made from bronze, of which many examples have been found (fig. 3.13). Records of quantities of arrowheads and javelin heads in Linear B texts suggest that the use of missile weapons, including the bow and arrow, was a more important feature of early warfare than the evidence otherwise indicates. It has even been suggested that armor was developed to provide soldiers with protection from missiles rather than from spear thrusts. The evidence suggests that the Minoans used a composite bow, but the few early representations of Mycenaean bows appear to be the simple one-piece "stave" or "self" bows, which continued in use in Greece for many centuries. Evidence for bows and arrows dating to the Dark Age is sparse, except in Crete where finds of arrowheads show that they were used throughout that period.

At some stage the Cretans switched from the stave bow to the composite bow. Both Scythian and Cretan archers used composite bows made from wood, horn, bone and sinew (fig. 3.13). Bowstrings were of dried gut or sinew. The Cretan composite bow was a simple bow in the shape of a segment of a circle, whereas the Scythian bow was doubly convex. The Scythian bow was more powerful than the Cretan and had a range of over 480 ft (146 m). Vase paintings show that Scythian archers carried a bow and arrows in a composite case slung from a belt.

Arrowheads were bronze and of various shapes, but Cretan arrowheads were generally larger and heavier than Scythian ones. Arrowheads were usually socketed so that the end of the arrow shaft fitted neatly to the head. Iron arrowheads may have been widely used, but few examples have survived. See also archers p. 92.

Slings

Slings were made from (or from materials reinforced with) dried gut or sinew. One end of the sling was looped around the slinger's wrist, who held the other end in his hand, with the shot held in the loop of the sling. The sling was whirled around to give the sling shot momentum, and the end of the sling was released to launch the sling shot. Sling shots were made of stone, baked clay and lead. Thousands of lead sling shots or bullets have been found. They were cast in clay molds and were plum shaped, sometimes with motifs and short inscriptions on the surface as part of the casting, such as *dexa* (take that). Lead shot generally weighed 0.7–1.7 oz (20–50 g), but much heavier weights were also used (fig. 3.14). Sling shots could not be seen in flight, and lead sling shots in particular could cause terrible wounds. Xenophon described how they could enter the body deep enough for the flesh to close over them.

A late Macedonian invention, around 170 BC, was a short bolt or arrow called the cestrosphendone (Greek *kestros*). This had a short iron bolt head attached to a short wooden shaft with flights attached. It was thrown by a sling with two loops in order to hold the cestrosphendone securely. A sling mounted on a long pole was a late Macedonian invention and enabled ordinary soldiers to throw large stones. See also slingers p. 93.

Artillery

The earliest known piece of artillery is the *gastraphetes* (belly bow), which was invented in Syracuse c. 400 BC, possibly at the instigation of Dionysius I, tyrant of Syracuse. The *gastraphetes* was a very powerful composite bow, mounted on a stock with a draw and release mechanism. This mechanism had a slider on a ratchet with a claw and trigger. To operate the *gastraphetes*, the slider was pushed forward along the stock, and the claw hooked the bowstring. The front of the stock was then placed on the ground, and the operator leaned on the back of the stock, which had a specially shaped transverse piece of wood. The slider was pulled back over the teeth of the ratchet until the bowstring was taut, and the arrow was loaded onto the stock, against the bowstring. The weapon could be fired by pulling the trigger, which allowed the claw to pivot upwards, releasing the bowstring. The advantage of the *gastraphetes* over an ordinary bow was its greater power and range. Because of its weight and slow rate of fire, it was used mainly in siege warfare.

A more powerful mechanical bow, the *oxybeles* (bolt-shooter) was developed c. 375 BC. This used a winch to draw back the bowstring. Because of the extra weight involved in building a more robust and powerful machine, the *oxybeles* was fixed to a stand. The use of an even more powerful bow than that of the *gastraphetes* gave increased range and accuracy.

A later development of the *oxybeles* was to replace the composite bow with a pair of torsion springs. Each spring was made by twisting a bundle of sinew ropes, into which was inserted a bar. The torsion of the sinews provided the power, forcing the bar forward. The two springs were mounted symmetrically, so that the bars of the springs could act as the arms of the bow. A bowstring was fixed between them and drawn back to the firing position. The springs were then drawn tight by further twisting of the sinew ropes. The general name for this machine was *katapeltes* (pl. *katapeltai*, shield piercers), because some were capable of penetrating a soldier's shield and armor at ranges of more than 1,320 ft (402 m).

The bolts that were fired from an *oxybeles* or *katapeltes* varied according to the size of the machine. A common length was about 27 in (0.68 m). The heads of these bolts also varied, but they frequently had a triple fin or barb.

As *katapeltai* increased in size some were adapted to throw stones. Depending on their size these machines could throw stones of 10–180 lbs (4.5–82 kg). They were usually used in sieges to batter fortified walls, often at a range of 450–600 ft (157–185 m). Such a machine was called a *lithobolos* (literally, stone-thrower). A machine capable of throwing the larger stones was sometimes called a *petrobolos*

(stone-thrower). The stones used in these machines were shaped into spheres to increase their accuracy, and several dumps of these stones have been found. Sometimes irregular stones were coated in clay to make them spherical, but this reduced their impact on the target.

Siege Engines

Before the mid-5th century BC siege engines were apparently rarely used, although devices such as battering rams may have been used from earliest times. It has even been suggested that the "wooden horse" of Troy was in reality a battering ram protected by a wooden superstructure. The siege of Plataea (429–427 BC) provides the first evidence of siege engines, with a battering ram being used. This and other tactics were unsuccessful, and the garrison had to be starved into submission. Dionysius I (tyrant of Syracuse, 405–367 BC) offered large rewards for new inventions of siege engines and artillery. The resulting inventions revolutionized siege warfare, but they seem to have been regularly used only under Philip II of Macedonia (4th century BC).

The "tortoise" type of battering ram was used for knocking down part of a wall. It was a beam of wood (the actual ram) mounted within a protective timber housing. The ram was either suspended so that it could swing back and forth or supported by rollers. The protective housing was mounted on wheels, so that it could be pushed into position, and the housing was covered with hide padded with seaweed. The front end of the ram had a bronze or iron head in order to cause maximum damage to the wall. The ram was operated by men inside the protective housing. They swung the ram back and forth manually or by a system of ropes and pulleys. A specialized form of ram was the drill, which knocked a hole in a wall, rather than shaking part of it down. The drill was a wooden beam with an iron point that moved on rollers within a wooden trough. The trough was mounted inside a protective housing, and the drill was moved back and forth by a system of ropes and pulleys attached to a windlass.

Siege towers provided the attackers with protected access to the top of a wall. Built of wood and covered with hides stuffed with wool or seaweed for

Fig. 3.15   Lion Gate, Mycenae, c. 1250 BC. Over the gateway are massive slabs of stone and a supporting lintel. The lintel probably weighs about 20 tons. Above is a relieving triangle with a carved slab 2 ft (0.61 m) thick. It has a relief of two lions either side of a column, but they have lost their heads.

protection, the towers were mounted on wheels so that they could be pushed up to the wall. Ladders or stairs inside the protective tower gave access to the top, and artillery and archers could fire from interior platforms. The towers sometimes had a drawbridge, which could be let down onto the wall being attacked. The Roman writer Vitruvius, quoting a lost work by Diades (an engineer that Alexander the Great took on his campaigns), gives the ideal dimensions of siege towers. The smallest one (10 floors) should be c. 88.5 ft (27 m) high and c. 24.5 ft (7.5 m) wide at the base, with the top 20 percent narrower than the base. The largest one (20 floors) should be c. 177 ft (54 m) high, c. 34.5 ft (10.5 m) wide at the base, with the top 20 percent narrower than the base. The larger towers, with only slightly tapering sides, would have been very unstable.

In 307 BC Demetrius I Poliorcetes (The Besieger) used a massive siege tower during his siege of Salamis. It was so large it was called the *helepolis*

(literally, city destroyer). In his attempts to take Rhodes in 305–304 BC, Demetrius built an even bigger *helepolis*, probably the largest siege tower constructed in ancient Greece. It was 130–140 ft (40–43 m) high and was built on a base 72 ft (22 m) square. The tower tapered upward and was about 29.5 ft (9 m) square at the top. It was mounted on wheels and had nine floors, all of which were armed with some kind of artillery—catapults on the lower floors and bolt throwers on the upper ones. It was built of wood, and all major joints were reinforced with iron plates. The front and sides were covered with iron plates to protect it from burning missiles, and it had ports at the front through which artillery could be fired. These ports were covered with shutters, which could be raised and lowered mechanically. The shutters were covered with hide stuffed with wool to protect against stone missiles.

At the siege of Delium in 424 BC, the Thebans used fire-raisers against a palisade held by the Athenians. The fire-raiser was a cauldron of burning coal, sulphur and pitch attached to one end of a long wooden beam. The beam had been split and hollowed out, so that an iron tube could be fitted inside. The two halves were bound together, and the cauldron end was protected with iron plating. A bellows was fitted at the other end of the tube inside the beam to provide a forced draught to the fire in the cauldron. The beam was fixed to two wooden carts, so that the cauldron could be pushed up against the palisade. The bellows were operated at a distance to force flames from the cauldron to spread to the palisade.

Scaling ladders were frequently used in attempts to break into besieged fortifications, but they were vulnerable to attack by the defending forces. An improvement on simple ladders was the sambuca (*sambuke*), a ladder covered by a reinforced roof and sides for protection. It was mounted on a wheeled carriage by a horizontal pivot near the base of the ladder, so that the top of the ladder could be raised to the top of the wall being attacked. At the base of the ladder was a compartment filled with stones. This was used as a counterweight to the weight of the ladder and the soldiers (about 10) who climbed into the protected top of the ladder before the attack. The sambuca was wheeled up to the wall. Aided by the counterweight, the top of the sambuca was raised to the height of the wall by applying pressure to the vertical arms of a capstan on the end of the pivot to which the ladder was attached.

Various types of movable wooden shelters were used to protect soldiers when they were close to the walls of a besieged town, attempting to fill in ditches or undermine walls. Several shelters could be placed together to provide a protective passage to the wall or to siege engines close to the wall.

FORTIFICATIONS

Bronze Age–Iron Age

Evidence for fortifications before the Third Palace Period is relatively rare and consists mainly of remains of town walls, watchtowers and cisterns (that might imply water storage in case of attack). In the Third Palace Period fortified settlements were

more common, but this may not be indicative of warfare until the end of the period. It has been argued that fortifications of the earlier Third Palace Period, such as those at Mycenae and Tiryns, were initially for prestige and control. A more serious threat is indicated at these sites by the later provision of water supplies and additional defended areas that could be used as refuge for the surrounding population and their livestock.

The citadels of the Mycenaean period were normally built on the tops of hills and were fortified by walls that followed the contours of the hills. The walls at Mycenae are typical of such fortifications; they are an average of 16.5 ft (5 m) thick and are built of massive stones weighing up to 10 tons. The method of construction has been labeled "Cyclopean" (fig. 1.4) from the later Greek explanation that these walls had been built by the Cyclops. The walls have flat surfaces built with close-fitting stones without mortar, but the stones are irregular. An exception is around gateways, which were often made more impressive by the use of more massive blocks, or (as at Mycenae) by the use of stones dressed into rectangular blocks (fig. 6.20). For thicker walls the gap between two outer layers of facing blocks was filled with earth and rubble. Gateways through the walls were constructed with a lintel supported by posts, all made from massive slabs of stone. Only at Mycenae has a sculpture been found surmounting the gateway (fig. 3.15). Walls of this type were used to enclose large citadels, settlements, small forts and apparently large areas of land. At Mycenae a bastion was built out from the side of the gate, so that the defenders could bombard attackers on their unshielded side. Mycenae had two gateways (Lion Gate and Postern Gate) and also two narrow sally ports to allow the defenders to go out and attack the enemy without having to open the main gates. At Tiryns the walls had galleries built into them. There is evidence that tops of the walls were finished off with mud-brick battlements.

Archaic and Classical

TOWN WALLS

Fortifications developed little from Mycenaean methods until the 6th century BC. The 7th-century-

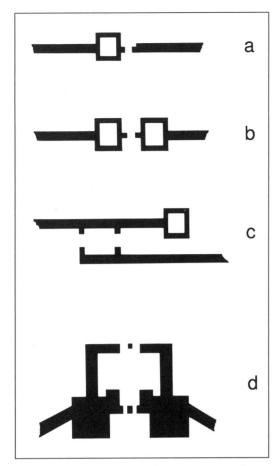

Fig. 3.16   Plans of fortification gateways dating from the Classical period: a. one flanking tower; b. two flanking towers; c. overlapping type with one tower; d. Hellenistic courtyard type.

ural defenses, such as steep slopes and cliffs. They were often pierced by sally ports. Earlier walls of mud brick or rubble masonry were now superseded by stronger walls of dressed rectangular or polygonal stone blocks, although mud brick may still have been used for battlements. Towers projecting outward from the walls were also introduced. Although bastions projecting from walls and separate watchtowers were used in Mycenaean times, the earliest use of projecting towers appears to have been in the 6th-century-BC fortifications at Burunkuk in Asia Minor. Initially such towers were used only to strengthen weak points in the circuit of the wall and at gateways, but by the 5th century BC two-story towers were normal at regular intervals along the wall.

GATEWAYS

Gateways did not undergo any significant development until the 4th century BC (fig. 3.16). Until then they were modified versions of Mycenaean types, guarded by one or two towers or bastions, or overlapping, with the outer wall parallel to the inner wall and ending in a tower. Attackers approaching the gate had to pass between these two walls, and their unshielded side was exposed to fire from the tower at the end of the outer wall. Gates usually had two leaves opening inward. Hinges were not used. Instead, the outer side of each gate had a pivot at each end set into holes in the floor and the roof of the gateway, allowing the gates to be opened and closed. Gates were secured by a wooden bar placed across the back of both gates and fitted into holes in the masonry on either side. This bar was sometimes held in position by a locking bar and pin, which prevented the main bar from being removed.

In the 4th century BC various gates that dropped into place from above seem to have been used as a second obstacle behind the traditional two-leaved gates. There is some evidence that a true portcullis was in use in the early 3rd century BC. This iron grating was raised and lowered from above, with its edges running in vertical channels in the masonry walls of the gateway.

LONG WALLS

In the 5th century BC, after the Persians retreated, the fortifications of Athens were rebuilt and extended to give fortified access to the harbors at Piraeus (fig. 3.17). Piraeus itself was fortified and

BC fortifications of Emporion on the island of Chios are very similar in concept to Mycenaean types, and fortifications were still concentrated on the citadel or acropolis. In the 6th century BC attempts were made to enclose entire towns with effective fortifications. Within (or sometimes outside) the walled city, an acropolis usually occupied the most commanding site, such as an isolated hill, serving as a refuge if an enemy force gained access to the walled city itself. Sometimes an acropolis served to hold a garrison, often against the will of the inhabitants of the city it dominated.

From the 6th century BC, town walls were built following natural contours and making use of nat-

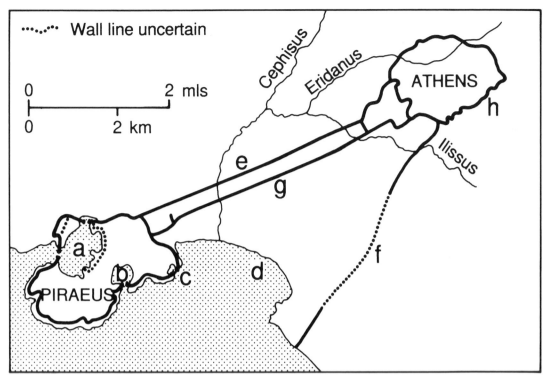

Fig. 3.17   The Long Walls between Athens and Piraeus: a. harbor of Cantharus; b. harbor of Zea; c. harbor of Munychia; d. Phalerum; e. northern wall; f. southern (or Phalerum) wall (line uncertain); g. middle wall; h. city wall.

connected to Athens by "long walls," which were strengthened at intervals by two-story towers. Initially the northern wall (completed about 456 BC) ran from Athens to Piraeus and the southern one from Athens to Phalerum, enclosing a triangle of land. A middle wall was later added about 327 ft (100 m) south of the northern wall, to form a defended corridor just over 4 miles (6.5 km) long. The southern wall from Athens to Phalerum was then allowed to decay.

Other seaboard cities, such as Corinth, also built long walls to connect them with their ports or the coast in order to ensure supplies when under siege. In some instances the distance between the city and the coast was too small for the connecting fortifications to be called long walls. At Megara the Athenians built long walls (completed in 459 BC) from the city to the port of Nisaea to ensure access to the Athenian garrison in the city. The effectiveness of long walls depended heavily on the number of soldiers available to defend them, but they prob-

ably would not have been capable of withstanding a determined siege. With the development of siege warfare, artillery and siege engines, long walls became increasingly obsolete.

A Mycenaean wall on the Isthmus of Corinth has been interpreted as an unfinished defensive wall. This may be one of the earliest instances of such fortified walls. They were often constructed to block passes during the Archaic and Classical periods. At various times from the 6th century BC, isthmuses, such as those at Gallipoli, Methana and Corinth, were blocked by walls and fortifications, and the pass at Thermopylae was blocked by a wall several times.

FORTS AND TOWERS

In the late 5th and early 4th centuries BC, Athens built a series of frontier forts to secure communications and serve as a first line of defense. Forts with a garrison were called *phrouria* (sing. *phrourion*) and could also act as a refuge for local inhabitants; fortified towns with garrisons were also sometimes called *phrouria*. One purpose of frontier forts was to make raids into enemy territory, and from 425 BC the Athenians built forts on enemy coasts as secure bases for raiding inland. In purely military forts, the garrison was housed in simple buildings, with each soldier allotted a regulation bed space. Such barrack blocks are known from Teke Kale in Turkey and Filla in Euboea.

A large number of individual towers are known from parts of mainland Greece and the Aegean islands. Those on the islands have been interpreted as part of a defense against slave raids by pirates, and some at least were used as residences. Mainland towers often appear to have been used as signaling towers and watchtowers.

Hellenistic

The development of artillery and siege engines could not easily be countered by modifications to walls and towers of fortifications. Once an enemy had reached the wall of a fort or town, it was only a matter of time before it was breached. Improvements to fortifications in the 4th and 3rd centuries BC therefore concentrated on preventing the enemy from reaching the walls. Walls were thickened, built higher and provided with shuttered loopholes and ports (instead of crenellations), through which artillery could be fired. Towers were built higher (often four or five floors), so that artillery fired from the towers would have a greater range. Towers had pitched roofs instead of crenellations to provide better protection from missiles, and sally ports allowed the defenders to attack besiegers and drive them back from the wall.

One or more large ditches were dug outside walls to deter mining and to provide an obstacle for siege engines. Outer ditches might have a palisade or thorn hedge outside them, and the inner ditch could be fronted by stone outworks, providing shelter for artillery emplacements. Outside the fortifications were various obstacles and traps, such as covered holes and artificial marshes. Gateways were massively reinforced, often with a complex system of outworks. The courtyard type of gateway was most common; it was made by indenting the line

of the walls as they approached the gate, so that a courtyard was formed outside the gate. A second outer gate was sometimes built, creating a closed courtyard.

Temporary Camps

The Greeks never valued the fortification of temporary camps as much as the Romans and usually did not fortify a camp unless they expected to stay for at least several weeks. No evidence for fortified camps exists before the 5th century BC, but Homer's *Iliad* describes the beached Greek ships being protected by a fortification. This consisted of a wall of stones reinforced by wooden beams, outside of which was a wide ditch; steep banks topped by palisades rose up on either side of the ditch. It appears that the defenses of a temporary camp depended on an assessment of the risk. A camp might be hurriedly fortified to keep out raiders, possibly with only a wall built with stones found in the vicinity. In places where there were not enough stones, mud bricks could be used, although these would take time to dry. In either case the result would be capable of refurbishment for many years, more like a fort than a camp.

Thucydides mentions a number of 5th-century-BC Athenian camps. Two were described as "walled" and others were "stockades." One description of a stockade shows that it consisted of a bank and ditch, with stakes revetting the outer face of the bank. On top of the bank, debris was piled, including stones, bricks from demolished buildings, and vine stumps. Wooden towers were built when necessary. Xenophon reports that one regulation in Spartan armies was that their camps should be circular in plan wherever topography permitted, with the weapons stored in the center. It seems that such camps were not fortified. The Spartans appear to have feared slave revolts more than anything, and so their first concern was to keep their weapons safe. There does not appear to have been a standard shape or plan for camps built by other Greek armies. In general, temporary camps and forts appear to have been built on an ad hoc basis, making best use of the terrain and available building materials. The result was usually a ditch backed by some kind of rampart and palisade.

SIEGES

The strength, size and complexity of Mycenaean fortifications suggest that they could have been besieged at times, although there is no evidence of siege warfare in this period. The siege warfare portrayed in Homer's *Iliad* is primitive. There appears to have been no encircling fortifications around Troy and no attempt to starve the city into surrender. Assaults were made on the gates, but not the walls, which was probably the main Greek tactic. Other legends record the fall of Troy by use of the wooden horse, which was possibly a battering ram used to demolish part of the wall.

The first evidence for Greek siege tactics occurs with the Spartans' siege of Plataea (429–427 BC) during the Peloponnesian War. They surrounded Plataea with a stockade to prevent anyone getting in or out. Against the wall they began to build an earth ramp reinforced with timber. The Plataeans responded by putting a screen on top of the wall, behind which they built the wall higher. When the ramp reached the wall, the Plataeans tunneled under the wall to try to undermine the ramp. A crescent-shaped emergency wall built behind the point being attacked by the Spartans allowed them to maintain the circuit of the town wall if it was breached. The Spartans brought battering rams up the slope and tried to demolish the wall, while the Plataeans lowered nooses in an attempt to grip and haul up the rams. They also dropped beams of wood suspended from chains to try to break the rams. Finally the Spartans tried to set fire to the town, but a thunderstorm extinguished the fire. Having failed to take the town by force, the Spartans reinforced the surrounding fortification with ditches, walls and a sentry walk with towers, and proceeded to starve the town into surrender. Since most Plataeans had escaped before the siege began, and others escaped later, the remaining small garrison held out for two years.

The siege of Plataea demonstrates the main problem of siege warfare: preventing supplies and reinforcements from reaching the besieged fortification. The success of subsequent sieges depended on the ability of the attacker to seal off the besieged fortification. If this was not done properly, as in the Athenian siege of Syracuse in 414–413 BC, there was a good chance that the attackers would be defeated. This situation changed with the development of sophisticated and powerful artillery and siege engines at the beginning of the 4th century BC.

In 379 BC Dionysius I (tyrant of Syracuse) besieged Motya, a town on an island off Sicily's coast. Having previously offered large rewards for inventions of new artillery and siege engines, he had the most sophisticated siege weapons at his disposal. Using a combination of artillery, battering rams and siege towers, Dionysius broke into and captured the town. Considering this success, it is surprising that the new siege weapons did not immediately come into common use. Not until the siege of Perinthus by Philip II in 340 BC was extensive use made of such engines. From then on the strength and power of the attackers' artillery and siege engines were often the determining factors in the success of a siege.

Alexander the Great made use of siege engines, most notably at the siege of Tyre (332 BC), but the use of siege engines to break into fortifications reached its peak after Alexander's death. In the siege of Salamis (306 BC), Demetrius I Poliorcetes (The Besieger) took the city with the aid of a huge siege tower nicknamed *helepolis* (city-destroyer). In 305–304 BC Demetrius earned his nickname attempting to take Rhodes by siege. He used a massive array of siege engines, including an even bigger version of the *helepolis*. Despite breaking down part of the curtain wall and towers, Demetrius failed to take the city. Never again were such massive siege engines used, although artillery and smaller siege engines were now established weapons. A well-fortified and well-equipped city could resist attack, but few could afford the expense. Nevertheless, besiegers sometimes had to fall back on the tactic of surrounding and starving out the defenders.

TROPHIES

Trophies (*tropaia*, sing. *tropaion*) were originally intended as a religious image or dedication to the *theos tropaios* (the god who caused the defeat). They usually consisted of a suit of enemy armor set up on a stake at the point on the battlefield

NAVIES

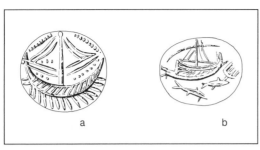

Fig. 3.18   Two types of possible warships of Bronze Age date, depicted on Minoan seals: a. symmetrical, with a single mast and several oars, c. 1800 BC; b. steeply rising stern and projecting forefoot on the bow, with a single mast, c. 2000 BC.

where the enemy had been routed. Trophies were also dedicated at the shrine of the deity who was thought to be responsible for the defeat of the enemy (usually at Olympia or Delphi). Several examples of such armor and weapons have been found at these sites. Trophies were depicted in artistic representations from the 6th century BC. In the 4th century BC trophies became permanent monuments, usually in the form of buildings, such as towers. The battle of Leuctra in 371 BC was commemorated by a tower with a trophy of arms at the top. Such trophies commemorated naval and land battles and became an increasingly common motif in art. By the time of Alexander the Great, captured enemy shields with a dedicatory inscription were the usual type of trophy dedicated at religious shrines. In the Hellenistic period, kings and other rulers decorated their buildings with sculptured trophies accompanied by statues representing the victors and their captives.

Function

Before the Classical period there is little evidence of the way in which navies were used. It is likely that the earliest use of ships in warfare was to carry troops on raids of coastal towns and of territory best approached from the sea. Although no doubt used primarily for transport, ships were probably equipped for fighting other ships. By the Archaic period, if not before, warfare was primarily at sea. Although warships may have been used for carrying troops in addition to their own marines, they were increasingly adapted to fighting other ships. In the Hellenistic period the warships were developed further to allow them to use artillery and carry more marines. Navies played an extremely important role in the history of Greece; without a strong navy the formation of Athens' overseas empire would have been impossible.

Warships

EARLY EXAMPLES

Before the Archaic period there is relatively little evidence for ships of any kind and what does exist comes mostly from artistic representations. It is usually unclear whether the vessel portrayed is a warship or not. It is likely that few, if any, specific warships existed at this time and that all ships were used for war when necessary. Two types of ship are

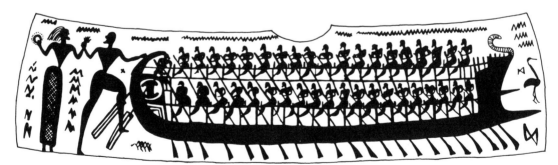

Fig. 3.19   A warship with two banks of oars (a bireme) depicted on a Geometric bowl from Thebes, dating to the second half of the 8th century BC. At the stern are two steering oars, while a ram is visible at the bow.

shown in Early Bronze Age representations. Both are powered by oars and have a mast with a single square sail (fig. 3.18). One type is approximately symmetrical, with a gently rising bow and stern giving a curved profile to the bottom of the vessel. The other type has a more steeply rising stern and a projecting forefoot on the bow. It is thought that this projection is a structural feature, probably a continuation of the keel beyond the stempost, but it is also probably the forerunner of the ram, which is a common feature of later warships. It is likely that these ships continued in use to the end of the Mycenaean period or beyond, but evidence that might show their development during this period is not available.

PENTEKONTERS

Good information about warships becomes available only in the Archaic period. Although Homer describes events some centuries earlier, the ships that he describes are 8th-century-BC types and cannot be taken as reliable descriptions of earlier vessels. Two types of ship are mentioned by Homer: light, fast ships powered by 20 oars, and heavier warships powered by 50 oars. These 50-oared galleys, known as pentekonters (literally, fifties; *pentekontoroi*, sing. *pentekontoros*), had oars on one level only. They appear to have been carvel built, mainly from pine wood, with oars of polished spruce. The stern was curved, with the end curving back over the ship like a scorpion's tail, while the bow terminated in a nearly vertical prow with a metal-sheathed ram at the waterline.

Pentekonters had a mast with a square sail that was taken down before going into battle, or perhaps even left ashore before a battle to lighten the ship, making it faster and more maneuverable. The ship was steered by two large paddles or steering oars lashed to the stern, and there was a stone anchor.

BIREMES

At the end of the 8th century BC the bireme was invented (fig. 3.19). This was a galley with two banks of oars on each side, one above the other. The bireme was developed by the Phoenicians or possibly by the Ionian Greeks, and was later generally adopted by the Greeks. Evidence about biremes is relatively scarce, and so it is not clear exactly how the banks of rowers were arranged, but the bireme

seems to have been developed to provide a more powerful vessel. Using two banks of oars meant that the vessel could be shorter and more maneuverable, but still have the same power as a pentekonter.

TRIREMES

In the 6th century BC, a third bank of oars was added to the bireme to produce the trireme (*trieres*, pl. *triereis*), and by the end of the 6th century BC this was the most common warship in the Mediterranean. There is still controversy over whether the triremes actually had three banks of rowers on each side, and alternative explanations have been given for its name. The warship could have had two banks of oars on each side, but three banks of rowers, with one bank being central to the ship and pulling two oars instead of one. While this scheme fits some surviving evidence, it does not explain it all, particularly the depictions of ships with three banks of oars along each side. Sea trials of a reconstruction of a trireme with three banks of oars and three banks of rowers (one to each oar) on each side have shown that such a ship is perfectly feasible, and it is now usually accepted that this is how Greek triremes were powered.

Excavations of ship sheds at Piraeus harbor have provided maximum dimensions of 121.5 ft (37 m) long and 9.9 ft (3 m) wide at the bottom for the triremes based there. Athenian naval records show that oars were 13.2–14.7 ft (4–4.5 m) long. There were three types of oars: thranite, zygian and thalamian. The lowest level of rowers were the thalamites (*thalamitai*). There were 27 thalamites on each side, and they worked their oars through ports close to the waterline. The second level of rowers were the zygites (*zygitai*), of which there were also 27 on each side. The top level of rowers were the thranites (*thranitai*). There were 31 thranites on each side, and they rowed through an outrigger, which was an extension from the side of the ship that provided greater leverage for the oars.

The trireme was steered by a pair of steering oars at the stern, and it had a pair of anchors at the bow. Triremes were carvel built, with a stern and prow of similar shape to those of pentekonters. They had a bronze-plated ram projecting from the bow at the waterline. Earlier triremes apparently had no deck or were only partially decked. Later they were decked right across to accommodate more armed men. Triremes still had a mast and sail like earlier ships, but before battle these were left ashore to lighten the load; the battle speed of a trireme depended only on the rowers. Because there was little room for supplies on board these ships, they were usually beached each night in order to obtain food and water.

LATER EXAMPLES

The trireme was the main Greek warship at least until the 4th century BC. At the beginning of that century several new galleys were introduced. Their names, such as *tetrereis* (fours, sing. *tetreres*) and *pentereis* (fives, sing. penteres), presumably relate to the number and arrangement of oars and rowers. These can be explained relatively easily, but by the mid-4th century BC there were apparently "sixes," with numbers rising progressively to 13. By the Hellenistic period in the 3rd century BC, there was a "sixteen," and by the end of that century there was a "forty" (*tessarakonteres*), a showpiece galley built by Ptolemy IV. Little evidence survives about these ships, and their names have proved difficult to interpret.

During this period ships were increasingly designed as platforms for artillery, so the sides were enclosed and they had a complete deck. Probably to cope with the extra weight, ships began to be designed with extra rowing capacity. The *tetrereis* (fours) probably had only two banks of oars, with two men to each oar. The term "four" probably referred to the number of men rowing each vertical group of oars (two oars, with two men at each oar). If this was the way that the names of the various galleys were derived, it can account easily for the lower numbers.

Ships of this type were depicted with up to three banks of oars, so that they were really just larger versions of the bireme and trireme with more than one rower per oar. From galleys used in the 17th and 18th centuries AD, it is known that the maximum number of men that can operate a single oar efficiently is eight, and so the largest efficient Greek vessel would have had three banks of oars with eight men per oar (a "twenty-four"). In fact a "sixteen" is one of the large galleys most frequently mentioned. This could have had two banks of oars on each side, with each oar operated by eight men. However, this theory still leaves the problem of the "forty" without a satisfactory explanation.

ANCHORS

The earliest anchors were anchor-stones with a hole through which a rope could be passed. Some stone anchors had extra holes for the insertion of sharpened stakes that would dig into the seabed, giving a more secure anchorage. These were superseded from c. 600 BC by the standard hook anchor (*agkura*, hook), although stone anchors continued in use until the Hellenistic period. Like some modern anchors, the hook anchor had a stock, shank and two arms (flukes). The stock fell to the bottom, causing one arm to dig in, holding the anchor cable at the correct angle. These anchors were of wood, with stocks of stone or lead. This type of anchor is sometimes called the "Admiralty type," although strictly the stock is removable on a true Admiralty-type anchor. Whenever possible, warships were beached at night, stern first, and propped upright with stones and lengths of wood.

Crews

EARLY WARSHIPS

Little is known about crews of early warships. References in the works of Homer imply that there was usually no distinction between the men who rowed and those who fought. Warships were also troopships. Homer mentions ships of 50 oars, probably referring to the pentekonters that were used in his own day, rather than warships that were used against Troy. The pentekonter had 50 rowers, as well as a helmsman, a captain, a time-beater to maintain the rowing rhythm, and probably four or five deck crew to handle the sail and anchor and do other tasks. It is not clear how biremes were manned; at least some appear to have had 28 oars per side, a total of 56 rowers. The number of rowers may have been the only significant difference between the crews of the pentekonter and the bireme. Both these warships also carried a number of soldiers to act as marines.

TRIREMES

At the battle of Salamis in 480 BC, when the Greeks defeated the Persians, the Greek triremes appear to have had a crew of 200. These consisted of 170 rowers (62 thranites on the upper banks of oars, 54 zygites on the middle banks and 54 thalamites on the lower banks), as well as 10 hoplites and four archers. Rowers were not slaves, but highly trained recruits from the poorer classes. In Athens rowers were usually *thetes*, the poorest class of free men. There was also a flute player (*trieraules*), who kept time for the rowers, possibly up to 15 deck hands who controlled the ship when under sail, and up to 40 marines, usually a mixture of hoplites and archers. For larger galleys, such as the *tetereis* and *pentereis*, there is little evidence for the size and composition of their crews. Triremes were usually commanded by a captain (trierarch: *trierarkhos*).

OFFICERS

Some indications of how a navy was commanded survive from Athens. Originally each of the local divisions of Attica (the *naukrariai*) was responsible for supplying and manning one ship, which was commanded by a *naukraros*. The *naukrariai* later became local administrative units, and their naval responsibilities were taken over by the boule and the trierarchs in the early 5th century BC.

Trierarchs were chosen from the wealthier citizens by the *strategoi*. The office of trierarch was a compulsory civic duty that entailed financial commitments (a liturgy). There was one trierarch for each of the triremes in service. Each trierarch served for one year and was provided with a trireme, as well as the pay and food of the crew. The trierarch served as captain and bore the cost of maintenance and repair. After 411 BC two citizens usually shared the cost of the office of trierarch, and after 340 BC the cost was spread more equally. The liturgy requiring chosen citizens to become trierarchs was abolished around 317–307 BC. In other Greek states the term trierarch merely meant a captain of a trireme, and in Hellenistic times it was the name for the captain of any warship.

Tactics

The need for warships to frequently put into shore (usually every night) to take on water and supplies restricted the possibilities for an elaborate and prolonged strategy. The two main methods of attacking a ship, ramming and boarding, determined

naval tactics. For example, the Athenian fleet carried relatively few marines, and the emphasis was on ramming rather than boarding. Tactics were generally simple, and the outcome of a battle depended on the success of individual ships.

For ramming, a ship would try to hit an enemy ship at a vulnerable point along the side and then pull away in order to get up sufficient speed to ram again. If the attacking ship could not pull away, marines from both ships would try to board the other and take it over in hand-to-hand fighting. For attempts at boarding, many methods of locking the two ships together were used, such as grappling hooks and ropes. As ships approached each other, missiles such as arrows and javelins were discharged.

Tactical maneuvers were developed to maximize the chances of ramming, while other maneuvers attempted to foil such tactics. The periplus (*periploos*; literally, sailing around) was the simplest form of maneuver and was carried out by a fleet that outnumbered its opponent. Its superior numbers were used to outflank the line of enemy ships. Most of the fleet retreated, keeping their rams facing the enemy ships. Meanwhile their flanking ships rammed the side of the outermost ship in the enemy line, leaving the next ship exposed to similar attack. Once this flanking maneuver had been carried out, the entire fleet would attack.

Another tactic was the diekplus (*diekploos*), which was used by a fleet of more maneuverable ships to break up a formation of enemy ships. This maneuver started with the attacking ships approaching the enemy line one after the other, in line-ahead formation. The leading ship would make a sharp turn into one of the enemy ships, shearing off its oars on one side and leaving it stranded for the next ship in the line to finish off. This maneuver could be forestalled if the formation under attack consisted of two lines of ships, one behind the other, so that the ships in the second line could deal with the attacking ships once they had lost their speed. However, dividing a fleet into two lines meant that it was vulnerable to the periplus.

The *kyklos* (circle) was a defensive formation adopted by slow or outnumbered fleets when attacked. The ships formed up in a circle with their rams pointing outward, making it very difficult for an attacking fleet to gain any advantage.

With the development of larger galleys with artillery mounted on their decks, there was more use of missiles in an attempt to cause casualties and drive the opposing marines off the deck before boarding. However, ramming and boarding were still the principal methods of fighting, and tactics remained much the same.

Harbors

Early warships were usually beached when not in use, but during the 6th century BC enclosed harbors began to be developed. A harbor at Samos was enclosed by a mole about 1,310 ft (400 m) long, which was built out into water about 100 ft (30 m) deep. At this time Athens beached its ships in the open bay between Piraeus and Phalerum, but in the 5th century BC Themistocles instigated their move to Piraeus. On the north side of Piraeus was a large inlet, which became the commercial harbor; two small inlets on the south side of Piraeus became the military harbors of Zea and Munychia (fig. 3.17). This whole area was surrounded by walls constructed of heavy limestone blocks, and the harbor entrances were narrowed by the construction of moles so that they could be closed with chains. The Zea harbor entrance was reduced to 114 ft (35 m). The moles at the harbor entrances had towers built on their seaward ends.

Within the military harbors at Piraeus were ship sheds, built in groups of four or eight. Each pair of sheds was covered by a single roof, and the sheds themselves were just less than 20 ft (6 m) wide and about 131 ft (40 m) long. The sheds were separated by rows of columns and sloped down to the water, with slipways projecting into the harbor so that the warships could be dragged up into the sheds, probably stern first. In the 4th century BC there were almost 400 ship sheds at Piraeus. The main military harbor was at Zea, where the naval stores were kept.

Fortifications known as the Long Walls were built joining Piraeus with Athens in an attempt to prevent hostile armies from cutting off Athens from the harbors during a siege. From this time on, many other coastal and island cities built harbors protected by moles with towers at the end. This was not always, as at Athens, because of the need to protect warships, but often because of the growing importance of trade, particularly in foodstuffs like grain.

READING

Several books deal with many aspects of Greek warfare, including Connolly 1988; Pritchett 1971, 1974, 1979, 1991a, 1991b; Rich and Shipley (eds.) 1993; and Warry 1980.

Armies

Bar-Kochva 1976: Seleucid army; Connolly 1988: hoplites and the phalanx, Sparta, armies of Macedonia; Engels 1978: Macedonian army; Heckel 1992, 237–370: Macedonian army; Lazenby 1985: Spartan army; Warry 1980: evidence for early organization and "Homeric" warriors, armies of Athens, Sparta and Macedonia.

Soldiers

Bowden 1993: early development of the hoplite; Best 1969: peltasts; Bugh 1988: history of the Athenian cavalry; Connolly 1988: hoplites, phalangites, cavalry, soldiers of the later Macedonian armies; Crouwel 1992: chariots; Greenhalgh 1973: cavalry and chariots; Griffith 1935: mercenaries in Hellenistic times; Hanson (ed.) 1991: hoplites; Pritchett 1971: various subjects concerning soldiers, including organization of the phalanx, pay and booty; Pritchett 1991b, 1–67: major source for slingers; Spence 1993: cavalry in the Classical period; Warry 1980: hoplites, archers, slingers, peltasts, cavalry, hypaspists and phalangites; Worley 1994: cavalry from Mycenaean to Macedonian times.

Training

Anderson 1970, 84–110: weapons and tactical training; Connolly 1988, 39–43: in Sparta; Hammond and Scullard (eds.) 1970, 386: 4th-century-BC Athens (under *Epheboi*); Pritchett 1974, 208–231: training in the Classical period.

Tactics

Anderson 1970; Connolly 1988; Hanson (ed.) 1991: hoplite tactics; Pritchett 1991a, 1–93: battles and tactics from historical sources; Scullard 1974, 64–100: use of elephants by Alexander and his successors, 120–145: use of elephants by the Seleucids and Ptolemies; Warry 1980.

Weapons and Equipment

Anderson 1970, 13–42: hoplite weapons and armor; Branigan 1967: Early Bronze Age daggers; Connolly 1988: armor, shields, helmets, weapons, artillery and siege engines; Dickinson 1994, 197–207: Bronze Age armor, shields, helmets, weapons; Fortenberry 1991: use of single greaves before 12th century BC; Hanson (ed.) 1991: hoplite weapons; Harding 1984, 151–187: Mycenaean weapons and armor; Marsden 1969: major source for artillery; Snodgrass 1964: early weapons and armor; Snodgrass 1967: armor, shields, helmets, weapons; Warry 1980: armor, shields, weapons, artillery, siege engines.

Fortifications

Connolly 1988; Lawrence 1979: major source; Ober 1987: early artillery towers; Pritchett 1974, 133–146: fortified camps; Winter 1971.

Sieges

Connolly 1988; Warry 1980; Whibley 1931, 562–566.

Trophies

Connolly 1988, 48, 83; Hammond and Scullard (eds.) 1970, 1,097; Pritchett 1974, 246–275: major source.

Navies

Bass 1972, 38–58: warships; Casson 1971: major source for warships; Coates et al. 1990: sea trials of reconstructed trireme; Connolly 1988, 267–268: tactics, harbors; Hammond and Scullard (eds.) 1970, 488: harbors, 1,094: officers (under *trierarchy*); Jordan 1975: organization of Athenian navy in 5th and 4th centuries BC; Morrison 1980: useful overview of warships; Morrison and Coates 1986: triremes; Morrison and Williams 1968: warships; Rodgers 1964: warships and tactics in Classical and Hellenistic periods; Shaw (ed.) 1993: sea trials of reconstructed trireme; Tilley 1992: an alternative view of rowing arrangements in a trireme; Tomlinson 1992, 68–71: Piraeus harbor; Warry 1980, 30–31: tactics, 18, 30: crews; Whibley 1931, 586–587: tactics.

4

GEOGRAPHY
OF THE
GREEK WORLD

LANDSCAPE

Greece is formed of limestone mountains, dividing up the country into large fertile plains in Thessaly, Boeotia and Attica, with some smaller plains elsewhere. The plains are almost entirely surrounded by mountains or have one side accessible to the sea. The mountains comprise the majority of the territory and often formed barriers with few passes and narrow valleys, so that transport by land was difficult. This type of landscape encouraged the development of independent states. The highest mountain is Olympus in Thessaly (9,750 ft, 2,972 m), and the mountains once had much decid-

uous forest, although the amount of deforestation and loss of fertility are disputed.

The coastline is deeply indented, and in the Aegean the submerged mountains form numerous islands. To the south of the Aegean is the large island of Crete. In the center of the Aegean are numerous small islands known collectively as the Cyclades, and off the west coast of Asia Minor are several larger islands, such as Lesbos and Rhodes.

In mainland Greece there were no navigable rivers. The rivers were often torrents in winter but dry in summer. There were many good harbors and anchorages, though few in Thessaly or on the west coast.

Mainland Greece is virtually split into two parts by the Saronic Gulf and Corinthian Gulf, which are

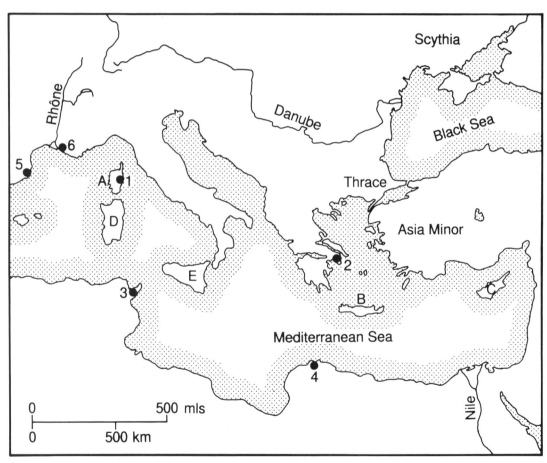

Fig. 4.1   Greek world from Spain to Egypt and Asia Minor: 1. Alalia; 2. Athens; 3. Carthage (Phoenician); 4. Cyrene; 5. Emporiae; 6. Massilia; A. Corsica; B. Crete; C. Cyprus; D. Sardinia; E. Sicily.

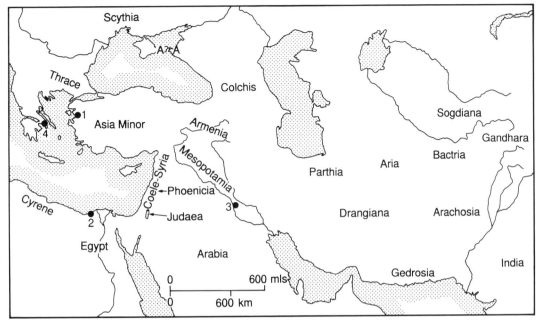

*Fig. 4.2   Regions of the Hellenistic Greek world. For districts in Asia Minor, see fig. 4.6. 1. Pergamum;
2. Alexandria; 3. Babylon; 4. Athens; A. Cimmerian Bosphorus.*

separated by a narrow isthmus (now cut by the Corinth canal). The southern mainland is the Peloponnese (island of Pelops). To the north of the isthmus is central Greece and northern Greece. Central Greece is a long peninsula between the Corinthian Gulf and the straits of Euboea (fig. 4.5).

Hellas was originally a small district of Phthiotis in Thessaly (and the people were Hellenes), but the name was extended to the rest of Greece. The names "Achaea" and "Argos" were also used for Greece or just for the Peloponnese. The Greek people were called Hellenes (and at times Achaeans, Argives or Danai). The Romans called Greece *Graecia*.

The climate of winters is severe in the mountains, but mild elsewhere, and in the hot summers there is very little rain. Most rain falls during five months in winter, with the greatest amount of rainfall in western Greece. The country is prone to earthquakes, especially in the Peloponnese, some of which have been devastating. An active volcano exists at the island of Thera.

Colonization and expansion of territory by conquest extended the Greek world westward into Spain, Sardinia, Corsica, Sicily, southern France and Magna Graecia (Great Greece: southern Italy).

Elsewhere the Greek world eventually extended into northern Africa (Cyrene), Egypt, around the Black Sea, Asia Minor, Cyprus and as far east as India and Afghanistan (figs. 4.1, 4.2).

CITY-STATES AND COLONIES

Poleis

In the Bronze Age during the Minoan and Mycenaean periods, settlement consisted of villas, towns and palaces (see chapters 1 and 6). The palaces may have been administrative centers of specific geographical regions, rather than royal residences. From c. 1200 BC there was widespread abandonment of many settlement sites, but at the end of the Dark Age self-governing states called *poleis* (sing. *polis*, city) emerged, some of which were very small. The Greek world was eventually divided into several hundred poleis. These city-states or self-governing communities consisted of only one city (also called a polis) with a citadel (acropolis) and marketplace (agora), surrounded by the countryside and its villages (hinterland). The term *asty* also referred to the city or town itself. The citizens lived in the countryside or in the city, but the government of the polis was concentrated in the city. The large number of poleis led to numerous conflicts between them, as well as civil war (*stasis*), particularly where there was a struggle concerning the type of government (oligarchy or democracy). Some poleis were very large, such as Sparta, while some islands were divided into several poleis.

FEDERATIONS AND ALLIANCES

The Greek mainland was divided into a number of regions, often distinct geographical entities. Tribal units, such as Aetolians and Boeotians, occupied these regions. When poleis began to develop, the tribal units in these regions were frequently retained. Cities within these regions often formed a loose or more formal confederation. City-states in alliance with each other were usually termed federal states, confederacies or leagues. These alliances first appeared in the 5th century BC. Alternatively

one city-state, such as Athens, became more powerful than other city-states in the region.

A symmachia (*symmakhia*, alliance in fighting) was often an informal alliance of city-states in war or for defense; it could also mean an alliance of city-states under the leadership (*hegemonia*) of one state. They were not federal states, and member city-states retained their individual freedom. Examples include the Peloponnesian League, Delian League, Second Athenian League and Hellenic League, some of which are also referred to as confederacies or alliances.

A *sympoliteia* (alliance in political life) was a true federal state in which city-states gave up some of their independence to a central federal government, so that power was divided between central and local governments. Citizens therefore often considered themselves as belonging to both a city-state and a federal state. Examples of *sympoliteiai* include the Achaean Confederacy, Arcadian Confederacy, Boeotian Confederacy and Aetolian Confederacy, although they are often referred to loosely as leagues. The term *koinon* (the state or commonwealth) is also used for a federal state, as is *ethnos* (pl. *ethne*, "tribe"). From c. 300 BC, federal states of Greece were classified as *ethne*.

Many federal states were dissolved at the King's Peace (386 BC). Particularly from the 3rd century

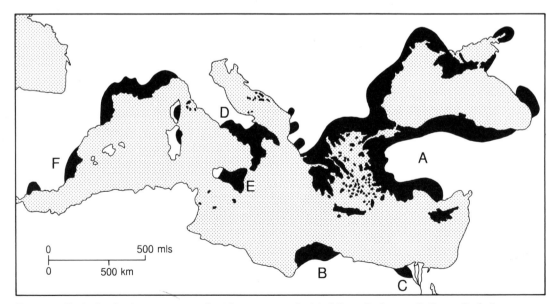

Fig. 4.3   Early Greek colonization up to the 6th century BC: A. Asia Minor; B. Cyrene; C. Egypt; D. Italy; E. Sicily; F. Spain.

BC, some federal states, such as the Achaean Confederacy, became so powerful that they incorporated cities and states from beyond their own regional boundaries. After the conquests of Alexander the Great in the late 4th century BC, the poleis lost much of their independence. Federal states were particularly numerous and powerful in the Hellenistic period, and continued in the Roman period in Asia Minor and Greece as forms of local government. See also chapter 1 for the government of poleis and chapter 6 for towns and town planning.

The Amphictyonic Council (or Delphic Amphictyony) managed the affairs of the Delphi sanctuary. It consisted mostly of states in the central and northern part of Greece, and its name derived from *amphictyones* (dwellers round about). Its original function had been the care of the temple of Demeter at Anthela near Thermopylae, but it acquired the care of the oracle and temple of Apollo at Delphi (fig. 8.27). Each member state sent one or two sacred representatives (*hieromnemones*) to the council meetings, which were held twice a year.

Fig. 4.4 *The colony of Heraclea in southern Italy was named after Heracles, who was an important figure there. The reverse of this silver stater of c. 350 BC from Heraclea shows Heracles in combat with the Nemean lion, with his club to one side and an owl below. The obverse shows the head of Athena (fig. 5.7).* Courtesy of Somerset County Museums Service.

Colonies

Colonization was the establishment of new settlements overseas by city-states of the Greek mainland, Aegean islands and Asia Minor. It was usually undertaken when an area could no longer support all its inhabitants (land hunger) or less frequently for reasons of trade, although the reasons for a particular colonization are rarely clear. The main period of colonization was c. 750–c. 550 BC (fig. 4.3), although Athens undertook no colonization, as the plains of Attica could support its people, while Sparta founded only one colony as it was supported by its helots and perioeci. Colonization was undertaken by sea and occurred in areas where the native people were politically weak and could offer little resistance. Some colonies established friendly relations with the native people and even had a mixed population of Greeks and native people, although elsewhere there was conflict. More politically advanced areas, such as the Syrian coast, Egypt and central Italy, were excluded. Colonization was mainly coastal and on islands, very rarely in the hinterland.

Colonization took place by appointing a founder (*oikistes*, oecist) from the mother city (*metropolis*), who consulted an oracle, usually Delphi or Didyma. The oecist then led a small group to a new site to found the colony (*apoika*, settlement far from home), taking with him the sacred fire from the hearth of the mother city. Additional settlers from the mother city would often arrive later on. Soldiers were included amongst the colonists if opposition from the native settlers was anticipated. There were often joint colonization ventures with other cities. The new colony was usually formed as a polis, independent of the mother city, but with certain ties, such as shared religious cults and political institutions. The colonists did not have the automatic right to return to their mother city. These new colonies could themselves found colonies, although the founder was usually appointed from the original mother city. Founders received heroic cults after their death.

The earliest colonization was undertaken by the Euboean cities of Chalcis and Eretria, followed by Corinth. Other main colonizing states were Miletus, Achaea, Megara and some Aegean islands. The first areas to be settled were Sicily and southern Italy (fig. 4.4), with other colonies around the Black Sea, Asia Minor, northwest Aegean, northern Greece and Illyria. Colonies numbered several hundred, although details such as foundation dates are not usually precisely known. In Sicily colonies were settled from many parts of Greece, including Chalcis, Corinth, Megara, Rhodes and Crete; Naxus was its earliest colony, founded by Chalcis in 734 BC, with Syracuse founded by Corinth in 733 BC. Corcyra was also colonized by Corinth in 733 BC. In Italy several colonies were founded by the Achaeans, including Sybaris and Croton; Tarentum in Italy was the only colony of Sparta, founded c. 706 BC. Phocaea founded Massilia in southern France c. 600 BC, which in turn established trading settlements in northeast Spain. Chalcis and Eretria founded several colonies in the 7th century BC in the promontory subsequently known as Chalcidice. Numerous colonies were founded around the shores of the Propontis and Black Sea, mainly by Miletus. Megara founded Byzantium (c. 667 BC) and Chalcedon (685 BC). Cyrene was founded by Thera c. 630 BC following a famine.

TRADING POSTS

Some settlements were established specifically as trading posts (*emporia*), not as poleis. Some colonies were also established on trade routes, which encouraged the expansion of trade and piracy. Trading posts included Al Mina in northern Syria, Naucratis in Egypt, Emporiae in Spain and Massilia in southern France. At Naucratis, land was presented to the Greeks as a trading center (not a colony) by the Egyptian pharaoh; numerous Greek states, particularly from Asia Minor, were involved in the settlement.

CLERUCHIES

A particular sort of colony (*kleroukhia*) was established by Athens from the end of the 6th century BC and through the 5th century BC in conquered Greek and non-Greek territory. The main period of establishing cleruchies was during the Athenian Empire in 450–446 BC, when Athenian settlements were imposed in allied territory. This policy of Pericles was bitterly resented by many allies, particularly in the islands, because local inhabitants were often dispossessed. Cleruchies were often established after the revolt of an ally. The cleruchs came

from Athens' two lowest citizen classes. Each cleruch was given a piece of land (*kleros*), which raised them to hoplite status and made them eligible for military service. The cleruchs retained their original citizenship, and the settlements were not politically independent. Places where cleruchies were established (some on existing settlements) include Chalcis (506 BC), the Chersonese, Chalcidice, Naxos, Andros, Lemnos and Lesbos. It is not always certain if a settlement was a colony or a cleruchy.

HELLENISTIC

From the time of conquest by Alexander, colonies of Greek settlers were established in Egypt and throughout the eastern territories of Asia. Alexander the Great founded many cities, named after himself, and the Seleucid kings (especially Antiochus I) also founded many new cities or refounded existing ones with Greek names, such as Antiokheia and Seleukeia. Alexandria in Egypt was founded partly for trade, but other colonies in Egypt were cleruchies founded for military reasons. In Asia many new cities also began as strategic military colonies, but developed into poleis, with Greek civilians and foreign settlers as well. Many eastern cities survived, even when they came under Parthian and Roman rule.

REGIONS AND ALLIANCES

For historical events and alliances, see chapter 1.

Acarnania

This region in the northwest coastal area of Greece is bounded by the Ionian Sea, the Gulf of Ambracia and the Achelous River (fig. 4.5). Coastal sites were colonized by settlers from Corinth in the 7th century BC. In the 5th century BC the Acarnanians formed a league, with its capital at Stratus. In

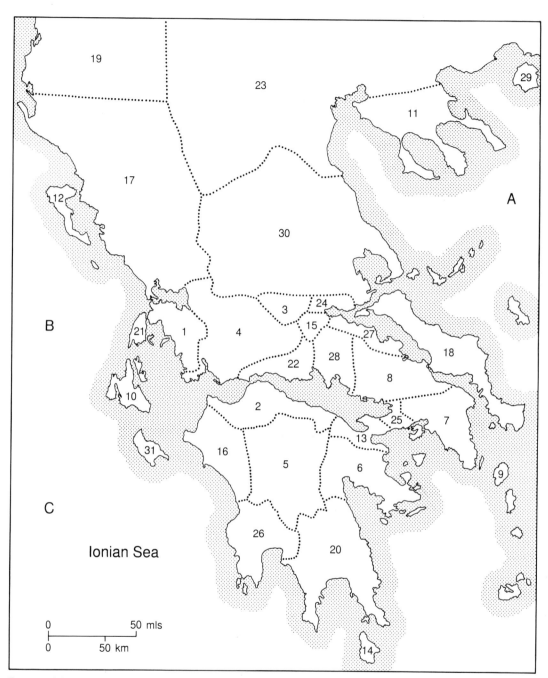

Fig. 4.5   Major states and islands of Greece: A. northern Greece; B. central Greece; C. Peloponnese; 1. Acarnania; 2. Achaea; 3. Aenis; 4. Aetolia; 5. Arcadia; 6. Argolis; 7. Attica; 8. Boeotia; 9. Ceos; 10. Cephallenia; 11. Chalcidice; 12. Corcyra; 13. Corinth; 14. Cythera; 15. Doris; 16. Elis; 17. Epirus; 18. Euboea; 19. Illyria; 20. Laconia; 21. Leucas; 22. Locris Ozolis; 23. Macedonia; 24. Malis; 25. Megara; 26. Messenia; 27. Opuntian Locris; 28. Phocis; 29. Thasos; 30. Thessaly; 31. Zacynthus.

432/431 BC, it sought help from Athens against Corinthian settlers at Ambracia and other colonies, and again in 429/426 BC against Sparta during the Peloponnesian War. In 390 BC Acarnania was conquered by Sparta under Agesilaus II, but in 375 BC it joined the Second Athenian League. It supported Boeotia against Sparta, and then Athens against Philip II of Macedonia. However, Acarnania came under the control of Macedonia. In 314 BC the Acarnanian League was replaced by a confederacy of newly founded cities. Around 255 BC Acarnania was split between Epirus and Aetolia, but at the downfall of the monarchy in Epirus, Acarnania regained its independence and acquired the island of Leucas. The Acarnanians sided with Philip V of Macedonia against Rome in 200 BC. Arcarnania lost Leucas in 167 BC, but was allowed by the Romans to retain its confederacy of city-states until 30 BC.

Achaea

The name Achaea (*Akhaia*) is derived from *Akhaioi* (Greeks), which occurs in Homer and also in Hittite and Egyptian texts of c. 1400–1200 BC. Greeks of the Mycenaean period are sometimes described as Achaeans by modern scholars. Two geographical areas were known as Achaea. The minor one was in southeast Thessaly (Achaea Phthiotis). The main territory of Achaea was in the Peloponnese along the coast of the Corinthian Gulf between Elis and Sicyon (fig. 4.5).

In the 8th century BC, this main territory of Achaea founded colonies in southern Italy, including Sybaris, Metapontum, Croton and Caulonia. Twelve small towns in Achaea, including Patrae, Aegium, Dyme, Cerynia and Leontium, were said to form a federal state that met at Helice (the sanctuary of Poseidon Heliconius), until Helice collapsed into the sea after an earthquake in 373 BC. The confederacy then met at Aegium. Achaea remained neutral in most Greek wars, including the Persian and Peloponnesian Wars. As an ally of Sparta the confederacy was not dissolved at the King's Peace (386 BC). A new confederacy was founded in 280 BC by four cities, joined later by other Achaean and non-Achaean cities, including Sicyon in 251 BC (after the expulsion of its tyrant). In the 3rd and 2nd centuries BC the Achaean Confederacy became the most important power in Greece, encompassing much of the Peloponnese and part of central Greece. Aratus of Sicyon was a powerful leader of the Confederacy, with Corinth as its main stronghold, initially against Macedonia. The admission of Arcadian cities, such as Megalopolis, led to conflict with Sparta, and the Confederacy became an ally of Macedonia against Sparta in 224 BC.

The Confederacy came into conflict with Rome, and after the battle of Pydna (167 BC), the Romans deported 1,000 eminent Achaeans to Italy, including the historian Polybius. They were released in 150 BC. In 148 BC further trouble again caused the Romans to intervene; after the Achaean War, the Confederacy was dissolved in 146 BC, with the Romans attaching Achaea to the Roman province of Macedonia. In 27 BC the name Achaea was used for a new Roman province, which comprised a large area of Greece.

Aenis

Aenis (*Ainis*) was a small region south of Thessaly (fig. 4.5), one of the original members of the Amphictyony centered at Anthela near Thermopylae and later at Delphi.

Aeolis

The northern part of the west coast of Asia Minor was known as Aeolis (*Aiolis*); it stretched from the Hellespont southward to Smyrna, and included the island of Lesbos (fig. 4.6). The speech of the country resembled that of Boeotia and Thessaly, from where the first settlers probably came in the 11th century BC. The Aeolian cities in the south were grouped in a league, possibly for religious purposes. Originally 12 in number, they were later reduced to 11 when Smyrna became an Ionian city. Cyme was the principal city.

Aetolia

This region of central Greece (fig. 4.5) was bordered on the west by Acarnania, on the north by Epirus and on the south by the Corinthian Gulf. A marshy coast without good harborage left Aetolia secluded, and it was still undeveloped in the 5th century BC, organized not in city-states but primarily in tribes

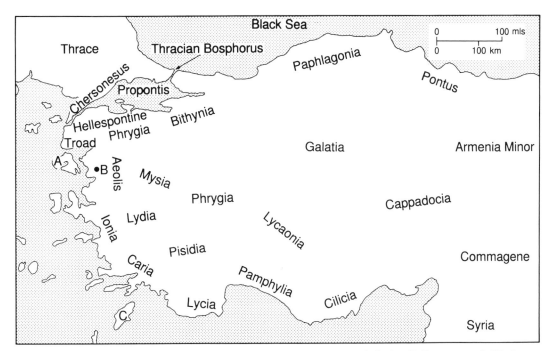

Fig. 4.6   Regions of Asia Minor before the rise of the Pergamum Kingdom. A. Lesbos; B. Pergamum; C. Rhodes.

under chieftains in remote unfortified villages. A federal state (*sympoliteia*) was formed by 376 BC (Aetolian Confederacy or League), which replaced the tribal system. In the late 4th century BC (after the death of Alexander the Great), this Confederacy became very powerful and extended its territory. By 220 BC it controlled all of central Greece (except Attica), including Delphi. It was a rival of Macedonia and became Rome's first ally in Greece, supporting Rome against Philip V of Macedonia in the Second Macedonian War (200–197 BC). However, Aetolia subsequently supported Antiochus III against Rome, and after his defeat by the Romans in 189 BC, the Aetolians were forced by Rome to accept a treaty. Although it was not dissolved, the Confederacy lost all its power. Its main towns were Calydon and Pleuron, with a religious center at Thermum, where Apollo was worshiped.

Arachosia

Situated in southern Afghanistan, Arachosia (*Arakhosia*) was formerly an eastern satrapy of the Persian Empire on a main route from Persia to India (fig. 4.2). Alexander the Great invaded it after defeating Darius at Gaugamela (331 BC). He subsequently gave Arachosia as part of a huge province to Sibyrtius, a Macedonian supporter. When that king died the territory passed to Seleucus I Nicator, although he probably ceded the eastern part in 301 BC to Sandracottus in return for war elephants. In the mid-3rd century BC, western Arachosia was split between the Greek kingdom of Bactria and the Parthian Empire.

Arcadia

A very mountainous and inaccessible region in the center of the Peloponnese (fig. 4.5). The archaic dialect of Arcadia (*Arkhadia*) was closest to that of Cyprus, probably indicating that the area was unaffected by the Dorian invasions. The language is known only from inscriptions and probably preserves elements of the Mycenaean language. The most prosperous areas were the eastern plains of Orchomenus, Mantinea and Tegea and also the valley of the Alpheus River. Its main rivers were the Alpheus, Stymphalus and Styx. Arcadia's most important towns were Tegea, Mantinea, Megalopolis and Orchomenus. The region was mainly one of villages, so it had little influence on Greek politics. Its main strength was its manpower, and Arcadian mercenaries were used from at least the 5th century BC.

From that time Arcadia came under Sparta's control, but an Arcadian Confederacy was formed under Epaminondas against Sparta between 370 and 362 BC. Epaminondas founded the city of Megalopolis as the Confederacy's center, and 40 villages were completely or partially abandoned. It became one of the largest cities in the Peloponnese. In 235 BC, Arcadia joined the Achaean Confederacy. Polybius the historian, a citizen of Megalopolis, was taken by the Romans as one of the 1,000 Achaean hostages after the battle of Pydna. Arcadia became part of the Roman province of Macedonia, and later part of the province of Achaea. The Roman poet Virgil idealized Arcadia's pastoral life by setting his bucolic poetry in the region. The notion of "arcadian" as a simple, bucolic life-style was not a Greek concept.

Argolis

Argos was a city in the northeast Peloponnese about 3 miles (4.8 km) from the sea; it was in the southern part of the Argive plain at the foot of the Larissa Hill. The name Argos also describes the territory of the city, itself also referred to as Argolis or the Argolid (fig. 4.5); its inhabitants were Argives. In Homer, "Argos" usually refers to the entire Peloponnese (with Hellas meaning all of northern and central Greece), and the word "Argives" frequently means "Greeks."

Argos was the leading power in the Peloponnese until challenged by Sparta in the 8th or 7th century BC. Sparta was defeated by Argos at the battle of Hysiae (669 BC), but the power of Argos soon waned. The city-state played a secondary and ineffective role in Greek politics, occasionally fighting with Sparta, but otherwise maintaining an apparent neutrality. In 461 BC Argos became allied with Athens against Sparta, and again in 420 and 395 BC. It sided with Philip II of Macedonia and was one of the last cities to join the Achaean Confederacy. The territory of Argos included Mycenae, Tiryns,

Nauplia and Asine. Its most important religious center was 6 miles (10 km) north of the city of Argos, where the goddess Hera was worshiped at the Heraeum.

Aria

This mountainous territory of northeast Persia (fig. 4.2), now western Afghanistan and eastern Iran, was bordered by Parthia, Margiana, Bactria and Drangiana. Alexander the Great subdued the land in 330 BC and appointed a Persian satrap in charge. From 316 BC Aria formed part of the Seleucid Empire, but came under Parthian control from c. 247 BC.

Armenia

A mountainous region to the northeast of Asia Minor (fig. 4.2), Armenia's inhabitants came under Median and then Persian control (forming a satrapy). Its boundaries, which extended either side of the Euphrates River, were subject to change, and there were numerous subdivisions. It formed part of the Empire of Alexander the Great from 331 BC and then the Seleucid Empire from 301 BC, when it was ruled by local governors. After Antiochus III was defeated by the Romans at the battle of Magnesia (189 BC), Armenia Major (the plateau region to the east of the Euphrates as far as the Caspian Sea) revolted and declared independence under King Artaxias. Armenia Minor was a small kingdom to the west (fig. 4.6), forming part of Asia Minor. Tigranes I of Armenia Major was an ally of Mithridates VI of Pontus against Rome in 69 BC. Tigranes surrendered, and Armenia became a protectorate kingdom of Rome.

Attica

The easternmost part of central Greece, Attica formed a triangular promontory of about 1,000 sq mi (2,500 sq km) in area (fig. 4.5). Its original name was possibly Acte (promontory). It is an arid and hilly region, divided by four mountain ranges

(Aegaleos, Hymettus, Pentelicus and Laurium) into three interconnecting plains (Thriasian, Attic or Athenian, and Mesogeia). The Attic Plain was often called the Plain (*Pedion*). The area's natural resources included its famous marbles (from Pentelicus and Hymettus), good-quality potters' clay, and lead and silver from Laurium. Laurium (*Laurion*) was a hilly district near Cape Sunium. It formed one of the largest mining districts in the Greek world, particularly for silver from the ore galena.

There were originally many separate independent communities (by tradition 12 in the time of the legendary king Cecrops), which had probably united into a single state by the 7th century BC (although tradition attributed this process to Theseus). Athens became the main city, both in terms of politics and religion. Other cities included Eleusis, Marathon, Aphidna and Thoricus. Aristocratic families remained influential and independent in the countryside, but their power was broken by the tyranny of Peisistratus (early 6th century BC) and by the reforms of Cleisthenes (late 6th century BC), which centralized the entire Attic government at Athens. In the Peloponnesian War, Attica was invaded annually by the Spartans, and the population retreated to the cities, notably Athens.

DIVISIONS OF ATTICA

Cleisthenes' political reforms (late 6th century BC) included the abolition of the four traditional Ionian tribes (*phylai*). Instead, Cleisthenes divided Attica

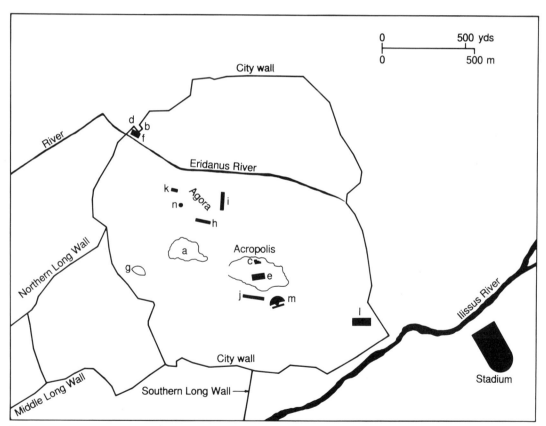

Fig. 4.7   Athens and its main monuments: a. Areopagus; b. Dipylon; c. Erechtheum; d. Kerameikos; e. Parthenon; f. Pompeium; g. Pnyx; h. South Stoa; i. Stoa of Attalus; j. Stoa of Eumenes II; k. temple of Hephaestus; l. temple of Olympian Zeus; m. theater of Dionysus; n. tholos.

Fig. 4.8   Athens Acropolis (center) with the Parthenon temple. At the foot of the Acropolis (left) is a Roman theater; to its right is the Stoa of Eumenes.

(including Athens) into 10 new tribes (*phylai*), each composed of three *trittyes*. A *trittys* was a group of at least three demes (the numbers varied), some selected from the city, some from the coast and some from inland (see chapter 1). There were 139 or 140 demes in all, some representing divisions of Athens and Piraeus, and others containing one or more centers of population, such as a village or town. Much progress has been made in identifying the location of demes. The largest Attic deme was Acharnae, situated in the northwest corner of the Attic Plain. The Acharnians were made famous as charcoal burners by Aristophanes. Cephisia was a deme situated northeast of Athens (modern Kephisia). Colonos was a small deme north of the Acropolis at Athens, near Plato's Academy; its territory included the hill Kolonos Hippios (not the Kolonos Agoraios on which the Hephaesteum stands overlooking the Acropolis).

ATHENS

Mycenaean Athens was centered on a heavily fortified prominent citadel (the Acropolis), probably similar in appearance to Mycenae, with a settlement below it. At the end of the Bronze Age, Athens did not decline, but continued to expand over the surrounding terrain in the Dark Age. Athens became the main city of Attica, situated within its largest plain, and was the center of communications. The Eridanus River was to the north, the Ilissus to the east and the Cephissus to the west (fig. 4.7). Athens had ready access to the sea at Phalerum and Piraeus (fig. 3.17).

In 480 BC Athens was destroyed by the Persians. In 478/477 BC the Delian League was established under Athenian leadership, with a treasury at Delos. In the mid-5th century BC this Delian League was gradually transformed into an Athenian Empire, with the treasury based at Athens. In 431 BC the Peloponnesian War broke out between Sparta and Athens, leading to the complete defeat of Athens, and its democratic government was temporarily replaced by an oligarchy that lasted until 399 BC. At the same time Athens' Long Walls were demolished and its empire dissolved. Athens established a Second Athenian Confederacy (377 BC), but was defeated by Philip II of Macedonia at the battle of Chaeronea (338 BC). From then on Athens was under the domination of Macedonia, and Alexandria became the cultural center of the Greek world. In 88–86 BC Athens supported Mithridates VI against Rome, and was sacked and partly destroyed by the Roman general Sulla in 86 BC.

It is uncertain if there was settlement on the Acropolis after the Mycenaean period, but by the 7th century BC the Acropolis was no longer of military importance, but was used for sacred buildings, particularly those dedicated to Athena. In the 6th century BC there was monumental building work on the Acropolis, which the Persians destroyed in 480 BC. Rebuilding work did not take place until the mid-5th century BC. This included a new precinct wall, which increased the terrace area. The new main gateway was the Propylaea, with the temple of Athena Nike on its southwest side (completed c. 420 BC). Other new temples included the Parthenon (which replaced the unfinished Peisistratid temple to Athena) and the Erechtheum (completed 407 BC) (fig. 4.8).

After the destruction of the city by the Persians, the ruined city below the Acropolis was surrounded by a substantial wall (attributable to Themistocles), surrounding an area about 0.9 by 0.9 miles (1.5 by 1.5 km) (fig. 4.9). It passed through the Kerameikos (Ceramicus) Cemetery, which had been used since the Bronze Age. Here a double gateway (the Dipylon) was built. A second wall was built outside the main one in the mid-4th century BC. Outside the city walls was the main city cemetery along the Eridanus River. The Academy was situated about 0.9 miles (1.5 km) from the Dipylon Gate.

The first agora at Athens was on the northwest slope of the Acropolis. The Sacred Way (Panathenaic Way) led from the Acropolis to the Kerameikos Cemetery and then to Eleusis. Here a new agora was developed from c. 600 BC where a cemetery once existed. This agora was an open space 218 by 273 yds (200 by 250 m) delimited by buildings, eventually including stoas on every side. On the north side were the Doric Stoa Basileos (Stoa of the

Fig. 4.9   City walls near the Dipylon Gate at Athens, where they passed through the Kerameikos Cemetery. The wall was probably originally constructed in the time of Themistocles (the two visible lower courses are early 5th century BC), with rebuildings attributable to Conon (the polygonal masonry, early 4th century BC) and later (upper courses). Excavation of this stretch has shown it to be c. 8 ft (2.5 m) wide; it was originally a stone wall with rubble infill, supporting a mud brick wall above.

GEOGRAPHY OF THE GREEK WORLD

King) and Stoa Poikile (Painted Stoa) with paintings of the battle of Marathon and the Trojan War. On the east side was the Stoa of Attalus (fig. 6.8), built in the mid-2nd century BC by Attalus II. On the south side was a fountain house, built c. 520 BC as part of a more extensive water supply project. On the west were mainly public offices, including the old bouleuterion, which was later used as the Metroon and archive store when it was replaced at the end of the 5th century BC by a new bouleuterion (fig. 1.14). Here a circular tholos (dated to c. 465 BC) also replaced the old *prytaneion* as a meeting and dining room for the *prytaneis*. The Stoa of Zeus was also built on the west side of the agora.

The Areopagus (Hill of Ares, *Areios Pagos*) was south of the agora; here the first council met (itself called the Areopagus). To the southwest was the Pnyx Hill, the meeting place of the Assembly, situated in the densely occupied Koile district of the city.

On the Kolonos Agoraios (a low hill to the west of the Acropolis) a temple was built dedicated to Hephaestus and Athena (Hephaesteum—erroneously called the Theseum), which was started about the mid-5th century BC. A limestone temple was also built to Apollo Delphinios about the same time, near the abandoned temple of Olympian Zeus (begun in the late 6th century BC and eventually completed by the Roman emperor Hadrian).

On the south side of the Acropolis was the theater of Dionysus (fig. 7.14), where theatrical performances were transferred from the agora after the collapse there of wooden scaffolding. Here the Attic tragedies were staged, with the audience sitting on wooden benches; in the 4th century BC this theater was substantially rebuilt with permanent seating. West of the theater was the Asclepieion, below which was the Stoa of Eumenes II (2nd century BC). Farther east was a stadium between two low hills. Surrounding the Acropolis was the street of the tripods, where numerous choregic monuments were erected.

Elsewhere in Athens, streets and alleyways were not laid out to a formal plan and varied in width (see chapter 6, p. 205), and there would have been various kinds of housing, shrines, shops and workshops, although little information is available compared with the vast amount of knowledge for public buildings. The potters' quarter was in the Kerameikos, and metalworking was probably around the Kolonos Agoraios.

The port of Athens was 4 miles (6.4 km) to the south of the city at Piraeus, where much commerce and industry took place. In the late 6th century BC the rocky hill of Munychia was fortified at Piraeus. From the time of Themistocles (late 5th century BC), a planned harbor city and naval base with a defensive wall were built, connected to Athens by the Long Walls (fig. 3.17). There were numerous harbors and slipways, and three harbors were incorporated: Cantharus, Zea and Munychia.

See also chapter 1 for the government of Athens.

Bactria

A flat fertile region between the Hindu Kush and the Oxus River, Bactria is now part of northern Afghanistan, southern Uzbekistan and Tadjikistan (fig. 4.2). It became a province of the Persian Empire in the 6th century BC. When the Persian satrap unsuccessfully resisted Alexander the Great, Bactria became part of the Seleucid Empire, although its governor Diodotus I Soter established an independent Hellenistic monarchy. Antiochus III was forced to conclude a treaty with Bactria. It became a very important state, eventually extending over western Pakistan and all of Afghanistan.

Bithynia

A region of northwest Asia Minor along the southern Black Sea coast (fig. 4.6), Bithynia was once just the Chalcedon Peninsula, but the territory expanded. It was largely mountainous, divided by the Sangarius River. The Bithynians were of Thracian origin, and the northern coast of Bithynia was called Thrace in Asia. Bithynia was in constant conflict with Greek colonies along the Black Sea coast. It repulsed Alexander the Great and his Seleucid successors, and became independent when its leader Zipoetes became king in 297 BC, establishing a Greek-style monarchy. The kingdom was bequeathed to the Romans in 75/74 BC by Nicomedes IV.

Boeotia

This was a district of central Greece bordered on the east and south by Attica and on the west by Phocis and Locris (fig. 4.5). It covered 1,119 sq miles (2,898 sq km). The south was rough and mountainous, and access to Corinthian Gulf harbors was blocked by mountains. The rich plains of Orchomenus and Thebes were suitable for horse breeding and cultivation of olives and wheat. Much of the northern plain was covered by the extensive shallow Lake Copaïs (now drained). Boeotia's rivers included the Asopus and the Cephissus.

The Boeotians (*Boiotoi*) migrated from Thessaly, possibly at the beginning of the Dark Age. They were perceived as dull and thick witted, especially by the Athenians. By the 9th century BC several poleis had formed, including Orchomenus, Thebes, Thespiae, Coronea, Haliartus, Plataea and Tanagra. Some of these disappeared and some absorbed less powerful neighbors. Early historians mention numerous towns and villages, but few have been securely identified. Twenty-nine towns are mentioned by name in the *Homeric Catalogue*. By about 520 BC there was a Boeotian Confederacy of city-states dominated by Thebes, possibly against Thessaly, although Orchomenus and Plataea failed to join. Boeotia was defeated by Athens and Plataea in 506 BC, after which Orchomenus joined the Confederacy, which was by now a federal state.

During the Persian Wars, Boeotia sided with the Persians and was defeated at the battle of Plataea. The Boeotian Confederacy continued to exist, although not under the domination of Thebes. In the Classical period, there were only about 12 independent cities, including Orchomenus, Thebes, Thespiae, Plataea, Haliartus, Chaeronea, Coronea and Tanagra.

In the mid-5th century BC, Athens invaded Boeotia and won a victory at the battle of Oenophyta in 457 BC, compelling all cities except Thebes to accept Athens' supremacy. Ten years later Athens was defeated at the battle of Coronea, and so Boeotia's independence was restored. In the 4th century BC Thebes extended its power over the rest of Boeotia. It defeated Sparta at the battle of Leuctra in 371 BC and again at Mantinea in 362 BC, and for a time Thebes was the dominant power in Greece. Orchomenus does not appear to have been a member of the Boeotian Confederacy at that time, and was destroyed by Thebes in 364 BC. Boeotia was unable to resist the rise of Macedonia under Philip II. Theban and Athenian forces were defeated at Chaeronea in 338 BC, and Thebes was destroyed in 335 BC by Alexander the Great, after which Boeotia rapidly declined. Thebes was reconstructed under Cassander (316 BC). By the Roman period, Boeotian cities were in ruins: only Tanagra and Thespiae remained as towns, with Thebes surviving as a village.

Bosphorus

Also known as Bosporus (cow's ford), the Cimmerian Bosphorus territory (fig. 4.2) was either side of the Maeotic Channel (Straits of Kerch) between the Black Sea and Sea of Maeotis (Azov). A kingdom was established in the 480s BC for protection against non-Greek neighbors, and the monarchy lasted for over 200 years. The main colonies were Panticapaeum, Nymphaeum and Phanagoria. The kingdom derived its wealth from fish processing, metalworking and huge exports of grain from Russia. From c. 250 BC there were increasing attacks from Scythians and Sarmatians. Ultimately Mithridates VI of Pontus was called on to help repulse the invaders, and he annexed the territory c. 110 BC, when the last Bosphoran king was killed. The Cimmerian Bosphorus is not the same as the Bosphorus Strait (Thracian Bosphorus) linking the Black Sea and the Sea of Marmara (Propontis).

Cappadocia

A mountainous region in Asia Minor, Cappadocia originally extended from the Black Sea to the Euphrates (fig. 4.6). The northern part became Pontus (or Pontic Cappadocia). Cappadocia was east of Galatia and Cilicia and was ruled as a Persian satrapy. It resisted Alexander the Great, and in 322 BC Ariarathes I, satrap of Cappadocia and Pontus, was killed by Perdiccas. Cappadocia then became part of the Seleucid Empire. After 301 BC Ariarathes II regained Cappadocia (but not Pontus), but remained subject to the Seleucids. Ariarathes III declared its independence c. 250 BC. It became an ally of Pergamum, but after Antiochus III was defeated by Rome at the battle of Magnesia (189 BC), Cappadocia became an ally of Rome.

Caria

Caria (*Karia*) was a mountainous region in southwest Asia Minor (fig. 4.6), south of the Maeander

River. The coast had some hellenized towns, such as Cnidus and Halicarnassus, but the interior was largely hilltop villages. It came under the control of King Croesus of Lydia and then the Persians, against whom the Carians fought in the Ionian Revolt (499–494 BC). Mausolus, son of the Persian satrap Hecatomnus, moved the capital of Caria from Mylasa to Halicarnassus. Under him, Caria was virtually a separate kingdom, and he extended its territory into Ionia and Lycia. He pursued a policy of hellenization, including building new cities. His sister Ada, who had been deposed, was reinstated by Alexander the Great. Caria subsequently formed part of the Ptolemaic Empire. Much of the territory was given to Rhodes for supporting Rome against Antiochus III in 188 BC. It became part of the Roman province of Asia (133 BC).

Chalcidice

A promontory in Macedonia (fig. 4.5), Chalcidice included the three smaller promontories of Pallene (Cassandra), Sithonia (Longos) and Acte (Athos). It was situated between the Thermaic and Strymonic Gulfs. The northern part was called Bottice. It gained its name Chalcidice (*Chalkidike*) from being first colonized by Chalcis in the 8th century BC. The colonists founded about 30 settlements and dispossessed the former Sithonian inhabitants. Eretria and Andros also founded colonies, as did Corinth (at Potidaea c. 600 BC). The cities joined the Delian League, coming under Athenian dominance, but in 432/431 BC they revolted by establishing their own Chalcidic (or Chalcidian) Confederacy (or League) with its capital at Olynthus. There were common laws and citizenship, and the Confederacy circulated its own coins. It expanded northwest into Macedonia in the 380s BC, taking over Anthemus and the capital Pella. Other threatened cities called on Sparta to intervene, and the Confederacy was forced to become allies in 379 BC. The Chalcidians joined the Second Athenian League, but then sided with Philip II of Macedonia in 356 BC. Philip dissolved the Confederacy and destroyed many of its cities, the last being Olynthus in 348 BC. Many cities were refounded in the Hellenistic period, such as Cassandrea, which was founded on the site of Potidaea in 316 BC.

Chersonesus

The Thracian Chersonesus or Chersonese (*Khersonesos*) was the Gallipoli Peninsula (fig. 4.6). It was an important wheat-growing area, and as it controlled the Dardanelles, it was also strategically important. It was colonized in the 8th and 7th centuries BC from Miletus and elsewhere. It came under Athenian control in the 6th century BC, but in 338 BC it was ceded to Philip II of Macedonia. It was subsequently fought over by Hellenistic rulers, until it was taken over by the kingdom of Pergamum in 189 BC.

The Tauric Chersonesus was the Crimea, which came under the control of the kingdom of the Cimmerian Bosphorus in 438 BC. A city named Chersonesus also existed in this area.

Cilicia

Cilicia comprised the southeastern coastal area of Asia Minor and its mountainous hinterland (fig. 4.6). It contained a western mountainous area called Cilicia Tracheia and a fertile plain to the east called Cilicia Pedias. The land became subject to the Persians, but was liberated unopposed by Alexander the Great. It became part of the Seleucid Empire, but was long disputed between the Ptolemies and Seleucids. In the late 2nd century BC pirates were based in Cilicia Tracheia, which led to it being occupied by the Romans.

Colchis

This region was at the east end of the Black Sea (now Georgia), south of the Caucasus Mountains (fig. 4.2). Here several colonies and trading posts were established by Miletus. Various goods were traded to the Greek world, and there were also commercial connections with the Scytho-Iranian world. The state was possibly established in the 6th century BC and was ruled by local chieftains. It was conquered by Mithridates VI c. 111/110 BC, and was later incorporated in the Roman province known as Bithynia and Pontus.

Commagene

A territory in northern Syria (now southeastern Turkey) extending to the Euphrates River (fig. 4.6). It became a client kingdom of the Seleucids, but declared its independence c. 162 BC. Subsequent Greco-Iranian kings claimed descent from Darius I and Alexander the Great.

Corinth

The city of Corinth, its acropolis (Acrocorinth) and its surrounding territory are situated by the Isthmus of Corinth, therefore controlling north-south communications between the Peloponnese and north Greece, and east-west communications between the Aegean and Ionian Seas (fig. 4.5). There was no canal across the isthmus, but it was easier to drag small ships across a special road (*diolkos*) (or to unload from one ship and load on to another) than to sail around the Peloponnese. Corinth's two ports (one on each gulf) were Lechaeum and Cenchreae.

Corinth is mentioned in Homer's *Iliad*, where it is also called Ephyre. It was probably occupied by Dorians c. 900 BC. Ancient tradition stated that the Dorian oligarchy of the Bacchiads ruled there from 747 to 657 BC. During that period Corinth founded the colonies of Syracuse and Corcyra (traditionally 733 BC). In 657 BC, the tyrant Cypselus overthrew the Bacchiads. Corinth's power and prosperity grew to its height under Cypselus and his son Periander (c. 625–585 BC). The colony of Potidaea was founded in Chalcidice c. 600 BC. The tyranny of Periander's successor and nephew Psammetichus was overthrown and replaced by an oligarchy friendly to both Sparta and Athens. Relations with Athens deteriorated in the later 5th century BC; disputes with Athens concerning Corcyra and Potidaea led to the outbreak of the Peloponnesian War in 431 BC, in which Corinth suffered badly due to the loss of trade, ships and colonies. Corinth defended Syracuse against Athens during its Sicilian Expedition (415 BC).

Corinth subsequently joined Athens, Argos and Boeotia against Sparta (Corinthian War, 395–386 BC), and again joined Athens against Philip II of Macedonia. When Athens and Thebes were defeated at the battle of Chaeronea (338 BC), Philip II summoned a congress of Greek states at Corinth to form the Hellenic League. It joined the Achaean Confederacy and later passed into Macedonian hands. When Macedonia was conquered by the Roman general Flamininus, Corinth became a free city and the main city of the Achaean Confederacy. It was destroyed by the Romans in 146 BC, and its people killed or enslaved. It was refounded by the Romans in 44 BC.

Crete

The largest island in the Aegean (fig. 4.1), which experienced the Minoan civilization (see chapter 1, p. 2–3). In historical times Crete was always outside mainstream events in Greece. Its social system seems to have been similar to that of Sparta (both were Dorian regions). Homer mentions 100 cities, and over 50 are known, the most important being Knossos, Gortyn, Lyttos and Cydonia. These many small city-states were often at war, and Cretans were often used as mercenary soldiers outside Crete, especially as slingers and archers. During the Persian Wars in the 5th century BC, Crete refused to assist Greece.

The island became notorious as a center of piracy, second to Cilicia. In the late 3rd century BC Philip V of Macedonia encouraged Crete to attack the fleets of his rival Rhodes. The pirates later supported Mithridates VI of Pontus against Rome. The Romans therefore captured the island in 68/67 BC and destroyed Knossos. Crete was attached to the Roman province of Cyrenaica, with Gortyn as its capital.

Cyprus

This island in the eastern Mediterranean, 50 miles (80 km) south of Cilicia Tracheia (fig. 4.1), traded copper and wood for shipbuilding. In the Late Bronze Age, Mycenaean settlements were established. Subsequently the island came variously under the control of Syria, Phoenicia, Assyria, Egypt and, from 525 BC, Persia. Each city on Cyprus retained its own king. Several cities joined the Ionian Revolt against Persia (499–494 BC), but this was crushed. The island supported Alexander the Great and helped him capture the Phoenician city of Tyre (333 BC). Cyprus was then ruled by the

Ptolemies, and the individual kingships were abolished. The island was ceded to Rome in 59 BC.

Cyrene

Also known as Cyrenaica, Cyrene was a fertile territory situated in the eastern part of Libya (fig. 4.2). The city of Cyrene was founded c. 630 BC by colonists from Thera under Battus, and established colonies of its own in the early 6th century BC. Cyrene was under Persian control 525–c. 479 BC. The Battiad monarchy came to an end c. 440 BC, when democratic reform took place. After the death of Alexander the Great, Cyrene was ruled by the Ptolemies. The coastal strip became known as the Pentapolis, with the five Greek cities of Cyrene, Ptolemais, Euesperides, Apollonia and Taucheira. In 74 BC it became a Roman province and merged with Crete seven years later (67 BC).

Doris

A small area of central Greece around the headwaters of the River Cephissus (fig. 4.5), its small plain contained the cities of Pindus, Erineus, Boeum and Cytinium. It came under the control of Onomarchus, the Phocian commander, in the 4th century BC, and later fell to Philip II of Macedonia.

Drangiana

This area (*Drangiane*), now largely comprising southwest Afghanistan (fig. 4.2), came under Persian control and formed part of the satrapy of Arachosia. In 330 BC Alexander the Great entered the region and detached it from Arachosia, joining it with Aria to the north. This territory then became part of the Seleucid Empire, but subsequently came under the control of Bactria (late 3rd century BC).

Egypt

Up to the time of Alexander the Great, Egypt (*Aigyptos*) was little affected by Greece, apart from the trading post at Naucratis (fig. 4.2). Alexander seized Egypt from the Persians in 332/331 BC and appointed Cleomenes (a Greek from Naucratis) as financial administrator. After Alexander's death Ptolemy was appointed as satrap, and he had Cleomenes assassinated. He became king (Ptolemy I) in 304 BC, and the Ptolemies ruled Egypt as hereditary monarchs for nearly 300 years, throughout the Hellenistic period. In addition they ruled other territories at various times, including Coele-Syria, Cyrene, parts of Asia Minor and Cyprus. There was also continual conflict with Seleucid Syria. At the end of the 3rd century BC, Nubia revolted. Internal dissension led to Egypt becoming a Roman province, with its last ruler (Cleopatra VII) committing suicide in 30 BC. Despite the lengthy rule of the Ptolemies, Greek culture never took root in much of Egypt. Even in Alexandria there were few Greeks by the 2nd century BC, according to the writer Polybius.

ALEXANDRIA

This city was founded by Alexander the Great in 331 BC, though possibly not intended as a capital city. It was on the Nile Delta, between the sea and Lake Mareotis, and may have been situated on an existing harbor and the village site of Rhacotis. It is the first known city to bear the name of its founder, and it became the wealthy center of the Hellenistic world and the largest of all Greek cities. It was inhabited by descendants of the Greek and Macedonian settlers, a substantial Jewish community, and people of numerous other races. Little survives today, but numerous ancient writers described it. It was planned by the Macedonian town planner/architect Deinocrates. It measured about 1.2 miles (2 km) north-south and 3.1 miles (5 km) east-west and was probably modeled on the plan of Pella. A royal palace was built in the northwest part of the town, adjacent to the sea, possibly occupying one-quarter or one-third of the city area. Next to the palace was the Akra (a fortified area but not an acropolis on a hill). There was an agora, probably in the city center. The city was divided into five *klimata* (strips), each of which was divided into rectangular blocks divided by streets.

On his death, Ptolemy I buried Alexander the Great at Alexandria, and the city subsequently underwent much development, with Ptolemy moving his capital there from Memphis. Little is known about Alexandria's public buildings, such as temples. The Museum became a center of Greek culture; it was a courtyard structure with a shrine to the Muses, and the nearby Library must have been substantial. There was a sanctuary of Sarapis in the southwestern part of the city, a theater, and a gymnasium next to the east-west street. The most famous building was the Pharos Lighthouse, which bears the name of the island on which it was built; it was connected to the mainland by a mole, which provided two harbors. Initially houses may have been very large, but these gave way to tenement blocks to house the rapidly increasing population. Cemeteries with substantial tombs exist, particularly on the east of the city.

Elis

A region in the northwest Peloponnese whose rich plain (in which Olympia is situated) was famous for horse breeding (fig. 4.5). Elis consisted of three distinct districts. Hollow Elis was in the north (named after its Plain of Peneus), and there were two other annexed districts—Pisatis in the center in the lower valley of the Alpheus (there may have been a town called Pisa) and Triphylia in the south. Elis was often in conflict with Pisatis (the district round Olympia) over control of Olympia. With Sparta as an ally, Elis regained control of the Olympic Games from Pisatis by the 6th century BC.

From 471 BC the city of Elis became the region's political and religious center. Although the state tended to remain neutral in politics, Elis was a close ally of Sparta until 420 BC, when Sparta supported the revolt and independence of Lepreum. Elis therefore became allied with Athens and Argos, and fought against Sparta at the battle of Mantinea (418 BC). In 399 BC Sparta punished Elis by the loss of Triphylia (which was united to Arcadia in 369 BC). Sparta gave Xenophon an estate near Olympia, but Elis forced him to move in 371 BC. In the 3rd century BC, the Eleans were allies of Aetolia and fought frequently with Arcadia. In 191 BC Elis was incorporated in the Achaean Confederacy, and in 146 BC became part of a Roman province, although still able to control the Olympic Games.

Epirus

Epirus (*Epeiros*, mainland) was a territory in northwest Greece and southern Albania (fig. 4.5). It was inhabited by three main groups of Iron Age tribes—the Chaones, Molossi and Thesproti. Along the coast were colonies founded by the Greeks, including the Corinthian colonies of Ambracia and the island of Corcyra. The Molossi under Alexander I (342–330 BC) unified much of Epirus. Pyrrhus I (297–272 BC) established his capital at Ambracia and expanded his kingdom, including the conquest of southern Illyria, the invasion of Italy and Sicily, and confrontations with the Carthaginians and Romans. Constant strife occurred between his successors, and the monarchy fell c. 232 BC. The Molossi alone subsequently supported Perseus of Macedonia against Rome. The Romans sacked much of the country and deported 150,000 inhabitants into slavery (167 BC). In 146 BC, Epirus was attached to the new Roman province of Macedonia.

Galatia

A large upland region in central Asia Minor, Galatia was formerly part of Phrygia and Cappadocia (fig. 4.6). It was occupied by Gauls (Galatians) who had crossed the Hellespont from Europe in the early 3rd century BC. They supported Antiochus III against the Romans, but became allies of Rome after the battle of Magnesia (189 BC). In 85 BC Galatia became a protectorate of Rome.

Gandhara

A territory now in northwest Pakistan, southeast of the Hindu Kush Mountains (fig. 4.2), it was under Persian rule for two centuries, but surrendered to Alexander the Great in 327 BC. Toward the end of the 4th century BC, western Gandhara was ceded to Sandracottus by Seleucus I in exchange for war elephants. Part of Gandhara was taken over in the early 2nd century BC by Bactria, which had also broken away from the Seleucid Empire.

Gedrosia

This was an area of southern Pakistan and southeast Iran that extended northward from the Arabian Sea (fig. 4.2). Its Persian satrap surrendered to Alexander the Great in 330/329 BC. It later fell to Parthia.

Illyria

Illyria comprised the northwestern part of the Balkan Peninsula to the north of Epirus and Macedonia (fig. 4.5). Its coast was settled by Greek colonists, such as at Epidamnus and Apollonia, but elsewhere it was populated by warlike Illyrians, who constantly harassed Epirus and Macedonia. Illyria fought wars with

Rome in the late 3rd century BC, and in the 2nd century BC it supported Perseus of Macedonia, but was defeated by the Romans in 168 BC.

India

Alexander the Great in his Indian Expedition of 327–325 BC took over parts of modern Pakistan and India as far as the Hyphasis (Beas) River (figs. 2.2, 4.2) and founded various cities. Seleucus I relinquished several of these eastern territories to the Mauryan king Sandracottus in 303 BC in exchange for war elephants. The Greco-Bactrian kings took control of many of the territories in northwest India, following the collapse of the Mauryan Empire in the early 2nd century BC. However, the rise of Parthia separated the Greek world from India.

Ionia

The central part of the west coast of Asia Minor (including islands), with Caria to the south and Aeolis to the north (fig. 4.6), this area began to be colonized before 1000 BC by migrations from mainland Greece, when the Dorians were pushing into Greece. By 700 BC a religious league was formed, known as the Panionion, and was based at Mycale. Twelve city-states emerged in the Archaic period and formed the Ionian League: Phocaea, Clazomenae, Erythrae, Teos, Lebedus, Colophon, Ephesus, Priene, Myus, Miletus and the islands of Chios and Samos. In the 7th century BC Miletus and Phocaea undertook much overseas colonization. Ionia came under the control of Lydia and then the Persians, against whom they revolted until defeated at Lade in 495/494 BC. They were liberated from the Persians after the battle of Mycale in 479 BC and joined the Delian League. After Athens was defeated in the Peloponnesian War, Ionia once again came under Persian domination. In 334 BC the Ionians (except Miletus) supported Alexander the Great, and subsequently came under Seleucid and Ptolemaic control, until the kingdom of Pergamum was formed. When Pergamum was bequeathed to the Romans (133 BC), Ionia became part of the Roman province of Asia.

The term Ionian is also used to cover Attica, Euboea, the Cyclades and the central part of western Asia Minor.

Judaea

One of the three main divisions of Palestine (the other two being Samaria and Galilee to the north), Judaea was part of Syria (fig. 4.2). It was in Persian control (538–332 BC) until taken by Alexander the Great. It later came under the control of the Ptolemies and then the Seleucids (200 BC). Antiochus IV attempted to hellenize Judaea, including substituting Zeus Olympias for the worship of Yahweh in the temple of Jerusalem. His persecutions of the Jews led to an insurrection. Judaea became the independent Hasmonaean state, largely outside Hellenistic influence, until it came under Roman control in 63 BC.

Laconia

This area of the southeastern Peloponnese was called Laconia or Laconica (fig. 4.5) (*Lakonia* or *Lakonike*). The area was also known as Lacedaemon (*Lakedaimon*), its most ancient name, which was used by Homer. This was the territory of Sparta (*Sparte*), itself also known as Lacedaemon. The name Sparta was applied only to the city. Laconia was bounded on the south and east by the Aegean Sea, on the west by Messenia and on the north by Arcadia and Argos. It is a mountainous limestone region, with Mt. Taygetus rising to 7,800 ft (2,377 m), overlooking the Plain of Sparta. The main rivers are the Eurotas and the Oenus (a tributary).

By the 12th century BC the Mycenaean kingdom was destroyed, and by 950 BC new Dorian settlements existed. By 700 BC one such settlement—Sparta—was in control of a large area of Laconia, which formed the territory of the *Spartiatai*. Various other territories were annexed, and the population was reduced to the level of either helots (serfs), who cultivated the land, or partially independent perioeci, but in reality they were under Spartan domination. Between c. 735 and 715 BC Sparta fought the First Messenian War against Messenia, annexing much of that state and reducing

(A)   (B)

Fig. 4.10   The colony of Taras was founded by Spartans c. 706 BC. The reverse (A) of this silver stater shows Taras riding on a dolphin; he was the mythical founder of the colony, who was saved from shipwreck by the aid of a dolphin sent by his father Poseidon. He holds a cantharus in his right hand, and there is a star behind him. The obverse (B) depicts a horseman, possibly Taras, riding over land.   Courtesy of Somerset County Museums Service.

its population to the level of helots. The Messenians later revolted, leading to the Second Messenian War.

Circa 706 BC a group of Spartans colonized Taras in south Italy (fig. 4.10). In the mid-6th century BC Sparta abandoned its policy of conquest and expansion, and concentrated on consolidation. A Peloponnesian League of states was formed under Sparta's leadership, including Corinth and Megara, but excluding Argos and Achaea. The states paid no tribute, but provided military assistance when needed. Sparta cooperated with Athens at the Persian invasion under Xerxes, particularly at the battles of Thermopylae and Plataea. Due especially to the disgrace of Pausanias, the leadership of the war against Persia passed to the Delian League under Athens, and Sparta was no longer the main power in Greece.

Sparta suffered a devastating earthquake (464 BC) and a revolt of the helots (Third Messenian War, 464–460 BC), but fear of Athenian expansion led to the Peloponnesian War against Athens (431–404 BC). Athens was defeated, leaving Sparta the dominant power in Greece. Sparta subsequently waged war against the Persians (400–390 BC) in support of the Ionian cities in Asia Minor. A league

of Thebes, Corinth, Athens and Argos was formed, which fought the Corinthian War against Sparta. It was brought to an end by the King's Peace (386 BC), leaving Sparta free and the Peloponnesian League in place. Sparta invaded Boeotia on several occasions from 378 BC, but was defeated by Thebes at the battle of Leuctra (371 BC). Sparta's power was weakened by the repeated invasions of the Theban commander Epaminondas (who also freed Messenia) and by the formation of a league of Arcadian cities.

By this time the number of Spartan citizens was diminished to only 2,000. When Philip II of Macedonia invaded the Peloponnese, Sparta's power and territory were further diminished, although the city itself was not captured. Sparta was later captured by Macedonia's Antigonus Doson and was enrolled in the Hellenic League, later being forced to join the Achaean Confederacy. When the Achaean Confederacy was abolished by the Romans, Sparta was joined to the Roman province of Macedonia (146 BC).

Sparta was different from all other states in several respects, including its constitution and its emphasis on a military life-style. The Spartans' reputation for terseness is responsible for the term "laconic." See also chapter 1 for the government of Sparta and its population.

SPARTA

Sparta was situated on low hills on the west bank of the Eurotas River (fig. 4.11). A group of at least four Dorian villages around the acropolis became united as a political entity in about the 10th century BC. The four quarters of the city were the villages known as Limnai, Pitane, Cynosura and Mesoa. The city continued to be a group of villages with no fine buildings. It was only partially walled by the end of the 4th century BC, and the city walls were only completed in 184 BC, enclosing an area 1.8 by 1.2 miles (3 by 2 km).

On the acropolis was a sanctuary of Athena Chalcioecus. Chalcioecus (*Khalkioikos*, living in a brazen house) was an epithet given to Athena Poliachos, the tutelary goddess of the city; it was derived from the metal shrine in which her statue stood. A theater of Hellenistic date was built into the foot of the acropolis. On the southeastern side of the acropolis was an agora. On the west bank of

the Eurotas was the Sanctuary of Orthia (later linked to Artemis), where over 100,000 lead figurines have been found. Contrary to normal Greek practice, burials were allowed inside the settlement area, although few have been found.

Locris

Two areas made up the territory of Locris (fig. 4.5), but these were separated by Doris and Phocis (probably as a result of invasions that divided Locris in two). The two areas played little part in history. One was Eastern Locris (Opuntian or Eoian Locris), which occupied the mainland coast of the Euboean Straits, from Thermopylae to Larymna. The center of the federal state was at Opus; it founded Locri Epizephyrii in Italy c. 700 BC. Opuntian Locris supported Greece against Persia, but still lost territory to its neighbors (such as Thermopylae to Thessaly and Daphnis to Phocis). The other area was Western Locris (Ozolian Locris or Locris Ozolis), which occupied the northern coast of the Corinthian Gulf and the Amphissa Valley. Ozolian Locris lost Naupactus to Athens c. 460 BC, and became involved in the Sacred Wars.

Lycaonia

Lycaonia (*Lykaonia*) was part of the uplands of central Asia Minor (fig. 4.6), whose people were not easily controlled. Perdiccas subdued them in 322 BC, and they became part of the Seleucid Empire (280–189 BC), with a capital at Iconium (Konya), which was once part of Phrygia. From 189 BC Lycaonia became part of the kingdom of Pergamum, and from 133 BC part of the Roman province of Asia.

Lycia

Lycia (*Lykia*) was part of mountainous southern Asia Minor between Caria and Pamphylia (fig. 4.6). Lycia was overrun by the Persians c. 540 BC, but the city-states were temporarily liberated by the Athenians under Cimon c. 468 BC. They joined the

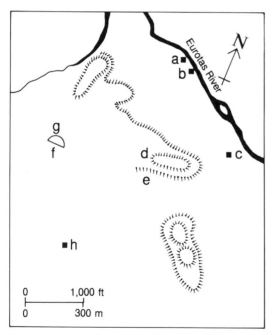

Fig. 4.11   Map of Sparta: a. altar of Lycurgus; b. heroon; c. sanctuary of Artemis Orthia (on banks of river tributary); d. acropolis; e. agora; f. theater; g. sanctuary of Athena Chalcioecus; h. temple.

Delian League for a brief period, but returned rapidly to Persian control. Lycia became part of the kingdom of Mausolus of Halicarnassus, but submitted to Alexander the Great. After Alexander's death, Lycia became part of the Ptolemaic and then the Seleucid Empires. Antiochus III defeated the region in 197 BC, but the territory was granted to Rhodes by Rome after his defeat at the battle of Magnesia in 189 BC. There was a Lycian Confederacy of city-states from at least 200 BC.

Lydia

This was an inland territory of western Asia Minor (fig. 4.6), centered on the Hermus and Cayster valleys (main east-west routes). Under the Mermnad dynasty (c. 700–550 BC), Lydia was a powerful kingdom, with a capital at Sardis. It was the first state to issue coinage. Its last king, Croesus (c. 560–546 BC), extended his Empire throughout Asia Minor but was defeated by the Persians. Lydia became the main Persian satrapy in Asia Minor. It was conquered by Alexander the Great and became part of the Seleucid Empire. From 189 BC it was part of the Pergamum Kingdom, and from 133 BC part of the Roman province of Asia.

Macedonia

Macedonia (*Makedonia*), also known as Macedon, was an area north of Greece, west of Thrace and south of Illyria, comprising a large Macedonian plain surrounded by hills and mountains (fig. 4.5). It was ruled by kings of the royal house of Argeads, a dynasty that claimed descent from Argos. Perdiccas I set up his capital at Aegae (modern Vergina) c. 640 BC. Macedonia became subject to Persia from the time of Darius I (512 BC) until Xerxes' retreat from Greece (480 BC). Archelaus moved the capital to Pella and hellenized and strengthened the country. Philip II gained control of Greece after defeating a Greek coalition at the battle of Chaeronea (338 BC). He established a Hellenic League at Corinth. Alexander the Great (336–323 BC) overthrew the Persian Empire and extended Macedonian control throughout the east as far as India (fig. 2.2). After his death there were

wars of succession, with the Antigonid monarchy in Macedonia. Philip V (221–179 BC) fought two wars against the Romans, who defeated him at Cynoscephalae (197 BC), confining him to Macedonia. His son Perseus was defeated by the Romans at the battle of Pydna (168 BC), and Macedonia was abolished and replaced by four autonomous republics. In 146 BC they became part of the Roman province of Macedonia.

PELLA

King Archelaus moved the capital of Macedonia here from Aegae. It was situated by a lake, and the river was navigable to the Thermaic Gulf of the Aegean Sea. Pella covered a large area and had a grid of substantial streets (fig. 4.12). Part of its northern area was devoted to the palace of the Macedonian kings, which seems to have consisted of a large structure with two rectangular peristyle courtyards side by side—possibly a public and private area. Also in the north part was an acropolis on a pair of hills. The agora was bounded by stoas on all four sides and was in the main area of the city. The houses seem to have been very large, with courtyards.

Malis

A small district in eastern Greece at the head of the Malian Gulf, Malis was surrounded on all sides by mountains, with Thessaly to the north (fig. 4.5). The first center of the Amphictyonic Council was at Anthela, Malis' southernmost town, although its first capital was at Trachis. It was forced to join the Persian army of Xerxes in his invasion of 480 BC, and Ephialtes (from Trachis) showed the Persians the way through Thermopylae (fig. 2.3). Malis supported Sparta in the Peloponnesian War, and Sparta established the military colony of Heraclea Trachinia there in 399 BC. This colony eclipsed Trachis, but was captured by Boeotians and Argives in the Corinthian War in 394 BC. It was destroyed by Jason of Pherae in 371 BC. Lamia then became the only important city of Malis. Malis sided with Sparta against Thebes, and in 338 BC joined the League of Corinth founded by Philip II. From c. 235 BC Malis joined the Aetolian Confederacy, but in 189 BC it became part of Thessaly.

Fig. 4.12   *Pella, capital city of Macedonia from the time of Archelaus. A view of the peristyle of the House of Dionysus (c. 300 BC), one of the larger, wealthier Hellenistic peristyle houses.*

Megara

A district centered on the Dorian city at the eastern end of the Isthmus of Corinth (fig. 4.5), its name was derived from *ta megara* (the temples). Its port was Nisaea on the Saronic Gulf, to which it was connected by its Long Walls. Megara controlled much of the isthmus. It was responsible for founding several early colonies, including Megara Hyblaea in Sicily and Byzantium and Chalcedon on the Bosphorus. Megara lost western territory to Corinth, and Salamis to Athens. It joined the Peloponnesian League before 500 BC and participated in the Persian Wars. Megara was then involved in territorial disputes with Corinth and left the Peloponnesian League to become allied with Athens. It then revolted from Athens, and in 433/432 BC Pericles decreed to block its trade, which was one of the causes of the Peloponnesian War. Megara did not play any important role in subsequent history. It regained some prosperity, came under Macedonian control and then joined the Achaean Confederacy.

Mesopotamia

An area of southeastern Turkey and Iraq between the Tigris and Euphrates Rivers (fig. 4.2), it was taken from the Babylonians by the Persians in 539 BC. Alexander the Great gained the territory after defeating Darius III at Gaugamela in 331 BC. Seleucus I made the new city of Seleucia on the Tigris his capital, and many other cities were founded here by the Seleucids. In 141/140 BC the area was overrun by Parthians.

Messenia

Also referred to as Messene (a name that gradually came to denote the town founded after the battle of Leuctra), this was a region in the southwestern Peloponnese, with Arcadia and Elis to the north and Laconia to the east (fig. 4.5). There was extensive occupation in the Mycenaean period, including the palace at Pylos. Between c. 735 and 715 BC Sparta fought against Messenia (First Messenian War) and conquered at least its central plain, reducing the population to the level of helots. Messenia later revolted, resulting in the Second Messenian War, when it held out under its leader Aristomenes. He was subsequently defeated, and all of Messenia came under Spartan control. There were several subsequent revolts, and in 370/369 BC the Theban commander Epaminondas freed Messenia from its state of servitude to Sparta, and founded Messene as the new capital. Messenia sided with Philip II of Macedonia in 344 BC, and Philip increased its territory. From c. 244 BC Messenia belonged alternately to the Aetolian and Achaean Confederacies. Forced to rejoin the Achaean Confederacy, it sent no troops to act against Rome and finally came under Roman control in 146 BC.

Mysia

This was a district in northwest Asia Minor, with Lydia to the south, Phrygia to the east and Propontis to the north (fig. 4.6). The Troad to the west was sometimes regarded as part of its territory. It came under the control of King Croesus of Lydia and then fell to the Persians. It was taken by Alexander the Great and became part of the Seleucid Empire. When Antiochus III was defeated by the Romans in 189 BC, Mysia was incorporated with the kingdom of Pergamum.

Pamphylia

This coastal plain of southern Asia Minor was between Lycia and Cilicia, with the Mediterranean on the south and the Taurus Mountains on the north (fig. 4.6). There was Greek colonization along the coast, but the area came under the control of Lydia and then Persia, until it surrendered to Alexander the Great (333 BC). Subsequently it became part of the Ptolemaic and then the Seleucid Empires. Antiochus III ceded the region to Rome in 189 BC.

Paphlagonia

This was an area of northern Asia Minor between Pontus and Bithynia along the Black Sea coast (fig. 4.6), where there were numerous Greek colonies. After Alexander the Great, it was divided between Bithynia and Pontus.

Parthia

This territory was part of the Persian Empire until it was overrun by Alexander the Great (fig. 4.2). It became a Seleucid satrapy, equivalent in area to modern Iran. Around 300 BC Scythian tribes moved from central Asia to Parthia. Circa 247 BC Arsaces I conquered the satrapy and established an independent kingdom, with Ecbatana as its capital. From that time the Parthian Empire began to expand, with territories divided into satrapies from the Euphrates to Turkmenistan and Afghanistan.

Peloponnese

This peninsula of southern Greece (*Peloponnesos*, Isle of Pelops; medieval Morea) was connected with central mainland Greece only by the Isthmus of Corinth (fig. 4.5). The main regions were Achaea, Elis, Arcadia, Argos, Messenia and Laconia. The main towns were Sparta, Argos and Corinth. The Peloponnesian League was a confederacy of Greek states, including Sparta and its allies.

Pergamum

A city in Asia Minor, about 15 miles (24 km) from the sea (fig. 4.6), it became the capital of the powerful Hellenistic Attalid kingdom in the 3rd century

Fig. 4.13 *Pergamum, capital of the Hellenistic kingdom ruled by the Attalids. Their greatest period of power was under Eumenes II. This huge theater was built against the western hillside of the acropolis.*

BC. The city itself was made one of the finest in the Greek world (fig. 4.13), with a library second only to Alexandria. It became part of the Seleucid Empire, but became independent under Eumenes I. The kingdom was bequeathed to Rome in 133 BC.

Persia

An area of about 1,000,000 sq mi (2,589,900 sq km), Persia extended from the Tigris to the Indus Rivers. The Persian Empire was established through conquest from the 6th century BC by Cyrus, who overthrew the Medes. Persia was then extended by Cambyses and Darius (late 6th–early 5th century BC) into Asia Minor, Bactria, India and Egypt, resulting in conflict with the Greeks (Persian Wars). Persia's administrative capital was at

Susa. The Empire was divided into a number of autonomous provinces called satrapies, each governed by a satrap (either a local ruler or a Persian). Each satrapy was required to pay tribute and provide supplies for the military. The Empire was conquered in the late 4th century BC by Alexander the Great, who maintained the satrapies. It later became part of the Seleucid Empire.

Phocis

A territory in central Greece, Phocis (*Phokis*) was organized as a confederation of small towns (fig. 4.5). It controlled Delphi until the early 6th century BC, when Delphi was brought under the control of the Amphictyonic Council in the First Sacred War. In the Persian Wars, Phocis was forced to take the side of the Persians, but fought against them at the battle of Plataea (479 BC). The Phocians regained Delphi in the Second Sacred War in 448 BC. They supported Sparta in the Peloponnesian War (431–404 BC) but joined the Boeotian Confederacy c. 380 BC.

In 356 BC Phocis seized the temple at Delphi, leading to the outbreak of the Third Sacred War. The Phocian leader Philomelus was killed (354 BC), and Onomarchus was defeated and killed by Philip II of Macedonia in 352 BC. Phocis surrendered in 346 BC and was considerably weakened, with the Phocian votes on the Amphictyonic Council transferred to Philip II. Phocis fought against Philip II at the battle of Chaeronea in 338 BC and against Antipater in the Lamian War (323 BC). In 279 BC the Phocians assisted in defending Thermopylae against the invading Gauls, and again became subject to Macedonia. In 196 BC they belonged to the Aetolian Confederacy, and after its dissolution by the Romans in 189 BC, they formed a Phocian Confederacy that lasted into the Roman period.

Phoenicia

An area largely equivalent to modern Lebanon (fig. 4.2), Phoenicia (*Phoinikia*) became part of the Persian Empire, but surrendered to Alexander the Great, except for Tyre, which was captured after a long siege (332 BC). The region was then fought over by the Ptolemies and Seleucids. In 200 BC it was part of the Seleucid kingdom of Antiochus III, forming part of Coele-Syria. It later became part of the Roman province of Syria.

Phrygia

A plateau region of Asia Minor, with Lycia and Pisidia to the south, Mysia and Lydia to the west, and Galatia and Lycaonia to the east (fig. 4.6), Phrygia came under the control of Lydia and then Persia. It was later occupied by Alexander the Great (333 BC), becoming part of the Seleucid Empire in 301 BC. The area to the east of the Sangarius River fell to the Gauls c. 275 BC and became Galatia, while western Phrygia became part of the Pergamum Kingdom.

The northwest part of Asia Minor was sometimes called Phrygia Minor or Hellespontine Phrygia.

Pisidia

An inland mountainous region of southern Asia Minor, bounded by Phrygia, Lycaonia, Lycia and Cilicia (fig. 4.6), it was a lawless area that resisted defeat by Lydia and Persia. Although it surrendered to Alexander the Great, it remained effectively independent.

Pontus

A region of northern Asia Minor including the southern shore of the Black Sea (fig. 4.6), Pontus (*Pontos*, sea) was originally regarded as part of Cappadocia, later termed Pontic Cappadocia, then just Pontus. In the 7th century BC Miletus established colonies along the coast at Amisus and Sinope, which established their own colonies. Pontus resisted Seleucid domination in the Hellenistic period, and Pharnaces I (186–169 BC) strove to expand the state all around the Black Sea coast. Mithridates V became the most powerful king in Asia Minor, and the kingdom reached its greatest extent under Mithridates VI. He came into conflict with the Romans, causing three Mithridatic wars.

Scythia

The name Scythia (*Skythia*) was used by the Greeks for the entire area between the Carpathians and the Tanais (Don) River, extending as far as the Caspian Sea (fig. 4.2). Scythians were nomadic people of central Asia, who traded with the Greek colonies of the northern Black Sea coast. They were expert horsemen, and with the use of mounted archers, they even defeated a force under Alexander the Great's general Zopyrion c. 325 BC.

Sicily

This is the largest island in the Mediterranean with 9,830 sq mi (25,458 sq km) (fig. 4.1). From c. 735 BC there was extensive Greek colonization of the island, beginning with Naxus and Syracuse (fig. 4.14). The western part of the island was controlled by Phoenicians from Carthage. In the Archaic period Gela and Syracuse dominated Sicily. In 480 BC Gelon and Theron defeated the Carthaginians at Himera, and in 474 BC an Etruscan fleet was destroyed by Hieron I off Cumae. Syracuse was now the greatest power in the Greek world. The indigenous Sicel people had been gradually displaced; in the 460s BC they unsuccessfully rebelled under their Sicel leader Ducetius. During the Peloponnesian War, Athens intervened in Sicily against Syracuse, but its expedition of 415–413 BC ended in disastrous defeat.

Dionysius I of Syracuse (406–367 BC) undertook four wars against the threatening Carthaginians. He ultimately controlled most of the island, and became the most powerful leader in the Greek world. On his death there were dynastic struggles. Syracuse appealed to Corinth for assistance against Dionysius II, and Timoleon was sent in 345 BC to repair the situation. However, after Timoleon's death, Agathocles became tyrant (to 289 BC). In 278/276 BC Pyrrhus of Epirus invaded Sicily, after which Hieron II established control. Syracuse supported Carthage in the First Punic War against Rome (264–241 BC), and Sicily came under Roman control, becoming the first Roman province in 211 BC.

Sogdiana

This region of central Asia between the Jaxartes and Oxus Rivers, forming part of Tajikistan and Uzbekistan (fig. 4.2), was a satrapy in the Persian Empire, and was conquered by Alexander the Great in 328/327 BC. He founded Alexandria Eschate (the farthest) on the Jaxartes River. Sogdiana later became part of the Seleucid Empire, but in the 3rd century BC it became part of the independent state of Bactria.

Syria

In ancient times Syria did not reflect the borders of modern Syria but was the whole fertile strip between the eastern Mediterranean and the desert of northern Arabia (fig. 4.2). The Greeks often called it Coele-Syria (literally, hollow Syria) to distinguish it from "Syria between the Rivers" (Mesopotamia). Within Syria the Phoenician cities of Byblus, Tyre and Sidon were established (an area known as Phoenicia), as well as the Greek trading stations of Al Mina and Poseidium. Syria became a satrapy of the Persian Empire c. 539 BC. In 332 BC Alexander the Great conquered Syria. After the battle of Ipsus (301 BC), Syria was split between Seleucus I in the north (Syria Seleucis) and Ptolemy I in the south (Coele-Syria, with the name now being used for just the southern region of Syria). Many cities were founded in the north by the Seleucids, including their capital Antioch by Daphne.

In Coele-Syria, the Ptolemies retained the existing system of local government. Syrian Wars were fought over this area, and in 217 BC the Seleucid

Fig. 4.14 *A late 6th-century-BC silver didrachm of Acragas, a city in Sicily founded in 582 BC by nearby Gela and the island of Rhodes. The eagle, the emblem of Zeus, was used for nearly a century from the end of the 6th century BC. The legend stands for Acragas. On the reverse is a crab (fig. 5.10).* Courtesy of Somerset County Museums Service.

king Antiochus III was defeated by Ptolemy IV at the battle of Raphia. In 200 BC Antiochus III won a victory over Ptolemy V at the battle of Panion, and finally took over Coele-Syria. Antiochus IV attempted to hellenize Judaea (part of Coele-Syria), which led to it becoming an independent state after an insurrection. After his death other states in Syria achieved independence, such as Ituraea and Commagene. In 83 BC the Armenian king Tigranes I occupied Syria until it was made a Roman province in 64/63 BC.

Thessaly

A region of northern Greece, south of Macedonia, east of Epirus and bordering the Aegean Sea (fig. 4.5), Thessaly (*Thessalia*) was a tetrarchy, divided into four regions: Thessaliotis, Hestiaeotis, Pelasgiotis and Phthiotis. There were two large plains surrounded by mountains. From the 7th century BC there was a Thessalian Confederacy under an elected military leader (*tagos*). During the 6th century BC Thessaly became the major power in northern Greece, although the people were regarded as backward. During the Persian Wars they supported the Persians. At the end of the 5th century BC a powerful unified state was created by the rulers of the city-state of Pherae. Jason of Pherae (tyrant c. 385–370 BC) took control of all Thessaly. He was succeeded by Alexander, but most Thessalian cities refused to recognize him as *tagos*. He came into conflict with Thebes, by whom he was defeated. In the Third Sacred War, Thessaly acted against Phocis, but Philip II of Macedonia defeated Phocis and Pherae at the battle of the Crocus Field in 352 BC. Thessaly then came under the domination of Macedonia, for whom the

Thessalian cavalry became very important. In 196 BC the Romans created a new Thessalian Confederacy detached from Macedonia, and in 146 BC it became part of the Roman province of Macedonia.

Thrace

Originally the area in the northern Balkans as far as the Danube, Thrace (*Thrakia*) was later regarded as the region of southeastern Bulgaria and European Turkey, with a western border at the Nestus River (fig. 4.2). The inhabitants were Indo-Europeans but not Greek in origin. From the 8th century BC the Aegean coastal areas were extensively colonized by the Greeks, forming independent city-states, but the interior was untouched. In 513 BC a large part of Thrace became a Persian satrapy until Xerxes retreated in 480 BC, when a dynasty of kings from the Odrysae tribe ruled. In 342 BC, Philip II of Macedonia took over Thrace and established Greek and Macedonian colonies. Lysimachus, a successor of Alexander the Great, reconquered the country and founded Lysimachia as a new capital in 308 BC. In 297 BC Gauls invaded Thrace, but were overthrown by the Thracians near the end of the 3rd century BC. In 201–200 BC Philip V of Macedonia overthrew the Thracian tribal states and occupied the Greek coastal cities. He was forced to retreat after being defeated by the Romans in 197 BC. Antiochus III then attempted to take Thrace. After the battle of Pydna (168 BC), western Thrace became part of the Roman territory of Macedonia, and the rest was ruled by native kings until the Roman province of Thrace was formed (AD 48).

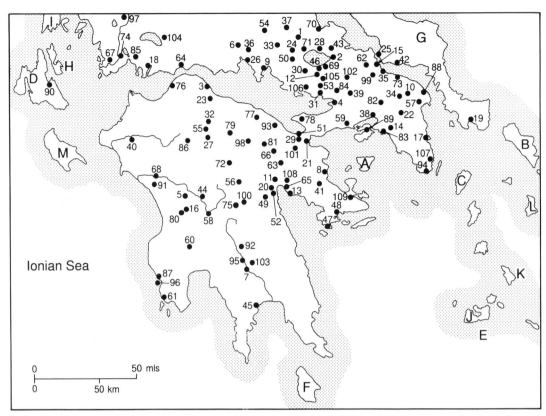

Fig. 4.15 Place-names and islands of southern and central Greece: A. Aegina; B. Andros; C. Ceos; D. Cephallenia; E. Cyclades; F. Cythera; G. Euboea; H. Ithaca; I. Leucas; J. Melos; K. Siphnos; L. Sirus; M. Zacynthus; 1. Abae; 2. Acraephia; 3. Aegium; 4. Aegosthena; 5. Aliphera; 6. Amphissa; 7. Amyclae; 8. Anthedon; 9. Anticyra; 10. Aphidna; 11. Argos; 12. Ascra; 13. Asine; 14. Athens; 15. Aulis; 16. Bassae; 17. Brauron; 18. Calydon; 19. Carystus; 20. Cenchreae; 21. Cenchreae; 22. Cephisia; 23. Cerynia; 24. Chaeronea; 25. Chalcis; 26. Cirrha; 27. Cleitor; 28. Copae; 29. Corinth; 30. Coronea; 31. Creusa; 32. Cynaetha; 33. Daulis; 34. Decelea; 35. Delium; 36. Delphi; 37. Elatea; 38. Eleusis; 39. Eleutherae; 40. Elis; 41. Epidaurus; 42. Eretria; 43. Gla; 44. Gortys; 45. Gythium; 46. Haliartus; 47. Halieis; 48. Hermione; 49. Hysiae; 50. Lebadea; 51. Lechaeum; 52. Lerna; 53. Leuctra; 54. Lilaea; 55. Lusi; 56. Mantinea; 57. Marathon; 58. Megalopolis; 59. Megara; 60. Messene; 61. Methone; 62. Mycalessus; 63. Mycenae; 64. Naupactus; 65. Nauplia; 66. Nemea; 67. Oeniadae; 68. Olympia; 69. Onchestus; 70. Opus; 71. Orchomenus; 72. Orchomenus; 73. Oropus; 74. Paeanium; 75. Pallantium; 76. Patrae; 77. Pellene; 78. Perachora; 79. Pheneus; 80. Phigalia; 81. Phlius; 82. Phyle; 83. Piraeus; 84. Plataea; 85. Pleuron; 86. Psophis; 87. Pylos; 88. Rhamnus; 89. Salamis; 90. Same; 91. Scillus; 92. Sellasia; 93. Sicyon; 94. Sounion; 95. Sparta; 96. Sphacteria; 97. Stratus; 98. Stymphalus; 99. Tanagra; 100. Tegea; 101. Tenea; 102. Thebes; 103. Therapne; 104. Thermum; 105. Thespiae; 106. Thisbe; 107. Thoricus; 108. Tiryns; 109. Troezen.

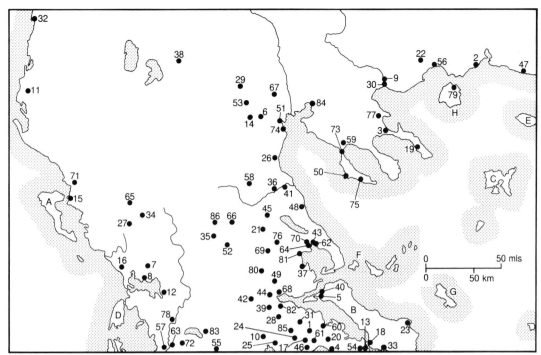

Fig. 4.16   Place-names and islands of central and northern Greece and southern Albania: A. Corcyra; B. Euboea; C. Lemnos; D. Leucas; E. Samothrace; F. Sciathus; G. Scyros; H. Thasos. 1) Abae; 2. Abdera; 3) Acanthus; 4. Acraephia; 5. Aedepsus; 6. Aegae; 7. Ambracia; 8. Ambracus; 9. Amphipolis; 10. Amphissa; 11. Apollonia; 12. Argos; 13. Aulis; 14. Beroea; 15. Buthrotum; 16. Cassope; 17. Chaeronea; 18. Chalcis; 19. Cleonae; 20. Copae; 21. Crannon; 22. Crenides; 23. Cyme; 24. Daulis; 25. Delphi; 26. Dium; 27. Dodona; 28. Drymaea; 29. Edessa; 30. Eion; 31. Elatea; 32. Epidamnus; 33. Eretria; 34. Eurymenae; 35. Gomphi; 36. Gonnus; 37. Halus; 38. Heraclea Lynci; 39. Heraclea Trachinia; 40. Histiaea; 41. Homolium; 42. Hypata; 43. Iolcus; 44. Lamia; 45. Larissa; 46. Lebadea; 47. Maronea; 48. Meliboea; 49. Melitaea; 50. Mende; 51. Methone; 52. Metropolis; 53. Mieza; 54. Mycalessus; 55. Naupactus; 56. Neapolis; 57. Oeniadae; 58. Oloosson; 59. Olynthus; 60. Opus; 61. Orchomenus; 62. Orminium; 63. Paeanium; 64. Pagasae and Demetrias (two sites); 65. Passaron; 66. Pelinna; 67. Pella; 68. Phalara; 69. Pharsalus; 70. Pherae; 71. Phoenice; 72. Pleuron; 73. Potidaea; 74. Pydna; 75. Scione; 76. Scotussa; 77. Stagirus; 78. Stratus; 79. Thasos; 80. Thaumaci; 81. Thebes; 82. Thermopylae; 83. Thermum; 84. Thessalonica; 85. Tithorea; 86. Tricca.

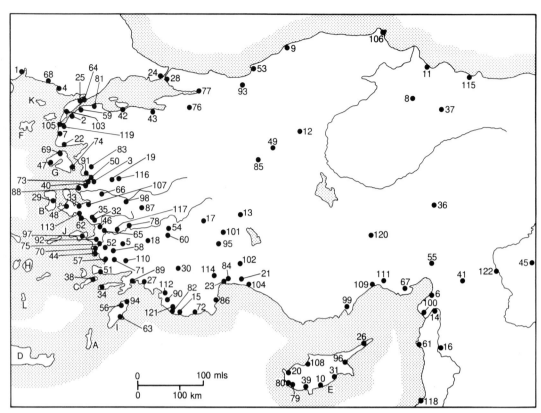

Fig. 4.17 *Main place-names of Asia Minor and Cyprus: A. Carpathus; B. Chios; C. Cos; D. Crete; E. Cyprus; F. Lemnos; G. Lesbos; H. Naxos; I. Rhodes; J. Samos; K. Samothrace; L. Thera. 1. Abdera; 2. Abydus; 3. Aegae; 4. Aenus; 5. Alabanda; 6. Alexandria ad Issum; 7. Alexandria Troas; 8. Amasea; 9. Amastris; 10. Amathus; 11. Amisus; 12. Ancyra; 13. Antioch in Pisidia; 14. Antioch (on the Orontes); 15. Antiphellus; 16. Apamea; 17. Apamea; 18. Aphrodisias; 19. Apollonis; 20. Arsinoë; 21. Aspendus; 22. Assus; 23. Attaleia; 24. Byzantium; 25. Cardia; 26. Carpasia; 27. Caunus; 28. Chalcedon; 29. Chios; 30. Cibyra; 31. Citium; 32. Clarus; 33. Clazomenae; 34. Cnidus; 35. Colophon; 36. Comana Cappadociae; 37. Comana Pontica; 38. Cos; 39. Curium; 40. Cyme; 41. Cyrrhus; 42. Cyzicus; 43. Dascylium; 44. Didyma; 45. Edessa; 46. Ephesus; 47. Eresus; 48. Erythrae; 49. Gordium; 50. Gryneum; 51. Halicarnassus; 52. Heraclea Latmus; 53. Heraclea Pontica; 54. Hierapolis; 55. Hieropolis Castabala; 56. Ialysus; 57. Iasus; 58. Labraunda; 59. Lampsacus; 60. Laodicea ad Lycum; 61. Laodicea ad Mare; 62. Lebedus; 63. Lindos; 64. Lysimachia; 65. Magnesia ad Maeandrum; 66. Magnesia ad Sipylum; 67. Mallus; 68. Maronea; 69. Methymna; 70. Miletus; 71. Mylasa; 72. Myra; 73. Myrina; 74. Mytilene; 75. Myus; 76. Nicaea; 77. Nicomedia; 78. Nysa; 79. Palaipaphos; 80. Paphos (Nea); 81. Parium; 82. Patara; 83. Pergamum; 84. Perge; 85. Pessinus; 86. Phaselis; 87. Philadelphia; 88. Phocaea; 89. Physcus; 90. Pinara; 91. Pitane; 92. Priene; 93. Prusias ad Hypium; 94. Rhodes; 95. Sagalassus; 96. Salamis; 97. Samos; 98. Sardis; 99. Seleucia ad Calycadnum; 100. Seleucia Pieria; 101. Seleucia Sidera; 102. Selge; 103. Sestus; 104. Side; 105. Sigeum; 106. Sinope; 107. Smyrna; 108. Soli; 109. Soli; 110. Stratonicea; 111. Tarsus; 112. Telmessus; 113. Teos; 114. Termessus; 115. Themiscyra; 116. Thyateira; 117. Tralles; 118. Tripolis; 119. Troy; 120. Tyana; 121. Xanthus; 122. Zeugma.*

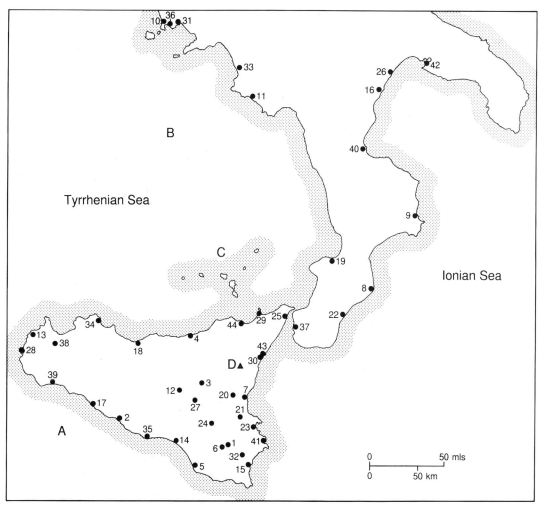

Fig. 4.18   Place-names of Sicily and Magna Graecia: A. Sicily; B. Magna Graecia; C. Lipari Islands; D. Mount Aetna; 1. Acrae; 2. Acragas; 3. Agyrium; 4. Caleacte; 5. Camarina; 6. Casmenae; 7. Catana; 8. Caulonia; 9. Croton; 10. Cumae; 11. Elea; 12. Enna; 13. Eryx; 14. Gela; 15. Helorus; 16. Heraclea; 17. Heraclea Minoa; 18. Himera; 19. Hipponium; 20. Hybla Geleatis; 21. Leontini; 22. Locri Epizephyrii; 23. Megara Hyblaea; 24. Menae; 25. Messana; 26. Metapontum; 27. Morgantina; 28. Motya; 29. Mylae; 30. Naxus; 31. Neapolis; 32. Netum; 33. Paestum; 34. Panormus; 35. Phintias; 36. Puteoli; 37. Rhegium; 38. Segesta; 39. Selinus; 40. Sybaris; 41. Syracuse; 42. Tarentum (Taras); 43. Tauromenium; 44. Tyndaris.

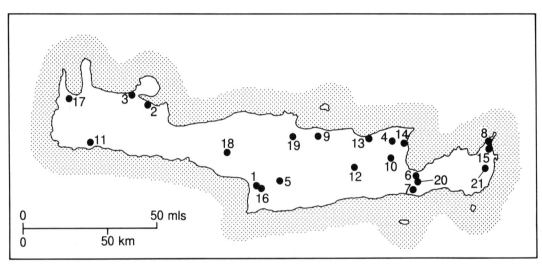

Fig. 4.19   Place-names of Crete: 1. Aghia Triadha; 2. Aptera; 3. Chania; 4. Drerus; 5. Gortyn; 6. Gournia; 7. Hieraptyna; 8. Itanus; 9. Knossos; 10. Lato; 11. Lissos; 12. Lyttos; 13. Mallia; 14. Olus; 15. Palaikastro; 16. Phaestus; 17. Polyrrhenia; 18. Sybrita; 19. Tylissus; 20. Vasiliki; 21. Zakros.

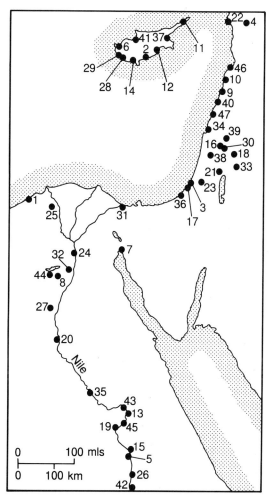

Fig. 4.20   Place-names of Egypt, Syria and Cyprus: 1. Alexandria; 2. Amathus; 3. Anthedon; 4. Apamea;
5. Apollinopolis Magna; 6. Arsinoë; 7. Arsinoë (Cleopatris); 8. Arsinoë (Crocodilopolis); 9. Berytus; 10. Byblus; 11.
Carpasia; 12. Citium; 13. Coptus; 14. Curium; 15. Eileithyia; 16. Gadara; 17. Gaza; 18. Gerasa; 19. Hermonthis;
20. Hermopolis Magna; 21. Jerusalem; 22. Laodicea ad Mare; 23. Marissa; 24. Memphis; 25. Naucratis; 26. Ombos;
27. Oxyrhynchus; 28. Palaipaphos; 29. Paphos (Nea); 30. Pella; 31. Pelusium; 32. Philadelphia; 33. Philadelphia; 34.
Ptolemais; 35. Ptolemais Hermiou; 36. Raphia; 37. Salamis; 38. Samaria; 39. Scythopolis; 40. Sidon; 41. Soli; 42.
Syene; 43. Tentyra; 44. Theadelphia; 45. Thebes; 46. Tripolis; 47. Tyre.

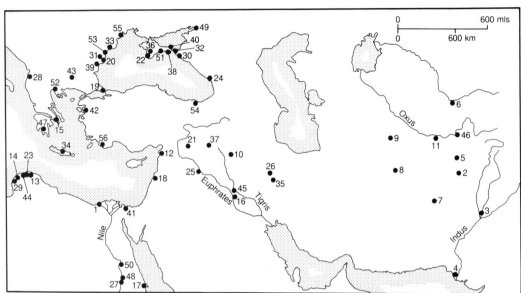

Fig. 4.21   Some major place-names in the Greek world (see also figs. 4.15–4.20): 1. Alexandria; 2. Alexandria (nr. Ghazni); 3. Alexandria (nr. Multan); 4. Alexandria (Patala); 5. Alexandria ad Caucasum; 6. Alexandria Eschate; 7. Alexandria in Arachosia; 8. Alexandria in Aria; 9. Alexandria in Margiana; 10. Alexandria of Mygdonia; 11. Alexandria Oxiana; 12. Antioch; 13. Apollonia; 14. Arsinoë (Taucheira); 15. Athens; 16. Babylon; 17. Berenice; 18. Berytus; 19. Byzantium; 20. Callatis; 21. Carrhae; 22. Chersonesus; 23. Cyrene; 24. Dioscurias; 25. Dura Europus; 26. Ecbatana; 27. Elephantine; 28. Epidamnus; 29. Euesperides; 30. Gorgippia; 31. Heraclea; 32. Hermonassa and Phanagoria (two sites); 33. Istrus; 34. Knossos; 35. Laodicea; 36. Neapolis Scythica; 37. Nisibis; 38. Nymphaeum; 39. Odessus; 40. Panticapaeum and Porthmeion (two sites); 41. Pelusium; 42. Pergamum; 43. Philippopolis; 44. Ptolemais; 45. Seleucia; 46. Seleucia on the Oxus; 47. Sparta; 48. Syene; 49. Tanais; 50. Thebes; 51. Theodosia; 52. Thessalonica; 53. Tomis; 54. Trapezus; 55. Tyras; 56. Xanthus.

PLACE-NAMES

Following is a list of major place-names in the Greek world (figs. 4.15–21). The name by which the place is usually known today is given first, generally the latinized or anglicized version. A transliteration of the ancient Greek name is given next, if known. This is followed by the modern place-name, which is often a transliteration of the modern Greek or Turkish. Many variant spellings are available for these transliterations, such as Eleusis, Elefsis and Elevsis. In addition, many modern places have changed their name to the ancient place-name in recent years. The final column provides the name of the country (or island in the case of Sicily and Crete) where the place is located.

Modern Version	Ancient Greek Version	Modern Place-Name	Country
Abae	Abai	nr. Exarcho	Greece
Abdera	Abdera	Avdira	Greece
Abydus	Abydos	nr. Canakkale	Turkey
Acanthus	Akanthos	Ierissos	Greece
Acrae	Akrai	Palazzuolo Acreide	Sicily
Acraephia	Akraiphia	Akraifnio, once Kardhitsa	Greece
Acragas (or Agrigentum)	Akragas	Agrigento	Sicily
Aedepsus	Aidepsos	Loutra Aidepsou	Greece
Aegae	Aigai	Vergina	Greece
Aegae	Aigai	Nemrud Kalesi	Turkey
Aegium	Aigion	Vostitsa	Greece
Aegosthena	Aigosthene	Aegosthena, once Porto Germano	Greece
Aenus	Ainos	Enez	Turkey
Aghia Triadha	unknown	Aghia Triadha	Crete
Agyrium	Agyrion	Agira	Sicily
Alabanda	Alabanda	nr. Saradar	Turkey
Alalia	Alalia	Aleria	Corsica
Alexandria in Arachosia	Alexandropolis	Qandahar	Afghanistan
Alexandria in Aria	Alexandreia Arion	Herat	Afghanistan
Alexandria	Alexandreia	nr. Ghazni	Afghanistan
Alexandria ad Caucasum	Alexandreia	nr. Kabul	Afghanistan
Alexandria Oxiana	Alexandreia	nr. Nakhshab	Afghanistan
Alexandria	Alexandreia	El-Iskandariya	Egypt
Alexandria	Alexandreia	possibly nr. Multan	India
Alexandria	Alexandreia	Patala	India
Alexandria of Mygdonia	Alexandreia	Arbil	Iraq
Alexandria the farthest, (Eschate), or Alexandria ad Tanais, later Antioch	Alexandreia Eskhate, later Antiokheia	nr. Khojend	Tajikistan
Alexandria ad Issum	Alexandreia	Iskenderun	Turkey
Alexandria Troas	Alexandreia (once Antigonia)	nr. Tenedos	Turkey
Alexandria in Margiana	Alexandreia	Merv	Turkmenistan
Aliphera	Alipheira	Alipheira	Greece
Amasia	Amaseia	Amasya	Turkey

Modern Version	Ancient Greek Version	Modern Place-Name	Country
Amastris	Amastris	Amasra	Turkey
Amathus	Amathous	nr. Limassol	Cyprus
Ambracia	Ambrakia	Arta	Greece
Ambracus	Ambrakos	Phidhokastro	Greece
Amisus	Amisos (also Peiraieus)	Samsun	Turkey
Amphipolis, once Nine Ways	Amphipolis, once Ennea Hodoi	Amphipole	Greece
Amphissa	Amphissa	Salona	Greece
Amyclae	Amyklai	Haghia Kyriaki	Greece
Ancyra	Ankyra	Ankara	Turkey
Anthedon	Anthedon	nr. Loukisia	Greece
Anthedon	Anthedon	Khirbet Teda	Israel
Anticyra	Antikyra	Antikhyra	Greece
Antioch (by Daphne or on the Orontes)	Antiokheia	Antakya	Turkey
Antioch in Pisidia	Antiokheia	nr. Yalvac	Turkey
Antiphellus	Antiphellos	Kas, once Andifli	Turkey
Apamea	Apameia	Qalaat al-Mudik	Syria
Apamea, once Celaenae	Apameia, once Kelainai	Dinar	Turkey
Aphidna	Aphidna	nr. Aphidnes	Greece
Aphrodisias	Aphrodisias	Geyre	Turkey
Apollinopolis Magna	Apollonos Polis	Idfu	Egypt
Apollonia	Apollonia	Pojani	Albania
Apollonia	Apollonia	Marsa Sousa	Libya
Apollonis	Apollonis	nr. Mecidiye	Turkey
Aptera	Aptera	Palaiokastro	Crete
Argos	Argos	Argos	Greece
Argos	Argos Amphilokhikon	nr. Loutron	Greece
Arsinoë, once Marium	Arsinoe, once Marion	nr. Polis	Cyprus
Arsinoë, once Crocodilopolis	Arsinoe, once Krokodilopolis	nr. Medinet-el-Fayum	Egypt
Arsinoë	Arsinoe, later Kleopatris	Ardscherud	Egypt
Arsinoë, once Taucheira	Arsinoe, once Taukheira	Tawqrah	Libya
Ascra	Askra	nr. Panayia (uncertain)	Greece
Asine	Asine	nr. Tolon	Greece
Aspendus	Aspendos	Belkis	Turkey
Assus	Assos	nr. Behramkale	Turkey
Athens	Athenai	Athina	Greece
Attaleia	Attaleia	Antalya	Turkey
Aulis	Aulis	Avlis	Greece
Babylon	Babylon (and Babylonia)	nr. Hillah	Iraq
Bassae	Bassai	Vasse	Greece
Berenice (of the Trogodytes)	Berenike	nr. Ras Benas	Egypt
Beroea	Beroia	Verria	Greece
Berytus	Berytos	Beirut	Lebanon
Brauron	Brauron	Vraona	Greece
Buthrotum	Bouthroton	Butrinto	Albania
Byblos/Byblus	Byblos	Jebeil	Lebanon
Byzantium	Byzantion	Istanbul	Turkey
Caleacte	Kalakta (or Kale Acte)	Caronia	Sicily
Callatis	Kallatis	Mangalia	Romania

Calydon	Kalydon	Kourtaga	Greece
Camarina	Kamarina	nr. Scoglitti	Sicily
Cardia	Kardia	nr. Gelibolu	Turkey
Carpasia	Karpasia	Haghios Philon	Cyprus
Carrhae	Karrhai	Altibasak, once Haran	Turkey
Carystus	Karystos	Palaichora	Greece
Casmenae	Kasmenai	Monte Casale	Sicily
Cassope	Kassope	Kamarina	Greece
Catana, later Aetna	Katane, later Aitne	Catania	Sicily
Caulonia	Kaulonia	nr. Punta di Stilo	Italy
Caunus	Kaunos	nr. Dalyan	Turkey
Cenchreae	Kenkhreai	nr. Paleo Skaphidaki	Greece
Cenchreae	Kenkhreai	nr. Corinth	Greece
Cephisia	Kephisia	Kephisia	Greece
Cerynia	Keryneia	Mamusia	Greece
Chaeronea	Khaironeia	nr. Khaironeia	Greece
Chalcedon or Calchedon	Khalkedon or Kalkhedon	Kadikoy	Turkey
Chalcis	Khalkis	Khalkida	Greece
Chania/Cydonia	Kydonia	Khania	Crete
Chersonesus	Khersonesos, or Kherronesos	nr. Sebastopol	Ukraine
Chios/Chius	Khios	Chios	Greece
Cibyra (Major)	Kibyra	Horzum	Turkey
Cirrha	Kirrha	Xeropigadi	Greece
Citium	Kition	Larnaca	Cyprus
Clarus	Klaros	nr. Ahmet-beyli	Turkey
Clazomenae	Klazomenai	Klazümen	Turkey
Cleitor	Kleitor	Kato Klitoria	Greece
Cleonae	Kleonai	nr. Mt. Athos	Greece
Cnidus	Knidos	Datca/Burgaz	Turkey
Colophon	Kolophon	Degirmendere	Turkey
Comana Cappadociae	Komana	Sar	Turkey
Comana Pontica	Komana	nr. Gümenek	Turkey
Copae	Kopai	nr. Stroviki	Greece
Coptus	Koptos	Keft	Egypt
Corinth	Korinthos	Korinthos	Greece
Coronea	Koroneia	Koroni	Greece
Cos	Kos	Kos	Greece
Crannon	Krannon	Palaio-Larisa	Greece
Crenides, later Philippi	Krenides, later Philippoi	Filippi	Greece
Creusa	Kreusa	Livadhostro	Greece
Croton	Kroton	Crotone	Italy
Cumae	Kyme	Cuma	Italy
Curium	Kourion	nr. Episkopi	Cyprus
Cyme	Kyme	uncertain (Euboea)	Greece
Cyme	Kyme	Namurtköy	Turkey
Cynaetha	Kynaitha	nr. Kalavryta	Greece
Cyrene	Kyrene	Shahhat	Libya
Cyrrhus	Kyrrhos	nr. Azaz	Syria
Cyzicus	Kyzikos	Belkis	Turkey
Damascus	Damaskos, later Demetrias	Esh-Sham	Syria
Dascylium	Daskyleion	Hisartepe	Turkey

Modern Version	Ancient Greek Version	Modern Place-Name	Country
Daulis	Daulis	Dhavlia	Greece
Decelea	Dekeleia	Dekelia	Greece
Delium	Delion	Dhilesi	Greece
Delphi	Delphi	Delfi	Greece
Demetrias	Demetrias	nr. Pagasai	Greece
Didyma, or Branchidae	Didyma, or Brankhidai	Didim, once Yoran	Turkey
Dioscurias	Dioskurias	Sukhumi	Georgia
Dium	Dion	nr. Malathria	Greece
Dodona	Dodone	Dodoni	Greece
Drerus	Dreros	nr. Neapolis	Crete
Drymaea	Drymaia	nr. Glounista	Greece
Dura Europus	Dura Europos	Qalat es-Salihiya	Syria
Ecbatana	Ekbatana, later Epiphaneia	Hamadan	Iran
Edessa	Edessa	Edessa, once Vodena	Greece
Edessa, later Antioch by the Callirhoe	Edessa, later Antiokheia Kalirrhoes	Urfa	Turkey
Eileithyia	Eileithyia	El-Kâb	Egypt
Eion	Eion	nr. Kerdilia	Greece
Elatea	Elateia	nr. Drachmani	Greece
Elea, later Velia	Elea/Yele	nr. Castellamare di Velia	Italy
Elephantine	Elephantis	nr. Aswan	Egypt
Eleusis	Eleusis	Elefsis	Greece
Eleutherae	Eleutherai	Gyphtokastro, or Myupolis	Greece
Elis	Elis	nr. Paliopolis	Greece
Emporiae	Emporion	Ampurias	Spain
Enna	Enna	Castrogiovanni	Sicily
Ephesus	Ephesos	nr. Selçuk	Turkey
Epidamnus, then Dyrrhachium	Epidamnos, then Dyrrakhion	Durrës	Albania
Epidaurus	Epidauros	Epidavros	Greece
Eresus	Eresos	Eresos	Greece
Eretria	Eretria	Eretria	Greece
Erythrae	Erythrai	Ildiri	Turkey
Eryx	Eryx	S. Giuliano	Sicily
Eu(h)esperides, later Berenice	Eu(h)esperides, later Berenike	Benghazi	Libya
Eurymenae	Eurymenai	Kastritsa	Greece
Gadara (also Antiochia, Seleucia)	Gadara (also Antiochia, Seleukeia)	Umm Qeis	Jordan
Gaza	Gaza	Gaza	Israel
Gela	Gela	Gela, once Terranova	Sicily
Gerasa, later Antiochia on the Chrysorrhoas	Gerasa, later Antiokheia	Jerash	Jordan
Gla or Gha	unknown	Gla	Greece
Glanum	Glanon	nr. St. Rémy	France
Gomphi	Gomphoi	nr. Muzaki	Greece
Gonnus	Gonnos	Gonni	Greece
Gordium	Gordion	Yassihüyük	Turkey
Gorgippia	Gorgippia	Anape	Russia

Gortyn(a)	Gortyn	Gortis	Crete
Gortys	Gortys	nr. Eliniko	Greece
Gournia	unknown	Gournia	Crete
Gryneum	Gryneion	Temasalik Burnu	Turkey
Gythium	Gytheion	Yithion	Greece
Haliartus	Haliartos	nr. Haliartos	Greece
Halicarnassus	Halikarnassos	Bodrum	Turkey
Halieis	Halieis	Porto Cheli	Greece
Halus	Halos	nr. Halmyrou	Greece
Helorus	Heloros	Eloro	Sicily
Heraclea Trachinia	Herakleia	nr. Lamia	Greece
Heraclea	Herakleia	Policoro	Italy
Heraclea Lynci	Herakleia Lynkestis	Bitola	Macedonia
Heraclea	Herakleia	Cernavoda	Romania
Heraclea Minoa	Herakleia Minoa	nr. Capo Bianco	Sicily
Heraclea on Latmus	Herakleia pros Latmo	nr. Bafa	Turkey
Heraclea Pontica, once Perinthus	Herakleia, once Perinthos	Eregli	Turkey
Hermione	Hermione	Hermione	Greece
Hermonassa	Hermonassa	Tamansk	Russia
Hermonthis	Hermonthis	Armant	Egypt
Hermopolis Magna	Hermou Polis Megale	Ashmûnein	Egypt
Hieraptyna	Hieraptyna	Ierapetra	Crete
Hieropolis/Hierapolis	Hieropolis/Hierapolis	Pamukkale	Turkey
Hieropolis Castabala	Hieropolis Kastabala	Bodrum	Turkey
Himera	Himera	Imera	Sicily
Hipponium	Hipponion	Vibo Valentia	Italy
Histiaea, later Oreus	Histiaia, later Oreos	Orei	Greece
Homolium	Homolion	nr. Laspochori	Greece
Hybla Geleatis	Hybla Geleatis	Paternò	Sicily
Hypata	Hypata	Hypati	Greece
Hysiae	Hysiai	nr. Achladokampos	Greece
Ialysus	Ialysos	nr. Ixia	Greece
Iasus, later Iassus	Iasos, later Iassos	Kiyi Kislacik	Turkey
Iolcus/Iolchus	Iolkos	nr. Volos	Greece
Issa	Issa	Vis	Croatia
Istrus	Istros	Histria	Romania
Itanus	Itanos	Eremoupolis	Crete
Jerusalem	Hierosolyma	Jerusalem	Israel
Joppa	Ioppe	Jaffa	Israel
Knossos/Cnossus	Knossos	Knossos	Crete
Labra(u)nda	Labra(u)nda	nr. Orta	Turkey
Lamia	Lamia	Lamia	Greece
Lampsacus	Lampsakos	Lapseki	Turkey
Laodicea, possibly Antioch in Persis	Laodikeia, possibly Antiokheia	nr. Nihavand	Iran
Laodicea ad Lycum	Laodikeia epi Luko (also Laodikeia tes Asias)	nr. Denizli	Turkey
Laodicea ad Mare	Laodikeia	Latakia	Syria
Larissa or Larisa	Larissa or Larisa	Larisa	Greece
Lato	Lato	nr. Haghios Nikalaos	Crete

Modern Version	Ancient Greek Version	Modern Place-Name	Country
Lebadea	Lebadeia	Levadhia	Greece
Lebedus, also Ptolemais	Lebedos, also Ptolemais	Doganbey	Turkey
Lechaeum	Lekhaion	nr. Corinth	Greece
Leontini	Leontinoi	Carlentini	Sicily
Lerna	Lerna	Myli	Greece
Leuctra	Leuktra	Lefktra, once Parapoungla	Greece
Lilaea	Lilaia	Kato Tithorea	Greece
Lindos	Lindos	Lindos	Greece
Lissos	Lisos	Agios Kyrkos	Crete
Locri Epizephyrii	Lokroi Epizephyrioi	nr. Gerace	Italy
Lusi	Lousoi	Kato Lousoi	Greece
Lysimachia	Lysimakheia	nr. Baklaburnu	Turkey
Lyttos	Lyttos	Xydas	Crete
Magnesia (ad Maeandrum)	Magnesia pros (or epi) Maiandron	nr. Ortaklar	Turkey
Magnesia (ad Sipylum)	Magnesia (pros Sipulo)	Manisa	Turkey
Mallia	Mallia	Malia	Crete
Mallus	Mallos	nr. Kiziltahta	Turkey
Mantinea, later Antignoeia	Mantineia, later Antignoeia	Mantinea	Greece
Marathon	Marathon	Plasi	Greece
Marissa	Marissa	Tell Sandahana	Israel
Maronea	Maroneia	Maronia	Greece
Massilia/Massalia	Massalia	Marseille	France
Mataurus	Matauros	Gioia Tauro	Italy
Megalopolis	Megalopolis	nr. Megalopolis	Greece
Megara	Megara	Megara	Greece
Megara (Hyblaea)	Megara	nr. Melilli	Sicily
Meliboea	Meliboia	nr. Polyendri	Greece
Melitaea	Meliteia	Meliteia, once Avaritsa	Greece
Memphis	Memphis	Mit Riheina	Egypt
Menae, later Menaenum	Menai, later Menainon	Mineo	Sicily
Mende	Mende	Kalandra	Greece
Messana, once Zancle	Messene, once Zankle	Messina	Sicily
Messene, once Ithome	Messene, once Ithome	Ithomi, nr. Mavromati	Greece
Metapontum	Metapontion	Metaponto	Italy
Methone (Macedonia)	Methone	Methone	Greece
Methone (Messenia)	Methone	Methone	Greece
Methymna	Methymna	Molybos	Greece
Metropolis	Metropolis	Mitropolis	Greece
Mieza	Mieza	nr. Edessa	Greece
Miletus	Miletos	Balat	Turkey
Morgantina (Murgantia)	Morgantina	Serra Orlando	Sicily
Motya	Motya	Mozia/S. Pantaleo	Sicily
Mycalessus	Mykalessos	Rhitsona	Greece
Mycenae, or Mycene	Mykenai, or Mykene	Mikini	Greece
Mylae	Mylai	Milazzo	Sicily
Mylasa	Mylasa	Milâs	Turkey
Myra	Myra	Kale, Demre	Turkey

Myrina	Myrina	Koca Cay	Turkey
Mytilene or Mitylene	Mytilene or Mitylene	Mitilini	Greece
Myus	Myous	nr. Avsar	Turkey
Naples	Neapolis	Napoli	Italy
Naucratis	Naukratis	Kom Gieif	Egypt
Naupactus	Naupaktos	Lepanto/Nafpaktos	Greece
Nauplia	Nauplia	Nauplio	Greece
Naxus	Naxos	Punta di Schisò	Sicily
Neapolis	Neapolis	Kavala	Greece
Neapolis Scythica	Neapolis	nr. Simferopol	Ukraine
Nemea	Nemea	Nemea	Greece
Netum (or Neetum)	Neeton	Noto	Sicily
Nicaea	Antigoneia, later Nikaia	Iznik	Turkey
Nicaea	Nikaia	Nice	France
Nicomedia	Nikomedeia	Ismid	Turkey
Nisibis	Nisibis	Nusaybin	Turkey
Nymphaeum	Nymphaion	nr. Geroevka	Ukraine
Nysa, once Athymbra	Nysa	Sultanhisar	Turkey
Odessus	Odessos	Varna	Bulgaria
Oeanthe(i)a, later Euanthe(i)a	Oiantheia	nr. Vitrinitsa	Greece
Oeniadae	Oiniadai	nr. Astrakos	Greece
Oloosson	Oloosson	Elassona	Greece
Olus	Olous	nr. Elounda	Crete
Olympia	Olympia	Olimbia	Greece
Olynthus	Olynthos	nr. Miriofita	Greece
Ombos	Ombos	Kom-Ombo	Egypt
Onchestus	Onchestos	nr. Aliartos	Greece
Opus	Opous	nr. Kiparissi	Greece
Orchomenus (in Boeotia)	Orkhomenos	Orchomenos (once Skripou)	Greece
Orchomenus (in Arcadia)	Orkhomenos	Kalpali	Greece
Orminium	Orminion	Goritsa	Greece
Oropus	Oropos	Skala Oropou	Greece
Oxyrhynchus	Oxyrynkhos	Bahnasa	Egypt
Paeanium	Paianion	nr. Mastru	Greece
Paestum	Poseidonia	Pesto	Italy
Pagasae	Pagasai	nr. Volo	Greece
Palaikastro	Dikta?	Palekastro	Crete
Pallantium	Pallantion	nr. Tripolis	Greece
Panormus	Panormos	Palermo	Sicily
Panticapaeum	Pantikapaion	Kerch	Ukraine
Paphos (Palaepaphos)	Paphos (Palaipaphos)	Kouklia	Cyprus
Paphos (Nea Paphos)	Paphos (Paphos Nea)	Kato Paphos	Cyprus
Parium	Parion	Kemer	Turkey
Passaron	Passaron	Radotovi	Greece
Patara	Patara	Kelemis	Turkey
Patrae	Patrai	Patras	Greece
Pelinna	Pelinna	Palaiogardiki	Greece
Pella	Pella	Khirbet Fahil	Jordan
Pella	Pella	Pella	Greece

Modern Version	Ancient Greek Version	Modern Place-Name	Country
Pellene	Pellene	nr. Zougra	Greece
Pelusium	Pelousion	Tell Farama	Egypt
Perachora	Peiraion	Perahora	Greece
Pergamum	Pergamon	Bergama	Turkey
Perge	Perge	nr. Aksu	Turkey
Pessinus	Pessinous	Balhisar	Turkey
Phaestus	Phaistos	Festos	Crete
Phalara	Phalara	Stylida	Greece
Phanagoria	Phanagoreia	Taman	Russia
Pharsalus	Pharsalos	Farsala	Greece
Phaselis	Phaselis	Tekirova	Turkey
Pheneus	Pheneos	nr. Kalivia	Greece
Pherae	Pherai	Velestinou	Greece
Phigalia	Phigalia	Phigaleia	Greece
Philadelphia	Philadelpheia	Darb Gerze	Egypt
Philadelphia	Philadelpheia	Amman	Jordan
Philadelphia	Philadelpheia	Alâshir	Turkey
Philippopolis	Philippopolis	Plovdiv	Bulgaria
Phintias	Phintias	Licata	Sicily
Phlius	Phlious	nr. Andonia	Greece
Phocaea	Phokaia	Foça	Turkey
Phoenice	Phoinike	nr. Sarande	Albania
Phyle	Phyle	Phyle	Greece
Physcus	Physkos	Marmaris	Turkey
Pinara	Pinara	Minare Köyü	Turkey
Piraeus	Peiraieus	Peiraias	Greece
Pitane	Pitane	Canderli	Turkey
Plataea	Plataiai	Plataies	Greece
Pleuron	Pleuron	nr. Messolongi	Greece
Polyrrhenia	Polyrrhenia	Polyrrhinia, once Epano Palaeokastro	Crete
Porthmeion	Porthmeion	nr. Zhukovka	Ukraine
Potidaea, later Cassandrea	Poteidaia, later Kassendreia	Nea Poteidaia	Greece
Priene	Priene	Turunçlar	Turkey
Prusias ad Hypium	Prusias	Üskübü	Turkey
Psophis	Psophis	nr. Tripotama	Greece
Ptolemais, once Ace	Ptolemais, once Ake	Acre	Israel
Ptolemais	Ptolemais	Tolmeta	Libya
Ptolemais Hermiou	Ptolemais Hermeiou	El-Manshah	Egypt
Puteoli	Pouteoloi	Pozzuoli	Italy
Pydna	Pydna	nr. Makrygialos	Greece
Pylos	Pylos	Palaiokastro	Greece
Raphia	Raphia	Rafah	Israel
Rhamnus	Rhamnous	Ramnous	Greece
Rhegium	Rhegion	Reggio di Calabria	Italy
Rhodes	Rhodos	Rodhos	Greece
Sagalassus	Sagalassos	Aglasun	Turkey
Salamis	Salamis	Salamis	Cyprus
Salamis	Salamis	Salamis	Greece

Samaria	Samaria	Shomeron	Israel
Same	Same	Sami	Greece
Samos	Samos	Tigani/Pythagoreia	Greece
Sardis/Sardes	Sardis/Sardeis	Sartmustafa	Turkey
Scillus	Skillous	nr. Krestaina	Greece
Scione	Skione/Skioni	nr. Paliuri	Greece
Scotussa	Skotoussa	nr. Soupli	Greece
Scythopolis	Skythopolis	Beth Shean	Israel
Segesta	Egesta	nr. Calatafimi	Sicily
Seleucia on Tigris	Seleukeia	Tell Umar	Iraq
Seleucia Pieria	Seleukeia Pieria	nr. Magharadjek	Turkey
Seleucia on the Oxus	Seleukeia	Aï Khanum	Afghanistan
Seleucia ad Calycadnum	Seleukeia	Silifke	Turkey
Seleucia Sidera	Seleukeia Sidera	Selef	Turkey
Selge	Selge	Sirk	Turkey
Selinus	Selinous	Selinunte	Sicily
Sellasia	Sellasia	nr. Palaiogulas (uncertain)	Greece
Sestus	Sestos	Akbasi	Turkey
Sicyon	Sikyon	Basiliko	Greece
Side	Side	Selimiye, once Eski Antalya	Turkey
Sidon	Sidon	Saida	Lebanon
Sigeum	Sigeion	nr. Yeniseri	Turkey
Sinope	Sinope	Sinop	Turkey
Smyrna	Smyrna	Izmir	Turkey
Soli	Soloi	Mezitli	Turkey
Soli	Soloi	Potamos tou Kambou	Cyprus
Sounion/Sunium	Sounion	Sounion	Greece
Sparta or Lacedaemon	Sparte or Lakedaimon	Sparti	Greece
Sphacteria	Sphakteria	Sfaktiria	Greece
Stagirus, later Stagira	Stageiros	Stayira	Greece
Stratonicea	Stratonikeia	Eskihisar	Turkey
Stratus	Stratos	Surovigli	Greece
Stymphalus	Stymphalos	Stymphalia	Greece
Sybaris, later Thurii	Sybaris, later Thourioi	nr. Sibari	Italy
Sybrita	Sybrita	Thronos	Crete
Syene	Syene	Aswan	Egypt
Syracuse	Syrakousai	Siracusa	Sicily
Tanagra	Tanagra	nr. Tanagra	Greece
Tanais	Tanais	nr. Taganrog	Russia
Tarentum	Taras	Taranto	Italy
Tarsus, later Antiochia	Tarsos, later Antiokheia	Tarsus	Turkey
Tauromenium	Tauromenion	Taormina	Sicily
Tegea	Tegea	nr. Tegea	Greece
Telmessus	Telmessos	Fethiye	Turkey
Tenea	Tenea	nr. Chiliomodhion	Greece
Tentyra	Tentyra	Dendera	Egypt
Teos	Teos	Sigacik	Turkey
Termessus	Termessos	Güllük Dag	Turkey

Modern Version	Ancient Greek Version	Modern Place-Name	Country
Thasos	Thasos	Thasos	Greece
Thaumaci	Thaumakoi	Dhomoko	Greece
Theadelphia	Theadelpheia	Batn-Ihrît	Egypt
Thebes Phthiae	Thebai Phthiotides	Mikrothivai, once Akitsi	Greece
Thebes	Thebai	Thivai	Greece
Thebes	Thebai	Luxor	Egypt
Themiscyra	Themiskyra	Terme	Turkey
Theodosia	Theodosia	Feodosya	Ukraine
Therapne	Therapnai	nr. Sparta	Greece
Thermopylae	Thermopylai	Thermopoli	Greece
Thermum	Thermon or Thermos	Thermon, once Kephalovrisi	Greece
Thespiae	Thespiai	Thespiai, once Erimokastro	Greece
Thessalonica (or Salonica)	Therme, later Thessalonike	Thessaloniki	Greece
Thisbe	Thisbe	Thisvi, once Kakosia	Greece
Thoricus	Thorikos	Thorikhos	Greece
Thyateira	Thyateira	Akhisar	Turkey
Tiryns	Tiryns	Tirins	Greece
Tithorea	Tithorea	Velitsa	Greece
Tomis	Tomis	Constanta	Romania
Tralles, later Seleucia	Tralleis, later Seleukeia	Aydin	Turkey
Trapezus	Trapezous	Trabzon	Turkey
Tricca	Trikka	Trikkala	Greece
Tripolis	Tripolis	Tripoli	Lebanon
Troezen	Troizen	Trizin	Greece
Troy/Ilium	Ilion	Hisarlik	Turkey
Tyana, later Eusebeia	Tyana, later Eusebeia	nr. Kemerhisar	Turkey
Tylissus	Tylissos	Tylisos	Crete
Tyndaris	Tyndaris	Tindari	Sicily
Tyras	Tyras	Belgorod Dniestrovsky	Ukraine
Tyre/Tyrus	Tyros	Es-Sur	Lebanon
Vasiliki	unknown	Vasiliki	Crete
Xanthus	Xanthos	Kinik	Turkey
Zakros	possibly Zakros	nr. Kato Zakros	Crete
Zeugma	Zeugma	Balkis	Syria

Islands

Modern Version	Ancient Greek Version	Modern Place-Name	Country
Aegina	Aigina	Aiyina	Greece
Amorgos	Amorgos	Amorgos	Greece
Andros	Andros	Andros	Greece
Carpathus	Karpathos	Karpathos	Greece
Ceos	Keos	Kea/Tzia	Greece
Cephallenia	Kephallenia	Kephallonia	Greece
Chios/Pityussa	Khios/Pityoussa	Khios	Greece

Corcyra	Kerkyra	Kerkira/Corfu	Greece
Cos	Kos	Kos	Greece
Crete	Krete	Krete	Greece
Cyprus	Kupros	Cyprus	Cyprus
Cythera	Kythera	Kithira	Greece
Delos	Delos	Dilos	Greece
Euboea	Euboia	Euboia	Greece
Ithaca	Ithake	Ithaki/Thiaki	Greece
Lemnos	Lemnos	Limnos	Greece
Lesbos	Lesbos	Lesbos	Greece
Leucas	Leukas	Lefkas	Greece
Melos	Melos	Melos	Greece
Naxos	Naxos	Naxos	Greece
Paros	Paros	Paros	Greece
Pithecusae	Pithekoussai	Ischia	Italy
Rhodes	Rhodos	Rhodos	Greece
Salamis	Salamis	Salamina	Greece
Samos	Samos	Samos	Greece
Samothrace	Samothrake	Samothraki	Greece
Sciathus	Skiathos	Skiathos	Greece
Scyrus/Scyros	Skyros	Skyros	Greece
Siphnus/os	Siphnos	Siphnos	Greece
Syrus	Syros	Siros	Greece
Tenos	Tenos	Tenos	Greece
Thasos	Thasos	Thasos	Greece
Thera	Thera	Santorini	Greece
Zacynthus	Zakynthos	Zakynthos	Greece

Seas

The name Adriatic (*Adrias*) described the gulf separating Italy and the Balkan Peninsula, including the sea east of Sicily. The term Ionian Sea (*Ionios*) was often used synonymously for the Adriatic, although later it came to mean just the sea from western Greece to Sicily and southern Italy. The Adriatic Sea was also described as the Ionian Gulf. The Aegean Sea (*Aigaios pontos*) was between Greece and Asia Minor down to Crete (or down to Thera, according to some ancient writers). The Euxine Sea was Pontos Euxeinos, from *euxeinos* (hospitable), a euphemistic name for the stormy Black Sea, which some authors called *axeinos* (inhospitable). The Bosphorus (or Bosporus) is a narrow strait joining the Euxine to the Propontis. This was different from the Cimmerian Bosphorus, which linked the Black Sea to the Sea of Azov (Lake Maeotis, *Maiotis*).

READING

Landscape

Hammond and Scullard (eds.) 1970, 477–478; Dickinson 1994, 23–29; Myers et al. 1992, 16–32: Crete; Pritchett 1965, 1969, 1980, 1982, 1985, 1989, 1991c, 1992: detailed topographical studies, relating in particular to towns and military campaigns.

City-States and Colonies

Boardman 1980: well-illustrated account of colonies; Boersma 1970: buildings of Athens; Graham 1964: colonization; Hammond and Scullard (eds.) 1970, 140–142: Athens; Holloway 1981: large section on Greek Sicily; Jeffery 1976: major source for city-states and colonies; Tomlinson 1992, 44–72: Athens and Piraeus, 96–108: Alexandria.

Regions

Buck 1979: Boeotia; Dawkins (ed.) 1929: Sparta's sanctuary of Artemis Orthia; Grant 1986: gazetteer includes descriptions of many regions; Hammond 1989: Macedonia; Sealey 1976: includes discussions of various regions; Whitehead 1986: demes of Attica.

Place-Names

Bell 1989: gazetteer of places with mythological associations; Burn and Burn 1980: descriptions of many places in Greece; Grant 1986: gazetteer and description of place names; Hammond 1981: several maps; Hammond and Scullard (eds.) 1970: includes discussion of the history of many places; Hope Simpson and Dickinson 1979: gazetteer of Bronze Age sites in the Greek islands and mainland; Levi 1971a and b: translation and commentary on Pausanias' visits to numerous places in central and southern Greece in 2nd century AD; Levi 1984: numerous maps; Myers et al. 1992: places in Crete; Schoder 1974: aerial views and explanations of many sites in Greece; Stillwell (ed.) 1976: description of numerous places, each with further reading; Talbert (ed.) 1985: numerous maps with text.

5

ECONOMY,
TRADE AND
TRANSPORT

ECONOMY AND INDUSTRY

The ancient Greek economy was primarily agricultural from at least the Bronze Age (when evidence is sparse). There was an expanding economy and increasing trade that lasted until the Dark Age disrupted this prosperity. From the 8th to the 3rd centuries BC the Greek world expanded greatly in geographical size, total population and total wealth. With some states richer than others and a large gap between the richest and poorest members of society, the expansion was uneven. The people who had least were the slaves.

The growth of towns and cities also affected the economy, encouraging crafts and trade. In many states endemic warfare also stimulated an expansion of the economy. Industry in the modern sense did not exist. Most goods were produced by local craftsmen, and industries were like large well-organized crafts. Crafts were labor-intensive, often very skilled and usually localized. Industries varied in their organization, from large-scale production for goods that were traded extensively to very small-scale production to meet local needs. Although quantity of output may not have been high, the quality of goods was often very high.

Very little is known of the working population. Slaves undertook a variety of work, including that of skilled craftsmen, but free citizens, metics and perioeci might also have been craftsmen, perhaps working in small family businesses. It is thought that some skilled craftsmen, such as construction workers on large public buildings, traveled from job to job. A large proportion of labor was slave labor, but with a few exceptions, both slave labor and free labor were engaged in the same occupations. Throughout the Greek period there was extremely little technical innovation that affected economic output, and labor-saving devices were rarely introduced.

Agriculture

The varied landscape determined the location of agriculture. The mountains of mainland Greece with prevailing westerly winds caused the highest rainfall to be in the west. Eastern Greece and the islands between Greece and Turkey were relatively arid, but the west coast of Turkey and nearby islands, such as Rhodes and Samos, were less so. Rainfall was often in the form of heavy downpours rather than steady light rain, making agriculture difficult, particularly cereal growing. Eighty percent of the country was mountainous, so agriculture was practiced in the plains and the small pockets of lower land between the mountains. Colonies were generally established in areas with good agricultural land, especially for growing grain. Agriculture was a major industry and was carried out by the inhabitants of towns and cities, as well as people living in isolated farms and villages. Market gardening also appears to have been widespread.

CROP PRODUCTION

Grain was an important crop, although there were relatively few areas where it could be grown successfully because of unsuitable climate and terrain. Wheat, emmer and barley were cultivated, and sowing was normally in the autumn, although some spring sowing took place for fast-ripening crops or as an emergency measure when the autumn sowing had not taken place or had failed. Millet was also grown. A crop rotation leaving land fallow for a year between crops appears to have been practiced, especially in the drier areas, allowing some fallow land to preserve moisture. The fallow land was plowed several times in the months before sowing took place. Seed grain was sown by hand from a container such as a sack or basket, and the seed could be covered by hoeing. Between sowing and harvesting some hoeing and weeding took place. With the variations in land and climate, there must have been great variations in the yield of cereal crops.

Another important crop was the vine. The grapes were mainly used for wine production, although some were eaten and some appear to have been dried as raisins. Once a vineyard was established, grapes were a perennial crop. The vines were tended throughout the year with pruning in winter and spring. Vines were either freestanding or were supported by stakes or other trees. The ground between the vines was often planted with other crops such as barley or beans.

The third most important crop was olives. It is uncertain how olive trees were initially grown—probably by cuttings and/or grafting. Olive trees

live for a long time, and once established they produce a regular crop with relatively little effort. Old
trees could be rejuvenated by cutting them down
and allowing shoots from the stump to form a new
tree. Olive trees required pruning, but apparently
not annually, and the ground around them was
tilled. The olives were picked from autumn until
early spring (fig. 5.1).

Various other fruit and nut trees were cultivated.
Apples, pears, plums, pomegranates, figs, almonds
and quinces were grown in orchards, but there is
little detailed evidence about their cultivation.
Some fruits such as figs, apples and pears were
sometimes dried to preserve them for storage. Nuts
from wild hazel, walnut and chestnut trees also
seem to have been harvested.

A variety of other crops were grown, such as
peas, beans, lentils, cabbage, onions, garlic, celery,
cucumbers, lettuces, leeks, artichokes, carrots,
pumpkins, beets and turnips, but it is unclear
whether they were grown on a large scale or as
market garden crops. Herbs appear to have been
gathered mainly from the wild rather than cultivated in the garden.

PLOWING AND HOEING

Plowing was usually done with an ard, which was a
simple plow without a coulter or moldboard. It was
drawn by one or two draft animals, normally oxen,
but in Homer's *Iliad* plowing with a team of mules
is mentioned. Such plows scratched a furrow, rather
than turned the soil over, and cross-plowing (plowing a second time at right angles) would have been
needed to provide a good seed bed. There is evidence that fields (particularly fallow fields) were
plowed several times to break up and air the topsoil
and to destroy weeds.

Land was also tilled using hoes, of which there
were several types, including two-pronged hoes and
broad-bladed hoes. Heavy hoes could be used instead of, or in addition to, the plow to break up the
topsoil, while lighter hoes were for weeding and
tilling after the crops had been sown. Little evidence exists for the use of spades.

OTHER TOOLS

Tools such as saws, hammers, knives, sickles, reaping hooks and bill hooks were also used in agriculture, and various containers, particularly baskets,

*Fig. 5.1 Picking of olives by beating the tree with
sticks. The olives are placed in a basket.*

were used in harvesting crops. As today, the division
between agricultural tools and general-purpose
tools is often difficult to define.

HARVESTING

Grain was harvested with a sickle or reaping hook.
These were like curved knives, and it is sometimes
difficult to distinguish them from pruning knives.
Once cut, the crop was transported to a threshing
floor, a circular area with a hard surface, often carefully paved with stones and with a low raised rim.
The crop was threshed by being trampled by draft
animals to break the grain from the husks. Usually
the animals were hitched to a pole set in the center
of the threshing floor, around which they walked as
the crop was strewn under their hooves. The resulting grain and chaff were separated by winnowing,
using a basket or shovel to throw the mixture into
the wind, so that the grain fell and the chaff blew
away. Other crops were harvested by hand, perhaps
aided by a knife.

ANIMAL HUSBANDRY

Ancient authors do not provide a great deal of information about farm animals, and evidence from
other sources is also sparse. Goats and sheep appear
to have been common in many areas, providing
milk, cheese and meat. Sheep also provided wool.
Pigs were raised for their meat, and poultry provided eggs. Horses were a luxury and a status symbol and were used only in battle, for racing and
sometimes for transport. Oxen, donkeys and mules

were bred as draft and transport animals. Cattle were mainly used for producing oxen and not for milk, since the Greeks preferred milk and milk products derived from sheep and goats. Bees were kept to provide honey, which was also gathered from hives of wild bees.

Because of the varying terrain, some areas were much more favorable to animal husbandry than others. Sheep, goats and, to a lesser extent, pigs were found almost everywhere. Thessaly and the Peloponnese were particularly known for horses, oxen, sheep and goats, while Euboea and Boeotia were noted for oxen, and Arcadia for sheep and mules. Transhumance was practiced, with herds of cattle and sheep exploiting mountain pastures in summer and lowland pastures in winter. However, there is little indication of the extent to which transhumance was practiced, or the areas in which it took place.

Sick animals were usually treated by the farmers, but there were veterinarians (*hippiatrikoi*) who could provide medical and surgical treatment to animals if required.

Hunting

The meat element in the diet was supplemented by hunting, but there is little evidence of its importance. Hunting was also regarded as a sport and entertainment, with apparently little or no restriction on who could hunt and what animals could be hunted. Various types of hunting are depicted in vase paintings and are described by ancient authors. Packs of dogs, nets, snares and bows and arrows were all used to catch wild animals, including birds, hare, deer and wild boar.

Fishing

Fish and other seafood were an important source of food, and a great variety of fish were consumed. Some types were gourmet dishes for the rich, while others were the staple diet of the poor. The majority of fish eaten were from the sea; freshwater fishing was relatively unproductive, although Lake Copais in Boeotia was known for its eels. Because of the difficulties in keeping fish fresh, there was no

wholesale trade in fresh fish. Coastal fishermen supplied only their local markets. Some fish, particularly tunny, was preserved by salting and drying and could be traded over a wider area. Some ancient authors give the impression that the Greeks were averse to fish, preferring roast meat, but this probably reflects the fact that roast joints of meat were a relatively expensive luxury, whereas cheaper fish was often the meat of the poor.

Food Processing

MILLS AND BAKING

The milling of grain into flour was initially a household occupation. Saddle querns were originally used. Grain was placed on a flat quernstone and was crushed by rubbing another stone back and forth over it. Rotary querns and mills were later developed. Rotary hand querns consisted of an upper concave stone and a lower convex one. Grain was fed through an aperture in the upper stone, which was simultaneously rotated. Although household milling and baking continued throughout the Greek period, commercial milling and baking were separate occupations by the 6th century BC. By the 2nd century BC these two occupations had merged. Large rotary mills powered by donkeys and mules became increasingly common.

To separate the flour from the bran, the meal was sieved. Flour that was finely sieved produced the best quality bread; coarsely sieved or unsieved flour produced lower-quality breads. The dough was kneaded in troughs, and there are records of bakers taking measures to prevent the slaves who were kneading the dough from contaminating it. Baking was done in simple ovens of fired clay, supported on legs, leaving room for a fire underneath. Various types of bread (both leavened and unleavened), biscuits, cakes and pastries were produced.

WINE PRODUCTION

Wine production was a major industry, giving rise to an export trade throughout the Greek world. Much of the grape harvest was used for wine. The grapes were collected in large wickerwork baskets and were either trodden in a vat or squeezed on a pressing board. The latter was a flat hard wood or stone surface with a spout, on which an open basket or sack of grapes was placed. This was trodden and squashed, so that the grape juice was separated from the grape skins and seeds; the grape juice ran down from the spout and was collected in a container. Juice recovered by treading made the best quality wine. More juice was then removed by using a simple mechanical press like that used for pressing olives. Juice from a second pressing, mixed with water, produced an inferior wine that was drunk only by the very poor.

The grape juice was fermented in large storage jars (*pithoi*), and the resulting wine was transferred to wine jars (amphorae). Perfumes and unguents were added to some wines to make them more highly flavored and increase their price.

OLIVE OIL PRODUCTION

To produce olive oil the flesh of the olives had to be crushed without crushing the kernels, which would give the oil a bitter taste. At some time during the Greek period a mill was invented for crushing olives, but it is not referred to by writers until the Roman period, when it is called a *trapetum*. It consisted of a large stone saucer with a central pillar, which supported the pivot for one or two millstones that could be rolled around the saucer to crush the olives (fig. 5.2). How olives were crushed before the invention of this mill is unknown, although the use of a roller, a mortar and pestle, or trampling with heavy shoes are all possibilities.

After crushing, the olives were pressed to extract the oil. This could be done by various means, such as placing a heavy weight on bags or baskets of olives. A simple mechanical press was also used, consisting of a large wooden beam that was anchored at one end and acted as a lever. Crushed olives were placed in a permeable container (possibly of cloth) on a hard surface beneath the lever, and the other end of the lever was forced downward to squash the container and its contents. This was done by ropes and levers, or a screw mechanism in Hellenistic times. The pressing was usually done on a wooden or stone pressing bed, with a channel and spout to collect the oil. Olive oil was used for various purposes, including food, lighting fuel, medicaments and skin oils.

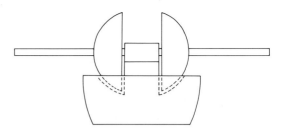

Fig. 5.2 A diagram of a trapetum *(olive mill), with stone saucer and two millstones.*

Salt

Salt was obtained by evaporating sea water or water from inland salt springs, since Greece has no deposits of rock salt that can be mined. The salt water was evaporated by the sun in shallow lagoons and was collected from the resulting salt pan. Megara specialized in salt production, and the best quality salt was produced there, as well as in Crete and Euboea. Salt appears to have been produced on the coasts of many other states. In addition to being used locally, it was traded inland to areas where salt production was not possible. Salt was used largely for preservation of foods.

Leather

Leather was produced from animal skins by a series of processes known collectively as tanning. The exact combination of processes depends on the type of leather. The raw hides had to be treated to prevent bacterial decay before they reached the tanyard. This was usually done by salting, but sometimes hides were merely sun dried, or they might be salted after drying. At the tanyard the hides were soaked in a solution, such as a mixture of urine and mulberry leaves, to make them more receptive to the tanning liquids and to loosen wool and hair, which were removed by scraping off the top layer of the hide (epidermis). Similarly, fat was scraped from the inner surface of the skin to leave the corium or derma that is made into leather. The hide was then tanned by soaking in a solution of wood and bark or a solution of alum and salt. A third method of tanning was treating the hide with oil or fat.

After tanning, leather underwent various processes, known collectively as finishing, to produce leather of the desired color, texture and surface appearance. Leather was an important material throughout the Greek world, used for a wide range of articles, such as saddles, shoes, harnesses, shields and some clothing. Leather articles were decorated in several ways. The leather could be cut into patterned shapes, such as on openwork sandals. Patterns could also be made with stamps and punches to produce pierced or relief designs, and leather could be colored by dyeing or painting. The supply of cowhide in particular was limited, and all leather was expensive. Parchment was also made from the skins of cattle, sheep and goats (see chapter 7).

Textiles

Most textiles were produced in the home. One of the principal occupations of women was making clothes, blankets, spreads and other cloths for the family, and this included spinning the yarn and weaving it into cloth. However, some processes of textile manufacturing, such as fulling, were carried out on a commercial basis by men, and some tex-

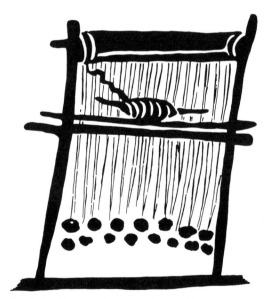

Fig. 5.3 Various elements of the upright loom, as depicted on a black-figure vase, including the vertical warp threads with weights.

tiles, such as cloaks, fine fabrics and cheap clothing for slaves, were produced commercially as well. Miletus was well known for its textiles and Megara for the production of cloaks.

Wool seems to have been the first fiber used for textiles. Linen made from flax was later introduced, probably from Egypt or the Near East, and by the time of Alexander the Great (and possibly as early as the 5th century BC) silk garments and cocoons of raw silk were being imported from the Far East. The manufacture of cloth consisted of three basic processes: fiber preparation, spinning and weaving.

FIBER PREPARATION

Raw wool sheared from the sheep was washed, and then the matted fibers were pulled apart and impurities removed by hand to produce a loose mass of fibers. Women did this over their knees with their feet propped up on a footstool, using a semicircular terra-cotta shield (*epinetron*) to protect their knees and thighs.

Flax was harvested in high summer by pulling up the complete flax plant by hand. The flax was retted by soaking it in stagnant or slow-flowing water for about three weeks, after which it was dried, pounded with a wooden mallet, and scutched. In scutching, the flax was bent over a narrow object and beaten with a wooden sword to loosen and separate the fibers. The fibers were combed (hackled) to remove impurities.

Cultivated silk imported from the Far East was a single fiber which did not need spinning. In the Hellenistic period mulberry trees were planted on the island of Cos, and wild silk was produced. It is likely that this silk was in short lengths and would have been spun, but otherwise no preparation was needed.

SPINNING

Spinning was a labor-intensive occupation, but the quality of the finished yarn could be almost equivalent to modern machine-spun yarn. Spinning was done with a spindle and a distaff, which was held in the hand. In its simplest form, the distaff was a forked stick supporting a mass of fibers. To spin yarn, fibers were drawn out from this mass and twisted into a thread, which was tied to the top of the spindle, which could have a hook for fastening. The spindle was a wooden or bone rod up to 8 in

(200 mm) long, thicker toward the lower end to hold a spindle whorl. Spindle whorls were of various materials, commonly stone, bone or pottery. They acted as flywheels to aid the rotation of the spindle. The spindle was set spinning, and fibers were drawn out by hand to add to the lengthening thread. When the spindle reached the floor, the thread was wound onto it, and the process was repeated.

WEAVING

The warp-weighted vertical loom (fig. 5.3) consisted of two wooden uprights with a horizontal beam across the top and a shed rod farther down to separate even and odd-numbered warp threads. This created the gap (shed) through which the horizontal weft thread was passed. A heddle-rod brought the odd-numbered warp threads back and forth to alternate the shed, so that the weft thread could be passed through as a single movement. The vertical warp threads were weighted with stone or baked clay weights (loomweights).

DYEING AND FULLING

It was more usual to dye unspun fiber than yarn or finished cloth. Vegetable dyes were common, but the highly prized and expensive purple dye came from two species of sea snail (*purpura* and *murex brandaris*), which were native to the coasts of Syria and Phoenicia. Yellow, also a popular color, was derived from saffron and red from madder. Violet could be otained from an insect similar to the Mexican cochineal insect.

Cloth was finished by fulling, which involved removing grease and dirt by treading it in a tub containing a solution of natron (natural soda from a deposit near Cairo in Egypt) or more commonly decayed urine. Fulling was then completed with fuller's earth, and the cloth was subsequently washed in clean water. Some cloth was finished by raising the nap with teasels and cropping it with shears.

Woodworking

WOOD

Good timber was scarce in Greece, and most timber, especially for shipbuilding, was imported.

Woodworking skills were highly developed, and specific types of wood were deliberately selected for different purposes. Wood was used in buildings (particularly for roofs), fortifications, boats, ships, carts, pit props and scaffolding. It was also used for smaller objects, such as furniture, boxes, tools, weapons and decorative carvings, including cult statues and figurines. There is evidence that wood was widely used for large sculptures and panel painting. Carved wooden objects are known from the Mycenaean period, but few survive from any period, although they were probably widely used.

TOOLS

From the Iron Age the range of woodworking tools was similar to the range of hand tools available today, and a high standard of craftsmanship was attained. What little is known of Bronze Age woodworking tools suggests that the range of tools was similar, but some would have been less effective and become blunt more frequently than iron tools.

Frame saws were of various kinds, the simplest being the bow saw. This had a saw blade fixed to the ends of a piece of wood that had been bent into a semicircle, so that the stress in the wood kept the saw blade taut. More commonly, an H-shaped wooden frame was used; the saw blade was fixed across the bottom of the "H," while a cord was fixed across the top and was tightened to keep the saw blade taut.

Axes, adzes and draw-knives were used for shaping wood, and planes for smoothing wood are mentioned by ancient authors. Chisels and gouges were used for the same purposes as they are used in modern carpentry and joinery. The lathe was probably introduced in the Bronze Age, and was employed for turning wood to produce objects such as parts of furniture. Holes in wood were made by bow drills or augers, and joinery techniques included mortise-and-tenon and dovetail joints. Pieces of wood were joined with wooden pegs, glue or iron nails.

Bone and Ivory

It is not known if specialist craftsmen made bone and ivory objects. It is more likely that bone and ivory were used as raw materials by a variety of craftsmen so that, for example, ivory pins were made by jewelers. There do not appear to have been any specialized tools used in the working of bone and ivory, which was generally cut, carved and shaped in a similar way to wood.

Animal bone was used for objects such as pins, seals, beads and other jewelry, and a variety of small tools and implements. It was also used for parts of other articles, such as hinges, handles and inlays. Pieces of boars' tusks were used as a protective inlay on some Bronze Age helmets (fig. 3.6).

Ivory working was very skilled in Minoan and Mycenaean times up to c. 1200 BC. In the later 8th century BC ivory carving was again borrowed from the Near East. Ivory was imported from Syria from the Bronze Age, but after the conquests of Alexander the Great much of it came from India. It was mainly from elephants, though some came from hippopotamuses. Ivory was used for figurines, as decorative inlay for furniture and boxes (including plaques with relief carvings), and in seals, jewelry, hinges, cosmetic boxes, mirror handles, gaming pieces, combs, and a variety of small tools and implements such as those used with toiletries and cosmetics. Ivory was also used in inlays to provide flesh-colored parts of chryselephantine (gold and ivory) cult statues, and was often combined with gold and silver. Ivory was sometimes tinted with colors.

Extractive Industries

QUARRIES

Most stone was quarried from opencast workings, but occasionally it was mined in underground galleries, such as the marble quarries on Paros (where a vein of special marble was exploited by tunneling), the limestone quarries in Syracuse and the selenite quarries in Spain. Early quarries usually worked isolated rock outcrops, but later quarries exploited specific types of stone for their appearance and could be very deep. Generally stone was cut from the parent rock in rectangular blocks. A piece of stone larger than the required block, but the same shape, was marked out by a channel or groove cut in the rock with a chisel. This groove was deepened with a pick to the required depth, and the resulting block was broken away from the rock face with wooden wedges. The wedges were fitted into prepared holes and saturated with water to make them swell, thus splitting the block from the rock face. Some rocks needed different techniques. Basalt blocks, for example, were cut from the parent rock by driving in iron wedges with heavy hammers rather than using wooden wedges.

Some stones had natural planes of cleavage and could be split, often into thin sheets. Other stones could be cut with saws, sometimes using an iron saw with teeth, but more often using a saw comprising a "blade" of taut wire. The latter saw used sand as a cutting agent: the sand was pressed into the cutting groove by the wire, which was moved back and forth to cut through the stone.

Limestone was the most common stone of the Greek world. It was readily available in many areas, and was used for buildings and sculpture. The general term *poros* described limestone and other soft, easily worked stones that were used in a similar way, such as calcareous tufa. The most famous limestone quarry was at Syracuse, which appears to have yielded over 112 million tons of stone.

The Greek word *marmaros* was used for stones that could take a high polish, including porphyry and granite, as well as the various types of marble. Major sources of marble were Mount Marpessa on Paros, Mount Pentelicus, Mount Hymettus and Spilia in Attica, and Naxos. Marble was also quarried at Doliana near Tegea in the Peloponnese, and green marble (actually porphyry) came from Croceae near Gythium in the Peloponnese. Other sources of *marmaros* were the island of Chios, and Thebes in Egypt. There were also various marble quarries in Asia Minor that served the needs of the cities on the west coast. *Marmaros* stone was generally chosen for the color of its finished surface: Parian marble was a glistening white, Naxian marble was gray and Hymettan marble was gray or bluish gray. Pentelic marble had traces of iron and acquired a golden patina as it weathered.

Blocks of stone were transported from the quarry to a stone yard near the building site for final dressing. The extra stone (*apergon*) left on the block helped to protect it during transport to the stoneyard. The architect appears to have been responsible for ordering the stone from the quarry and ensuring its suitability; there is evidence for blocks being returned to quarries at Eleusis and Didyma because they were not what had been ordered.

Blocks of stone were transported in wagons drawn by teams of oxen, which was adequate for blocks weighing up to about 12 tons. Column drums above this weight were pulled by rolling. In Sicily there is evidence that very heavy blocks had huge wooden wheels built around them so that they too could be rolled along.

MINES

Apart from a few mines for stone, most mining was to exploit metal ores. Three types of mining were used: placer, opencast and deep vein mining. The general word for a mine or quarry was *metallon*.

Placer mining was the recovery of mineral grains from alluvial deposits. Gold and silver were recovered by this method in suitable rivers. Greasy sheep fleeces were pegged in the river, and heavier grains of gold and silver stuck to the grease on the fleece and were recovered. Lighter materials were carried away by the water.

The Greeks had no detailed knowledge of geology, so they located sources of minerals by looking for surface outcrops of suitable rock. It was then exploited by opencast mining, usually in the form of simple pits. Deep mining, following veins of minerals, probably developed from some opencast workings. Opencast pits were often abandoned when the ore was exhausted, but sometimes mine passages (adits) were dug into a hillside to follow a vein of ore. The technique of digging adits was also adopted as an exploratory measure; if the adit failed to find ore, it was abandoned, but if ore was found, a gallery was dug to remove it.

Where ore was known to be present, vertical shafts could be dug to reach the vein of ore, and then a gallery would be dug to exploit it. At Laurium in Attica over 2,000 mine shafts are known, the deepest being 390 ft (119 m). Here the shafts were square or rectangular, averaging 6 ft by 4 ft (1.83 m by 1.22 m). They were dug in stages until the ore was reached. Holes in the sides of the shaft were apparently for insertion of horizontal pieces of wood, which could be climbed like a ladder.

At the bottom of the shaft, a gallery was dug to remove the ore. Occasionally this would follow the vein of ore exactly, but usually galleries were rectangular, square or trapezoidal. The height of the

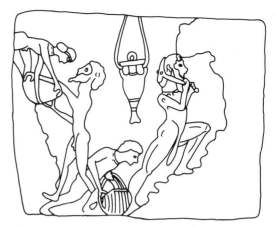

Fig. 5.4   A painted clay votive tablet of the 7th or 6th century BC, depicting the working of an ancient mine.

galleries was no more than 3 ft 4 in (1 m), and could be as little as 2 ft (0.6 m), with a width of 2–3 ft (0.6–0.9 m). Shoring was not often necessary, but pit props and lintels were used in some mines.

Tools used in mining included picks, hammers and chisels for breaking up the rock. A kind of mattock or shovel was used for raking up the rock after it had been dislodged, and rock was collected in baskets or other containers (fig. 5.4). Torches of resinous wood, and stone and pottery lamps burning olive oil were used for lighting. The ore appears to have been removed from the workings by boys and was either hauled up the shaft in containers or passed to the surface by a chain of miners.

Most information about how mines were operated comes from the Laurium mines, which were owned by the city-state of Athens, and it is usually assumed that most or all mines were state owned. The miners (*metalleutai*) were mainly slaves, who were leased to work in the mines by their owners (Athenian citizens and metics). These owners received an obol for each day's work by a slave. Finds of skeletons with iron fetters on their legs show that at least some miners were chained.

Although the approximate locations of some mines are known from ancient authors, the Laurium mines have provided the greatest amount of historical and archaeological evidence. Silver was the main product of the Laurium mines, although some of the lead (a byproduct of silver production) was also used, and to a lesser extent copper and iron were also mined here. Evidence of ore processing has been found in the area immediately surrounding the mine shafts.

Stoneworking

Stone was used for a large number of purposes, particularly in public buildings (see chapter 6). It was also used for objects such as statues, figurines, boxes, lamps, vessels, altars, tombstones and other monuments. Many different stones were used for their decorative effects. Amber and various precious and semiprecious stones were used in jewelry, for rings, beads, pendants and inlays, and various stones were used for making seals. Limestone was predominantly used in buildings and for carvings, as was marble, and all were painted in bright colors.

Masons used a wide range of tools. Points, punches and chisels were commonly employed in sculpture, with the bow-drill for finer details, such as on seals. Small Bronze Age vessels were made by chiseling and drilling the interior and hammering the exterior, polishing with the abrasive emery or sand. Large stone statues were probably first modeled in clay by master sculptors, and then copied in stone by their assistants. See also masonry walls, chapter 6.

Metalworking

Converting ores into metal involved several processes, including smelting with charcoal in a fire or furnace. Smelting was usually undertaken as close as possible to the mines, unless charcoal was unavailable nearby. Iron ore smelting required more sophisticated techniques, using bowl furnaces and shaft furnaces. Silver was obtained from lead by a further process known as cupellation.

The smelted metals were poured into molds to form ingots, which were transported to manufacturing centers for the production of artifacts. In the Bronze Age, distinctive "oxhide" ingots of copper (so-called because of their shape) were traded throughout the central and eastern Mediterranean and to Crete. Some came from Cyprus, but the majority came from elsewhere, possibly from Anatolia.

GOLD

Gold is the only metal that occurs in usable form in reasonable quantities. It was extracted by crushing the rock and washing the resultant powder in a stream of water to separate the gold from impurities—similar to the collection of alluvial gold. Gold is generally found as an alloy with silver or copper. If silver formed a large proportion of the alloy, it was regarded as electrum. Gold could be refined by heating it with lead in a porous clay crucible. A current of air across the top of the crucible oxidized the lead and the impurities, which became attached to the walls of the crucible, leaving a residue of gold or electrum. This process was called cupellation, and others separated silver from gold.

Most objects were made from sheet gold, which was formed by hammering a gold ingot on an anvil. Other techniques included filigree—thin gold wire for manufacturing decorative objects such as chains and earrings. Occasionally, gold objects were cast. Granulation involved globules of gold (or silver) soldered onto jewelry. Jewelry was the main product of gold, including necklaces, rings, signet rings, bracelets, earrings, pendants and pins. Gold was also used for death masks, wreaths, vessels, seal mounts, and coins, as well as for gilding in the form of gold leaf. Gold was used with ivory and silver (chryselephantine) for cult statues. Decorative gold work was particularly common at Mycenae in the Bronze Age, and from the later 4th century BC in the Hellenistic period, it became widely used due to exploitation of the Thracian mines. Gold jewelry in particular became common among the wealthy, with many new shapes being manufactured.

SILVER

Silver was derived mainly from the ore galena, which was crushed, washed and sieved. It was then roasted to remove some of the sulphur content, and smelted to produce a mixture of lead and silver. The silver could then be purified by cupellation in the same way as gold. Techniques of silver working are similar to those used today. Silver could be hammered into shape, with all traces of hammering removed by polishing. Decoration was done by repoussé work, engraving, granulation, chasing and gilding, and niello inlay.

Silver was used for jewelry, wreaths and vessels, and the same range of objects was probably made in silver as in gold. Silver was also used for coins and for some luxury tableware. As with gold, few large objects have survived, because they tended to be melted down.

BRONZE

Copper was obtained from smelting copper-bearing ores, such as malachite, in a simple furnace. Copper and tin were most commonly used together as the alloy bronze. Tin is a relatively rare metal occurring in the ore cassiterite and can also be recovered by smelting the ore in a simple furnace. Bronze was used for a diverse range of objects, including tableware, coins, weapons, figurines, statues, tripods, cauldrons and jewelry.

Bronze was sometimes worked cold but was usually cast, lead being added to increase its fluidity. Solid objects were cast in stone molds, and open vessels were formed by casting in stone molds or by hammering and shaping sheet bronze around a mold. Early votive offerings were made by being cut from bronze or copper sheet. Some early cult statues were made of bronze plates fixed to or beaten over a wooden core. Solid objects could also be made by the lost-wax (*cire perdue*) method: A beeswax model was covered in clay and fired, melting the wax; molten bronze was poured into the hollow, and when solidified, the clay was removed.

Later on, particularly from the 6th century BC, larger hollow objects were made by core casting (hollow casting), similar to the lost-wax method. One method was to make a rough shape in clay with a sculpted wax model around it, which was covered with clay. Bronze pins were inserted so that the clay core remained in place after the wax was melted in the firing. Molten bronze was poured into the gap left by the wax. The outer clay mold was removed, sometimes in pieces so that it could be reused as a piece mold. The clay core could be left in place or removed through a hole, which was then sealed with bronze. Very large objects might be cast in several pieces in molds set in pits, which were soldered or riveted together.

ENAMELING

Enamel is a vitreous material fused to a metallic surface (mainly gold and electrum, occasionally silver) as a means of decoration in various bright colors. Areas of metal were cut out or cast as hollows, filled with glass powder and heated so that the glass powder fused with the metal to form enamel.

LEAD

Lead was mainly obtained as a byproduct of the process of obtaining silver. Various objects were made of lead, such as anchors, sheathing for ships' timbers, joining materials in building, figurines, cheap jewelry and weights.

IRON

Iron was obtained by smelting iron ore in a furnace. Unlike the other metals used by the Greeks, iron did not become molten at the temperatures achieved by their furnaces. The result of smelting was a hard spongy metallic mass that had to be repeatedly forged (reheated and hammered while red-hot) in order to turn it into a piece of metal.

Iron was worked by blacksmiths in forges with a variety of tools. Anvils were roughly squared blocks of iron. Most shaping and finishing of objects was done with variously shaped hammers, and holes were made with punches. Smithing was a common industry, and many objects were produced, especially tools, weapons and fittings. Ancient authors refer to specialist blacksmiths such as manufacturers of spears, swords, knives and nails.

Jewelry Manufacture

The best quality jewelry was made from gold and silver, using precious and semiprecious stones, enamels and glass for a variety of color and texture. Cheap jewelry was made from bronze, iron and even lead. A great range of jewelry was produced, including pins and brooches for fastening clothing, rings, beads, necklaces, bracelets, armbands, earrings, headbands and diadems.

Most Greek jewelry was manufactured from several parts made from sheet metal, wire and sometimes cast metal pieces. A jeweler's workshop had an open charcoal fire with some means of creating a forced draft, such as a blowpipe or bellows. This heated metal to the required temperature. There would also be a metal or stone anvil, hammers, punches, stamps and engraving tools, as well as formers for beating sheet metal to shapes and molds for casting. Files, abrasives and burnishing stones were used in the finishing processes.

Sheet metal was made by a repeat process of hammering an ingot flat on the anvil, bringing it to a red heat and then rapidly cooling it in water to stop it from becoming brittle. Sheet metal was shaped by being hammered over a former or into a mold, and was decorated using punches and gravers. Wire was made by hammering a thin strip of metal and rolling it between two metal plates or two stones until it had been reduced to the desired thickness. Jewelry workshops dating from the Mycenaean period have been found. Some specialized in particular materials, such as glass and gold.

Faience and Glass

Glass and faience are related materials using quartz or silica. Faience consisted of crushed quartz or silica grains covered with a layer of glaze, usually blue or green in color. The basic paste was modeled by hand, usually around a core that would burn away, or in clay molds. Its use dates from c. 1900 BC in Crete and a little later on the mainland. Faience was used for various objects in the Bronze Age, including beads, amulets, inlays, bowls, figurines, pendants and vases (fig. 9.10). In the Hellenistic period objects of faience included vases and wine jugs with portraits of Ptolemaic queens.

Initially glass in the form of ingots and glass products was imported into Greece, probably from Mesopotamia and Egypt. There is a little evidence for glassworking within Greece, and it is unclear how much Greek glass resulted from local glassmaking and glassworking, and how much was imported. Throughout the Greek period, glass vessels were luxury items, mainly because their production was a highly skilled and slow process, and therefore costly. Glass vessels were made by building up molten glass over a core, by casting glass in a mold, or by grinding and carving vessels from blocks of glass. Beads, seals and jewelry were also made from glass. It was in use by c. 1450 BC in Crete and on the mainland. The art of glassmaking and faience was lost at the end of the Bronze Age, but reappeared around the 6th century BC, when the repertoire included figured vases of glass.

Pottery Manufacture

Clay for pottery and other terra-cotta objects was dug from selected deposits and allowed to weather. Clay may then have been refined by levigating—mixing it with water so that coarse particles sank and organic debris floated and could be skimmed off. It was then puddled (mixed and blended with temper and water). Different mixes of clay and filler (sand or various sizes of crushed rock) were used for different pottery vessels, with larger filler added to strengthen large and heavy-duty vessels.

The potter's wheel began to be used in the Middle Minoan period, initially a slow wheel or turntable, but soon after a fast potter's wheel was also introduced. The fast wheel appears to have been a broad flat wheel set near the ground, with the potter sitting or squatting by it. The wheel was kept spinning by an assistant. The later type of fast wheel had a smaller potter's wheel set on a spindle attached to a flywheel. This could be kept spinning by being kicked by the potter. It appears to have been introduced in the Hellenistic period.

Before the introduction of the wheel, all pottery was hand made. This was done by pinching and pulling a ball of clay into shape, forming the shape from coils or slabs of clay and then smoothing the sides to remove the ridges. Alternatively a slab of clay was pounded over a pattern or former, such as an inverted bowl. Even after the introduction of the fast potter's wheel, some pottery was still made by hand; large pots in particular, such as storage jars, were built up from coils or slabs of clay. Some intricately shaped vessels, as well as decorative elements (such as animal heads) for addition to vessels, were formed in molds.

Many pots were decorated using stamps or by painting designs using clay slips (solutions of fine clay particles), which provided the desired colors when the pot was fired. See chapter 9 for pottery types.

After drying, pots were fired in kilns. Coarsewares were sometimes fired in simple bonfire kilns, with the pots stacked and baked in a pit under a bonfire. For most wares the single-flue updraft kiln was used. The pots were stacked inverted within an oval or circular chamber, supported on clay fire bars over the fire. A stokehole or stoking tunnel was on one side, and the hot gases rose from the fire around the pots and out a vent at the top of the kiln. The kiln's superstructure is uncertain, but some may have had a temporary covering, and others a permanent dome. The fuel was probably mainly wood, including olive prunings, thorn bushes and other brushwood, and the dry residue from olive oil production could have been used.

Not all pottery was made on a commercial basis. Some would have been made by members of a family to supply domestic requirements, perhaps on an annual basis. Commercial pottery was made by specialist potters, some of whom may have been itinerant workers, setting up a temporary production to supply local needs, and then moving to another community.

Apart from pottery vessels, terra-cotta was used for many other purposes, such as lamps, seals, relief sculpture, figurines, statues, molds, model objects, votive plaques, cult statues, coffins and bathtubs.

TRADE OF GOODS

Raw materials and manufactured goods were produced both for the home market and for export over varying distances. Trade was originally conducted as a barter system, but goods could later be exchanged for precious metals and eventually coinage.

Bronze Age

Movement of goods between Bronze Age communities has traditionally been interpreted as commercial trade. Since the earliest evidence consists only of movement of goods, the assumption that all or even any were actually traded has been questioned. It is quite possible that many items were transported for reasons other than trade. For example, they may have been carried as exchange goods for diplomatic purposes, for bribes, as containers or for religious purposes, and they may even reflect the actual movement of peoples. However, the quantity and distribution of some goods suggest that commercial trade was being carried on at least as early as the First Palace Period, and that the variety of goods and the area over which they were traded increased from that time.

PREPALATIAL PERIOD

The distribution of various artifacts in the Aegean area demonstrates that patterns of contact and exchange were being established in the Prepalatial Period. Professional merchants and traders are identifiable in Egypt by the 2nd millennium BC, and traders could also have operated in Greece.

FIRST PALACE PERIOD

In this period there is evidence for patterns of exchange in the Aegean involving the Cyclades and the island of Aegina. These patterns suggest that certain sites, such as Kolonna on Aegina, acted as centers of exchange at the heart of a web of settlements involved in exchanging goods. The various patterns of exchange appear to have been largely independent of each other, so that exchange of goods was usually confined within a pattern of settlements. Pottery was the most frequently exchanged item, but probably only certain categories of pottery. The pots were primarily containers for the goods being exchanged. Other items known to have been exchanged within different exchange patterns include millstones (thought to be of andesite from Aegina), silver, copper and lead from Laurium, and tin, gold, ivory and exotic stones from the Near East.

SECOND PALACE PERIOD

In this period Minoan influence throughout the Aegean dominated exchange patterns. New centers of wealth on the mainland also became involved, and the Near East increased its involvement in the Aegean area. There is also evidence for contacts elsewhere in Europe at this time, with a general increase of wealth in the Aegean area. The overall impression is one of a widening pattern of exchange, and an increase in the amount and variety of goods being exchanged. Goods such as silver, lead and copper from Laurium, and various items of bronze appear to have circulated widely. Some fine stones and metals, including gold, seem to have originated in Laconia, and gold, ivory and exotic stones came from the Near East. Lapis lazuli from Asia and Egyptian alabaster were brought to mainland Greece, and amber came from Europe. Tin and copper were imported, possibly from Anatolia. At least a portion of the goods being exchanged seem to have been the subject of commercial trade, particularly with the Near East.

THIRD PALACE PERIOD

Shipwreck cargoes of this period demonstrate the very wide trading contacts. These cargoes consist of a mixture of goods with various places of origin, such as Egypt, Syria and Cyprus. Such a mixture of imported goods is paralleled by finds from contemporary settlement sites, and settlements in Cyprus and Syria appear to have been centers of long-distance trade within the Mediterranean area. Mycenaean pottery was exported widely in the Dodecanese, Cyclades, Near East, Sicily and other parts of the Mediterranean. Some of it may have served as containers for high-quality goods such as perfumed oil.

In the later 13th century BC trade in the Mediterranean seems to have deteriorated. Trade continued over a wide area, but not at the previous level. In particular, the eastward export of Mycenaean pottery appears to have greatly diminished. The disruptions at the end of the Bronze Age caused a collapse of trading, and contact with settlements outside the Aegean was lost or continued only intermittently.

Dark Age and Archaic Period

Little evidence for trade exists for the Dark Age, but from the 8th century BC there are indications of a gradual revival of trade. Greek colonies were founded from the mid-8th century BC. Sites were usually chosen for their ability to provide natural resources. As colonies became established they often produced a surplus that could be traded for other goods. Some colonies acted as staging posts on a trade route, while others acted as a focus for trade with their hinterland. Greek city-states were also developing at this time. Despite warfare between city-states, there is good evidence that trade continued and probably increased.

In the second half of the 7th century BC increased seafaring established contacts in the Black Sea area, Egypt and on the north coast of Africa. The introduction of coinage from the 6th century BC is likely to have had a beneficial effect on trade,

and there appears to have been a gradual increase of trade up to the Classical period.

Classical and Hellenistic Periods

There is more evidence of trade from the Classical period, with an impression of an overall increase in trade and a greater diversity in the goods being traded. Literary sources provide information mainly about Athenian trade, but it is thought that most others cities were similarly involved, although usually to a lesser extent. By the Hellenistic period, trade had increased to such a level that some states depended upon it. Merchants selling particular wares were known by that product, such as cattle merchants and leather merchants. Retail merchants of this sort were called *kapeloi*, and entrepreneurs and middlemen *palinkapeloi*. Merchants engaged in long-distance trade were called *emporoi* (sing. *emporos*), and trade was also carried out by shipowners (*naukleroi*).

Trade Routes

Most cities of the Mediterranean world were on the coast, and materials could be traded between them fairly easily by sea, although in some cases it was cheaper to transport goods overland. For example, Thucydides records that before Decelea in Attica was occupied by the Spartans in 413 BC, it was cheaper to transport goods overland from Oropus to Athens than to transport them by sea around Cape Sounion. This was probably the situation with many capes and headlands, where adverse winds could cause considerable delays to merchant shipping and so increase transport costs.

The sparse evidence suggests that Piraeus was the busiest and most important of all the island and mainland ports in the Classical period. Its predominance probably stemmed from the large amount of grain that was imported through this port. Through the hold it had on the Delian League, Athens came to control the supply of imported grain and timber for shipbuilding, thereby maintaining dominance over other states.

The pattern of Greek trade routes was therefore dominated by the need for imported grain, which resulted in three main shipping routes—northeast to the Black Sea, southeast to Crete, Cyprus and Egypt, and west to southern Italy, Sicily and beyond. A fourth main route, dominated by Corinth, was through the Gulf of Corinth to ports in the Adriatic, but it is uncertain whether the Adriatic was a major trading destination. Other basic supplies, such as metals and timber, were traded over long distances as well, but local trade within Greece also used the many coastal shipping routes.

In Hellenistic times trade routes to the east were expanded. Again, these were largely shipping routes, as land transport was still difficult and expensive. The major land routes were the two Silk Roads running north and south of the region east of the Black Sea, and shipping routes extended to the Red Sea, Persian Gulf and the Indian Ocean. Trade with the coastal cities of western Asia Minor flourished, and in the 4th century BC Rhodes became an important trading center. Rhodes later declined and was finally eclipsed by the establishment of Delos as a free port in 166 BC. Increased contact led to continued development of trade with Syria, the Middle East and beyond.

Containers

Particularly from the 6th century BC amphorae were used as all-purpose containers for transporting liquid and semiliquid goods. These large pottery jars were frequently used for transporting wine by sea, as well as other goods such as olives, olive oil, and a variety of preserved and fresh foodstuffs. Different city-states made different shapes of amphorae, and even the amphorae of a single state changed shape over a period of time. Shipwreck cargoes often include a great variety of amphora shapes, probably reflecting their different origins and contents. Many amphorae were stamped with control marks on their handles. Stamped amphorae were largely issued by Greek states that were important wine producers, although some important producers of oil may also have used stamped amphorae. See also pp. 373–374 and fig. 9.1.

Grain was generally transported in sacks. Barrels do not appear to have been used as containers, possibly because the scarcity of wood made them uneconomic.

Exports and Imports

Greece exported a number of commodities such as olive oil and wine, as well as a range of manufactured goods including pottery, furniture, weapons, personal ornaments and jewelry. The major imports were grain, timber, hides and slaves, as well as fish and fish products, nuts, raisins, figs, cheese and tallow. Raw materials, such as various types of metal and stone, were also imported.

GRAIN

Grain was the principal import of Athens and many other states, usually transported in sacks. While some states imported grain only when the need arose, Athens appears to have become dependent on such imports. Within Greece, the area around Sparta and Messenia was very fertile, but did not produce grain for export. Thessaly and Euboea were important grain exporters, and Lemnos, Thasos and Sciathus also exported grain. Other major sources of grain were outside Greece, the main ones being southern Russia near the Black Sea, Pontus on the southern coast of the Black Sea, Thrace, Egypt, southern Italy and Sicily. At times grain was also exported from the west coast of Turkey and possibly Cyprus. Rather than a major grain producer, Cyprus was probably mainly an intermediate point on the shipping route from Egypt.

Within the Athenian Empire, Athens kept a tight control on the grain trade, laying down regulations about who could trade in grain and who was allowed to transport it. It was also essential for Athens and its allies to maintain good relations with the Black Sea region and to control the Aegean and Black Sea approaches, in order to ensure the grain supply from this area. At times Athens exported grain that it had imported. During the Peloponnesian War, Athens attempted to intercept grain ships to the Peloponnese, mainly from Egypt, Cyprus and Crete. The vast majority of imported grain was wheat, which was preferred but could not be efficiently grown in many parts of Greece.

WINE

Wine was an important export from Greece. Many Greek states produced wine, although not all had a regular surplus for export, unless the harvest had been good. The main exporters of wine included Peparethus, Cos, Thasos, Mende, Rhodes, Cnidus, Chios, Leucas, Lesbos, Corcyra and Paros. Thasos, Rhodes, Cnidus, Paros and Chios used stamped amphorae for exporting their wine, and the distribution of these amphorae adds to the evidence from ancient literary sources about the wine trade. Wines were traded within Greece; for example, wines such as those from Thasos, Rhodes and Cnidus were exported to Athens. Wines were also exported to places outside Greece, the major destinations being southern Russia, Egypt and Pontus.

OLIVE OIL

In Greece olive oil served as a food, fuel and lubricant, and it was also used in place of soap. Olive oil was exported in amphorae from various parts of Greece including Attica. Miletus was also an important oil producer. Although Athens generally exported oil, there is some indication that oil was imported in some periods of population growth when domestic demand exceeded supply.

TIMBER

Timber, particularly that suitable for shipbuilding and large structures such as temples, was in short supply in Greece, and much had to be imported. Various types of wood were used in shipbuilding, including fir, cedar, pine, mulberry, elm and sometimes sycamore and acacia. Oak or beech were often used for the keels of warships. Cedar was imported from Crete, Cyprus, Africa, Syria and Lebanon, and fir was imported from Thessaly and Macedonia. Continuous efforts were made to conciliate the Macedonian kings in order to obtain supplies of Macedonian fir wood. Pontus was a source of good pine wood, and various woods were exported from western Turkey. Southern Italy and Sicily also supplied fir and pine. It is uncertain how timber was transported, but it was probably as deck cargo on merchant ships.

FISH

Fish were often preserved by drying, salting, smoking or pickling, which enabled them to be traded. Fresh fish were only traded locally. Imports of preserved fish from Pontus were important, because these provided good supplies of tunny and sturgeon. The Black Sea coast of southern Russia was another important exporter of preserved fish, and many places in Greece itself were involved in this fish trade. Miletus had a flourishing fishing industry, as did many cities in the western Mediterranean, such as Syracuse and Messana. Pickled fish were transported in pottery jars, and the trade in preserved fish of all kinds was handled by wholesale fish merchants called *tarikhemporoi* or *tarikhegoi*, who supplied retailers called *tarikhopolai*.

HIDES

Hides were a major import into Greece where a shortage of cattle made leather a scarce commodity. The most important sources were southern Russia and Cyrene. Hides were transported as deck cargo on merchant ships.

STONE

Various types of marble were traded for decorative use in building construction and for sculpture. White marble from Paros was considered the best for sculpture, and gray marble from Naxos was also of high quality. The marble from Pentelicus in Attica was of lesser quality, as was that from Hymettus. Marbles from Thasos, Lesbos, Proconnesus and Carystus were also used, as well as spotted and variegated marble from Chios. In the Classical period plain marbles were generally used, but colored marbles became popular in the Hellenistic period, particularly for interior decoration. Because overland transport of stone was so difficult and expensive, it was transported by sea wherever possible. Sometimes it was more efficient to open up a new quarry near a building than to transport stone from a distance. See also quarries.

TEXTILES

Textiles were apparently an important item of trade, but little detailed evidence is available because textiles rarely survive. Linen was made from imported flax, which probably came from Egypt, western Turkey and Colchis, although some may have come from Macedonia and Thrace. Silk was introduced to Greece before the conquests of Alexander the Great. Cotton was probably unknown until the very end of the Greek period. Wool was a common textile, as sheep were common in mountainous districts within Greece. It was also imported from western Turkey, the Black Sea coast and Italy.

Megara was famous for the production of coarse garments for slaves, and Pellene was famous for woollens (Pellene cloaks were sometimes given as prizes at local games), but little evidence exists for other exports of clothing. Miletus was a wool market well known for fabrics and tapestries used as wall hangings, and Amorgos was also famous for fabrics. Carpets were imported from Cyprus, and hemp ropes were probably imported from the area north of the Black Sea.

METALS

The trade in various metals must have been very important. Although there is some evidence for the mining of metal ores and the production of metal artifacts, little is known about how metals were traded. See also mines and metalworking.

POTTERY

Apart from amphorae and pottery vessels that were used as containers to transport other goods, there was some trade in pottery itself, usually high-quality ware, finely decorated by the best artists. All the finest decorated types of pottery appear to have been exported at some time, but there is some controversy over the nature of the pottery trade. Because many pottery vessels were highly prized as works of art, doubt has been cast on whether they were always objects of commerce. When found at some distance from Greece, they may have been used as diplomatic gifts, tribute, bribes or they may even have been looted.

Another question has been raised concerning the centers of pottery production, since some potters may have traveled outside Greece making high-quality wares. It would therefore be difficult to distinguish between exported pottery and that made locally by a Greek potter. There seems little doubt, however, that most fine pottery was made in Greece and exported. High-quality Greek pottery is found throughout the Mediterranean world and in neighboring regions. It is one of many imported luxury items found in Scythian graves, and it is also found in Etruscan tombs in Italy. See also chapter 9, pottery.

SLAVES

Slaves were an important commodity, providing labor in many industries, as well as personal and public servants. The main sources of slaves were captives taken in war and piracy. In war, the victors might enslave the defeated population, as well as the defeated army. Piracy is a term that appears to have covered organized trading in slaves who were kidnapped or captured in non-war situations. Sometimes the difference between warfare and piracy is difficult to distinguish. Children of slaves were born into slavery, so providing another supply of slaves, and some slaves were obtained from unwanted newborn babies exposed to die. The exact proportion of slaves that came from these three sources is unknown. Ancient literary sources rarely mention the slave trade, which left few recognizable archaeological traces. It is known that a major slave market existed at Ephesus for over 400 years. After Delos became a free port in 166 BC, it became a major transshipment center for slaves, who were largely supplied by the pirate slave trade in southwest Asia Minor.

COMMERCE

Wages

Evidence for wages during the Greek period is sparse, and consists of records of particular wages at a specific period. This makes it impossible to see any trends in wages over time, and generalizations are difficult. The surviving evidence only allows indications of wage levels. There is also little indication of how the labor of slaves, who could be bought or leased, and the labor of dependent tenants affected the wages of free laborers.

In the late 5th century BC there was apparently no distinction between skilled and unskilled labor. Each workman received about 1 drachma a day, and an assistant received 3 obols. Agricultural laborers earned 4 obols and their food (valued at 2 obols).

In the 4th century BC wages seem to have risen. At the beginning of the century the foreman of a gang of bricklayers received 2 drachmas a day, while at Delphi in the middle of the century, plasterers were paid between 1 and 2½ drachmas. Near the end of the century, bricklayers, carpenters and plasterers at Eleusis received 2½ drachmas, sawyers 2 drachmas and laborers 1½ drachmas. Wages gradually became based on piecework rather than a daily rate. At the beginning of the 4th century BC bricklayers at Eleusis were paid at a rate of 12 to 15 drachmas per 1,000 bricks, but toward the end of the century the price had risen to 17 drachmas per 1,000.

As might be expected there are indications that professional services were paid at a higher rate. Physicians, musicians, actors, hetaerae, the best teachers and some highly rated artists received wages above the average, but few precise figures are known.

The *theorika* were probably introduced by Pericles. They were state allowances paid to poor Athenian citizens to visit the theaters. Theoric magistrates were in charge of its administration.

Taxation

In Crete taxes were apparently exacted during the Minoan and Mycenaean periods, probably in the form of produce and forced labor, but as yet the evidence is unclear and has been disputed. There is little other evidence for systematic tax collection before the Archaic period. With the introduction of coinage and increasing economic sophistication of the city-states, taxes began to be levied on a regular basis. Although some tyrants levied heavy taxes to pay for mercenary troops, taxes appear to have been relatively light before the Persian Wars (early 5th century BC).

In the Classical period taxation became the main method of raising money in city-states. The majority of evidence comes from Athens. Direct taxation on citizens and regular taxes on their property were regarded as degrading, although such taxes had been levied by some of the tyrants. However, it was considered reasonable to tax noncitizens. Metics were subject to an annual poll tax (*metoikion*) of 12 drachmas per man and 6 drachmas for a woman without a working husband or son.

Food and goods sold in the market were subject to a market tax, which fell heavily on metics. An excise tax (*eponia*), effectively a sales tax, was levied on some transactions, mainly those conducted in the agora. The tax varied according to what was being sold. The general level of this tax was around 1 percent of the value of the goods, although some goods were taxed more heavily. Evidence from other city-states shows that taxes were also levied on foreign-

ers trading in the agora, on the right of unloading, on fishing rights and on anchorage. Cities often had gate tolls as well. Brothel keepers paid an excise tax called *pornikos telos*.

Although direct taxation of citizens was not approved of in Athens, some direct taxes did exist. One means of raising revenue at Athens was through the liturgy (*leitourgia*), a burdensome public duty that wealthier individual citizens discharged at their own expense. These public duties were numerous and were associated particularly with festivals. They included the choregia (*khoregia*: production of a chorus at a drama festival), *hippotrophia* (maintaining a horse for military purposes), *arkhitheoria* (leading a state group to foreign festivals) and *hestiasis* (providing a public banquet for the tribe). The trierarchy (acting as trierarch for a year) was a liturgy for naval purposes. Originally a voluntary honor, by the early 4th century BC liturgies were effectively compulsory.

The *eisphora* was a direct property tax levied on citizens and metics in times of emergency, such as war. It was reformed in 378/377 BC, and a fixed rate was levied on all but the poorest class of citizens. The tax was levied intermittently, apparently well into Hellenistic times.

The *epidosis* was a voluntary contribution to state revenues, particularly in time of war, usually following an appeal for funds. Wealthy citizens felt it their duty to contribute, and in the 5th century BC such contributions seem to have been genuinely voluntary; in the 4th century BC they were virtually compulsory.

In the Hellenistic period, with the establishment of Empires by the successors of Alexander the Great, tribute from cities and other political bodies within the Empires became a major source of revenue. New taxes were introduced, such as a tax on salt, which was a government monopoly in both the Seleucid and Ptolemaic Empires, and on other goods such as leather, spices and perfumes. Within Greek cities there was little change to the existing tax system apart from the increased use of liturgies. The choregia was replaced by the *sitonia*, which obliged rich citizens to purchase grain for the city. When the city was not rich enough for liturgies to operate properly, money for grain, olive oil and fish was raised by subscriptions called *epidoseis*. Technically voluntary, these subscriptions were effectively a compulsory tax.

Taxes were generally collected by tax farming. The right to collect a tax was auctioned to the highest bidder. The state set the tax at a fixed rate or a percentage of the value of the contract. The amount that the tax farmer managed to collect in addition to what he paid in the auction and his expenses was profit. The system was open to corruption and abuse, and tax farmers were generally feared and hated.

Customs

Because Greek states imported only the goods that they needed but could not manufacture, customs duties were not protectionist in the modern sense of protecting home industries from rival imports. The straightforward purpose of customs duties was to make money for the state, and several Greek cities became very rich from this source of income. Corinth benefited from its position on the isthmus by controlling commerce between mainland Greece and the Peloponnese. Ports regularly exacted a toll on all incoming goods, and some if not all cities apparently imposed a tax on goods leaving the port as well as entering it.

Customs duties varied, but most commonly they were about 2 percent of the value of the goods. This was the case in Athens after the disastrous Sicilian expedition of 413 BC. At this time the tax for allies of Athens was 5 percent on their imports and exports, replacing the tribute previously paid to Athens by members of the Delian League. When Athens controlled the Hellespont, a 10 percent tax on traffic was introduced in 410 BC, which was later abolished, reimposed, and finally withdrawn in 386 BC. Under Roman domination Delos became a possession of Athens and a free port in 166 BC. It was a thriving trading center for a century, but it declined after devastation by pirates in 69 BC.

Markets

Retail goods were generally sold in markets and in areas (quarters) of cities occupied by specific craftsmen. In these city quarters, craftsmen lived and carried on their business, and specialized quarters for retailers such as honey sellers, cheese sellers and tanners are known. Some craftsmen's quarters were outside the city walls, such as the Kerameikos (potters' quarter) outside the walls of Athens. Sometimes it is difficult to distinguish between a craftsman's quarter and a market, since in Athens and probably many other cities specialized markets existed for different commodities, including wine, olive oil, bedding, cheese and even soft cheese. Markets were probably not all held within the agora, but ones in the agora were probably divided by speciality into separate spaces within the market area. In many states officials were elected by lot as overseers of the market (*agoranomoi*). They kept order in the market, collected market dues, and inspected the quality and correct weight of goods on sale. In Athens there were 10 *agoranomoi*, five for the city itself and five for Piraeus.

In Athens and other large port cities, *deigmata* (sing. *deigma*, literally "sample") were specialized market halls, set up by the state to enable foreign merchants to display samples of their wares. This was effectively a wholesale market where city merchants could test samples of foreign goods before buying them for resale. It is uncertain whether city merchants could also display samples of their own wares for foreign merchants to buy. However, it is likely that foreign merchants generally purchased a return cargo so that their ships did not return home empty. At Athens it is thought that the *deigma* was located in a part of Piraeus accessible to the sea.

Weights and Measures

There was a variety of standards of weights and measures. Pheidon of Argos apparently fixed the standard measures used by the Peloponnesians, and Solon fixed the Attic standards of weights and measures. Most measures of length were named after parts of the human body, the basic unit being the foot. The foot measure (*hekatompedos*) was mentioned by Homer, but its length is unknown. In historic Greece there were many foot standards, such as 12.6 in (320 mm) at Olympia, 13.1 in (333 mm) at Aegina and 12.9 in (330 mm) at Pergamum, while the Attic standard was 11.6 in (295.7 mm). The main units of measurement were:

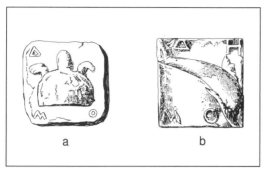

Fig. 5.5   Examples of two Attic weights: a. half-tortoise (equivalent to one-eighth stater); b. dolphin weight (equivalent to one mina).

2 fingers (*daktyloi*) = 1 *kondylos* (middle joint of finger)
4 fingers = 1 *palaste* (palm)
12 fingers = 1 *spithame* (span of all fingers)
16 fingers = 1 foot (*pous*)
18 fingers = 1 *pygme* (short cubit, elbow to knuckles)
20 fingers = 1 *pygon* (short cubit, elbow to first joint)
24 fingers = 1 *pekhys* (normal cubit, elbow to fingertips)
2.5 feet = 1 *bema* (pace)
6 feet = 1 *orgyia* (fathom: stretch of both arms)
100 feet = 1 *plethron* (also used for "acre")
600 feet = 1 *stadion* (stade)
30 stades = 1 *parasanges* (parasang, adopted from Persia)

Area measurements were based on speeds of plowing and sowing. A strip of land that could be plowed by oxen in one day in Greece was a *plethron*. One square *plethron* was 10,000 square feet.

There were dry and liquid measures of capacity or volume. The smallest unit was a *kyathos* (about 0.08 pints, 0.4 liters), possibly originally a gourd. The main measurements of capacity were:

1.5 *kyathoi* = 1 *oxybathon*
3 *kyathoi* = 1 *hemikotylion*
6 *kyathoi* = (in Attica) 1 *kotyle* (a kind of cup)
6 *kyathoi* = (elsewhere) 1 *tryblion* or *hemina*

Liquid measures continued as:

6 *kotylai* = 1 *hemikhous*
12 *kotylai* = 1 *khous*
12 *khoes* = 1 *metretes*

The *metretes* was the measure of the large wine amphorae, containing 8 gallons 5 pints (38.88 liters).

Dry measures continued as:

4 *kotylai* = 1 *khoinix* (at Athens, one person's daily grain ration)
4 *khoinikes* = 1 *hemiekton*
8 *khoinikes* = 1 *hekteus* or *modios*
48 *khoinikes* = 1 *medimnos*

The Attic *medimnos* contained 11 gallons 4 pints (51.84 liters), the Spartan 15 gallons 6.5 pints–17 gallons (71.16–77.88 liters).

Weighing was done using a balance scale (*stathmos*), in use from the Bronze Age. Actual weights in the Bronze Age were usually flattened stone or metal cylinders, inscribed with a symbol denoting the weight, and various weight standards were in use. In historic times the main weight standards were Aeginetic (apparently introduced by Pheidon of Argos) and Euboic (or Attic-Euboic), adopted in Attica and Corinth. Many weight standards were used in the various city-states, connected with gold, copper and silver. Actual weights were usually square and of lead or bronze, inscribed with a symbol denoting the weight, and sometimes the name of the city and the denomination. The most common Attic weights used the astragal symbol (stater), dolphin (mina, Greek *mna*), amphora (one-third stater) and tortoise (one-quarter stater) (fig. 5.5). See also coinage, below.

Trade between states was complicated by the many weight standards used in different cities, which also had to be correlated with the eastern system of staters and minae. Solon adopted a system of weights for coinage at Athens comprising 1 obol (12 measures of barley, 0.72 gm), 1 drachma (6 obols, 4.31 gm), 1 mina (100 drachmae, 431 gm) and 1 talent (60 minae, 25.86 kg). In the Aeginetic standard, a talent was 83 lb (37.8 kg). A talent represented a person's load. The stater was another common standard of weight.

Coinage

ARCHAIC

Early civilizations undertook trade by barter or exchange based on units of value such as weighed silver. In Homer, money mainly took the form of axes. Other metal objects were also used as currency, such as tripods, cauldrons, nails and rings. Particularly well known is the use of currency based on the iron cooking spit, *obelos* or *obolos*, about 3 ft (1 m) long. In Sparta, spits were the only permitted currency until the 3rd century BC, long after other states had introduced coinage. Coins were a development from the use of objects, and were minted with a regulated weight.

The first coins were minted in Lydia from the mid-7th century BC and were flat pebble-shaped staters of electrum (a gold and silver alloy). The first ones had a grooved surface on one side and an incuse punch mark on the other, and later ones were of pure gold and of pure silver. The early coins of Lydia were copied in mainland Greece and the islands, although silver coins were preferred. They were struck by hand using two dies or a die and a punch, and initially had an obverse design (with a symbol or badge of the issuing city) and a deep punch mark on the reverse.

Aegina was probably the first Greek state to mint coins in the early 6th century BC, with the badge of a sea turtle (the city's emblem) on one side and an incuse punch mark on the other. This was followed by coins from Athens and Corinth (late 6th century BC). The first Athenian coins used a diverse series of heraldic devices relating to Athena. These one-sided 6th-century-BC Athenian stater-didrachms are termed *Wappenmünzen* (heraldic coins) and date to c. 575–525 BC. In the late 6th century BC Athens minted new double-sided coins termed "owls." On the obverse was the helmeted head of Athena, and on the reverse the sacred owl of Athena, the city's name and an olive branch (fig. 5.6). They had a wide distribution, from India to Spain. The tetradrachm (*tetradrakhmon*) began to be struck, and the didrachm (*didrakhmon*) was no longer regularly struck at Athens.

The first coins of Corinth appeared c. 575 BC; they were silver staters (*stateres*, sing. *stater*), with the initial letter of *Korinthos* (archaic koppa) and the winged horse Pegasus. They became double-sided coins, with the head of Athena in a Corinthian helmet on the reverse. These coins were commonly called "colts."

Minting spread rapidly throughout the Greek world, including the city-states of Italy and Sicily, and most city-states minted coins by 500 BC. In northern Greece silver was available from the many

mines, and the coins here were very large, such as the octodrachm (eight-drachma piece) of the Macedonian Orrescii tribe. In Italy the late 6th-century-BC coins had a thin metal flan or disk, with the main design in relief on one side and the same design in intaglio on the other. Examples include the barley ear on coins of Metapontum. The more normal double-sided coins were adopted in Italy and Sicily.

CLASSICAL

Coins from the early 5th century to the late 4th century BC were usually double sided, with the head of a deity on one side and a related design on the other. There were some very fine designs throughout the Greek states and colonies, particularly in Sicily. However, in cities like Aegina, Corinth and Athens, the types (the design, indicating the origin of the coin) changed little for centuries. Athens retained its archaic design of the head of Athena (obverse) and owl (reverse); with only small variations in design, this coin lasted to the Roman period. Most coins had designs relating to a deity, either an

Fig. 5.6   *A silver tetradrachm of c. 450 BC, one of the so-called owls of Athens. This reverse shows an owl, a symbol of Athena, with the first three letters of the city's name. Above the owl are portrayed olive leaves and a waning moon. For the obverse see fig. 1.6.*   Courtesy of Somerset County Museums Service.

Fig. 5.7   Obverse of a silver stater from Heraclea in Italy, depicting the head of Athena with Scylla on her helmet. The reverse (fig. 4.4) depicts Heracles strangling a lion.   Courtesy of Somerset County Museums Service.

Fig. 5.8   Gold stater of Philip II of Macedonia. This reverse shows a two-horse chariot (biga), with the driver holding a staff or rod. Underneath are the trident symbol and the letters PHILIPPOU (of Philip). The obverse (fig. 8.2) shows Apollo.   Courtesy of Somerset County Museums Service.

oblique reference, such as a deity's favorite animal, or the head or figure of the deity (fig. 5.7).

There was an increase in the production of small change from c. 450 BC. For domestic use at Athens there was a great range of denominations, and copper coins known as chalkoi (khalkoi) were introduced in the late 5th or early 4th century BC. Circa 449 BC Athens issued a decree that Athenian coinage and weights and measures should be adopted by all allies within the Delian League, and that they should not strike their own silver coins, although other coinage continued to flourish. In Macedonia the coinage of individual cities ceased once they fell to Philip II. He himself extensively issued silver tetradrachms with the head of Zeus and a racehorse reverse, and also gold staters with the head of Apollo and a chariot on the reverse (fig. 5.8). The gold staters found their way into western Europe, and were even copied by the Celtic coinage of Gaul and Britain in the 1st century BC.

HELLENISTIC

The coins of Alexander the Great had worldwide circulation, and he adopted the Euboic-Attic standard for both gold and silver. His coinage was minted in gold, silver and bronze. Gold coins were primarily staters, with the head of Athena on the obverse and Nike on the reverse. The tetradrachm was the main silver coin, with the head of Heracles on the obverse (similar to the head of Alexander the Great), and an enthroned Zeus on the reverse (fig. 5.12). Bronze coins had Heracles' head and club and bow symbols. Alexander's main mints were in Macedonia, but mints were also established to produce this uniform coinage throughout his empire, at places such as Miletus, Tarsus, Side, Cyprus and Babylon. It was still produced after his death, until the end of the 4th century BC, when his successors began to produce their own individual coinage.

With the rise of Hellenistic kingdoms, coins were rarely minted by individual city-states, but by much larger regions, such as the Aetolian and Achaean Confederacies and kingdoms. Athens and Rhodes were the only two major city-states to mint continuously to the 1st century BC. Only bronze coinage was produced by individual city-states. The first portraits of Alexander appeared on coins after his death. Portraits of other rulers also began to appear, such as Philip V and his son Perseus on Macedonian silver tetradrachms. At the end of the

Fig. 5.9   Bronze litra *from Syracuse in Sicily of c. 344* BC. *The obverse (left) shows Athena in a wreathed Corinthian helmet, and the reverse (right) shows two dolphins and a starfish.*

4th century BC, portraits of rulers appeared on Egyptian coins, initially of Ptolemy I, and portraits of the deified royal family were also used, particularly the veiled head of the deified Arsinoë II.

The numerous smaller Hellenistic kingdoms, including those that broke away from the Seleucid Empire (such as Bactria), produced coins with very fine regal portraits, especially on silver tetra-drachms. Greek-type coinage was gradually eliminated with the expansion of Roman power, initially in Italy and Sicily, then mainland Greece and Asia Minor.

COIN DEMONINATIONS

Early coin values were mainly of high denominations, little better than ingots, and so were too large for domestic usage. They may have been used when large payments were needed, such as in trade between rulers, and in payment for taxation and mercenaries. Smaller denominations in the form of very small silver coins gradually appeared, and in the 4th century BC bronze and gold coins became more common. The value of coins depended on the value of the metal from which the coins were made. The ratio of silver to gold was 1:13 in 6th-century-BC Lydia and 1:10 in Athens during the Peloponnesian War, while the ratio of bronze to silver was 1:110 in the 5th century BC, and 1:50–70 in the late 4th to late 3rd centuries BC.

Trade between states was complicated by the many weight standards in different cities, which also had to be correlated with the eastern system of staters and minae. The two main standards were Aeginetic (used from Thessaly to the Peloponnese) and Euboic-Attic, the latter being more complex. Units of money had the same names as units of weight, because they denoted weights of metal. Despite the differences in weight standards, the same money values were used in the different city-states, based on the *obelos* (iron spit). The values of coins were not stated on the actual coins.

The smallest silver coin was the obol (*obolos*, equivalent to one spit), and six obols constituted a drachm(a); the name of the drachm (*drakhme*) was apparently derived from *drax* (handful) of six iron spits (*obeloi*)—as many spits as could be held in one hand. In Sicily the drachma was not divided into six obols, but five litras (*litrai*, sing. *litra*, fig. 5.9). An *obkia* was an ounce, one-twelfth of the Sicilian bronze litra. Large sums of money were represented as weights in silver, sometimes gold. A talent (*talenton*) was about 57 lb (26 kg) in the Euboic-Attic system. The main Greek money values were:

12 chalkoi = 1 obol
6 obols = 1 drachma
1 stater = 2, sometimes 3, drachmas
100 drachmas = 1 mina (*mna*)
60 minas = 1 talent

Common coins included a two-drachma piece (didrachm, fig. 5.10) and four-drachma piece (tetradrachm). Also known are a half-drachma (hemidrachm), three-drachma (tridrachm), five-drachma (pentadrachm), eight-drachma (octodrachm), ten-drachma (decadrachm), twelve-drachma (dodekadrachm), quarter-obol (tetartemorion—a very thin coin), one-and-a-half tetartemorion (trihemitetartemorion), three-tetartemorion coin (tritartemorion), half-obol (hemiobol), one-and-a-half obols (trihemiobol), two-obol coin (diobol), three-obol coin (triobol), four-obol coin (terobol), three-onkia coin (trias), two-litra coin (dilitron), and a half-litra bronze coin (hemilitron).

MINTING

Coins were always struck with dies, never cast in molds. A design (device) was engraved on the obverse die, which was situated in a recess on the anvil. A flan or blank of the required weight was heated and shaped to fit the die. It was placed on the die by tongs, and a short stout bar (a punch) was hit by a hammer, which then struck the blank on the die (fig. 5.11). The coin received the design in relief on the obverse and an incuse impression on the reverse. By the late 6th century BC, the punch also carried the reverse die, so double-sided coins could be produced. Dies were usually of bronze or iron, and were cut in intaglio. Artists' signatures are found on some designs, especially those of Italy and Sicily of the 5th and 4th centuries BC.

Each state usually appointed a magistrate for one year in charge of the mint, and his name or monogram appeared on many of the later coins (fig. 5.12). The presumed artists' signatures may possibly be those of the mint official. Overstriking is found, where new coins were struck on existing coins—usually a foreign coin or one that had been withdrawn, including coins of defeated enemies. Evidence of the previous coin is often visible.

Fig. 5.10   Reverse of a silver didrachm of Acragas. The crab possibly represented the emblem of Poseidon, but may have been a freshwater crab. The obverse (fig. 4.14) was an eagle, and these two emblems were used for nearly a century in Acragas from the end of the 6th century BC. Courtesy of Somerset County Museums Service.

Banking

Banking could not properly develop before the invention of coins. At first, temples such as that of Artemis at Ephesus effectively had regional monopolies on banking, storing valuables and providing loans. Between 433 and 427 BC the temple of Athena at Athens lent the city-state finance at an interest rate of 6 percent. In the Classical period much of the banking trade was taken over by private individual bankers (*trapezitai*), many of whom were money changers, operating at temples and markets. Such bankers were usually metics. In addition to changing money, they held deposits and provided loans. Often banking was an adjunct to other business. Pasion (died 370 BC) was a famous banker in Athens who also had a flourishing shield manufacturing business.

Bankers took cash deposits, on which interest was paid, and provided safekeeping for valuables, mainly for merchants in foreign cities. Most citizens kept their wealth hidden at home rather than at a bank. Loans were made to individuals (but apparently not to the state) for various commercial ventures, such as mortgages, and as a form of shipping insurance called bottomry loans. These loans had a high rate of interest and were repayable only if the voyage was successful, but not if the ship or cargo was lost through accident. The terms of such loans were set out in a written contract, and interest rates varied according to the particular voyage. For example, in the 4th century BC the interest on a bottomry loan for a voyage from Byzantium to Athens was about 10–12 percent, whereas from Athens to Pontus and back it was about 30 percent. There are a few recorded instances where other types of insurance were provided by banks.

Money changing (conversion from one currency to another) was a high-risk business, which appears to be one of the reasons why money changers took up banking, although banking also had its risks. A panic among depositors could cause a run on a bank, resulting in bankruptcy for the banker.

Despite the rise of individual bankers, temples continued to operate as banks, some being controlled by city-states. Some cities established public banks which performed some of the functions of a private bank, but primarily handled the money from the city's taxes and spent it in accordance with the city's budget. In Hellenistic times, temples, private banks and cities continued their banking businesses

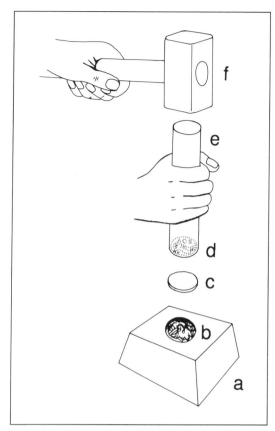

Fig. 5.11   Striking a coin: a. anvil; b. obverse die; c. coin blank; d. reverse die; e. punch; f. hammer.

with little change, but in the region controlled by the Ptolemies a public banking system was created. A network of royal banks spread throughout Egypt, with a central bank at Alexandria. Branches in outlying areas were leased to private bankers under the control of the state bank.

TRAVEL AND TRANSPORT

Maps and Itineraries

Little evidence survives for ancient Greek maps, perhaps because they may have been normally drawn on perishable materials. The evidence sug-

gests that they were usually painted on wood but occasionally engraved on bronze. The Greeks thought that the first mapmaker was a philosopher, Anaximander of Miletus (c. 611–546 BC). Ancient authors record him making a map of the known world, although their descriptions do not provide an idea of its appearance. It was drawn on a *pinax* (pl. *pinakes*), a term meaning a painted panel and sometimes a bronze panel. Other world maps are mentioned by authors such as Herodotus, and it appears that many were circular, with the land masses of Europe and Asia surrounded by ocean. Greece seems to have been at the center of these early maps, with Delphi at the center of Greece. Delphi is near the center of the Greek mainland, but more importantly it was the religious center and main religious meeting place of the Greeks. Delphi claimed to be the *omphalos* (navel) of the world.

The reference by Herodotus to maps implies that when he was writing (c. 444–430 BC) maps were not a rarity. The overall impression given by ancient historical sources is that the position of

Fig. 5.12   Silver tetradrachm of Alexander the Great. This reverse is of enthroned Zeus, holding a scepter in his left hand and an eagle in his right. The letters BASILEOS (king) and ALEXANDROU (of Alexander) are present, as well as the initials of the magistrate or official for minting the coinage. The obverse (fig. 8.12) is of the head of Heracles.   Courtesy of Somerset County Museums Service.

countries around Greece was known, and the approximate size and shape of islands. Although the coasts of Europe, Asia and Africa were known, the extent of these land masses remained unknown, and there was generally little detailed information about any particular place.

Alexander the Great regarded his expedition against the Persians as not only a military campaign but also an exploratory one. Before setting out, his secretaries gathered all available information, and Alexander took with him various scholars and technicians to record new discoveries. It is not known if these people made maps, but the group did include two "road measurers" whose job was to record distances between places, geography, soil, vegetation and wildlife.

Eratosthenes (c. 280–c. 194 BC) greatly improved the potential accuracy of world maps by estimating the circumference of the Earth, from which lines of latitude and longitude could be calculated. He drew his main axes of latitude and longitude to intersect at Rhodes. Eratosthenes wrote *On the Measurement of the Earth* and *Geographica*, neither of which have survived. He drew a map of the world that was presented to the Ptolemaic court of Egypt. This was the first properly scientific Greek map and greatly influenced world maps in succeeding centuries.

A *periplus* (a sailing round, pl. *periploi*) was the name given to records of coastal voyages. These were verbal instructions or textual records rather than maps, and fragments have been preserved in the works of ancient Greek and Roman authors. The surviving fragments are from journeys of exploration on the edges of the Greek world and so are probably exceptional. Most sea journeys were coastal, or island to island, with ships traveling from point to point and generally keeping within sight of land. Most *periploi* probably covered frequently traveled routes, listing landmarks, distances and hazards.

Land Transport

The landscape of Greece and the poor state of the roads did not encourage travel or transport by land. Travelers by land often went on foot or horseback, and pack animals were frequently used for carrying loads. Porters were sometimes used for light loads

of around 50–60 lbs (23–27 kg) over very short distances. Transport of goods by land was insignificant in comparison with sea transport.

ROADS

Unlike the Romans the Greeks did not systematically build networks of roads. Most roads in ancient Greece were little more than tracks. The road surface was often the surface of the natural limestone, but parts of a road might be paved where the underlying rock was not suitable. Some stretches of paved road have survived, particularly near important sites such as Delphi, and some date to the Mycenaean period. River beds could be used as roads, as they provided a naturally gravelled road surface, and river gorges gave access through mountainous areas.

Some roads had cartwheel ruts, which may have been worn into the rock surface by traffic. Many ruts, however, were deliberately cut in the surface of roads to facilitate the passage of vehicles, although erosion may have subsequently deepened them. Without the extra grip and stability provided by these ruts, it is thought that many roads would have been impassable to wheeled traffic. They are found particularly on sloping grades and where the rock surface was uneven. The average distance between wheel ruts is 4.6 ft (1.4 m), although there is some variation. These roads appear to date from the Archaic period, although some roads with wheel ruts may be Mycenaean. The use and construction of this type of road continued into the Roman period.

Some paved roads with wheel ruts were sacred roads, usually leading from a city to a nearby religious sanctuary. They provided easy passage for pilgrims, and were also processional ways. Many processional ways followed routes believed to have been taken by particular deities, and their main purpose was for the vehicles carrying statues of gods and other sacred objects that accompanied processions.

"Wagon roads" are occasionally mentioned in ancient sources, presumably meaning all the roads with cartwheel ruts. But such roads were in the minority. Most roads were designed for pedestrians, horses and pack animals, and were generally impassable for wheeled vehicles.

One particular road for which there is good evidence is the *diolkos* across the Isthmus of Corinth. This road ran from Schoinous on the Saronic Gulf across the isthmus to the Gulf of Corinth. It was built specifically for the transport of ships across the Isthmus. Paved with stone slabs, it was 11.8–13.8 ft (3.6–4.2 m) wide. It had two parallel ruts 4.9 ft (1.5 m) apart for the wheels of the vehicle that transported the ships. This road was built in the 6th century BC and was still in use in the 9th century AD.

BRIDGES

Little is known about bridges, but it is assumed that timber ones were used from an early date. Some bridges with corbeled stone arches have been found associated with Bronze Age roads. It is thought that bridges with this type of construction continued in use into the Classical period. Bridges supported on stone pillars spanned by stone lintels were used from the 5th century BC, and Hellenistic bridges were sometimes supported on masonry piers designed to disturb the flow of water as little as possible. Some bridges were constructed with removable wooden roadways rather than permanent stone ones. Masonry bridges using true arches, rather than lintels or corbeling, do not seem to have been constructed until the Roman period.

MILESTONES

Very few milestones have survived, which no doubt reflects the poor state of ancient Greek roads. Milestones were probably never common. Even after absorption into the Roman Empire, there were fewer milestones in Greece than elsewhere. Milestones appear to have been simple in form, inscribed with the names of places and relevant distances. Hipparchus, the son of Peisistratus, is recorded as having set up herms in Attica marking the halfway point between Athens and each surrounding village. It has been estimated that there must have been around 100 of these herms, although only one has been discovered.

PACK ANIMALS

Donkeys were probably the most common method of transporting goods and could probably carry loads of 220 lbs (100 kg). Mules (a cross between a male donkey and a female horse) were hardier, stronger and more sure-footed than horses, and could carry loads of 198–441 lbs (90–200 kg). Both mules and donkeys were also used for riding. Horses were luxury items, status symbols affordable only by the rich. Apart from horses used for cavalry or in sports such as chariot racing, a few were used for riding, but rarely for transport.

Loads could be secured onto a mule or donkey with ropes, or a pack saddle could be used. Pack saddles had a wooden frame covered with cloth or leather to which the load could be secured. Panniers, usually made of soft basketry, were probably often used. They are shown in ancient artistic representations and are still used in parts of Greece today. Slings to carry a pair of pottery jars or other vessels were also common. Pack animals could cope with the poorest of tracks and roads, and the majority of goods transported by land were carried by pack animals.

WHEELED VEHICLES

The date of the introduction of chariots into Greece is uncertain. They were probably introduced from Syria and were used from at least the Mycenaean period. Very few actual remains of chariots have survived, and most evidence comes from texts of ancient authors and from artistic representations. Chariots were light vehicles with two spoked wheels, usually drawn by a pair of horses (sometimes four) and designed to travel fast. They carried only one or two people, usually standing (fig. 5.13), and were probably not greatly used for general transportation. They were mainly for warfare and later for racing (see chapter 3).

Two-wheeled carts were for the transport of goods too heavy or bulky for pack animals. Four-wheeled wagons were for even heavier or more unwieldy loads. Both types of vehicle were of relatively simple wooden construction and had solid, spoked or cross-bar wheels, also of wood. They were usually drawn by a pair of mules or oxen, with a neck yoke and a harness to keep the yoke in place. This type of harness is more suitable for oxen than mules. It is very inefficient if used with horses as it tends to obstruct their windpipes. The continued use of this type of harness and the failure to develop a more efficient type are sometimes taken as a measure of the lack of importance of land transport in Greece. Both carts and wagons were all-purpose vehicles and might carry passengers or a variety of types of load (fig. 5.14).

Shipping

TYPES OF MERCHANT SHIPS

Little is known about merchant ships before the 5th century BC, and even then the evidence is sparse. There were undoubtedly various shapes and sizes of merchant ships, but relatively little evidence about their design has survived. Few ancient representations of merchant ships exist, although evidence has recently come from surveys and excavations of shipwrecks. Unlike warships (see chapter 3), the design of merchant ships does not appear to have greatly changed during the Greek period, except that later ships tended to be larger than earlier ones. Greek merchant ships relied on sails for power. They usually carried some oars, but there were generally not enough oars or crew to move the ships much distance.

Sailing ships were known as *strongyla ploia* (sing. *strongylon ploion*, round ships) or *holkades* (sing. *holkas*, merchant ship). *Holkas* comes from a word meaning "tow," because these ships relied almost completely on sails and were generally towed in and

Fig. 5.14   A two-wheeled cart with passengers pulled by a mule, depicted on a Boeotian black-figure vase.

out of harbors. They were broad, deep vessels with a curved prow, unlike the characteristic ram on warships. Also unlike warships, they could carry large amounts of cargo, maintain better stability in bad weather, and continue sailing both day and night over long distances without intermediate stops. The few representations depict merchant ships with differing deck arrangements, but they all had decks and usually some kind of housing on the deck. The earliest ships appear to have had a single mast, but by the Roman period two and three masts had been developed.

The merchant galley was a hybrid of the sailing ship and warship. They were used to carry dispatches, passengers and cargo, in particular, cargo needing rapid transport. *Ploia* (sing. *ploion*, ship) was a general term for merchant ships and merchant galleys. The galleys were wider than warships and had a curved or straight prow, although some had a prow similar to a warship. Smaller galleys probably relied wholly on oars, but larger ones relied more on sails, using oars only when needed. There were many more merchant ships than oared galleys, but the latter often had an auxiliary role in warfare. There is therefore more information about them in the texts of ancient authors, who mention various types of galleys.

Merchant ships were not built for speed and could be rather slow, but they were generally cheaper and quicker than land transport. They could not make reasonable progress without a following wind and could be substantially affected by an adverse wind, making journeys take three or four times longer than those with favorable winds. If a contrary wind was met, a sailing ship would set its sails as close to the wind as possible and proceed by a zigzag course.

Fig. 5.13   Silver tetradrachm of Syracuse of 474–450 BC. This obverse shows a quadriga chariot, with the four horses walking. Beneath is a sea monster (ketos), possibly alluding to the sea victory by Hieron at Cyme in 474 BC. The reverse shows Arethusa and four dolphins (fig. 10.5).   Courtesy of Somerset County Museums Service.

SHIP CONSTRUCTION

A passage in Homer's *Odyssey* describes Odysseus building a ship on Calypso's island and has been interpreted as a reasonably accurate account of the construction of a merchant ship, apparently confirmed by excavated shipwrecks. A hull-first (shell sequence) of construction was used, in which the watertight shell was built or partly built before the internal timbers were inserted for support. Later ships had a keel, but probably not earlier ships.

In shell construction the longitudinal planks (strakes) were fastened to each other edge-to-edge by mortise-and-tenon joints to form a complete hull or shell. The mortises were cut into opposing edges of planks, which were held together by tenons and fixed firmly in place by wooden pegs. The frames (ribs) were then shaped and inserted in this hull. Each frame was secured to the planking of the hull with treenails, which were themselves held in place with bronze spikes that were hammered into them. A lining of wooden planks was then nailed over the frames.

The hull was waterproofed by smearing the seams and sometimes the entire exterior with pitch. Generally, little waterproofing was necessary due to the tightness of the mortise-and-tenon joints. The underwater surface of the hull was then often sheathed in lead as protection against marine worms, with thin lead plates nailed over a tarred fabric layer. As merchant ships were normally kept afloat, not hauled ashore, they would have been especially vulnerable to worms without the lead sheathing. In some cases a false timber keel was nailed onto the hull over the lead sheathing, presumably to provide protection if the ship was beached.

Most merchant ships apparently had a main deck that ran from stem to stern. Larger ships probably had a lower deck as well, but whether this was a full or partial deck is unknown. A deckhouse at the stern appears to have had a flat roof, which could be used as a raised afterdeck. The ships were steered by long oars operated by a tiller.

SIZE OF SHIPS

Evidence for physical dimensions of ancient Greek ships is rarely available, but records indicate the size of cargoes. The smallest seagoing ships appear to have been able to carry 70–80 tons of cargo, and from the 5th century BC 100–150 tons were commonly carried. Even at this early date cargoes of 350–500 tons were not rare, although they were considered very large. Hellenistic merchant ships were even larger, and the largest recorded ship was built in the 3rd century BC for Hieron II, king of Syracuse. It was so large that Archimedes was required to devise the method of launching. This ship was apparently unique. It was a massive grain carrier with three decks and three masts and an estimated carrying capacity of 1,700–1,900 tons. The carrying capacity of a ship was only loosely related to its physical size. A vessel designed to carry bulky but relatively light types of cargo would obviously be much larger than one carrying the same weight of denser material such as stone.

SAILS

Merchant ships had sails, rarely using oars because far too many crew members would be needed for rowing. The two types of sailing rigs were square rigs and fore-and-aft rigs. With square rigs the mainsail was a broad square sail on a single central mast, with occasionally a topsail above. Some ships also had a foremast with a square foresail. In representations of ships the foremast is shown sloping forward rather than upright. Some Hellenistic ships may also have had a mizzenmast, with sails behind the mainmast. Square rig was the usual method of rigging, with sails at right angles to the axis of the hull, gaining full power when the wind was directly astern.

With fore-and-aft rigs the sails were set in line with the hull, which enabled the ship to tack and therefore sail into the wind. Fore-and-aft rigs were not commonly used until the medieval period.

Sails (*histia*, sing. *histion*) were usually made of square and rectangular pieces of linen cloth sewn together, the edges protected by a boltrope and the corners reinforced by leather patches. Ropes were of flax, hemp, papyrus or esparto grass.

PASSENGERS AND CREW

Compared with warships, merchant ships had a relatively small crew. The smallest ships might have only three or four men, although larger ships would require more. Unlike warships, crews on merchant ships were often slaves. Late Greek and Roman authors provide names for some types of men controlling merchant ships. The most important was the *naukleros* (shipowner or charterer). If the cargo belonged to the *naukleros*, he or his representative probably sailed with the ship. A professional captain (*kybernetes*, literally "helmsman") was hired to run the ship, although occasionally the *naukleros* would take the role of captain. The actual working of the ship was carried out by sailors (*nautai*, sing. *nautes*).

No ships were specifically passenger ships. Anyone wanting to travel by ship went to the harbor and made inquiries, until they found a merchant ship going to their required destination. Most ships were designed for cargoes only and had little accommodation other than for the captain, although there were sometimes a few cabins for important passengers, such as the shipowner, and for those who could afford them. Passengers (like most of the crew) generally lived on deck or under tent-like shelters and ate food they had brought with them. Water was generally provided for passengers, who were allowed use of the galley for cooking food. Only the humblest people traveled without at least one servant. These servants took turns using the galley to prepare food for their masters. A small all-purpose boat was usually towed behind the ship, but there were no lifeboats. Because merchant galleys tended to travel close to the shore, they were regarded as safer for passengers than the ships that sailed across open water.

NAVIGATION

Throughout the Greek period navigation was by observation of the sun and stars. Stars seem to have been mostly used, and captains of ships presumably had a good working knowledge of astronomy. They must also have had a good knowledge of winds, since in the Mediterranean winds blow from different directions at various times of year, or in some places at various times of day. This knowledge would have been crucial for merchant shipping, which relied on sail power.

It is likely that some charts existed, although none have survived. For coastal navigation *periploi* provided lists of landmarks, with distances, to assist a ship's captain in plotting a course. The only instrument available as a navigational aid was a lead line, which was a lead weight on the end of a line used to measure the depth of water beneath the ship. Wax in a hollow on the bottom of the lead weight could pick up material from the seabed to give an idea of the ship's position.

RIVERBOATS

River transport was much less important than sea transport within Greece, because of the lack of easily navigable rivers. River transport increased in importance in the Hellenistic period when inland waterways, such as the Nile in Egypt, came under Greek control. Indeed, most evidence for river craft relates to those used on the Nile. All types of merchant galleys were used on this waterway, and the smaller types were probably used on other rivers. The Nile also had a variety of river craft, ranging from canoes to the large *thalamegoi* (cabin carriers), which were expensive barges for transporting the nobility and officials. A particularly grandiose *thalamegos* was built by Ptolemy IV and was effectively a floating palace. Simple small boats powered by paddles, oars or a single sail, as well as boats and barges towed by other vessels, were probably commonly used on many rivers.

HARBORS

It is assumed that early ships were beached when not in use, propped upright with timber and stones. For winter storage they might be covered with coarse cloth or branches for protection from the weather. Some possible Bronze Age harbor works have been found in Crete, but the evidence is inconclusive.

Enclosed harbors began to be developed in Greece from the 6th century BC. At this time a harbor at Samos was enclosed by a mole about 1,310 ft (400 m) long, built out into water about 100 ft (30 m) deep. Other harbors are not precisely dated, but appear to have been developed during the 6th to 3rd centuries BC. At Mytilene on Lesbos a citadel was located on a peninsula that provided a natural harbor on either side. A similar situation occurred at Cyzicus and Smyrna. At Aegina harbors were formed by building thick stone walls out from the shore, with towers on the end to protect the harbor entrance. On the north side of Piraeus was a large inlet, which became the commercial harbor (fig. 3.17), and at other places, such as Syracuse, Nisaea or Cnidus, offshore islands, reefs and projecting headlands were adapted to form harbors.

In Hellenistic times many ports were expanded and new ones created. In many cases, such as

Alexandria in Egypt, the port had been established before the Greek period and continued in use through the Roman and Byzantine periods to the present day. In such cases the archaeological remains of Hellenistic harbors are often inaccessible, and any remains are often difficult to interpret or date accurately.

LIGHTHOUSES

As early as the 5th century BC the harbor at Piraeus was marked at night by fires on columns, and beacon towers were apparently used at other harbors. The first true lighthouse was at Alexandria in Egypt. Known as the Pharos, its name derives from the island of Pharos in front of the harbor. It was apparently begun under Ptolemy I in the late 3rd century BC, and was a three-tiered polygonal structure about 328 ft (100 m) in overall height. The light was provided by a huge fire in the base, which was said to be reflected by mirrors (probably of burnished bronze) at the top of the structure, which increased the intensity of the light. The Pharos came to be regarded as one of the Seven Wonders of the World and was the model for later Hellenistic and Roman lighthouses.

Pirates

Piracy was endemic in the Greek world. In the works of Homer, piracy is accepted as natural, and from the Archaic period the distinction between acts of war and acts of piracy was often not at all clear. Pirates not only attacked shipping, but also sometimes attacked coastal towns and operated as wreckers. A major part of their occupation was kidnapping people for ransom. At various times Greek city-states with an interest in protecting shipping and possessing a powerful navy made attempts to suppress piracy, but piracy was never completely eradicated.

READING

Economy and Industry

AGRICULTURE

Bolkstein 1958, 12–35; Burford 1993: agriculture, land tenure and land management; Hopper 1979,

147–163; Isager and Skydsgaard 1992: major source; Mitchell 1940, 38–88; Pullen 1992: early evidence for plowing; Sallares 1991, 294–389: especially olive production and cereals; White 1978: contains translations of extracts about agriculture and country life from ancient authors; White 1988, 211–218.

HUNTING AND FISHING

Bolkstein 1958, 35–40; Brothwell 1988, 259–260: fishing; Hammond and Scullard (eds.) 1970, 533: hunting.

FOOD PROCESSING

Brothwell 1988; Hammond and Scullard (eds.) 1970, 748–749: olive oil, 1,138–1,139: wine; Mitchell 1940, 190–196: wine, olive oil, milling and baking.

EXTRACTIVE INDUSTRIES

Hammond and Scullard (eds.) 1970, 689–690: mines; Healy 1978: mining; Healy 1988: mines and quarries; Hopper 1979, 164–189: mining; Jones 1987: Laurium mining area; Meiggs 1982: includes timber trade; Mitchell 1940, 89–124: mining.

MANUFACTURING

Bonfante and Jaunzems 1988: textiles; Fitton (ed.) 1992: ivory; Grose 1984, 9–22: glass; Hammond and Scullard (eds.) 1970, 561: ivory, 676–677: metalworking, 1,137–1,138: weaving; Harden 1968: glass; Hemelrijk 1991: pottery; Higgins 1961: major source for jewelry of various materials; Jones 1987: silver and lead; Mitchell 1940, 124: salt, 170–173: leather, 173–179: pottery, 179–190: textiles, 196–202: woodworking, 204–209: metalworking; Sparkes 1991, 8–27: pottery.

Trade of Goods

Dickinson 1994, 234–256: Bronze Age; Hammond and Scullard (eds.) 1970, 55–56: stamped amphorae, 1,074–1,075: timber; Hopper 1979: most aspects of trade of goods; Meiggs 1982: includes timber trade; Mitchell 1940: still very useful (despite its age) for many aspects of trade; Smith 1987: Mycenaean trade in Sicily, Italy and Sardinia; Sparkes 1991: pottery trade; Talbert (ed.) 1985, 51–53: trade routes.

COMMERCE

Carson 1988: coins; Davis 1967: coins of individual city-states; Hammond and Scullard (eds.) 1970, 160–161: banking, 436–437: taxation; Jenkins 1990: coins; Jones: useful dictionary of coins; Kagan 1982: earliest coins; Kraay 1966: coins; Littman 1988: taxation; Mitchell 1940, 131–132: wages, 333–351: banking, 352–393: taxation; Thompson 1988: taxation; Whibley (ed.) 1931, 528: wages.

Travel and Transport

MAPS AND ITINERARIES

Dilke 1985, 21–38, 130–137, 196; Hammond and Scullard (eds.) 1970, 645, 802.

LAND TRANSPORT

Armstrong et al. 1992: bridges in Laconia; Crouwel 1981: major source for Bronze Age transport; Crouwel 1992: major source for Iron Age chariots and carts, 21–22: roads; Hammond and Scullard (eds.) 1970, 180: bridges, 925: roads; Hill 1984, 78–79: sacred roads; Landels 1978, 170–185: pack animals, porters and carts; Piggott 1983: major source for chariots and carts; Pritchett 1980, 143–196: major source for roads, 158–167: milestones.

SHIPPING AND PIRATES

Casson 1971, 157–168: merchant galleys, 170–173: size of cargoes, 314–321: crews of merchant ships, 331–335: riverboats; Casson 1988: pirates; Casson 1994, 119–120: anchors, 121–122: cargo size, 124–126: passengers, 131–137: riverboats; Clayton 1988, 138–157: the Pharos; Hammond and Scullard (eds.) 1970, 488: harbors, 609: lighthouses, 724–725: navigation, 834–835: pirates; Hopper 1979, 195–197: pirates; McKechnie 1989, 101–141: pirates; Morrison 1980, 55–58: ship construction; Shaw 1972, 88–112: harbors; Throckmorton 1972, 78: navigation; Tomlinson 1992, 104–105: lighthouses.

6

TOWNS AND COUNTRYSIDE

The attention of archaeologists and historians has tended to focus on urban centers, particularly in the Classical and Hellenistic periods, because of the large amount of evidence readily available. Until recently features of the countryside have been neglected. This has resulted in much more information about urban life than about rural settlements, although rural villages and farms must have been a constant feature of the Greek landscape from the Bronze Age.

The surviving history of the Classical period is dominated by the often hostile relations between the major city-states (poleis). However, the poleis were largely confined to central and southern Greece, the Aegean islands, Italy, Sicily and the colonies on the west coast of Turkey. In other areas political and social structures were not always based on the concept of the polis, and many areas were effectively nonurbanized. The polis was a city-state, a political unit, with an urban center and surrounding territory. The urban center (or even the upper town) was the *asty*.

The terms "town" and "city" are used synonymously by most authors, and the two terms do not necessarily imply different types of government or reflect different sizes. The term town planning (rather than city planning) is common usage.

TOWNS AND THEIR PLANNING

A variety of settlements developed throughout the very long history of the Greek world. These included the palaces and associated settlements of the Minoan and Mycenaean periods, the poleis and the colonies. Alexander the Great and his successors founded a large number of new towns. Numerous Classical and Hellenistic towns continued to flourish throughout the Roman period.

Unplanned Towns

BRONZE AGE

Towns and cities originated in Mesopotamia many centuries before they developed in Greece, but evidence of Eastern influence on the development of Greek towns and cities is minimal. Towns that were not deliberately laid out to a pattern, but were the product of unrestricted or partially restricted development, had a variety of plans. Settlements recognizable as towns are evident during the Bronze Age, particularly on Crete and some other Aegean islands. Bronze Age towns show a degree of controlled development, with a fairly regular plan to the main streets that divide the towns into blocks of buildings. The impression is that the towns evolved and developed, rather than being originally subject to a detailed plan. The blocks of buildings were irregular and were divided by alleyways, small open spaces and squares. Some apparently had a public square as their focus, some centered on an important building or a citadel, and others appear to have been a ribbon development, following a street line that served much of the settlement. Buildings were separated by a basic network of main streets and many small alleyways, which often provided routes for drainage channels as well. Buildings in these towns varied in size and complexity, but generally had several rooms and two floors. On the mainland it appears that towns were often fortified, but evidence for this is lacking in Crete.

DARK AGE

With the collapse of the Mycenaean civilization, the settlement pattern seems to have changed. Although recent evidence suggests that the concentration of population in towns was not as great during the later Mycenaean period as was once thought, there still seems to have been a move toward a less dense settlement pattern during the Dark Age. Easily defended hills were fortified and surrounded on the lower slopes by scattered villages, some of which later developed into towns and cities. Villages were linked by a network of paths that became the basis for city streets. They gradually developed into unplanned towns with irregular streets and unrestricted development clustered around a citadel. A good example of this type of development is Athens, where sporadic settlement around the Acropolis eventually resulted in a cramped and overcrowded city, with irregular blocks of buildings divided by narrow winding streets.

Synoecismus (*synoikismos*) was the amalgamation of villages into a single city-state, which the Greeks regarded as a single act or event. For example, the synoecismus of Athens was allegedly performed by Theseus. In reality such amalgamation of villages took place over a considerable period of time. The term synoecismus was also applied to the bringing together of a rural population into a fortified town, or the amalgamation of two cities by a superior force (usually a Hellenistic king). In such cases the word referred to the actual movement of the population.

Town Planning

ORIGINS

There is controversy over the origins of Greek town planning, but there is no doubt that by the 5th century BC town planning was firmly established in Greece. In the Near East, town planning occurred earlier and despite the lack of direct evi-

dence, the Near East was probably the source of inspiration for town planning in Greece. Greek colonization of the western coast of Turkey began in the 11th century BC, and many of the early towns established here were on elevated, easily defended sites. Of these towns, Smyrna and Miletus provide the earliest evidence for Greek planned towns. After destruction by an earthquake at the end of the 8th century BC, Smyrna was rebuilt with a completely new layout. The peninsula on which it was built was divided into strips by a system of parallel streets. Little evidence for streets at right angles has been discovered, but lanes and alleys most likely provided access into and through the building blocks, within which houses were generally free-standing and aligned in the same direction. At the north end of the town the existing public area was enlarged to create a religious and civic zone. The development at Smyrna took place over several centuries; new fortifications were built near the end of the 7th century BC, just before the town was sacked by Alyattes in 600 BC.

At Miletus evidence of the early layout of the town is fragmentary, but there seem to have been deliberately planned districts with regular street

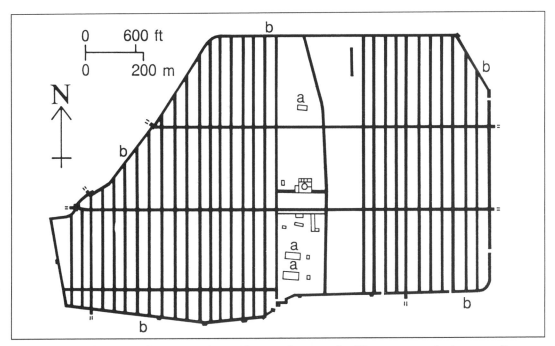

Fig. 6.1   *Plan of the town of Paestum with its grid system of streets and public areas: a. temples; b. town walls.*

T O W N S   A N D   C O U N T R Y S I D E

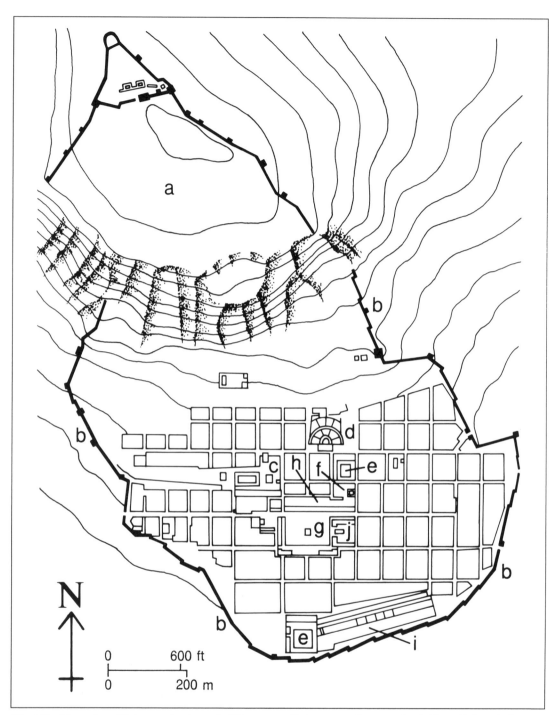

Fig. 6.2   Town plan of Priene on the slopes of a hill: a. acropolis; b. town walls; c. temple of Athena Polias; d. theater; e. gymnasia (two); f. bouleuterion and prytaneion; g. agora; h. sacred stoa; i. stadium; j. temple of Zeus.

plans. The dating of these planned districts is unclear, but their development may have begun before the end of the 8th century BC. However, the street plans of these different districts were not on the same alignment, implying that the town was not built to a unified plan at that date.

The imposition of town plans on existing settlements could be carried out only during rebuilding after destruction, as at Smyrna. However, increasing colonization from the 8th century BC enabled town planning to be more frequently used. Colonies were generally laid out in an orderly way, but not all conformed to a preconceived pattern. The superimposition of plans on existing settlements was often based on one or two main streets running across the site, which formed the axis for new development, whereas planned towns had one or more grids of streets dividing the town into blocks or insulae. Paestum in Italy is an example of the developed form of town planning (fig. 6.1). The colony was established in the 7th century BC, but the town planning probably dates to the end of the 6th century BC. Here an eastern and a western residential area were separated by an area for public use, containing temples (fig. 8.11) and civic buildings. The residential areas were divided into parallel strips of land by three regularly spaced avenues running east–west right across the site. They were also divided by more than 30 regularly spaced cross streets running north–south across the site, creating insulae 115 by 984 ft (35 by 300 m). Similar gridded town plans are found in many colonies, and the use of a regular street grid and different zones for different functions became the most important features of town planning.

CLASSICAL

While the political unit of the polis remained relatively unchanged, the urban center continued to develop. Town plans were not confined to a particular system of planning but were adapted to each situation, and sometimes the opportunity for planning a city was not adopted. For example, after Athens was destroyed by the Persians in 480 BC, it was rebuilt on the old irregular pattern rather than on a new planned grid of streets. In the 5th and 4th centuries BC there was a great increase in the number of cities in Greece, most of which had regular plans.

Little is known about Greek town planners and surveyors. It is likely that town planners were usually architects, and they were probably responsible for overseeing a number of surveyors who actually laid out the pattern of the town on the chosen site. Considering the amount of work in which they would have been involved, it is likely that there would have been a large number of surveyors (*geometrai*, sing. *geometres*; literally, "land measurer").

The first recorded town planner was Hippodamus of Miletus, who lived in the 5th century BC and has come to dominate the history of Classical town planning. His native city of Miletus was destroyed by the Persians in 494 BC, and the new city was rebuilt with a grid layout. It was once thought that Hippodamus invented this system of planning, but this has been disproved, and it is unlikely that he was responsible for the new layout of Miletus. Relatively little is known about Hippodamus, and there is even controversy over the planning of Piraeus. Aristotle states that Piraeus was planned by Hippodamus, but there is disagreement over the date when the city was laid out. Hippodamus is definitely associated with only three cities, Piraeus, Thurii and Rhodes, although it has been conjectured that he was involved with the planning of other cities. It is more likely that the similarity between cities such as Miletus and those with which Hippodamus was associated arose from his knowledge of the new layout of Miletus.

Despite their plans being adapted to local needs, cities of this period had certain common characteristics, such as the division of the city into large areas demarcated by wide main roads or avenues (*plateiai*). These areas were subdivided by a grid system of narrow streets (*stenopoi*). In most grids the streets intersected at right angles (orthogonal grids). In addition, cities associated with Hippodamus display an integrated design beyond the simple use of zoning, not usually evident in other cities; different districts were designated for specific purposes, such as commercial districts, residential districts, public and religious zones, and in the case of ports, harbor areas. Even within districts there is evidence for an integrated plan, such as the way public buildings were grouped together. Hippodamus appears to have based his plans on theoretical and mathematical principles, and at Rhodes, at least, the plan was made up of square areas of land of uniform and predetermined size.

This rigidly geometrical approach goes beyond the more pragmatic methods of land division used elsewhere.

In the later Classical period, town planning continued to be based on a grid system, but remained essentially functional. The ideas of Hippodamus do not seem to have greatly influenced the plans of later Classical cities. Town planning was not confined to a particular rigid system, and plans continued to be adapted to meet local conditions (fig. 6.2). The distance between avenues (*plateiai*) was reduced, and often town plans were laid out to give insulae of equal dimensions. One element that may have originated with Hippodamus was the attempt to use landscape for visual effect. In some cities built on sloping terrain, public buildings were not merely situated in commanding positions, but were positioned for visual effect.

HELLENISTIC

The conquests of Alexander the Great transformed Greece and the East. He and his successors founded many cities as centers of control and administration and as a means of spreading the Greek way of life. The element of propaganda was also important and not only were new cities founded, but established cities were also transformed with new designs and monumental architecture to provide visually impressive townscapes. Deinocrates of Rhodes was Alexander the Great's architect, responsible for building the new city of Alexandria in Egypt. Little else is known about him; indeed, Deinocrates and Hippodamus are the only two ancient Greek town planners whose names are known.

Hellenistic town plans continued to use a grid system as the quickest and most convenient method of establishing a new city, which resulted in a greater degree of uniformity in town plans. There was much greater exploitation of topography and careful placing of monumental buildings to produce an impressive city landscape. The most spectacular example was Pergamum in Turkey, which was greatly expanded from the time of Eumenes II (early 2nd century BC). Situated on the summit of a steep hill (fig. 4.13), complex and extensive terraces were needed to accommodate the city. The result was a unified plan of buildings, rising in tiers, that was visually extremely impressive.

Pergamum is often regarded as the high point of Hellenistic town planning.

PALACES

Bronze Age

In Bronze Age Crete sites that have been identified as "palaces" were built from the end of the 3rd millennium BC. The term "palace" has been used indiscriminately to describe both large establishments and also buildings that might be better described as "mansions" or "villas." The term is now generally used for very large sites, giving rise to what has been called the "palace economy." Palaces appear to have been at the center of an economic and administrative system that was at first local but eventually extended beyond Crete. These palaces were at the heart of towns and were often repeatedly rebuilt, making them difficult to interpret. Although palaces were administrative centers, the identification of the administrators is uncertain. Some palaces were originally assumed to be royal residences, but as yet no evidence supports this.

FIRST PALACE PERIOD

Palaces of this period are known at Knossos, Mallia, Phaistos and Chania, all built around a central courtyard. The best preserved example is Phaistos, which had a monumental paved courtyard crossed by raised walkways and flanked on the north by stepped stone benches. The courtyard was surrounded on other sides by buildings, beyond which there were other paved courts.

SECOND PALACE PERIOD

Palaces of this period provide more evidence for their structure and layout. The largest was at Knossos and covered approximately 15,550 sq yds (13,000 sq m). A central courtyard was again a major feature, surrounded by a continuous range of buildings and with a courtyard to the west. The ground floor of the west wing was used for storage (fig. 6.3), and the remains of the upper floor show that there were more imposing rooms above. Other important rooms opened off the west and north sides of the courtyard, and to the south the building may have had three or four floors.

The construction of the building was high quality, with carefully dressed stone used for foundations. The walls were strengthened by timber beams. Many walls were faced with large sheets of gypsum or were finished with plaster, and they were often decorated with elaborate frescoes. Other architectural features included the use of light wells and monumental stairways, frequent use of supporting pillars, and multiple doorways to form partitions. In a chamber off the "Queen's Megaron" was a bathroom and toilet, and the site was drained by channels and baked clay pipes. Some clay pipes possibly supplied water to the site. The building produced evidence for religious and ceremonial functions, but the use of many rooms is purely conjectural.

The other palace sites of this period, such as at Phaistos and Mallia, were generally similar to Knossos, but differed in architectural detail and were not quite so magnificent. The palace at Zakros differed most from that at Knossos. It had a central courtyard, but none to the west, and evidence for upper floors is sparse. It also seems to have been separated from the surrounding town by a wall. Around the palaces (particularly Knossos) were other buildings of a much smaller scale, but showing the same architectural quality.

Later writers located the legendary labyrinth (the maze-like building made by Daedalus for King Minos of Crete) at Knossos or at Gortyn, and it has sometimes been suggested that this identification was inspired by the complicated ruins of Knossos. Other possible connections with later legend include the use of the bull motif (echoing the half-man, half-bull Minotaur) and paintings of young men and women leaping over the horns of charging bulls. Although many objects and painted scenes from Knossos and other Minoan sites are believed to be of religious significance, virtually nothing is certain about Minoan religion or its place within the palace sites. What does seem certain is that the palaces controlled production of manufactured goods and food, and there was sufficient wealth for the production of luxury goods as well.

Fig. 6.3   The west magazines at Knossos, Crete, in the Second Palace Period. The clay jars (pithoi) stand nearly 6.56 ft (2 m) high and were used for the storage of wine, olive oil and grain. Lead-lined stone chests set in the floor held more valuable goods.

T O W N S   A N D   C O U N T R Y S I D E

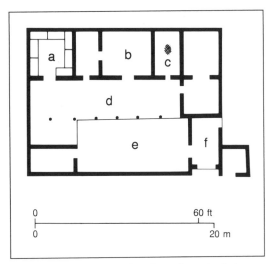

Fig. 6.4 *Ground plan of the Dema house in Attica: a.* andron *(with couches); b. kitchen; c. hearth; d. pastas;* e. courtyard; f. vestibule.

THIRD PALACE PERIOD

Palaces of this period continued on Crete, and are also found on mainland Greece at such places as Mycenae, Tiryns and Pylos. They are Mycenaean rather than Minoan, but like the Minoan palaces, they were surrounded by towns. Much smaller than the palaces on Crete, Tiryns is 76.5 by 65.6 yds (70 by 60 m), and Pylos is only 59 by 32.8 yds (54 by 30 m), which is about the same size as the central courtyard at Knossos. The main element of these palaces was the *megaron* (pl. *megara*), a large hall, often with a central hearth. It was entered from a smaller room or vestibule, which was itself entered from a porch. All three rooms shared the same side walls. This simple building unit often formed the basic structure of temples, and it has been identified as an element of other Greek buildings, from the later palace at Knossos to a Hellenistic town house at Priene.

While some of these identifications may be correct, the form of the megaron is so simple that it is relatively easy to discern approximations to it within many complicated building plans. The megaron halls in Mycenaean palaces measured about 14.4 sq yds (12 sq m) and had a central hearth and four columns to support the roof. Those at Pylos and Tiryns had a base for a throne. The porch of the megaron opened onto a courtyard, which was surrounded by a portico with wooden columns at Tiryns. Despite differences in architectural detail, the approach to the megaron in all these palaces was designed to be impressive.

The best-preserved palaces at Tiryns, Pylos and Mycenae had elaborate frescoes and stuccoed and painted floors. Wall foundations consisted of well-laid rubble set in clay, and walls were built of mud brick or rubble strengthened with timber beams. The buildings may have had two or three floors. As with Minoan palaces, the Mycenaean ones were administrative centers. In addition to providing evidence for storage rooms, Linear B clay tablets also give an idea of the control of some industries and of various classes of workers.

Hellenistic

Although a few tyrants are known to have built palaces for themselves while they held power, palaces were not commonly used until the Hellenistic period. Evidence for the palaces of Hellenistic rulers is limited, because only plans of the buildings have survived in the few excavated examples. These palaces were relatively simple, with rooms arranged around one or more courtyards. They are similar in plan to houses of the period, and it is only their size and the remains of rich decorative features that distinguish them from houses of the wealthy.

RURAL SETTLEMENTS

Until recently towns and cities have been the focus of study by historians and archaeologists. Relatively little is therefore known about settlements in the countryside. Surveys have revealed the existence of many villages, country houses and farmsteads, but few have been studied in detail, even though they must have performed an important function.

Villages

Surveys and excavations of Bronze Age sites in Crete suggest that there were a few large settlements with estimated populations of several hundred people, and many more small villages with populations of probably less than 100 people. The economy was essentially agricultural, and these villages would have played an important part in food production. Many inhabitants of the larger settlements were probably also engaged in farming. Surveys elsewhere in Greece suggest that this settlement pattern was prevalent during the Bronze Age, but at present there is insufficient evidence to present a coherent picture.

The situation regarding Archaic and later villages is to some extent less clear. Villages are mentioned by some ancient authors, and the impression is of towns and cities surrounded by a network of villages, with farming carried on by people from both the villages and towns. Surveys have located village sites, but very few have undergone even partial excavation. Many other village sites appear to lie beneath modern villages, so that opportunities for investigation are greatly reduced.

Country Houses and Farms

BRONZE AGE

During the Bronze Age on Crete there were a number of large structures that have sometimes been called "villas," because they were thought to be a type of country house for the wealthy. But recent work has provided evidence for settlements associated with some of these sites, so their exact status and function are unclear. These "villas" often have high-quality architecture with features such as frescoes and rooms for storage and ceremonies, which demonstrates close similarities with palace sites. They appear to have been high-status residences; they were possibly local administrative centers rather than country houses for wealthy individuals. However, these two functions are not

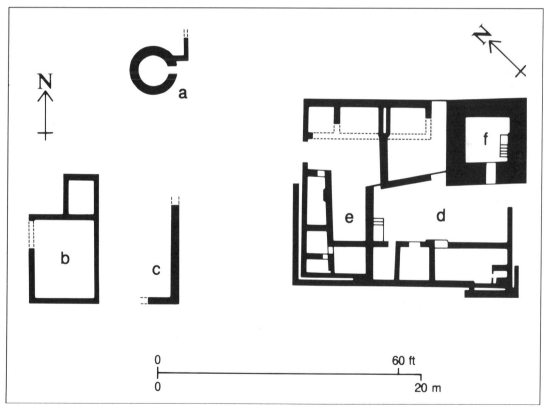

Fig. 6.5   Plans of tower farmsteads. At Cliff Tower in Sounion, Attica, is a separate circular tower (a), a farmstead (b) and possible terrace wall (c). At Lighthouse Peninsula in the Chersonese is a tower and court complex, with courtyard (d), farmstead (e) and integral tower (f).

incompatible, and the sites may also have served as religious centers or performed other functions. These sites do not seem to have been used during the Third Palace Period, and there are no similar contemporary sites on mainland Greece.

CLASSICAL AND LATER

As a result of the distorted view given by ancient authors and the modern attention centering largely on towns, it was previously thought that from the Classical period the population was concentrated in towns, or in surrounding villages closely connected to towns. It now appears that there were many country houses and farmsteads, with surveys revealing a large number of such sites. Relatively few have been studied in detail, and it is often hard to distinguish between a country house and a farmstead: both were probably agricultural establishments. Differences may result from the varying wealth or status of the occupants (free people or slaves). Many structures usually termed "houses"

rather than "farms" are broadly similar to contemporary town houses. For example, a late 5th-century-BC house 7.45 miles (12 km) northwest of Athens, called the Dema house, was built around a courtyard and had a colonnaded porch (*pastas*) on its north side (fig. 6.4). On the ground floor the various rooms included a men's room (*andron*) and kitchen, with the women's quarters (*gynaikonitis*) and bedrooms above.

Another type of structure that is more often identified as a farmstead rather than a country house is the "tower and court complex." All towers were once regarded as military installations, but evidence suggests that many were part of a farmstead that consisted of a tower, courtyard and house (fig. 6.5). Towers were either round or rectangular in plan and may have served as places of refuge, among other functions. Some sites with towers appear to have been very simple, but elsewhere towers formed part of a structure with a courtyard, *pastas* and other features associated with country houses. The tower structure and the country house some-

Fig. 6.6   View of the agora at Athens from the Areopagus. On the far right is the restored Stoa of Attalus and on the far left the temple of Hephaestus.

Fig. 6.7 Tholos at Delphi, c. 375 BC. The architect may have been Theodorus of Phocaea, who apparently wrote a book on this tholos. There was an outer ring (pteron) of 20 Doric columns and an internal circular wall of a cella, with a ring of 10 adjoining Corinthian columns. The diameter of the entire building was 49 ft (13.5 m) and the diameter of the cella was 28 ft (8.41 m). Its dedication and purpose are unknown.

times share many features and display numerous variations, demonstrating the difficulty in trying to differentiate between such sites. The current evidence does not allow a full interpretation of these rural sites.

TOWN BUILDINGS AND STRUCTURES

Much information in towns is derived from publicly financed and prestigious buildings, such as temples, stoas, theaters and fortifications. Very little is known about private houses and industrial com-

plexes, which nevertheless formed an essential element of towns. Some buildings found in towns, such as theaters and hippodromes, were also constructed in rural sanctuaries.

Acropolis

The acropolis (*akropolis*, literally "highest part of the city") was originally a citadel. It was the most easily defended and most highly fortified part of a city, often providing the last place of refuge in a siege. Because of constant warfare in the Greek world, the majority of cities were divided into an acropolis and a lower town. The acropolis was sometimes a garrison for foreign troops when a city was under foreign control. During the Classical period the military importance of the acropolis in cities gradually diminished, and it became a location for religious buildings. The most well-known acropolis is that at Athens, which lost its military importance; in the 5th century BC it was transformed by the rebuilding of old temples and the construction of new ones, which made it the most magnificent in Greece.

Agora

This open space within the city provided a focal point for civic life. Agoras varied in size and shape, although they were often square or rectangular, and a city might possess more than one. In its simplest form an agora was an open space with roads leading into it, but in its developed form it contained structures such as honorific statues, fountain houses, shrines and even small temples (fig. 6.6). These were usually sited on the periphery of the agora so as not to impinge too much on the open area. The agora provided space for political and legal business and public gatherings, as well as for commerce. It was often used for markets and could also be used for festivals and athletic events. It was sometimes demarcated by boundary stones (fig. 7.12), and was surrounded by public buildings such as the bouleuterion, prytaneion and stoas. In the Hellenistic period stoas commonly surrounded agoras (fig. 6.8).

Fig. 6.8A (left)   This imposing Hellenistic stoa at Athens defined the east of the agora. It was given to the city by Attalus II of Pergamum in the mid-2nd century BC. It had two floors with two aisles and rooms behind. Below are Doric columns, with Ionic columns above. It was restored by its American excavators.

Fig. 6.8B (below)   Plan of South Stoa I in the agora at Athens, which consisted of two rows of columns, a row of rooms and an upper floor. At least two rooms had couches for dining. The stoa was constructed at the end of the 5th century BC.

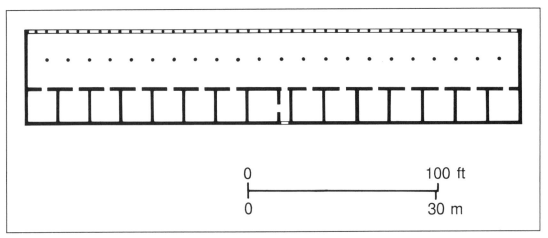

0   100 ft

0   30 m

Fig. 6.9   The theater at Epidaurus was built in the later 4th century BC. *It consisted of seating set in the hillside, a circular orchestra with doorways at each end of the* parados, *and (left) a* skene, *which was originally very tall.*

Public Buildings

BOULEUTERION

The council (*boule*) of a Greek city usually met in a *bouleuterion* (council house). The bouleuterion was generally an uncomplicated rectangular (often square) building. It had a single chamber or auditorium for council debates, with tiers of seats around three sides and probably internal columns supporting the roof. Earlier ones were apparently simple buildings without distinctive architecture and with wooden seats. The New Bouleuterion built at Athens in the late 5th century BC for the boule of 500 members had wooden seats. These were later replaced by a semicircle of marble seats, and a porch

was also added (fig. 1.14), possibly in the late 4th century BC. Several excavated examples from the 3rd and 2nd centuries BC also had porches. The 2nd-century-BC bouleuterion at Miletus was more elaborate and had over 1,200 seats. It was a large rectangular hall with a porch. The tiers of seats were arranged in a semicircle at one end, behind which staircases were fitted into the two corners, and the roof was supported by pillars or wooden posts.

PRYTANEION

The *prytaneis*, an executive committee of the boule (council), met in a building called a *prytaneion* (pl. *prytaneia*). In effect, it was the headquarters of the city administration. It had offices for the magistrates, and ambassadors were entertained there.

Somewhere within the prytaneion a fire sacred to the goddess Hestia was always kept burning, since the prytaneion was the symbolic "home" of the city-state. A flame from the sacred fire was taken to kindle the fire in the prytaneion of a new colony. It is not known whether early examples had a distinctive architecture, but some Hellenistic ones resembled a type of private house with an inner courtyard surrounded by rooms, while that at Athens was circular (a tholos, fig. 1.14).

THOLOS

Tholos (pl. *tholoi*) was the name given to a circular building (fig. 6.7). Most known tholoi had a circular roof supported on pillars in a style very similar to that of temples, but usually with more elaborate decoration. The purpose of these tholoi is not always known, although some housed statues. At Athens a tholos was constructed in the agora c. 465 BC next to the New Bouleuterion (fig. 1.14), to replace an earlier structure. This tholos appears to have been a larger, simpler, more utilitarian building, where the *prytaneis* dined at public expense and made sacrifices and libations. It therefore had to accommodate about 50 diners. There was a kitchen annex to the north. The official weights and measures were kept in this tholos.

STOA

This was a long roofed colonnade with a wall on one long side (sometimes with rooms behind) and an open single or double row of columns on the other. Sometimes a short projecting wing was added to both ends. Athough stoas are known from the mid-7th century BC, they became a standard civic building from the 5th century BC. They were situated near temples or gymnasia or most commonly around the sides of an agora, with the colonnade opening onto the agora itself. Walls of stoas were often decorated with paintings or inscriptions. In the Hellenistic period, stoas were built to be architecturally impressive, and some had two floors (fig. 6.8). Stoas were sheltered places in which to walk and talk, teach or hold meetings. The philosopher Zeno and his followers were named the Stoics because they frequented stoas.

BALANEIA

Baths (*balaneia*, sing. *balaneion*) were used from at least the 5th century BC, but the Roman concept of public baths as social centers was alien to the Greeks. The evidence from literature suggest that steam baths were common by the mid-5th century BC. However, evidence from artistic representations and excavations of baths suggest that bathtubs were more commonly used. Bathtubs were made of terra-cotta or of stone waterproofed either with stucco or with a surface of glazed brick cubes. The floor of the tub might be at two or three different levels, providing differing depths of water. In public baths, bathtubs were set in a regular pattern, often in parallel rows, or around the wall of a circular room, with the axis of each bathtub aligned with the center of the circle. Running water could be supplied at shoulder height for someone sitting in a tub, and water was sometimes heated. There were also footbaths and high spouts to provide showers. By the 3rd century BC some houses in many cities had their own bathroom complete with bathtub and sometimes a wash basin and toilet.

TEMPLES AND ALTARS

Religious structures, such as temples and altars, were often situated on the acropolis or near the agora. Large religious sanctuaries were also situated away from cities. In addition to temples and altars, these rural sanctuaries had a variety of buildings, such as theaters, stoas and gymnasia. For temples and altars, see chapter 8.

THEATERS

Theaters (*theatra*, sing. *theatron*, literally "a place for watching") were built from the 6th century BC. Most religious sites had a theater, originally designed for festivals of Dionysus (fig. 7.14), from which Greek drama eventually developed. Early theaters could consist of a temporary structure of wooden scaffolding. In Athens performances took place in such a structure in the agora until a collapse c. 497 BC. Performances were then transferred to the site of the theater of Dionysus, which was then just a hillside with wooden benches.

Theaters were built into the slope of a hillside or natural hollow, or else a deliberately built bank of earth provided support for the tiers of seats. Theaters were generally D-shaped, or just over half a circle in plan. All theaters (other than *odeia*) were open-air structures. Originally spectators stood on the hillside or sat on wooden seats, but from the

4th century BC theaters were provided with tiers of permanent stone seats (fig. 6.9).

Three main components of a theater were the *koilon* (or *theatron*), *orkhestra* and *skene*. The *koilon* was where the spectators (*theatai*) sat. The row of seats nearest the orchestra was reserved for priests and officials. The tiers of stone seats were divided into two by a horizontal walkway (*diazoma*), providing access for the audience, as did a walkway at the very top of the tiers of seats. The orchestra was a level circular area of hard earth at the foot of the tiers of seats, where the chorus and actors performed. On either side of the orchestra was a passage called a *parados*, which provided access for spectators and performers. On the opposite side of the orchestra from the seating was the *skene* (literally, "hut"). This was originally a building provid-ing storage and changing rooms for the performers, but it developed into a low stage with changing rooms behind and a *proskenion* in front. The *proskenion* was a kind of portico that provided a backdrop for the action in the orchestra. Later the stage was enlarged and incorporated into the performing area, so that actors had more scope with their roles.

ODEION

An *odeion* (music hall) was a small roofed theater for musical recitals and contests, poetry readings and similar performances. The term is used in a general sense for any small theater, most of which were roofed, but it may have originated with the odeion built at Athens by Pericles in the 5th century BC. This was a large, distinctive, rectangular building

Fig. 6.10   Palaestra at Olympia. Olympic competitors did their training here, especially wrestling. It was an open court surrounded by porticoes, and it adjoined the gymnasium.

Fig. 6.11   Stadium at Delphi, constructed in the 5th century BC and refurbished in the 2nd century AD. It is the best-preserved stadium in Greece. It had seating for 7,000. The course was 525 ft (160 m) long.

with a wooden pyramidal roof supported by a great number of internal columns.

Athletics and Sports Facilities

See also chapter 10, entertainment.

GYMNASIUM

The gymnasium (*gymnasion*) was a school that derived its name from the fact that men and boys did physical exercises naked (*gymnos*). The Greek idea of education was that of combined intellectual and physical training, usually in preparation for war. Gymnastics were practiced by all ages, so the gym-nasium catered to the education of boys and men taking exercise. A public institution run by the state, the gymnasium's focal point was an open court for wrestling and similar sports, and a running track. Architecturally, the buildings of the gymnasium were largely established by the late 4th century BC, varying little after that date. The open space of the gymnasium was often bordered by one or more stoas and a covered running track very similar to a stoa in appearance. There might be provision for jumping practice and throwing ranges, and there were various rooms where athletes oiled or dusted themselves, bathrooms, rooms for ball games, and lecture rooms. Some gymnasia became famous centers of philosophy, and by the Hellenistic period the gymnasium was an essential part of Greek culture.

PALAESTRA

This institution was somewhat similar to the gymnasium. The Latin word *palaestra* is sometimes used loosely for gymnasium, but in reality the Greek palaestra (*palaistra*, wrestling school) was quite different. A school that taught boys athletics (mainly wrestling and boxing), it was, unlike the gymnasium, often privately owned. The palaestra usually consisted of an open courtyard covered in sand, which provided a practice area, surrounded by a rectangular colonnade behind which were changing rooms and bathrooms (fig. 6.10). A palaestra often formed part of a gymnasium.

STADIUM

The stadium (*stadion*) was a running track primarily for foot races, although other athletic events also took place there. The track was straight, just over 200 yds (183 m) long and about 30 yds (27 m) wide. The foot race called the *stadion* was one length of the track, but other races involved several lengths, with competitors having to turn around a pillar at each end. The sides of the track were embanked, and the banks were held in place by retaining walls. Later stadia had tiers of stone seats for spectators (fig. 6.11).

HIPPODROME

A track or stadium for chariot and horse racing was called a hippodrome (*hippodromos*). Chariot and horse racing were usually the most prestigious of the athletic contests at festivals, but little is known about

hippodromes until the Roman period. Earlier hippodromes were apparently little more than a track, possibly with some structures from which important
spectators could view the races. No actual hippodrome has been identified in Greece, and only at
Olympia is there reasonable evidence of where a hippodrome was situated. The Roman circus (a stadium
for chariot racing) is thought to have been modeled
on the Greek hippodrome and perhaps gives an idea
of what Greek hippodromes were like. The Roman
circus was U-shaped, with a barrier down the middle
and tiers of seats for spectators. The starting line was
at the open end of the U, and races consisted of several laps around a central barrier.

Fortifications

Evidence for Bronze Age fortifications before the
Third Palace Period is relatively rare and consists

mainly of the remains of town walls and watchtowers. From the Third Palace Period fortified settlements became increasingly common, and many
towns and cities had fortifications throughout much
of their history. For fortifications, see chapter 3.

Gateways

A *dipylon* was a double gateway in a city wall with
gateways side by side. The most famous example
was at Athens, where it was the principal gateway
on the northwest side of the city (fig. 4.7). A *propy-
lon* (also referred to by its Latin name *propylaeum*)
was a monumental gateway that formed the entrance to a city or a sacred precinct. At Athens the
most famous example of this type of gateway is
the entrance to the Acropolis, usually referred to in
the plural as the Propylaia (fig. 6.12). It was con-

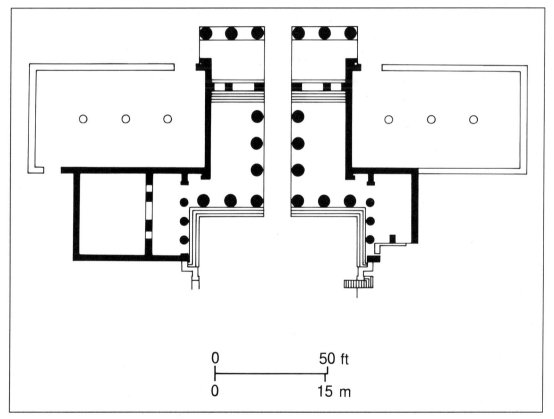

0   50 ft

0   15 m

*Fig. 6.12   Plan of the Propylaia, the monumental gateway to the Acropolis at Athens, constructed between 437 and
432 BC. This is the original plan, although it was abandoned at the outbreak of the Peloponnesian War and never
completed. The architect was Mnesicles.*

Fig. 6.13   Middle Bronze Age houses well preserved by a volcanic eruption at the town of Akrotiri on Thera. They had up to three floors and were made of ashlar masonry, mud brick and timber-laced rubble, with evidence of doors, windows and wall paintings.

structed as part of Pericles' building program between 437 and 432 BC.

Town Houses

Available evidence for Bronze Age town houses is uneven because extensive excavation of house sites has rarely been undertaken; excavation has largely concentrated on more spectacular sites. The resulting evidence for houses does not allow many generalizations, because the excavated houses vary in size, complexity and to some extent architectural quality. Houses usually had many rooms on two floors. In what are assumed to be the poorer houses, the plan of rooms is extremely irregular, with curving walls meeting at any angle. The well-preserved houses at Akrotiri on Thera show that walls could be of mud brick, roughly faced stone, or rubble reinforced with timber (fig. 6.13). Mud-

brick walls were sometimes reinforced with stone blocks at the corners, and window frames were of stone or timber. Elsewhere it can be difficult to be certain which rooms formed a single structure or which structure was a town house rather than some other type of building, particularly where only foundations survive. Except where evidence exists for storage, it is often impossible to do more than make conjectures about the function of rooms.

Very little evidence exists for town houses during the Dark Age. In the Archaic period, some houses are very similar to those in Mycenaean towns, while others are an early version of the courtyard house that became prevalent in the Classical period: the most regular version of this type of courtyard house is seen in houses of Olynthus, which were built in the late 5th century BC (fig. 6.14). In a new part of the town planned on a grid system of streets, houses were built in blocks of 10. Each block consisted of two parallel rows of five adjoining houses, and each house occupied a plot approximately 20 by 20 yds (18 by 18 m).

Although each house had a different plan, the resulting similarities are noticeable.

Various elements of the Olynthus houses can often be distinguished. The entrance from the street usually led into a courtyard, which had a colonnaded porch (*pastas*) on its north side, facing south for maximum sunlight. Also at ground level was a living room (*oikos*) with a central hearth. This was adjacent to the kitchen and bathroom. A men's room (*andron*) could usually hold about seven couches for dining, and there were also storage rooms. On the upper floor above the northern half of the house were the women's quarters (*gynaikonitis*) and bedrooms. These houses at Olynthus were built of mud brick and roofed with baked clay tiles. The earth floors were sometimes surfaced with pebbles or a patterned mosaic. Walls were sometimes stuccoed and painted with bands of color. Rectangular houses of similar type were built in other cities. A few larger houses had a courtyard with a colonnade on all four sides.

The courtyard house continued into the Hellenistic period, when more elaborate house types also appeared. Wealthier Hellenistic houses were more often of the peristyle type, having a colonnade on all four sides of the courtyard (fig. 4.12). There was a greater use of stone in their construction, and floors of main rooms might be covered with elaborate mosaics. Walls were stuccoed and painted to resemble high-quality masonry such as marble. These wealthier houses existed alongside poorer ones. At Priene there is evidence for a late Hellenistic house that included a feature resembling a megaron. In this house the main room opened off a porch with two columns (probably wooden posts) between side walls, giving a plan similar to a megaron. No other town houses with such a feature have yet been found.

Water Supply and Drainage

Although springs and wells were used as water sources throughout the Greek period, water was also supplied to settlements from distant sources at least as early as the Mycenaean period. Very little evidence exists for water supply or drainage during the Dark Age. The sophisticated provisions for water supply and drainage that are common from the Classical period appear to have developed dur-

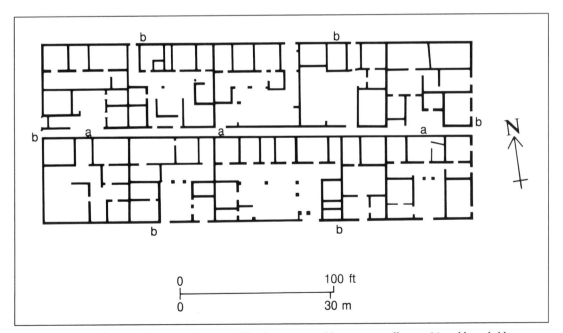

Fig. 6.14   *Plan of a block of two town houses at Olynthus, separated by a narrow alleyway (a) and bounded by streets (b).*

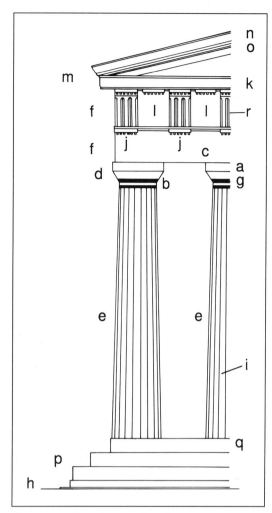

*Fig. 6.15 Main elements of the Doric order: a. abacus;
b. annuli; c. architrave; d. capital; e. columns; f. entablature; g. echinus; h. euthynteria; i. fluting; j. guttae; k.
horizontal cornice; l. metope; m. pediment; n. sima; o.
slanting cornice; p. steps; q. stylobate; r. triglyph.*

WELLS AND CISTERNS

Private domestic water supplies came mainly from
wells and cisterns. Cisterns were large waterproof
underground tanks for water storage, often of rainwater. In suitable areas wells were dug. Well heads
gave access to both wells and cisterns and prevented
people and animals from falling into the well shaft.
They were stone or terra-cotta cylinders about 2 ft
(0.6 m) high, set over the opening of a well or cistern. Many surviving well heads have deep grooves
caused by friction from the ropes that hauled up
vessels of water. Some well heads had a superstructure supporting a pulley, making it easy to haul up a
vessel on the end of a rope. In some cities private
cisterns were supplied with water from pipes.

AQUEDUCTS AND PIPES

In the Bronze Age, places such as Mycenae and
Tiryns had tunnels cut through rock to reach
sources of water, probably as a precaution against
sieges; elsewhere, aqueducts conducted water from
springs to nearby settlements. They were usually
constructed by lining a ditch with stone slabs to
form a channel, which was itself roofed over with
stone slabs. It is possible that baked clay pipes were
also used for water supply, but it is sometimes unclear whether excavated pipes were for water supply
or for drainage. Clay pipes and channels were certainly used for drainage as early as the First Palace
Period at Knossos, and clay pipes of the Second
Palace Period at Knossos may have supplied water
and been used for drainage. In Classical cities aqueducts often brought water from distant sources. In
the Hellenistic period aqueducts were increasingly
used to supply water to cities, and the use of clay
pipes to distribute water continued from the
Classical period. Some Hellenistic cities had large
reservoirs on their outskirts.

FOUNTAIN HOUSES

Fountain houses providing a public water supply
appear to have been built around springs as early as
the 6th century BC. The main element of fountain
houses was a stone tank or tanks filled by water
from a spring. In many cases the facade of the fountain house had an appearance similar to a temple,
with a gable roof and supporting columns. The

ing the 8th–6th centuries BC. Classical cities obtained their water from springs, wells and aqueducts. Apart from drinking, water was used for such
activities as washing, bathing, laundry, cooking,
cleaning and industrial manufacturing processes.
Public baths had bathtubs and showers, and some
houses had bathrooms with a bathtub and wash
basin. Basins in kitchens were also used for washing
and for laundry.

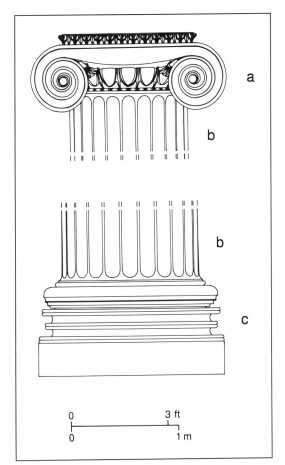

Fig. 6.16A *Ionic capital with (a) spiral scrolls; it is supported by a tapering column, greater in circumference at the bottom. The column has deep fluting (b) and stands on a base (c). This type of column stood in the temple of Athena Polias, Priene.*

Fig. 6.16B (right) *Column of the Naxians, Delphi, an Ionic column once supporting a sculpture of a sphinx. It was dedicated c. 570–560 BC. The entire column was once 32.2 ft (9.9 m) high. The Ionic capital and part of the upper column with its fluting survive.*

water flowed from ornamental bronze spouts, or in some cases water could be taken by dipping vessels into open water tanks. Some fountain houses were supplied by aqueducts. There are also examples of underground public water sources, reached by flights of steps, either in a cistern or where there was access to an underground spring.

WASTE WATER

Drains were used as early as the First Palace Period. Greek cities developed a system of drains to get rid of surface water, wastewater and overflows from springs and fountain houses. These drainage systems became increasingly sophisticated and complex, with clay drainpipes and open drainage channels feeding into larger drains and sewers. Public toilets are known to have existed, from which wastewater was carried away in large drains. Houses often had some kind of toilet; at Olynthus a surprisingly modern-looking terra-cotta toilet was found, which was part of a bathroom also equipped with a bathtub and wash basin. The toilet appears to have been connected to the local drainage system, and it was found in a house dating to the 4th century BC. In Athens toilets in 5th-century-BC houses emptied into stone-lined cesspools, and in the 4th century BC they were connected to the drainage system. In houses without any toilet it is assumed that some kind of chamber pot was employed.

ARCHITECTURE AND ARCHITECTS

Civil and domestic architecture generally developed late in Greece. Most architectural excellence was lavished on temples and related religious buildings. This has resulted in temple sites being the best surviving examples of the architectural orders, and it is largely from temples that the development of Greek architecture has been reconstructed. Apart from the different architectural orders, the various plans of Doric and Ionic temples demonstrate the diversity of Greek architecture from the Archaic period. See also temples in chapter 8.

Architectural Orders

From the 7th century BC the three major Greek architectural orders gradually developed: Doric, Ionic and Corinthian. Sometimes only two major orders (Doric and Ionic) are recognized, because Corinthian is a later variation of Ionic. The styles of these three orders are most easily distinguished by their columns.

DORIC

Doric columns had no base and rose directly from the floor, with a maximum diameter of about one-fifth or one-sixth the column height. The column had wide shallow flutings and tapered slightly from about one-quarter of its height from the floor. At the top of the column was a capital consisting of a basin-shaped circular molding and a plain square slab.

The Doric order evolved in the 7th century BC and became the normal style in mainland Greece, Sicily and Magna Graecia. The main elements of a Doric building (fig. 6.15) were the foundation and leveling course (*euthynteria*), three steps up to the platform on which the structure was built, and the columns and their capitals supporting the architrave (plain stone blocks spanning the gaps between the columns), above which was the frieze. The frieze consisted of alternating triglyphs and metopes. The triglyphs were divided into three bars by vertical

grooves. The metopes were square slabs, set back from the surface of the triglyphs. The architrave and the frieze made up the entablature, on top of which was the cornice, the gutter and the eaves of the roof. At the gable ends of the building, a horizontal cornice was at the same level as the cornice on the sides, but above that there was a pediment

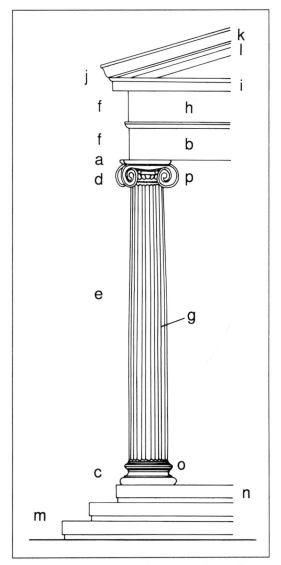

Fig. 6.17 Main elements of the Ionic order: a. abacus; b. architrave; c. base; d. capital; e. column; f. entablature; g. fluting; h. frieze; i. horizontal cornice; j. pediment; k. sima; l. sloping cornice; m. steps; n. stylobate; o. torus; p. volute.

surmounted by slanting cornices under the edges of the roof.

IONIC

The Ionic column had a maximum diameter of one-eighth or one-ninth of the column height, giving it a more slender appearance than a Doric column. It also had deeper fluting, stood on a base, and had a capital decorated with spiral scrolls (fig. 6.16).

The Ionic order developed in the late 6th century BC (fig. 6.17). The main differences between an Ionic and Doric building are the columns with bases and different capitals. These supported an entablature in which the architrave consisted of three bands, each one projecting a little from the one below. Above this was an egg-and-tongue molding. The triglyphs and metopes of the Doric order were now replaced by a row of small projecting blocks called "dentils", and/or by a continuous frieze of sculptured decoration.

A variant on the Ionic capital was the Aeolic capital (fig. 6.18), which appears to have developed earlier than the true Ionic capital, in the early 6th or even late 7th century BC. This type of capital is similar to the usual Ionic capital, but is more ornate and shows distinctive Eastern influence. Similar capitals have been found in Palestine, Phoenicia and Syria dating to the 8th–7th centuries BC. The use of the Aeolic capital was largely confined to Aeolia in northwest Turkey.

CORINTHIAN

The Corinthian order developed from the Ionic in the later 5th century BC; the main change was to the capitals of the columns, which became an inverted bell shape, decorated with acanthus leaves (fig. 6.19). Corinthian became the dominant architectural style in the 1st century BC.

Architects

An architect (*arkhitekton*) had the role more of a master builder than an architect. After he served an apprenticeship and worked as a master craftsman, he would eventually be selected to draw up a design (*syngraphe*) and supervise the construction of a

Fig. 6.18   A restored Aeolic capital from the temple at Neandria, northwest Asia Minor, c. 600 BC.

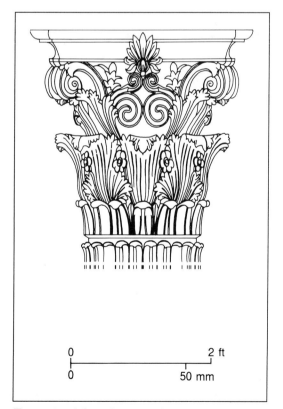

Fig. 6.19   A Corinthian capital.

Fig. 6.20   The Postern Gate from inside the citadel at Mycenae, late 13th century BC. This entrance was made in the north wall long after the completion of the Lion Gate (fig. 3.15). The double door was over 6 ft (1.83 m) high.

building. Most building commissions were for public rather than private buildings, and the majority were official commissions on behalf of the state. Even when a private individual paid for a building, it was mostly on behalf of his city. Until the rise of Macedonia most patrons of architects were therefore city-states, after which Macedonian and Hellenistic rulers became the main patrons.

Architects working for city-states were closely controlled. In some places two or three architects were elected to oversee repairs and regulate build-ing work. For large projects architects might have to compete by submitting estimates for programs of work drawn up by the city-state. Projects such as the Parthenon had more than one architect. Historical sources show that the architect and building contractors were bound by detailed regulations, and in some cases rules were laid down to deal with conflicts between the architect and contractors. The architect was also bound by other restrictions; complex regulations often governed the possession of sacred ground and what could be done with it. Architects also had to take into account the foundations of earlier buildings. Material from earlier buildings often had to be reused to reduce costs. Even in the choice of architectural order, architects had to take into account traditional local preferences. The names of some architects are known from historical sources: Callicrates, Hermogenes, Hippodamus, Ictinus, Mnesicles, Philon, Pythius and Scopas (see chapter 9).

BUILDING TECHNIQUES

Greeks generally built in stone wherever it was readily available, and dressed stones were held together using a number of techniques. Where good stone was unavailable, stone rubble was used or walls were built of mud brick. In the 2nd century BC the Romans began using concrete, and it was only under Roman influence at the very end of the Greek period that mortar and some concrete were used in Greek buildings.

Foundations

From the Minoan period most buildings had stone foundations, irrespective of the materials used for the walls. Mud brick walls, used throughout the Greek period, were generally set on a foundation of a few courses of stone rubble as a precaution against damp. For the same reason walls of mud brick were set on foundations of well-dressed masonry in some Hellenistic buildings. Structures built of stone rubble were set on foundations of the same material. Monumental buildings constructed from large masonry blocks needed substantial foundations, not only because of the weight of the masonry, but also because even minor subsidence could cause serious problems. Such foundations were built on rock or undisturbed subsoil and were usually one-and-a-half or two times the width of the walls that they supported. Foundations were usually provided only for individual walls; buildings constructed on solid

rafts of masonry were rare. On top of the foundation was a more carefully laid leveling course of stone blocks called the *euthynteria*. The top of this course was dressed as accurately as possible to provide a guide for the walls or columns above it.

Walls

The three main materials used for wall construction were masonry, mud brick and stone rubble, but sometimes a mixture of materials was used. For example, a building might have stone walls for rooms at ground level and mud brick for upper floors. Some wide walls, such as those in early fortifications, had two parallel wall faces of dressed stone with a core of stone rubble. Walls were constructed on foundations.

MUD-BRICK WALLS

In many areas suitable stone was not readily available, and mud brick was the normal building material. The bricks were made from a mixture of clay, water and a suitable tempering material such as straw, which was worked into a malleable consistency and pressed into molds. The finished bricks were turned out of the molds and dried in the sun. A few rare Bronze Age examples of fire-burnt bricks are known. When dry, mud bricks were laid in courses to form a wall. The surfaces of the wall were smoothed and sealed with clay or plaster in order to prevent water seeping into the wall, causing it to disintegrate. The top of the wall was kept dry by the overhanging eaves of the roof. These walls were often reinforced with timber. Walls of mud brick were commonly 1.5–2 ft (0.5–0.6 m) thick.

RUBBLE WALLS

These walls were made with locally available stone. If it was easily and neatly split, walls were less uneven than in areas where the stone broke into irregular pieces. The stone was rarely shaped after quarrying, apart from specific pieces such as bases for posts. Larger pieces could be used in the lower part of a wall, but stones were generally around 0.5–1.5 ft (0.15–0.46 m) long. Each stone was placed so that its best side formed one face of the

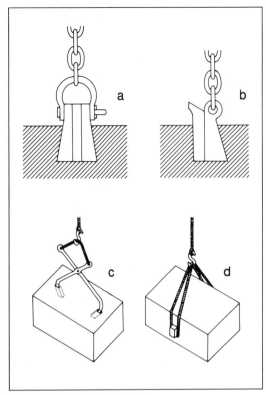

Fig. 6.21 Methods of lifting masonry blocks: a. lewis iron wedged in a lewis hole, attached to an iron chain and pulley system (not shown); b. side view of another shape of lewis iron; c. lifting tongs inserted into holes in a stone block and being hoisted by a rope; d. a stone block being lifted by a sling attached to projecting pieces of stone.

wall. Individual stones rarely showed on both faces of the wall. Gaps in the wall were filled with earth and smaller stones.

MASONRY WALLS

Citadels of the Mycenaean period had masonry walls that have been labeled "Cyclopean," from the later Greek explanation that these walls had been built by the Cyclops. Cyclopean walls have flat surfaces built with close-fitting irregular stones, using no mortar (fig. 1.4). An exception is around gateways, which were often made more impressive by using more massive blocks or (as at Mycenae) stones dressed into rectangular blocks (fig. 6.20). On average the blocks weighed 5 or 6 tons, but they could

weigh up to 10 tons. For thicker walls, the gap between two outer layers of facing blocks was filled with earth and rubble. Such walls were used for fortifications to enclose large citadels, settlements, small forts and apparently large areas of land.

From the 7th century BC carefully dressed stone replaced rubble and mud brick in the construction of temples and important public buildings. This method of using such dressed stone is sometimes called monumental masonry, because it formed a large part of the monumental system of construction that is associated with the characteristic forms of Greek architecture. In the centuries following its introduction, this type of masonry was adopted for most other types of building.

Monumental masonry required each block to be quarried separately, so that it could be dressed to the required size for its position in the building. A masonry wall was constructed on the top course of the foundation (*euthynteria*). The first course was usually two blocks thick, set upright. These rectangular blocks each measured about 1 yd (0.9 m) long and were called *orthostatai* (sing. *orthostates*). On top of these orthostats, stone blocks of the normal smaller size were laid in approximately regular courses. Before a block was laid, all the faces except the top were given the final dressing. The top of the block was not given a final dressing until its entire course was completed. The course was then dressed to provide a continuous surface on which to lay the next course of blocks.

Masonry blocks were raised into position using hoisting gear with a system of pulleys. The rope from the pulley system was attached to the block by various means (fig. 6.21). Holes were sometimes drilled into the top of the block. For example, ropes could be passed through U-shaped holes or attached to a lewis iron wedged into lewis holes with packing materials. A lewis iron was an iron plug shaped like half a dovetail, with the bottom end wider than the top. Similar holes could also enable lifting tongs to achieve a grip. In some cases projecting pieces of stone were left on the sides of the block to help secure a sling for lifting. They were usually removed after the block was built into the wall, but some walls still have these handling bosses in place (fig. 6.22). Once a block had been hoisted onto the top of the wall, it was levered into position with crowbars.

Fig. 6.22   A lifting boss on a stone block on the Megarian Treasury at Delphi.

The earliest buildings had no pegs or clamps holding the blocks together, but from the second half of the 6th century BC, buildings in Ionia and on some Aegean islands used wooden dowels in holes in the blocks, which were usually held in place by pouring molten lead around them. These dowels were used to join blocks above and below and for strengthening corners. Dowels continued to be used in Ionia and the Aegean islands until the Hellenistic period, but were rarely used elsewhere.

The earliest type of clamp for holding two blocks of stone together was the dovetail clamp, made of wood or lead and shaped like a bowtie. At the end of the 6th century BC, an iron clamp shaped like an H, but with an elongated central bar, came into use (fig. 6.23). This became the main shape of clamp on mainland Greece during the 5th century BC. Other shapes of iron clamp were also used (fig. 6.24). Clamps were set in holes in the tops of blocks and were held fast by being set in lead.

Walls were constructed with masonry blocks according to one of several possible systems (fig.

6.25). The most regular was the isodomic, in which all courses above the orthostats were of equal height, and the vertical joints of alternate courses were on the same vertical alignment. This system was popular from the 6th century BC, particularly in mainland Greece and the western colonies. Another commonly used system was the pseudoisodomic, which differed from the isodomic in having alternating deep and shallow courses in a regular pattern, rather than all courses having a uniform depth.

For fortification walls and retaining walls, other systems were sometimes used, including trapezoidal masonry. In walls built from trapezoidal rather than rectangular blocks, the blocks were still laid in courses, but the vertical joints were sloping rather than absolutely vertical. Polygonal masonry was also popular for this type of wall (fig. 10.3); there were no courses, and the polygonal stones were dressed to fit their position in the wall. Lesbian polygonal was a particular type of polygonal masonry, with curved rather than straight joints between blocks.

Columns

With the introduction of monumental masonry in the 7th century BC, stone columns replaced wooden ones. Columns were built in sections (drums), the blocks for which were cut roughly to shape at the quarry and then transported to the stone yard for final dressing. Columns were assembled by stacking drums on top of each other (figs. 8.20, 8.22). To prevent columns moving sideways and toppling, the drums were joined together. This was often done with wooden pegs about 2–2.75 in (50–70 mm) square, which fitted into sockets cut in the center of the top and bottom of the drums. Round rather than square pegs were sometimes used. In the second half of the 5th century BC an improved system of joining drums came into use in Athens. Instead of a square peg, a roughly cubical plug (*empolion*) was hammered into the central sockets of the drums. Holes were then bored in the plugs, into which a cylindrical peg (*polos*) was fitted, joining the two drums. At first plugs and pegs were of wood, but later they were made of bronze, with the *empolia* being sealed in place with lead. From the 4th century BC this type of joining was reinforced by adding extra metal dowels, usually of square or flat sections, set in other holes in the drums.

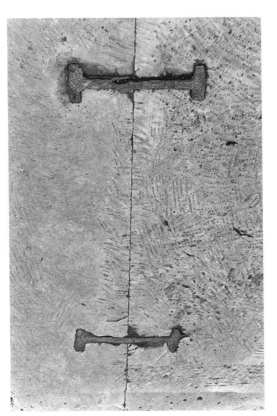

Fig. 6.23   *Dressed blocks of stone joined by H-shaped iron clamps.*

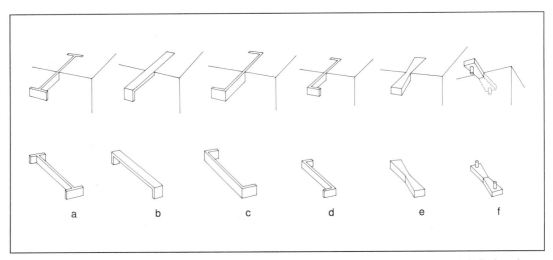

Fig. 6.24   *Types of masonry clamps: a. H-shaped (or double T); b. flat staple (or hook); c. U-shaped; d. Z-shaped; e. dovetail (or swallow tail); f. reinforced dovetail.*

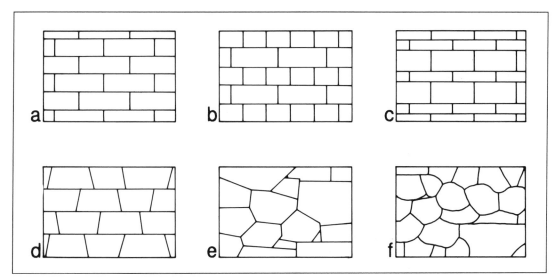

Fig. 6.25 *Types of bonds used in masonry construction: a. and b. isodomic (or ashlar); c. pseudoisodomic; d. trape-zoidal; e. polygonal; f. Lesbian polygonal.*

Roofs and Vaults

Evidence for Bronze Age buildings suggests that flat roofs were common. They were probably of the same construction as used later in Greece; timber beams supporting the roof were covered with brushwood, which in turn was covered with clay packed hard to make it waterproof. Thatched roofs may also have been used, and at least one example exists of a roof covered with baked clay tiles. All these types of roofs continued in use, but from the Archaic period thatch was used mainly for temporary buildings. Flat clay roofs continued where the climate was suitable, but tiled roofs became common.

Tiled roofs did not require as steep a pitch as thatched roofs to remain watertight—generally a slope of 10 to 15 degrees. The wooden framework of beams, rafters and battens was covered with two types of tile. Large, fairly flat pantiles were laid edge to edge, with the bottom of a tile overlapping the top of the one below to allow rainwater to run off. Small gaps between the edges of adjacent tiles were protected from the weather by narrow cover tiles. Pantiles were usually 2–3 ft (0.65–0.95 m) long and 1.5–2 ft (0.50–0.65 m) wide, and the cover tiles were made the same length as the pantiles, but were only 8–10 in (0.2–0.25 m) wide.

The two main forms of tiled roof were known as Laconian and Corinthian (fig. 6.26). The Laconian had slightly concave pantiles with convex cover

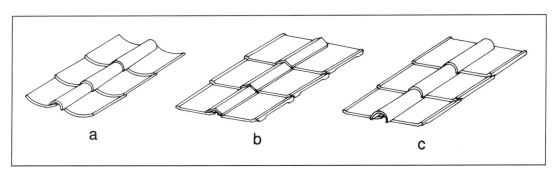

Fig. 6.26 *Types of roof tiles: a. Laconian; b. Corinthian; c. Sicilian.*

tiles, while the Corinthian had flat pantiles with raised edges and angular cover tiles. The names of these roofs reflect their places of origin. Because the Laconian type was easier to manufacture, they were generally used for houses, whereas the Corinthian type was preferred for public buildings. A combination of the two types, using Corinthian-type pantiles and Laconian-type cover tiles, was used on some buildings in Sicily.

Special tiles covered the ridge, eaves and gable ends of roofs. These tiles were often decorated architectural features, used to enhance the appearance of the roof. Some roofs, such as conical or hipped, also required special forms of tiles. Except at the eaves, tiles were rarely fixed to roof timbers. The tiles interlocked and were held in place largely by their own weight, although sometimes clay was laid between the tiles and the roof timbers to help secure them.

Vaults were not extensively used by the Greeks, and most vaults were underground rather than integral parts of buildings. The Greeks made little use of the masonry arch, preferring to use massive stone lintels for spanning gaps in buildings, even when it proved necessary to reinforce such lintels with iron rods. This may have been because arches would not readily suit their architectural styles, and also because they were unsure about counteracting the lateral forces produced by arches. Nevertheless, arches were used underground, where the pressure of earth counteracted all lateral forces and the style of architecture was not on view. Barreled vaults were commonly used for tomb chambers in Macedonia from the 4th century BC, and earlier examples are known. Corbeling was also used for arches and vaulting. The Bronze Age tholos tombs are some of the best surviving examples of underground vaults constructed using the corbeling technique. Above ground, the most common use of both true arches and corbeled arches was for small gateways through fortification walls.

Doors and Windows

The surviving evidence for doors and windows in Minoan buildings appears to show that they were were simple rectangles or squares. Doorways appear to have been rectangular, with a timber or stone frame. Doors were made of wood, and the usual method of installing them was by wooden pivots that projected at the top and bottom of the inner edge of the door. The pivots fitted into sockets in the lintel and threshold of the door frame, allowing the door to open and close as the pivots turned in the sockets. The bottom pivot, which took the weight of the door, was sometimes encased in bronze. In Minoan palaces, double doors were apparently common.

Windows generally had timber frames, and faience plaques from Knossos depict house fronts with two types of windows. One type is rectangular with vertical long sides and with a central beam dividing the window into two lights. The other type is square, with a horizontal and a vertical beam forming a cross to divide the window into four lights. Some windows possibly had wooden shutters, but no definite evidence exists for them or for translucent window coverings; windows appear to have just been framed openings in walls. Doors and windows in Mycenaean buildings were apparently very similar to Minoan ones.

In the Classical period doors and windows continued to be rectangular openings, with wood or stone frames. Windows in houses often had wooden shutters, and in public buildings bronze lattices were sometimes used as screens in windows and doors, allowing ventilation and light. Similar grilles or lattices may also have been made of wood . Glass was not used for windows until the Roman period, but in winter windows may have been covered with an oiled cloth or some other translucent material. Doors were still generally made of wood, but in public buildings some doors were wood covered with bronze.

The exterior door was secured by a bolt passing through staples on the inner side of the door. This was locked from the outside by pulling the bolt into position with a strap that passed through a hole in the door. The door was unlocked by passing a key (a bent metal rod or bar) through another hole in the door and engaging the end of it in a groove in the bolt. Pulling the key released the bolt and unlocked the door. Later refinements improved the security of such locks, but the type of lock where the key is rotated to withdraw the bolt was not invented until the Roman period. Decorative bronze key plates were sometimes fitted around keyholes in doors, and other ornamental door fittings included discs, nail heads and door knockers.

Floors

Various materials were used for floors in Bronze Age buildings, the most common being packed earth floors, particularly in houses. In palaces, floors were sometimes paved with stone, and sheets of white alabaster or gypsum were used in the finest rooms. Some floors were made of plaster or cement, usually where they needed to be water resistant. These floors might be decorated by painting or have inset colored pebbles, but not to form a pattern as in a mosaic. Wood was probably used for upper floors.

With the introduction of monumental masonry in the 7th century BC, stone was commonly used for floors of temples and other public buildings. Packed earth floors continued to be used in most houses, but mosaic floors began to be used for some rooms from about 400 BC (see chapter 9). Wood continued to be used for most upper floors.

INTERIORS AND EXTERIORS

Mosaics

Apart from a few wall mosaics that might be very late Hellenistic in date (or possibly Roman), Greek mosaics were floor mosaics. In addition to their decorative function, these floors were smooth, cool and water-resistant. They were most commonly used for floors of dining rooms. The earliest mosaics, made from pebbles, date mainly to around 400 BC, although pebbled floors had been used in earlier contexts, such as the Bronze Age. In the early or mid-3rd century BC, pebble mosaics were replaced by tesselated mosaics. See also chapter 9, mosaics.

Painted Decoration

Interior rooms of Minoan palaces were highly decorated, possibly using the fresco technique. Paint, usually earth pigments, was brushed onto plaster before it had dried (although it is thought that much may have been painted on dry). Some of the painting, particularly details, was probably added afterwards. Some rooms had walls painted in one or more colors, while others had life-size scenes or miniatures, or a mixture of scenes and solid color. Some painting imitated stonework, and floors could be painted. Mycenaean palaces were also highly decorated with wall paintings. Evidence from both Crete and the mainland suggests that some larger houses also had wall paintings. Although paintings on wooden plaques are known from the Archaic period, little evidence of wall paintings of this period has survived. They were certainly a feature of interior decoration from the 5th century BC to the Roman period, and a number of painters' names are known from historical sources, but virtualy no evidence of the paintings has survived. See chapter 9, wall paintings.

From at least the 7th century BC paint was also used to enhance the exterior of public buildings, for example to pick out details above the columns of temples and as a colored background to sculptural elements such as friezes. Because very little direct evidence has survived, it remains unclear exactly how much of the exterior of these buildings was painted. It is thought that a great deal of exterior architecture was painted in bright colors.

Sculpture and Stucco

The exterior of masonry buildings was often decorated with sculpture and moldings. While moldings were used on all types of buildings, sculpture was used only on religious buildings such as temples and treasuries. On Doric-style buildings the pediments on the gable ends were sometimes decorated with sculpture; on Ionic and Corinthian-style buildings, the pediments and the frieze were often decorated with sculptures and carved moldings. The blocks for such moldings and sculptures were not completely finished before installation—usually a certain amount of surplus stone was left on these blocks until they were in position on the building. This helped to protect them against damage during handling and to ensure that carvings continuing over two or more blocks matched properly. Any necessary adjustments to achieve continuity of carving could be made during the final finishing of the blocks.

Some types of stone were given a stucco coating in which any fine detail was picked out, but marble was usually just given a final smoothing of its surface. Columns were treated in a similar way, with the fluting being cut after the column was assembled, since any minor inaccuracies in the fluting from badly fitting drums would be immediately apparent. A particular form of column, the caryatid, was decorated with sculpture. The columns were sculpted in the form of draped females, the most famous examples being from the Erechtheum at Athens (fig. 8.25). Other examples are known from Delphi. Much architectural sculpture and stucco were painted in bright colors. See also chapter 9, architectural sculpture.

Stucco (decorative plasterwork) was also used for interior decoration. Patterns and pictures were raised in low relief from a flat plaster background, the designs being either formed in molds or done freehand.

Roofs on religious buildings were often decorated with ornamental tiles. The edges of the roof tiles at the eaves were finished off with antefixes with molded decoration, such as animal heads or foliage patterns. There were decorative water spouts (*akroteria*, sing. *akroterion*) at the corners of roofs, and decorative ridge tiles were also used.

Heating

Throughout the Greek period the most common method of heating was with braziers, generally made of baked clay or bronze. In Minoan palaces braziers and portable hearths of baked clay are known, and there were a few fixed hearths. Hearths were a central feature of the megaron in Mycenaean palaces, but houses of later periods had hearths confined mainly to the living room and kitchen area, the latter more for cooking than heating. Sometimes wood was used as fuel, but charcoal was apparently more common and probably more effective. Smoke was left to find its own way out through windows and gaps under the eaves, since buildings did not have chimneys.

Lighting

Braziers were apparently used as a source of light as well as heat, but the most common source of artificial light from the Bronze Age was the simple oil lamp (fig. 6.27). These were made in many sizes and many forms, but were essentially an open bowl for the oil, with a handle, and a nozzle for the wick. Body shapes changed in time, and later types of lamps were enclosed rather than having open bowls. From the 3rd century BC lamps were made in two-piece molds, often with decoration.

Open lamps were of pottery, stone or bronze, and the enclosed type mainly of pottery. Lamps burned olive oil and could be placed on flat surfaces, on tripods or suspended from wall brackets. Torches, made from a burning branch or bundle of twigs, were mainly used for outdoor lighting.

Furniture and Furnishings

Very little evidence for furniture and furnishings has survived from the Bronze Age. Much of the evidence is associated with the palaces and is unlikely to be representative of most houses. Decorative ivory inlays from boxes have been found, and boxes and chests are shown in some artistic representations; remains of wooden chests have also survived. Inlays for furniture are known, including ivory and faience, and possible ivory chair legs have been rec-

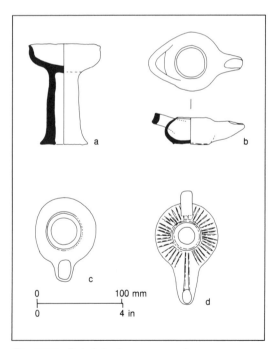

Fig. 6.27   Baked clay lamps: a. open lamp on a pedestal; b. 5th-century-BC lamp with handle; c. 5th-century-BC lamp with no handle; d. Hellenistic lamp with longer nozzle and decoration.

ognized. Furniture inlaid with ivory and precious metals is mentioned in Linear B texts, but most furniture must have been of perishable materials, such as wood and textiles. Smaller household items of the Bronze Age included lamps and braziers, bathtubs and stone basins for washing, and bronze vessels such as cauldrons.

By the time of the Classical period much more is known about furniture and furnishings. Walls of rooms might be painted in single colors or with elaborate designs, or pictures painted on wooden panels might be hung on the walls. Furniture was sparse by modern standards and generally simple in design. Most houses had chairs with backs and armrests, four-legged and folding stools, benches, and easy chairs with curved backs (see fig. 7.13). Beds and dining couches were made of wood and had mattresses and pillows. Soft furnishings such as mattress covers, cushions, rugs and bedspreads were often woven with richly colored patterns or dyed in solid bright colors. Dining couches were frequently accompanied by small rectangular tables, generally with three legs to give stability on uneven floors. Three-legged round and oval tables are also known. Lamps were sometimes supported on special stands or tripods, or hung from wall brackets, and there were braziers for heating. Chests and boxes of various sizes were used for storage, as there were no cupboards. Items such as containers and utensils were hung on walls when not in use. Interior doors were not common, and doorways to bedrooms usually had a curtain. The average household would have had a selection of pottery and bronze containers for storing, cooking and serving food.

Hellenistic houses appear to have been more richly furnished than earlier ones, and those of the wealthy might have had sculptures and portrait paintings, as well as pools, gardens and orchards.

READING

Towns and Their Planning

Boyd 1988, 1,692–1,693: surveyors; Dickinson 1994, 50–69: Bronze Age towns; Dilke 1985, 87–88: surveyors; Owens 1991: major source for town planning; Tomlinson 1992: town planning, with studies of specific sites.

Palaces

Dickinson 1994; Graham 1987: major source for Cretan palaces, with many illustrations, although some interpretations have since been challenged; Lawrence 1983, 42–70, 87–109; Wardle 1994: useful summary.

Rural Settlements

Dickinson 1994, 69–71, 73–76: "villas"; Isager and Skydsgaard 1992, 67–82: farmsteads; Jones 1975: country houses and farms in Attica; Pecírka 1973: country houses and farms.

Town Buildings and Structures

Boersma 1970: buildings of Athens; Coulton 1976: major source for stoas; Crouch 1993: major source for water supply, drainage and related subjects; Crouwel 1992, 62–63: hippodromes; Lang 1968: water supply in Athens; McKay 1988: town houses; Miller 1978: major source for prytaneia; Pedley 1993: includes information on towns; Shaw 1987: early Bronze Age houses; Tomlinson 1992, 17–29: types of buildings.

Architecture and Architects

Allsopp 1965: architecture of all periods; Boardman (ed.) 1993: includes chronological descriptions; Coulton 1977: architects; Coulton 1988b: useful summary of architecture; Dickinson 1994, 144–164: Bronze Age architecture; Lawrence 1983: useful discussion of architecture of all periods and architects; Pedley 1993: includes information on architecture; Robertson 1943.

Building Techniques

Camp and Dinsmoor 1984: in Athens; Coulton 1988a: useful summary; Winter (ed.) 1990: contains papers on roof tiles; Winter 1993: roof tiles.

Interiors and Exteriors

For mosaics and painting, see reading in chapter 9, Art.

Bailey 1975: lamps; Dickinson 1994, 130–143, 164–168: Bronze Age furniture and frescoes; Graham 1987, 210–219: furnishings in Cretan palaces; McKay 1988, 1,369–1,371: Classical furnishings; Richter 1926, 1–100: furniture; Richter 1966: furniture and furnishing from Minoan times; Whibley 1931, 661–663: furnishings; Winter (ed.) 1990: includes papers on terra-cotta architectural decorations; Winter 1993: terra-cotta.

7

WRITTEN
EVIDENCE

GREEK LANGUAGE

Dialects

Although Greece was divided into numerous regions and states, the same language was spoken, distinguishing Greeks from barbarians (a word they applied to all non-Greek speaking people, especially the Persians in the 5th century BC). Greeks were therefore monoglots. Greek is an Indo-European language, originating at the end of the 2nd millennium BC with the migrations of Indo-European people into Greece. During the 17th and 16th centuries BC the Greek language began to develop and is recognizable in the Linear B script written on clay tablets in the Mycenaean period. From about 1200 BC there were widespread movements of people throughout Europe, including a Dorian invasion into parts of Greece. This was an invasion of Greek people who spoke a Doric dialect and came from northwest Greece (Epirus and Macedonia). Some settled in the region known as Doris, and others moved into the Peloponnese via Delphi and Naupactus. In the central Peloponnese the Arcadian dialect was similar to pre-Dorian Greek, so the Dorians probably failed to penetrate much of Arcadia. During the Dark Age people migrated from Greece to other parts of the Greek world. This included the migration of Ionian Greeks to western Asia Minor.

These events may have resulted in the distribution of various dialects in historic Greece. The differences between the dialects were fairly small, and speakers of one dialect could be understood by speakers of another. The main dialects were West Greek, Attic-Ionic, Aeolic and Arcado-Cyprian. West Greek dialects included North-West Greek (spoken in Phocis, Locris, Elis and Aetolia) and Doric (spoken throughout the Peloponnese and places colonized from there, such as the southern Aegean islands, Crete, southwest coast of Asia Minor, Rhodes and parts of Sicily and Italy). Other dialects are categorized as East Greek: Ionic was spoken in the Ionic colonies of Asia Minor, Euboea and some Aegean islands, with its offshoot, Attic, spoken in Attica and Athens. Aeolic was spoken in Lesbos and neighboring Aeolis, with a variant in Thessaly and Boeotia (actually a mixture with North-West Greek). The dialect of epic poetry is an artificial dialect based on Ionic, but with fundamental differences such as $\bar{e}$ being used instead of $\bar{a}$.

Arcado-Cyprian (a modern term) was an archaic dialect used in Arcadia, Pamphylia and Cyprus that possibly preserved Mycenaean Greek; it is not found in extant literature. Aeolic and Arcado-Cyprian have many common elements and are classed as Achaean. They are similar to the language of Linear B texts. The Attic dialect later predominated.

Dialects used by authors were not necessarily their native tongue or that of the city in which they wrote, but that of the genre. For example, choral lyric poetry originated in a Doric-speaking region, and so all such poetry was composed in a literary form of Doric. While tragedy and comedy at Athens were written in Attic, the choral lyric parts were written in Doric. Homer wrote in an artificial combination of Ionic and Aeolic, as did later epic writers.

With the unification by conquest of many parts of Greece by Philip II of Macedonia, and many parts of the east by Alexander the Great, local dialects declined, and a new uniform Greek dialect emerged known as *koine* (common dialect). It was based on the Attic dialect rather than the semibarbarous Macedonian dialect. Its use spread throughout the Greek Empire, and Xenophon was the first writer to use the *koine*.

Basic Rules of Greek

In English and other Romance languages, the pronouns *I*, *you*, *we* and *they* are used with verbs to make the sense clear, and the definite and indefinite articles, *the*, *a/an*, are used with nouns. Only the definite article is used in Greek. The use of pronouns is not essential, as verbs have personal endings to indicate their meanings. Pronouns such as *I* and *you* are used only for special emphasis or to make a meaning clear. The sense of a sentence depends on a combination of word endings and word order.

VERBS

Verbs can be classified into two groups (called conjugations), depending on whether the first person present tense ends in -*ō* (omega) or -*mi*. Most verbs belong in the first group, such as *luō* (I set free), *pherō* (I carry) and *graphō* (I write). The second group forms a very small class, such as *phēmi* (I say). When conjugated, *luō* becomes:

luō	I set free
lueis	you (singular) set free
luei	he/she/it sets free
luomen	we set free
luete	you (plural) set free
luousi(n)	they set free (the *n* is used before a vowel or at the end of a sentence)

Different forms of the verb can indicate different tenses, and there are numerous modifications to the stem, such as adding *-so* to a stem for a future tense. There are also verbs with irregular patterns. In the case of *luō*, the stem is *lu*. Examples are:

eluomen	we were setting free
lusō	I will set free
lusousi(n)	they will set free
elusas	you set free
leluka	I have set free
elelukei	she had set free
luein	to set free
luomai	I ransom (passive present, with slight change of meaning)

NOUNS

Greek nouns have various endings (called cases) that demonstrate their role in a sentence. The various cases are:

Nominative:	The subject of the verb.
Vocative:	Calling to or addressing a person or thing, such as "Oh Muse!".
Accusative:	The direct object of the verb.
Genitive:	Denotes possession, such as "the altar of the god"—"of the god" is genitive. It is also used where Latin uses the ablative, to denote separation with prepositional phrases such as "away from" or "out of."
Dative:	Indirect object of the verb, translated as "to" or "for." For example, "The priest gave the offering to the god"—"to the god" is dative. It is also used where Latin uses the ablative.

Adjectives have similar endings and agree with the nouns to which they are attached. Greek, unlike Latin, uses a definite article. It is declined like an adjective and also agrees with the noun to which it is attached, reflecting the gender, number and case. There is no definite article for the vocative case.

Nouns belong to one of three classes, called declensions. Nouns ending in *-ē* (eta) or *-a* are usually first declension feminine. Examples are *timē* (honor), *khōra* (country), *thea* (goddess), *Mousa* (Muse) and *stratia* (army).

SINGULAR

Nominative:	*hē Mousa*	the Muse
Vocative:	*ō Mousa*	O Muse!
Accusative:	*tēn Mousan*	the Muse
Genitive:	*tēs Mousēs*	of the Muse
Dative:	*tē Mousē*	to the Muse (actually ends in *-i*, which is usually shown as a subscript)

PLURAL

Nominative:	*hai Mousai*	the Muses
Vocative:	*ō Mousai*	O Muses!
Accusative:	*tas Mousas*	the Muses
Genitive:	*tōn Mousōn*	of the Muses
Dative:	*tais Mousais*	to the Muses

With *timē*, the nominative ends in *-ē*, which is retained throughout the singular: *timē, timē, timēn, timēs, timē*, but plural: *timai, timai, timas, timon, timais*. If the nominative singular ends in *-a* after *e, i* or *r* (as in *khōra, stratia* and *thea*), then the *a* is retained throughout the singular: *khōra, khōra, khōran, khōras, khōra*, and plural: *khōrai, khōrai, khōrai, khōras, khōrōn, khōrais*. If the nominative ends in *-a* after any consonant except *r* (such as *Mousa*, but not *khōra*), then the accusative singular ends in *-an*, the genitive in *-ēs* and the dative ends in *-ē*.

First declension masculine nouns end in *-as* or *-ēs* such as *neanias* (young man) and *kritēs* (judge). Second declension nouns end in *-os* and are masculine and feminine. Second declension neuter nouns end in *-on*, such as *dendron* (tree) and *ergon* (deed). In the plural, neuter nouns use a singular verb. Third declension nouns have stems that end in a consonant, such as *phylax* (guard), whose stem is *phylak-*, and *sōma* (name), whose stem is *sōmat-*.

They decline, for example, as: *phylax, phylax, phylaka, phylakos, phylaki*, and in the plural as *phylakes, phylakes, phylakas, phylakon, phylaxi(n)*. They comprise masculine, feminine and neuter nouns.

GENDER

In English the gender of a noun is determined by its meaning, so that "man" is masculine, "mother" is feminine and "house" is neuter, although there is an archaic tendency to treat things like a country or a ship as feminine. In Greek the gender of a noun does not necessarily reflect what it denotes. For example, *biblos* (book) is feminine, *potamos* (river) is masculine and *dendron* (tree) is neuter. Adjectives and definite articles also carry different

endings that relate to the number, gender and case of the noun.

WORD ORDER

In Latin the verb is nearly always at the end of a sentence, but in Greek the order is very similar to that seen in English, with words occasionally brought to the beginning for emphasis. A genitive is usually placed between the definite article and noun on which it depends. For example: *he tou kritou oikia* is "the judge's house," but literally "the of the judge house."

ETYMOLOGY

The derivation of words was a study pursued by the Greeks, which became subject to speculation by

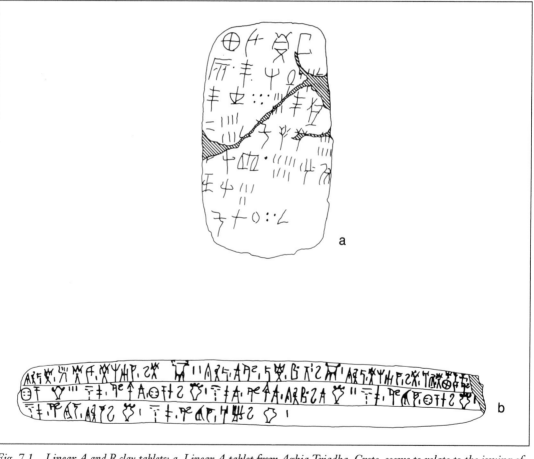

Fig. 7.1   Linear A and B clay tablets: a. Linear A tablet from Aghia Triadha, Crete, seems to relate to the issuing of wine; b. the Linear B "tripod tablet" from Pylos carries symbols relating to tripod-cauldrons, and other vessels are also shown with their precise number of handles.

sophists and philosophers. Grammar was also a subject of study, initially by sophists in the 5th century BC.

WRITING

Alphabet

LINEAR A AND B

In Minoan Crete in the 2nd millennium BC a pictographic form of writing (found mainly on sealstones or sealings) emerged, sometimes miscalled hieroglyphic. The small number of symbols probably represented open syllables. From this script Linear A probably developed early in the Second Palace Period. Linear A was a syllabic script used throughout Crete and some other Aegean islands c. 1700–c. 1450 BC, and it is only partly deciphered. It seems to have been used for administrative documents and on religious sites, and is found on clay tablets, stone vases and double axes (fig. 7.1).

During the Mycenaean period a syllabic script known as Linear B was used 1450–1200 BC. It was written on clay tablets and has been deciphered by Michael Ventris as an early form of Greek. As many of the signs are similar or identical, Linear B probably developed from Linear A at Knossos during the early Third Palace Period. Thousands of clay tablets with Linear B script have been found at major palace sites—at Knossos in Crete and on the mainland at Thebes, Mycenae, Tiryns and Pylos. Over 90 signs were used, written left to right, each representing an open syllable, and the script was used for official accounts and inventories. It seems that writing was not widespread, but done mainly by bureaucratic officials associated with palaces; it was not used for, or suitable for, literary purposes. Virtually all the inscriptions relate to administration (lists of people, produce and manufactured goods); only 1 percent relate to other matters, such as some possible personal inscriptions on vases. A few storage stirrup jars have painted Linear B inscriptions, denoting the origin or producer.

In Bronze Age Cyprus, Cypro-Minoan syllabic script was used from the 15th century BC. It was de-

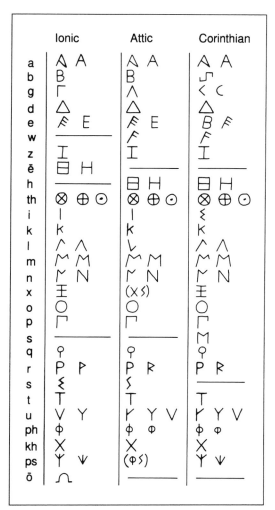

Fig. 7.2 *Examples of different letters used in alphabets in Archaic Ionia, Attica and Corinth.*

rived from Linear A and was probably an ancestor of the later Classical Cypriot Syllabary. It was used on baked clay tablets, bronze votives, ivories and seals.

LATER ALPHABETS

After the Mycenaean period the art of writing was lost. Evidence suggests that it reappeared by about 750 BC in all parts of the Greek world (but probably existed earlier than this), with a new alphabet derived from a Semitic alphabet (Phoenician script). The word for letters was *phoinikeia* (Phoenician things). The letters alpha to tau were the same, although some characters were adapted as vowels (the Semitic alphabet wrote only consonants). In Greek the names of letters were merely labels, but in Phoenician they had meaning (such as *aleph*, ox, and *beth*, house). Initially there were several local variants of the alphabet to suit the local Greek dialects (fig. 7.2). All share similar errors, such as using

wrong Phoenician names for letters. This implies a common origin, possibly as a consequence of early trading with Syria.

Local alphabets lasted for centuries. Some dialects had an extra letter resembling *F* between epsilon and zeta (called *vau* and later *digamma*, double gamma); it was pronounced like an English *W*, but the sound disappeared from the Attic-Ionic dialect before 1000 BC and a little later from other dialects. Its use is supported in Homer's poetry. Other letters were added, such as those to represent the sounds *ph* and *kh*.

Most local alphabets have been conventionally categorized into two groups, labeled "red" and "blue," with letters in one group of alphabets representing a different sound-value in the other. However, some overlap exists, with some "blue" alphabets using "red" signs and vice versa. The distribution of "red" and "blue" is mainly geographical (red in the western colonies and western mainland, and blue in the eastern colonies and eastern mainland), although colonies tended to use the alphabet of their metropolis. Blue alphabets used chi for *kh*, and psi (or phi and sigma) for *ps*, and most used xi for *x*. "Red" alphabets used psi for *kh*, and chi (and occasionally chi and sigma) for *x*. Corinth had a "blue" alphabet, but used the letter san for an *s* rather than a sigma (fig. 7.2), which was later universal. Differences also existed in the way letters, such as sigma, lamda and gamma were written.

The letters from alpha to chi were used by the Athenians to the end of the 5th century BC (Attic script). At this time in Athens epsilon was used for all types of *e*, and omicron for all types of *o*. Eta was used for the aspirate *h*. In 403 BC Athens officially adopted the more developed Ionic (East Ionic or Milesian) alphabet (fig. 7.3), which ultimately prevailed throughout Greece and is still used today. The Ionic alphabet distinguished between long and short *o* sounds by using omicron and omega (the latter an open letter *o*). Similarly, short and long *e* sounds were distinguished by epsilon and eta. Diphthongs (double sounds) were also used. The letter eta was not used in Ionic dialects as an aspirate, which was ignored in writing. Occasionally the left half of the upper case eta (⊢) was used to express the aspirate, and the right half to express absence of the aspirate, known as "rough breathing" and "smooth breathing." From these signs developed the later signs ' and ', and the aspirate is transliterated as *h*.

Fig. 7.3 Inscription from Sigeum in northwest Asia Minor. The upper text is written in the Ionic dialect and alphabet. The text is given below in Attic in smaller letters and with more details. This stele was probably erected after the Athenian conquest of the area in the mid-6th century BC. It records the presentation of a wine bowl, stand and strainer for civic use in the town hall at Sigeum. It was written as boustrophedon.

The Cypriot Syllabary (or Classical Syllabary) is the system of writing used in Cyprus from the early 7th to the end of the 3rd century BC. It consisted of 56 signs, including five vowels. It represented the Cypro-Arcadian dialect and the unintelligible Eteo-Cypriot dialect. Over 800 texts are known, and it is subdivided into Paphian (confined to Paphos and Curium) and the Common Cypriot (used elsewhere in the island).

The standard Greek alphabet still in use today is:

Lower case	Upper case	Greek name	English equivalent
α	A	alpha	a
β	B	beta	b
γ	Γ	gamma	g
δ	Δ	delta	d
ε	E	epsilon	e (short)
ζ	Z	zeta	z (pronounced ds)
η	H	eta	e (long)
θ	Θ	theta	th
ι	I	iota	i
κ	K	kappa	k or c
λ	Λ	lam(b)da	l
μ	M	mu	m
ν	N	nu	n
ξ	Ξ	xi	x (pronounced ks)
o	O	omicron	o (short)
π	Π	pi	p
ρ	P	rho	r (or rh)
σ, s, or c	Σ, C	sigma	s
τ	T	tau	t
υ	Y	upsilon	u (usually transliterated y)
φ	Φ	phi	ph
χ	X	chi	kh (sometimes transliterated ch)
ψ	Ψ	psi	ps
ω	Ω	omega	o (long)

A cursive script was developed for everyday letters and accounts, which made use of lowercase letters. Otherwise there was no distinction between lower- and uppercase letters until the 9th century AD. Papyri mainly used a majuscule (large letters) script known as uncial, with very little change over that time. There was little, if any, division between words, little punctuation and no enlarged initial letters. Even lyric poetry was written as if prose. A rough breathing sign was sometimes added if a misunderstanding might arise. From the 4th century BC a short stroke (*paragraphos*) was placed below the line to indicate a break, and the same symbol was used in drama to indicate a change of speaker.

Manuscripts at the Library at Alexandria were largely copies rather than original texts, and so inevitably contained errors. The librarians and scholars there tried to restore them to the version originally intended by the authors and added various notes (scholia) to the texts. There were difficulties in interpretation, because of the method of writing, with few aids to readers. They therefore invented and added various critical signs to indicate, for example, omissions or corruption in the text. Some of these critical signs are still used today. Aids to the reader became more common only in the Roman period.

Numerals

In Linear B there was a decimal system of numerals, using upright strokes for units, horizontal bars for tens, circles for hundreds, circles with rays for thousands, and a symbol for 10,000. Each sign could be repeated nine times.

The later names of Greek numerals were:

Numeral	Greek Name
1	*heis*
2	*duo*
3	*treis*
4	*tessares* or *tettares*
5	*pente*
6	*hex*
7	*hepta*
8	*okto*
9	*ennea*
10	*deka*
11	*endeka*
12	*dodeka*
13	*triskaideka*
14	*tessareskaideka*
15	*pentekaideka*
16	*hekkaideka*
17	*heptakaideka*
18	*oktokaideka*

Number	Symbol	Number	Symbol
1	α´	100	ρ
2	β´	200	σ
3	γ	300	τ
4	δ	400	υ
5	ε	500	φ
6	ς	600	χ
7	ζ	700	ψ
8	η	800	ω
9	θ	900	ϡ
10	ι	1,000	͵α
11	ια		
12	ιβ	2,000	͵β
13	ιγ		
14	ιδ	3,000	͵γ
15	ιε		
16	ις	4,000	͵δ
17	ιζ		
18	ιη	5,000	͵ε
19	ιθ		
20	κ	10,000	͵ι or Μ
21	κα		
30	λ		
40	μ	20,000	β͞Μ
50	ν		
60	ξ	31,000	γ͞Μ, α
70	ο		
80	π	42,528	δ͞Μ, βφκη
90	ϙ		

Fig. 7.4 *Alphabetic system of numerals. For numerals up to 999, an acute accent was often used, shown here for 1 and 2.*

19	*evveakaideka*
20	*eikosi*
30	*triakonta*
40	*tessarakonta*
50	*pentekonta*
60	*hexekonta*
70	*hebdomekonta*
80	*ogdoekonta*
90	*enenekonta*
100	*hekaton*
200	*diakosioi*
300	*triakosioi*
400	*tetrakosioi*
500	*pentakosioi*
1,000	*khilioi*
10,000	*myrioi*
20,000	*duo myriades*

There were two systems of writing numerals. The older system used the alphabet (with a few additions) to represent numerals. For example, 1 to 5 was represented by alpha to epsilon. This notation system is known as "alphabetic" or "Milesian" (fig. 7.4) and may have originated in Ionia by the 6th century BC, to judge from the obsolete signs used. For 6, a lower case *digamma* was used, and *koppa* was used for 90 and *sampi* for 900. This method of writing numbers was used on early Attic vase inscriptions and replaced the acrophonic system in Greek states other than Attica in the 3rd century BC. It is virtually the only system used in papyri and other manuscripts. An acute accent is usually added to letters representing numerals up to 999. Higher numerals in the thousands are written with a diacritical sign on the left, above or below the line. Multiples of 10,000 have their multiplier written above the M. For example, 20,000 would have the letter beta written above it.

A later (acrophonic) system of expressing numerals used acronyms (fig. 7.5), particularly on public inscriptions in Attica when representing money. It was used on private Attic inscriptions from the 5th century BC. The system seems to have been current to c. 100 BC and occasionally later on, but was otherwise replaced by the alphabetic system. It was also used in other Greek states from the 5th to 3rd centuries BC, when it was replaced by the alphabetic system. Apart from the unit I (representing 1), other numerals were represented by the initial letters of the numeral words. Quintuples of 10, 100, 1,000 or 10,000 were a combination of their own signs with the sign for 5. Other multiples were expressed by repeating these signs. When expressing money, drachmas were understood if no other symbol was used.

A zero sign is found in astronomical papyri and manuscripts. There was also a system for expressing fractions, with 1 as the enumerator. There were special signs for one-half and two-thirds, but there were no special symbols for ordinal numerals such as dates. Archimedes used an artifical system for expressing very large numerals.

Writing Materials

CLAY TABLETS

Linear A and B scripts have been found on thousands of unbaked, sun-dried clay tablets (fig. 7.1).

The signs were written on damp clay with a sharp instrument. Records other than accounts and inventories may have been on more perishable materials, but the evidence is slight.

PARCHMENT AND PAPYRUS

Skins or parchment may have been used for writing from an early date (possibly for the earliest versions of Homer and Hesiod), although one story relates that in the 2nd century BC an embargo was placed on the supply of papyrus to Pergamum, and so parchment (or vellum) was invented there. Parchment (*pergamene*) was made from skins of cattle, sheep and goats, and manufacture may certainly have been improved at Pergamum. It was made up into leather rolls known as *diphtherai*. Its use may never have been as widespread as papyrus.

The earliest papyrus roll is Egyptian, dating to c. 3000 BC. In Greece papyrus was probably in general use from the early 7th century BC (fig. 7.6), imported from the Phoenician town of Byblos (from which the Greeks took their name *biblos* for papyrus, hence bible). Papyrus was made from the pith of a water plant growing mainly in the Nile River. The pith was sliced vertically into thin strips, and one layer of strips with fibers running vertically was superimposed on another layer with fibers running horizontally. The two layers were hammered together and adhered by means of the plant's natural gum. The sheet was dried and the surface polished. The sheets were about 16 in (0.4 m) wide and 9 in (0.23 m) high and were pasted side by side to form a continuous roll (*khartes*) (as papyrus does not fold well). In good-quality rolls seams were barely visible. Papyrus production was later organized by the Hellenistic kings.

Writing was usually done on the side with horizontal fibers, but sometimes the back was also used. Writing was done in vertical columns 2 to 4 in (55 to 100 mm) wide, with a margin between the columns and a broader margin at top and bottom. Titles were written at the end of the papyrus roll (the part least liable to damage), and the roll was usually identified by a label (*sillybos*) of papyrus or vellum. A roller (*omphalos*) could be attached to the end of the roll. A roll of papyrus seems to have cost the equivalent of one or two days' wages (possibly six days for a laborer). Papyrus has survived mainly in Egypt, with a few finds elsewhere.

Skytales were a secret method of communicating between Spartan magistrates in times of war. Each magistrate had a stick of equal size. A message was written on a strip of leather wound around one stick. The leather strip was then detached, and the message could be read only if wound round the other stick.

WOODEN TABLETS

From the time of Homer the wooden tablet (*deltos* or *pinax*) was used. Tablets consisted of two or more pieces of wood, hinged on a ring or leather thong. They were used for notes or letters and could be used with an ink pen (*kalamos*). They were secured with thread or tape and sealed with wax and the impress of a seal. Alternatively they could be hollowed out and filled with wax, which was incised with a sharp pen (*graphis*); the wax could be smoothed again with the blunt end of the pen for reuse. From the 5th century BC wooden tablets whitened with gypsum (*leukomata*) were used for temporary public notices.

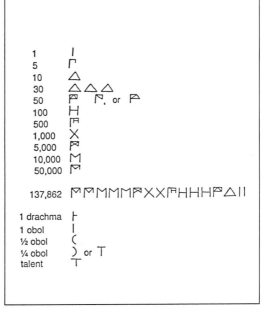

Fig. 7.5 Acrophonic system of numerals. The letter for 5 is from pente, *for 10 from* deka, *for 100 from* hekaton, *for 1,000 from* khilioi *and for 10,000 from* myrioi.

Fig. 7.6 Graeco-Egyptian papyrus of the 3rd–2nd centuries BC, length 5 in (0.13 m). Courtesy of Somerset County Museums Service.

METAL AND STONE

Inscriptions of various kinds could be written on stone or metal. See Inscriptions, below.

INK

There were two types of ink. One was made from carbon mixed with a thin vegetable gum to give it adhesive properties. Most writing on papyrus rolls was done with this type of ink. As it was water soluble, papyrus surfaces could be cleaned and used again. Parchment could also be cleaned in this way, but palimpsests of previous writings could survive. Later, iron-tannin inks were used. Pens were made of reed, and a stylus was used for wax tablets.

SEALS

Seals were used for administrative purposes on documents and other items from earliest times in Greece; they provided authentication, identification and security. Seals were cut from various materials, usually stone, precious metal, precious stones, sometimes ivory and glass, and possibly wood. Most seals were used by stamping a soft clay sealing to the object being secured, for example a box. The clay sealing could not be broken without detection. From the Archaic period, sealings for documents were of lead or wax, while clay was used for larger commercial items.

Although seals were used for decorative purposes since Neolithic times, their uses in the Aegean from the Bronze Age Prepalatial Period were also administrative; they were used for monitoring the storage and movement of goods. Seals are among the most common small artifacts of the Bronze Age, and are usually less than 0.78 in (20 mm) in size (rarely more than 1.18 in [30 mm]). The two main types were the cylinder seal and the stamp seal (fig. 7.7). A cylinder seal had a design or inscription carved on a cylinder, which was rolled across the sealing, producing a single or repeated impression of the design. A stamp seal was pressed into the sealing rather than being rolled across it. The shape of stamps varies, but the most common is lentoid. The designs range from geometric patterns to extremely detailed groups of animals and humans. The finest examples are from the Second Palace Period.

Seals reappeared in the Archaic period, and the scarab form adopted from Egypt was popular in the 5th century BC. Seals were usually worn as signet rings, though they were sometimes hung from the neck or kept in a case. The main design (device) was usually a deity, hero or animal, and Greek cities had civic seals for documents. Engraving of sealstones was a fine art.

BOOKS

The first literature was composed and handed down orally, even after the development of the alphabet from the 8th century BC. The tyrant Peisistratus in the mid-6th century BC apparently initiated an official written text of Homer, and prose works must have been written down from the late 7th century BC, as it would have been difficult to transmit them orally. Books (papyrus or parchment rolls) were not common until the 5th century BC, and a book trade developed at Athens from the middle of that century; books could then be bought in the agora for less than one drachma each, and personal libraries could be formed. Some books were illustrated, particularly scientific treatises, but also literary works. Book rolls were themselves depicted on Attic vases from the early 5th century BC. Books on papyrus rolls could be stored vertically in boxes, buckets, shelves or pigeon holes, with the rolls themselves placed in a vellum cover (*diphthera*).

By the 4th century BC private reading (that is, reading aloud) of books was well established. From the 3rd century BC many educated slaves were used for copying vast numbers of books, a process facilitated by the improved organization of the papyrus and parchment trade. It is unknown if scribes copied by sight or by dictation, but both methods may have been practiced. Most surviving works of literature are copies that date from the 9th to 15th centuries AD. A few surviving texts date back to the 5th century BC, but most Greek texts date to the Roman period.

Libraries

Early owners of collections of books included the tyrants Polycrates of Samos and Peisistratus (both 6th century BC). Euripides also owned books. Books read by people, other than by performers such as actors and singers, probably did not exist until the end of the 5th century BC. Owning books continued to be uncommon, and Aristotle in the 4th century BC may have been the first to collect books and arrange them systematically in a library at the Lyceum at Athens. His library provided a model for the great library at Alexandria, which was founded by Ptolemy I (ruled 323–283 BC) in conjunction with a museum. It was greatly extended by Ptolemy II (ruled 285–246 BC), who is often considered to be the real founder. It contained between 100,000 and 700,000 volumes (papyrus rolls), and numerous scholars became head of the library or else worked there. It became a center of Hellenistic scholarship, and classified catalogs (*pinakes*) of its contents were compiled under Callimachus. A second smaller library was founded at the Serapeum. The main library may have been destroyed in 47 BC by Julius Caesar.

Another great library was established at Pergamum by Eumenes II (197–159 BC), which apparently contained 200,000 volumes in the 1st century BC. Pliny states that Ptolemy V (205–182 BC)

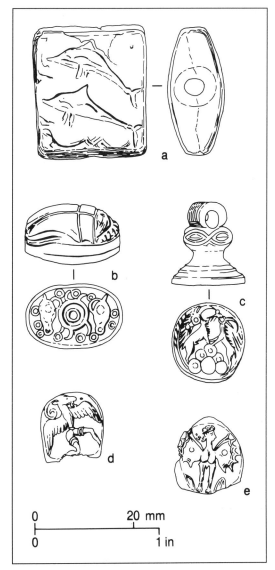

Fig. 7.7 Minoan stone seals and clay sealings: a. flattened cylinder seal, Middle Bronze Age; b. scarab stamp seal, MMI; c. MMII handled stamp; d. and e. clay sealings (with impressions of seals).

prevented the export of papyrus in order to restrict the growth of the rival library at Pergamum. The Seleucid king Antiochus the Great (223–187 BC) had a library at Antioch, and the Macedonian king Perseus also owned a library at Pella. A public library was only established at Athens in the 2nd century BC by a gift of a Ptolemy, and was called the Ptolemaion. There are likely to have been libraries in other main Hellenistic towns, and specialist libraries were attached to institutions, such as those at Asclepieia. There is little mention of private libraries by ancient authors, but finds of papyri suggest that they certainly existed.

Archives

The Greek word for archives (*arkheion*) derives from the term for "magistrates's office." From the Archaic period temple officials kept records of dedications and property. From the 6th century BC secular records were kept, a practice that reached its greatest extent in Hellenistic times. In Athens records of magistracies were kept on *pinakes* (writing tablets), *leukomata* (whitened boards) or papyri. At the end of the 5th century BC these archives were housed in the metroon.

INSCRIPTIONS

Epigraphy is the study of the form and content of inscriptions. It generally deals only with inscriptions cut, scratched or impressed on durable materials such as metal and stone, either in an official form or casually by an individual (a graffito). The Greek word for inscription is *epigraphe*. The term

Fig. 7.8   Hairpin bend type of boustrophedon inscription. It was written on a block of sandstone at Olympia and reads Bubon teterei kheri hyperkephala m' hyperebaleto ho ph... *(Bubon threw me over his head with one hand). It dates to the mid-6th century BC. The last letters are missing.*

epigraphy does not usually include coin legends, painted inscriptions (such as on pots) and texts written in ink (such as on papyrus). Paleography is the study of handwriting on manuscripts such as papyri, parchment and writing tablets. Papyrology is the study of papyri and writing tablets.

Unlike literature, which could have been copied many times with the original version no longer extant, inscriptions provide an original record of writing. Many provide additional information on contemporary historical events. They have been found on various types of monuments throughout the Greek world, although most are no longer in situ or were reused in ancient times (incorporated into city walls, for example). Many inscriptions are fragmentary and mutilated, and new ones are constantly discovered. Tens of thousands of Greek inscriptions survive.

Dating

The earliest inscriptions are those in Linear A and B. Inscriptions using the Greek alphabet date from the later 8th century BC and continue through the Roman period. The earliest of these inscriptions are on potsherds of the later 8th century BC. More formal inscriptions occur from the early 7th century BC, either on gravestones or as dedications to deities. Greek inscriptions are difficult to date with accuracy, quite often only to the nearest century or to the Roman period. Some can be dated by reference to known events or people, and some inscriptions do incorporate a precise date, with a record of the day, month and year, primarily in official decrees and lists. Many cities identified the year by the name of the chief magistrate: in Athens the eponymous archon dated the year (see chapter 10, calendar). An inscription can be dated if the name of the archon was included and if he can be identified. Some inscriptions in the Ptolemaic Empire can be dated by the inclusion of the regnal year of the particular Ptolemy. At times an inscription can be dated only by the style of lettering and writing, but this is unreliable.

Writing

Greeks originally wrote from right to left (retrograde), and most (but not all) early inscriptions

Fig. 7.9   Inscription on the Great Altar of Apollo (or Altar of Chios) at Delphi, displaying the use of stoikhedon. *The inscription records its dedication in the 470s BC by the people of Chios in gratitude for deliverance from the Persians.*

follow this pattern. Later on, if a second line was required, it was done from left to right like a hairpin bend. The earliest examples of Greek inscriptions have these alternate lines running from right to left, then left to right, known as *boustrophedon* (as the ox turns—signifying the ox pulling the plow in successive furrows). Even the letters are turned around to face the appropriate direction (fig. 7.8). This provided an easy method of reading. Some 7th- and 6th-century BC inscriptions were vertical, such as those written on vases to identify figures. The *boustrophedon* style of writing persisted to the 5th century BC, such as in the Gortyn law code.

A left-to-right system of writing was virtually universal by the 5th century BC. In the 6th century BC the Athenians in particular adopted a system of writing inscriptions known as *stoikhedon* (in a line). The letters were aligned exactly, both vertically (in columns) and horizontally, irrespective of their width (fig. 7.9). Virtually all Athenian inscriptions in the Classical period were cut in this way, but the system went out of use by the end of the 3rd century BC. Ligatures (combining letters) were not used until Roman times.

There was no spacing between words, clauses and sentences in inscriptions, although in dedications and epitaphs a natural break between words often occurred at the end of a line. In inscriptions of public documents, though, the wording was continuous. Some punctuation was used, especially in the Archaic period, such as a colon or three superimposed dots to divide a group of words (not individual words), but the practice died out and was not revived until Roman times. Uppercase letters were mainly used, although a cursive type of writing developed for everyday use, with lowercase letters increasing the speed of writing.

Stone-cut inscriptions were often colored with paints (which rarely survive). These were usually red, but sometimes alternate lines were colored in red and black, a practice that was possibly widespread.

Types of Inscriptions

There were numerous types of inscriptions, both public and private. Public ones recorded official transactions of the state, including law codes, treaties with cities, decrees of the assembly, war memorials, financial accounts, items dedicated in temples, lists of magistrates, lists of *epheboi*, winners of competitions, and Athenian tribute lists (fig. 7.10). The most numerous public documents come from Athens. Private documents largely consist of gravestones, but also include contracts and other legal documents, manumissions, dedications to gods, wills, property contracts, and graffiti.

Many inscriptions were on stone slabs and bronze plaques, and their purpose was to display information to the people of a city-state, particularly in democracies. Not all were permanent records; many were temporary notices written on whitened boards (*leukomata*) and displayed in the agora. In Athens some records were on papyrus and were stored in the metroon, which served as a public record office. Athens used marble for many inscriptions, but where marble was not readily available, cities used bronze plaques, often with holes so that they could be attached to a wall (fig. 7.10). The most famous Greek inscription is on the Rosetta Stone, which also contains translations into the hieroglyphic and demotic Egyptian scripts.

Athens in particular recorded a good number of decrees of the Assembly and boule on stone slabs and displayed them on the Acropolis or elsewhere in the city. The decrees used a standard formula, including an introduction, the name of the prytany tribe, the names of the archons and other officials,

the date and the proposer of the decree. After democracy was reestablished at Athens in 307/306 BC, annual tablets were inscribed listing all 600 members of the boule, each with patronymic and deme.

Many inscriptions recorded honors awarded to men in their own lifetimes, often in the form of honorary decrees issued by the council or in the name of the people. Large numbers of these honorary decrees survive. In time the wording became increasingly verbose. It was also an annual custom in Athens in times of war to commemorate those who had died in battle.

Didaskaliai were official records of dramatic performances, giving the festival name, the eponymous archon, names of plays and dramatists (in order of

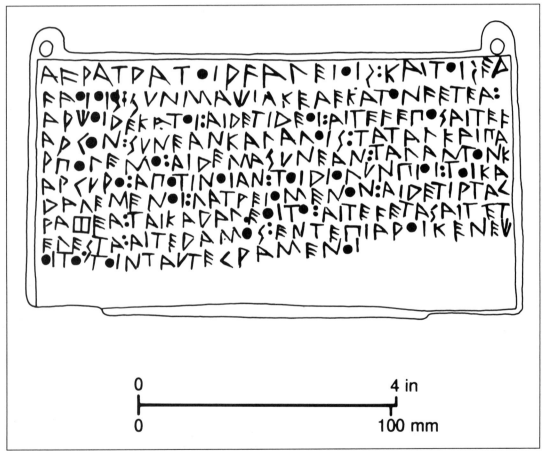

Fig. 7.10   *Inscription on a bronze plaque dating to c. 500 BC and found at Olympia. It records a treaty between Elis and Heraea. It contains various archaic features of the dialect, including use of digamma and rhotacism (use of rho for sigma).*

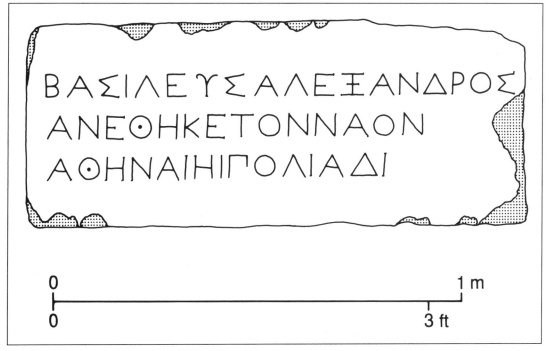

Fig. 7.11 *Inscription recording Alexander the Great's dedication of the temple of Athena Polias in Priene in 334* BC: Basileus/Alexandros/anetheke/ton/naon/Athenaiei/Poliadi *(King Alexander dedicated the temple to Athena Polias).*

success), best actor, *khoregoi* and (in the case of dithyrambic competitions) the name of the victorious tribe and best flute player. In the 4th century BC Aristotle compiled a book of *didaskaliai*, which has not survived, but some inscriptions on stone do survive.

One class of inscription includes inventories, catalogs, building accounts and financial accounts. These mainly consisted of lists with financial information. For example, inventories were maintained of the contents of temple treasuries. At Athens valuable gifts were regularly given to Athena, and annually appointed commissions of citizens were responsible for the treasures. Each year an inventory was taken before handing over responsibility to the next commission. Every four years the lists seem to have been recorded permanently on stone. They were very repetitive, with each year's acquisitions added at the end, and contained many examples of the acrophonic system of numerals (fig. 7.5). Similar in format are building records, which listed expenditure item by item for a particular year; information about the building of public monuments can be gained from such records.

Dedicatory inscriptions to deities can be very simple, such as "of Zeus." Many dedicatory inscriptions contain the word *anetheke* (dedicated), although the verb can be omitted (fig. 7.11). Dedications normally contain the dedicator's name (in the nominative), object being dedicated (in accusative, although this is not always present) and the recipient's name (in the dative). A reason for giving the dedication may also be included. Some are in verse and some in prose. Where inscriptions record the dedications of buildings, such as a temple, a list of the officials involved in the construction may be included. Unlike other inscriptions, dedicatory inscriptions often use spacing between words and symmetry in layout, rather than continuous unspaced text.

Inscriptions on boundary stones are of various types; they record the limits of a sanctuary, public area or privately owned property (fig. 7.12); some are mortgage stones, which mark private property pledged as security on a dowry or mortgage.

Funerary inscriptions on the numerous types of gravestones form the largest class of inscription.

Fig. 7.12 An inscription on a boundary stone reading "I am the boundary of the Agora." It is inscribed in Attic lettering and dates to c. 500 BC. It marked the boundary of the sacred precinct.

The earliest surviving inscriptions occur scratched on potsherds from the later 8th century BC and are found across the Greek world (Magna Graecia to the Black Sea). They consist of names or brief personal comments. Inscriptions scratched on pots or potsherds after manufacture are known as graffiti, while painted ones are called *dipinti*. The latter usually represent commercial information, such as indication of quantity and quality of contents, and are on the underside of pots; they are usually too faint to read. Thousands of such informal inscriptions on pots and potsherds are known, including the simple practice of writing the alphabet, names of owners and complicated messages. Many contain obscene remarks and sexual insults. Ostraka record the names of politicians a person wished to ostracize (fig. 1.15). Inscriptions were also painted on pots during manufacture, such as signatures of potters and painters and the names of the figures.

Epitaphs commonly consist only of a person's name (usually in the nominative, sometimes in the genitive, occasionally dative). The deceased person's deme and patronymic may also be mentioned. For women, the father's name and deme might be added and, if married, the husband's name and deme as well. The exact age of the deceased is rarely mentioned. In the Hellenistic period the name was often accompanied by *khaire* (farewell) and an adjective might be added, the most common being *khrestos* (*khreste* if female; good or upright). In some parts of Greece it was common for the deceased to be described as *heros* (deceased). Longer epitaphs also occur, some with a long account in verse of the life of the deceased. Prose eulogies were not used. Painted commemorative inscriptions occur on cinerary urns (Hadra vases) from Alexandria in Egypt.

Manumission inscriptions record the means by which a slave was liberated. They are sometimes fairly brief but can be lengthy. Numerous "freedom by dedication" manumission inscriptions are known at the sanctuary at Delphi (fig. 10.3).

Modern Conventions

In printing Greek inscriptions today, the text can either be written continuously or with a division of lines corresponding to that of the actual inscription. The following conventions are used to represent various aspects of the inscription, especially when it is being published for the first time:

[ ]   Brackets represent restoration of lacunae and enclose letters that are illegible or totally lost.

[[ ]]   Double brackets indicate letters that have been erased.

( )   Parentheses are used to expand an abbreviation, or more commonly to provide a word needed to make sense of the Greek original. For example, "Cimon of Miltiades" means "Cimon (son) of Miltiades."

‹ ›   Angular brackets enclose letters that were omitted or written in error by the stonecutter.

{ }   Hooked brackets indicate duplicated (too many) letters or words.

A̤   A dot placed beneath a letter indicates that it is not fully legible, due to decay or erasure, but identification is reasonably certain.

| A vertical stroke indicates the beginning of a fresh line on the inscription.

|| Two vertical strokes can indicate the beginning of every fifth line, sometimes with a number in the margin (5, 10, 15 etc.).

. . . . The number of dots on or below the line indicates the precise number of missing letters.

– – – Dashes can indicate where an uncertain number of letters is missing.

vvv The number of *v*s indicates the precise number of uninscribed letter spaces.

Arrows are used to indicate the direction of writing.

PERSONAL NAMES

Men and women usually had only one personal name, given at birth. On marriage women did not change their names. It was customary for the eldest son to be named after his father's father. In Homer a hero was often called not by his own name but by a form of his father's name (patronymic)—Agamemnon is sometimes called Atreides (son of Atreus).

If identification needed to be clarified, the father's name in the genitive could be added, such as "Cimon of Miltiades" (a practice of the historians Herodotus and Thucydides), or the deme name or city, such as "Pericles, of Xanthippus, Cholargeus" (son of Xanthippus, from the deme of Cholargos). These additions were not used as a form of address. Slaves could be given ordinary names, but more commonly received names indicating their place of origin, appearance or qualities.

Thousands of names are known, particularly at Athens where over 30,000 citizens are known by name (more than in any other ancient state). Most names were a compound of two honorific words, such as "Megacles" (of great fame), or a shortened version, such as Nicias (victorious), while some names reflected personal characteristics, such as Plato (broad-shouldered). Many names incorporated the name of a deity (theophoric), such as

Apollodorus, Dionysius and Demetrios. In these names, deities of ill-omen (such as Pluton) and ones of insufficient dignity were excluded. Boys could be named after goddesses and girls after gods. By the Classical period, patronymics had become actual personal names, such as Miltiades. A patronymic was sometimes added to indicate the clan (*genos*) of a person, so Philiades indicated someone from the clan of the Philaidae. Nicknames were not hereditary. They were often given to Hellenistic rulers, along with honorific surnames, such as Philadelphus and Soter.

Prosopography is the listing of names of people, usually derived from inscriptions.

EDUCATION

Although writing was reintroduced from the later 8th century BC, there is no evidence for schools until at least the mid-7th century BC. Up to then training must have been given to certain parts of the community in numeracy, poetry and religious ritual.

Sparta

From the 7th century BC a militaristic type of education (*agoge*) was established at Sparta, adapted entirely to maintaining military strength. Between the ages of 7 and 20, boys were removed from their families and housed in state barracks, where the emphasis was on sports and physical education, as well as dancing and music (because of their military uses), but only basic reading and writing (see also chapter 3, training.). Girls, as future mothers of warriors, also undertook physical training, gymnastics, dancing and music.

Classical Athens

Early education may have been for priests, scribes and poets. Evidence for general literacy occurs from the introduction of ostracism, when citizens wrote names on potsherds (fig. 1.15), and by the 5th century BC most male citizens seem to have been literate. Schools existed from the end of the 6th century BC. Boys attended school from the age of six or seven; fees were relatively low because teachers were poorly paid. Most teachers were slaves, but were sometimes freedmen, with the head teacher usually being a freedman. Boys were accompanied to school by a slave called a *paidagogos*.

The three main branches of education were writing, music and gymnastics, although it is uncertain if they were taught in one or more buildings. Girls could receive the same sort of education, although it is unclear if they attended the same schools or received education in the seclusion of their homes. Girls tended to be taught domestic skills at home by their mothers. Reading, writing, arithmetic and literature were taught by a *grammatistes*; literature involved reciting and memorizing passages from poets, especially Homer, for moral training. Music and lyric poetry were taught by a *kitharistes* (lyre player), and physical education by a *paidotribes* (trainer).

In the 5th century BC no organized system of higher education existed. Sons of wealthier parents usually continued their children's education to the age of 18 with specialist teachers in medicine, law, rhetoric or the increasingly popular courses given by the sophists. In the late 5th century BC sophists (*sophistes*) were itinerant intellectuals, mainly from Ionia and southern Italy, who went from city to city giving instruction and lectures in a wide range of subjects for a fee. These included the new subjects of geography, mathematics and science. Many sophists concentrated on language and literature and trained their pupils in public speaking. Sophists met a need for higher education, and some amassed large fortunes. The word "sophist" does not refer to a school of thought but to professional teachers.

Later on the best-known schools at Athens were Plato's Academy (*Akademia*, founded c. 385 BC), Aristotle's Lyceum (*Lykeion*, founded 335 BC) and Isocrates' school of rhetoric and philosophy (founded c. 392 BC). At Plato's Academy on the outskirts of Athens, the instruction was mainly in science and philosophy, with no fixed curriculum or fixed age. Its goal was the pursuit of knowledge. It was the site of a public gymnasium dedicated to the hero Academus (or Hekaemus), surrounded by gardens and groves. Here Plato's school lasted until AD 529.

Aristotle's Lyceum was a research establishment to the east of Athens, with a grove and gymnasium. It was established in a grove sacred to Apollo, Lyceius and the Muses. It was founded to systematically collect, organize and preserve human knowledge. Its library was an essential element of the establishment. The scholars were called Peripatetics, probably from *peripatos*, a shaded walk. It was modeled on Plato's Academy, but in the 3rd century BC the field of study was reduced to biography and literary criticism. Isocrates' school concentrated on rhetoric, which was reputedly developed in Sicily in the mid-5th century BC and was refined by the sophists. It was the learning of the art of oratory, and it became essential for men embarking on a political career, particularly in Roman times. Isocrates ran his school for 50 years and charged 1,000 drachmas for a course of three or four years. See also chapter 9, philosophy.

Hellenistic

By c. 335 BC at Athens young men (*epheboi*) of age 18 spent two compulsory years attending an ephebic college (*ephebia*) in physical and military training. After 305 BC military service was no longer compulsory, and the *ephebia* became an educational establishment for the wealthy. By the end of the 2nd century BC it had become a school primarily of literature and philosophy. From c. 332 BC annual lists of *epheboi* undergoing military training were produced, and these lists continued into the Roman period even after military training had ceased.

In the Hellenistic period education remained private, but it was under greater state control. Education was now split into three main groups: *paides* (up to the age of 14), *epheboi* (up to the age of 18) and *neoi* (over 18), with girls apparently receiving the same education in the same establishments. At Athens the term *epheboi* was used for those over 18; there were no *neoi*. Elementary education remained unchanged, but a system of secondary education emerged. Most cities had at least one gymnasium with an attached public library, supervised by a *gymnasiarkhos*, a public official elected for one year. At the gymnasia, physical training was taught as well as philosophy, literature, music, mathematics and science, forming a general education (*enkyklios paideia*), which was a forerunner of the medieval Seven Liberal Arts.

After the age of 18 some education continued in schools, but those with sufficient wealth went to the great centers of learning at Alexandria, Rhodes and Pergamum for philosophy and rhetoric, and to Cos, Pergamum and Ephesus for medicine.

LITERATURE

Poetry

Greek poetry was generally intended to be sung or chanted to the accompaniment of music. Professional reciters of poetry included rhapsodists (from *rhapsodos*, song stitcher). They often recited Homer, but also other poetry, and were especially common in the 5th and 4th centuries BC competing at public festivals and games. They originally accompanied themselves on the lyre, but later declaimed poems unaccompanied. Homeridae were a guild of reciters of Homer's poetry in Chios.

Anthologies of poems were collected from the 4th century BC, but most have been lost. The first known anthology was by Meleager in 80 BC, called the *Garland*. Anthology (*anthologia*) originally meant "bouquet," but from Byzantine times came to mean a collection of poems. Collections of epigrams have survived in the *Greek Anthology*. Alexandrian poetry is the term commonly given to Greek poetry (other than the New Comedy of Athens) composed between c. 300 BC and c. 30 BC. At that time Alexandria was the literary capital of the Greek world.

METER

Unlike English verse, which relies on stressed and unstressed syllables, Greek verse did not rely on accent but on quantity—the number of long and short syllables in a line. The various meters have different patterns of long and short syllables, which in analysis are indicated by the signs ‾ and ˇ. For example, there was a long *ē* (eta) and a short *ĕ* (epsilon), which would form part of long and short syllables respectively. Examples of meters include

iambic, pentameter and hexameter. The latter was the meter of epic poetry, some hymns and bucolic poetry.

EPIC POETRY

This was secular poetry on a grand scale, relating at length the heroic deeds of men or gods. It usually focused on events that were believed to have taken place in the region's past. An epic poet (*epopoios*) was literally one who composed hexameter verses (*epe*). The earliest surviving Greek epic poems are Homer's *Iliad* and *Odyssey* (8th century BC). Epic poetry probably had its origins in prehistoric oral epic narrative. Such epic poetry would have been recited or chanted by a bard to the accompaniment of a lyre. It was written in an Ionic dialect with some Aeolic elements.

The *Epic Cycle* is a collection of epic poetry (excluding the *Iliad* and *Odyssey*) written by different poets in the 7th and 6th centuries BC and sometimes attributed to Homer. These poems were arranged in chronological order of subject, extending from the beginning of the world to the end of the heroic age. They were well known in the 5th and 4th centuries BC, and were a source for dramatic and lyric poets. They were little read later on, and only 120 lines now survive. The *Epic Cycle* included a Trojan and a Theban cycle. The poetry of Panyassis (5th century BC) represents the end of this phase of epic poetry. It continued to be written but was no longer of the same quality. Antimachus of Colophon (c. 400 BC) wrote long epic poems, and in the 3rd century BC Apollonius Rhodius wrote an epic *Argonautica* in four books.

EPYLLION

This was a very small epic poem (*epyllion*) of a few hundred hexameter lines, usually on the life of a hero or heroine, particularly on the subject of love. *Epyllia* were popular during Hellenistic times, from c. 300 BC (Theocritus onward).

LYRIC POETRY

This type of poetry (*lyrikos*) was sung to the accompaniment of a musical instrument, usually a lyre. Only the poetry exists today, as evidence for the musical accompaniment has been lost. The two types were monody (*monodia*, solo song) and choral song, both of which were known to Homer. Monody consisted of short poems written in various meters. The subjects were of a personal nature, and this type of poetry was probably performed on private occasions. The lyric poetry of Sappho, Alcaeus and Anacreon was largely monody.

Scolia (*skolia*, sing. *skolion*) were drinking songs, mainly Attic, performed at banquets or drinking parties and accompanied by the lyre. A guest holding a myrtle branch would sing and then pass that branch to another guest. The term derives from *skolios* (crooked), because the scolia were sung in random (crooked) order. There is evidence for some choral scolia. Terpander was traditionally the orginator of scolia. They were apparently popular in the 6th and 5th centuries BC, but then stopped being composed.

Choral lyric poetry was sung by a chorus, accompanied by music and sometimes by dancing (*khoros* means dance, although not all choral music seems to have been accompanied by dancing). The music was usually the lyre, sometimes the *aulos* (flute). It was performed from earliest times on public religious occasions. The poems could be quite long. There are many types of choral lyrics, some mentioned as early as Homer. This genre of poetry became increasingly secular. Poets included Alcman, Stesichorus, Simonides of Ceos, Pindar and Bacchylides. It was written in Doric dialect.

Maiden songs (*partheneia*, sing. *partheneion*) were a form of choral lyric; they were processional hymns sung by a chorus of girls on religious occasions. The earliest example is by Alcman (7th century BC). The procession song (*prosodion*) existed by the mid-8th century BC. The hyporchema (*hyporkhema*, pl. *hyporkhemata*; "dance song") was a lively form of choral lyric accompanied by dancing with mime. A hymenaeus (*hymenaios*, pl. *hymenaioi*) was a wedding song sung by the attendants accompanying the bride to the groom's house. The epithalamium (*epithalamion*, literally "at the bedroom") was a wedding song performed by young men and girls outside the bedroom on the wedding night.

The dithyramb (*dithyrambos*, a word of unknown origin) was a choral lyric sung to the god Dionysus. It was developed by Arion of Corinth in the late 7th century BC and became especially popular when it was made the subject of competition in the festivals of Dionysus from 509 BC. Poets composing dithyrambs included Lasus, Simonides, Pindar and Bacchylides. The subject matter was not necessarily connected with Dionysus. Dithyrambs were performed by a choir without masks who danced and sang in the orchestra of the theater. At the City Dionysia at Athens, each tribe entered two choruses (one of boys, one of men) for the dithyrambic competitions. They were staged at the expense of a wealthy choregos (*khoregos*, pl. *khoregoi*) appointed from each tribe. The winning choregos (not the poet) would receive a tripod, which was then dedicated to the gods. At Athens there was a "street of the tripods" where winning tripods were erected (fig. 7.13).

In the early 5th century BC the nature of dithyrambs began to change, with the music becoming more important than the words (against which Pratinas protested in one poem), and lyric solos were introduced. By 300 BC the expenses of the production were borne by the state. Dithyrambic competitions lasted into the Roman period, although they had lost their importance after the 4th century BC.

The nome (*nomos*, pl. *nomoi*) was originally a tune or melody. It was a term applied to the type of melody invented by Terpander for epic poetry. In the 5th century BC it was used for a type of choral lyric poetry similar to the dithyramb (such as Timotheus' *Persae*).

An encomium (*enkomion*) was a choral hymn celebrating a person rather than a god. Encomia were often sung at the end of banquets. A type of encomium was the epinician ode (*epinikion*), a victory or triumphal ode sung in honor of the victor at one of the great games. They were usually sung when the victor returned home. The major poets of this genre were Pindar and Bacchylides. Another type of encomium was the *threnos*, a lament for a dead person.

A paean was originally a hymn sung to Apollo in his role as healer, but it came to be used for any hymn to Apollo and to other gods, and was also sung on other occasions, such as by the guests after the libation before the symposium. In Hellenistic times, paeans were addressed to successful individuals. Greek armies going into battle sang a paean to ask support from a god and to help maintain order while approaching the enemy. A hymn (*hymnos*) was a song in honor of a god or hero. The Homeric Hymns were a collection of literary epic-style hexameter poems addressed to various gods and relating their deeds; they were written in the 8th–6th centuries BC and were originally attributed to Homer. Some were short, some very long, and they may have been recited at the festivals of particular gods. Later, hymns became devotional lyric poems sung by choruses; they gave the names and epithets of the god, a recital of his deeds and a short prayer. Many cult hymns must have existed but few survive. Poets included Pindar, Alcaeus, Alcman and Bacchylides. The 5th century BC marked the end of the major phase of lyric poetry, after which the choruses in drama became preeminent.

ELEGIAC POETRY

This verse composed in elegiacs (elegiac couplets) is sometimes classified as lyric poetry. The word *elegos* may have derived from a word meaning "flute," which possibly originally accompanied its recitation. It was composed of alternate hexameter lines (the meter of epic poetry) and pentameter lines. Elegiacs date from the late 8th century BC and were used for various types of poetry, such as for expressing personal sentiments, love poems, military exhortations, laments, and inscriptions commemorating the dead (epigrams). Elegiac poets included Tyrtaeus, Mimnermus, Solon, Phocylides, Callinus and Theognis.

EPIGRAMS

The word *epigram* is derived from *epigramma*, "inscription." Epigrams as inscriptions commemorating the dead (epitaphs) date from the 7th century BC. They were initially written in hexameters and then in elegiac couplets, in the local dialect. Elegiac epigrams became popular from the mid-6th century BC, especially in Attica, the most famous being by Simonides. Epitaphs were often written in the first person, as if the dead person were addressing the passerby, and they were inscribed on gravestones or votive tablets. They were inscribed without the poet's name, so the certain attribution of epigrams to specific poets is uncertain. They continued in use for centuries.

From the 4th century BC the word *epigram* was also used for brief poems not intended for inscription on stone. They were usually elegiacs and usually about a single event; themes of wine and love were extremely popular. It was only in the 1st century AD (Roman period) that the characteristic feature of an unexpected or witty ending was added. The *Greek Anthology* is a collection of 16 books of epigrams. It was based on two anthologies, one of which is known as the *Palatine Anthology* and con-

Fig. 7.13   The Choregic Monument of Lysicrates at Athens, which stood in the Street of the Tripods. It originally supported a victory tripod won by Lysicrates, who was the winning choregos in 335–334 BC. The monument consists of a square base and a tall cylinder with engaged Corinthian columns. The frieze has carvings of a narrative of Dionysus.

tains 3,700 epigrams. The other was a collection made around AD 1300 and includes 400 epigrams not in the *Palatine Anthology*.

IAMBIC POETRY

This poetry was mainly in the iambic meter; the word *iambos* is of unknown derivation, but was first used by Archilochus for his satirical poems (7th century BC). The rhythm was apparently closest to speech, and poems were often satirical, abusive, political or moral in tone, spoken or chanted, but not sung to music. It became the standard meter for the spoken dialogue in tragedy and comedy.

BUCOLIC POETRY

The genre of bucolic or pastoral poetry (*boukolika*) was first used by Theocritus (3rd century BC), although it probably had earlier origins. The name is derived from *boukoloi* (herdsmen). This type of poetry continued to be written by minor poets throughout the Hellenistic period. It was similar to the earlier epic poetry, as it was written in hexameters, but was short in length. It described the life of ordinary country people, such as herdsmen and laborers, rather than the heroes of epic.

Drama

Drama had its origins in choral lyric, and although actors were used, the chorus remained a major element, playing the role of groups of people within the play (such as people of the city) or the role of narrators. The chorus both danced and sang, and Greek tragedy and comedy were musical productions. Plays were performed in theaters, in a large circular area (orchestra) surrounded by seats. They were staged as competitions in religious festivals. Most comic poets wrote only comedies, and tragic poets only tragedies. Prefixed to each play was a *hypothesis*, an introductory note giving an outline of the plot and other information.

TRAGEDY

The word *tragedy* is from *tragoidia* (goat song), possibly because the chorus wore goat skins, or a goat was sacrificed or there was a prize of a goat. Only tragedy written in Athens (Attic tragedy) survives. Tragedy seems to date from the mid-6th century BC, and the earliest surviving play is Aeschylus' *Persians* (472 BC). Tragedy may have developed from the productions of dithyrambs, and it was believed to have had an Attic or Peloponnesian origin. The inventor of tragedy was allegedly Thespis (c. 535 BC), who introduced an actor to deliver prologues and converse with the chorus, marking a change from choral productions to drama. Another view held in antiquity was that tragedy evolved

from satyr plays, although any link with goat skins is unlikely.

Tragic plays consisted of choral song in lyric meters (accompanied by the flute) interspersed with dialogue, mainly in iambic trimeters. Little is known of the type of dancing performed. By the end of the 5th century BC the role of the chorus had diminished. Early choruses may have been large (possibly 50 members, although this is disputed), but in most plays there were 12 or, later, 15 singers in the chorus. Choruses continued to be used in tragedy throughout the 5th century BC and part of the 4th. At first only a single actor (protagonist) was used (introduced by Thespis), so that the spoken parts were monologues. Aeschylus added a second actor (deuteragonist), and Sophocles a third (tritagonist). There were rarely more than three actors in tragedies, although an actor could play several parts. The word for an actor was *hypokrites* (one who answers, or an interpreter). Poets occasionally acted in their own plays. All actors and the chorus wore masks appropriate to the part, but the flute player was not masked. Female parts were played by men. Nonspeaking actors or "extras" were called spear carriers (*doryphoremata*).

The theme of the plays was tragic, and nearly all were based on myth, rarely on contemporary themes or recent history. Very occasionally there was a happy ending, but these were regarded as inferior. Performances were confined to competitions at the festivals of Dionysus until the Hellenistic age, so that tragedies were performed on only a few occasions each year. Any particular play was performed only on one occasion. The most important festivals for staging tragedies were the City Dionysia and the Lenaea (fig. 7.14). Some plays could be produced for a second time at the Rural Dionysia, but at the City Dionysia they could be produced for a second time only if they had been previously unsuccessful and had been revised. After the death of Aeschylus an exception was made with a decree that anyone could produce his plays at the City Dionysia. From 386 BC, earlier tragedies were allowed to be produced.

Festivals were organized by the state, with the City Dionysia under the control of the eponymous archon. Three tragic poets were selected by the archon and were allocated an actor, but the main costs of the chorus were the responsibility of the choregos. The tragic poets each submitted three tragedies, originally a trilogy of closely related

Fig. 7.14   Theater of Dionysus at Athens where the City Dionysia was celebrated. Here were performed comedies, tragedies, satyr plays and dithyrambs.

themes, but later, three distinct themes. They were also required to submit a satyr play (p. 260), the four plays being known as a tetralogy. The winning poet received a wreath, and from 449 BC the best protagonist actor also received a prize. Money prizes were probably also given. The judges of the contest were drawn by lot from each tribe. The arrangements at the Lenaea and Rural Dionysia were similar, although metics could also participate. Tragedy was introduced to the Lenaea c. 432 BC, held under the auspices of the archon basileus. Two poets competed with two plays (there was no satyr play).

Tragic plays normally consisted of a prologue (*prologos*), with a monologue or dialogue introducing the play before the entrance of the chorus. Earlier tragedies began with the entrance of the chorus who provided the prologue. Next came a *parados*, a song performed by the chorus as it entered. This was followed by *epeisodia* (sing. *epeisodion*), scenes or episodes with the actors and chorus. These were divided by *stasima*, songs per-

formed by the chorus "standing in one place" in the orchestra. After the last *stasimon* came the final scene or *exodos*. By the end of the 4th century BC tragedy was declining, and very little is known of later tragic poets. At Alexandria in the 3rd century BC a Pleiad of seven tragic poets was at the court of Ptolemy II (including Homerus, Lycophron, Philicus, Sositheus and Alexander).

COMEDY

The word comedy is from *komoidia*, derived from *komos*, a procession of revellers singing and dancing. Only Attic comedy—that written in Athens—survives. Comedy seems to date from at least the 6th century BC, and the earliest surviving play is Aristophanes' *Acharnians* (produced in 425 BC). Comedy may have developed from the chorus of men who accompanied the phallic symbols in the Dionysiac festival processions at Athens, but the date at which this evolved into drama is uncertain.

Comedy may also have had early roots in Sicilian and Megarian drama. Early comedy was composed in Sicily, but the earliest Attic comedy is known as "Old Comedy" (or Aristophanic Comedy), which refers to plays produced in the 5th century BC. The only surviving complete plays of this period are by Aristophanes, but there were earlier comic poets. Other authors of Old Comedy include Cratinus, Crates, Pherecrates, Eupolis and Plato.

Old Comedy plays consisted of choral song alternating with dialogue, but with a less regular pattern than tragedy. The chorus was composed of 24 men, and there were three or, more often, four actors and several extras. The chorus was of particular importance, often characterized as animals and birds, and many plays took their titles from the chorus, such as *Babylonians*, *Birds* and *Wasps*. The actors wore grotesque costumes with artificial exaggeration.

The plays were humorous and uninhibited, with many of the jokes based on sex and excretion. They ridiculed, parodied and exaggerated contemporary characters and issues, as well as gods, myths and religious ceremonies. Performances were staged at competitions at the City Dionysia under a magistrate from 488/487 or 487/486 BC (and possibly staged by volunteers before then). At the Lenaea they were first included just before 440 BC. Originally five comedies were produced at the City Dionysia and Lenaea, but only three during the Peloponnesian War. Comedies were also performed at the Rural Dionysia in the 4th century BC.

Old Comedy plays could consist of a prologue (*prologos*), before the entrance of the chorus, followed by a *parados*, a song performed by the chorus as it entered. Next came the *agon* (contest), a debate or physical fight between the two adversaries, punctuated by choral songs. The actors then left the stage, and in the *parabasis* the chorus came forward and addressed the audience, often on subjects of no relevance to the plot. There followed various *epeisodia*, scenes or episodes, and then the final scene or *exodos*.

Middle Comedy is Athenian comedy from c. 400 to c. 323 BC, developing from the end of the Peloponnesian War. It was a time of experimentation, and no single play represents the type. The role of the comic chorus diminished greatly, and the *parabasis* disappeared, as did the grotesque padded costume and enlarged phallus. Plots based on mythology and political satire gradually gave way to less abrasive humor concerned with ordinary lives and issues, including mistaken identity, and they were more cosmopolitan in nature. No complete play from Middle Comedy survives. Authors (many non-Athenian) included Antiphanes, Eubulus, Anaxandrides, Timocles and Alexis. From 339 BC comedies that had been previously staged only once at competitions were allowed to be produced again.

New Comedy is Athenian comedy from the death of Alexander the Great (323 BC) to the death of Philemon (c. 267/263 BC). Plays were divided into five acts, with unconnected choral interludes. They were set in Athens, but writers were drawn to Athens from other cities. Actors still wore masks, but otherwise wore everyday dress. Themes were no longer political, but probably developed from Middle Comedy, which was concerned with family relationships, including love, mistaken identity, intrigues of slaves and long-lost children. Plays had stock characters, such as pimps, courtesans, soldiers, young men in love, genial old men and cross old men. They continued to be popular into the Roman period, but little New Comedy has survived, although there have been recent papyrus discoveries of Menander's plays. Dramatists included Menander, Diphilus and Philemon.

SATYR PLAYS

Each tragedian was required to submit a satyr play with three tragedies for the City Dionysia. They were short, almost comic pieces, but only one has survived complete—Euripides' *Cyclops*. They were farces, with a chorus of satyrs led by a Silenus, wearing horses' tails and ears. From the mid-4th century BC the satyr play was largely dropped, with just one being performed at the beginning of each festival.

History

The writing of history (historiography) began in Ionia in the late 6th century BC, coinciding with the development of science and philosophy. Prose works were therefore written in Ionic. These early historians of the 6th and 5th centuries BC were called logographers (*logographoi*). They were prose writers, as distinct from poets, the most notable being Hecateus of Miletus of c. 500 BC. The term *logographer* was also used for those who wrote speeches for others to perform. Very little work of these historians survives. They created a historical science, writing in prose about local history and more general history, particularly mythology and the traditions of poetry. In order to compile a chronological framework, they also kept lists of annual magistrates, Olympian victors, priests, priestesses and other similar regular occurrences.

Throughout the 5th and 4th centuries local histories continued to be written. Those writing about Attica were called *atthidographers*. A history of Attica is called an *Atthis* (pl. *Atthides*), literally, *Atthis historia* (history of Attica). This type of history was particularly popular from c. 350 BC to c. 250 BC, in an attempt to relive the glories of Athens' past.

Greek history proper (*historiai*, inquiries) began with Herodotus ("father of history") c. 490 BC, and other major historians included Thucydides and Xenophon. As written by Herodotus, history included other topics, such as archaeology, ethnography, religion and geography. From c. 300 BC the Hellenistic historians aimed at being popular rather than accurate. From the time of Polybius in the 2nd century BC, Roman history preoccupied Greek historians.

Biography

Some earlier historians undertook partial biographies or sketches of notable people, such as in the writings of Thucydides and Xenophon, but the whole life of a person was not explored. The first work approaching true biography was Isocrates' *Evagoras* (c. 365 BC). The writing of biography proper developed under Aristotle in the 4th century BC, when he encouraged the writing of *bioi* (lives, or ways of life). There was particular interest in information about authors, because of the light it could throw on their writings. Alexandrian scholars continued this tradition in the 3rd century BC.

Letters

A letter (*epistole*) was written to someone either on wooden tablets or papyrus. It had to be carried by a private messenger. The earliest letters survive in Egypt on papyrus from the 3rd century BC. They have an address mark on the back, and begin and end with formulas that varied little over the centuries. Surviving letters before the Roman period are usually either private or concerned mainly with administrative details. They were not letters possessing literary merit, nor were they intended for subsequent publication. Letters were also used to express ideas, such as ideas on philosophy by Epicurus and on science by Archimedes. Surviving letters attributed to famous Greeks are nearly all spurious.

Novels

Greek novels were long, romantic, fictional prose compositions, which developed from Hellenistic times. They may have originated in rhetorical training, where imaginary situations were used in declamation, although other origins are possible. Novels could extend to several books. Several papyrus fragments have survived. The genre flourished in the Roman period.

Literature: Timetable of Events (All dates are BC.)

by 750	Phoenician script was adapted to create Greek alphabet throughout the Greek world.
c. 700	Homer and Hesiod active.
676–673	Terpander won a competition at the Carnea.
c. 632–629	Stesichorus was born.
c. 620	Alcaeus was born.
c. 612	Sappho was born.
c. 570	Anacreon was born.
557/556	Simonides was born.
c. 556–553	Stesichorus died.
c. 550	Hecateus of Miletus was born.
545	Anaximander died.
534	First tragedy performed at the City Dionysia in Athens.
525/524	Aeschylus was born.
c. 520	Melanippides was born.

518	Pindar was born.
498	Earliest surviving poem of Pindar.
c. 496	Sophocles was born.
490	Hellanicus was born.
487	First comedies were performed at the City Dionysia at Athens (contest won by Chionides).
c. 485	Euripides was born.
484	First victory of Aeschylus. Herodotus was born.
476	Pindar's first *Olympian Ode* and Bacchylides' fifth *Ode* for the victory of Hieron at Olympia.
472	Aeschylus' tragedy, the *Persians*.
470	Pindar's first *Pythian Ode*.
468	Sophocles' first tragic victory (over Aeschylus).
468/467	Simonides died.
467	*Seven against Thebes* of Aeschylus.
c. 460–455	Thucydides was born.
459	Lysias was born.
458	Aeschylus' trilogy *Oresteia*.
c. 457	Aristophanes was born.
456/455	Aeschylus died.
455	First production at the City Dionysia by Euripides.
c. 450	Bacchylides died. Timotheus was born.
450	Victory by Crates at the City Dionysia.
c. 447	Agathon was born.
446	Pindar's last ode. Callias won first prize at the City Dionysia.
c. 446	Pindar died.
441	Euripides' first victory with a tragic play.
c. 441	*Antigone* of Sophocles.
438	*Alcestis* of Euripides.
436	Isocrates was born.
435	Victory by Hermippus at the City Dionysia.
435/434	Philoxenus of Cythera was born.
431	Euripides' *Medea*. Euphorion beat Sophocles and Euripides.
c. 430	Philistus was born.
c. 430/428	*Children of Heracles* of Euripides.
429	First play of Eupolis was produced.
428	*Hippolytus* of Euripides (won first prize).
c. 428/427	Xenophon was born.

427	*Banqueters* of Aristophanes.
426	*Babylonians* of Aristophanes.
c. 426/425	*Andromache* of Euripides.
425	*Acharnians* of Aristophanes.
424	*Knights* of Aristophanes. Aristomenes won first prize at the City Dionysia.
c. 424	*Hecuba* of Euripides.
423	*Clouds* of Aristophanes.
422	*Wasps* of Aristophanes.
c. 422	*Suppliant Women* of Euripides. Ion died.
421	*Peace* of Aristophanes.
420	Herodotus died.
c. 420	Isaeus was born.
c. 417	*Electra* of Euripides. *Madness of Heracles* of Euripides.
416	Agathon's first victory at the Lenaea.
415	*Trojan Women* of Euripides.
414	*Birds* of Aristophanes. *Amphiaraus* of Aristophanes.
c. 414/413	*Iphigeneia in Tauris* of Euripides.
412	*Helen* of Euripides.
411	*Lysistrata* and *Thesmophoriazusae* of Aristophanes.
c. 410	*Ion* of Euripides.
409	*Philoctetes* of Sophocles.
c. 409	*Phoenician Women* of Euripides.
408	*Orestes* of Euripides. *Wealth* of Aristophanes.
c. 406	Euripides died.
c. 406/405	Sophocles died.
405	*Frogs* of Aristophanes. Hellanicus died. *Bacchae* of Euripides.
402/401	Victory by Telestes at Athens.
401	*Oedipus at Colonus* of Sophocles produced posthumously.
c. 401/400	Agathon died.
c. 400/399	Thucydides died.
395	Thucydides' *History* published.
c. 392–c. 388	Last plays of Aristophanes.
c. 392	Isocrates opened a school for rhetoric at Athens.
391/390	*Against the Sophists* of Isocrates.
c. 388	*Spartan Consitution* of Xenophon.
c. 385	Aristophanes died.
380	Lysias died.
c. 380	*On Horsemanship* of Xenophon.
380/379	Philoxenus of Cythera died.
c. 377	Theopompus was born.

c. 375	Alexis was born.
c. 370	Callisthenes was born.
c. 364	Hieronymus was born.
c. 360	Timotheus died.
356	Philistus died.
c. 356	Timaeus was born.
355	*On the Peace* of Isocrates.
c. 354	Xenophon died.
353	*Antidosis* of Isocrates.
c. 350	Megasthenes was born. Isaeus died.
346	*Philippus* of Isocrates.
342/341	Menander was born.
c. 340	Douris of Samos was born.
339	*Panathenaicus* of Isocrates.
338	Isocrates died.
327	First victory at the Dionysia by Philemon. Callisthenes was executed by Alexander.
c. 325	Zenodotus was born.
321	*Orge* of Menander.
320	Theopompus died.
c. 320	Lycophron was born.
317/316	*Dyscolus* of Menander performed (won first prize).
c. 315	Alexander Aetolus and Aratus were born.
c. 300	Hermesianax, Theocritus and Herodas were born.
c. 295	Apollonius Rhodius was born.
290	Megasthenes died.
290/289	Menander died (or 293/292).
c. 280	Eratosthenes was born.
c. 285	Zenodotus was first head of the Alexandria Library.
c. 275	Alexis died. Rhianus was born.
270	Douris of Samos died.
c. 270	Euphorion died.
260	Hieronymus of Cardia died, age 104. Timaeus died, age 96.
c. 260	Theocritus died.
250	Herodas died.
c. 240	Callimachus died.
240/239	Aratus died.
215	Apollonius Rhodius died.
c. 215	Aristarchus of Samos was born.
c. 200	Aristophanes of Byzantium became head of the Alexandria Library.
c. 194	Eratosthenes died.
167	Polybius the historian arrived in Rome.
145	Aristarchus of Samos and other intellectuals fled from Alexandria on the accession of Ptolemy VIII.
c. 143	Aristarchus of Samos died.

MUSIC AND DANCE

Music (*mousike*, art of the muses) was an essential element of everyday life, including literature, religion, festivals, funerals, marriages and banquets. Music and dance were vital components of a child's education, especially lyre playing. The value of music was emphasized by philosophers such as Plato and Aristotle. There were also professional musicians. Until the mid-5th century BC Sparta was the musical center of Greece, and Terpander is said to have founded a school of music there, where the flute and lyre were taught.

The main function of music was as an essential accompaniment to poetry and dance. Most poetry, such as epics, lyrics and the choruses in tragedy and comedy, was sung or chanted to the accompaniment of some sort of music. The words were as important as the music, which was composed by the poet. Leading composers were Archilochus, Sappho, Pindar and Sophocles, but little is known of their compositions. Homeric poetry was chanted to the accompaniment of a lyre, lyric poetry was sung to the lyre, and choral lyric was accompanied by dancing and music. Solo lyre playing and duets of flute and lyre were also practiced. Virtually all of the games, but especially the Pythian Games, had music competitions as well as athletic ones. These included instrumental solos and singing to the accompaniment of an instrument. Winners of such contests were honored as much as athletes. Pericles built the Odeum at Athens to house the musical contests of the Panathenaic Games. At the Dionysia and Thargelia festivals, choirs of 50 men from the 10 Attic tribes competed, mainly in singing nomes.

In the 4th century BC music became more important than the words in lyrical performances, a trend that met with opposition. Likewise, the songs of the chorus in tragedies were replaced with musical interludes only.

Fig. 7.15 A marble relief of a Muse playing a cithara.

Instruments

A few musical instruments (*organa*) have survived. The main ones were the lyre and flute. The two types of lyre were the *lyra* and *kithara*, the latter a more substantial instrument. The lyre was considered to be the superior instrument and mainly accompanied lyric poetry. Unlike a harp, the lyre and cithara (fig. 7.15) had seven vertical strings of equal length, which were plucked with the left hand and with a plectrum held in the right hand (no bow was used). The lyre rested against a person's body. The strings were stretched over a bridge to a crossbar where there were pegs for tuning. The pitch was regulated by the tension and possibly the thickness of the strings. The sound box was originally a tortoise shell, later replaced by a box made of wood and ox hide. Sappho and Alcaeus used a type of lyre with longer strings and lower pitch known as a *barbitos* (or *barbiton*). Homer used a simple lyre with only three to five strings, known as a *kitharis* or *phorminx*. Minoan and Mycenaean citharas had seven strings or more, and seven strings were apparently reintroduced by Terpander in the 7th century BC.

The misnamed flute (*aulos*, pl. *auloi*) was actually an instrument with a single or double reed, similar to a clarinet or oboe, allegedly invented by the goddess Athena. The cylindrical or conical pipe was made of reed, wood, bone or ivory, originally with three holes, which had increased to six by the early 5th century BC. By the late 5th century BC a longer pipe with up to 16 holes was used. The *aulos* was mainly used to accompany dithyrambs and dramatic choruses of tragedy and comedy. It was also used to accompany Pindar's odes. It was played mainly in pairs by one person, possibly at the same time or separately. The pipes were not always of the same length.

The *syrinx* (Pan pipes) was an instrument of seven or fewer pipes bound together and blown with a mouthpiece. The pipes were of the same length but were stopped internally at graduated intervals. The familiar stepped shape is Etruscan and Roman. Based on the same principle was the water organ (*hydraulis*) with rows of graduated pipes; this instrument was invented in the 3rd century BC by Ctesibius of Alexandria.

Cymbals, rattles and castanets were also played. Brass instruments were used mainly for military purposes, such as the *salpinx* (trumpet) and *keras* (horn).

Scores

Music was based on a large number of scales or modes (*harmoniai*), with names such as Aeolian, Ionian and Dorian. The modes were associated with particular emotions. Music was almost all melodic, with virtually no harmonization. Choruses, for example, sang in unison, with no deviation from the melody, although the accompanying musician may sometimes have deviated from the melody. Surviving scores (on papyrus and stone) are very fragmentary, but the rhythms seem to have reflected the meter of the poetry. There were two types of alphabetic notation, one for the voice and one for the instruments. Treatises on music have survived, the earliest being part of a 4th-century-BC treatise on music theory by Aristoxenus of Tarentum.

Dancing

The art of *mousike* included poetry, dancing and music. Dancing was a popular form of entertainment from at least the time of Homer, taking place at weddings, funerals, harvests and religious occasions. Public religious festivals were accompanied by music and dancing, with simple rhythmical movements performed by a chorus (*khoros*, dance). By Archaic times the male chorus sang as well as danced in performances of choral lyric poetry, usually under the direction of a leader. Choruses also had a role in tragedy and comedy. Dithyrambs were also sung and danced in honor of Dionysus.

Dancing was part of a child's education and also part of gymnastic training as preparation for war, particularly in Sparta. War dances with weapons were performed, the best known being the Pyrrhic dance. Dancing was for groups of people, not couples. Professional dancers (usually slaves and prostitutes) often entertained at dinner parties. Over 200 names of dances have survived, including particular dances in tragedy and comedy, such as a lewd *kordax* in comedy and a stately *emmeleia* in tragedy.

AUTHORS

ACHAEUS OF ERETRIA (*Akhaios*): Born 484/481 BC. Athenian tragic poet. Little is known of his work, but critics regarded him as one of the five great tragedians. The philosopher Menedemus believed his satyr plays second only to those of Aeschylus. He possibly wrote 44 plays; titles of 19 are known.

ACUSILAUS OF ARGOS (*Akousilaos*): He lived just before the Persian Wars, c. 500 BC. His three

books, called *Genealogies* or *Histories*, were accounts of epic heroes.

AENEAS TACITUS (*Aineias, Aeneas,* the Tactician): Fourth century BC. A writer of handbooks on military practice, of which one survives on besieging cites. He is sometimes identifed as Aeneas of Stymphalus, leader of the Arcadian Confederacy in 367 BC.

AESCHYLUS (*Aiskhylos*): 525/524–456/455 BC, born at Eleusis. The earliest Greek tragic poet whose work survives. He fought in the battle of Marathon (490 BC) and possibly at the battle of Salamis (480 BC). He was said to have been unsuccessfully prosecuted for divulging the secret rites of the Eleusinian Mysteries in one of his plays. He visited Syracuse to produce plays for Hieron I and died at Gela. He wrote 80–90 plays (including satyr plays), of which over 70 titles are known. He won at least 13 victories (the first in 484 BC) in the competitions at Athens, and had the unique honor, after his death, of having his plays produced with a chorus.

Aeschylus is believed to have been the real founder of Greek tragedy, responsible for increasing the number of actors and reducing the role of the chorus. He added a second actor, and Sophocles a third, seen in his later plays. Seven plays survive: *Persians* (*Persai*, produced in 472 BC and his only surviving tragedy on an historical subject), *Seven against Thebes* (467 BC), the *Oresteia* trilogy of 458 BC (*Agamemnon, Choephori* [libation bearers] and *Eumenides*), the *Suppliants* (or *Suppliant Women*, possibly 463 BC) and *Prometheus Bound* (uncertain date; possibly not by Aeschylus). Some fragments of satyr plays also survive. Aeschylus took the leading role in many of his own plays (normal for that time) and was himself portrayed as a character in Aristophanes' *Frogs*.

AESOP (*Aisopos*): A slave from Thrace who lived on Samos in the early 6th century BC. Ancient tradition made him the inventor of fables, a short story in prose or verse ending in a moral, and a collection of fables was attributed to him.

AGATHARCHIDES OF CNIDUS (*Agatharkhides*): Second century BC. He was a historian, geographer and grammarian, and served as a private secretary in the court of Ptolemy VI. He was also a prolific writer, and his surviving works include *Events in Asia, Events in Europe* (histories) and *On the Red Sea*, a collection of five books. He was forced to flee Alexandria because of the persecution of scholars by Ptolemy VIII in 145 BC.

AGATHON (*Agathon*):   c. 447–c. 401/400 BC. One of the most important Athenian tragedians, though less than 40 lines of his poetry survive. He was the first to construct an imaginary subject with imaginary characters, rather than use mythology. He also introduced changes in the music, making choral odes mere interludes not essential to the plot. His first victory in the dramatic competitions was at the Lenaea in 416 BC. Toward the end of the Peloponnesian War c. 407 BC, Agathon (like Euripides) abandoned Athens for the Macedonian court of Archelaus, where he died. Agathon appears as a character in Plato's *Symposium*, which represents a feast held at Agathon's house to celebrate his first victory, and in Aristophanes' *Thesmophoriazusae*.

ALCAEUS (*Alkaios*):   Born c. 620 BC, date of death unknown. A lyric poet from Mytilene in Lesbos, Alcaeus was closely involved in the politics of Mytilene when, allied with Pittacus, his brothers overthrew the tyrants there and later fought the Athenians for possession of Sigeum (a key stronghold on the Hellespont) c. 606 BC. Pittacus turned against them, forcing Alcaeus into exile in Egypt. He was apparently allowed to return to Lesbos. Alcaeus mainly wrote lyrical songs about contemporary politics, and also love songs, drinking songs and hymns to the gods. He used a variety of meters that were later adapted to Latin poetry by Horace. His work survives only as fragments.

ALCAEUS OF MESSENE (*Alkaios*):   c. 200 BC. He was an epigrammatist, and composed some biting epigrams on Philip V of Macedonia, one of which was apparently repeated all over Greece. Fifteen epigrams survive in the *Greek Anthology*.

ALCIDAMAS (*Alkidamas*):   Early-4th-century-BC sophist and rhetorician from Elaea in Aeolis. He taught rhetoric mainly at Athens. A pupil and follower of Gorgias, he opposed the theories of Isocrates. He emphasized the importance of improvisation. One speech survives (*On Those Who Write Written Speeches, or On the Sophists*) and fragments survive of his textbook on oratory (*Mouseion*).

ALCMAN (*Alkman*):   A lyric poet of c. 610 BC, he was probably Laconian (but possibly from Sardis) and lived in Sparta. His work consisted mainly of choral lyrics for festivals. His poems appeared in six books, all lost except for some fragments. His *partheneia* (maiden songs) were especially popular, and the longest surviving fragment (and the earliest piece of choral lyric poetry) is from a *partheneion*.

ALEXANDER AETOLUS (*Alexandros*):   Born c. 315 BC, he was from Pleuron. A versatile poet, known particularly as a tragic poet, he was contemporary with Aratus at the court of Antigonus II Gonatas (c. 276 BC), and also worked for Ptolemy II sorting out the tragedies collected for the Alexandria Library. Of his own tragedies, only one title survives (*Dice-players*).

ALEXANDER POLYHISTOR (*Alexandros*, very learned):   c. 105–c. 50 BC. A historian, born at Miletus and brought to Rome as a prisoner of war, he was freed by the Roman general Sulla c. 80 BC and took the Roman name Lucius Cornelius Alexander, becoming a pedagogue. He wrote copiously on a wide range of subjects. He died in a fire at Laurentum in Italy.

ALEXIS (*Alexis*):   c. 375–c. 275 BC, from Thurii. He was a comic poet at Athens, spanning Middle and New Comedy. He apparently wrote 245 plays, and his popularity continued into the Roman period when his plays were adapted by Roman comedians.

ANACREON (*Anakreon*):   Born c. 570 BC. A lyric poet from Teos, Ionia. He may have moved with colonists to Abdera and later moved to the court of Polycrates, tyrant of Samos. At the fall of Polycrates (523 BC) he was brought to Athens, where he had many patrons. He wrote lyric songs to be performed at symposia, as well as elegiac and iambic poems, collected in five books. Only a few poems survive.

ANAXANDRIDES (*Anaxandrides*):   Possibly of Rhodes, active c. 380 to after 349 BC as a Middle Comedy poet. He won first prize 10 times from 376 BC, three times at the Lenaea. He apparently wrote 65 plays, of which 41 titles and many fragments survive.

ANDROTION (*Androtion*):   c. 410–340 BC. An Athenian politician, he was exiled to Megara where he wrote in eight books a history of Attica (*Atthis*) down to 343 BC. His history, now lost, was the major source for the *Atthis* of Philochorus and for Aristotle's *Constitution of Athens*.

ANTICLEIDES (*Antikleides*): Floruit early 3rd century BC. He was from Athens and wrote a history of Alexander the Great, a mythological and historical account of homeward journeys (*Nostoi*) and an account of Delos.

ANTIGONUS OF CARYSTUS (*Antigonos*): Late 3rd century BC, from Carystus. He was apparently a bronzeworker and a biographer of contemporary philosophers (for which he gained popularity). He also wrote about works of art.

ANTIMACHUS OF COLOPHON (*Antimakhos*): Floruit c. 400 BC. A poet and scholar. Five poems are known: *Thebais* (an epic on Thebes), *Lyde* (a long poem in elegiac couplets on the misfortune of heroes), *Deltoi* (possibly *Tablets*), *Artemis* and *Iachine*.

ANTIPATER OF SIDON (*Antipatros*): Floruit c. 145/120 BC. About 75 epigrams of this poet survive in the *Greek Anthology* and one on papyrus, including poems on the Roman destruction of Corinth (146 BC).

ANTIPHANES (*Antiphanes*): Active from 385 BC. Middle Comedy poet. He won 13 victories (eight at the Lenaea) and wrote 260 to 365 plays, of which 134 titles and many fragments survive.

ANTIPHON (*Antiphon*): c. 480–411 BC. An Attic orator, he seldom spoke in public but wrote speeches for others. His work includes oratorical exercises called tetralogies. Three speeches also survive, as well as fragments of others.

ANYTE (*Anyte*): Early-3rd-century-BC poetess from Tegea, one of the first to write pastoral poetry on wild nature. About 20 epigrams survive, mostly sepulchral and including the first ones for animals.

APOLLODORUS OF ARTEMITA (*Apollodoros*): Floruit c. 100–70 BC. A historian who wrote a history of Parthia in at least four books, including an account of Bactria and the Greek conquest of India.

APOLLODORUS OF ATHENS (*Apollodoros*): Floruit c. 140 BC. A scholar at Alexandria (pupil of Aristarchus), he moved to Pergamum c. 146 BC, then to Athens. He dedicated his *Chronica* to Attalus II of Pergamum—a chronological history from the fall of Troy to 144 BC in iambic trimeters. He also wrote a prose work *On the Gods* (account of Greek religion in 24 books) and *Bibliothe* (study of Greek heroic mythology).

APOLLODORUS OF CARYSTUS (*Apollodoros*): c. 285 BC. New Comedy poet, sometimes called "Athenian." He wrote 47 plays and won five victories. Terence adapted two of his plays (in *Hecyra* and *Phormio*).

APOLLODORUS OF GELA (*Apollodoros*): New Comedy poet, contemporary with Menander.

APOLLONIUS RHODIUS (*Apollonios*): c. 295–215 BC. Poet and scholar from Alexandria, where he was head of the Library. He was a pupil of Callimachus with whom he quarreled and so retired to Rhodes. His main work (which survives) was *Argonautica* (an epic poem in four books on the story of Jason and the Argonauts). He also wrote numerous minor poems and works on Homer, Hesiod and Archilochus.

ARATUS (*Aratos*): c. 315–240/239 BC. A poet, possibly from Soli in Cilicia, he went to Athens and then to the court of Antigonus II Gonatas at Pella, with some time at the court of Antiochus I in Syria. His one surviving work *Phaenomena* (*Astronomy*) was a didactic poem in 1,154 hexameters, based on a prose work by Eudoxus of Cnidus. It achieved immediate fame.

ARATUS OF SICYON (*Aratos*): 271–213 BC. Military leader. He wrote his *Memoirs* to c. 220 BC in over 30 books, a major source for Polybius. It survives only in quotes.

ARCHILOCHUS (*Arkhilokhos*): Poet, mid-7th century BC, from Paros. Little is known of his life, but he colonized Thasos and fought there and was later apparently killed in battle. He quarreled with Lycambes over marrying his daughter Neobule, and his invective poems allegedly led to their suicide. He wrote short poems, often innovative in nature, in a variety of meters (elegiac, iambic, trochaic), many on the subject of his own affairs. Much survives in quotations by later writers and in some papyrus fragments. He was ranked alongside Homer.

ARCTINUS (*Arktinos*): Epic poet from Miletus, possibly 8th or 7th century BC. Author of *Aethiopis* (sequel to the *Iliad*) and *Iliupersis* (both part of the Epic Cycle) and probably *Titanomachia*. All are lost.

ARION (*Arion*): Possibly late 7th century BC. Lyric poet from Methymna who spent most of his life at the court of Periander (tyrant of Corinth). He was the first composer of dithyrambs, which he taught Corinthian choirs to perform, and he was also linked to the birth of tragedy. None of his work survives.

ARIPHRON (*Ariphron*): Lyric poet from Sicyon, 5th–4th century BC, famous for his *Paean to Health* (*Hygieia*).

ARISTARCHUS OF SAMOTHRACE (*Aristarkhos*): c. 215–c. 143 BC. A scholar, tutor of Ptolemy VII and head of the Alexandria Library (c. 153 BC). His name was often used to personify fine scholarship. He wrote numerous commentaries on grammar and on various authors, and was known particularly for his study of Homer. He fled to Cyprus in 145 BC and died shortly afterwards. Fragments of his work survive.

ARISTARCHUS OF TEGEA (*Aristarkhos*): Mid-5th-century-BC contemporary of Euripides. He wrote 75 tragedies and won two victories. His plays included *Tantalus*, *Achilles* and *Asclepius* (in thanks for recovery from illness).

ARISTEAS OF PROCONNESUS (*Aristeas*): Possibly 7th century BC. He was a hexameter poet and devoted servant of Apollo. He wrote an epic poem in three books (*Arimaspeia*) on his travels beyond the Black Sea. It was later a source of geography and history, and fragments of it survive.

ARISTIDES OF MILETUS (*Aristeides*): Second century BC. Author of *Milesiaka* (*Milesian Tales*), erotic, often obscene short stories. Only one fragment survives, but the Parthians were apparently shocked on finding a copy amongst spoils captured from the Romans in 55 BC. This genre of literature became known as Milesian Tales.

ARISTOBULUS OF CASSENDREA (*Aristoboulos*): A technician in Alexander the Great's army. Circa 300 BC he wrote a history of Alexander's reign and was a source for Arrian and Strabo.

ARISTOMENES (*Aristomenes*): Athenian comic poet who competed during the years 439–388 BC. He won first prize at the City Dionysia in 424 BC and had two victories at the Lenaea. Five titles survive.

ARISTOPHANES (*Aristophanes*): c. 457–c. 385 BC. Comic poet, the greatest of Old Attic Comedy; his were the only Greek comedies to survive in medieval manuscripts. He was from Athens, but possibly lived or owned property on Aegina, and was the son of Philippus and father of Araros. Eleven of his plays survive, and titles of 32 others (some possibly alternative titles); nearly 1,000 fragments survive. In all he wrote about 40 plays. Some were performed at the City Dionysia and others at the Lenaea. Datable plays are:

427 BC *Daitaleis* (*Banqueters*) Now lost. Produced by Callistratus. It won second prize.
426 BC *Babylonians* Now lost. Produced by Callistratus at the City Dionysia. Aristophanes was prosecuted (apparently unsuccessfully) for its attacks on magistrates. Possibly won first prize.
425 BC *Acharnians* (*Men of Acharnae*) First prize at the Lenaea). Produced by Callistratus.
424 BC *Knights* Lenaea, first prize.
423 BC *Clouds* City Dionysia, third prize—i.e., last.
422 BC *Wasps* Lenaea, second prize.
421 BC *Peace* City Dionysia, second prize.
414 BC *Amphiaraus* Produced by Philonides at the Lenaea. Now lost.
414 BC *Birds* Produced by Callistratus at the City Dionysia, second prize.
411 BC *Lysistrata* Produced by Callistratus, probably at the Lenaea.
411 BC *Thesmophoriazusae* (*Women Celebrating the Thesmophoria*) Probably at the City Dionysia.
408 BC *Plutus* (*Wealth*) First play of this name, now lost.

405 BC *Frogs* Lenaea, first prize.
c. 392 BC *Ecclesiazusae (Women Holding an Assembly)*
388 BC *Plutus (Wealth)* Second play of this
  name.
Probably posthumous: *Aiolosikon* and *Cocalus*.
  Produced by his son Araros; now lost.

ARISTOPHANES OF BYZANTIUM (*Aristoph-anes*): Born c. 260 BC. A scholar and head of the
Alexandria Library (c. 200 BC), he undertook the
first critical editions of several Greek poets, formulated symbols for manuscript criticism and devised
a system of accentuation. He wrote a grammatical
treatise and produced books of proverbs and a
Lexeis (Glossary) on dialect.

ARTEMIDORUS OF EPHESUS (*Artemidoros*):
Second half of 2nd century BC. Geographer and
traveler to many parts of the Mediterranean, Egypt,
Africa, Red Sea, Arabia and Ethiopia. He wrote 11
geographical books, with distances, navigation and
main routes.

ASCLEPIADES OF SAMOS (*Asklepiades*): Also
called Sicelidas. Floruit c. 300 BC. Major Hellenistic
epigrammatic poet, particularly of love epigrams.
He gave his name to the asclepiad meters, which he
revived.

ASTYDAMAS (*Astydamas*): Father and son by
the same name. 4th-century-BC poets (of tragedy).
The father produced his first play in 398 BC and
lived to the age of 60. The son probably won his
first victory in 372 BC, with subsequent victories
recorded in 341 and 340 BC. Less than 20 lines survive.

BACCHYLIDES (*Bakkhylides*): Late 6th century
BC to c. 450 BC. Lyric poet from Ceos, who wrote
in Thessaly, Macedonia, Sicily and then in the
Peloponnese. He was nephew of the poet
Simonides and was employed by the same patrons.
Bacchylides wrote odes, dithyrambs, encomia,
paeans, hymns, processional songs, maiden songs
and hyporchemata. Very little survives, although
some work was discovered in 1896 and a few more
fragments since then.

BION (*Bion*): Floruit c. 100 BC, from Phlossa
near Smyrna. A pastoral poet about whom very little is known. Seventeen fragments survive.

CALLIAS (*Kallias*): Athenian comic poet who
won first prize at the City Dionysia in 446 BC and
was active to at least 430 BC. Eight titles and some
fragments survive.

CALLIAS OF SYRACUSE (*Kallias*): Historian
who probably lived at the court of Agathocles
(tyrant of Syracuse) from 316 to 289 BC and wrote
the first known history of his reign in 22 books.
Very little survives, but it was apparently favorable
to Agathocles, and Callias may have been bribed.

CALLIMACHUS (*Kallimakhos*): c. 310–305 BC
to c. 240 BC. A poet and scholar from Cyrene, often
called Battiades (allegedly descended from Cyrene's
founder Battus). He went to Alexandria as a schoolteacher, then worked in the Library, producing a
120-volume catalog of its books (*Pinakes*). His many
scholarly prose works (including *Rivers of the World*,
About Nymphs, *A Chronological Register of the
Athenian Dramatic Poets*) have not survived. His surviving poems are six *Hymns* and about 60 *Epigrams*.
Other poetry survives in fragments. The best
known was *Aetia (Origins)*, an elegiac poem of about
7,000 lines in four books, which included the *Lock
of Berenice (Plokamos)*. Other poetic works included
Hecale, *Iambi*, *Apotheosis of Queen Arsinoë* and *Victory
of Sosibius*. Callimachus apparently produced 800
volumes. He greatly influenced later Roman poets.

CALLINUS (*Kallinos*): First half of 7th century
BC. Elegiac poet from Ephesus, the apparent inventor of elegiac couplets. A few fragments survive, including exhortation to take up arms to defend one's
country.

CALLISTHENES (*Kallisthenes*): c. 370–327 BC.
A historian from Olynthus and a relation of
Aristotle. His lost works include a monograph on
the Sacred War (355–346 BC), a history of Greece
in 10 books (386–355 BC) and *Achievements of
Alexander*, whose expedition he accompanied. A virtually fictitious and romantic biography of
Alexander (*Alexander Romance* or *Pseudo-Callisthenes*)
is wrongly ascribed to Callisthenes.

CARCINUS (*Karkinos*): A tragic poet who was
ridiculed by Aristophanes. His grandson was also a
tragic poet in the 4th century BC. He apparently
wrote 160 plays and won 11 victories. He worked at
the court of Dionysius II of Syracuse.

CERCIDAS (*Kerkidas*): c. 290–c. 220 BC. A poet, philosopher and statesman. He was much influenced by Cynic philosophy, and his best-known work was the *Meliambi* (lyric poems, satirical in nature). Only a few fragments of his work survive.

CHAEREMON (*Khairemon*): Mid-4th-century-BC tragic poet. His work included the *Centaur*, which (according to Aristotle) was better suited to reading than performance.

CHARES OF MYTILENE (*Khares*): Fourth century BC. He was Alexander the Great's chamberlain and wrote an account of Alexander and his court.

CHARON OF LAMPSACUS (*Kharon*): Fifth-century-BC logographer. Possibly earlier than Herodotus. Author of several works, but none survive.

CHIONIDES (*Khionides*): Possibly one of the earliest Attic poets (along with Magnes). He won a victory at the City Dionysia in 487 BC.

CHOERILUS OF ATHENS (*Khoirilos*): Tragic poet who wrote plays from c. 523 BC. He won 13 victories and competed against Aeschylus.

CHOERILUS OF SAMOS (*Khoirilos*): Late 5th-century-BC epic poet, author of the famous *Persica*, which was still read in the 3rd century AD. He died at the court of Archelaus of Macedonia.

CINESIAS (*Kinesias*): c. 450–c. 390 BC. Athenian lyric (especially dithyrambic) poet criticized by Aristophanes, Pherecrates, Plato and Lysias. Nothing survives of his work.

CLEIDEMUS or CLEITODEMUS (*Kleidemos* or *Kleitodemos*): Floruit c. 350 BC. One of the oldest atthidographers. His *Atthis* was in about four books but was superseded by later versions.

CLEITARCHUS OF ALEXANDRIA (*Kleitarkhos*): c. 350–c. 300 BC or later. A historian who wrote a lost history of Alexander the Great in about 12 books, and was possibly from Alexandria. Although popular in the Roman Empire, his work was criticized for inaccuracy.

CORINNA (*Korinna*): Lyric poetess from Tanagra. She was possibly a rival of Pindar (5th century BC), but may actually have written in the 3rd century BC or later. Her poems were often based on local Boeotian myths, including a singing contest between two mountains—Cithaeron and Helicon.

CRATES (*Krates*): Athenian comic poet (previously an actor) who won three victories at the City Dionysia, the first in 450 BC. Six titles survive.

CRATES OF MALLUS (Cilicia) (*Krates*): 2nd-century-BC scholar and first head of the Pergamum Library. His works included commentaries on Hesiod, Homer, Euripides, Aristophanes and Attalus. He visited Rome in 168 BC as an envoy from Pergamum and made a great impression on Roman scholars, despite breaking his leg in the Cloaca Maxima.

CRATINUS (*Kratinos*): Active c. 450–c. 423 BC. Leading writer of Old Comedy. He won first prize six times at the City Dionysia and three times at the Lenaea. Surviving are 27 titles and over 460 fragments. Cratinus was inventive and renowned for invective, as well as drunkenness.

CRATIPPUS (*Kratippos*): Possibly early-4th-century-BC historian from Athens who wrote a continuation of Thucydides' history (from 410 BC) to Conon's victory at Cnidus (394 BC). He is sometimes regarded as a late Hellenistic writer or possibly the Oxyrhynchus Historian.

CTESIAS (*Ktesias*): Early-4th-century-BC historian from Cnidus. He was a physician employed in the Persian court of Artaxerxes from 405 BC, and was sent as an envoy to Conon. Returning home, he wrote an unreliable history of Persia (*Persika*) in 23 books (written in Ionic), as well as a geographical treatise in three books and the first book on India (*Indika*). A few fragments survive.

D(E)INARCHUS (*Deinarkhos*): c. 360–c. 290 BC. An Attic orator who lived at Athens. Corinthian by birth (not an Athenian citizen), he was debarred from addressing the Assembly. He wrote many speeches for others, of which 60 or 64 were known in the Augustan period. Three surviving speeches are *Against Demosthenes*, *Against Aristogiton* and *Against Philocles*, and three others are sometimes attributed to him. He spent 15 years at Chalcis, returning in 292 BC.

DEMOSTHENES (*Demosthenes*): Lived 384–322 BC. He was regarded as the greatest of the Attic orators. See chapter 2.

DIAGORAS (*Diagoras*): Late-5th-century-BC lyric poet from Melos. He was renowned for his atheism and fled after being condemned to death. The surviving fragments do not reflect his atheism.

DIONYSIUS CHALCUS (*Dionysios*): Fifth-century-BC elegiac poet who took part in the colonization of Thurii. Fragments of poems written for symposia survive. His nickname (*Khalkous*, of bronze) was obtained after advising Athenians to adopt bronze coinage.

DIONYSIUS THE THRACIAN (*Dionysios Thrax*): c. 170–c. 90 BC. Son of Teres, a Thracian from Alexandria. He was a pupil of Aristarchus and later a teacher of grammar and literature at Rhodes. He wrote many works, but only a Greek grammar survives (*Tekhne grammatike*); it influenced Latin grammar books, and its popularity lasted to the Renaissance.

DIOSCORIDES (*Dioskourides*): Floruit 230 BC. A writer of epigrams who possibly lived at Alexandria. About 40 epigrams survive in the *Greek Anthology*.

DIPHILUS (*Diphilos*): c. 360/350 to c. 300 BC (?). A New Comedy poet from Sinope who lived mostly at Athens but died at Smyrna. He wrote about 100 plays, of which about 60 titles are known. He won three victories at the Lenaea (after 318 BC).

DOURIS OF SAMOS (*Douris*): c. 340–270 BC. Historian and critic, and pupil of Theophrastus; also tyrant of Samos after 322 BC to after c. 300 BC. He was a prolific writer, whose works include a *Chronicle of Samos* covering 370–281 BC, a *Life* of Agathocles of Syracuse, and various works on literature, music, law and the history of art.

EPHORUS (*Ephoros*): A 4th-century-BC historian from Cyme (Asia Minor). Little is known of his life. He wrote a 30-volume history of the cities of Greece and Asia Minor (edited and completed by his son Demophilus) covering the Dorian invasion to the sack of Perinthus (341 BC). It was arranged by subject. He was a very influential historian, known to Polybius and extensively used by Strabo and Diodorus.

EPICHARMUS (*Epikharmos*): A 6th–5th-centuries-BC comic poet from Sicily (probably Syracuse). He worked at the court of Hieron I. Some titles and fragments of plays survive, indicating a burlesque treatment of myths. Several plural titles suggest that he used a chorus. He wrote in Sicilian Doric. Epicharmus was later regarded as author of several philosophical and quasi-scientific works, which is unlikely.

ERATOSTHENES (*Eratosthenes*): c. 280–c. 194 BC. From Cyrene, the first to call himself *philologos* (scholar). He became head of the Alexandria Library (after Apollonius Rhodius), and was a versatile scholar in astronomy, geography, mathematics, poetry, philosophy, grammar and chronography. Only quotations from his work survive, which included *On Ancient Comedy* (in at least 12 books), the *Chronographia* (in which he presented dates of literary and political history free of myth), *On the Measurement of the Earth* (in which he fairly accurately calculated the circumference of Earth) and *Geographica* (a scientific geography).

ERINNA (*Erinna*): Probably 4th century BC poetess from Telos near Rhodes who died at the age of 19. She was famous for *The Distaff* (*Elakate*) of 300 hexameter lines, of which fragments survive. It was written in memory of her friend Baucis.

EUHEMERUS (*Euemeros*): c. 300 BC, from Messene. Author of an influential novel *Sacred Scripture* (*Hiera anagraphe*) about an imaginary journey to utopian islands in the Indian Ocean, chief of which was Panchaea. The mythological gods, such as Zeus, Cronus and Uranus, were once great kings of this island, deified by their grateful people (hence, "euhemerism"). This theory was very relevant to Hellenistic rulers of the time. Only fragments survive.

EUMELUS (*Eumelos*): Floruit c. 730 BC. An epic poet from the ruling Bacchiad family in Corinth. He wrote *Corinthiaca*, in which he describes mythical and heroic figures of Corinth's history, and a famous *Prosodion* (procession song) for the Messenians to sing at the festival of Apollo on Delos. Other works are doubtfully attributed to him.

EUPHORION (*Euphorion*):   Fifth century BC. He won four victories in the drama festivals with tragedies written by his father Aeschylus, but not produced in his lifetime; he defeated Sophocles and Euripides in 431 BC.

EUPHORION (*Euphorion*):   Born c. 270 BC. A poet from Chalcis in Euboea. He became wealthy through a liaison with the widow of Alexander of Corinth (died c. 245 BC) and subsequently took up the post of librarian to Antiochus the Great at Antioch. He mainly wrote epic-type poetry on mythological subjects, especially the hexameter epyllion. His works were much praised at Rome by poets in the 1st century BC.

EUPOLIS (*Eupolis*):   Active c. 429–412 BC. One of the most famous Old Comedy poets, along with Aristophanes and Cratinus. He produced his first play in 429 BC and won three victories at the Lenaea and at least one at the City Dionysia. Nineteen titles and over 460 fragments survive.

EURIPIDES (*Euripides*):   c. 485–c. 406 BC. This Athenian tragedian is regarded as one of the greatest, but little is known of his life. He was not active in politics, although he went on an embassy to Syracuse. His family came from Phyle and was probably wealthy. He was apparently acquainted with Anaxagoras, Socrates and Protagoras. He used to compose in a cave on Salamis, and in 408 or 407 BC, allegedly embittered by lack of success, he went to the court of Archelaus of Macedonia to produce plays, where he died c. 406 BC.

Euripides wrote 92 plays, of which about 80 titles are known. He competed 22 times at the City Dionysia (the first time in 455 BC). He won first prize only in 441 BC, in 428 BC (with *Hippolytus*), twice more and posthumously (possibly 405 BC). Nineteen plays survive, of two groups. The following group of 10 was selected c. AD 200 for use in schools, accompanied by notes:

Alcestis (438 BC, second prize)
Medea (431 BC, third prize)
Hippolytus (428 BC, first prize)
Andromache (c. 426/425 BC)
Hecuba (c. 424 BC)
Trojan Women (415 BC, second prize)
Phoenician Women (c. 409 BC; concerning the sons of Oedipus)

Orestes (408 BC)
Bacchae (405 BC; notes lost; posthumously produced)
Rhesus (probably not genuine)

Other plays are from an alphabetic group (letters *E* to *K* in Greek survive):
Helen (412 BC)
Electra (c. 417 BC)
Children of Heracles (*Heracleidae*) (c. 430/428 BC)
Madness of Heracles (c. 417 BC)
Suppliant Women (c. 422 BC; on the burial of the Seven against Thebes)
Iphigeneia in Aulis (405 BC; posthumously produced)
Iphigeneia in Tauris (c. 414/413 BC)
Ion (c. 410 BC)
Cyclops (a satyr play, not a tragedy; date unknown, probably late)

Some other plays survive as papyrus fragments, which are at times substantial.

HECATEUS (*Hekataios*):   c. 550–490 BC or later, from Miletus. One of the earliest Ionian logographers, writing about the past in prose. Initially he opposed the Ionian revolt against Persia (499–494 BC), knowing the extent of the Persian Empire from his travels, but was later one of the leaders of the revolt. He wrote a *Periegesis* (a guide) to illustrate a map he had compiled (possibly of the world); over 300 fragments survive, and it was used extensively by Herodotus. He also wrote *Genealogies* (or *Histories*), tracing families back to mythical times, only fragments of which survive.

HECATAEUS OF ABDERA (*Hekataios*):   Floruit c. 315–285 BC (?). He trained as a philosopher and lived in Egypt under Ptolemy I. He wrote a history of Egypt, a large part of which is preserved in book one of Diodorus Siculus.

HEGEMON (*Hegemon*):   Fifth-century-BC parodist from Thasos, probably the first to establish parody as a literary genre.

HEGESIAS OF MAGNESIA (*Hegesias*):   Third-century-BC orator and historian. His speeches do not survive, but he was criticized in the Roman period by Cicero and others. Fragments remain of his *History of Alexandria*.

HELLANICUS (*Hellanikos*): Traditional dates 490–405 BC. A logographer from Lesbos who wrote prolifically on various subjects. Twenty-four titles and extensive fragments are known. His work included the genealogies of epic heroes, various regional and local histories, the first history of Athens (*Atthis*), a list of the priestesses of Hera at Argos and a list of victors at the Carnea.

HERMAGORAS OF TEMNOS (*Hermagoras*): Floruit c. 150 BC. The most influential rhetorician of Hellenistic times, who compiled a lost handbook on rhetoric.

HERMESIANAX (*Hermesianax*): Early-3rd-century-BC poet (born c. 300 BC) from Colophon. He was a pupil of Philetas. His works included *Persica*, as well as *Leontion* in three books, which were erotic love elegies named after his mistress Leontion.

HERMIPPUS (*Hermippos*): Active c. 436/435–c. 415 BC. Athenian comic poet and brother of Myrtilus. Ten titles and 100 fragments survive. Hermippus won one victory at least at the City Dionysia (435 BC) and four at the Lenaea (the first c. 430 BC).

HERMIPPUS OF SMYRNA (*Hermippos*): Late-3rd-century-BC biographer of lawgivers, famous writers and philosophers. He worked in Alexandria and was imaginative rather than historically accurate.

HERODAS or HERONDAS (*Herodas/Herondas*): c. 300–250 BC, from Cos or Miletus. Writer of literary mimes (*mimiamboi*) in the iambic scazon meter. Eight mimes and the beginning of a ninth are known from papyrus discoveries: *The Bawd, The Pimp, The Schoolmaster, The Women Worshippers, The Jealous Mistress, The Private Conversation, The Shoemaker, The Dream* (mutilated) and *Women Breaking a Fast* (fragmentary).

HERODOTUS (*Herodotos*): Traditional date 484–420 BC. Historian, son of a distinguished family from Halicarnassus (fig. 7.16). He withdrew or was exiled to Samos in the political troubles of the 460s BC and then traveled extensively before joining the Athenian colony at Thurii (founded 443 BC) where he died. He is author of *Histories* (*Historiai*)— nine books on the Persian War, with numerous digressions on various topics. It covers the struggle between Greece and Asia from the time of Croesus (mid-6th century BC) to the withdrawal of the Persians from Greece after their defeats at Plataea and Mycale. Herodotus was regarded as the "father of history" by Cicero and others.

HESIOD (*Hesiodos*): c. 700 BC. Epic poet, one of the earliest known Greek poets. His father gave up unprofitable seafaring business and left Aeolian Cyme for Ascra, a village near Mount Helicon in Boeotia. Hesiod tended sheep on Mount Helicon where he heard the Muses call him to write poetry and sing of the gods. He won a tripod at the funeral games of Amphidamas in Chalcis with a hymn (possibly the *Theogony*). Hesiod was author of *Theogony* (dealing with the origin and genealogies of gods) and *Works and Days* (advice on undertaking honest work, including much practical instruction on agriculture). The *Shield of Heracles* is probably not by him, but other poems (now lost) have been ascribed to him.

HIERONYMUS OF CARDIA (*Hieronymos*): c. 364–260 BC. Historian from the death of Alexander the Great (323 BC) to the death of Pyrrhus (272 BC) or perhaps to 263 BC. He was a general and statesman for Eumenes of Cardia, and after his death in 316 BC, Hieronymus served Antigonus I, his son Demetrius and his grandson Antigonus II Gonatas. He had firsthand knowledge of many of the events he related, and his history (now lost) was much used by later writers. He died at the age of 104.

HIPPONAX (*Hipponax*): Floruit c. 540–437 BC. Iambic poet from Ephesus, exiled to Clazomenae. He wrote satirical, scurrilous and even abusive poetry, and invented the scazon meter. He has been credited with the invention of parody. His poems survive only in fragments. A story relates that he quarreled with the sculptors Bupalus and Athenis, who made a caricature statue of him; he abused them with such offensive poetry that they hanged themselves.

HOMER (*Homeros*): Probably 8th century BC. Epic poet, generally regarded as the greatest and earliest Greek poet. His place of origin and date were disputed by the Greeks. It is now thought that he cannot be earlier than the 8th century BC or later than c. 700 BC. He may have originated from Chios

Athens. He was known mainly for tragedies, but also wrote other types of poetry and possibly comedies. He was defeated by Euripides' *Hippolytus* (428 BC) but later won first prize at the City Dionysia for tragedy and dithyramb. He was variously reported as having written 12, 30 or 40 plays, and a few titles are known. He also wrote some prose works, including *Epidemiae* (*Visits*), *Founding of Chios* and *Triagmos* (on Pythagorean philosophy).

ISAEUS (*Isaios*): c. 420–c. 350 BC. Attic orator, possibly from Chalcis (Euboea). He was a logographer, composing speeches for others to deliver. Fifty speeches were known, of which 11 and part of a 12th survive, all on issues of inheritance.

ISOCRATES (*Isokrates*): 436–338 BC. Athenian orator of importance. He played no direct part in politics, but wrote speeches as a logographer for others to perform in the courts. He opened a school at Athens c. 392 BC to train others in rhetoric; it became famous, attracting pupils from all over the Greek world, including Androtion, Hyperides, Isaeus, Ephorus, Theopompus and Timotheus. Several of his political writings and rhetorical exercises survive, as well as six speeches and nine letters. They include *Against the Sophists* (391 or 390 BC) and *Antidosis* (353 BC), both on education; *Panegyricus* (festival oration, published in 380 BC); *Plataicus* (written as a plea for retaliation after Thebes destroyed Plataea in 373 BC); *On the Peace* (denouncing imperialism and advocating a Common Peace and colonization of Thasos, written in 355 BC just before the end of the Social War); *Philippus* (346 BC, written after the Peace of Philocrates, calling on Philip II of Macedonia to unite the entire Greek nation against the Persians); and *Panathenaicus* (339 BC, comparing the achievements of Sparta and Athens).

Fig. 7.16 A Roman copy of a sculpture, possibly the head of Herodotus.

(home of the Homeridae, a guild of reciters) or Smyrna; he certainly came from an Ionian-speaking region. He is regarded as the author of the epic poem *Iliad* and its sequel the *Odyssey*, although there is a possibility that they were written by different people; perhaps they were the result of oral tradition. The title of the *Iliad* is derived from Ilion (Troy); it is about a single episode in the Trojan War—the wrath of Achilles. The poem is divided into 24 books, as is the *Odyssey* (*Odysseia*). The latter records the return of Odysseus to Ithaca from the Trojan War. Other epic poems were sometimes attributed to Homer in antiquity, including *Margites* and *Batrachomyomachia*.

IBYCUS (*Ibykos*): Sixth century BC (floruit 564 or 536 BC). A lyric poet from Rhegium. He apparently refused to become tyrant and went to work at the court of Polycrates on Samos. Originally his work was collected in seven books, mainly choral songs, encomia and personal love songs in various meters. Fragments survive. He was allegedly killed by robbers and buried at Rhegium.

ION OF CHIOS (*Ion*): c. 490/480–c. 422 BC. Poet and prose writer who spent much time in

ISTER (*Istros*): c. 250–200 BC. Historical researcher and atthidographer, possibly from Cyrene. He was a pupil of Callimachus. His main work was *Attika* in 14 books, which dealt only with mythical Attic history. His *Atakta* also dealt with Attic history.

LASUS (*Lasos*): Born c. 548–545 BC, from Hermione (Argolis). An early lyric poet and musician. He worked under the patronage of Hipparchus (brother of the tyrant Hippias). He wrote hymns and founded Athenian dithyrambic poetry. He exposed Onomacritus as a forger of oracles of Musaeus. Most of his poetry is lost.

LEONIDAS OF TARENTUM (*Leonidas*): First half of 3rd century BC (possibly later). Writer of epigrams who apparently led a poor wandering life. He was one of the best and most imitated poets of his time. About 100 epigrams survive, most of which are highly pessimistic; some were genuine dedications and others imaginary. He wrote about the poor rather than love and feasting (about which his contemporaries Asclepiades and Posidippus wrote).

LYCOPHRON (*Lykophron*): Born c. 320 BC. Tragic poet from Chalcis who went to Alexandria c. 285–283 BC to work in the library, initially sorting the comedies. He was author of 64 or 46 tragedies, of which 20 titles are known. His only surviving work is *Alexandra*, a dramatic monologue of 1,474 lines in iambic trimeters, although its authorship is disputed. Lycophron was one of the Pleiad of tragic poets.

LYSIAS (*Lysias*): Traditional dates 459–380 BC. Attic orator. Son of a Syracusan living at Athens, he went to Thurii for some years with his brothers. Returning to Athens, they ran a successful shield-manufacturing business but were proscribed by the Thirty Tyrants in 404 BC. Lysias escaped to Megara but returned in 403 BC. From then on, he became a professional speechwriter (*logographos*) and reputedly wrote over 200 speeches for others to perform. He could not speak in court, being a metic. Thirty-five speeches survive (23 complete).

MACHON (*Makhon*): Mid-3rd century BC. New Comedy poet who moved from Corinth or Sicyon to Alexandria, where he staged comedies. He also wrote in iambic verse a book of anecdotes (*Chreiai*) about notorious Athenian prostitutes and their associates.

MANETHO (*Manethon*): Floruit c. 280 BC. Historian and Egyptian high priest at Heliopolis under Ptolemy I and II. He wrote a history of Egypt (possibly dedicated to Ptolemy II) from mythical times to 323 BC. He is the first native Egyptian known to have written in Greek. He divided the kings into dynasties and kingdoms. Parts of his work are preserved by later historians and are valuable for establishing biblical chronology.

MEGASTHENES (*Megasthenes*): c. 350–290 BC. An Ionian envoy of Seleucus I, sent on several occasions to the court of the Indian king Sandracottus. He also spent time at Sandracottus' capital at Pataliputra. He traveled widely in northern India and was the first Greek to write about India authoratively. His *Indika* was a history in four books, including geography, peoples, cities, government, religion, history and legends.

MELANIPPIDES (*Melanippides*): c. 520–after 450 BC. Dithyrambic poet from Miletus who died at the court of Perdiccas II of Macedonia. He changed the structure of dithyrambs by introducing lyric solos. Little of his work survives.

MENANDER (*Menandros*): 342/341 to 293/292 or 290/289 BC. The leading writer of New Comedy poetry. He was of a good Athenian family, a pupil of Theophrastus and acquainted with Demetrius of Phalerum. His first play *Orge* (anger) was in 321 BC (now lost). He wrote over 100 plays, and nearly 100 titles (some possibly alternatives) are known. In the 7th and 8th centuries AD his plays were lost: they had been excluded from the school curriculum of the 5th century AD and later because they were written in dialect, not Classical Attic Greek. Over 900 quotations did survive. In the 20th century numerous finds of papyri have yielded one complete play, *Dyskolos* (*The Bad-Tempered Man*) and many substantial fragments from *Samia* (*The Samian Woman*), *Epitrepontes* (*The Arbitrants*), *Perikeiromene* (*The Shorn Girl*), *Aspis* (*The Shield*), *Sicyonios* (*The Sicyonian*), *Georgos* (*Farmer*) and *Dis exapaton* (*Twice a Swindler*). He won only eight victories, including *Dyskolos* in 317/316 BC. His plays were set in contemporary Greece, usually Athens or Attica, and most were written in iambic trimeters.

MIMNERMUS (*Mimnermos*): Floruit 632–629 BC. An elegiac poet and musician from Colophon or Smyrna. He mainly wrote love poems in elegiacs, which were collected in two books; the book called *Nanno* (possibly after a flute player he loved) contained a collection of poems on various themes, possibly including his *Smyrneis* (historical poem on Smyrna).

MOSCHUS (*Moskhos*): Floruit c. 150 BC. A poet from Syracuse. A pupil of Aristarchus of Samothrace and possibly also a grammarian. Five short hexameter poems survive; three are from his *Bucolica*, one comparing the pleasures of the countryman with the hard life of the fisherman. An epyllion in hexameters called *Europa* is also attributed to Moschus. The *Lament for Bion* is unlikely to be by him.

NICANDER (*Nikandros*): Second-century-BC didactic poet from Colophon (or nearby). Two didactic poems in hexameters survive complete: *Theriaca* (on poisonous snakes and other creatures, with bite remedies) and *Alexipharmaca* (on miscellaneous poisons and their antidotes). Fragments of other poems also survive. There is confusion between this poet and the mid-3rd-century-BC epic poet Nicander of Colophon.

NOSSIS (*Nossis*): Early 3rd-century-BC poetess from Locri Epizephyrii. Her lyric poetry has not survived, but several epigrams still exist; in one she compares herself to Sappho.

ONESICRITUS (*Onesikritos*): Floruit 320s BC. A historian and seaman who accompanied Alexander the Great's expedition to India. He wrote a work on the campaign in India and won a reputation as a liar.

ONOMACRITUS (*Onomakritos*): Late-6th-century-BC poet and oracle editor. An Athenian who lived at the court of Peisistratus, he collected and edited the oracles of Musaeus and was exposed by Lasus for forgery. On the expulsion of the Peisistratids, Onomacritus went to Susa and presented Xerxes with oracles favorable to an invasion of Greece. He was later thought to have been author of other poems.

OXYRHYNCHUS HISTORIAN: A historian of unknown name (possibly Cratippus), fragments of whose work were discovered on papyri at Oxyrhynchus in 1906 (*Hellenica Oxyrhynchia*). The fragments cover in detail the years 396–395 BC.

PANYASSIS (*Panuas[s]is*): Fifth-century-BC epic poet from Halicarnassus. He was uncle or cousin of Herodotus and author of *Heracleia* (14 books on Heracles) and *Ionica* (on the foundation of the Ionian cities). A few fragments of the *Heracleia* survive. He was executed in the 460s or early 450s BC for his political activities.

PHANODEMUS (*Phanodemos*): Fourth-century-BC historian from Athens. He wrote a history of Athens (*Atthis*) in at least nine books, and a history of the island of Icus. He played a prominent part in public life and was a member of the Athenian boule. Inscriptions record the granting of civic crowns for his services. He was a supporter of Lycurgus and was connected with the restoration of the cult of Amphiaraus.

PHERECRATES (*Pherekrates*): Mid-5th-century-BC Athenian comic poet. He was the rival of Aristophanes and won his first victories at the City Dionysia and Lenaea between 440 and 430 BC. Nineteen titles of plays survive and 250 fragments, one being a speech adversely criticizing contemporary musicians.

PHERECYDES (*Pherekydes*): Early-5th-century-BC logographer from Athens who wrote a mythological and genealogical history in 10 books, of which fragments survive. He is sometimes confused with Pherecydes of Syrus, a philosopher.

PHILEMON (*Philemon*): c. 368/360–c. 267/263 BC. New Comedy poet, probably from Syracuse. He became an Athenian citizen before 307 BC. Over 60 titles of his 97 comedies are known, and over 200 fragments survive. He won three Lenaean victories after 320 BC, and his first victory at the Dionysia was in 327 BC. He won more victories than Menander, but his popularity diminished after his death.

PHILETAS or PHILITAS (*Philetas*): Born before 320 BC. A poet and scholar from Cos who became tutor to the future Ptolemy II. Other pupils were Zenodotus and Theocritus. Philetas wrote love poems and was particularly famous for his elegies. His works included *Demeter*, *Hermes* (an epyllion), *Telephus*, *Epigrammata* and *Paegnia* (*Playful Poems*). He also wrote the prose work *Miscellaneous Glosses*, a lexicon of rare words. Very little of his work survives.

PHILICUS (*Philikos*): c. 275 BC. A tragic poet from Corcyra who lived at Alexandria. He was one of the "Tragic Pleiad" and a priest of Dionysus. He wrote 42 tragedies, but not even one title survives. A papyrus fragment of his *Hymn to Demeter* is in the choriambic hexameter meter, which he claimed to have invented.

PHILISTUS (*Philistos*): c. 430–356 BC. Historian and statesman from Syracuse who helped Dionysius I become tyrant but later quarreled with him and was exiled. He was recalled by Dionysius II. Philistus exiled Dion (uncle of Dionysius II) and became admiral. However, he was defeated in a naval battle by Dion and committed suicide. Philistus is best known for an unfinished history of Sicily in 11 to 13 books from earliest times to 406 BC, written when he was exiled. It became a major source for later historians and was much praised by Cicero and others.

PHILOCHORUS (*Philokhoros*): Before 340 BC–c. 262 BC. An atthidographer (the best and most famous). He was of a distinguished family and held official religious posts. Twenty-seven titles are known, the most important being *Atthis* (*Attic History*) in 17 books. The last seven books are lost. It was a history of Athens to the Chremonidean War. Philochorus was executed by Antigonus II Gonatas for supporting Ptolemy II.

PHILOXENUS OF CYTHERA (*Philoxenos*): 435/434–380/379 BC. Dithyrambic poet who worked at the court of Dionysius I of Syracuse. His most famous dithyramb was *Cyclops*, in which the Cyclops sang a solo to the lyre, an innovative feature parodied by Aristophanes. He is often confused with a Philoxenus who wrote a lyric poem *The Banquet* (*Deipnon*).

PHOCYLIDES (*Phokylides*): Mid-6th century BC. An elegiac and hexameter poet from Miletus, known particularly for gnomic couplets with a moral observation.

PHOENIX OF COLOPHON (*Phoinix*): 3rd-century-BC iambic poet who wrote moralizing choliambics and *Coronistae*, a version of a beggar's song.

PHRYNICHUS (*Phrynikhos*): Athenian tragic poet, 6th–5th centuries BC. Ancient authors regarded him and Thespis as the originators of tragedy. His first victory for a tragedy was between 511 and 508 BC. Only a few fragments of his plays survive. They included one on the capture of Miletus by the Persians (probably produced 492 BC), for which Phrynichus was heavily fined for upsetting the Athenians. Another historical play was *Phoenician Women* (*Phoenissae*), possibly 476 BC.

There were also plays on mythological subjects. He was apparently the first tragic poet to introduce female characters (by using a female mask).

PHYLARCHUS (*Phylarkhos*): Later-3rd-century-BC historian who wrote several works, of which only the titles are known, and also a 28-book *History*. It covered the period between the death of Pyrrhus (272 BC) and the defeat of Cleomenes III (222 BC). It was not arranged chronologically and survives only in quotations. He was a supporter of Cleomenes and apparently displayed a bias in the history.

PINDAR (*Pindaros*): 518–after 446 BC. A lyric poet from Cynoscephalae in Boeotia. Little is known of his life, but he was a member of the aristocratic Aegeidae clan. He was particularly known for his Epinician (victory) Odes written to celebrate victors at the Olympian, Pythian, Nemean and Isthmian Games. His earliest known poem was in 498 BC, and the last datable ode celebrates a victory in 446 BC. Pindar traveled in various parts of the Greek world and in 476 BC went to Sicily, later writing odes for Hieron I. He became famous in his lifetime, and wrote many poems in all the main types of choral lyric. They were grouped into 17 books by Alexandrian scholars, who divided them by type: epinicians, encomia, dirges, hymns, paeans, dithyrambs, prosodia, hyporchemata and partheneia. Only the four books of Epinician Odes survive (45 odes) and other fragments, mostly from paeans.

PLATO (*Platon*): Floruit c. 420–c. 390 BC. Athenian comic poet who won his first victory at the City Dionysia c. 410 BC; a rival of Aristophanes. Thirty titles and 270 fragments of his plays survive, which were apparently political in nature.

POLEMON OF ILIUM (*Polemon*): c. 190/180 BC. A geographer and antiquarian. He traveled throughout the Greek world, recording monuments, inscriptions and artistic material, especially at Sparta, Athens and Delphi.

POLYBIUS (*Polybios*): c. 200–after 118 BC. Born at Megalopolis, he was among 1,000 Achaeans taken to Rome after the Roman victory at the battle of Pydna in 168 BC. He was author of *Historiai*, a 40-volume history from 220 to 146 BC. The first five volumes and fragments of others survive.

POLYCLEITUS or POLYCLITUS OF LARISSA (*Polykleitos*): Floruit 320s BC. A historian of Alexander the Great who probably accompanied his army. He wrote a *Historiai* that was used by Strabo and Eratosthenes.

POSEIDIPPUS or POSIDIPPUS (*Poseidippos*): Floruit 275 BC. An epigrammatic poet from Pella who lived on Samos and later at Alexandria. With Asclepiades and Hedylus, he published an anthology called *Soros* (the *Heap*). He wrote erotic poems.

PRATINAS (*Pratinas*): A poet from Phlius, 6th–5th centuries BC, who was the first writer of satyr plays. Thirty-two of his 50 plays were satyric, and he also wrote tragedies, dithyrambs and hyporchemata. He competed at Athens at the beginning of the 5th century BC. In one substantial fragment a chorus attacks flute players who drown the words of the dithyramb.

PRAXILLA (*Praxilla*): Mid-5th-century-BC lyric poetess from Sicyon who wrote dithyrambs, hymns and drinking songs. Little survives, but one line in a *Hymn to Adonis* was proverbial for its silliness.

RHIANUS (*Rhianos*): Born c. 275 BC. Poet and Homeric scholar from Crete who may have originally been a slave in charge of a wrestling school. He wrote epigrams and epic poems. His historical epics include *Achaica*, *Thessalica*, *Eliaca* and *Messeniaca*. Most of the epigrams are pederastic. Rhianus also produced an edition of Homer's *Iliad* and *Odyssey*.

SACADAS (*Sakadas*): Early-6th-century-BC musician and elegiac poet from Argos who won three flute competitions at the Pythian Games of 586, 582 and 578 BC. He also wrote elegiac poems set to tunes and was connected with the music school at Sparta. Nothing survives of his work.

SAPPHO (*Phsappho*): Born c. 612 BC. A lyric poetess, possibly the greatest in antiquity, from Lesbos (fig. 7.17). As a child she lived in exile in Sicily but eventually returned to Mytilene. She mentions three brothers, one of whom, Charaxus, was involved with a courtesan in Egypt. Sappho married Cercylas and had a daughter Cleis. Little is known of Sappho's life. She apparently committed suicide for love of Phaeon but this may have been an invention of New Comedy. Sappho was a contemporary of Alcaeus, and seems to have been the leading figure of a group of women and girls who formed her audience. She knew them intimately and wrote about her love for them (and sometimes her hate). Despite no certain evidence for physical intimacy, the poet Anacreon later accused the island of female homosexuality, from which the terms lesbianism and sapphism derive. Sappho's poems were divided into nine books according to meter, nearly all monody, sung to the lyre accompaniment and of an intimate nature.

SEMONIDES (*Semonides/Simonides*): Mid-7th century BC. An iambic and elegiac poet. Although from Samos he is associated with Amorgos (being part of the Samian colony). He wrote two books of elegiacs on the history of Samos. Another piece of elegiac verse is on the brevity of life. He apparently wrote one book of iambic verse, but very little survives.

SIMIAS or SIMMIAS OF RHODES (*Simias*): c. 300 BC poet who wrote four books of miscellaneous poems, including epyllia, epigrams and lyrical poems. Three *teknopaegnia* survive (*Wings*, *Ax* and *Egg*), poems that imitated the shape of the object on the page. Simias was also a grammarian and wrote three scholarly books.

SIMONIDES (*Simonides*): 557/556–468/467 BC. A lyric and elegiac poet from Ceos who was uncle of the poet Bacchylides. He worked as a poet throughout Greece: at the court of Hipparchus at Athens, in Thessaly (from c. 514 BC), at Athens (by 490 BC) and at the court of Hieron I of Syracuse (c. 476 BC until his death). He wrote hymns, scolia, encomia, epinicians and elegies, but he was especially famous for his dirges and sepulchral epigrams (possibly nearly all written for tombstones and other monuments). He wrote an epitaph on the Athenian dead at the battle of Marathon, which was preferred to that of Aeschylus. Simonides won 56 victories in dithyrambic competitions. His poetry is now largely lost.

SOPHOCLES (*Sophokles*): c. 496–406/405 BC. An Athenian tragedian from a wealthy family. He wrote 123 plays (over 110 titles are known). He won 24 victories with 96 plays; 18 victories (72 plays) were at the City Dionysia and the rest at the

Lenaea. In the other contests he was second, never third. His first victory was in 468 BC, when he defeated Aeschylus at the City Dionysia. Sophocles may have introduced the third actor and increased the chorus from 12 to 15. Seven plays survive: *Ajax*, *Antigone* (possibly 441 BC), *Women of Trachis* (*Trachiniae*), *Oedipus Tyrannus* (*Oedipus Rex*), *Electra*, *Philoctetes* (409 BC) and *Oedipus at Colonus* (produced posthumously 401 BC). A satyr play *Ichneutae* (trackers) concerned the infant Hermes. Sophocles also wrote paeans to Asclepius and Herodotus, an elegiac poem to the philosopher Archelaus, and a prose work *On the Chorus*. He abandoned the idea of connected plays; instead, each play had a self-contained plot. He took an active part in public life and refused invitations to work away from Athens. After his death he was honored as a hero because he had received the sacred snake representing Asclepius in his house until the temple was ready.

SOPHRON (*Sophron*): Fifth-century-BC writer of mimes on events of everyday life. He was from Syracuse.

SOTADES (*Sotades*): c. 280 BC. An iambic poet from Maronea. He invented a flexible "sotadean" meter that was used for centuries. Most of his work is lost, including a rewritten *Iliad*. He wrote moralizing sotadeans for the education of Greek children in Egypt. His abusive attack on Ptolemy II's incestuous marriage with Arsinoë (276/275 BC) may have led to his imprisonment and death.

STESICHORUS (*Stesikhoros*, choir-setter): c. 560 BC, possibly 632–629 to 556–553 BC. Lyric poet whose real name was Teisias—Stesichorus may have been a title. Born at Mataurus or Locri Epizephyrii, he lived at Himera. He was a choral poet, writing long narrative lyric poetry where singing was accompanied by a lyre. He was even credited with inventing this type of poetry. His poems were collected in six books, but only fragments survive. They included *Geryoneis* (over 1,800 lines), *Oresteia* (in two books), *Funeral Games of Pelias*, *Boarhunters*, *Eriphyle*, *Iliupersis* (sack of Troy) and *Helen*. His most famous poem was *Palinode*, in which he denied that Helen ever went to Troy and asserted that she went to Egypt instead.

STESIMBROTUS (*Stesimbrotos*): Fifth-century-BC sophist and biographer from Thasos who taught at Athens. He wrote about Homer and the Mysteries of Samothrace, as well as a work *On Themistocles, Thucydides and Pericles*. A few quotes from the latter work survive, but none concern Thucydides (son of Melesias).

SUDA (*he Souda*, fortress): The name of a lexicon not an author; a historical and literary encyclopedia compiled at the end of the 10th century AD. It contains works of various authors, including texts with scholia, as well as many later abridgments of authors. It made use of other encyclopedias, including the *Palatine Anthology*. Nevertheless, it preserves in some form many works of ancient Greek authors.

SUSARION (*Sousarion*): 6th-century-BC iambic poet, believed by ancient writers to be from Icaria in Attica (but possibly from Megara) and the inventor of comedy. He may be a fictitious figure.

TELESILLA (*Telesilla*): 6th–5th-centuries-BC lyric poetess from Argos. Nine fragments of hymns

Fig. 7.17   Head of the poetess Sappho.

survive. The Telesilleion meter is named after her. She was famous for saving her city by arming its women after the defeat of the men by Cleomenes III.

TELESTES (*Telestes*): Floruit c. 400 BC. A dithyrambic poet from Selinus. He won a victory at Athens in 402/401 BC. His dithyrambs included *Argo*, *Asclepius* and *Hymenaeus*.

TERPANDER (*Terpandros*): Mid-7th-century-BC poet and musician from Antissa in Lesbos. Nothing certain is known of his life; he won a musical competition at the Carnea 676–673 BC and founded the "First School" of music at Sparta. He added a seventh string to the lyre (cithara). He composed nomes (epic poetry set to lyre music, using his own or Homer's lines) and also scolia (drinking songs).

THALETAS (*Thaletas*): Seventh-century-BC poet and musician from Gortyn in Crete, allegedly called to Sparta by the Delphic oracle to rid it of a plague by appeasing Apollo with his poetry. At Sparta he established a Second School of music and the Gymnopaedia festival (665 BC), and composed paeans and hyporchemata. None of his work survives.

THEAGENES OF RHEGIUM (*Theagenes*): Floruit c. 525 BC. A scholar and rhapsode. He wrote a book on Homer and was the first to give allegorical interpretations.

THEOCRITUS (*Theokritos*): Possibly c. 300–c. 260 BC. A poet from Syracuse but who lived in southern Italy, eastern Aegean and then Alexandria during the reign of Ptolemy II. His poems are known collectively as *Idylls* (short poems), but his fame rested on those of a bucolic or pastoral nature (hence, "idyllic"). The bucolic poems may have been written in Cos and contain references to numerous plants. He also wrote epyllia, epithalamia, hymns, love poems and epigrams. His poetry was written mainly in hexameters. Of his surviving poems, about seven are bucolic, and they influenced Virgil and later European poetry. Thirty poems, fragments and epigrams survive.

THEODECTES (*Theodektes/Theodektas*): Active c. 375–334 BC. A tragedian and orator from Phaselis. He studied under Plato, Isocrates and Aristotle and became famous as an orator, as well

as a writer of tragedies, of popular riddles in verse and of prose work on rhetoric. He wrote 50 tragedies and won eight victories at 13 competitions (seven at the City Dionysia). They included *Lynceus*, *Mausolus* and *Philoctetes*. He died at the age of 41.

THEOGNIS (*Theognis*): Sixth century BC, possibly floruit 544–541 BC. An elegiac poet from Megara with 1,389 lines surviving in a manuscript. Divided into two books of short poems, the work's authenticity is disputed. The two books are probably an anthology based on and around poems of Theognis. Those addressed to Cyrnus appear genuine.

THEOPOMPUS (*Theopompos*): c. 377–320 BC. A historian from Chios from where he was banished by Alexander the Great with his father Damasistratus c. 334 BC for supporting Sparta. He was later restored, but fled to the court of Ptolemy I in Egypt after Alexander died. Theopompus wrote numerous books, although only fragments survive from *Hellenica* and *Philippica*. The former was in 12 books and continued Thucydides' history from 411 BC to the battle of Cnidus (394 BC). *Philippica*, a world history in 58 books, described events at the time of Philip II of Macedonia (359–336 BC), with numerous digressions.

THESPIS (*Thespis*): c. 535 BC. A poet from Icaria (Attica), famed as the inventor of tragedy and also credited with introducing an actor to deliver prologues and converse with the chorus (a change from a choral production to a drama). He may also have invented the mask. Surviving fragments from his plays may not be genuine.

THUCYDIDES (*Thoukydides*): c. 460–455 to c. 400/399 BC. Historian. Between 430 and 427 BC he caught the plague but recovered. In 424 BC he was *strategos* and lost Amphipolis to the Spartan Brasidas; for this he was exiled, returning 20 years later. He was probably related to Cimon and to Thucydides the politician, and he owned property in Thrace. He wrote an incomplete history in eight books of the Second Peloponnesian War between Athens and Sparta (431–404 BC). It stops in mid-sentence in winter 411/410 BC, but was intended to go as far as 404 BC. It was later completed by Theopompus and Cratippus.

TIMAEUS (*Timaios*): c. 356–260 BC. Historian from Tauromenium who lived in exile at Athens for 50 years from c. 317 BC, probably returning under Hieron II. He wrote a history of Sicily (called *Historiai* or *Sicelica*) in 38 books from earliest times to 264 BC. It also dealt with events in Italy, north Africa and elsewhere.

TIMOCREON (*Timokreon*): First half of the 5th century BC. A lyric and elegiac poet from Rhodes who was banished, apparently for supporting the Persians when they occupied the island. He was an enemy of Themistocles and Simonides. Only fragments of his work survive.

TIMOTHEUS (*Timotheos*): c. 450–c. 360 BC. A poet from Miletus famous for his nomes and dithyrambs. He was innovative and unpopular. Most of his 18 books are lost, but a 4th-century-BC papyrus has preserved over 200 lines of his lyric nome *Persae* (*Persians*), describing the battle of Salamis and ending with a defense of his own music. Euripides (his friend) wrote the prologue.

TYRTAEUS (*Tyrtaios*): Seventh-century-BC elegiac poet, possibly (but unlikely) originally an Athenian schoolteacher. By the Second Messenian War he was living at Sparta, and encouraged the Spartans with war songs and exhortations in elegiac verse to capture Messene. His poems were collected in five books.

XANTHUS (*Xanthos*): Fifth-century-BC historian who wrote a four-book history of Lydia (*Lydiaka*).

XENOPHON (*Xenophon*): c. 428/427–c. 354 BC. Historian and soldier, born of a wealthy Athenian family and associated with Socrates. He was regarded in antiquity as a philosopher. He joined the army of Cyrus the Younger and campaigned in Asia Minor. He was exiled c. 399 BC and became a soldier under Agesilaus II of Sparta, being present at the battle of Coronea against Athens in 394 BC. His family was given an estate at Scillus near Olympia, and he was elected Spartan *proxenos*, responsible for entertaining Spartans visiting Olympia. Elis claimed Scillus in 371 BC, and Xenophon went to live near Corinth. He returned to Athens in 366/365 BC after the decree of his banishment was lifted.

Xenophon was very prolific and wrote on numerous topics. *Hellenica* was a history of Greece from 411 to 362 BC in seven books (mostly written in the 350s BC). *Anabasis* was an account of the Greek mercenaries under Cyrus the Younger (401–399 BC). *Cynegeticus* was a treatise on hunting. *Spartan Constitution* was written c. 388 BC in praise of Sparta. *Apologia* was a defense of Socrates. *Oeconomicus* was a dialogue with Socrates on estate management. *Memorabilia* were recollections of Socrates in four books. *Symposium* was an imaginary party with Socrates as a guest. *Vectigalia* gave advice to Athenians on increasing their revenue. *On Horsemanship* is the oldest such treatise to survive, written c. 380 BC. *Cryopaedia* was an imaginative work in eight books on Cyrus the Great. *Hieron* was a dialogue between Hieron I and Simonides on tyranny. *Hipparchicus* (*Cavalry Commander*) was on the duties of an Athenian cavalry commander. *Agesilaus* was written in praise of the Spartan king. *Ways and Means* offered a policy of peace through strength. *The Constitution of Athens* was a pamphlet possibly written by Xenophon.

ZENODOTUS (*Zenodotos*): Born c. 325 BC. Scholar from Ephesus who became royal tutor and first head of the Alexandria Library c. 285 BC. He undertook the classification of epic and lyric poets and wrote a *Homeric Glossary*. He apparently divided both the *Iliad* and *Odyssey* into 24 books.

READING

Greek Language

Hammond and Scullard (eds.) 1970: 334–336: dialects, 411: etymology; Joint Association of Classical Teachers 1978a and b: learning Greek; Langslow 1988: languages and dialects.

Writing

Chadwick 1987: early scripts; Dickinson 1994, 189–197: seals, Linear A and B; Hammond and Scullard (eds.) 1970, 741: numerals; Immerwahr 1990: Attic script; Jeffery: early writing; Kitzinger

1988: alphabet and writing; Lang 1976: graffiti; Stephens 1988: writing materials; Woodhead 1992, 12–23: alphabet, 108–112: numerals.

Libraries

Hammond and Scullard (eds.) 1970, 172–175, 607–608; Stephens 1988: book production.

Education

Beck 1964; Dewald 1988; Drever 1912; Hammond and Scullard (eds.) 1970, 369–371.

Inscriptions

Cook 1987; Lang 1976: graffiti and *dipinti*; Woodhead 1992 (few illustrations, but numerous references).

Personal Names

Fraser and Matthews (eds.) 1987: lexicon giving detailed listings of names in the Aegean islands and elsewhere; Hammond and Scullard (eds.) 1970, 720–722.

Literature

Arnott 1988: drama; Bowie 1988: lyric and elegiac poetry; Green 1994: theater, with extensive notes and bibliography; Griffiths 1988: literary criticism; Hainsworth 1988: epic poetry; Halperin 1988: bucolic poetry; Hammond and Scullard (eds.) 1970, 679–684: meter in poetry; Lane Fox 1988: literature after Alexander; Levi 1988: drama; Murray 1988: history; Russo 1988: lyric and elegiac poetry; Sullivan 1988: epigrams and satire; Usher 1988: history and biography; Ussher 1988: letters; Winkler 1988: novels.

Music and Dance

Borthwick 1988; Hammond and Scullard (eds.) 1970, 705–713: music.

Authors

Bowder (ed.) 1982: short biographies of many authors; Griffin 1988: history; Hammond and Scullard (eds.) 1970: biographies of many authors; Levi 1985: discusses many different authors in chronological order; Levi 1988: discusses several dramatists; Murray 1988: historians; Talpin 1988: Homer; Warner 1972: chapters on Aeschylus, Sophocles, Thucydides, Aristophanes and Euripides.

8

RELIGION AND MYTHOLOGY

CHRONOLOGY AND DEVELOPMENT

Concept of Religion

The Greeks had no word for religion. Gods were thought to be everywhere, and religion was part of everyday life: it was not divorced from mundane activities, and therefore no word categorized it. It was believed that the gods could see all human activities, provide for all human needs, protect against danger and heal the sick. In return, they were worshiped according to their functions and spheres of influence. People offered sacrifices, votive offerings and prayers, and looked after the gods' sacred places. Except for a few specific cults, the Greeks did not expect the gods to provide salvation after death (as in the Christian sense), but rather rewards and favors during life in return for piety, service and sacrifice to the gods.

Religious observance accompanied all important private and public events and transactions. During the Classical period no significant private or public undertaking was started without consulting a god, and no successful outcome went without a votive offering, vow of thanks or public dedication. In Athens religious observance was usually further organized within membership of groups, such as a deme, professional organization, phratry or family.

Minoan Religion

In mainland Greece evidence for religion is uncommon before the Late Helladic, but evidence exists, mainly on Crete, for religion in the Minoan period. The archaeological evidence was once interpreted as representing a unified religion based on the worship of one or more mother goddesses, and finds of female figurines were interpreted as images of deities. It is now recognized that this did not take account of other archaeological evidence, particularly figurines representing human males and various animals. Some figurines also represented

people worshiping a deity, not the deity itself. The idea of a single unified religion based on worship of one or more mother goddesses is no longer valid.

A reassessment of religion in early Crete has led to a picture of greater diversity in religious practice (and probably belief). Some religious practices were possibly more like those in the Near East than in later Greek religion. In particular it seems that individual communities tended to recognize different, very local gods and were not part of a unified and fairly uniform religion. The evidence is still undergoing detailed reappraisal, and so the present picture of early religion is necessarily incomplete and to some extent confused.

Although some artifacts from the Prepalatial Period are interpreted as having religious significance, more evidence from the First and Second Palace Periods gives the first real indications of how religion was developing. Priests and priestesses are represented, and rituals appear to have included processions and dances, offerings, sacrifices and practices apparently designed to cause the immediate appearance of a deity. Religious practices were conducted in outdoor settings, where a tree or rock was apparently of central importance in the ritual, but rituals also took place in caves and buildings. Religious sanctuaries on or near mountain peaks were possibly important communal religious centers, but other sites show the diversity of religious practice. One common religious practice was the offering of clay artifacts: Human figurines are often in poses of worship or invocation, while animal figurines and models of food on plates may represent sacrifices. Anatomical models, such as heads and limbs, may have been votive offerings to healing deities. Also commonly associated with religious practices are models of double-headed axes and horns (sometimes called "horns of consecration"), as well as cylindrical ceramic objects labeled "snake tubes," decorated with other religious symbols. Symbols such as snakes and horns found on "snake tubes" also decorated some figurines.

Evidence for Minoan religious practices has been found at Aegean sites other than Crete. In the Third Palace Period there were major changes in religious practice, with the increased Mycenaean influence.

Mycenaean Religion

How Mycenaean religion developed is unclear, but some continuity from Minoan religion is evident. Earlier evidence is sparse, but by the later Mycenaean period a distinctive religion had developed. Mycenaean religion was polytheistic, and the names of some gods are known: Zeus, Poseidon, Enyalios, Paean, Eileithyia, Hera, Dionysus and Hermaias (Hermes). There were also numerous goddesses, many of whom had the title *potnia* (lady). A goddess whose name translates as "Lady of Athana" may be the same as the goddess Athena.

The evidence for worship of gods in Mycenaean times suggests some similarity to the forms of worship practiced later in the Classical period; offerings were made to the gods, and similar commodities and animals were sacrificed. Religion of the Classical period is generally regarded as having roots in Minoan and Mycenaean religion, but it is apparent that great changes in ritual (and perhaps belief) took place during the intervening Dark Age.

Dark Age Religion

In the Dark Age there still appears to have been some religious continuity, although evidence for the continued use of a sacred site from Mycenaean times through the Dark Age and into the Classical period is extremely rare. The open-air altar and temple with cult image are features of Classical religion that appear to have arisen during the Dark Age. Some authorities do regard Classical religion as a development from Minoan and Mycenaean religion, with influences from the Near East, but there is insufficient evidence to trace its development through the Dark Age.

Classical Religion

In the Classical period there were numerous deities, and every locality, river or spring had its own god or nymph. Gods were anthropomorphic, regarded as essentially like humans in their motives and behavior, but differing from humans in their superior power and their immortality. A complicated mythology developed around the gods, and many myths and legends were concerned with relationships between gods and other gods, and between gods and mortals. The Greeks tried to rationalize some of the myths, and some myths were adjusted or invented in order to create genealogies for particular peoples, because of the prestige in being descended from a god. This often resulted in differing versions of particular myths, or conflict between two or more myths.

Worship of deities was generally done outdoors, and hymns, prayers, sacrifices, vows and votive offerings all played a part. There were religious festivals in honor of the gods, sometimes accompanied by sporting and artistic contests. As city-states expanded and admitted foreigners, foreign gods became established and accepted, often being equated with existing Greek gods. Because religion formed part of most everyday activities, it provided virtually a common factor among all Greeks.

Hellenistic Religion

After the Classical period religion lost some of its popularity among the educated classes, although it still thrived among peasants. Religion was partly supplanted by philosophy, and after Alexander the Great the Eastern practice of ruler worship became increasingly common. Alexander demanded and received divine honors from the Greeks, but his successors and their descendants seem to have been granted divine honors voluntarily. Kings were worshiped as gods by the cities they had founded, and other cities might enroll a king among their official deities. In time the monarchies of the East developed their own official cults, such as that of the Ptolemies at Alexandria. Ruler worship was usually political rather than truly religious; examples of offerings dedicated to rulers are known, but not prayers. It was generally regarded as an expression of loyalty to the state.

GODS AND GODDESSES

Groups of Deities

The major Greek gods and goddesses were often thought of in groups. According to mythology these groups formed several levels of gods, possibly an attempt to explain the relationships of the gods. Much evidence for the groups of deities and their levels comes from the poet Hesiod. According to him there was originally Chaos, then Gaia (Earth) and Eros. Gaia first bore Uranus (the heavens), and then from a union with Uranus and Gaia, she bore the Titans, then the Cyclopes and finally the Hecatoncheires. The offspring of the two Titans, Cronus and Rhea, formed another level of gods: Hestia, Demeter, Hera, Hades, Poseidon and Zeus. Zeus led a rebellion against his parents, and he became the chief god in the level of gods known as the Olympians (so-called because they lived on Mount Olympus). According to Hesiod there were 12 Olympians: Zeus, Poseidon, Hera, Athena, Apollo, Artemis, Aphrodite, Hermes, Demeter, Dionysus, Hephaestus and Ares. Not all sources agree with Hesiod; for example, Hades, Hestia, Pan and Asclepius sometimes appear to have been regarded as Olympians as well.

Myths

The Greeks had no central collection of sacred texts (such as the Bible). This role was filled by an extensive collection of myths, which were stories about gods, heroes and fantastic monsters. Gods were considered similar to humans, but possessing supernatural powers and immortality. The myths explained the origin of the world; they also provided the Greeks with a fabulous early history and an understanding of their gods. Originally the stories were transmitted by oral tradition, but eventually they were written down and used as themes and reference points in poetry and drama. Knowledge of the myths is largely derived from these written sources. Because they originated in oral tradition, there were often different versions of the same story, frequently conflicting. Characters common to two or more stories may be portrayed as being in two or more places at the same time, or as having lived in different centuries. Despite later attempts by the Greeks to rationalize their myths, many incongruities still exist in those that have survived to the present day.

Descriptions of Gods, Heroes and Mythological Beings

The following descriptions are of the main deities of Greek religion and of other main characters in Greek myths. They are given in alphabetical order. They are known mainly from the Classical period, sometimes earlier. Some of these deities were adopted from other cultures or were local deities of prehistoric origin, but all were tolerated within Greek society. The name by which they are most commonly known is given, with the Greek version in parentheses.

ACHELOUS (*Akheloos*):   God of the Achelous, the longest river in Greece, part of it forming the border between Acarnania and Aetolia. In mythology Achelous was the son of Oceanus and Tethys. A sacrifice to Achelous by the Attic deme Erchia took place on the 27th day of the month Boedromion.

ACHILLES (*Akhilleus*):   A hero, son of King Peleus of Thessaly and the Nereid Thetis. He had a prominent role in Homer's *Iliad*, and probably because of this, he was worshiped in a hero cult that was widespread in several regions of Greece. See also PATROCLUS, ZEPHYRUS.

ACTAEON (*Aktaion*):   Grandson of King Cadmus of Thebes and a legendary huntsman who accidentally found the goddess Artemis bathing. Offended at being seen naked by a man, Artemis turned Actaeon into a stag, and he was killed by his own pack of hounds.

ADONIS (*Adonis*): A god of vegetation and fertility, whose cult originated on Cyprus and was generally connected with the cult of Aphrodite. In mythology Adonis was a beautiful youth loved by Aphrodite, but he was killed while hunting. The rites of his cult included women mourning his death, and subsequently rejoicing at his rebirth. However, the idea of his resurrection seems to have been absorbed from another cult, probably that of Osiris. Festivals of Adonis (*Adonia*) were held at Athens and Alexandria.

ADRASTUS (*Adrastus*): This mythological king of Argos took part in the "Seven Against Thebes," which was the failed attempt to restore Polynices, son of Oedipus, to the throne of Thebes.

AEACUS (*Aiakos*): The son of Zeus and Aegina (daughter of the river god Asopus), father of Peleus and grandfather of Achilles and Ajax. He was king of the island of Aegina. In some legends Aeacus is one of the judges of the dead in the underworld.

AEGAEON (*Aigaion*): One of the Hecatoncheires, and also known as Briareus.

AEGEUS (*Aigeus*): In mythology, an early king of Athens and father of Theseus. One legend describes how the Aegean Sea was named after him. See THESEUS.

AEGISTHUS (*Aigisthos*): The seducer of Agamemnon's wife, Clytemnestra, and the killer of Agamemnon, for whose murder he was himself killed by Orestes.

AELLO (*Aello*, storm wind): Also called Nicothoe. One of the Harpies.

AENEAS (*Aineias, Aineas*): A Trojan hero, son of Anchises and the goddess Aphrodite. He plays only a small part in Homer's *Iliad*, but later legends told of his escape from Troy and his subsequent wanderings. He became associated with the mythical founding of Rome, a theme developed by the Roman poet Virgil in the *Aeneid*.

AEOLUS (*Aiolos*): God of the winds. According to legend he lived on a floating island called Aeolia with his six sons and six daughters, who had married each other. He kept the winds in a sack or a cave when he wanted to prevent them from blowing.

AETHER (*Aither*): In mythology the personification of the upper sky.

AGAMEMNON (*Agamemnon*): The son of Atreus and brother of Menelaus was married to Clytemnestra and was the father of Orestes, Electra and Iphigenia. He was a king of Mycenae (or in some legends, of Argos) and led the Greek forces in the Trojan War. On his return he was killed by Clytemnestra's lover, Aegisthus. See also CHRYSEIS.

AGATHOS DAIMON (*Agathos Daimon*, Good Spirit): In Athens the second day of every month was sacred to this deity. See also DAIMON.

AGLAURUS (*Aglauros*): In mythology two women had this name. The first was the daughter of Actaeus, the first king of Athens. She married Cecrops and had a daughter also called Aglaurus, who was worshiped as a deity. A sacrifice to Aglaurus by the Attic deme Erchia took place on the third day of the month Skirophorion.

AJAX (*Aias*): A hero and son of Telamon, king of Salamis, Ajax played a major role in Homer's *Iliad*. There was a cult of Ajax in Salamis, Attica and the Troad. A lesser hero, also called Ajax, appears as leader of the Locrian forces in the *Iliad*. According to another legend this latter Ajax dragged Cassandra from the altar of Athena, and for this sacrilege Athena drowned him in a storm as he sailed home to Greece. See also CASSANDRA.

ALCESTIS (*Alkestis*): The daughter of Pelias and the wife of Admetus (king of Pherae in Thessaly). According to one legend Admetus, helped by Apollo, won the hand of Alcestis by being the only suitor to drive a chariot pulled by wild beasts. In another legend Admetus offended Artemis at their wedding feast and was condemned to die, but the intervention of Apollo allowed someone else to die instead. The only willing person was Alcestis, but after she died, Heracles brought her back from the underworld as a favor to Admetus.

ALCINOUS (*Alkinoos*): In mythology the king of the Phaeacians. He was grandson of Poseidon, husband of his own sister Arete and father of Nausicaa. In Homer's *Odyssey*, Alcinous helped Odysseus on his way to Ithaca. In another legend he entertained the Argonauts on their return from Colchis, and refused to return Medea, who escaped with Jason, to her Colchian father.

ALCM(A)EON (*Alkmaion, Alkmeon*): Son of Amphiaraus and Eriphyle. After the failure of the Seven against Thebes and the death of his father, he led the *Epigonoi* (Successors) and captured Thebes. He killed his mother in revenge for the death of his father, for which the Erinyes made him mad and drove him from Argos. He settled in Psophis and married Arsinoë, daughter of King Phegeus. When famine struck he left this area to settle in western Greece, by the mouth of the Achelous River. Here he married Callirhoe (daughter of the river god Achelous) and was later killed by the brothers of Arsinoë.

ALCYONE (*Alkyone*): The daughter of Aeolus and wife of Ceyx (the son of Eosphorus and king of Trachis). On hearing of Ceyx's death by drowning, she flung herself into the sea. Both Alcyone and Ceyx were changed into birds and reunited. They apparently kept the Aegean Sea calm while they were building and sitting on their nest. These days of calm at the time of the winter solstice were known as "halcyon days."

ALEXANDER (*Alexandros*): Son of King Priam and Hecuba, also known as Paris.

AMALTHEA (*Amaltheia*): A nurse of Zeus, she was sometimes regarded as a Nymph, sometimes a she-goat, and in one legend she was transformed

into the star Capella. In another legend one of her goat's horns was broken off; it was filled with fruits and given to Zeus as the original cornucopia (horn of plenty), a frequent motif in art.

AMMON: The Greek name for the Egyptian god Amun, who was identified with the Greek god Zeus as Zeus Ammon. He became known to the Greeks after colonizing Cyrene in north Africa c. 630 BC. The cult of Zeus Ammon at the Siwa oasis in the Libyan desert had an oracle, which was consulted by Greeks (the most famous being Alexander the Great), and Ammon was portrayed on Greek coins and in Greek art, usually as the head of Zeus with the addition of curling ram's horns.

AMPHIARAUS (*Amphiaraos, Amphiareos*): A prophet who foresaw the failure of the Seven against Thebes, Amphiaraus refused to join the expedition until tricked by his wife Eriphyle. Previously he had charged his children to avenge his death, later resulting in Alcmaeon killing Eriphyle. In the attack against Thebes, Zeus saved Amphiaraus by opening a cleft in the ground into which he drove his chariot. He emerged at Oropus in Boeotia, where he founded a famous oracular and healing shrine, later described by Pausanias. See also ALCMAEON.

AMPHITRYON (*Amphitryon*): In mythology the king of Thebes, son of Acaeus (king of Tiryns), husband of Alcmene (daughter of Electryon) and father of Iphicles. His uncle Electryon was king of Mycenae, and after the death of his sons, the kingdom of Mycenae was given to Amphitryon. While helping to recover stolen cattle, he killed Electryon and so took refuge with Alcmene in Thebes. Amphitryon carried out Alcmene's wish to avenge her brothers before marrying her. However, Zeus fell in love with her, and just before Amphitryon's return, he visited her disguised as Amphitryon. Alcmene subsequently gave birth to twins: Heracles (fathered by Zeus) and Iphicles (fathered by Amphitryon).

ANANKE (*Agnagke*): A goddess who personified necessity or obligation. She was sometimes invoked in curses and charms. In mythology she was the daughter of Cronus.

ANCHISES (*Ankhises*):   In mythology a Trojan prince, known mainly for his union with the goddess Aphrodite who bore his son Aeneas. His brother was Laocoön.

ANDROMACHE (*Andromakhe*):   The wife of the Trojan hero Hector and mother of Astyanax. After the sack of Troy Astyanax was killed by the Greeks, and Andromache was carried off as Neoptolemus' slave. She bore him a son, Molossus, from whom the royal family of the Molossi in Epirus claimed descent. After Neoptolemus' death she became the wife of Helenus.

ANDROMEDA (*Andromede*):   The daughter of Cepheus (king of Ethiopia) and Cassiope, who boasted that Andromeda was more beautiful than the Nereids. This angered Poseidon, who flooded the land and sent a ravaging sea monster that could be placated only by a sacrifice. On consulting Ammon, Cepheus learned that Andromeda should be sacrificed to the monster; she was chained to a rock on the seashore but was rescued by Perseus. He fought her uncle Phineus (who was betrothed to her) and won Andromeda's hand in marriage. Their children were Perses, Alcaeus, Sthenelus, Heleius, Mestor, Electryon and Gorgophone.

ANTAEUS (*Antaios*):   A giant living in Libya, the son of Poseidon and Gaia. He compelled all comers to wrestle with him, killing them when they had been beaten, until Heracles fought and killed him.

ANTIGONE (*Antigone*):   In mythology three women had this name:

1. The daughter of Eurytion (son of King Actor of Phthia) and the wife of Peleus.
2. The daughter of King Laomedon of Troy. Hera changed this Antigone's hair to snakes, because she rivaled her in beauty. Later, Antigone was changed into a stork.
3. The best known Antigone was the daughter of King Oedipus of Thebes and Jocasta. She appar-

Fig. 8.1   Marble head of the goddess Aphrodite, found at Ephesus.

ently held no significant role in the legends of Oedipus until the works of Sophocles; in these she looked after the blinded Oedipus in his exile and returned to Thebes to defy her uncle Creon, insisting on burying her brother Polynices. Consequently Creon condemned her to be buried alive, but she committed suicide instead.

ANTILOCHUS (*Antilokhos*):   In mythology the son of King Nestor of Pylos. In Homer's *Iliad* he is portrayed as a fine runner, brave warrior and skillful

Fig. 8.2 Apollo portrayed on the obverse of a gold stater of Philip II of Macedonia. The head was possibly copied from the coins of Olynthus that Philip destroyed in 348 BC. Courtesy of Somerset County Museums Service.

charioteer. In another legend he was killed by Memnon while defending his father.

ANTINOUS (*Antinoos*): The son of Eupeithes and chief suitor to Penelope. He was killed by Odysseus.

ANTIOPE (*Antiope*): In mythology the daughter either of the Asopus River or of King Nycteus of Boeotia. She was loved by Zeus (in the form of a satyr) and gave birth to twin sons, Amphion and Zethus. She fled from her father to Sicyon, where she married Epopeus. Nycteus, committing suicide, sent his brother Lycus to punish Antiope. He killed Epopeus and imprisoned Antiope. She was then tormented by Lycus and his wife Dirce, but eventually escaped and was avenged by her sons.

APHAEA (*Aphaia*): A goddess worshiped on Aegina, where the ruins of her temple stand. She was identified with the Cretan goddess Britomartis.

APHRODITE (*Aphrodite*): Goddess of love, beauty and fertility, and one of the Olympians (fig. 8.1) She was worshiped thoughout almost all the Greek world. She may originally have been a Hellenized version of the Asian goddess Astarte. She was associated with Adonis, who was sometimes regarded as Astarte's consort. In Hellenistic times she was sometimes identified with Isis. Primarily Aphrodite was a goddess of sexual love, generation and fertility, but some evidence suggests she was sometimes regarded as a goddess of vegetation. Aphrodite was also widely worshiped as a goddess of the sea and of seafaring. She was the patron goddess of prostitutes, and there was sacred prostitution at her sanctuary at Corinth. Particularly in Sparta, Cyprus and Cythera, she was worshiped as a goddess of war. Aphrodite had close connections with Cyprus, where she had two major sanctuaries at Paphos and Amathus. She was associated with the hero Hippolytus, and they had a shrine on the Acropolis at Athens.

Aphrodite had many epithets, such as Aligena (sea born), Urania (heavenly), Pandemos (popular), Area (like Ares, that is, armed for war), Kourotrophos (nurse) and Epipontia (on the sea). The myrtle and dove were sacred to Aphrodite. In mythology she has two alternative origins. In one legend she sprang from the foam in the sea that gathered around the severed organs when Uranus was castrated by Cronus. In another legend she was the daughter of Zeus and Dione and husband of Hephaestus. Aphrodite favored the Trojan cause in the siege of Troy, and Aeneas was her son by the Trojan Anchises. In some legends she was the mother of Eros by Ares, in others the mother of Harmonia by Ares. In Athens the fourth day of every month was celebrated as the birthday of Aphrodite.

APOLLO (*Apollon, Appollon*): A god worshiped throughout the Greek world, and the embodiment of moral excellence and of young, but mature, male beauty (fig. 8.2). He had many diverse functions: he was a god of music (especially the lyre), of prophecy, healing, archery (but not war or hunting) and of the care of herds and flocks. He was also a god of light (sometimes being identified with the sun and with the god Helios). Despite being a god of healing and medicine, he was also the god of plague. He was usually associated with what were regarded as the higher developments of civilization, such as moral and religious principles, philosophy and law.

As a god of prophecy, there were important oracles at several of Apollo's sanctuaries, such as Branchidae and Clarus. The most important was at Delphi. The island of Delos was sacred to Apollo. He had many epithets, including Pythian (the name of Apollo at Delphi), Phoebus (bright) and Nomius (belonging to shepherds). On Cyprus there was a sanctuary of Apollo Hylates (Apollo of the Woodland) (fig. 8.3).

In mythology Apollo was an Olympian, the son of Zeus and Leto and the twin brother of Artemis. Many legends concerned Apollo's numerous spheres of influence. One related how he seized Delphi by destroying the Python, an early deity that appears to have been absorbed by Apollo, giving rise to the Pythian Apollo of the Delphic Oracle. Apollo was generally regarded as politically neutral, but he is shown favoring the Trojans in Homer's *Iliad*. The Delphic Oracle was not always neutral, however, and favored the Persians during the Persian Wars and the Spartans during the Peloponnesian War.

In Athens the seventh day of every month was celebrated as Apollo's birthday. The Pythian Games were held every four years at Delphi in his honor. A sacrifice to Apollo Apotropaeus (Apollo who averts evil) and to Apollo Nymphegetes (Apollo who looks after the Nymphs) was undertaken by the Attic deme Erchia on the eighth day of the month Gamelion. A sacrifice to Pythian Apollo by the deme Erchia also took place on the fourth day of the month Thargelion. In Sparta and other Doric states, the Carnea festival was celebrated in honor of Apollo in the month of Karneios (August–September).

ARES (*Ares, Areus*):   The god of war, a personification of the warlike spirit or warlike frenzy. He was not a very popular god but was more important in Thebes, northern and western Greece and possibly in Athens. In mythology he was one of the Olympians, son of Hera and Zeus. Ares was portrayed as an unchivalrous instigator of trouble and strife. He was frequently associated with Aphrodite

(wife of Hephaestus), by whom (in some legends) he had a daughter Harmonia or (in other legends) a son Eros. He also fathered numerous other children, usually sons, most of whom came to unhappy ends.

ARETHUSA (*Arethousa*):   In mythology one of the Hesperides and also the name given to a Nymph of Arcadia. The latter Arethusa (fig. 10.5) bathed in the Alpheus River in Arcadia; the river god (Alpheus) fell in love with her. She fled from him and became a spring in Syracuse, but Alpheus flowed under the sea to be joined with her. In antiquity it was believed that there was an actual connection between the two, and that something thrown into the Alpheus River might be recovered from the spring in Syracuse.

Fig. 8.3   Restored temple in the sanctuary of Apollo Hylates at Curium, Cyprus. The cult was celebrated here from the 8th century BC, but most remains date to c. AD 100, when the temple was rebuilt after an earlier earthquake.

RELIGION AND MYTHOLOGY

Fig. 8.4 Marble statue of Artemis, a copy of a 4th-century-BC original.

ARGES (*Arges*, Bright):   One of the Cyclopes.

ARGONAUTS (*Argonautai*):   Heroes who were led by Jason in his journey to Colchis to bring back the Golden Fleece. Their name (sailors of *Argo*) is derived from their ship, called *Argo*. The legend of the Argonauts is one of the oldest Greek legends and may derive from an actual expedition from Boeotia to the Black Sea. The Argonauts had many adventures during the voyage. See also JASON.

ARGOS (*Argos*):   The names of several characters in mythology. One was a craftsman who built the ship *Argo* with the help of Athena. Another was the faithful dog of Odysseus, who recognized his master after 20 years' absence, and then died. The third Argos was a giant with 100 eyes, used as a herdsman to keep careful watch over Io, after Zeus changed her into a heifer. Hermes killed Argos, and Hera placed his eyes in the peacock's tail.

ARIADNE (*Ariadne*):   In mythology the daughter of King Minos of Crete and Pasiphae. When Theseus arrived in Crete, Ariadne fell in love with him and gave him a ball of thread with which he guided himself out of the labyrinth after killing the Minotaur. Theseus fled with Ariadne but abandoned her on the island of Naxos. In some legends Theseus left her pregnant and she died in childbirth. In another version Ariadne was found by Dionysus who married her. She then became immortal or else was given a crown of seven stars by Dionysus, and the stars became a constellation after her death. See also THESEUS.

ARIMASPEANS or ARIMASPIANS (*Arimaspoi*):   A legendary people whose land bordered that of the Hyperboreans. They were one-eyed and were continually fighting with griffins who guarded a hoard of gold.

ARISTAEUS (*Aristaios*):   A hero or god who was a protector of cattle and fruit trees, and a deity of hunting, husbandry and beekeeping. His cult originated in Thessaly, but he was also worshiped in Boeotia, Ceos, Cyrene and elsewhere. In mythology he was the son of Apollo and Cyrene (daughter of King Hypseus of the Lapiths). Aristaeus fell in love with Eurydice and pursued her; as she tried to escape, she trod on a snake and was fatally bitten. To avenge her the Nymphs killed all his bees. Aristaeus tried to ascertain what was wrong from Proteus, who told him to sacrifice all his cattle to the Nymphs. This he did, and returning after nine days he found bees swarming in the cattle carcasses.

ARTEMIS (*Artemis*, *Artamis*):   A goddess, originally a deity of wildlife, wild places and fertility, who came to be worshiped in cities as a goddess of fertility and a protector of women in childbirth (fig. 8.4). Artemis was the daughter of Zeus and Leto and the twin sister of Apollo. She was one of the Olympians and was usually portrayed as a virgin huntress with bow and arrows. Sudden and painless deaths of women were thought to be the result of being struck by the arrows of Artemis. In Athens the fifth day of every month was celebrated as her birthday, and a sacrifice to Artemis by the Attic deme Erchia took place on the 12th day of the month Hekatombaion. The festival of Munichia was celebrated in her honor at Athens on the 16th day of the month Mounichion. She had a major cult center at Brauron, where a festival (Brauronia) was held in her honor. Artemis was sometimes identified with the goddesses Hecate and Selene, the Cretan goddess Britomartis, and the great mother goddess of Ephesus (usually known now by her Roman name "Diana of the Ephesians"). Artemis had several epithets, including Potnia Theron (mistress of wild animals), Cynthia (after her birthplace on Mount Cynthus in Delos), Kourotrophos (nurse), Agrotera (huntress) and Locheia (helper in childbirth).

ASCLEPIUS (*Asklepios*):   A hero and god of healing (fig. 8.5). He was worshiped throughout Greece and had several major healing shrines (Asclepieia), the most important being at Epidaurus. His five daughters, Aceso, Iaso, Panacea, Aglaea and Hygieia, were associated with his cult, although Hygieia (health) appears to have been the most important after Asclepius himself. His symbols were snakes twined around a staff, crowns of laurel and pine cones. Asclepius was the son of Apollo and Coronis and was taught his art by Chiron. He appears to have originally been regarded as a hero (he is a mortal in Homer's *Iliad*) but was later regarded as a god. Asclepius knew how to bring the dead to life and restored Hippolytus, but Zeus, fearing that Asclepius would upset the natural order, killed him

with a thunderbolt. At Athens the Epidauria (a festival in honor of Asclepius) probably took place on the 17th or 18th day of the month Boedromion. See also HEALING SANCTUARIES and SHRINES.

ATALANTA (*Atalante*):   In mythology daughter of either Iasos (son of Lycurgus) or Schoeneus (son of Athamas) and Clymene (daughter of Minyas). Atalanta was a huntress and averse to marriage. She refused to marry any man who could not defeat her in a race, and those who failed were killed. She took part in the Calydonian boar hunt with Meleager, who fell in love with her. Aphrodite gave Meleager three golden apples, which he carried in the race, dropping them at intervals. Atalanta could not resist stopping to pick them up, and so Meleager won and married her.

Fig. 8.5   Head of the god Asclepius, a 4th-century-BC sculpture from Thessalonica.

Fig. 8.6 Athena Chalinitis depicted wearing a Corinthian helmet on a 4th-century-BC silver stater from Corinth. Athena's head is depicted on the reverse of coins from Corinth and its colonies, as she assisted Bellerophon to capture Pegasus and kill the Chimaera.

ATARGATIS (Aramaic, *Atar-Ata*): A Syrian earth and vegetation goddess whose cult spread to a number of Greek cities in the 2nd century BC. She was sometimes identified with the Ephesian Artemis. Atargatis was worshiped as a fertility goddess at her temple at Hierapolis—the greatest and holiest in Syria. Originally her consort was apparently Dushara or Dusares; he was regarded as subordinate to Atargatis and was thought to be a king who had died and was reborn. He became identified with Dionysus. Later on Atargatis had a second consort called Hadad, a Syrian thunder god (also called Baal Shamin) who became identified with Zeus. He was also subordinate to Atargatis.

ATE (*Ate*): The personification of infatuation or moral blindness.

ATHENA (*Athena, Athene, Athenaia*): Patron goddess of Athens in Attica and of Athens in Boeotia. She was also worshiped in many other places in Greece (figs. 1.6, 3.9, 5.7, 5.9, 8.6). In Athens (Attica) the third day of every month was celebrated as the birthday of Athena. A festival of Chalceia also took place on the 30th day of the month Pyanopsion at Athens; it was celebrated in honor of Athena in her role of mistress of technology and in honor of Hephaestus, god of the smiths. The festival of Callynteria was the spring cleaning of the temple of Athena at Athens, which took place in the month of Thargelion (probably the 24th day). On the 25th day of Thargelion, the Plynteria (Festival of Washing) took place at Athens, when the image of Athena (and possibly her robe) was ceremonially washed. A sacrifice to Athena was undertaken by the Attic deme Teithras on the 27th day of the month Boedromion, with another sacrifice by the Attic deme Erchia on the ninth day of the month Gamelion. The deme Erchia also made a sacrifice to Athena Polias (Athena protector of the city) on the third day of the month Skirophorion. Athena had three main festivals: the Arrephoria, the Scirophoria and the Panathenaea.

In addition to being protector of citadels and cities, Athena was regarded as a virgin war goddess, a patron of arts and crafts and the personification of wisdom. She is usually portrayed in armor with a spear and shield, often with an owl on her shoulder. She was sometimes known as Pallas Athene, an obscure name possibly meaning "maiden" or "brandisher of weapons." She had several epithets, including Glaukopis (owl-faced or bright-eyed), Parthenos (virgin), Promachos (fighter in the front ranks), Alalcomeneis (repulses the enemy), Ergane (working woman), Hippia (protector of horses), Nike (victorious), Agoraia (goddess of the assembly) and Tritogeneia (meaning unclear, but appears to link Athena with water). As Athena Parthenos she had a major temple on the Acropolis of Athens, now known as the Parthenon (fig. 2.7). At Corinth she was worshiped as Chalinitis (the Bridler, fig. 8.6), and at Sparta Athena Poliachos (protector of the city) was worshiped as Chalcioecus (living in a brazen shrine).

In mythology Athena was an Olympian, the daughter of Zeus and Metis (the latter being the wisest of all deities). Because it was destined that Metis would first bear Athena and then a god who would rule Mount Olympus (and thus be a threat to Zeus), Zeus swallowed Metis before Athena was born. This resulted in Athena emerging, in full armor, from the head of Zeus. Athena was identified with several other deities including the Egyptian goddess Neith. See also CASSANDRA.

ATLAS (*Atlas*):   In mythology one of the Titans, a son of Iapetus and Clymene. In Homer's poetry he is the father of Calypso, but in other legends he is the father of the Pleiades, Hyades and Hesperides. He was guardian of the pillars of heaven (which held up the sky), but for his part in the revolt of the Titans against Uranus, he was condemned to hold up the sky by himself. He helped Heracles fetch the golden apples of the Hesperides. See HERACLES.

ATREUS (*Atreus*):   The son of Pelops, king of Mycenae and father of Agamemnon and Menelaus. He was married to Aerope. After Myrtilus cursed Pelops, each generation of his family met with disaster. Pelops' brother, Thyestes, seduced Aerope and tried to usurp the throne of Atreus. Atreus banished Thyestes, but later pretended to be reconciled. At a banquet Atreus cooked and served Thyestes' children to him. Varying versions of this legend existed.

ATROPOS (*Atropos*, Inflexible):   One of the Fates who cut the thread at the moment of death.

ATTIS or ATYS (*Attis*):   An Anatolian god who was the consort of the goddess Cybele. Phrygian myth states that Attis was the son of Nana, daughter of the river god Sangarius (a river in Asia Minor). Nana conceived him after gathering an almond or almond tree blossom that had risen from the severed male organs of Agdistis (Cybele), who was born both male and female and had been castrated by the gods. Agdistis, now purely female, loved Attis. When Attis wished to marry someone else, Agdistis was jealous and drove him mad. He castrated himself and died beneath a pine tree. Agdistis was so distressed that the other gods granted that his body would not decay.

In another legend Zeus, having tried in vain to marry Cybele, let some of his semen fall on a rock, from which the hermaphrodite Agdistis was born. Dionysus castrated Agdistis, and a pomegranate tree grew from the blood. Nana became pregnant

by inserting one of the fruits of the tree in her womb and gave birth to Attis, but at Sangarius' wish she abandoned Attis, who was adopted by some passersby. He grew to be very handsome, and King Midas of Pessinus wanted him to marry one of his daughters. Attis and his attendants became very frenzied during an argument between Agdistis and Cybele. He castrated himself beneath a pine tree and died. Cybele buried Attis and the daughter of Midas, who had killed herself in despair. Violets grew around the pine tree where the blood of Attis and of Midas' daughter had fallen, and an almond tree grew over the daughter's grave. Zeus granted Agdistis that the body of Attis should not decay, and that his hair would continue to grow and his little finger move. According to legend a festival and community of priests were founded by Agdistis at Pessinus in honor of Attis.

Attis was a minor part of Cybele's cult, and he was variously regarded as a mortal or as a god of vegetation, although his status increased until, in the Roman period, he was an equal deity with Cybele. See also CYBELE.

AUGEAS or AUGIAS (*Augeias*):   In mythology a king of Elis, the cleaning of whose stables was one of the labors of Heracles. Augeas' treasury was said to have been built by the legendary architects Trophonius and Agamedes. See also HERACLES and TROPHONIUS.

AUTOLYCUS (*Autolykos*):   In mythology the grandfather of Odysseus and a master of thieving and trickery. He was taught his skills by Hermes, who, in some versions of the legend, is said to be his father.

AUXO: One of three goddesses of the seasons (Horae) in Attica.

BASILE (*Basile*):   A deity associated with the legendary hero King Codrus and his ancestor Neleus. The Attic deme Erchia sacrificed to Basile on the fourth day of the month Boedromion. Little else is known about this deity.

BELLEROPHON (*Bellerophon, Bellerophontes*):   In mythology the son of Glaucus and grandson of

Sisyphus. He was the hero of an old legend of Corinth retold in Homer's *Iliad*. Because he repelled the advances of Anteia (queen of Argos), she denounced him, and her husband (King Proetus) sent him to the king of Lycia with a sealed letter demanding Bellerophon's death. In Lycia he was given a number of potentially lethal tasks, which he successfully performed, earning the right to marry the king's daughter. Later versions of the legend relate that he was helped to perform the tasks by a magic winged horse called Pegasus, and that afterward he affronted the gods by trying to ride Pegasus up to heaven. The gods made him mad, and he died a wandering outcast. See also CHIMAERA.

BENDIS (*Bendis*):   A Thracian goddess, for whom there was a festival at Athens on the 19th day of the month Thargelion.

BITON and CLEOBIS (*Biton, Kleobis*):   In a legend recounted in Herodotus' history, Biton and Cleobis were sons of a priestess of Hera. When no oxen could be found, they pulled their mother's chariot several miles to the temple. She prayed for the best possible gift as their reward, and consequently they died in the temple. In Herodotus the story is given as an illustration of the saying "call no man happy until he is dead."

BOREAS (*Boreas*):   God of the north or northeast wind. Like all wind gods, he was often thought to take the form of a horse. He seems to have been particularly worshiped in Attica, and a state cult of Boreas was established in Athens after he allegedly destroyed the Persian fleet at the battle of Artemisium in 480 BC. Boreas was the son of Eos and Astraeus. Legend says that he carried off the Nymph Oreithyia (daughter of king Erechtheus of Athens) to be his wife, for which he was described as "son-in-law of the Athenians." In Homer's *Iliad* he is described as a begetter of horses, probably reflecting the speed of the wind and the common belief that mares could be impregnated by the wind.

BRIAREUS (*Briareos*, also known as Aegaeon by men, Briareos by gods):   Son of Uranus and Gaia and one of the Hecatoncheires. He was a giant with 100 hands who, with his brothers, helped Zeus in his battle against the Titans (Titanomachia). As a reward he was given the task of guarding the Titans in Tartarus (part of the underworld where the wicked were punished for their evil deeds). When Zeus was about to be put in chains by the other Olympian gods, Thetis summoned Briareus to save him.

BRITOMARTIS (*Britomartis*, sweet maid in the Cretan language):   A Cretan goddess identified with the goddesses Artemis, Aphaea and Dictynna. In mythology Minos fell in love with Britomartis. To escape him, she jumped over a cliff into the sea and made her way to Aegina, where she was subsequently worshiped as Aphaea.

BRONTES (*Brontes*, Thunderer):   One of the Cyclopes.

BUBASTIS: A cat-headed Egyptian goddess. She was originally the local goddess of the city of Bubastis in Egypt and became identified with Isis. The Greeks identified her with Artemis. She was a goddess of pleasure and of protection against evil spirits and disease.

CABIRI or CABEIRI (*Kabeiroi*):   Deities of fertility and of protection of sailors, whose cult was centered on Samothrace. They were probably originally Phrygian deities, and different traditions record different numbers of Cabiri. One tradition recorded four Cabiri and named them as Axierus, Axiocersa, Axiocersus and Cadmilus. The Cabiri were part of a mystery cult. Probably because of this, they were not usually individually named but were generally referred to as the "great gods." See also Oriental and Mystery Religions, p. 357.

CADMUS (*Kadmos*):   In mythology the son of King Agenor of Tyre, brother of Europa and Phoenix and legendary founder of Thebes. After Europa was abducted by Zeus, Cadmus was sent to look for her, but abandoned the search on the advice of the Delphic Oracle. Instead, he followed a cow in order to found a city where it lay down. This took him to a spring guarded by a dragon, which he killed. On the instructions of the goddess

Athena, Cadmus sowed half the dragon's teeth, which became fighting men who fought among themselves until only five were left; these were the *Spartoi* (sown men) whom the Theban nobility claimed as ancestors. The city of Thebes was founded beside this spring, and its acropolis was called the Cadmea. Cadmus married Harmonia (daughter of Ares and Aphrodite), and they had several children including Semele. Eventually Cadmus and Harmonia withdrew to Illyria, where Zeus changed them into snakes and carried them off to Elysium. Cadmus was credited with civilizing the Boeotians and teaching them writing.

CALCHAS (*Kalkhas*):   In mythology a Greek seer who took part in the Trojan War. In Homer's *Iliad*, he revealed the reason for the plague in the Greek camp and also foretold the length of the war. In other legends he was associated with the sacrifice of Iphigenia and with the Argonauts.

CALLIOPE (*Kalliope*):   One of the Muses, thought in late Roman times to preside over heroic epic.

CALLISTO (*Kallisto*):   A Nymph who was a daughter of Lycaon. She was loved by Zeus and they had a son, Arcas, who was the mythical ancestor of the Arcadians. Callisto was changed into a bear, either in anger by Hera or by Zeus to protect her from Hera's anger. She wandered as a bear until her son (or in some versions, Artemis) pursued her with a spear. To save her Zeus changed both into constellations, so that Callisto became the constellation of the Great Bear and Arcas became the Little Bear.

CALYDONIAN BOAR: In mythology a monstrous boar that ravaged the lands of King Oeneus of Calydon. It was sent by Artemis because Oeneus had not offered her proper sacrifice. It was hunted and killed by Meleager during the Calydonian Boar Hunt.

CALYPSO (*Kalypso*):   A goddess or Nymph who was the daughter of Atlas. She lived on an island called Ogygia, where Odysseus was shipwrecked. Calypso kept him there for seven years, promising to make him immortal if he married her. Zeus sent Hermes to order her to release Odysseus, and she gave him materials to build a boat and released him. In some legends Calypso had a son by Odysseus, called Auson, who was the eponymous ancestor of the Ausonians in Italy.

CAPANEUS (*Kapaneus*):   One of the heroes of the Seven against Thebes and husband of Evadne. He boasted that not even Zeus could stop him from scaling the walls of Thebes; for this blasphemy, Zeus killed Capaneus with a thunderbolt. Evadne committed suicide by throwing herself on his funeral pyre.

CASSANDRA (also known as Alexandra) (*Kassandra*):   In mythology a prophetess, the daughter of King Priam of Troy and Hecuba. No mention of Cassandra's ability to prophesy occurs in Homer's works, but in a later legend she was loved by Apollo and was given the art of prophecy. When she refused Apollo's love, he condemned her true prophecies to be always disbelieved. When Troy fell she was found by Ajax the Locrian clinging to the statue of Athena in her temple. He dragged her away and raped her, for which sacrilege the Locrians were obliged annually to send two maidens to serve as slaves in the temple of Athena at Troy. If the inhabitants caught them before reaching the temple, they were killed. After the sack of Troy Cassandra was given as a concubine to Agamemnon, with whom she was murdered by Aegisthus. See also AJAX.

CASTOR and POLYDEUCES (*Kastor, Polydeukes*):   Gods known collectively as the Dioscuri.

CECROPS (*Kekrops*):   In mythology the first king of Athens, believed to have "sprung from the earth" as a native of Attica. He was often represented as a human above the waist and a serpent below, indicating his origin, since serpents were thought to dwell within the earth. During his reign a contest for Attica took place between Athena and Poseidon, and Cecrops was appointed judge; he awarded Attica to Athena.

CELAENO (*Kelaino*, dark):   One of the Harpies.

Fig. 8.7   A triumphal procession including a pair of centaurs pulling a chariot in which the baby Dionysus (barely visible) is carried. A Roman mosaic from Paphos Nea, Cyprus.

CENTAURS (*Kentauroi*):   A race of monsters with the chest, head and arms of a man, but the legs and body of a horse (fig. 8.7). They were variously described as the offspring of Ixion and Nephele or the offspring of Centaurus (son of Ixion and Nephele) who had mated with mares. See also CHIRON, NESSUS and THESEUS.

CEPHALUS (*Kephalos*):   A hero of Attica. In mythology he was the husband of Procris (daughter of Erechtheus). The goddess Eos fell in love with Cephalus, causing dissension between him and Procris, but Artemis gave Procris a hound that always caught its quarry and a spear that never missed its target. Procris gave these to Cephalus, and the two were reconciled. However, Eos made Procris jealous of the amount of time Cephalus spent hunting. Procris hid in a bush to spy on Cephalus; mistaking her for an animal, Cephalus killed Procris with his spear.

CERBERUS (*Kerberos*):   A monstrous dog that guarded the entrance to the underworld. It was the offspring of Typhon and Echidna and had three (in some versions, 50) heads and a tail or mane of snakes. One labor of Heracles was to capture Cerberus and take him back to King Eurystheus. See also HERACLES.

CHAOS (*Khaos*, gaping void):   In mythology the first being to be created. Chaos was scarcely a personification, being generally regarded as the nothingness that existed before the rest of creation. Gaia was the daughter of Chaos.

CHARON (*Kharon*):   An aged ferryman who conveyed the souls of the dead across the rivers of the underworld to their final resting place. He would ferry them only if the funeral rites had been properly performed, and if they paid a fee of one obol. The Greeks put a coin in the mouth of the dead person before burial as his fee.

CHARYBDIS (*Kharybdis*):   A whirlpool in a narrow channel of water (often identified as the Straits of Messina). It was sometimes regarded as a female monster, the daughter of Poseidon and Gaia. Charybdis was situated opposite Scylla, creating two hazards between which Odysseus had to choose, since he could not avoid both. He chose Charybdis and escaped from the resulting shipwreck by clinging to a tree growing above the whirlpool.

CHIMAERA (*Khimaira*): A fire-breathing monster with a lion's head, a she-goat's body and the tail of a snake. It was the offspring of Typhon and Echidna and was killed by Bellerophon.

CHIRON (*Kheiron*): A centaur who was wise and kind (unlike other centaurs). He was sometimes said to have different parents (Cronus and Philyra) from the other centaurs. Chiron was known for his knowledge of archery, music and medicine and taught heroes such as Achilles, Jason and Asclepius. He was accidentally killed by Heracles and became the constellation Sagittarius.

CHRYSEIS (*Khryseis*): In mythology the daughter of Chryses (priest of Apollo on the island of Chryse, near Troy). When the Greeks overran the island, she was taken prisoner and given to Agamemnon as a concubine. Agamemnon refused to ransom her, preferring her to Clytemnestra. Apollo therefore answered the prayers of Chryseis' father and sent a plague to the Greek camp. Agamemnon refused to return Chryseis unless he was given Briseis, who had been allotted to Achilles, thus starting their quarrel.

CIRCE (*Kirke*): In mythology a goddess and sorceress who lived on the mythical island of Aeaea. In Homer's *Odyssey* she is the daughter of Helios and Perse. She changed Odysseus' men into pigs, but Odysseus managed to resist the spell, aided by a herb given to him by Hermes. He forced her to restore his men, and they lived on Aeaea for a year. Circe then gave Odysseus advice about his journey to the underworld and his return home. In other legends she had two children (Agrios and Latinus) by Odysseus and received Jason and Medea on their return from Colchis. Some legends said Telegonus was the son of Circe and Odysseus, and in other legends Circe married Telemachus after Odysseus' death.

CLIO (*Kleio*): One of the Muses, thought in the late Roman period to preside over history.

CLOTHO (*Klotho*, spinner): One of the Fates who spun the thread of life.

CLYTEMNESTRA or CLYTAEM(N)ESTRA (*Klytaim(n)estra*): Daughter of King Tyndareus of Sparta and his wife Leda, and sister of Helen of Troy and the Dioscuri. She married Agamemnon and was the mother of Iphigenia, Chrysothemis, Electra and Orestes. While Agamemnon was at the siege of Troy, Clytemnestra took Aegisthus as a lover. When Agamemnon returned with Cassandra as his concubine, Aegisthus killed them both. When Orestes reached manhood he killed Clytemnestra and Aegisthus in revenge for Agamemnon's death.

CODRUS (*Kodros*): A legendary king of Athens, thought to have reigned in the 11th century BC. He was worshiped as a hero in association with Neleus and the obscure deity Basile. In mythology Codrus was of the Neleid family and was expelled, with his father Melanthus, from his kingdom of Pylos by the Dorians. He went to Attica, killed King Xanthus of Boeotia in single combat, and was accepted as king of Athens in place of the existing king who was of the Theseid family.

COEUS (*Koios*): In mythology one of the Titans.

CORONIS (*Koronis*): The daughter of Phlegyas and mother of Asclepius. While pregnant by Apollo, Coronis fell in love with an Arcadian, Ischys (son of Elatus). A crow informed Apollo, who sent Artemis to kill Coronis; when her body was on the funeral pyre, Apollo took the unborn child (Asclepius) to be raised by Chiron.

COTTUS (*Kottus*): In mythology one of the Hecatoncheires.

COTYS, COTYTO or COTYTTO (*Kotys, Koty[t]to*): A Thracian goddess associated with Cybele. She had an orgiastic cult that eventually spread throughout Greece.

CREON (*Kreon*, Prince): The name of several figures in mythology, of whom two were particularly important. One was the king of Corinth with whom Jason and Medea took refuge. Jason abandoned Medea in favor of Creon's daughter; in revenge Medea killed Creon (in some versions, Creon's daughter as well). Another Creon was the brother of Jocasta (wife of Oedipus). Creon ruled Thebes on three occasions: after the death of Laius (father of Oedipus), on the downfall of Oedipus and at the death of Eteocles.

CREUSA (*Kreousa*, Princess): The name of several figures in mythology, of whom two were particularly important. One was the daughter of King Erechtheus of Athens and mother (by Apollo) of Ion, from whom the Ionians were allegedly descended. Another Creusa was daughter of King Priam of Troy and Hecuba. This Creusa was wife of Aeneas and mother of Ascanius and died fleeing Troy after its capture.

CRIUS (*Kreios*): In mythology one of the Titans.

CRONUS (*Kronos*): One of the Titans and the youngest son of Uranus and Gaia. He castrated Uranus in order to gain his throne and married his sister Rhea. Their children were Hestia, Demeter, Hera, Hades, Poseidon and Zeus. Because he was fated to be overthrown by one of his children, he swallowed each one after they were born, except Zeus, who was smuggled to Crete. Instead, Cronus was tricked into swallowing a stone wrapped in swaddling clothes, and later he vomited up all those he had swallowed. In Athens a festival in honor of Cronus was on the 12th day of the month Hekatombaion.

CURETES (*Kouretes*): The half-divine beings who lived in Crete. The infant Zeus was given to their care, to protect him from his father Cronus. To conceal Zeus they danced around him clashing weapons to drown his cries. They were later confused with the Corybantes who attended the goddess Cybele.

CYBELE or AGDISTIS (*Kybele, Kybebe*): Anatolian mother goddess whose cult was known in Greece by the 5th century BC. She was sometimes identified with Demeter or with Rhea, and also with the local "mother of the gods." Her cult was centered at Pessinus in Phrygia, where she was known as Agdistis. Her consort was Attis, and a great deal of mythology surrounded them both. She was considered to be the mother of all living things—an earth mother goddess and a goddess of fertility and wild nature. She was often portrayed wearing a turreted crown, seated on a vehicle drawn by lions or on a throne attended by lions. A characteristic of her cult consisted of states of ecstasy, inducing prophecy and insensibility to pain. She was also said to cause and to cure disease.

The rites of Cybele and Attis included the *taurobolium* (a ritual where a worshiper stood in a pit, while a bull was sacrificed on a slatted floor above, bathing the person in its blood), self-flagellation and castration of the priests (*galloi*) and ecstatic dances. The Corybantes were priests associated mainly with the cult of Cybele. A temple or sanctuary of Cybele was known as a *metroon* (from *meter*, mother). See also ATTIS.

CYCLOPES (sing. Cyclops) (*Kyklopes*): Gigantic one-eyed beings, the offspring of Uranus and Gaia. There are conflicting traditions about the Cyclopes. According to Hesiod there were three Cyclopes called Brontes, Steropes and Arges, who were craftsmen and made thunderbolts. They were sometimes regarded as the workmen of Hephaestus, and the Greeks often attributed ancient fortifications to them. However, in Homer's *Odyssey*, the Cyclopes are represented as savage, pastoral creatures and one of them, Polyphemus (a son of Poseidon), imprisoned Odysseus in a cave.

DAEDALUS (*Daidalos*, literally "artful" or "cunning worker"): In mythology an inventor and craftsman living at the time of King Minos of Crete. Born in Athens he was forced to leave after he killed his nephew Perdix, who was a more skillful craftsman. Daedalus went to Crete where he made the labyrinth to house the Minotaur. He also made Ariadne's thread and the hollow wooden cow for Pasiphae. Enraged that he had helped Pasiphae, King Minos imprisoned Daedalus and his son Icarus, but they escaped from Crete by flying on wings of wax and feathers. Icarus was killed, but Daedalus successfully flew to Sicily, where he made many marvelous creations. See also ICARUS.

DAIMON (*Daimon*): A supernatural being, intermediate between gods and men. A man was believed to have a good and evil Daimon that followed him through life and influenced his actions. It does not appear to have been equivalent to "fate." The term *Daimon* was also applied to some minor gods. See also AGATHOS DAIMON.

DAMOCLES (*Damokles*): In mythology a courtier of Dionysius I, tyrant of Syracuse. When Damocles excessively praised the life of luxury of Dionysius, the latter gave a banquet during which a sword was suspended by a thread above the head of Damocles to make him understand the precarious nature of the luxury enjoyed by the tyrant. This gave rise to the expression "sword of Damocles."

DANAE (*Danae*): The daughter of King Acrisius of Argos. Because a prophecy foretold that Acrisius would be killed by his daughter's son, he imprisoned Danae in a bronze tower to keep her away from men. However, Zeus descended on her as a shower of gold, and she bore him a son called Perseus. Acrisius set Danae and Perseus adrift on the sea in a chest, but they safely reached the island of Seriphos and were sheltered by King Polydectes. The king persuaded Perseus to fetch the Gorgon's head; returning with the head, he used it to turn Polydectes to stone for molesting Danae. Perseus then returned to Argos with Danae. See also PERSEUS.

DANAUS (*Danaos*): In mythology the son of King Belus of Egypt and brother of Aegyptus. Aegyptus wanted his 50 sons to marry the 50 daughters of Danaus. There was a dispute between them, but Danaus finally agreed to the mass marriage. However, he told his daughters to kill their husbands on the wedding night. All obeyed except Hypermestra, who spared her husband Lynceus. Danaus imprisoned Hypermestra, but she was later spared (in some versions, by Aphrodite's intervention). Danaus married off the other daughters by standing them at the end of a racecourse and letting their suitors run for them. After their deaths these daughters were punished in the underworld by being made to fill leaking jars with water. The myth of Danaus is an attempt to establish Egyptian origins for the Danaans, a general name for early Greek people inhabiting the Argos region. It was sometimes used to mean the Greek nation as a whole.

DAPHNE (*Daphne*, laurel): A Nymph who was daughter of the river god Ladon in Arcadia. Pursued by Apollo she prayed to the river god Peneus for help and was turned into a laurel tree.

DEIANIRA (*Deianeira*): The daughter of Oeneus and Althea, sister of Meleager and wife of Heracles. Heracles met Meleager's spirit in the underworld, and the spirit asked him to marry Deianira who was without support after Meleager's death. Heracles won Deianira in combat with Achelous, but on the way home Heracles trusted the centaur Nessus to carry her across a river. Nessus tried to assault her, and Heracles killed him with one of his poisoned arrows. The dying Nessus gave Deianira some of his blood (or a blood-stained shirt) telling her it was a love charm. Years later, after Deianira had borne Heracles several children, Heracles brought home Iole. To regain his affection Deianira gave him a garment smeared with the blood of Nessus (which was poison); when Heracles put it on, the poison killed him. Deianira killed herself when she realized what had happened.

DEIDAMIA (*Deidameia*): In mythology the mother of Neoptolemus by Achilles.

DEMETER (*Demeter*): The goddess of grain crops who presided over agriculture and who was a central deity in the Eleusinian Mysteries. She was sometimes identified with the Egyptian goddess Isis and the Phrygian goddess Cybele. Demeter was one of the Olympians. Apart from her worship at Eleusis, she was worshiped throughout Greece. A three-day festival (Thesmophoria) in her honor was celebrated throughout most of the Greek world. At Athens it took place on the 11th–13th days of the month Pyanopsion. Also at Athens a fertility festival (called Haloa) in honor of Demeter and Dionysus took place on the 26th day of the month Poseideon. The Stenia was a women's festival at Athens in honor of Demeter and Persephone. In mythology Demeter was daughter of Cronus and Rhea, and mother of Persephone by Zeus and of Plutus by Iasion. Most myths concerning Demeter also relate to Persephone. See also PERSEPHONE.

DEUCALION (*Deukalion*):   The name of several characters in mythology, the most important being the son of Prometheus. When Zeus was so angry at the crimes of mortals and decided to destroy them with a flood, Deucalion was warned by Prometheus. Deucalion built a boat for himself and his wife Pyrrha. They sailed on the flood until they grounded on Mount Parnassus. Advised by an oracle to throw their mother's bones over their shoulder, they realized that this meant "mother earth" and threw stones. Those thrown by Deucalion became men and those thrown by Pyrrha became women. They later became the parents of Hellen, the eponymous ancestor of the Greeks (Hellenes).

DICTYNNA (*Diktynna*):   A goddess identified with Britomartis and Artemis. She was probably a goddess of Mount Dicte in Crete, but her cult is also known from places on mainland Greece. She was usually portrayed as a huntress. Due to confusion over the origin of her name (from Mount Dicte, rather than from *diktyon*, fishing net), a myth existed that she fled from King Minos, who was in love with her, but became entangled in fishermen's nets.

DIOMEDES (*Diomedes*):   In mythology two characters were called Diomedes. One was a king of Thrace, son of Ares and Cyrene, whose man-eating horses were captured by Heracles as one of his labors. The other Diomedes was a son of Tydeus and Deipyle, the daughter of Adrastus. He took part in the siege of Troy and, with the help of Athena, managed to wound Aphrodite and Ares. He behaved chivalrously to Glaucus, who fought for the Trojan side. With Odysseus he raided the

Trojan camp and went to fetch Philoctetes from Lemnos. See also GLAUCUS.

DIONYSUS (*Dionysos*):   God of nature, who became god of the vine and of wine. He was also a god of mystic ecstasy, and his cult was one of the mystery religions. In mythology Dionysus was the son of Zeus and Semele and was one of the Olympians. Semele asked Zeus to show himself to her in all his glory, but she was struck dead by the sight. Zeus took Dionysus, only in his sixth month, from Semele's womb and sewed the infant inside his thigh. At the proper time Dionysus emerged from the thigh, alive and perfectly formed, to become "the twice-born god." Other legends describe Dionysus as driven mad by Hera and cured by the goddess Cybele, into whose rites he was initiated. He was said to have descended into the underworld, where he restored Semele to life. Hades agreed to release the shade of Semele if Dionysus gave him something that he held very dear, so Dionysus gave up the myrtle plant. On his way to the underworld he had asked a man named Prosymnus (or Polymnus) for directions, and the man had asked for certain sexual favors from Dionysus on his return. When Dionysus returned, he could not fulfill his promise because Prosymnus had died; the best he could do was to plant a phallus-shaped stick in the tomb of Prosymnus.

The cult of Dionysus reflected elements of these varying myths. There were two Dionysia (festivals of Dionysus) celebrated at Athens. The lesser festival was the Rural Dionysia (celebrated in the month Poseideon). The greater festival was the City or Great Dionysia, which apparently took place between the 10th and 17th of the month Elaphebolion. Also at Athens a fertility festival (Haloa), in honor of Dionysus and Demeter, took place on the 26th day of the month Poseideon, and a festival in honor of Dionysus (the Lenaea) on the 12th day of the month Gamelion. A sacrifice to Dionysus by the Attic deme Erchia took place on the second day of the month Anthesterion. The Anthesteria was a festival in honor of Dionysus, widely celebrated by Ionian Greeks; at Athens it was celebrated on the 11th–13th of the month Anthesterion. A meeting of the Attic deme Myrrhinus took place on the 19th day of the month Poseideon on matters concerned with Dionysus. See also Mysteries of Dionysus, Oschophoria, Rural Dionysia, Lenaea, Anthesteria, City Dionysia, LYCURGUS, SILENUS.

DIONYSUS ZAGREUS (*Dionysos Zagreus*): The Greek god Dionysus linked with the Cretan god Zagreus. In mythology he was the son of Zeus and Demeter. The other Greek gods were jealous of him and arranged that he was torn to pieces. The goddess Pallas Athene saved his heart and took it to Zeus, who used it to create the god Dionysus. This story of death and resurrection appears to have played an important part in the cult of Orphism.

DIOSCURI (*Dioskouroi*, Sons of Zeus): The gods Castor and Polydeuces (Pollux to the Romans) were known collectively as the Dioscuri. It is uncertain whether they were originally heroes who became regarded as gods, or gods whose cult had been diminished. The Dioscuri were sometimes identified with the Cabiri, Oriental deities (probably of Phrygian origin), who promoted fertility and protected sailors. Castor and Polydeuces came to be regarded as gods of salvation and protectors of sailors at sea. In mythology they were twin brothers of Helen and sons of Leda. They were notable horsemen and took part in the expedition of the Argonauts. They carried off Hilaera and Phoebe (daughters of King Leucippus of Messenia), whose brothers Idas and Lynceus fought to rescue them and killed Castor. However, Polydeuces was allowed to take Castor's place in the underworld on alternate days. A sacrifice to the Dioscuri by the Attic deme Erchia took place on the fourth day of the month Thargelion. They were important deities at Sparta.

DIRCE (*Dirke*): In mythology the wife of Lycus who was regent of Thebes. She persecuted Antiope, and in revenge the sons of Antiope killed Dirce by tying her to the horns of a bull. After her death she was changed into the stream that then bore her name.

ECHO (*Ekho*): A Nymph who engaged Hera in conversation when she was trying to spy on Zeus.

As punishment Hera deprived Echo of normal speech so that she could only repeat the words of others. Echo fell in love with Narcissus, but when he rejected her, she pined away until only her voice was left.

EILEITHYIA (*Eileithyia*): Goddess of childbirth, occasionally worshiped as a guardian deity of a city. She appears originally to have been a Mycenaean mother goddess. She was later identified with Artemis and Hera, and her name was sometimes used as a title of Hera. She was sometimes regarded as the sister of Artemis and daughter of Zeus and Hera. She was sometimes addressed in the plural— Eileithyiae (*Eileithyiai*), who were goddesses of childbirth.

ELECTRA (*Elektra*): Three mythological characters had the name Electra:

1. A daughter of Atlas, one of the Pleiades and mother of Dardanus and Iasion.
2. A daughter of Oceanus, wife of Thaumus and mother of Iris and the Harpies.
3. The best known Electra was the daughter of Agamemnon and Clytemnestra. She was not mentioned by Homer, but appears first in a work by Stesichorus and is a central figure in later Greek tragedies, where she is represented as the driving force behind her brother Orestes' revenge on their mother.

ELPENOR (*Elpenor*): In mythology a companion of Odysseus who fell to his death from the roof of Circe's palace while sleeping and was left unburied. He was the first shade met by Odysseus in the underworld, and successfully begged Odysseus to have his body cremated and buried beneath a barrow with his oar planted on top.

ENDYMION (*Endymion*): In mythology a very beautiful youth who was a shepherd. Selene (the moon) fell in love with him because of his beauty while he was sleeping on Mount Latmus in Caria. Selene (or in some versions, Zeus) made him sleep there forever. In another version Hypnos (god of

Fig. 8.8 *Ionic columns supporting an entablature in the Erechtheum at Athens. This temple housed various cults, including those of Athena, Poseidon and Erechtheus.*

sleep) fell in love with Endymion and made him sleep with open eyes, while another legend relates that Endymion was king of Elis and founder of the festival at Olympia. Selene was said to have borne 50 daughters by him (probably corresponding to the 50 months of an Olympiad).

ENYO (*Enyo*): Goddess of war, second in importance to Ares. In mythology Enyo was also a name of one of the Graiae.

EOS (*Eos*): Goddess of the dawn, who appears to have been a purely mythological rather than cult figure. In mythology she was sister of Helios and Selene, and each morning she drove a chariot across the sky. Most stories about her concern beautiful young men that she carried off to be her lovers. See also TITHONUS.

EPOPS (*Epops*, literally a "hoopoe"): A sacrifice to Epops by the Attic deme Erchia took place on the fifth day of the month Boedromion.

ERATO (*Erato*): One of the Muses, thought in late Roman times to preside over hymns.

ERECHTHEUS (*Erekhtheus*): Believed by the Greeks to be an early king of Athens. Homer mentions that he was worshiped with Athena on the Acropolis at Athens (fig. 8.8). In mythology Erechtheus was a son of Gaia but was reared by Athena. Creusa and Procris (who married Cephalus) were his daughters.

ERINYES (*Erinyes*): Spirits of punishment and vengeance, sometimes invoked in oaths and curses. They avenged wrongs done to kindred, especially murder of one family member by another. They were sometimes thought to act on the conscience or remorse of the wrongdoer, making the person mad. They were the offspring of Gaia and Uranus.

EROS (*Eros*): God of love and fertility, worshiped in many parts of Greece. He had an ancient fertility cult at Thespiae and a joint cult with Aphrodite at Athens. He was sometimes worshiped in the plural (*Erotes*) and symbolized all attractions that provoked love, including heterosexual and homosexual attractions. In Athens the fourth day of every month was sacred to Eros. In mythology he was often regarded as the companion and sometimes the son of Aphrodite. In some legends he is the son of Iris and Zephyrus. In other legends he was one of the oldest gods, all-powerful over every god and mortal.

ETEOCLES (*Eteokles*): In mythology the elder son of Oedipus and Jocasta, the brother of Polynices, Antigone and Ismene. After Oedipus went into exile, Eteocles and Polynices agreed to rule Thebes in alternate years, but at the end of his year Eteocles refused to give up the throne, which led to the action called the "Seven Against Thebes."

EUMAEUS (*Eumaios*): Odysseus' faithful swineherd who entertained Odysseus in his hut when the latter returned home. He recognized Odysseus and helped him destroy Penelope's suitors.

EUMENIDES (*Eumenides*, literally "kindly ones"): A euphemistic name for the Erinyes.

EUROPA (*Europe*): A goddess worshiped in Crete. She appears to have been a mythological figure who became conflated with a Cretan goddess, and had a festival called the Hellotia. In mythology Europa was a daughter of King Agenor of Tyre. Zeus fell in love with her and, disguised as a bull, carried her off to Crete. There she had three sons by Zeus called Minos, Rhadamanthys and Sarpedon.

EURYDICE (*Eurydike*): The name of several women in mythology, including the wife of King Creon of Thebes. The best known Eurydice was the wife of Orpheus. While pursued by Aristaeus, Eurydice was bitten by a snake and died. She descended into the underworld. Orpheus followed her and persuaded Hades to let her follow him out of the underworld. This was on condition that Orpheus did not look back at Eurydice before reaching the upper world, but he broke this condition and lost her forever.

EUTERPE (*Euterpe*, well-pleasing): One of the Muses, thought in the late Roman period to preside over flutes and music.

EVANDER (*Evandros*): A god worshiped in Arcadia, connected with the worship of Pan. In mythology Evander was the son of Hermes and Themis.

FATES (*Moirai*): In early Greek literature fate appears to be an impersonal concept—something that ruled people's destinies and was stronger than the gods. The concept of a trio of goddesses developed (*Moirai*, sing. *Moira*), who were variously regarded as daughters of Nyx (night), or of Zeus and Themis (justice), but Plato made them daughters of Ananke (necessity). The three Fates were regarded as old women engaged in spinning: Clotho (spinner) spun the thread of life, Lachesis (apportioner) drew off the length of thread and Atropos (inflexible) cut the thread at the moment of death.

GAIA or GE (Latin, *Gaea*; Greek, *Gaia* or *Ge*): A goddess who personified the earth. She was worshiped throughout Greece in early times, but later was often superseded by other gods. For example, she originally provided the oracle at Delphi, before Apollo. A sacrifice to Gaia by the Attic deme Erchia took place on the 27th day of the month Boedromion. In mythology Gaia was the daughter of Chaos and the mother and wife of Uranus (heaven). Among her offspring were the Titans, Cyclopes, Giants, Erinyes and Hecatoncheires.

GALATEA (*Galateia*, literally "milk-white"): A Nereid wooed by the Cyclops Polyphemus. In a later legend, she loved a Sicilian shepherd called Acis. Polyphemus pursued them, and Galatea escaped into the sea. Acis was crushed by a rock thrown by Polyphemus, so Galatea changed him into the Acis River in Sicily.

GANYMEDE (*Ganymedes*): In mythology a Trojan prince who was son of King Tros (in some versions, Laomedon). Because of his beauty Ganymede was carried off to be the cupbearer to Zeus. In exchange Zeus gave Ganymede's father a pair of divine horses (or in later legends, a golden vine). In other versions Ganymede was carried off by an eagle (or by Zeus in the shape of an eagle) because Zeus desired him. He came to symbolize homosexuality.

GERYON (*Geryones* or *Geryoneus*): A three-headed (or three-bodied) monster who lived on Erytheia, an island in the extreme west. One of the labors of Heracles was to steal Geryon's herd of marvelous cattle and drive them back to Greece. In mythology Geryon was son of Chrysaor and Callirhoe.

GIANTS (*Gigantes*): In mythology the sons of Gaia (earth) conceived from the blood of Uranus that fell to earth when he was castrated. They had great strength and monstrous appearance and rebelled against the Olympians. The Olympians called in Heracles to assist them, because they learned that they could not win without the help of a mortal.

GLAUCUS (*Glaukos*): The name of several mythological figures. Three are of particular importance:

1. A Boeotian fisherman who pursued Scylla (the sea monster) and became immortal by eating a magic herb. He became a sea god and continued to woo Scylla in vain.
2. The father of Bellerophon, who kept horses at Potniae in Boeotia and fed them on human flesh. For some reason (several explanations exist), the horses went mad and killed and ate Glaucus.

3. The second-in-command of the Lycians, who were allies of the Trojans at the siege of Troy. In Homer's *Iliad*, Glaucus tells the story of his grandfather Bellerophon. Because the grandfather of Diomedes was bound by ties of hospitality to Bellerophon, Diomedes and Glaucus (despite being on opposite sides at the siege of Troy) exchanged sets of armor as a sign of friendship. Glaucus received the worst of the bargain—bronze armor for gold.

GORGON or MEDUSA (*Gorgo, Medousa*): Medusa was the name of a particular gorgon, but was also used as a general term meaning "gorgon." She was a female monster that had snakes instead of hair and eyes that could turn people to stone. In some legends there was one Gorgon, and in others three Gorgons (*Gorgones*): Medusa, Sthenno and Euryale who were sisters. The Gorgon lived in the far west with Poseidon. Perseus went in search of the Gorgon and killed her with the aid of Athena. He cut off her head and it was used to adorn the aegis of Athena (or in some versions, the aegis of Zeus). The image of the Gorgon's head was a popular charm for averting evil. The Graiae were also sisters of the Gorgons. See also PERSEUS, PEGASUS.

GRACES (*Kharites*): Goddesses personifying charm, grace and beauty. They had various names such as Kale (beautiful), Thaleia (flowering), Auxo (the grower), Aglaia (radiant) and Euphrosyne (joy). Originally of indeterminate number, later there were thought to be three Graces. They were worshiped in various parts of the Greek world, particularly Orchomenus, Paphos, Athens and Sparta. In mythology they were daughters of Zeus, although their mothers vary from legend to legend. They were associated with many deities and played minor parts in numerous myths.

GRAIAE or GRAEAE (*Graiai*): In mythology three daughters of Phorcys and Ceto, and sisters of the Gorgons. The names of the Graiae were Pemphredo, Enyo and Deino, and they personified old age. They had gray hair from birth, with one tooth and one eye between them. Perseus stole their eye to make them inform him where the Gorgon lived.

GYES or GYGES (*Gyes*):   In mythology one of the Hecatoncheires.

HADES (*Haides*):   A god also known as Plouton or Pluton (meaning "rich," since all metals are found underground). He was brother of Zeus and god of the underworld, ruling over the dead with his wife Persephone. Hades was regarded as a severe punisher of evil, although not himself evil (not like the Christian devil). The underworld was thought of as being underground. The underworld was the realm of Hades, but was not *called* Hades (the term is often incorrectly used today). See also chapter 10, afterlife.

HARPIES or HARPIAE (*Harpyiai*, snatchers): Originally wind spirits, they appeared in Homer carrying people off to their deaths. In later mythology they were winged monsters who snatched away food or people and were generally blamed if something could not be found. They were represented as birds with the faces of women and were regarded as daughters of Thaumas and Electra. Their names were Aello (storm-wind), Ocypete (swift-flying), Celaeno (dark) and Podarge (swift-footed).

HARPOCRATES (Horus the child):   The name generally used by the Greeks for the Egyptian god Horus. He was the son of Isis and Osiris. Horus was identified with Apollo by Herodotus, but others identified him with Heracles and Eros. His cult was closely connected with the worship of Isis, and he became particularly popular during the Hellenistic period. In Egyptian myth he was a heroic figure who avenged his father Osiris, who had been killed and dismembered by the evil god Seth and then restored to life by Isis.

HEBE (*Hebe*):   A goddess who was the personification of youth. Her cult was not important, although she was sometimes worshiped in association with other deities, such as Heracles and Aphrodite. In mythology she was a daughter of Zeus and Hera

and cupbearer (serving nectar) to the gods. In some legends she was the wife of Heracles after he became a god.

HECATE (*Hekate*):   An ancient goddess of the underworld, later often identified with Artemis and sometimes confused with Selene. Hecate was generally regarded as an attendant of Persephone, and associated with ghosts, demons, sorcery and black magic. At night she sent demons and ghosts into the world and wandered with the souls of the dead. She was worshiped at crossroads and road junctions, where she was represented as a statue with three heads or three bodies. Dishes of food were left for her as a purificatory ritual at the end of each month. The animal usually sacrificed to her was a dog. Hecate had several epithets and was occasionally regarded as a goddess of women and nurturer of children, performing similar functions to Artemis. She was thought by some to provide her adherents with a variety of blessings, such as success in law courts, athletics and war. In mythology she was a daughter of the Titans Perses and Asterie, although other legends give different genealogies.

HECATONCHEIRES (*Hekatoukheires*):   Three monsters each with 100 hands and 50 heads, the offspring of Uranus and Gaia. They were called Briareus, Cottus and Gyes. See also BRIAREUS.

HECTOR (*Hektor*):   A hero who had a cult in several places, including Thebes, where his bones were supposed to have been buried by the Thebans after removing them from Troy in response to an oracle. In mythology Hector was the eldest son of King Priam and Hecuba, and bravest of the Trojan heroes during the siege of Troy. He was husband of Andromache and father of Astyanax. He led the Trojans in battle and fought Ajax. In revenge for killing Patroclus, Hector was killed by Achilles and his body dragged around the walls of Troy and back to the Greek ships. Priam begged for the return of his body, and the funeral of Hector is the closing episode of Homer's *Iliad*.

HECUBA (*Hekabe*):   The chief wife of King Priam of Troy and mother of 19 of his children, including Hector, Paris, Cassandra and Polyxena. Hecuba has only a background role in Homer's *Iliad*, as the queen who survives the fall of Troy but loses her husband and most of her children. She was developed as a character in later Greek tragedies.

HELEN (*Helene*): A goddess associated with birds and trees, and probably originally a goddess of vegetation and fertility. She was regarded as daughter of Zeus and Leda. She was worshiped as an important deity at Sparta, with her twin brothers the Dioscuri, and she was worshiped elsewhere in Greece. She is better known as Helen of Troy, wife of Menelaus, whose abduction by Paris triggered the Trojan War. It seems likely that Helen was originally a goddess, but her cult dwindled, and in many legends she came to be regarded as a mortal. In mythology, she has a key role in Homer's *Iliad*, and in the *Odyssey* she is reconciled with her husband Menelaus. Other legends recount her great beauty, her abduction by Theseus and her subsequent rescue by her brothers. See also THESEUS.

HELENUS (*Helenos*): In mythology a warrior and prophet, the son of King Priam of Troy. In Homer's *Iliad*, he was wounded by Menelaus. He was captured by Odysseus and prophesied the fall of Troy if Philoctetes was brought to Troy with his bow. After Troy fell he was given as a captive to Neoptolemus, along with Andromache who eventually became the wife of Helenus.

HELIOS (*Helios*): The sun god, who was particularly worshiped in Rhodes where a festival (Halieia) was held in his honor. Evidence of his worship elsewhere in Greece is sparse. He was sometimes identified with Apollo and was often invoked as a witness in oaths because he was in the sky all day, where he saw and heard everything. In mythology Helios was son of the Titans Hyperion and Thea, brother of Selene and Eos and father of Aeëtes, Circe, Pasiphae and Phaethon. Homer occasionally called him Hyperion, a practice adopted by other poets. Helios was generally regarded as a charioteer driving across the sky from east to west each day

and floating back on the ocean from west to east at night in a golden cup. The Colossus of Rhodes (one of the Seven Wonders of the World) was a gigantic statue of Helios.

HEPHAESTUS (*Hephaistos*): God of fire, particularly the smithy fire, and also of smiths and of crafts, especially those using fire. He was associated with volcanoes and may originally have been a volcanic deity from Asia Minor. In mythology he was the son of Zeus and Hera, and one of the Olympians. However, because he was born lame, he was cast out of Olympus and became a smith on Lemnos. He was a superb craftsman and subsequently made various items for the gods. He was generally regarded as the husband of Aphrodite, but in some legends he has other wives instead. His cult was mainly confined to industrialized areas of Greece (fig. 8.9) and was particularly prominent in Athens. The festival Chalceia was celebrated on the 30th day of the month Pyanopsion in honor of Hephaestus and Athena (in her role of mistress of technology).

HERA (*Hera*): Wife of Zeus and queen of the Greek gods (fig. 8.10). Hera was a goddess of marriage and of the life (particularly sexual) of married women, rather than of motherhood. She was never invoked or portrayed as a mother, although she was sometimes connected with the birth and nurture of children. Occasionally Hera was worshiped as patron deity of particular cities and identified with the goddess Eileithyia (her daughter). In mythology she was one of the Olympians. She was the daughter of Cronus and Rhea, making her the sister and also wife of Zeus, by whom she had the children Hephaestus, Ares, Hebe and Eileithyia. She often had the title Argeia (of Argos), and Argos may have been her earliest place of worship, although she was worshiped over much of Greece and beyond, both in partnership with Zeus and on her own (fig. 8.11).

Sacrifices to Hera by the Attic deme Erchia were undertaken on the 27th day of the month Gamelion, and to Hera Thelchinia by the same deme on the 20th day of the month Metageitnion. At Athens a festival (Theogamia or the Gamelia) in

Fig. 8.9   Temple of Hephaestus and Athena (the Hephaesteum, also referred to as the Theseum), the most complete example of a Doric temple. It was built in 449 BC.

the month Gamelion celebrated the sacred marriage between Hera and Zeus. At Argos the Heraea was a festival held every fourth year in honor of Hera, and on Mount Cithaeron the festival of Daidala was celebrated every 59 years.

HERACLES (*Herakles*):   The most popular and most widely worshiped of Greek heroes, who was occasionally worshiped as a god (fig. 8.12). Heracles was at times identified with non-Greek gods. He was famous for courage, strength, endurance, compassion and good nature, but also for gluttony and lust. He had many epithets and was commonly invoked under the epithet Alexikakos (averter of evil). His other epithets include Misogunus (woman-hater) and Soter (savior). In Athens the fourth day of every month was celebrated as the birthday of Heracles.

Heracles was the son of Zeus and Alcmene, a descendant of Perseus and of Danaus, and husband of Megara (daughter of Creon) and later of Deianira. There were many legends concerning him, but the most important were those concerning the "Twelve Labors of Heracles." These were tasks imposed upon Heracles by King Eurystheus of Argos to expiate Heracles' guilt after he had killed his own wife and children in a fit of madness caused by Hera. The 12 labors were:

Nemean Lion: This monster was sent by Hera to plague Nemea. It was the offspring of Echidna and of Typhon or Orthrus. The lion's skin was invulnerable, so Heracles choked the lion to death (fig. 4.4) and skinned it using the beast's claws (the only thing that would pierce its hide). Heracles wore the lion's skin as clothing, and it was one of the symbols used in representations of Heracles (fig. 8.12).

Lernaean Hydra: This was another monstrous offspring of Echidna and Typhon—a poisonous snake with many heads. When one head was cut

Fig. 8.10   Silver drachm of the head of the goddess Hera.

off, another grew in its place. It lived in the marshes of Lerna near Argos. Hera sent a monstrous crab to help it against Heracles, who summoned his comrade Iolaus for assistance. They fought the Hydra together, and as Heracles cut off its heads, Iolaus seared the stumps with burning brands until the Hydra was dead. Heracles killed the crab by crushing it underfoot, and it became the constellation Cancer. He dipped his arrows in the Hydra's poison blood, so any wound made by the arrows was incurable.

Erymanthian Boar: Heracles had to catch this boar alive. It lived on Mount Erymanthus in Arcadia. He caught it by driving it into a snowfield and then throwing a net over it. While searching for the boar Heracles was entertained by the centaur Pholus, who gave Heracles wine in his cave. Other centaurs were attracted by the smell of wine. When drunk, they attacked Heracles. Defending himself Heracles killed many of the centaurs with his poison arrows.

Cerynitian Hind: This hind was one of five that Artemis had seen grazing on Mount Lycaeus. They were bigger than bulls and had gilded horns. She captured four, but the fifth took refuge on Mount Ceryneia. Because the animal was sacred to Artemis, it was an act of impiety to kill it. After a chase lasting a year, which took Heracles to the

land of the Hyperboreans, he eventually managed to capture it alive.

Stymphalian Birds: These infested the woods around Lake Stymphalus in Arcadia, eating the fruit and the crops. In some versions they even killed and ate people and animals using their bronze-tipped feathers as arrows. Heracles killed some of them with his arrows and drove the rest away with a special rattle made by Hephaestus.

Augean Stables: Heracles was required, in a single day, to clean out the stables of King Augeas of Elis, who kept enormous herds of cattle. The stables had never been previously cleaned. Heracles performed this task by diverting the Alpheus River to flow through the stable yard.

Cretan Bull: Different legends record that this was the bull with which Pasiphae fell in love, or the one that carried Europa to Crete (contradicting the legend of Europa being carried to Crete by Zeus disguised as a bull). Heracles' task was to bring the bull to Eurystheus alive, after which it was released and wandered throughout Greece, finally settling near Marathon.

Horses of Diomedes: King Diomedes of Thrace owned four mares that fed on human flesh, and the task was to bring them to king Eurystheus alive. In one version Heracles was attacked by local inhabitants as he led the mares away. Heracles entrusted them to Abderus (son of Hermes), but he was killed by the local inhabitants. Heracles therefore killed King Diomedes and the local inhabitants and founded a city called Abdera in memory of Abderus. When he returned to Eurystheus the mares were released and were devoured by wild beasts on Mount Olympus. In another version Heracles killed Diomedes and fed him to the mares, whereupon they became tame.

Girdle of Queen Hippolyta: The girdle given by her father Ares was worn by Queen Hippolyta of the Amazons. Eurystheus' daughter Admete persuaded her father to give Heracles the task of capturing the girdle, which she wanted. Hippolyta was willing to give the girdle, but Hera (disguised as an Amazon) provoked a battle between the followers of Heracles and the Amazons, during which Heracles killed Hippolyta and captured the girdle. In another version Heracles captured Hippolyta's

Fig. 8.11 *Early or mid-5th-century-BC Doric temple at Paestum, the best preserved in the Greek world. It was dedicated to Hera (but traditionally called the Temple of Neptune). It measures 79.5 by 196.75 ft (24.26 by 59.98 m).*

second-in-command, Melanippe, and Hippolyta exchanged the girdle for her release.

Cattle of Geryon: These lived on the mythical island of Erytheia in the extreme west. By threatening to shoot Helios with his arrows, Heracles obtained a loan of Helios' golden cup. This allowed Heracles to cross the ocean and reach Erytheia, where he killed the dog Orthrus and the herdsman Eurytion with single blows of his club. Heracles then killed the three-headed monster Geryon with his arrows and returned to King Eurystheus with the cattle. On the journey back he set up two pillars of rock on either side of the Straits of Gibraltar (rock of Gibraltar and rock of Ceuta), which became known as the Pillars of Heracles, to commemorate his journey.

Golden Apples of the Hesperides: Eurystheus ordered Heracles to bring him the apples given by Gaia to Hera as a wedding present. They were kept in a garden in the extreme west, guarded by a dragon called Ladon and three Nymphs of the evening called the Hesperides. Heracles first had to discover where the apples were kept. Some river Nymphs said that only Nereus could identify the place. Heracles fought with Nereus, who constantly changed his shape, but he managed to tie him up

Fig. 8.12 *Silver tetradrachm of Alexander the Great depicting the head of the young Heracles dressed in his lion's skin. It acknowledges Heracles as the legendary ancestor of the Macedonian royal house and is thought to resemble Alexander the Great. The reverse (fig. 5.12) shows the enthroned Zeus.* Courtesy of Somerset County Museums Service.

RELIGION AND MYTHOLOGY

and force him to reveal the location of the garden of the Hesperides. On his way there Heracles fought a giant in Libya, narrowly escaped being sacrificed in Egypt and killed Emathion, son of Tithonus in Arabia. Heracles journeyed to the foot of the Caucasus Mountains using Helios' cup. While climbing the Caucasus he freed Prometheus who told him that only Atlas could collect the apples. Reaching the country of the Hyperboreans, Heracles found Atlas holding up the sky. Atlas agreed that Heracles should take his place while he fetched the apples. When Atlas returned with the apples he offered to take them to Eurystheus if Heracles continued to support the sky. Heracles pretended to agree, but asked Atlas to take the weight for a moment while he put a cushion on his shoulders. Heracles then took the apples and fled. In an alternative legend Heracles took the apples himself, without the help of Atlas.

Cerberus: The final labor was to bring back the dog Cerberus that guarded the entrance to the underworld. Heracles was initiated into the Eleusinian Mysteries and, helped by Hermes and Athena, he descended into the underworld by a path in Laconia. There he found Theseus and Pirithous, still alive but in chains. He freed Theseus but could not free Pirithous. Heracles met the spirit of Meleager who asked him to marry Deianira, left without support after Meleager's death. Heracles eventually encountered Hades, who let him take Cerberus if he could overcome the dog without weapons. Accomplishing this, he returned to Eurystheus who was so frightened by Cerberus that Heracles had to return the dog to the underworld.

Although in legend Heracles was killed by poison, he was generally regarded as immortal. In later times the legend of him successfully returning from the underworld may have reinforced the popularity of his cult. In art he was normally represented as bearded, with a bow and arrows, club and lion skin. See also DEIANIRA, GIANTS, LAOMEDON.

HERMAPHRODITUS or APHRODITUS

(*Hermaphroditos*): A bisexual deity worshiped in Attica and Cyprus. He was possibly a deity invented to explain certain marriage rites in which the different sexes exchanged clothing. Hermaphroditus was portrayed either as a beautiful young man with developed breasts or as Aphrodite with male genitals. In mythology Hermaphroditus was the son of Hermes and Aphrodite. He was loved by the Nymph Salmacis, who embraced him and prayed to the gods to make them one body. This the gods did, resulting in the bisexual Hermaphroditus.

HERMES (*Hermes, Hermeias*): Originally a phallic god represented by a stone set up by the roadside, Hermes came to be a god of fertility and good fortune, as well as of roads and boundaries. He was regarded as the herald of the gods, and as such conducted the souls of the dead to the underworld. Hermes was patron of merchants and thieves, as well as of oratory, literature and athletics. In art he was represented with wings on his sandals, a winged cap or broad-brimmed hat, and the staff of a herald (*kerykeion*; Latin, *caduceus*) on which two serpents were entwined in an approximate figure-of-eight shape. The god was also represented by herms (*hermae*), which were stone or bronze pillars, square or rectangular in section; on top was the bust of Hermes with a beard, and lower down were carved male genitals (fig. 8.13). Herms were set up in various parts of Greece, especially Athens, as boundary markers to avert evil. Later, heads of gods other than Hermes were carved on the tops of herms.

In Athens the fourth day of every month was celebrated as the birthday of Hermes, and sacrifices to him by the Attic deme Erchia took place on the 27th day of the month Boedromion, and on the fourth day of the month Thargelion. In mythology Hermes was the son of Zeus and Maia, and one of the Olympians. As a newborn baby he invented the lyre and stole Apollo's cattle. Hermes placated Apollo by presenting him with the lyre. Hermes became messenger of Zeus, and Zeus gave him his hat, winged sandals and herald's staff. Hermes generally appears in legends as a guide conveying people to the underworld or as a messenger giving mortals instructions from Zeus. Hermaphroditus, Abderus and Pan are cited as his offspring.

HEROES, HEROINES: Dead men and women (real or imaginary) who were worshiped as superhuman. Their cults were usually centered on their actual (or supposed) burial place, although sometimes a cult proliferated because more than one place claimed to possess a particular tomb. Exceptions included heroes such as Heracles, whose worship was widespread, often more like a god than a hero. Methods of worship and sacrifice to heroes and heroines were similar to that for gods of the underworld, so that dark-colored animals were usually chosen for sacrifice, and libations and sacrifices were performed in a pit or on a low altar. Sometimes gods and goddesses whose cults had dwindled came to be regarded as heroes and heroines instead. Not all heroes and heroines appear in myths, and any myths are often irrelevant to their cults. Sacrifices to "the heroines" by the Attic deme Erchia took place on the 19th day of the month Metageitnion, and on the 14th day of the month Pyanopsion.

HESPERIDES (*Hesperides*):   In mythology the Nymphs of the evening and daughters of Nyx and Erebus, although some legends say Atlas was their father. The Hesperides lived in the extreme west guarding a tree of golden apples for Hera, subsequently stolen by Heracles. The number of Hesperides varied from three to seven (between different legends), and their names include Aigle, Arethusa, Erytheia, Hespere and Hesperethusa. See also HERACLES.

HESPERUS (*Hesperos*):   In mythology the evening star.

HESTIA (*Hestia*):   Goddess of the hearth and the household fire. The hearth was the symbol of home and family, and the prytaneion in many cities had a public hearth dedicated to Hestia, with a fire kept constantly burning. If a city founded a colony, fire was taken from the public hearth to the colony. One of Hestia's titles was Boulaia (of the council), and many bouleuteria had public hearths. Sacrifices began with libations to Hestia, and she was generally mentioned first in prayers and oaths. Meals began with small offerings thrown into the domestic fire. Pigs and occasionally cows were sacrificed to Hestia. At five days old children were formally accepted into the family; as part of the ceremony

Fig. 8.13   Hermes, depicted on a typical herm, with a rectangular pillar, a bust of the god and male genitals.

someone carrying the child ran around the hearth. Temples dedicated to Hestia were characteristically circular in form. In mythology Hestia was a virgin daughter of Cronus and Rhea.

HIPPOLYTUS (*Hippolytos*): A hero whose cult was associated with Aphrodite. They had a shrine on the Acropolis at Athens. At Troezen (where he died), a ritual was carried out in his honor, including laments for him and offerings of hair from girls about to marry. In mythology he was the son of Theseus and the Amazon queen Hippolyta. After Hippolyta's death Theseus married Phaedra, but she fell in love with Hippolytus who rejected her advances. Phaedra told Theseus in a letter that she had been seduced by Hippolytus and then hanged herself. Believing the accusation, Theseus used one of three curses given him by Poseidon. As Hippolytus was driving his chariot, a monster from the sea terrified the horses, and Hippolytus was killed. Theseus later learned of his error from Artemis.

HORAE (*Horai*): Goddesses of the seasons, worshiped in Athens, Argos and Olympia. They were associated with many deities, such as Demeter, Pan, Apollo and Dionysus, but always as subordinate companions. In mythology they were the daughters of Zeus and Themis. Their numbers (generally three or four) and their names varied from region to region. In Attica their names appear to have been Karpo, Thallo and Auxo.

HORUS: An Egyptian god, usually known to the Greeks as Harpocrates (Horus the child). See HARPOCRATES.

HYACINTHUS (*Hyakinthos*): An ancient god worshiped at Amyclae near Sparta. In mythology he was represented as a beautiful youth of Amyclae, loved by both Apollo and Zephyrus. Apollo accidentally killed Hyacinthus with a discus that he had thrown; in some versions, Zephyrus blew the discus aside to strike Hyacinthus because he was jealous that Hyacinthus preferred Apollo. Where Hyacinthus' blood fell on the earth, a flower sprang up that was named after him. A festival at Sparta (Hyacinthia) was held in his honor.

HYGIEIA (*Hygieia*, health): Daughter of Asclepius. A goddess worshiped as part of the cult of Asclepius.

HYPERBOREANS (*Hyperboreioi*): A race of worshipers of Apollo living in a distant and inaccessible land to the north. Their name has been interpreted as "dwellers beyond the north wind" or "dwellers beyond the mountains." They were thought to live in perpetual sunshine, and Apollo spent the three winter months with them. Some offerings at the shrine of Apollo at Delos were allegedly sent by them. According to some legends those especially favored by the gods might spend their afterlife with the Hyperboreans.

HYPERION (*Hyperion*): In mythology one of the male Titans.

HYPNOS (*Hypnos*): God of sleep, worshiped in Troezen. In mythology he was the son of Nyx, brother of Thanatos and father of the three gods of dreams: Morpheus, Icelos (or Phobetor) and Phantasus. Hypnos was usually thought of as a winged youth who poured sleep-inducing liquid from a horn or touched the foreheads of the tired with a branch. He appears in few legends, but apparently fell in love with Endymion and made him sleep with open eyes.

IAPETUS (*Iapetos*): In mythology one of the male Titans. He was husband of Clymene (daughter of Oceanus) and father of Prometheus, Epimetheus and Atlas.

ICARUS (*Ikaros*): Son of Daedalus the craftsman who lived in the age of King Minos. Having constructed the labyrinth for Minos, Daedalus was forbidden to leave Crete, so he constructed wings from wax and feathers for himself and Icarus. They escaped from Crete, but Icarus disobeyed Daedalus and flew too near the sun. The wax melted, the wings disintegrated and Icarus fell to his death. Daedalus buried him on an island that became known as Icaria, and the surrounding sea was named the Icarian Sea.

IDOMENEUS (*Idomeneus*):   In mythology the leader of the Cretans who were allies of the Greeks in the siege of Troy. He was grandson of Minos and distinguished himself fighting at Troy, despite being older than most of the other warriors. A later legend (but possibly reflecting an earlier Cretan legend) recounted how Idomeneus made a vow to Poseidon to sacrifice the first living thing he encountered on reaching home in Crete, if he was saved from a shipwreck. He first encountered his son, and fulfilled or tried to fulfil his vow. Consequently a plague broke out and Idomeneus was forced into exile by the Cretans.

ICELOS or PHOBETOR (*Ikelos*):   One of three gods of dreams who were sons of Hypnos (god of sleep). Icelos was responsible for sending dreams of animals. See also MORPHEUS and PHANTASUS.

INO (*Ino*):   In mythology the daughter of Cadmus and wife of Athamas. She incurred the wrath of Hera, who drove Ino mad so that she threw herself into the sea, but then Ino was changed into a sea goddess. She was identified with the goddess Leucothea.

IO (*Io*):   A mythological Greek figure, sometimes identified with the Egyptian goddess Isis. In mythology Io was daughter of Inachus (legendary first king of Argos). She was a priestess of Hera and was loved by Zeus. To hide her from Hera's anger, Zeus turned Io into a heifer, but Hera was not deceived. She made a gadfly torment Io continually, so that she was not still long enough for Zeus to make love to her. Goaded by the gadfly, Io eventually wandered into Egypt, where Zeus restored her to human form. She bore him a son called Epaphus, the ancestor of Danaus and Aegyptus. According to one legend Io was worshiped as Isis in Egypt, and Epaphus was identified with the Egyptian god Apis.

ION (*Ion*):   The eponymous ancestor of the Ionian Greeks. He was the son of Creusa, but legends give his father as Apollo or Xuthus (son of Hellen). Ion appears in various legends, mostly concerned with the origin of the Ionians. These legends seem to be products of the ethnological theories of early narrators, rather than remnants of a folk tradition. In most Ion survives various adventures and settles in Athens. He divides the people into the four traditional Ionian tribes: Hopletes, Geleontes, Argadeis and Aegicoreis.

IPHIGENIA (*Iphigeneia*):   In mythology the daughter of Agamemnon and Clytemnestra, and sacrificed by Agamemnon. When contrary winds prevented the Greek fleet from sailing to besiege Troy, the seer Calchas revealed that Artemis required Iphigenia's sacrifice. She was therefore summoned, on the pretext that she was to marry Achilles. In some legends Iphigenia was sacrificed, but in others Artemis substituted a deer as the sacrifice and carried her off to the land of the Tauri (the Crimea); here, as priestess of Artemis, Iphigenia's duty was to prepare all strangers for sacrifice. Her brother Orestes was ordered by Apollo to bring to Attica the image of Artemis belonging to the Tauri, but he and his companion Pylades were captured by the Tauri and were sent to be sacrificed. Iphigenia learned who they were, and they all escaped to Attica with the image of Artemis. The image was set up at Halae (or in some versions, Brauron). Iphigenia was made priestess of Artemis there, with the title Tauropolos.

IRIS (*Iris*):   Goddess of the rainbow. She was apparently a purely mythological figure, with no cult. She was the daughter of Thaumas and Electra, and sister of the Harpies. Iris was a messenger of the gods (particularly Hera), and in some legends she was mother of Eros by Zephyrus.

ISIS (*Isis*):   An Egyptian goddess, wife of Osiris, and mother of Horus. By Hellenistic times she was an important deity in the Greek world. Isis was a mother goddess, and a goddess of fertility and marriage, represented as loving and compassionate to individual suppliants. She was identified with Demeter by Herodotus, and was regarded as representing the female productive force of nature, but in the Hellenistic period she was identified with Aphrodite. Along with Osiris she was considered to be a ruler of the underworld.

Worship of Isis was similar to a mystery religion, including initiation ceremonies, processions, music and dance designed to arouse religious fervor. Isis was usually portrayed in a long garment with a characteristic knot of drapery on her breast and an ancient Egyptian headdress. Her symbol was a cow. Isis was served by professional Egyptian priests. Her worship was established in Piraeus by the 4th century BC. The cult spread throughout the Greek world, initially regarded as the cult of Sarapis, even though it included Harpocrates, Isis, Sarapis and other Egyptian gods. The emphasis changed by Roman times, when it was generally known as the cult of Isis. A shrine or temple dedicated to Isis was called an *Iseion*. See also SARAPIS and Oriental and Mystery Religions (p. 357).

ITYS (*Itys*): In mythology the son of King Tereus of Thrace and Procne. He was killed and cooked by Procne and served to Tereus. See PHILOMELA.

IXION (*Ixion*): In mythology the king of the Lapiths and the first Greek to murder a kinsman. He married Dia (daughter of Deioneus or Eioneus), and Pirithous was their son. When Deioneus came to fetch the bride-price for Dia, Ixion murdered him. Ixion obtained ritual purification from Zeus for this act, but then attempted to seduce Hera, who complained to Zeus. Zeus formed a cloud called Nephele in the likeness of Hera, and the offspring of Ixion and Nephele was Centaurus (father of the Centaurs). For his crimes Zeus had Ixion fixed to a fiery wheel that constantly revolved in the underworld.

JASON (*Iason*): In mythology the son of King Aeson of Iolchus in Thessaly and leader of the Argonauts. While Jason was still a child Aeson's brother Pelias usurped the throne of Iolchus. Jason escaped and was reared by the centaur Chiron. Returning as an adult to claim his inheritance, Jason arrived in Iolchus with only one sandal, having lost the other during the journey. Pelias had been warned by an oracle that a stranger with only one sandal would kill him, and so he sent Jason to fetch the Golden Fleece. To accompany him, Jason assembled a group of heroes, the Argonauts. Later

legends added other heroes to the Argonauts, because families liked to claim descent from an Argonaut. Heracles was said to have joined the Argonauts after killing the Erymanthian boar, but then stayed at Chios to look after Hylas.

In their quest for the Golden Fleece, Jason and the Argonauts had many adventures, including a long stay on Lemnos, where the women, led by Queen Hypsipele, had murdered their husbands and were eager to welcome the Argonauts. Sailing on, they rescued Phoineus from the Harpies and, with the aid of Orpheus' music, stilled the Clashing Rocks that guarded the entrance to the Bosphorus. At Colchis King Aeëtes set Jason the task of sowing the dragon's teeth. With the help of the witch Medea (daughter of Aeëtes), he yoked a pair of fire-breathing bulls to plow a furrow and accomplished the task. By Medea's sorcery he managed to take the Golden Fleece from the dragon who guarded it and sailed for home with Medea and the fleece. The legends then concentrate on Medea. After Medea had tricked the daughters of Pelias into killing their father, Medea and Jason were driven from Iolchus and fled to Corinth, where Jason was later killed as he slept beneath his ship *Argo* and part of it fell on him. See also CREON, MEDEA.

JOCASTA, IOCASTE or EPICASTE (*Epikaste*): In mythology the wife of King Laius of Thebes and mother of Oedipus. She later unknowingly became the wife of Oedipus, and hanged herself when she discovered the truth of her incestuous marriage. In Homer's *Odyssey*, she is called Epicaste, and Odysseus sees her shade in the underworld. See also OEDIPUS.

KARPO (*Karpo*): In Attica one of three goddesses of the seasons (Horae).

KOUROTROPHOS (*Kourotrophos*, Nurse): A title given to several deities, including Aphrodite, Artemis and Hecate, but Kourotrophos was sometimes regarded as a separate deity. Some uncertain references in literature and inscriptions have been interpreted as the goddess Gaia, but others remain unclear. Sacrifices to the deity Kourotrophos by the Attic deme Erchia took place on the 12th day of the month Hekatombaion, 27th day of the month Gamelion and third day of the month Skirophorion.

LACHESIS (*Lakhesis*, apportioner):   One of the Fates who drew off the length of thread.

LAESTRYGONES (*Laistrygones*):   A race of cannibal giants. They appear in Homer's *Odyssey*, where they sink all but one of Odysseus' fleet of 12 ships. The land of the Laestrygones was said to have summer nights so short that shepherds taking out their flocks in the morning met those returning at sunset. This was probably the reminiscence of some traveler in the far north, but some tried to locate their land in Magna Graecia.

LAOCOÖN (*Laokoon*):   In mythology a Trojan prince, brother of Anchises and priest of Apollo (or priest of Poseidon). He tried to prevent the Trojans opening the city gates and bringing in the wooden horse, and so two great sea serpents sent by Apollo (or in some versions, Athena) killed him and his sons.

LAODAMIA (*Laodameia*):   A name shared by two mythological women. One was a daughter of Bellerophon, who had a son called Sarpedon by Zeus. She was killed while still young, shot by Artemis. The other was daughter of Acastus and wife of Protesilaus (the first Greek hero to be killed). She begged the gods to be allowed just three more hours with him alive. The request was granted, and at the end she killed herself because she could not bear to be parted from him.

LAOMEDON (*Laomedon*):   In mythology the king of Troy and father of King Priam and Tithonus. Laomedon was famous for his treachery. When he failed to pay Apollo and Poseidon for helping to build the walls of Troy, they sent a sea monster to eat his daughter Hesione, but she was rescued by Heracles. Laomedon then refused to give Heracles the promised horses, and so Heracles sacked Troy and killed all his sons except Priam.

LAPITHS (*Lapithai*):   In mythology a primitive tribe inhabiting the mountains of Thessaly. They were related to the centaurs by common descent from Ixion, who was king of the Lapiths and father of Centaurus.

LEDA (*Leda*):   The daughter of King Thestius of Aetolia, wife of King Tyndareus of Sparta and mother of Clytemnestra, Helen and the Dioscuri. Leda was loved by Zeus who took the form of a swan to mate with her (fig. 8.14). Legends vary as to which of her children were fathered by Zeus. See also NEMESIS.

LETO (*Leto*):   A goddess generally worshiped in connection with her children Apollo and Artemis, although several temples were dedicated to Leto. In mythology she was one of the Titans, a daughter of Coeus and Phoebe. She was loved by Zeus and gave birth to the twin gods Apollo and Artemis. A sacrifice to Leto by the Attic deme Erchia was undertaken on the fourth day of the month Thargelion.

LEUCASPIS (*Leukaspis*, the Deity of the White Shield):   A sacrifice to Leucaspis by the Attic deme Erchia took place on the 20th day of the month Mounichion. Nothing else is known about this deity.

LEUCIPPUS (*Leukippos*, literally "person who keeps white horses"):   The name of many different characters in Greek mythology, perhaps the most important being King Leucippus of Messenia. His daughters Hilaera and Phoebe were carried off by the Dioscuri. Their brothers, Idas and Lynceus, fought to rescue them and killed Castor, but Polydeuces was allowed to take Castor's place in the underworld on alternate days. See DIOSCURI.

LEUCOTHEA (*Leukothea*, probably meaning "white goddess," or less likely "runner on white foam"):   A goddess of the sea who was identified with Ino (daughter of Cadmus and wife of Athamas).

LOTOPHAGI (*Lotophagoi*, Lotus-eaters):   A fabulous people who lived on the lotus fruit, which induced forgetfulness. Anyone eating the lotus forgot about returning to their own country and remained

Fig. 8.14 A copy of a Roman mosaic at Palaipaphos, Cyprus, showing Leda and Zeus disguised as a swan.

in the land of the lotus-eaters. According to Herodotus they lived in what is now western Libya.

LYCURGUS (*Lykourgos*): In mythology Lycurgus attacked the young Dionysus, driving him and his nurses forward until Dionysus took refuge in the sea. Consequently Lycurgus was struck blind and died soon after. In some versions Lycurgus is king of the Edones in Thrace; for his crime he is driven mad, so that he kills his own son and is later eaten alive by wild horses.

MAIA (*Maia*): In mythology the daughter of Atlas and one of the Pleiades. She was also mother of Hermes.

MARSYAS (*Marsyas*): A satyr or Silenus who was associated with the Marsyas River, a tributary of the Maeander in Turkey, and was possibly a local deity. In mythology Marsyas was a flute player who challenged Apollo to a music contest. Apollo won and had Marsyas flayed alive for the presumption of challenging a god (fig. 8.15). The Maeander River sprang from his blood, or alternatively from the tears of the woodland gods and animals that mourned him.

MEDEA (*Medeia*): In mythology the daughter of Aeëtes (king of Colchis) and his wife Eidya, granddaughter of Helios, and niece of Circe. She was generally regarded as a witch, but some evidence suggests she was possibly once worshiped as a deity. Various legends recount how she helped Jason to win the Golden Fleece. She returned with him to Iolchus, and rejuvenated his father Aeson by boiling him with magic herbs. She persuaded the daughters of Pelias (Jason's uncle) to try to rejuvenate their father in the same way. However, in order to avenge the wrong Pelias had done to Jason's family, Medea ensured that the process killed him. Medea and Jason were then driven from Iolchus and fled to Corinth where they had two children. In the play *Medea* by Euripides, she murders her children in a jealous rage when hearing Jason is to leave her. Medea also appears in other legends. See also THESEUS, CREON.

MELEAGER (*Meleagros*): In mythology the son of Oeneus (king of Calydon) and his wife Althaea (in some versions, son of Ares and Althaea), brother of Deianira and husband of Atalanta. In Homer's *Iliad*, Meleager is presented as a hero of the past (dead before the start of the Trojan War) who killed the Calydonian boar, a monster sent to ravage Calydon after Oeneus failed to sacrifice to Artemis.

In another legend the Fates decreed that he would not die as long as a firebrand remained unburnt. His mother kept the firebrand safe, but after Meleager killed her brothers in a quarrel, she flung it on a fire and he died. See also ATALANTA, DEIANIRA, HERACLES.

MELPOMENE (*Melpomene*, the songstress): One of the Muses, thought in late Roman times to preside over tragedy.

MEMNON (*Memnon*): In mythology the son of Tithonus and Eos, king of the Ethiopians, and brother of King Emathion of Egypt. He fought with the Trojans at the siege of Troy, killed Antilochus and was later killed by Achilles. His body was carried away by Eos, and Zeus made him immortal. According to a legend from Thebes in Egypt, he survived the siege of Troy and ruled in Ethiopia for five generations. A colossal statue (one of two seated statues outside the temple of Amenophis III at Luxor) was thought to represent Memnon.

Fig. 8.15 Marsyas about to be flayed alive for daring to compete with Apollo in a music contest. His son Olympus begs Apollo (seated, far right) for mercy. A Roman mosaic from Paphos Nea, Cyprus.

RELIGION AND MYTHOLOGY

MENEDEIUS (*Menedeios*, the one who stands his ground):   A sacrifice to Menedeius was performed by the Attic deme Erchia on the 19th day of the month Thargelion. Nothing else is known about this deity.

MENELAUS (*Menelaos, Meneleos*):   A hero who was occasionally regarded as a god. He was worshiped at a shrine at Therapne, near Sparta. In mythology he was a son of Atreus and younger brother of Agamemnon. Menelaus was king of Sparta and the husband of Helen whose abduction caused the Trojan War. He has a prominent role in Homer's *Iliad*, where he agreed to settle the dispute by single combat with Paris. He was prevented from killing Paris by Aphrodite, and Athena then prompted Pandarus to wound Menelaus to provoke a continuation of the war. In Homer's *Odyssey* the adventures of Menelaus after the siege of Troy are described, with him eventually reaching his home, Sparta, safely with Helen.

MENTOR (*Mentor*):   A friend of Odysseus who was too old to take part in the siege of Troy and instead stayed in Ithaca to look after Odysseus' household. Athena took the form of Mentor when she accompanied Telemachus in the search for Odysseus, which gave rise to the use of the term "mentor" for a trusted guide or counselor.

MIDAS (*Midas*):   In mythology a king of Phrygia (not to be confused with the historical King Midas of Phrygia of the 8th–7th centuries BC). The mythical Midas featured in various legends and reputedly had wonderful rose gardens, where he entertained a Silenus who had been left behind after a drunken rout led by Dionysus. In gratitude Dionysus granted him a wish, and Midas asked that everything he touch turn to gold. On finding this also applied to food and drink, he asked to be rid of the gift. He was told to bathe in the Pactolus River, which thereafter had sands containing gold. On another occasion Midas had to judge a music contest between Apollo and Pan (in some versions, Marsyas). He decided against Apollo who therefore gave Midas the ears of an ass to denote his stupidity. Midas hid these ears under a headdress, and only his barber

knew about them, but he was sworn to secrecy. Unable to prevent himself from telling the secret, the barber dug a hole, whispered the secret into it and filled in the hole. Reeds grew over the hole, and whispered the secret as they moved in the wind.

MINOS (*Minos*):   The son of Zeus and Europa, and a king of Crete who became a judge of the dead in the underworld. The legends about him vaguely reflect the Cretan civilization that has (in modern times) been labeled "Minoan." His name, Minos, may have been a title or a dynastic name. In Homer's *Odyssey*, Minos is represented as a just ruler, whereas the Athenian legend of Theseus represents him as a villain. Minos was husband of Pasiphae and had many children, including Phaedra and Ariadne. See also DAEDALUS, NISUS, PASIPHAE and THESEUS.

MINOTAUR (*Minotauros*):   A monster on Crete, half-man and half-bull, and the offspring of Pasiphae and a bull. He lived in the labyrinth on Crete and was killed by Theseus. See also DAEDALUS, PASIPHAE, THESEUS.

MNEMOSYNE (*Mnemosyne*):   In mythology one of the female Titans. She was mother, by Zeus, of the Muses.

MORPHEUS (*Morpheus*):   One of three gods of dreams who were sons of Hypnos (god of sleep). Morpheus was responsible for sending dreams of human forms. See also ICELOS and PHANTASUS.

MUSES (*Mousai*):   Deities of poetry, literature, music and dance, who later presided over philosophy, astronomy and all intellectual pursuits. They were worshiped throughout the Greek world. There were generally considered to be nine Muses, but their individual spheres of influence were not distinguished until the late Roman period, when each one presided over one of the arts or sciences: Calliope (heroic epic), Clio (history), Euterpe (flutes, music), Terpsichore (lyric poetry, dancing), Erato (hymns), Melpomene (tragedy), Thalia (comedy), Polhymnia (mime) and Urania (astronomy). These attributed spheres of influence vary among ancient authors, and some other names for Muses are known. In mythology the Muses were daughters of Zeus and Mnemosyne. They were born at the foot of Mount Olympus, and Mount Helicon was sacred to them.

NARCISSUS (*Narkissos*): In mythology the son of Cephissus (a river in Boeotia) and the Nymph Liriope. He was a beautiful youth who fell in love with his own reflection in a pool. He rejected Echo, who wasted away with grief until only her voice was left. Narcissus also wasted away and was changed into a flower. Pausanias visited the pool on Mount Helicon where these events allegedly took place. He related a local version of the legend in which Narcissus was in love with his twin sister, who died. He looked at his own reflection to be reminded of her.

NAUSICAA (*Nausikaa*): In mythology the daughter of Alcinous, king of Phaeacia. Nausicaa appeared in Homer's *Odyssey*, where she was told by Athena in a dream to go to the mouth of the river with her handmaids to do the family washing. Afterward they played ball, and Odysseus (who had been shipwrecked) found them. The handmaids fled, but Nausicaa gave Odysseus food, drink and clothing, and showed him the way to her father's city, from where he continued his homeward journey.

NELEUS (*Neleus*): A legendary king of Pylos who was worshiped as a hero in association with Codrus and the obscure deity Basile. In mythology Neleus was son of Poseidon and Tyro (daughter of Salmoneus). Neleus married Chloris (daughter of Amphion of Orchomenus), who bore him several sons including Nestor. Because Neleus would not purify Heracles after killing Iphitus, Heracles attacked Pylos and killed all sons of Neleus except Nestor.

NEMESIS (*Nemesis*): A goddess who personified retribution or righteous indignation—usually retribution by the gods for the presumption or insolence (hubris) of mortals. Her main cult was centered around her shrine at Rhamnus. A cult of Nemesis Adrasteia (Unescapable Nemesis) in Boeotia identified her with the Phrygian goddess

Ida. In mythology Nemesis assumed a variety of shapes, especially fish, to avoid the attentions of Zeus. In one legend she finally changed into a goose, whereupon Zeus mated with her in the form of a swan (rather than with Leda, as in other legends). She subsequently laid the egg that was found by a shepherd and given to Leda to hatch.

NEOPTOLEMUS or PYRRHUS (*Neoptolemos*): In mythology the son of Achilles and Deidamia. After Achilles died in the siege of Troy, the Greeks sent for Neoptolemus, as his presence was necessary for the capture of the city. Neoptolemus was one of the Greeks who entered Troy in the wooden horse. After the war he returned home and married Hermione, daughter of Menelaus. In later legends Neoptolemus incurred the anger of the gods by killing Priam at the altar of Zeus Herkeios. He was consequently prevented from returning home and was killed.

NEREIDS (*Nereides*): The sea Nymphs, daughters of the sea god Nereus and the Oceanid Doris. There were said to be 50 or 100 Nereids, the most famous being Amphitrite (wife of Poseidon) and Thetis (mother of Achilles).

NEREUS (*Nereus*): An ancient sea god. Only slight evidence exists for his worship as a deity. In mythology he was the son of Pontus and father of the Nereids (by the Oceanid Doris). He lived in the depths of the sea with the Nereids. He was thought to have great wisdom and the power of prophecy, and could transform himself into various shapes. In a contest with Heracles he transformed himself into many shapes, including fire and water.

NESSUS (*Nessos*): A centaur who assaulted Deianira and was killed by Heracles. His blood-soaked shirt later caused the death of Heracles. See DEIANIRA.

NESTOR (*Nestor*): In mythology the son of King Neleus of Pylos and Chloris. Nestor lived to a great age. In Homer's *Iliad* he is represented as an elder statesman, full of often ineffectual advice and having outlived two generations. In Homer's *Odyssey* he had returned safely to Pylos from Troy and entertained Odysseus' son Telemachus. Nestor was father of Antilochus.

NIKE (*Nike*):   Goddess and personification of victory, both in war and in athletic contests. In mythology she was daughter of the Titan Pallas and of Styx. She is frequently portrayed in vase paintings with wings and holding a victory wreath (fig. 9.7). The sculptor Archermus (6th century BC) is said to have been the first to represent her with wings, which became a common image.

NIOBE (*Niobe*):   In mythology the daughter of Tantalus and wife of Amphion. She had six or seven children and boasted of her superiority to the goddess Leto who had only two. Leto's children (Apollo and Artemis) then killed all Niobe's children with their arrows. Niobe wept for them until she turned into a pillar of stone, which was identified by local inhabitants as a column of stone on Mount Sipylus in Lydia. It was still visited by travelers in the Roman period.

NISUS (*Nisos*):   In mythology the son of Pandion and king of Megara. The safety of the city of Megara depended on a lock of the red hair of Nisus. Megara was besieged by King Minos, but was safe as long as the lock of red hair remained unharmed among Nisus' white hair. For the love of Minos his daughter Scylla cut it off, which killed Nisus. Megara fell to King Minos, who was horrified at Scylla's deed and drowned her (in some versions she drowned herself). She was turned into a seabird and was forever pursued by her father Nisus, who had been changed into a sea eagle.

NYMPHS (*Nymphai*):   Female spirits of nature, often considered personifications of natural features, such as trees, springs, rivers and even regions and cities. Nymph (*Nymphe*) meant "young unmarried woman," so Nymphs were usually regarded as young and beautiful, with a taste for dancing and music. They had the power of inspiring mortals with prophetic powers and poetry, and were mostly benevolent to mortals. As spirits of natural features there were numerous types and classifications of Nymphs, such as Hamadryades (tree Nymphs), Orestiads (mountain Nymphs), Alseides, Napaeae and Dryades (categories of Nymphs of forests and groves), Leimoniads (meadow Nymphs) and various water Nymphs such as Hydriads, Naiads, Potameids and Creneids. The cult of the Nymphs was widespread throughout Greece, and they were often worshiped in caves. Sacrifices to the Nymphs by the Attic deme Erchia took place on the 27th day of the month Boedromion, and on the eighth day of the month Gamelion.

NYX (*Nyx*):   A goddess who personified night. She was regarded more as a mythological figure than a cult deity, but a dedication to her is known from the temple of Demeter at Pergamum.

OCEANUS (*Okeanos*):   A personification of the ocean, represented in Homer as a river that encircled the earth and from which all other rivers originated. In mythology he was a Titan, the son of Uranus and Gaia. He was married to Tethys. His sons were the river gods and his daughters the Oceanids.

OCYPETE (*Okypete*, swift flying):   One of the Harpies who were daughters of Thaumas and Electra.

ODYSSEUS (*Odysseus*):   A hero and legendary king of Ithaca. He was occasionally worshiped in parts of Greece, although apparently not in Ithaca. In mythology he was the son and successor of King Laertes of Ithaca, husband of Penelope and father of Telemachus. He played a prominent role in Homer's *Iliad*, where he fought on the side of the Greeks, took part in the embassy to Achilles (which attempted to reconcile Achilles with Agamemnon) and carried out the night raid on the Trojan camp with Diomedes.

Homer's *Odyssey* is devoted to the adventures of Odysseus returning home to Ithaca after the Trojan War. On his eventual return Odysseus killed the suitors of Penelope, who had thought him dead, and founded a shrine to appease the god Poseidon, his last enemy. Odysseus was unwittingly killed by

Telegonus, his son by Circe, who had traveled to Ithaca to find his father. Apart from his roles in the Homeric poems, Odysseus appears as a character in works by several Greek playwrights. See also CALYPSO, CHARYBDIS, CIRCE, CYCLOPES, DIOMEDES, ELPENOR, EUMAEUS, HELENUS, JOCASTA, LAESTRYGONES, NAUSICAA, POLYPHEMUS.

OEDIPUS (*Oidipous*, swollen-footed): A hero who had various cults. In mythology he was the son of King Laius of Thebes. Having taken refuge with Pelops, Laius carried off Pelops' son Chrysippus. As punishment Apollo warned Laius that if he had a son, he would be killed by that son. Laius ignored the warning, and the unwanted newborn baby Oedipus was left to die with a spike through his feet. The baby was taken by a shepherd to King Polybus of Corinth and his queen Merope, who were childless. They reared Oedipus as their own son (his name derived from his deformed feet). As an adult Oedipus questioned the Delphic Oracle about his true parents, but was told only that he would kill his father and marry his mother. Deciding never to return to Corinth, he went toward Thebes. Meeting, but not recognizing, his father Laius, they quarreled and Oedipus killed him. At Thebes he destroyed the Sphinx that had been terrorizing the city and won the throne of Thebes and Jocasta in marriage, not knowing that she was his mother. They had two sons, Eteocles and Polynices, and two daughters, Antigone and Ismene. When it was discovered what had happened, Jocasta hanged herself and Oedipus blinded himself (or was blinded). No longer able to be king, he went into exile.

ORESTES (*Orestes*): In mythology the son of Agamemnon and Clytemnestra, and brother of Iphigenia and Electra. When Agamemnon returned from the siege of Troy with Cassandra as his concubine, Aegisthus killed them both. When Orestes reached manhood, he killed Clytemnestra and her lover Aegisthus in revenge for Agamemnon's death. See also ELECTRA and IPHIGENIA.

ORPHEUS (*Orpheus*): A mythical poet and hero from Thrace who was the founder of Orphism, a mystery religion connected with the mysteries of the god Dionysus. According to legend Orpheus was a pre-Homeric Greek poet and marvelous lyre player. He went down to the underworld to recover his wife Eurydice. On leaving the underworld with Eurydice following, he disobeyed the condition imposed by Hades that he should not look back, and so Eurydice was lost forever. A different myth relates how he was torn to pieces, either by the women of Thrace or by Maenads. His mythology is complex and varied, but the common theme is his return after death. There are several variations in the legend, which was often used as a theme by poets and artists. See also Orphic Mysteries, p. 358.

OSIRIS: An Egyptian god, the husband of Isis and father of Horus. Osiris represented male fertility in nature and was identified with Dionysus. His worship was closely connected with the cult of Isis. According to Egyptian myth Osiris was killed and dismembered by the evil god Seth, but was restored to life by Isis and was avenged by Horus. Along with Isis he was considered a ruler of the underworld. A conflation of Osiris and the sacred bull Apis was worshiped as Sarapis.

PAN (*Pan*): A god of flocks, herds and fertility, and patron of shepherds and herdsmen. He originated in Arcadia where goats were more abundant than cattle. Pan was usually depicted with a human body with goats' legs, ears and horns. He was believed capable of striking terror ("panic") among people, like that in stampeding animals. He apparently inhabited mountains, caves and deserted places, and was musical (fig. 8.16). His cult spread from Arcadia in the 5th century BC, and he was sometimes worshiped in the plural (Panes). In mythology Pan was the son of Hermes, and most legends relate his amorous affairs with Nymphs. The best known story is that of the Nymph Syrinx in Arcadia, who was loved by Pan. To escape him she begged Gaia (in some versions, river Nymphs) to change her into a bed of reeds; out of these reeds Pan made a set of pipes known as Pan pipes (*syrinx*).

PANDARUS (*Pandaros*): In mythology a Trojan, son of Lycaon. In Homer's *Iliad*, Pandarus was an

Fig. 8.16 Votive marble relief of the Cave of Pan, portraying various gods including Pan and the Nymphs. This cave has an altar in the foreground and so represents a sanctuary.

archer urged by Athena to break the truce between the Greeks and Trojans by shooting an arrow and wounding Menelaus. He was later killed by Diomedes.

PANDORA (*Pandora*): In mythology the first woman. She was created by Zeus to punish man after Prometheus had created and helped mankind. She was made by Hephaestus from clay and was brought to life by Athena. Pandora was endowed with every charm by the other gods, hence her name meaning "all gifts." She was sent by Zeus with a sealed storage jar to Prometheus' brother Epimetheus, who married her. When she opened the jar all the evils and diseases of humankind flew out and spread through the world, leaving only hope inside the jar as consolation. In post-Classical mythology the jar became a box, possibly because of confusion with another story.

PARIS or ALEXANDER (*Paris, Alexandros*): In mythology the son of King Priam and Hecuba. Paris is a prominent character in Homer's *Iliad*, where he is held responsible for the Trojan War because he abducted Helen. Incidents concerning Paris (related in other legends) include the judgment of Paris, where he was forced to judge who was the most beautiful of the goddesses Hera,

Athena and Aphrodite. Bribed by the promise of Helen for himself, he chose Aphrodite and thus insulted Hera and Athena. (In another version, he chose Helen as the most beautiful woman in the world, in a contest between her and these three goddesses.) Paris killed Achilles and was himself fatally wounded by an arrow fired by Philoctetes. Oenone, a Nymph who lived on Mount Ida and whom Paris had deserted in favor of Helen, refused to help him. Paris died, and Oenone was stricken with remorse and killed herself. In other legends Paris killed Philoctetes.

PARTHENOPE (*Parthenope*): In mythology one of the Sirens whose body was said to have been washed ashore on the site of Neapolis (modern Naples), a Greek colony in Italy.

PASIPHAE (*Pasiphae*): The daughter of Helios, wife of King Minos of Crete, and mother of Ariadne and Phaedra. To resolve who should be king of Crete, Minos appealed to Poseidon to send him a victim to sacrifice. He sent him a bull from the sea, thus confirming Minos' right to be king. However, Minos refused to sacrifice the bull to Poseidon as promised, and so Poseidon made Pasiphae fall in love with the bull. With the help of Daedalus, who made a hollow wooden cow for her to get inside, Pasiphae mated with the bull and gave birth to the Minotaur, a monster that was part bull and part man.

PATROCLUS (*Patroklos*): In mythology the son of Menoetius. In Homer's *Iliad*, he is the attendant and favorite companion of Achilles. Offended by Agamemnon, Achilles retired from the siege of Troy, taking with him his men and Patroclus, after which the fighting went against the Greeks. Patroclus then obtained permission from Achilles to borrow his armor and help the Greeks. Mistaken for Achilles, Patroclus was killed by Hector. Maddened by grief Achilles reclaimed his body and, with new armor forged by Hephaestus, fought and killed Hector in revenge.

PEGASUS (*Pegasos*): A winged horse (fig. 8.17) that was born from the blood of Medusa when she was killed by Perseus. Bellerephon captured Pegasus with a magic bridle given by Athena, while Pegasus was drinking from the spring of Pirene in Corinth. Pegasus was reputed to have created many famous springs, including Hippocrene on Mount Helicon, by stamping his hoof.

PELEUS (*Peleus*):   In mythology the son of Aeacus. Peleus appears in several legends. When he and his brother Telamon killed their half-brother Phocus, Aeacus expelled them. Peleus went to Phthia in Thessaly where he was given the king's daughter, Antigone (not the Antigone of the Oedipus legend), in marriage and a share of the kingdom. However, he accidentally killed someone during the Calydonian boar hunt and was again banished. Acastus (son of Pelias) had a wife called Astydameia who fell in love with Peleus, but he rejected her. She therefore sent a message to Antigone that Peleus was about to marry another woman, and so Antigone hanged herself. Astydameia also told Acastus that Peleus had made advances to her, and so Acastus left Peleus unarmed on Mount Pelion, so that he could be attacked by the centaurs. However, the centaur Chiron gave Peleus his sword, and Peleus then captured Iolchus, cut Astydameia to pieces and marched his army through the pieces as an act of ritual purification.

Peleus was given the goddess Thetis as wife. Although Zeus was in love with her, she was fated to bear a son more powerful than his father, so Zeus thought it prudent to marry her to a mortal. The child she bore was Achilles, and Peleus took him to Chiron to be reared. Many incidents in the legends about Peleus became favorite subjects for artistic portrayal.

PELOPS (*Pelops*):   A hero worshiped at Olympia (fig. 8.18). In mythology he was the son of Tantalus, king of Sipylus in Lydia. He was founder of the Pelopid family after whom the Peloponnesus (Isle of Pelops) was named. In childhood Pelops was killed, cooked and served to the gods by Tantalus, to discover if they could distinguish human flesh from animal meat. Pelops was brought back to life by the gods when they found out, and his shoulder (inadvertently eaten by Demeter) was replaced by

one of ivory. As a youth Pelops was loved by Poseidon who gave him a wonderful team of horses and great driving skill. Reaching manhood he won the hand of Hippodamia in a chariot race against her father Oenomaus by bribing Myrtilus (the charioteer of Oenomaus) to sabotage his chariot. Instead of paying Myrtilus, he killed him. Although Pelops prospered and had six sons by Hippodamia, his descendants were cursed.

PENELOPE (*Penelope*):   In mythology the daughter of Icarius of Sparta (brother of Tyndareus) and wife of Odysseus. In Homer's *Odyssey* Penelope, beset by numerous suitors, faithfully waited 20 years for Odysseus to return from the siege of Troy. She stalled them by saying she must first weave a shroud for Odysseus' father Laertes, but unraveled her work each night. A maid betrayed her, and so Penelope was forced to complete it. She then

Fig. 8.17   Pegasus shown on the obverse of a Corinthian silver stater of c. 360 BC from Leucas (a colony of Corinth). The obverse of all Corinthian coins carries Pegasus (and Athena on the reverse) because Pegasus was captured by Bellerophon with the aid of a magic bridle given to him by Athena.   Courtesy of Somerset County Museums Service.

RELIGION AND MYTHOLOGY

Fig. 8.18   Excavations taking place in the sanctuary of Pelops at Olympia. Pausanias described this sanctuary in the 2nd century AD, when it consisted of a grove surrounded by a stone wall and one entrance. Inside was an altar of Pelops and several statues.

promised to marry the suitor who could bend the bow of Odysseus. At this point Odysseus returned in disguise and used the bow against the other suitors. He then revealed his identity, and Penelope welcomed him back.

PENTHEUS (*Pentheus*):   The son of Echion and Agave (daughter of Cadmus). Pentheus doubted the divinity of the god Dionysus. He was subsequently torn to pieces by a group of Maenads, including his mother who, in her frenzy, did not recognize him.

PERSEPHONE, PHERSEPHONE or KORE (*Persephone, Phersephone, Persephassa, Persephatta, Kore*):   A goddess of grain seed. In religious obser-

vance she was usually known as Kore, but as Persephone in mythology and modern times. The daughter of Demeter, she was seldom worshiped other than in association with Demeter, with whom she was closely concerned in the Eleusinian Mysteries. In mythology Persephone was the daughter of Zeus and Demeter. She was snatched by Hades to be his wife and queen of the underworld. Demeter searched, lamenting, for her daughter, and finally Zeus pitied her. However, Persephone could not be completely released from the underworld because she had eaten there (some pomegranate seeds). It was arranged that she should spend eight (in some versions, six) months in the world and the rest of the year with Hades. This myth was understood as an allegory of grain seed, which must descend into the earth and disappear in order to germinate and reappear as grain crops. At Athens a women's festival (Stenia) was held in honor of Persephone and Demeter, but was overshadowed by the festival in honor of Demeter (Thesmophoria) on the 11th–13th days of the month Pyanopsion.

PERSEUS (*Perseus*): In mythology a hero who was son of Zeus and Danae. After Danae and Perseus arrived at Seriphos, Polydectes (king of the island) fell in love with Danae. To remove Perseus, Polydectes persuaded him to bring back the head of Medusa. After many adventures, aided by various gods and goddesses, Perseus managed to kill Medusa. He returned to Seriphos just in time to save Danae from the violence of Polydectes. He turned Polydectes to stone with Medusa's head and left his brother Dictys as king. Perseus then returned to his native Argos with Danae in search of his grandfather Acrisius, but found that he had gone to Larissa; following him there, Perseus accidentally killed Acrisius by striking him with a discus thrown during funeral games. He thus fulfilled the prophecy that he was destined to kill Acrisius. Perseus refused to rule his grandfather's kingdom, to which he was heir, but instead became king of Tiryns and founder of the dynasty of Perseidae. In other versions he went to Asia, where his son Perses became ruler of the Persians. See also GRAIAE, DANAE.

PHAEDRA (*Phaidra*): In mythology the daughter of King Minos of Crete and Pasiphae, sister of Ariadne, and second wife of King Theseus of Athens. Rejected by Hippolytus, son of Theseus by Hippolyta, she brought about his death and killed herself. See also HIPPOLYTUS.

PHAETHON (*Phaethon*): In mythology the son of Helios and the heroine Clymene. Learning that his father was the sun, he set off to find him in the East. Arriving at the palace of Helios, Phaethon asked for a favor. Helios said he would grant him anything he wished, and Phaeton asked to drive the chariot of the sun for a day. However, he could not control the horses, and there was a danger that he would set the world on fire. Zeus therefore killed him with a thunderbolt.

PHANTASUS (*Phantasos*): One of three gods of dreams who were sons of Hypnos (god of sleep). Phantasus was responsible for sending dreams of inanimate objects. See also ICELOS and MORPHEUS.

PHILOCTETES (*Philoktetes*): A hero with centers of worship in Magna Graecia. In mythology he was a Greek leader in the Trojan War who was left behind on Lemnos suffering from a snake bite. Odysseus discovered that Troy would not fall unless Philoctetes was present, so he went with Diomedes to fetch him. In some versions Philoctetes was killed by Paris, in others he killed Paris. Because he had hero cults in Magna Graecia, it was also said that he survived the fall of Troy, wandered to Magna Graecia and founded cities there. See also HELENUS.

PHILOMELA (*Philomela*): In mythology a daughter of King Pandion of Athens who had another daughter, Procne (married to King Tereus of Thrace). Pretending Procne was dead, Tereus persuaded Pandion to send Philomela to him. Tereus raped her, cut out her tongue and hid her, to prevent her revealing what had happened. She managed to send a message to her sister, woven on tapestry. Procne took revenge by killing and cooking their son Itys and serving him up to Tereus. When Tereus realized what had happened, he pursued the two sisters, but the gods changed Procne into a nightingale, Philomela into a swallow and Tereus into a hoopoe.

PHOEBE (*Phoibe*, bright one): In mythology one of the Titans, daughter of Uranus and Gaia, wife of Coeus, and mother of Leto. She was thus grandmother of Apollo and Artemis. Her name later came to be used for the moon (Selene). Another Phoebe was daughter of King Leucippus who was carried off with Hilaera by the Dioscuri. See also DIOSCURI.

PHOENIX (*Phoinix*): Two mythological characters had this name. One was the son of King Agenor of Tyre and the brother of Cadmus and Europa. He was sent to look for Europa, but did not return. Instead he founded the people called Phoenicians. The other Phoenix was a son of Amyntor (king in Thessaly) who was persuaded by his jealous mother to seduce his father's concubine. When Amyntor found out he cursed Phoenix with childlessness. Phoenix went to Phthia and was welcomed by Peleus, who put him in charge of the youthful Achilles. Phoenix accompanied Achilles to the Trojan War and was one of the ambassadors sent to offer Achilles reconciliation with Agamemnon after their quarrel. Phoenix was also the name of a mythical bird that reproduced itself by dying in a fire. From its ashes a new Phoenix arose. It was thought to live in Ethiopia but traveled to Egypt to reproduce. Since it was extremely long-lived, Phoenix rising from the ashes was a rare event.

PHRIXUS and HELLE (*Phrixos, Helle*): In mythology a brother and sister who were the children of Athamus and his first wife (the cloud goddess Nephele). Ino, second wife of Amathus, jealously hated Phrixus and Helle. She persuaded Athamus to sacrifice them, but they escaped on a golden ram sent by Zeus (in some versions, by Hermes). Helle fell into the sea, which became known as the Hellespont, but Phrixus arrived safely in Colchis. In gratitude he sacrificed the ram to Zeus, and its golden fleece was hung up and guarded by a dragon. It was this Golden Fleece that the Argonauts sought.

PIRITHOUS (*P[e]irithoos*): In mythology the king of the Lapiths and son of Ixion and Dia. With other Lapiths, Pirithous appeared in several myths, the main one concerning his marriage to Hippodamia. For various reasons the Centaurs were invited to the wedding feast but abused the hospitality of Pirithous. They threatened Hippodamia, causing a great battle between the Centaurs and the Lapiths, which the Lapiths eventually won. See also HERACLES, THESEUS.

PLUTUS (*Ploutos*): A god who personified wealth, which originally took the form of abundant crops. He was probably connected to the under-world deity Pluton (another name for Hades), since several forms of wealth sprang from under the earth. Plutus was associated with Demeter at Eleusis. In mythology he was son of Iasion and Demeter.

PODARGE (*Podarge*, swift-footed): One of the Harpies, who were daughters of Thaumas and Electra.

POLHYMNIA (*Polymnia*): One of the Muses, thought in late Roman times to preside over mime.

POLYPHEMUS (*Polyphemos*): In mythology a Cyclops and son of Poseidon, who appeared in Homer's *Odyssey*. Polyphemus captured Odysseus and his men and shut them in his cave. He ate two men each evening, until they managed to blind him and escape. Polyphemus called on Poseidon for help, and consequently Poseidon delayed Odysseus' return home. See also GALATEA.

POLYXENA (*Polyxene*): In mythology the daughter of King Priam of Troy and Hecuba. She is not mentioned by Homer, but in other legends she was sacrificed to the shade of Achilles by his son Neoptolemus, as they were about to sail home from Troy.

POSEIDON (*Poseidon*): Originally a god of earthquakes and water, he also came to be a deity of the sea and to be associated with horses. In mythology Poseidon was son of Cronus and Rhea and brother of Zeus and Hades. He was one of the Olympians. His wife was Amphitrite, and they had a son, Triton. Poseidon also had children by numerous other goddesses and mortals, some of whom were giants and monsters. As a god of the sea he was worshiped throughout Greece, particularly on occasions connected with the sea and with navigation. He was also worshiped as god of fresh water. He was considered a tamer of horses as well and was often worshiped as Poseidon Hippios (Poseidon of Horses). In Athens the eighth day of every month was sacred to Poseidon. The Isthmian Games were held every two years on the Isthmus of Corinth in his honor. Sacrifices to Poseidon by the

Attic deme Erchia were held on the 27th day of the month Gamelion and on the third day of the month Skirophorion. See also PELOPS.

PRIAM (*Priamos*):   In mythology the son of Laomedon and husband of Hecuba. He was king of Troy during the Trojan War. He had 50 sons and many daughters, some by Hecuba and many by other wives or concubines. His best known children were Hector, Paris, Polydorus, Creusa and Cassandra. In Homer's *Iliad*, Priam is depicted as an old man lamenting the misfortunes of the Trojans and the death of many of his sons. After Hector's death he went to the Greek camp with the help of Hermes to ransom Hector's body. Other legends tell how, when Troy fell, he took refuge at the Altar of Zeus Herkeios (Zeus the household god) and was killed there by Neoptolemus.

PRIAPUS (*Priapos*):   A god of the fertility of crops and of protection against harm. Originally worshiped in the Lampsacus region, his cult spread to Greece in the Hellenistic period. He was apparently regarded with amusement rather than awe (although still treated as a deity), and he became primarily a god of gardens. His symbol was a phallus, and his secondary role was probably linked to the more general use of phallic symbols as protective charms, particularly against the evil eye. Priapus was usually portrayed as a small, sometimes misshapen man with enormous genitals. In some myths Priapus was son of Dionysus, and he was sometimes worshiped as part of the rites of Dionysus.

PROCRUSTES (*Prokroustes*):   Also called Damastes he was a legendary robber and son of Poseidon. He lived somewhere in Attica (in some versions, alongside the Athens–Eleusis road) and preyed on strangers. He would measure them against a bed, and if too short, he put them on a rack or hammered them out to the right length. If they were too long, he cut off their legs. Theseus caught him and cut off his head because Procrustes was too long for the bed.

PROMETHEUS (*Prometheus*, forethinker):   A Titan who was the son of Iapetus and Clymene

(daughter of Oceanus), and in some versions, son of Iapetus and Themis. His son was Deucalion. Prometheus was regarded as a champion of mortals against the hostility of the gods. In some myths Prometheus created the first men from clay. Zeus hid fire from men, but Prometheus stole a spark and gave it to them in a stalk of fennel. Prometheus was also regarded as a craftsman who gave mortals all kinds of arts and sciences. He also tricked Zeus into choosing the worst part of sacrificed animals (bones covered with fat), leaving the best part for mortals. In revenge Zeus had Hephaestus create Pandora and sent her to Epimetheus, brother of Prometheus, with a jar containing all the evils and diseases of humankind. Prometheus also knew the secret of the marriage of Thetis (she was destined to bear a child greater than its father) but refused to tell Zeus, who wanted to marry her. Zeus therefore chained Prometheus to a rock where an eagle ate his liver by day, and it grew back at night. He was eventually released by Heracles (or, in another version, by revealing the secret of Thetis). See also PANDORA.

PROTEUS (*Proteus*):   A sea god who was herdsman of flocks of the sea, such as seals. He was given the power of prophecy by Poseidon. He also had the power to change his shape. If held firmly to retain his true shape, he would answer questions, for he possessed the gift of prophecy.

PSYCHE (*Psykhe*):   The soul, sometimes considered by Greeks as a butterfly or bird. Different notions of the soul were developed by poets and philosophers. Later, Psyche was regarded as female and was portrayed as a young woman.

PYGMALION (*Pygmalion*):   In mythology a king of Cyprus who made an ivory sculpture of a woman. He fell in love with the statue, and Aphrodite breathed life into it, forming a woman who bore Pygmalion a daughter called Paphos.

PYRRHUS (*Pyrros*):   One of the Greeks involved in the Trojan War, also known as Neoptolemus.

PYTHON (*Python*): A dragon that guarded the sacred place at Delphi, and a deity that personified the underworld's dark forces. Apollo killed the dragon and established his oracle at Delphi, where he became known as Pythian Apollo, and his priestess was called Pythia. Python was probably an ancient deity whose oracle was transferred to Apollo.

RHADAMANTHYS (*Rhadamanthys*): The son of Zeus and Europa, and brother of Minos and Sarpedon. He became a ruler and judge of dead souls in the underworld, noted for his justice.

RHEA (*Rheia*): In mythology one of the Titans. She was sister and wife of Cronus, and mother of some of the Olympian gods. She was sometimes identified with Cybele. See also CRONUS.

SALMONEUS (*Salmoneus*): In mythology the son of Aeolus and father of Tyro. He was a king of Elis who pretended to be Zeus by making a noise like thunder with his chariot, and throwing torches about to mimic lightning. For this blasphemy Zeus struck him with a thunderbolt, destroying him and his city. Salmoneus was cast into Tartarus in the underworld.

SARAPIS: Greek word for the Egyptian god who was a conflation of the god Osiris and the sacred bull Apis. The cult of Sarapis seems to have arisen at Memphis in Egypt, in the temple where Apis was kept. According to tradition Ptolemy I effectively created the god as a new cult to accompany his own power, establishing the cult at Alexandria. Sarapis was a god of the underworld, sky and healing, regarded as above fate. He also performed miracles and was equated with many gods, such as Dionysus, Zeus, Asclepius, Hades and Helios. The cult was usually known as that of Sarapis, even though it included Isis, Harpocrates and other Egyptian deities. By Roman times Isis was usually the chief deity. Sarapis was generally portrayed with a benign and bearded face like that of Zeus, with a *modius* (fertility symbol) on his head. He was sometimes shown seated, with Cerberus at his right knee. A shrine or temple dedicated to Sarapis was known as a

Sarapeion. See also ISIS, Oriental and Mystery Religions, p. 357.

SARPEDON (*Sarpedon*): A hero worshiped in Lycia. In mythology, he was son of Zeus and Laodamia. He commanded the Lycian allies of the Trojans at the siege of Troy. In Homer's *Iliad*, he was killed by Patroclus and was mourned by Zeus. He was then carried to Lycia by Hypnos and Thanatos for burial. Later legends make him the son of Zeus and Europa and uncle of Glaucus, but he would therefore have lived for three generations: two Lycian heroes with the same name may have been conflated. To explain the problem Diodorus Siculus (writing 1st century BC) constructed a genealogy in which Sarpedon (son of Zeus and Europa) had a son called Evander. He married Laodamia, and their son Sarpedon took part in the Trojan War.

SATYRS (*Satyroi*): The boisterous half-bestial spirits of woods and hills, who were attendant on the god Dionysus. They were usually portrayed in human form with some animal part, such as a horse's tail. From about the 4th century BC they were portrayed with a human body and goat's legs. They were constantly confused with Sileni by ancient authors. Satyrs had goat's legs and were generally young, but Sileni were portrayed as old men with horse's ears. Satyrs were lustful and fond of revelry, and were often portrayed chasing Nymphs.

SCYLLA (*Skylle, Skylla*): The name of two mythological figures. The better known Scylla was a daughter of Phorcys and Hecate, and a sea monster in the Straits of Messina. She had six heads, each with a triple row of teeth, and 12 feet. She lived off fish, but also took men from nearby ships and devoured them. This sea monster was sometimes confused with Scylla, daughter of King Nisus of Megara. See also GLAUCUS, NISUS.

SELENE (*Selene*): Goddess of the moon, identified with Artemis. Selene does not appear to have had much cult following, although there was an oracle at the shrine of Selene Pasiphae near Thalamae in Laconia. In mythology Selene was daughter of the Titans Hyperion and Theia, and sister of Helios and Eos. She appears in a few myths, the best known being that of Endymion. In later times she may have been identified with Phoebe, since the latter name came to be used for the moon.

SEMELE (*Semele*; sometimes called Thyone): In mythology the daughter of Cadmus and mother of Dionysus by Zeus. Hera was jealous that Semele was loved by Zeus. She disguised herself and advised Semele to test the divinity of her lover. Consequently Semele asked Zeus to show himself to her in all his glory, but she was struck dead by the sight. Dionysus brought Semele back from the underworld to become a goddess. See DIONYSUS for his birth.

SEVEN AGAINST THEBES: In mythology the action of seven Argive leaders to retrieve the throne of Thebes. When Oedipus cursed his sons (Eteocles and Polynices) and went into exile, they agreed to rule Thebes in alternate years. At the end of his year Eteocles refused to give up the throne, precipitating the episode called the Seven Against Thebes. The seven are usually named as Polynices, Adrastus, Tydeus, Parthenopaeus, Capaneus, Hippomedon and Amphiaraus, with Adrastus as their leader. Other versions name Eteocles (son of Iphis) instead of Adrastus, and Mecisteus (brother of Adrastus) instead of Polynices. They attacked Thebes, and Eteocles and the seven (except Adrastus) were killed.

SILENUS (*Seilenos*): A god who represented the spirit of untamed nature. He was represented in art as half-man and half-animal, with ears and sometimes legs and tail of a horse. Silenus was often regarded as plural (Sileni). Sileni were frequently confused with Satyrs by ancient authors, and sometimes with the god Pan. It can be difficult to distinguish between portrayals of Sileni and Satyrs in art, although Satyrs had goat's legs and were generally young, and Sileni were portrayed as old men with horse's ears. Silenus was associated with the cult of Dionysus and was sometimes regarded as his tutor.

SIRENS (*Seirenes*): In mythology the female creatures who had the power of luring men to destruction at sea by their singing. In Homer's *Odyssey* the Sirens inhabited an island near Scylla and Charybdis. Sailors charmed by their song would land on the island and perish in a meadow full of corpses. The Sirens were sometimes considered daughters of Gaia. In some legends they had to die if a mortal escaped their power. They drowned themselves after Odysseus passed by safely. In art Sirens were usually represented as half-women and half-birds, although male, bearded versions predominated in early art. See also PARTHENOPE.

SISYPHUS (*Sisyphos*): A mythological character who had a shrine at Corinth and was allegedly buried on the Isthmus at Corinth. In mythology he was the son of Aeolus and was tormented in Hades by having to push a rock up a hill, which rolled down again when he reached the top. One explanation for his punishment was that he offended Zeus by telling Asopus where Zeus had taken his daughter Aegina. Sisyphus is portrayed in other myths as a trickster, and his name was used as a nickname for a cunning person.

SPHINX (*Sphinx*): A monster with a human head and lion's body. It originated in Egypt but was absorbed into Greek mythology at an early date. In Greek literature the Sphinx was always female, although some bearded male Sphinxes were portrayed in art. The image of the Sphinx was used as protection against evil. The Sphinx appears in several myths, including Theban examples about the House of Oedipus where she preyed on Thebans and devoured those who could not solve her riddle. Oedipus destroyed the Sphinx by correctly solving the riddle, and the Sphinx committed suicide.

STENTOR (*Stentor*): In mythology a man with a "brazen voice" who could shout as loud as 50 men. He appears in Homer's *Iliad* but in few other myths. One later myth related that he died after losing a shouting match with Hermes.

STEROPES (*Steropes*, Lightener): In mythology one of the Cyclopes.

SYRINX (*Syrinx*): A Nymph of Arcadia with whom the god Pan fell in love. She ran away from Pan and begged the river Nymphs (in some versions, Gaia) to turn her into a reed bed. It was with reeds from this bed that Pan made a set of Pan pipes (*syrinx*).

TANTALUS (*Tantalos*): In mythology the king of Sipylus in Lydia, son of Zeus and father of Niobe and Pelops. Various legends recount different crimes he allegedly committed. These included stealing food from the gods and giving it to mortals, and killing and cooking his son Pelops for a banquet for the gods, who found out and brought Pelops back to life. For his crime he was punished with everlasting torment, usually in Tartarus (part of the underworld), where he is "tantalized" by food and water that constantly moved out of his reach. See also PELOPS.

TEIRESIAS or TIRESIAS (*Teiresias*): A blind Theban seer. Various legends explain his blindness, including one that says he saw Athena bathing and she blinded him. In compensation she gave him the power of prophecy. He appears in many myths, including Homer's *Odyssey*, with Odysseus being sent into the underworld to consult him.

TELEGONUS (*Telegonos*): According to legend, the son of Odysseus and Circe. He was possibly an invention of the author of the *Telegony*, a lost epic of the 6th century BC. See also ODYSSEUS.

TELEMACHUS (*Telemakhos*): In mythology the son of Odysseus and Penelope. He has a prominent role in Homer's *Odyssey*, developing from a youthful and dutiful but unenterprising son to a warrior who helped to destroy the unwanted suitors of Penelope. In another legend he married Circe after Odysseus' death.

TERPSICHORE (*Terpsikhora*): One of the Muses, thought in late Roman times to preside over lyric poetry and dancing.

TETHYS (*Tethys*): In mythology one of the Titans. She was wife of Oceanus, and mother of Achelous and the Oceanids.

THALIA (*Thalia*): One of the Muses, thought in late Roman times to preside over comedy.

THALLO (*Thallo*): In Attica one of three goddesses of the seasons (Horae).

THANATOS (*Thanatos*): In mythology the personification of death.

THEIA (*Theia*): In mythology one of the female Titans.

THEMIS (*Themis*): Originally a goddess similar to Gaia, she came to be regarded as a personification of justice. In mythology she was one of the Titans. She was mother, by Zeus, of the Horae and the Fates, and in some legends mother of Prometheus by Iapetus.

THERSITES (*Thersites*): In mythology the only nonheroic character in Homer's *Iliad*, described as meanspirited, ugly, foul-mouthed and low-class. He accused Agamemnon of prolonging the Trojan War for his own ends, and was beaten into silence by Odysseus. In another legend, where he was described as from a good family, he insulted Achilles who then killed him.

THESEUS (*Theseus*): The national hero of Athens, his cult center. He was believed by Athenians to be an early king of Athens. In mythology he was son either of Poseidon or of King Aegeus of Athens and Aethra (daughter of King Pittheus of Troezen). Aegeus left Aethra at Troezen, telling her that when Theseus reached manhood, he was to lift a certain large rock and take the sword and sandals hidden underneath to Athens. Theseus embarked for Athens by the dangerous land route, enduring adventures on the way. At Athens he was recognized by Medea, who had taken refuge with King Aegeus. In an attempt to destroy Theseus, Medea persuaded Aegeus to send him to kill the bull of

Marathon. Theseus accomplished this task, so Medea tried to poison him on his return to Athens. However, Aegeus recognized his son in time to prevent his death. Medea was sent back to Colchis, along with her son Medus, whose father was either Aegeus or an Asian king who married Medea after she was driven out of Athens.

Theseus then heard about the tribute that Athens had to pay Minos of Crete—seven girls and seven youths to be eaten by the Minotaur. Theseus volunteered to be one of the youths, and with the help of Ariadne and her thread he managed to kill the Minotaur in the labyrinth and find his way out. Theseus, the other Greeks and Ariadne sailed from Crete. He abandoned Ariadne on the island of Naxos and returned to Athens. Theseus had arranged with his father that he would change his black sail for a white one if his mission had been successful, but he forgot. On seeing the black sail, Aegeus threw himself from the cliffs into the sea in despair. Some legends cite this as the origin of the name, Aegean Sea. Theseus then became king of Athens. He was credited with unifying the Attic communities into a single state, with Athens as the capital.

With Heracles, Theseus took part in an expedition against the Amazons and married the Amazon queen Hippolyta (in some versions, the Amazon Antiope). The Amazons invaded Attica to recover her but were defeated. Theseus was present at the wedding feast of King Pirithous of the Lapiths and the subsequent battle between the Lapiths and Centaurs. He later helped Pirithous to invade the underworld to try to carry off Persephone. Theseus also apparently abducted Helen, who was then rescued by her brothers the Dioscuri. When Creon, king of Thebes, refused burial of the bodies of the Seven against Thebes, Theseus marched with Adrastus and the sons of these Argive leaders to bury the dead. After Hippolyta died, by whom he had a son, Hippolytus, Theseus married Phaedra (sister of Ariadne). Theseus was finally driven from Athens by rebellions. He took refuge in Scyros, where he died, but he was seen in the form of a giant fighting for the Greeks at the battle of Marathon in 490 BC. See also ARIADNE, HIPPOLYTUS, PROCRUSTES.

THETIS (*Thetis*): One of the Nereids who was destined to bear a son greater than his father. When this was revealed to the gods, Zeus and Poseidon decided to marry her to a mortal. She was married to Peleus and gave birth to Achilles. In one legend she left Peleus after he tried to prevent her from dipping Achilles in the river Styx to make him immortal. In Homer's *Iliad* she is portrayed as a mother who is only concerned for her son.

TITANS (*Titanes*): In mythology the older gods who existed before the Olympians. They were the offspring of Gaia and Uranus. According to Hesiod there were six male Titans (Oceanus, Coeus, Crius, Hyperion, Iapetus, Cronus) and six female Titans (Thea, Rhea, Themis, Mnemosyne, Phoebe, Tethys). Some other legends cite other characters as Titans, such as Atlas, Leto, Perses and Asterie. When Cronus castrated Uranus and took his throne, the Titans seized power. Cronus married Rhea, but knowing that he would be overthrown by his children, he tried to prevent this by swallowing them. His children finally escaped, and led by Zeus, they fought and overcame the Titans and took power for themselves. This struggle against the Titans was sometimes called Titanomachia.

TITHONUS (*Tithonos*): In mythology the son of King Laomedon of Troy and brother of Priam. Eos fell in love with Tithonus, and their children were Emathion and Memnon. Eos asked Zeus to make Tithonus immortal, but forgot to ask for eternal youth. He therefore became so old and shriveled that little more than his voice was left.

TRITON (*Triton*): The son of Poseidon and Amphitrite, with a human head and shoulders and a fish tail from the waist down. He was commonly portrayed as blowing on a conch shell. In some myths there were several Tritons.

TRITOPATORES or TRITOPATREIS (*Tritopatores, Tritopatreis*): Obscure deities worshiped in Attica. Their name seems to mean "great-grandfathers," and they were said to be ancestors. They were also sometimes regarded as wind gods. These deities were invoked in prayers for children before a marriage. The Attic deme Erchia sacrificed to them on the 21st day of the month Mounichion, and they were worshiped at Marathon on the eve of the Scira festival.

TROILUS (*Troilos*): In mythology a younger son of King Priam of Troy. In Homer's *Iliad* he had already been killed, but other legends relate how he was slain by Achilles.

TROPHONIUS (*Trophonios*): A hero who became god of the oracular shrine at a cave at Lebadea. This was an important oracle, and the method of consulting it was recorded by Pausanias in Roman times. In mythology Trophonius and his brother Agamedes were sons of Erginus of Orchomenus in Boeotia. They were architects and allegedly built the temple of Apollo at Delphi and a treasury, either for King Hyrieus of Boeotia or King Augeas of Elis. They tried to rob the treasury by means of a movable stone in the wall, but the king caught Agamedes in a trap. To avoid Agamedes being identified, Trophonius cut off his head. He himself was subsequently swallowed up by the earth at Lebadea. Having consulted the Delphic Oracle because of a drought, the Boeotians were told to consult Trophonius' oracle. They were led to a cave by a swarm of bees, where one Boeotian had a vision of Trophonius.

TYCHE (*Tykhe*): A goddess who personified chance or fortune. She became increasingly popular in the Hellenistic period, when a number of cities adopted their own version of Tyche as patron deity.

TYPHON or TYPHOEUS (*Typhon, Typhoeus*): In mythology a monster who was often confused with the Giants. Typhon had 100 dragon-shaped heads and powerful hands and feet. Zeus overcame him with thunderbolts and cast him into Tartarus, setting Mount Aetna on fire on the way. In other myths Typhon is the power below the volcano on Mount Aetna. See also CERBERUS, CHIMAERA, and HERACLES.

URANIA (*Ourania*): One of the Muses, thought in late Roman times to preside over astronomy.

URANUS (*Ouranos*): In mythology the personification of the heavens. Gaia gave birth to Uranus, who fathered a number of children on Gaia. He prevented them being born until Cronus (another son of Gaia) castrated Uranus, which apparently allowed the children to be born. The children included the Titans, Giants, Erinyes and Hecatoncheires.

ZEPHYRUS (*Zephyros*): God of the west wind; like all wind gods, he was often thought to take the form of a horse. He was son of Eos and Astraeus and sometimes considered to be the husband of the goddess Iris and father of Eros. In Homer's *Iliad* he is the father of the talking horses of Achilles (called Xanthus and Balius), which had been a present from Poseidon to Achilles' father, Peleus.

ZEUS (*Zeus*): Originally a weather god, Zeus was chief of all the Greek gods and came to be regarded as father of gods and mortals (fig. 8.19). He was one of the Olympians and the supreme ruler who controlled thunder, lightning and rain, and upheld justice, law and morals. In mythology the power of Zeus was based on supreme strength and wisdom, a limited power because he was unable to oppose the will of the three Fates. They controlled the destinies of people, and fate was the law of the universe, a law made by Zeus himself. Before the Dark Age Zeus was regarded as protector of the king and his family, but after the abolition of monarchies, Zeus became protector of the polis and of political freedom.

Zeus appears in various myths, where he is usually regarded as the youngest son of Cronus, overthrown by Zeus in the struggle against the Titans (Titanomachia). Afterward Zeus and his brothers divided the universe among them, with Zeus obtaining the heavens, Hades the underworld and Poseidon the sea. Zeus lived on mountaintops, particularly Mount Olympus, the highest mountain in Greece. His power was symbolized by the thunderbolt, which only he could wield. Zeus had various children: deities including Apollo, Ares, Artemis, Athena, Hebe, Hephaestus, Hermes, Dionysus,

Eileithyia and Persephone, and mortals including Heracles, Helen, Perseus and Minos.

In the Hellenistic period Zeus was frequently identified with the chief god of any non-Greek area, such as Ammon in Libya. Zeus had more than 150 epithets, such as Zeus Xenios (Zeus, god of hospitality and protector of guests) and Zeus Ktesios (Zeus, god of the household).

The Nemean Games were held every two years at Nemea in honor of Zeus, and the Olympic Games were held every four years at Olympia in honor of Olympian Zeus (fig. 8.20). At Athens there were several festivals celebrated in honor of Zeus: in the month Gamelion, the Theogamia (or Gamelia) festival celebrated the sacred marriage between Hera and Zeus; the Diasia festival on the 23rd day of the month Anthesterion in honor of Zeus Meilichios (gracious Zeus); the Pandia festival on the 17th day of the month Elaphebolion; the Olympieia festival in honor of Olympian Zeus on the 19th day of the month Mounichion; and the Bouphonia festival in honor of Zeus Polieus (Zeus, guardian of the city) on the 14th day of the month Skirophorion. The Lycaea was a festival in honor of Zeus, celebrated at Mount Lycaeus. Several sacrifices to Zeus were undertaken by the Attic deme Erchia: to Zeus Epoptes (tutelary Zeus) on the 25th day of the month Metageitnion; to Zeus Horios (Zeus of the boundary) on the 16th day of the month Poseideon; to Zeus Teleius (perfect Zeus, as a deity who is both perfect and who provides perfection) on the 27th day of the month Gamelion; to Zeus on the fourth day of the month Thargelion; to Zeus Epacrios (Zeus of the heights) on the 16th day of the month Thargelion; and to Zeus Polieus (Zeus, protector of the city) on the third day of the month Skirophorion.

PRIESTHOODS

Function

Religion was intertwined with politics, and religious matters took precedence in state business. Most

Fig. 8.19   Hellenistic marble head of Zeus, 3rd–2nd century BC.

priests and priestesses were state officials whose duty was to perform religious observances on behalf of the whole state or part of it.

The duties of priesthood varied from cult to cult, and some cults had specialized priests performing different tasks. Duties might include presiding over rituals and sacrifices, preparing and participating in festivals, officiating at wedding and funerals, purifying houses after a birth or a death, administering oaths, looking after cult property, and administering of the cult's affairs.

The earliest historical evidence for priests and priestesses in Greece comes from Linear B tablets of c. 1200 BC, which depict them in specialized roles, such as workers of sacred bronze and keepers of temple keys. This indicates that by this date priesthoods were fully developed. Priests continued to retain respect and authority until the Roman emperor Theodosius I banned pagan cults in AD 391.

Officeholders

Traditionally goddesses were served by priestesses and gods by priests, although some cults had both

Fig. 8.20   Early Classical Doric temple of Zeus at Olympia. It was begun c. 470 BC and was the work of a local architect, Libon of Elis. It measures 91 by 210.5 ft (27.68 by 64.12 m).

priests and priestesses, and there were exceptions. For example, some cults of Athena were served by boy priests, while some cults of Apollo had priestesses, such as the Pythia, who gave the oracles at Delphi.

There were hereditary priesthoods, such as that of Poseidon Erechtheus at Athens. So strong was this tradition, that some priesthoods remained hereditary for over 1,000 years. Inheritance through the male line had priority, but if not possible, inheritance was through the female line. The exact method of inheritance varied, and complicated patterns of inheritance are known. Sometimes priesthoods were passed on by wills and testaments, while others were obtained by election (apparently rare), lottery, purchase or appointment. Election, lottery and appointment were methods largely confined to mainland Greece, whereas purchase of priesthoods was confined largely to eastern Greek islands and Asia Minor.

Eligibility for priesthoods varied from cult to cult, but generally candidates needed to have a suitable family background. This often meant being able to demonstrate citizenship of a city for several generations, so priests frequently came from elite families. Other factors included age and family status. For example, priests of Athena at Rhodes were boys (not men), the virgin goddess Artemis was served by virgin priestesses, and Hera (goddess of marriage) was served by married priestesses. The length of time priesthoods were held also varied from cult to cult, but this often reflected the method by which the priesthood was acquired. Hereditary and purchased priesthoods were usually for life, while those obtained in a lottery tended to be for between two and four years, or from festival to festival.

Priests and priestesses frequently had high social status, as well as a legal status that was particularly beneficial to priestesses, who could act on their own behalf and were not under the guardianship of a father, husband or brother. Priests and priestesses were entitled to parts of animals slaughtered for sacrifice and sometimes to housing. The priestess of Demeter at Eleusis, for example, had a private house. Other rewards for priests included free meals and privileges, such as front seats at the theater, but salaries were apparently uncommon. The value of the rewards generally reflected the status of the priesthood.

Types of Priesthood

Various types of priesthood are recorded in inscriptions. The most common are the *hiereus* (priest) and *hiereia* (priestess), who looked after the sacred things (*hiera*) stored in the sanctuary; many temples had a single *hiereus* or *hiereia*. Larger temples had a staff with specialists that could include *spondophoroi* (libation bearers), *loutrophoroi* or *hydrophoroi* (carriers of holy water), *manteis* (prophets), an *auletes* (musician), *exegetai* (interpreters or expounders of sacred law), *kleidoukhoi* (key holders), an *oinokhoos* (wine pourer), a *grammateus* (scribe) and a *mageiros* (sacrificer). A *neokoros* originally meant "temple sweeper," but it later became a less humble post, perhaps "temple assistant" or "caretaker." The *diakonos* (deacon) was responsible for some chores, and temple slaves were called *hierodouloi*. Other specialist priests known from inscriptions are the *dadoukhos* (torch bearer) and *hierokeryx* (a herald who announced the ritual), as well as *hierothytai* (sacrificing priests) and *rhabdophoroi* (responsible for keeping order at festivals).

At the Asclepieion in Athens the priest was assisted by a *zakoros* (senior attendant), and there was also a male sacristan, a male fire bearer (*pyrphoros*), a female basket bearer (*kanephoros*) and a female "bearer of holy secrets" (*arrephoros*).

At oracular shrines the words of the god were usually proclaimed by a *chresmologos*, *mantis* or *prophetes* (prophet), and at Eleusis the *hierophantes* was the presiding priest who showed initiates the sacred objects. In some temples special names were used for priests and priestesses. For example the child priestesses of Artemis at Brauron were called

"bears," and the priestesses of Artemis at Ephesus were called "bees." In the cult of Dionysus at Smyrna a *theophantor* had some connection with the god appearing to mortals. At Pergamum the staff of priests included a *thyroros* (janitor), and on Crete a *hiarorgos* (performer of sacred acts) sometimes took the place of the normal priest.

Sibyl (*Sibylla*) was a general name given to various prophetesses, some of whose individual names have survived as well (fig. 8.21). Sibyls were present in various places. They prophesied in a state of ecstasy, possessed by a god (usually Apollo). Their prophecies were sometimes written down, collections of which were used as oracles.

The Ptolemaic dynasty from the late 4th century BC introduced Greek traditions to Egypt. Under the Ptolemies the priesthood remained largely unchanged, and double names of priests quite often included a Greek name. Priests in Egypt were full-time officials of high standing in society. Generations of families followed the priesthood, and wives were often priestesses. The new ruler cult of the Ptolemies required traditional priests to become priests of this cult as well. In 196 BC Ptolemy V Epiphanes conferred great benefits upon the priesthood and set aside revenues for the maintenance of temples. In gratitude the priests met at Memphis and ordered statues of the king to be erected and copies of the decree to be set up, of which the Rosetta Stone is a surviving example, inscribed in hieroglyphic, demotic and Greek.

SACRED PLACES

Types

In both rural and urban areas land sacred to the gods (*hieron*, literally "filled with divine power") was subject to restrictions. Such sacred land might be an enclosed or delineated area (*temenos*), a sanctuary (*hieron*) with or without a building, or a natural feature such as a cave, spring or grove. The term "shrine" is often used loosely to mean a place

Fig. 8.21   Below the terrace of the temple of Apollo at Delphi is Herophile's rock, where the Sibyl Herophile sang her oracles.

of worship, such as a sanctuary or a temple. Temples were built within sacred areas.

Religious Pollution

Regulations about entry to some specific sacred areas are known from inscriptions and show considerable variation. In Athens the agora had many temples and altars. Here the *perirranteria* was an area marked off by lustral basins where people could ritually purify themselves before entering the sacred area. People tainted with some forms of religious pollution were not allowed into the sacred area, which could restrict their participation in the political life of Athens. Of the many types of religious pollution that precluded entry to sacred areas, the only universal ones were childbirth, contact with childbirth and contact with a dead person. Other types of pollution that prevented entry

to specific sacred areas included the wearing of certain clothes, recent sexual intercourse, eating certain foods and carrying particular types of weapons or certain types of metal. Sexual intercourse, birth and death were activities prohibited within sacred areas.

Temples

FUNCTION

Temples were built within sacred areas and were primarily considered as places where the gods lived, rather than places where congregations assembled for worship. They often served other purposes, such as sheltering sacred places or objects (for example, an ancient sacred image or sacred tree) and storing offerings made to the temple deity. Many temples became wealthy and to some extent operated as banks and as keepers of records (see chapter 5). Acts of worship were usually carried out at outdoor altars near temples, although acts of worship and sacrifice did sometimes take place within temples.

The basic component of a temple was the *naos* (or cella), which was the room that housed the cult statue of the deity. Temples were constructed with a great variety of orientations, but around 80 percent were oriented approximately eastward, often so that the rising sun shone into the temple on the festival day of the deity to which the temple was dedicated.

EARLY TEMPLES

Temples apparently developed from the 8th century BC, and these early temples had a certain amount of variation in their form. They were most commonly based on three types of contemporary house plans. The simplest temple was square or rectangular in plan, with a stone bench at the rear for offerings to the deity. Another type had a hairpin plan, consisting of a long hall with a narthex (porch) at one end and an apse at the other. The third type of early temple was most common and was similar to a *megaron*. It was rectangular in plan, with an entrance at one end, and the side walls often projected to form a porch.

Early temples of the 8th–7th centuries BC appear to have been constructed mainly of wood, but stone was also used at an early date. Temple plans developed from the *megaron* type, usually with the addition of columns to form facades, porches and colonnades. In larger temples there were interior columns (usually in two parallel rows) to support the roof. After the experimentation of the early period the basic plan of temples remained relatively constant, although there were many variations of proportion, detail and decoration. The cella became a central hall, almost always with a columned porch (pronaos) at the front, and often a symmetrical structure to the porch at the rear of the cella, called an *opisthodomos*. The cella side walls often projected to form the side walls of the pronaos and *opisthodomos*, and terminated in columns called antae. Rows of columns were placed in front, at the rear and sometimes all the way around the temple to form a colonnade (*peristylon*).

ARCHAIC TEMPLES

Doric temples of the late 7th century BC are known from places such as Delphi and Cyrene, but have not survived in any substantial form. One of the earliest Doric temples of the Archaic Age with substantial elements remaining is the temple of Hera at Olympia (fig. 8.22), built around 590 BC. It appears to mark the end of the transition from wood to stone for temple building. It had a cella, pronaos and *opisthodomos*, surrounded by a colonnade with a row of six columns at the rear and at the front, and a row of 16 columns on each side. The pronaos and *opisthodomos* both have two columns *in antis* (sited between the columns called antae that terminate the side walls). The columns of this temple were originally wooden but were gradually replaced in stone.

The temple of Apollo at Corinth provides a good example of a Doric temple of c. 560 BC. It was basically similar to the temple of Hera but had two chambers instead of the single cella, and these chambers had two interior rows of columns. In eastern Greece Ionic temples of this period were often larger and more elaborate than mainland Doric ones, probably due to Near Eastern influences. Examples of this Ionic type include the temple of Apollo at Didyma and the temple of Artemis at Ephesus. The latter temple was built c. 530 BC; it was a dipteral temple (having a colonnade with two parallel rows of columns surrounding the temple), with two rows of 21 columns on both sides. It had a triple row of columns on the facade and was a massive structure, 164 ft (50 m) wide and 377 ft (115 m) long. The temple of Apollo at Didyma, built in the mid-6th century BC, was also a large dipteral temple. Its interior was open to the sky, and within it was a small shrine.

CLASSICAL TEMPLES

In the early Classical period (c. 480–450 BC), most temples appear to have been built in the Doric style, although some Ionic ones are known. A Doric example is the temple of Zeus at Olympia (fig. 8.20), which had a pronaos, *opisthodomos* and peristyle, with two rows of columns within the cella. The pediments and metopes were richly decorated with marble sculptures, many fragments of which have survived. Another example of an early Classical Doric temple is that of Zeus Olympios at Acragas, which had a cella and narrow *opisthodomos* but no pronaos. There were two rows of columns in the interior, and the peristyle had engaged columns set along a continuous wall.

In the second half of the 5th century BC (sometimes called the High Classical period), there was much building on the Acropolis at Athens, including the Parthenon (temple of Athena Parthenos) (figs. 2.7, 8.23). This temple, which replaced an earlier temple, had a cella and two shallow porches. A room behind the cella may have served as a treasury. It was the largest Doric temple on the Greek mainland. At Sounion the Doric temple of Poseidon was built about the same time, as were other examples, such as the temple of Nemesis at Rhamnus and the temple of Ares in the agora at Athens. Examples of Ionic temples of this period include the temple of Athena Nike (figs. 8.23, 8.24) and the Erechtheum (figs. 8.8, 8.23, 8.25), both on the Acropolis at Athens.

The 4th century BC was marked by the introduction of the Corinthian column (see chapter 6), which gradually gained popularity, but Doric and Ionic temples still continued to be built. Corinthian columns were often incorporated as an additional feature into an otherwise Doric, or sometimes Ionic, building. The temple of Asclepius at Epidaurus is an example of a Doric temple of this period. It had a cella and pronaos but no *opisthodomos*, and it had a surrounding peristyle. Grandiose Ionic temples were built in Asia Minor, such as the temple of Apollo at Didyma and the temple of Athena Polias at Priene (figs. 6.16A, 8.26, 9.14).

HELLENISTIC TEMPLES

Most examples of architecture of this period are found in Asia Minor, as mainland Greece no longer had resources for much major building. The Doric order was not popular for Hellenistic temple construction, although it was used for other buildings.

Fig. 8.22 Archaic temple of Hera at Olympia. The cella walls were of limestone, and the upper part was of sun-dried bricks. The rest was of wood, apart from the tiled roof. The wooden columns were replaced in stone from time to time.

HANDBOOK TO LIFE IN ANCIENT GREECE

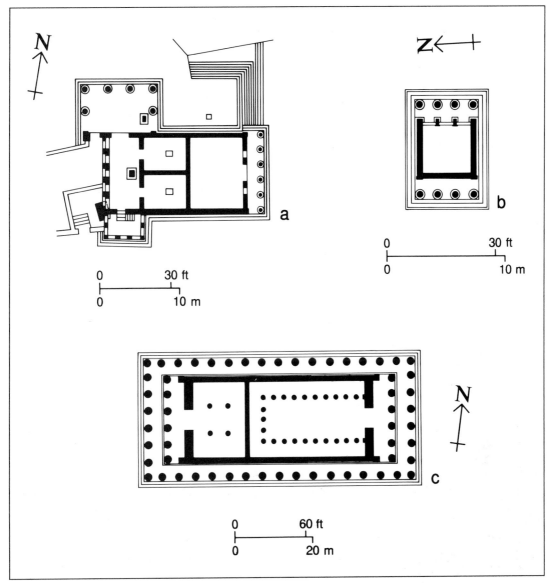

Fig. 8.23 Plans of temples at Athens: a. Erechtheum; b. Athena Nike; c. Parthenon.

The Ionic order continued to be used, and the first instance of the Corinthian order for the exterior of a temple appears to have been on the temple of Olympian Zeus at Athens. In addition to using the Corinthian order, some temples showed Oriental influences, such as the temple of Sarapis in Alexandria, whose architecture was a mixture of Greek and Oriental features.

CULT IMAGES

Cult images were representations of gods, goddesses and heroes, often forming the center of cult sites such as temples (where the cult image occupied the cella). Images were either statues or reliefs, usually of stone or bronze, although early ones may often have been made of wood. Images of gold and chryselephantine (part gold and part ivory) are also known. It is usually impossible to be certain that a surviving statue or fragment was originally a cult image, particularly as many were deliberately destroyed in the early Christian period.

Treasuries

Offerings to the gods were usually stored within a temple, or sometimes in ancillary buildings within temple precincts. In the larger, more famous sanctuaries, treasuries (*thesauroi*, sing. *thesauros*) were also built. These structures were designed to protect and display offerings of individual cities. The buildings themselves also performed the function of a votive offering, marking the devotion and gratitude of the builders. Treasuries were normally very simple in plan, consisting of a rectangular room fronted by a porch with a two-column facade. They were built in both Doric and Ionic orders and were often highly ornamented and embellished to honor the deity and reflect the prestige of the city that had donated them (fig. 2.4).

Altars

Altars were sited in sacred places. They were used as sacrificial tables and were indispensable in the

Fig. 8.24   The Ionic marble temple of Athena Nike, constructed c. 425 BC. It has an almost square cella. The temple measures 17.75 by 26.75 ft (5.39 by 8.16 m). There are four prostyle columns at each end.

cult of most gods (the exception being underworld gods, to whom offerings were made in pits). Since nearly every religious act was accompanied by a sacrifice, altars were a focus of worship that predated the use of temples. When temples were built the altar usually stood outside, often at the front. Altars were sometimes situated inside temples. There were altars in domestic houses, often in a courtyard, where the household could worship and perform sacrifices.

An altar was a raised place, and the earliest altars may have been of earth. The great altar of Zeus at Olympia was made of the ashes of sacrifices that took place there. Altars were usually of stone, the simplest being a single stone slab. They were usually rectangular or square, occasionally circular. In time they became increasingly elaborate, and eventually became independent buildings, the most elaborate being the Hellenistic altar of Zeus at Pergamum. Built on a platform 120 by 112 ft (36.44 by 34.2 m), it had a podium reached by a great flight of steps and was ornamented by high-relief sculptures. The podium had an Ionic portico with two projecting sides. This type of altar is sometimes called a stepped monumental altar and was built to give increased honor to the god to whom it was dedicated. The largest known altar was found at Syracuse and was 650 by 74 ft (198 by 23 m).

Not all altars were designed to have sacrifices burnt on them, although some had a metal fire pan on top for that purpose. Some altars had a deep depression in the center of the upper surface, and these were usually dedicated to deities of the underworld. Small altars of stone or terra-cotta were possibly intended to be portable.

RELIGIOUS OBSERVANCE

Purpose

The Greeks had no central collection of sacred texts, such as a bible, nor a universal caste of priests

Fig. 8.25   The Erechtheum on the Acropolis at Athens. In front are the still visible ruins of the older temple of Athena, which was destroyed by the Persians. Various cults were apparently housed in the Erechtheum, including Athena, Poseidon and Erechtheus. It is an Ionic temple, begun in 421 BC and finished in 405 BC. Both the plan and elevation are unique.

to interpret and define orthodox religion. They demonstrated their beliefs and communicated with their gods largely through prayers, hymns, divination, sacrifice and votive offerings. It was believed that gods could intervene in human affairs and could be influenced by rituals, even though there was a distinction between the realm of gods and that of humans. Such influence and intervention might be sought by simple prayers or by a combination of prayer, ritual and sacrifice. The religious festival was an example of such a combination and could include all methods of communicating with gods and propitiating them. Devotion to the gods was seen as regular performance of rituals, including various forms of prayer and sacrifice. Piety was defined by correct performance of these rituals, rather than by moral behavior.

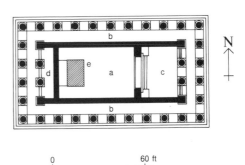

Fig. 8.26   Plan of the temple of Athena Polias at Priene, dedicated by Alexander the Great. Its architect was Pythius, who wrote a book on this temple. a. cella reached by steps from the porch; b. peristyle; c. deep porch with two columns in antis; d. opisthodomos with two columns in antis; e. pedestal for a cult image.

R ELIGION AND M YTHOLOGY

Prayers

Prayers are known from ancient literature and inscriptions. They generally followed a formula and were highly structured, usually with three parts. They began with an invocation of the deity, referring to the relevant function or functions of that deity. This was followed by reasons why the deity should answer the prayer, often citing what the suppliant had done for the deity in the past, such as sacrifices, votive offerings and worship. The final part of the prayer was a particular request to the deity.

Personal prayers were usually offered at the start of new projects, the beginning of a new day and the beginning of the farming season. Public prayers were offered at the start of military campaigns, athletic or dramatic contests, and political meetings. The division between prayers and curses could be very narrow; often the only difference was in what was being requested from the deity. It was believed that gods could provide protection and success for the living. Prayers were not concerned with the afterlife and tended to be requests for benefits for the living, such as success in war and love, a good harvest, good health and fortune, wealth and children. Prayers were often accompanied by sacrifice, and the gods were expected to listen and help.

Hymns

Hymns were sung to the gods as prayers set to music, and there were several types of hymns, including paeans. The dithyramb was a choral hymn to Dionysus. For paeans and dithyrambs, see chapter 7 (lyric poetry). There were also hymns for particular occasions, such as processions, and some were written to address a particular god about a specific subject. Singing of hymns by a trained chorus appears to have been a common element of communal worship, and it is likely that each sanctuary had its own set of hymns, probably used for festivals and special events, rather than as an act of daily worship.

Votive Offerings

PURPOSE

Votive offerings were token gifts to the gods in gratitude for favors received and to ensure continuing attention from the gods. Some inscriptions give thanks for a gift or favor received, and also constitute a prayer for similar gifts or favors in the future. Votive offerings could be a part of what had been requested from the god or closely connected. For example, victorious soldiers often donated some spoils captured from the enemy, and winners of contests often dedicated part of their prizes. Votive offerings were made to mark important stages in life, such as births and marriages, to give thanks for having survived disasters, such as earthquakes and shipwrecks, and in gratitude for recovery from illness.

TYPES OF OFFERING

A great variety of votive offerings existed. Almost everything could be used, from seeds and grains to massive statues, but some objects were specifically made as votive offerings. Linear B records show that votive offerings were made to the gods as early as the Mycenaean period, with honey commonly offered, as well as other foodstuffs such as oil, wine, barley and figs.

Votive offerings reflected the increase in prosperity from the 8th century BC. A variety of pottery containers were used (including specially made miniature pots), probably of less importance than the offerings of perishable foodstuffs or wine contained in them. These pots were often ritually broken to prevent them being taken back into everyday use after having been given to the gods. Other types of pottery were used as offerings, such as painted rectangular plaques and other terra-cotta models.

Personal possessions were often dedicated to the gods. Soldiers might dedicate arms and armor, poets might give copies of their poems, athletes might dedicate athletic equipment, and women might offer spinning and weaving equipment. Jewelry was commonly offered, more to goddesses than gods, and the size of some extremely large jewelry indicates that it was specially manufactured for votive offerings. Figurines in pottery and bronze were also popular, and some religious sanctuaries had their own manufacturing workshops. Human figurines predominated, sometimes representing deities, but more often representing the worshiper. Figurines of animals such as bulls, deer, sheep and goats, were also common. Foodstuffs and other perishable offerings, such as flowers, continued to be dedicated, but have left no trace unless mentioned in surviving records. Hair was another perishable offering, frequently made at puberty and at times of crisis to a river god.

A particular form of votive offering, commonly made at healing sanctuaries in gratitude for a successful cure, consisted of anatomical models of parts of the body, such as hands, feet, legs and heads. These represented the afflicted part that had been healed. Of those that survive, the majority are of pottery, but wood and various metals were used as well. Also given as offerings were images of the person cured and images of the deity that presided over the shrine.

Most votive offerings were relatively small and were stored within the religious sanctuary where they had been dedicated. Thousands of offerings could accumulate, and special buildings were often constructed to house them. There were also larger and more elaborate votive offerings, such as sculptured reliefs dedicated to heroes, which were carved to portray scenes from the hero's life, scenes of rituals and scenes of feasting. Another type of large votive offering was a bronze cauldron on a tripod; these cauldrons were everyday objects, but ones specially made for the gods were much larger and elaborately decorated.

Sacrifice

Sacrifice to the gods was a major component of Greek religion and consisted of blood sacrifices, libations and other offerings. The most common word for sacrifice, *thusia* (pl. *thusiai*), came to be synonymous with "festival" and "cult." A sacrifice was a gift to the gods, to heroes or to the dead. Sacrifice could also be a private offering or a public one on behalf of the people.

WASHING

Before any sacrifice took place, the sacrificer needed to be ritually cleansed, which usually took the form of washing the hands or sprinkling with water. Hand washing was an essential part of the ritual of animal sacrifice; in Classical times a distinctive metal vessel (*khernibeion*) was used for holding water for ritual washing and is portrayed in artistic representations of sacrifice. *Peirrhanteria* were raised stone basins holding water for ritual washing, commonly found in religious sanctuaries.

ANIMAL SACRIFICE

One of the most important parts of Greek religion was the sacrifice of animals to gods. Abundant references to such sacrifices exist in ancient literature and inscriptions. Animal sacrifices were also portrayed in art. However, relatively little evidence survives of how such sacrifices were performed. Some evidence comes from writers criticizing sacrifices, and so has an inevitable bias.

Animal sacrifice formed the heart of the vast majority of Greek religious cults. Animals selected for sacrifice had to be without blemish. They comprised domesticated and wild animals, birds and sometimes even fish. Generally male animals were sacrificed to gods and female ones to goddesses. Light-haired victims were chosen for sacrifice to "bright" (celestial) deities, and black-haired victims were sacrificed to the dead and to the gods of the underworld, although there were many exceptions. Animals unfit (or not used) for human food were sacrificed to specific deities. For example, horses were sacrificed to Poseidon and dogs to Hecate.

Homer gives details of the performance of an animal sacrifice. The sacrificer ritually washed his hands, and water was sprinkled on the victim. After a holy silence was declared, followed by a prayer by the officiant, unground barleycorn was sprinkled over the victim, altar and possibly the participants. Hair was cut from the victim's head and burned on the altar. The victim was then killed with a blow from an ax, and its throat was cut. Blood was collected in a bowl and splashed on the altar. The animal was then butchered, and the portion selected for the god was burned on the altar (apparently usually thigh bones wrapped in fat—worthless as food), while wine was simultaneously poured into the flames. The entrails were cooked separately and tasted first, then the remaining meat was cooked and eaten by the participants in a sacrificial feast at which the god was regarded as an honored guest.

The sacrifice took place in a sacred area, where the sacrificial meat often had to be consumed, although evidence suggests that sometimes the participants took home portions of sacrificial meat. The sacrifice was accompanied by music, and in post-Homeric times the entrails of the victim were examined for purposes of divination. In purificatory sacrifices and those sacrifices designed to propitiate the gods, the whole animal (or other offering) was completely destroyed. The complete burning of a sacrifice is known as a holocaust; such a ritual was usually performed to propitiate gods of the underworld, although in times of crisis it was offered to any deity who was thought able to alleviate the problem. A hecatomb (*hekatombe*) was literally an offering of 100 oxen, but more often referred to a great public sacrifice, not necessarily of 100, nor of oxen.

Oath sacrifices were made to consecrate oaths. This was effectively a magical ritual, since oath takers made a conditional curse upon themselves that specified penalties if the oath was violated. Such a sacrifice is described in Homer's *Iliad*, where those taking the oath first cut hair from the victims' heads and invoked the relevant gods. They then stated the terms of the oath, cut the victims' throat and poured libations of wine on the ground. Finally they prayed to the gods and buried the victims or threw them into the sea.

Although there are accounts of human sacrifice in Greek mythology, no definite evidence exists for human sacrifice, and the Greeks appear to have regarded the practice as barbaric.

LIBATIONS

Libations (offerings of a liquid as a sacrifice) were very common. Liquids were poured into a container and deposited in a sacred spot, or else poured on an altar, a rock or the ground. A distinction was made between a *sponde*, where a small part of the liquid was poured from a drinking vessel before the rest was drunk by the worshiper, and a *khoe*, in which all the liquid was poured out. *Spondai* were particularly associated with solemnizing treaties and *khoai* with the dead. The most common liquid for libations was wine, quite often mixed with water (as normally drunk by the Greeks). Water, milk, oil and honey were mainly for specific rituals, and libations of oil, perfumes and ointments were smeared on sacred objects. A distinctive vessel called a *phiale*, usually of metal, was employed for pouring libations and was itself a common offering at religious sanctuaries. In the 5th century BC in Athens, decorated flasks (*lethykoi*) containing oil were often deposited as grave goods and offerings.

OTHER SACRIFICIAL OFFERINGS

Apart from blood sacrifices of animals and libations, various other commodities were used as offerings to the gods. Incense, in the form of native herbs or expensive herbs imported from the East, were burnt on their own (as a modest sacrifice) or with other offerings. Flowers were used as offerings, as well as to decorate sacrificial victims and adorn participants in rituals. Branches of trees, such as olive and laurel, were similarly used, sometimes draped with fillets (decorative bands) of wool. All kinds of raw and cooked foods were used as offerings and in rituals. The *panspermia* (all-seeds) was an offering of a collection of different grains, and pots of cooked beans were deposited when an altar was set up and used as regular offerings. *Pelanos* was an offering made of flour mixed with liquids, and cakes in various shapes (often animals) were given as offerings. The "first fruits" of the harvest from fields and orchards were another popular offering. The idea also applied to meals, so that part of the meal was offered to the gods.

Divination

It was thought that gods revealed their will to people in the form of signs or omens. Some might be fairly obvious, such as natural phenomena or meaningful words uttered by chance, but most signs were less obvious and needed proper interpretation. Divination was the art of reading such signs to predict the future. The Greeks had various methods of divination, which can be divided into artificial and natural divination.

ARTIFICIAL DIVINATION

Artificial divination was based on external observation of animals, plants, objects or phenomena, and on the observation of the entrails of sacrificed animals. Augury was divination by the observation of the behavior of birds, and was one of the most ancient methods of divination. Generally augury was performed by recognized augurs, but many aspects of augury were well known; for example, a bird appearing from the right during observation of the augur was taken as a good omen, but a bird from the left was a bad omen, as was a crow settling on a half-built house. Lecanomancy was divination by looking into water (usually in a bowl or basin) in the hope of seeing future events, and took place at some oracles. Cleromancy was divination by lots, and both the drawing of lots and throwing of dice were used to predict the future. Divination by cleromancy, regarded as an inferior method, was apparently sometimes available as a cheaper option at some oracles for those who could not afford to consult the oracle proper. Divination by the examination of the entrails of sacrificed animals was practiced but was not particularly common.

NATURAL DIVINATION

Natural divination included the interpretation of dreams, either by the dreamer or by a professional interpreter. The rite of incubation was the process of sleeping in a sacred place in the hope of receiving guidance from a god in a dream. This method was often used to obtain guidance on how to cure a particular affliction and was commonly employed at healing sanctuaries. Necromancy, divination by communication with the dead, was practiced, but was generally regarded as less than respectable. Cledomancy was divination by the interpretation of chance remarks or sayings. A very important method of divination was prophecy. Prophets were thought, at certain times, to be possessed by a deity, so that the deity could speak through the mouth of the prophet. Sometimes the power of prophecy was considered to reside in a particular place, where oracles would be established: the deity might speak through a succession of prophets or seers over many generations.

ORACLES

Oracles were a form of natural divination in which a god gave a response to a question by a worshiper. It was the most prestigious method of divination, and oracular shrines were scattered across the Greek world. The deity at such shrines (often Apollo) was usually approached through the medium of a priest or priestess; inspired by the god, the medium gave advice to the person consulting the oracle. There were different ways in which the priest or priestess delivering the oracle achieved the state of inspiration (often a trance) to receive and deliver the words of the deity. For example, the Pythia at Delphi sat on a tripod with a laurel twig in her right hand and a bowl in her left. Unless the bowl contained a drug or a substance giving off intoxicating fumes, it is difficult to understand how her apparent trance was achieved. In some cases the prophet at an oracle drank holy water before prophesying.

The term "oracle" has come to be used both for the response of the deity and the shrine at which the deity was consulted. Oracles were consulted on personal, religious and political matters by men and women, both rich and poor, by slaves and by delegations from groups and communities. Each oracle made certain demands on those consulting it (usually sacrifices and rituals of purification); each also had its own rituals to be performed by the priests or priestesses at the oracle as well as by the worshipers. Records also existed of oracular sayings by prophets and prophetesses (some possibly mytho-logical rather than real people), which were thought to predict the future.

The most famous oracle was that of Pythian Apollo at Delphi (fig. 8.27). Here the responses of the god were given by an elected and elderly priestess with the title Pythia. Despite its mountainous location, Delphi was easily accessible by sea and attracted enquiries from beyond the Greek world. It continued to be consulted well into the Roman period. Other oracles of the god Apollo included Delos, Corope (Thessaly), Abae, Tegyra, Thebes and Mount Ptoon in Boeotia, and Clarus, Gryneum, Patara and Branchidae (Didyma) in Asia Minor.

An oracle of Zeus was at Dodona in northwest Greece, and one of Zeus Ammon was at the oasis of Siwa in north Africa. Gaia had oracles at Olympia and at Agae near Corinth, Dionysus had ones in Thrace and at Amphicleia in Phocis, and there was an oracle of Hermes at Pharae in Achaea. Other gods also had oracles, as did some heroes, the most famous being that of the hero Trophonius at Lebadea.

Healing Sanctuaries and Shrines

These were particular kinds of oracular shrines that people visited in order to consult the deity about curing ailments. The most common method of consulting a deity at a healing shrine was by incubation. After various rituals, such as sacrifices and ritual purification, the person seeking a cure slept at the shrine (often in a special dormitory, the *abaton*), in the hope that the deity would heal them or give instructions in a dream that would lead to their cure. At some healing sanctuaries people may have been given drugs or herbs before they slept to increase the possibility of dreams. Official interpreters of dreams were often present at these sanctuaries. Such official interpretations might include the prescription of drugs, a special diet and/or a regime of bathing and excercise, so that there could be a degree of overlap between religious healing and that attempted by physicians.

Those cured of ailments left votive offerings to the deity, which sometimes took the form of a model of the afflicted part of the anatomy. People could also visit such sanctuaries in order to preserve good health. Most healing sanctuaries were dedicated to Asclepius (called Asclepieia: fig. 8.28), the most famous being the Asclepieion of Epidaurus (fig. 6.9). There were other well-known healing centers, such as the sanctuary of Amphiaraus at Oropus in Boeotia. Other deities, such as Ino and Isis, were believed to possess healing powers. Despite their specialization in healing, such sanctuaries were still religious sites, and worship of the deity took place there as at other sacred places.

FESTIVALS

Type and Number of Festivals

Religious festivals varied in importance, size and popularity, and present knowledge of festivals is uneven: there is more surviving evidence about Panhellenic and Athenian festivals than others. The Panhellenic festivals were great interstate events that attracted people from all parts of the Greek world. Local festivals were organized and celebrated on a city-state, deme or even village basis, and their significance was generally limited to the area in which they were held. Most Panhellenic festivals were celebrated at only one center, but a few were celebrated at several places. The Thesmophoria, for example, was celebrated in at least 30 cities throughout the Greek world.

Each festival had its own events and rituals, but common elements included a formal procession to the shrine of a deity (with ritual stops along the way), decorating wooden objects symbolizing the deity, singing of hymns by choirs, athletic, music and drama contests, and the sacrifice of an animal in front of the shrine of the deity.

Fig. 8.27   The most famous oracle of the Greek world was at the sanctuary of Apollo at Delphi. View looking down on the theater and the temple of Apollo beyond.

The number of festivals celebrated during the year was probably quite high. In Athens, for which information is relatively complete, it has been estimated that just under half the days in each year were festival days. However, the boule remained in session on all except the annual festival days, although the Assembly did not meet on monthly festival days. It is assumed that most citizens conducted their normal business on most festival days, and that much the same schedule for festivals existed elsewhere in Greece.

Panhellenic Festivals

The Panhellenic festivals (Panhellenic Games) comprised four events recognized as national Greek festivals: Olympic Games, Pythian Games, Isthmian Games and Nemean Games. These games took place at different intervals within a four-year

cycle. Each four-year period was known as an Olympiad. Within an Olympiad the games were held in the following sequence: Olympic, Nemean, Isthmian, Pythian, Nemean and Isthmian Games. Thus it was possible to compete in each of the four games in the course of 25 months, rather than four years. The four games were known as the circuit (*periodos*), and a winner of all four games was known as a circuit victor (*periodonikes*).

OLYMPIC GAMES

Traditionally these games were thought to have been founded in 776 BC. Originally a local festival held at Olympia, the Olympic Games became a Peloponnesian and eventually a national event. The festival took place once every four years, and the four-year interval was known as an Olympiad (later used as a dating system). The games were in honor of Olympian Zeus. Originally they lasted only one day and consisted of running and wrestling con-

Fig. 8.28   The Asclepieion healing center at Pergamum. Looking to the theater and the acropolis from the Doric colonnade.

tests. Later horse and chariot races were included, but the foot race of one length of the stadium (fig. 8.29) remained the principal event. Other contests were added, and the games then took place over five days. The first day was for sacrifices and festivities, while judges and competitors took oaths of fair dealing. The second day had horse and chariot races and the men's pentathlon. Boys' contests took place on the third day, and men's running, jumping, wrestling, boxing and *pankration* contests occupied the fourth day, with the last event being the race for men in armor. The final day was for sacrifices, and in the evening a banquet was held for the winners. The prizes were chaplets of wild olive. The games were abolished by the Roman emperor Theodosius I in AD 393.

PYTHIAN GAMES

These took place at Delphi in honor of Apollo. From very early times there was a musical festival here. Originally held every eight years, it was con-

nected with the oracle of Apollo. In 582 BC the festival was reorganized and was then celebrated every four years, in the third year of each Olympiad. From that time both music and athletic contests took place. The athletic contests were modeled on those at Olympia, and there were competitions in singing, instrumental music, drama, and verse and rose recitation. The prize was a crown of bay leaves cut from the valley of Tempe.

ISTHMIAN GAMES

These were celebrated on the Isthmus of Corinth in honor of Poseidon. There was probably an ancient local festival on the Isthmus, but the Panhellenic festival dated from 581 BC and was held every two years, in the first and third years of each Olympiad. The games consisted of various athletic contests, and the prize was a wreath of dry celery (differentiating it from the crown of fresh celery awarded at Nemea).

NEMEAN GAMES

These were held in honor of Zeus in the sanctuary of Zeus at Nemea in Argolis. According to tradition, the games had been founded either by Heracles after killing the Nemean Lion, or by the Seven Against Thebes to commemorate the death of the Opheltes (infant son of Lycurgus). The Panhellenic festival dated from 573 BC and was held every two years in the second and fourth years of each Olympiad. The games consisted of athletic contests, with a greater number of boys' events than at Olympia. The prize was a crown of fresh wild celery (differentiating it from the wreath of dry celery awarded at the Isthmian Games).

Athenian and Attic Festivals

The calendar of festivals and religious sacrifices in Athens and Attica is the only one that can be reconstructed in any detail. Apart from the annual festivals there were a number of days in the first part of each month on which monthly festivals took place. The first day of the month was new moon day (*noumenia*), recognized as a holy day throughout the Greek world. It was so holy that at Athens no other festival ever took place that day. It was celebrated by a public ritual on the Acropolis and by private offerings of frankincense to statues of the gods.

The second day of the month was sacred to the Agathos Daimon. The third day of the month was the birthday of Athena; it may also have been sacred to the three Graces. The fourth day of the month was the birthday of Heracles, Hermes and Aphrodite, and was also sacred to Eros. The fifth day of the month was the birthday of Artemis, recognized throughout Greece. The seventh day of the month was Apollo's birthday, which was celebrated widely in the Greek world, and at Athens no other festival was held on this day. The eighth day of the month was sacred to Poseidon.

The main annual festivals and some annual sacrifices in Athens and Attica are listed below, under the names of the months of the Athenian calendar during which they took place. For the calendar, see chapter 10.

HEKATOMBAION (MONTH OF)

12th day: Festival in honor of Cronus (*Kronia*). Also a sacrifice by the Attic deme Erchia to Kourotrophos and Artemis.

16th day: Synoecia (*Synoikia*), a celebration of the coming together of the peoples of Attica. It appears to have been an annual sacrifice, although sometimes recorded as biennial. The sacrifice was not accompanied by public meetings.

17th and 18th days: A private celebration by Orgeones, a general term used mainly in Attica for a religious organization or group of worshipers, irrespective of what deities were worshiped.

28th day: Panathenaea (*Panathenaia*), a major festival that appears to have been celebrated at Athens on a varying number of days between the 23rd and 30th days of Hekatombaion, with the main celebration on the 28th. The festival was in honor of the birth of the goddess Athena, and the focal point was the presentation of a new robe (*peplos*) to the goddess. This robe was set up on a mast on a cart in the form of a ship. It was carried in a religious procession to the temple of Athena on the Acropolis. This procession was depicted on the frieze of the Parthenon temple (Elgin Marbles) now in the British Museum. There were numerous animal sacrifices, which were subject to complex regulations. The parts of the meat not offered to Athena were distributed to the people in the Kerameikos district. Every fourth year a much larger celebration took place called the Great Panathenaea (Panathenaic Games), which included horse racing, chariot racing (fig. 8.30) and a regatta; on the other three years the festival was known as the Lesser Panathenaea.

METAGEITNION (MONTH OF)

15th–18th days: Eleusinia, a festival of games celebrated at Eleusis (not the celebration of the Eleusinian Mysteries). The Eleusinia took place on four days between the 13th and 20th days of Metageitnion (probably 15th–18th). This festival was celebrated on the fourth year of every Olympiad and, on a lesser scale, every second year of the Olympiad. The festival included a religious procession and sacrifices, as well as the games. The winner's prize was a quantity of grain.

16th day: A sacrifice by the Attic deme Erchia to Kourotrophos, Hecate and Artemis.

19th day: A sacrifice by the Attic deme Erchia to "the Heroines."

20th day: A sacrifice by the Attic deme Erchia to Hera Thelchinia.

25th day: A sacrifice by the Attic deme Erchia to Zeus Epoptes.

BOEDROMION (MONTH OF)

The major celebration of the Eleusinian Mysteries (the Greater Mysteries) was held in this month. See also Oriental and Mystery Religions (p. 357).

4th day: A sacrifice by the Attic deme Erchia to Basile.

5th day: Genesia, a public festival for the dead. There was also a sacrifice by the Attic deme Erchia to Epops. The sacrifice was a holocaust without

Fig. 8.29 The stadium at Olympia where the Olympic Games were held. It dates to the 4th century BC. Both ends are straight, and it had earth banks that could hold 45,000 spectators.

wine and may have been connected with the festival of Genesia.

6th day: A festival in honor of Artemis Agrotera.

12th day: Democratia, a festival in honor of democracy, established after the restoration of democracy in Athens in 403 BC following the rule of the Thirty Tyrants. It probably took place on the 12th day of this month.

17th or 18th day: Epidauria, a festival in honor of Asclepius.

27th day: A sacrifice by the Attic deme Erchia to the Nymphs, Achelous, Alochus, Hermes and Gaia. Also a sacrifice by the Attic deme Teithras to Athene.

PYANOPSION (MONTH OF)

6th (?) day: Proerosia, an agricultural festival, literally "the preliminary to the plowing." It involved an offering of first fruits in gratitude for deliverance from a legendary plague. There is doubt as to whether it was an official festival of the Athenian state.

7th day: Pyanopsia, a festival in honor of Apollo.

8th day: Theseia, a festival in honor of Theseus.

8th (?) day: Oschophoria (*Oskhophoria*), a festival of the vintage. The main ritual was a procession carrying vine branches with clusters of grapes from the shrine of Dionysus at Athens to the shrine of Athena Sciras at Phalerum. The branches were carried by two young men dressed in female robes, followed by a choir singing hymns.

9th day: Stenia, a women's festival at Athens in honor of Demeter and Persephone. It was celebrated by sacrifice and a ritual exchange of verbal abuse. It was overshadowed by the festival of Thesmophoria.

11th–13th days: Thesmophoria, a three-day festival in honor of Demeter, celebrated not only in Athens, but also virtually everywhere in the Greek world. It was a women's festival from which men were excluded. At Athens it took place on the 11th to 13th days of Pyanopsion, and the celebration ceremonies were a mystery known only to the participants. On the first day shelters with couches of plants were erected for participants to camp in. The

Fig. 8.30   Chariot racing in the Great Panathenaea, in which an apobates *jumped on and off a moving chariot. The race was held in the agora at Athens on the Panathenaic Way. Fourth-century-BC sculpture.*

RELIGION AND MYTHOLOGY

second was a fast day, ending in a ritual exchange of verbal abuse. The third day was known as Calligeneia (day of fine offspring), but the rituals that took place are unknown. The main focus of the festival seems to have been the retrieval of the remains of piglets and other fertility symbols that had been thrown into pits or caves earlier in the year, probably during the festival of Scirophoria. These were laid on an altar, mixed with grain seed and later buried. The festival appears to have been a fertility ritual to ensure the success of the cereal crops sown in the autumn. The play *Thesmophoriazusae* (women celebrating the Thesmophoria) by Aristophanes is a parody of this festival.

14th day: A sacrifice by the Attic deme Erchia to "the Heroines."

19th–21st or 26th–28th days: Apaturia (*Apatouria*, probably meaning the festival of common fatherhood), a three-day festival of the phratries. Sacrifices were made to Zeus Phratrios and Athena Phratria. The three days of the festival were called Dorpia (Supper), Anarrhyrsis (Sacrifice) and Cureotis (Day of the Youths). On the last day (Cureotis) children, young adult men and newly married wives were enrolled in the phratries.

30th day: Chalceia (*Khalkeia*), a festival in honor of Athena in her role as mistress of technology, and in honor of Hephaestus, god of the smiths. During this festival the loom was set up for weaving the robe presented to Athena in the Panathenaea festival.

MAIMAKTERION (MONTH OF)

Pompaia was a festival that took place some time during this month. A sheepskin from a sacrifice to Zeus was carried in procession along with the staff of Hermes, possibly to avert evil at the onset of winter.

POSEIDEON (MONTH OF)

The Rural Dionysia (or Rustic Dionysia) took place this month. The name Dionysia was given to any festival in honor of Dionysus at which dramatic performances took place. Because the dramatic per-

formances became very popular, such festivals rapidly spread from Athens where this type of festival appears to have originated. Two Dionysia were celebrated at Athens, the lesser one being the Rural Dionysia. In addition to dramatic performances and the sacrifice of a goat, fruit in a basket and a ceremonial phallus were carried in procession. See also ELAPHEBOLION on p. 355.

5th day: Plerosia, a festival celebrated by the Attic deme Myrrhinus.

16th day: A sacrifice to Zeus Horios by the Attic deme Erchia.

19th day: A private sacrifice to the wind gods is recorded for this day. A meeting of the Attic deme Myrrhinus on matters concerned with Dionysus also took place.

26th day: Haloa, a fertility festival in honor of Dionysus and Demeter.

GAMELION (MONTH OF)

8th day: A sacrifice to Apollo Apotropaeus, Apollo Nymphegetes and the Nymphs by the Attic deme Erchia.

9th day: A sacrifice to Athena by the Attic deme Erchia.

12th day: Lenaea, a festival in honor of Dionysus. It took place on the 12th but appears to have lasted at least four days. Among the Ionian Greeks the festival gave its name to the month, which was Lanaeon in their calendar. Little is known about the rituals of the festival, but there were dramatic performances and a procession. From about 440 BC drama competitions took place in which comedy seems to have been particularly important.

27th day: Theogamia, a festival celebrating the sacred marriage between Hera and Zeus, also called the Gamelia, may have taken place on this day. Also on this day there was a sacrifice to Kourotrophos, Hera, Zeus Teleius and Poseidon by the Attic deme

Erchia. This may·have been connected with the Theogamia festival.

ANTHESTERION (MONTH OF)

2nd day: A sacrifice to Dionysus by the Attic deme Erchia.

11th-13th days: Anthesteria, a festival in honor of Dionysus, involving flowers, wine and spirits of the dead, from which the month Anthesterion took its name. At Athens it was celebrated on the 11th to 13th of this month. It was also widely celebrated among Ionian Greeks. Children took part in the festival and three-year old children were garlanded with flowers. The first day was the Pithoigia (Opening of the Jars), when the new wine was tasted and offered at the shrine of Dionysus. The second day, called Choes (Wine Jugs), saw much drinking and a procession in which Dionysus (perhaps an image or a masked actor) was carried in a cart in the form of a ship with wheels. Dionysus was then united in a sacred marriage with the wife of the archon basileus. The third day was called Chytrai (Pots), because pots containing a mixture of boiled vegetables were offered to Hermes Chthonios (Hermes of the underworld) to placate the hostility of the dead. It was a day of ill-omen, when spirits of the dead were thought to roam the city. At the end of the day they were banished with the cry "away, dread spirits; Anthesteria is over."

20th–26th days: A smaller festival (Lesser Mysteries), in preparation for the Eleusinian Mysteries, was held at Agrae, a suburb of Athens, probably between the 20th and 26th of this month.

23rd day: Diasia, a festival in honor of Zeus Meilichios.

ELAPHEBOLION (MONTH OF)

10th–17th days: City Dionysia (or Great Dionysia), an important festival in honor of Dionysus. The festival lasted five days, and appears to have taken place between the 10th and 17th of this month. It was celebrated from at least 534 BC, when Peisistratus brought the cult to Athens from Eleutherae (on the Attica-Boeotia border). Just before each festival the image of Dionysus was removed to a temple outside Athens, so that a procession carrying the image could reenact the god's original arrival from Eleutherae. The procession was performed with a great deal of pomp, and images of phalli were carried in the god's honor. The god's image was then placed in the old temple of Dionysus within the theater precinct, and sacrifices and libations were offered. Then the god's image was carried to the theater and was present for the performance of the comedies, tragedies, satyr plays and dithyrambic competitions.

15th day: A private sacrifice to Cronus.

17th day: Pandia, a festival in honor of Zeus about which little is known.

MOUNICHION (MONTH OF)

16th day: Munichia (*Mounikhia*), a festival in honor of Artemis. It involved special cakes with candles said to be moon symbols, and a sacrifice of a she-goat dressed as a girl.

17th day: The religious association of the Thiasotai is recorded as meeting on this day.

18th day: The religious association of the Eranistai is recorded as meeting on this day.

19th day: Olympieia, a festival in honor of Olympian Zeus. It was instituted by Peisistratus and was associated with the inauguration of the temple of Olympian Zeus at Athens, which was not completed until Roman times. The festival included a procession of cavalry.

20th day: A sacrifice to Leucaspis by the Attic deme Erchia.

21st day: A sacrifice to the Tritopatores by the Attic deme Erchia.

THARGELION (MONTH OF)

4th day: A sacrifice to Leto, Pythian Apollo, Zeus, Hermes and the Dioscuri by the Attic deme Erchia.

7th day: Thargelia, a festival in honor of Apollo.

16th day: A sacrifice to Zeus Epacrios by the Attic deme Erchia.

19th day: A festival of the Thracian goddess Bendis (Bendideia). It included an all-night festival with a torch race on horseback. Also a sacrifice to Menedeius by the Attic deme Erchia.

24th day: Spring-cleaning of the temple of Athena probably took place on the 24th day. It was known as the Callynteria.

25th day: Festival of Washing (Plynteria), during which the image of Athena, and possibly her robe, was ceremonially washed. It was regarded as a dangerous day, because the goddess was preoccupied and might not afford her usual degree of protection.

SKIROPHORION (MONTH OF)

3rd day: Arrephoria (or Arrhetophoria), a festival in honor of Athena.

3rd day: A sacrifice to Kourotrophos, Athena Polias, Aglaurus, Zeus Polieus, Poseidon and possibly to Pandrosus by the Attic deme Erchia. Athena Polias and Zeus Polieus were both "protectors of the city."

12th day: Scira (*Skira*), a predominantly, but not exclusively, women's festival. A procession included the priestess of Athena, priest of Poseidon and possibly the priest of Apollo, all under a large parasol. The festival included a women's fertility ritual in honor of Demeter. The Tritopatores were worshiped at Marathon on the eve of this festival.

14th day: Bouphonia (also known as Dipolieia), a festival in honor of Zeus Polieus. It included a strange ritual. Barley and wheat were placed on a altar, and when the sacrificial bull moved to eat the grain, a priest killed the bull, threw down the poleax and fled. The poleax was then formally tried for murder.

Other Festivals

ASCLEPIEIA

Festivals in honor of Asclepius, held at various sanctuaries (also called Asclepieia) of the god. A major festival of this kind took place at Epidaurus every four years, nine days after the Isthmian Games (Great Asclepieia). At Epidaurus the worshipers were ritually cleansed before entering the sanctuary, and a series of rituals preceded games and musical contests in honor of Asclepius. The festival culminated in a sacrifice to Asclepius, followed by a banquet.

GYMNOPAIDIAI

"Festival of the naked youths" at Sparta. It was established as an annual festival soon after the crushing defeat of Sparta by Argos at the battle of Hysiae in 669 BC. It was held in July and lasted several days, during which there were gymnastic displays and dancing by boys and men. Hymns were sung in honor of the gods and Spartan heroes.

CARNEA (*KARNEIA*)

A festival celebrated by Sparta and other Doric states in the month of Karneios (August–September), which derived its name from the festival. It was held in honor of Apollo, but it may have originally been in honor of a more ancient, unknown god, perhaps with the name Karnos or Karneis. In part it reflected Sparta's military life, and a meal was taken in shelters in a military fashion, but there were rural aspects to the celebration as well, including a race between boys carrying bunches of grapes. There were other races, as well as a musical contest that drew musicians and poets from all parts of the Greek world.

HERAEA

A festival in honor of Hera at Argos, held every fourth year. In a procession to the Heraeum the priestess of Hera rode in a chariot drawn by oxen. There was a hecatomb, and athletic contests took place in the stadium near the temple of Hera, with a bronze shield as the prize.

DAIDALA

A festival in honor of Hera, celebrated in Boeotia every 59 years. *Daidala* (intricately worked things) were wooden images. One was dressed as a bride and carried in procession to the top of Mount Cithaeron. Here a sacrifice was performed, and several *daidala* were burned in a great bonfire. According to the myth that explained this curious festival, Zeus and Hera quarreled, and Hera hid on Mount Cithaeron. Zeus therefore dressed a doll as a bride, which he said he was going to marry. Hera rushed out to attack her rival but, realizing the trick, was reconciled with Zeus, and the doll was burned.

ELEUTHERIA

A festival celebrated at Plataea every four years in thanksgiving for the Greek defeat of the Persians in the battle of Plataea (479 BC).

LYCAEA

A festival in honor of Zeus, celebrated at Mount Lycaeus.

HYACINTHIA

A festival celebrated at Sparta in honor of Hyacinthus. The first half of the festival was a solemn event, with no garlands worn or hymns sung and only extremely plain food being eaten. Halfway through the festival, a hymn was sung, the nature of the festival changed to one of celebration, and a large procession occurred.

ORIENTAL AND MYSTERY RELIGIONS

Many foreign cults were absorbed into Greek religion by the process of identifying foreign gods with existing Greek ones. However, some foreign cults were adopted rather than absorbed, usually because their cults offered the worshiper more than the existing Greek cults. Generally these foreign cults were partly or wholly mystery religions, which had secrets (mysteries) that were revealed only to initiates. Their teachings were supposed to illuminate the mystery of achieving immortality; the teachings themselves were kept as a mystery, to which the faithful were initiated. Mystery religions involved participation by the individual, unlike worship of traditional Greek gods. They involved initiation rites, purification, sacred symbols, sacred rites and a promise of a happy afterlife. Because so much of a mystery religion was kept secret, modern knowledge of the beliefs and rituals of these religions is far from complete.

Eleusinian Mysteries

The Eleusinian Mysteries were claimed to guarantee initiates a happy afterlife. The cult was celebrated each year at Athens in the month Boedromion (September) at the time of sowing, when every participant bathed in the sea for purification and sacrificed a piglet. Then the sacred and secret objects, which had been brought from Eleusis to Athens a few days previously and stored in the Eleusinion (a temple below the Acropolis at Athens), were taken back to Eleusis accompanied by a great procession of initiates. At a certain place on the procession route, obscenities were shouted as a reenactment of the abusive joking of a mythical woman (called Iambe), who was supposed to have made Demeter smile. The shout of *Iakch' o Iakche* was raised regularly during the procession, and was usually regarded as referring to Iacchus (an obscure deity, sometimes identified with Dionysus or said to be a son of Demeter or Persephone). The ritual was supposed to represent the myth of Demeter and

Persephone and the symbolic death and rebirth of the grain seed. On the following day the initiates fasted (as Demeter fasted when mourning the loss of Persephone). They broke their fast with a special drink of barley water flavored with pennyroyal (called *kykeon*). The culmination of the festival took place in the *telesterion* (initiation hall) at Eleusis (fig. 8.31), where a priest showed the sacred objects to the initiated. The cult appears to have existed for more than 1,000 years, until it was suppressed by the Roman emperor Theodosius I in AD 393.

Mysteries of the Cabiri

The cult of the Cabiri was centered on Samothrace. The Cabiri were deities of fertility and of protection for sailors, probably originally Phrygian deities. Different traditions recorded different numbers of Cabiri. One tradition recorded four Cabiri and named them as Axierus, Axiocersa, Axiocersus and Cadmilus. The Cabiri were part of a mystery cult; probably because of this they were not usually individually named and were generally referred to as the "great gods." In the Hellenistic period the cult spread rapidly throughout the Greek world. The Cabiri were often confused with the Dioscuri, who also had the function of protecting sailors. This confusion was helped by the fact that the Cabiri came to be portrayed in art as a pair of gods: an old, reclining, bearded one, and a younger, standing one. Later they were depicted as a pair of youths almost indistinguishable from portrayals of the Dioscuri.

Mysteries of Dionysus

These mysteries were the rites (*orgia*) of the worship of Dionysus. The cult appears to have originated in Asia Minor, or possibly Thrace, and spread rapidly throughout Greece from Thrace. The *orgia* do not appear to have been associated with specific cult sites, but were performed wherever there was a group of worshipers. Adherents to this cult were mainly women and were called Maenads. Inspired by Dionysus they surrendered to an ecstatic frenzy in order to achieve a sense of freedom and well-being; this appears to have been at the heart of these mysteries, although there were also promises of an afterlife.

The Maenads were believed to roam mountains with music and dancing, performing supernatural feats of strength, such as uprooting trees and catching and tearing apart wild animals, sometimes eating the flesh raw. Maenads were often depicted wearing the skins of fawns or panthers, with wreaths of ivy, oak or fir, and carrying a *thyrsos* (wand wreathed in ivy and vine leaves and topped with a pine cone). This aspect of the religion symbolized the triumph of unfettered nature over man-made order. Less wild forms of the worship of Dionysus, similar to worship offered to other Greek gods, took place at shrines and temples dedicated to Dionysus and at festivals in his honor. See also DIONYSUS.

Orphic Mysteries

From about the 6th century BC there are indications of mystery cults associated with Orpheus (see p. 323), but it is doubtful whether there was ever a unified cult that could be called "Orphism." The Derveni papyrus, an ancient book of the late 4th century BC found at Derveni in Macedonia, gives a commentary on an Orphic religious poem. It indicates that good and evil in human nature were explained by the myth of Dionysus Zagreus (which involved death and resurrection, and punishment of the wicked). Men were regarded as bearing the guilt of the death of Dionysus Zagreus and had to pay a penalty to Persephone after death before rising to a higher existence. This Greek myth was different in having as its central doctrine the punishment of individuals after death.

The Orphic cult also recognized reincarnation. After three virtuous lives as defined by Orphic doctrine, individuals were supposed to dwell in the Isles of the Blessed forever. The mysteries continued to have a following into the Roman period, but the high ethical tone and ascetic practices of some adherents of Orpheus in Greece later became debased and ridiculed. There appear to have been some links between the Orphic Mysteries and the mythology of Dionysus, but some hostility evidently existed between the adherents of Orpheus and those of Dionysus.

Cult of Isis and Sarapis

Isis was an Egyptian mother goddess whose son Horus (usually called Harpocrates in the Greek world) is an heroic figure who avenged the death of his father Osiris (usually known to the Greeks as Sarapis). Their worship was virtually a mystery religion. The triad of Isis, Harpocrates and Sarapis represented the power of creation. The cult of Isis involved initiation ceremonies, baptism and service, and processions of music and dance designed to arouse religious fervor. It also promised eventual salvation. See also HARPOCRATES, ISIS and SARAPIS.

Judaism

Judaism was originally an ancient monotheistic Oriental mystery religion of Judaea and Babylonia. Of all religions in the ancient world before Christianity, Judaism was exclusive in insisting on the worship of only one God (Yahweh), based on the temple at Jerusalem. The Jews built their second temple at Jerusalem when the Persian king Cyrus allowed them to return there from exile in Babylon. It was dedicated in 516 BC, and Judaism was centered on this temple, whose high priest and priests ruled Judaea and collected taxes. In 167 BC under the reign of Antiochus IV, it was rededicated to Olympian Zeus, but after the Maccabean Revolt it was reconsecrated to Yahweh in 164 BC. Herod the Great replaced this small temple with a massive third temple; the building work took place from 19 BC and was largely completed by 9 BC. It was destroyed by Titus during the Jewish revolt against Roman rule in AD 70.

Jews regarded their God as the one and only creator of all things and the giver of natural and moral law. They also regarded the Jewish nation as the

Fig. 8.31 Excavations at Eleusis c. 1860, the sanctuary sacred to Demeter and where the Eleusinian Mysteries were worshiped.

RELIGION AND MYTHOLOGY

people especially chosen by God to receive his revelation and to play the central role in human salvation. Judaism was not exclusive to the Jewish nation, since non-Jews could convert to the religion, but no active missionary work took place to encourage such conversions. Judaea was under Persian domination from 538 to 332 BC, when it became part of the empire of Alexander the Great. From that time it continued to be influenced by the Greeks until after it came under Roman control in 37 BC.

In the early years of Greek rule, Jews were encouraged to settle in the newly founded cities of Alexander the Great's empire; this greatly increased the dispersion (diaspora) of Jews, which had begun as early as 587 BC when Nebuchadnezzar sacked Jerusalem and captured the inhabitants. Settlement in the new Hellenistic cities spread Jews and the Jewish religion throughout the Greek world. Jewish communities were organized in officially recognized corporations (*politeumata*), as were other minority groups. This gave Jews the freedom to live under their own laws and privileges such as exemption from worship of rulers and pagan gods, and freedom to keep the Sabbath as a day of rest. In return Jews were generally loyal to their foreign rulers.

MAGIC AND SUPERSTITION

Superstition is the irrational fear of the unknown allied to a false idea of the causes of events. Magic is the attempt to control such events by direct actions and rituals. Superstition and magic spring from the same origin as religion—a belief in supernatural forces that control the lives of people. The dividing line between a religious ritual (asking the gods for something to happen) and a magic ritual (directly attempting to make that thing happen) was often very fine. A strong element of magic was present in Greek religion. For example, at a sacred well on Mount Lycaeon in Arcadia, a priest performed a ritual to induce rain in time of drought. Having offered a sacrifice to Zeus, he stirred the waters with a twig and summoned mist and rain clouds.

There were apparently no magicians in Classical Greece, although evidence suggests that they existed in earlier periods. As Greek civilization developed magic appears to have been suppressed, but many magical rituals appear to have been absorbed into Greek religion. Also, many superstitions survived that were mainly concerned with averting evil, often by warding off the evil eye. Various charms, spells and rituals were used to avert evil. For example, care had to be taken in the disposal of nail-parings and hair-clippings, in case they were used in black magic to cause harm to the body from which they had come. Necromancy, the summoning of spirits of the dead for various purposes, was practiced, although not considered respectable.

RITUAL ARTIFACTS

Several groups of artifacts were connected with ritual and religious use, including cult images, altars, implements, vessels, votive offerings, materials used for curses, charms and amulets. There was some overlap between these groups. For instance, an altar may have been a votive gift as well as an object used in rituals. Many artifacts are often conveniently assumed to have had a religious or ritual connection, when no other interpretation can be suggested.

Ritual Vessels and Implements

Various vessels were used in religious rituals, although it is not always certain whether special vessels were used, or whether everyday vessels were consecrated for religious use. In art a distinctive vessel called a *phiale* is often depicted for pouring libations, as are cups and similar vessels. In Athens in the 5th century BC flasks (*lekythoi*) containing oil were placed in graves as offerings. In the Classical period a distinctive metal vessel known as a *khernibeion* was used for holding water for ritual washing. It is portrayed in artistic representations of sacrifices. Raised stone basins holding water for ritual washing (*peirrhanteria*) were commonly found in religious sanctuaries.

Musical Instruments

Music played a part in religious observance, particularly at festivals and games, where there were musical contests. See chapter 7, music.

Processional Objects

Processions were a major part of Greek festivals and usually consisted of worshipers walking to a temple or taking an image of a deity from one place to another. Sacred implements relating to the deity were often carried in procession. For example, virtually no procession in honor of Dionysus was without at least a few phallic symbols. Special vehicles were sometimes present, such as the ship on wheels that carried the new robe of the goddess to the temple of Athena on the Acropolis at Athens in the Panathenaea festival. A cart in the form of a ship formed part of the procession during the Anthesteria festival.

Charms, Amulets and Curses

Various charms and amulets were used to bring good luck and as protection against evil, and the division between superstition and religion in their use is often unclear. For example, one of the titles of Heracles was "Averter of Evil" (Alexikakos), so wearing his image, perhaps on a ring, could be interpreted as both religious and superstitious. Amulets were used to protect the wearer against witchcraft and the evil eye. They were also used to protect buildings, particularly houses and other structures such as walls. Amulets were of virtually any material, and rings were often worn for this purpose. The potency of amulets might be enhanced by having a charm inscribed on them.

Charms were used to bring good luck and ward off evil. They were used on their own, sometimes worn around the neck in a bag on a string, and consisted of magic formulas, words and anagrams.

Curses were used for a variety of purposes, such as revenge against an enemy or to protect a grave against violation; the difference between a vow and a curse was often negligible. Curses could be spoken or else written down on a variety of objects such as papyrus, lead tablets and amulets of various kinds. See also votive offerings, cult images, altars.

READING

Chronological Development

Several books deal with many aspects of Greek religion over time, including Bremmer 1994, Burkert 1985, Ferguson 1989, Garland 1995, Hammond and Scullard (eds.) 1970, Howatson (ed.) 1989, and Pritchett 1979.

Gods and Goddesses

Antonaccio 1994: aspects of the development of hero cults; Bourgeaud 1988: Pan; Farnell 1921: hero cults; Ferguson 1988a; Ferguson 1989: chapter on gods and goddesses; Grant and Hazel 1973: myths; Griffin 1988: myths; Hammond and Scullard (eds.) 1970; Howatson (ed.) 1989; Kerényi 1951; Morford and Lenardon 1971: myths; Simpson 1988: has useful overview of Greek mythology; Soren (ed.) 1987: Apollo Hylates; Vermaseren 1977: Cybele and Attis.

Priesthoods

Ferguson 1989: chapter on priesthood; Garland 1990: priests in Classical Athens; Hooker 1990: Mycenaean cult personnel; Thompson 1990: Ptolemaic priests at Memphis; Turner 1988: useful summary of priesthoods.

Sacred Places

Carter 1983: sanctuary of Athena Polias at Priene; Ferguson 1989; Gesell 1985: Minoan; Levi 1971a and b: translation and commentary on Pausanias' visits to numerous sacred places in 2nd century AD; Marinatos & Hägg (eds.) 1993: aspects of sanctuaries; Robertson 1943: descriptions and plans of temples; Tomlinson 1976: temples, sanctuaries; Trell 1988: temple of Artemis at Ephesus; Yavis 1949: altars.

Religious Observance

Bruit Zaidman and Schmitt Pantel 1992: ritual; Cole 1988; Ferguson 1989: chapter on votive offerings; Hammond and Scullard (eds.) 1970; Howatson (ed.) 1989; Hughes 1991: evidence for human sacrifice; Jameson 1988: contains useful summary of sacrifice and ritual; Levi 1971a and b: translation and commentary on Pausanias' firsthand accounts of visits in the 2nd century AD to oracles, including Delphi, and his own consultation of the oracle of Trophonius; Parke 1985: oracles; Parke 1988: Sibylline prophecy; Pollard 1988: contains useful summary of divination.

Festivals

Bruit Zaidman and Schmitt Pantel 1992; Ferguson 1989: chapter on games and festivals; Garland 1988; Hammond and Scullard (eds.) 1970; Howatson (ed.) 1989; Parke 1977: Athenian festivals; Robertson 1992: deals with some major festivals at Athens, Sparta, Argos, Messenia and Phigaleia; Simon 1983: festivals of Attica.

Oriental and Mystery Religions

Alderink 1981: Orphism, with English translation of the Derveni Papyrus and useful bibliography; Carpenter and Faraone (eds.) 1993: aspects of the cult of Dionysus, with useful bibliography; Ferguson 1989; Hammond and Scullard (eds.) 1970; Howatson (ed.) 1989; Kerényi 1967: Eleusinian Mysteries; Mylonas 1961: Eleusinian Mysteries; Schwartz 1988: deals with Judaism in the Greek world, particularly in Hellenistic times.

Magic and Superstition

Ferguson 1988b; Ferguson 1989: chapter on magic; Luck 1985.

Ritual Artifacts

Ferguson 1989.

9

ART, SCIENCE
AND PHILOSOPHY

ART

What is today termed "art" or "applied art" encompasses a wide range of materials and techniques in the Greek world, including pottery, sculpture (from miniature objects to immense statues and architectural sculpture), metalwork (especially bronze and gold), frescoes and wall paintings, and floor mosaics. In the Greek world there was no Muse for art or architecture, only for arts such as music, dancing and literature. Artists were artisans, and the only word for art was *tekhne* (craft). Roman collectors of art date from the later Republic, and they were particularly attracted to objects from Greece.

Contrary to perceptions of Greek art today, much Greek art was very colorful and gaudy, with architectural sculpture, columns, walls, ceilings, gravestones and sculptures all being brightly painted.

Pottery

Many types of Greek pottery have distinctive decoration and are usually discussed in terms of art history, in particular black-figure and red-figure vases. Pottery is the most common artifact in archaeological sites and was first developed in the Neolithic period. Particularly for the prehistoric period many types of pottery are named after the sites where they have been found (such as Kamares ware). The study of pottery has tended to concentrate on decorated wares, but in nearly all periods plain wares existed alongside decorated wares.

SHAPES

Pottery (baked clay or terra-cotta) was used for a vast range of vessels with varying and sometimes overlapping shapes and functions (fig. 9.1). Not only were containers such as jugs, drinking vessels and dishes produced, but also items such as large tubs, buckets, kettles, frying pans, mortars for grinding, ovens, cosmetic boxes, coffins, figurines, statues, architectural decoration and lamps.

A great deal is known about the finer pottery wares with artistic decoration, because they can sur-

vive relatively intact in tombs; far less is known about everyday coarse wares, such as those used in the kitchen, although these latter vessels were probably more common in all periods. Pottery containers were also used in trades, industries and public life, such as for liquid and dry measures, water clocks and voting urns. Pottery vessels, such as black-figure Panathenaic prize amphorae, were also given as prizes in games. Greek names of some shapes of pots are known, largely of Attic fine wares. The same shape could be used for a fairly plain vessel and a highly decorated one. Some shapes were also made in other materials, such as stone and metal. The following were the most common shapes:

Alabastron (pl. *alabastra*): Small flask for oil or perfume, with a narrow neck, sagging base (no foot) and no handles.

Amis (pl. *amides*): A portable urinal, possibly in the form of a wide-mouthed jug.

Amphora (pl. *amphorae*): A tall vessel (Greek *amphoreus*) carried by two handles, used for transporting and storing wine, olive oil and other goods, for serving wine at the table, and as cremation urns. There were three main kinds: transport amphorae, neck amphorae and belly amphorae. Amphorae were also given as prizes in games.

Amphoriskos (pl. *amphoriskoi*): A small amphora for perfumed oil.

Aryballos (pl. *aryballoi*): A small rounded oil flask with one, two or no handles, used by athletes.

Askos (pl. *askoi*, literally "a wine skin"): A small, wide flat vase or flask for oil, with a narrow sloping spout and an arched handle meeting the spout.

Bolsal: An invented name for a broad shallow cup with two horizontal handles.

Bottle: A vase with a narrow neck, rounded body, shallow foot and no handle.

Bowl: A plain open vessel with no handles.

Chalice: A deep cup with conical foot, and horizontal handles.

Chous (pl. *choes*, Greek *khous* from the verb meaning "to pour"): A bulbous jug with a low handle and trefoil mouth, supported on a stand. Choes were used in the Anthesteria festival. Small choes were given to children.

Chytra (pl. *chytrai*): (Greek *khytra*) Footless cooking pot, with one or two handles at the rim. Some have a lid.

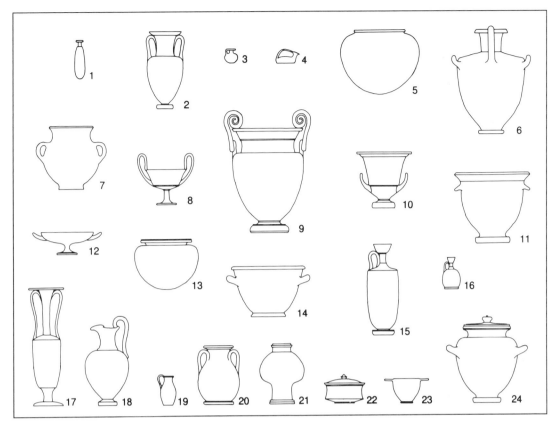

Fig. 9.1 Types of pottery shapes: 1. alabastron; 2. neck amphora; 3. aryballos; 4. askos; 5. dinos; 6. hydria; 7. kados; 8. kantharos; 9. volute krater; 10. calyx krater; 11. bell krater; 12. type B kylix; 13. lebes; 14. lekane; 15. lekythos; 16. squat lekythos; 17. loutrophoros; 18. oinochoe; 19. olpe; 20. pelike; 21. psykter; 22. pyxis; 23. skyphos; 24. stamnos.

Cup: A general term for a two-handled drinking vessel.

Dinos (pl. *dinoi*): Literally, a drinking cup, although now used to denote a large, open round-bottomed bowl supported on a stand and used for mixing wine and water.

Epichysis (pl. *epichysides*): (Greek *epikhysis*) One-handled jug with a long narrow neck, mainly from south Italy.

Epinetron (pl. *epinetra*): Also miscalled an *onos* (pl. *onoi*), this was a long semicircular cover or shield for the knees and thighs, over which wool was worked.

Exaleiptron (pl. *exaleiptra*, from the verb meaning "to anoint"): A vase with a low or high foot, usually lidded. It was used for perfumed oil in women's rooms and at graves. There were no handles. It was also called a plemochoe or kothon.

Feeder: Small footed vessel with a flat top and spout on the side, for feeding infants or invalids.

Fish-plate: Plate with a low foot, often decorated with fish.

Frying pans: Flat pans about 2.5 in (60 mm) high, sometimes thought to be prehistoric fertility charms representing a womb.

Guttus (pl. *gutti*): Latin name for a narrow-necked vessel, usually an oil pot.

Hydria (pl. *hydriai*): A large oval water jar with three handles—two horizontal and one vertical. Hellenistic Hadra hydriai were used as cremation urns.

Kados (pl. *kadoi*): A coarse ware bucket for getting water from a well. It had a wide mouth and two small vertical handles.

Kalathos (pl. *kalathoi*): Literally a basket, such as for wool; the pottery versions were small handleless conical vessels.

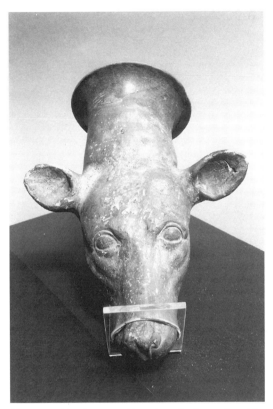

Fig. 9.2 Drinking cup (rhyton) in the shape of a calf. It has one handle. Its length is 6.3 in (0.16 m), 4th century BC. Courtesy of Somerset County Museums Service.

Kalpis (pl. *kalpides*): A type of fine ware hydria.

Kantharos (pl. *kantharoi*): A deep drinking cup with tall vertical handles.

Kernos (pl. *kernoi*): Small bowls attached to the rim of a large bowl on a foot. This was a multiple vase for making offerings to a deity.

Kothon (pl. *kothones*): A term used for various shapes of pottery vessels, such as (incorrectly) the exaleiptron, as well as a deep one-handled drinking cup used by soldiers and travelers.

Kotyle (pl. *kotylai*): An alternative name for a skyphos.

Krater (pl. *krateres* from the word meaning "mix"): A large open bowl for mixing wine with water, particularly common as Attic and south Italian red-figure vessels. The main forms were a volute krater, calyx krater and bell krater.

Kyathos (pl. *kyathoi*): A vessel with a single long handle, used as a ladle or cup.

Kylix (pl. *kylikes*): A wide shallow drinking cup with two horizontal handles and a tall stem above a foot. Many forms exist, such as Siana cups, Type A and Type B. There were also stemless examples, which had a ring foot instead.

Lagynos (pl. *lagynoi*): A jug with a squat bulbous body, tall narrow neck and long vertical handle.

Lakaina (pl. *lakainai*): A drinking cup with a deep body and two horizontal handles near the base.

Lebes (pl. *lebetes*): A mixing bowl with a spherical body, no handles or foot, supported on a stand.

Lebes gamikos (pl. *lebetes gamikoi*): Like the lebes, but with two tall vertical handles at the shoulder, a lid and a stand or foot. Used in weddings for the bridal bath.

Lekane (pl. *lekanai*): Basin or bowl with two horizontal handles. Used for food preparation.

Lekanis (pl. *lekanides*): A shallow lidded dish with a foot and two horizontal handles.

Lekythos (pl. *lekythoi*): A tall cylindrical flask for oil, with a foot and single handle. Another version was the squat lekythos.

Lopas (pl. *lopades*): A shallow cooking pot with lid.

Louterion (pl. *louteria*): A bowl with two handles and a spout.

Loutrophoros (pl. *loutrophoroi*, literally "carrying to the bath"): A tall slender ritual vessel like a neck amphora with two very tall vertical handles. It was used in weddings and at funerals of the unmarried.

Lydion (pl. *lydia*): A handleless perfume bottle.

Mastos (pl. *mastoi*, literally "breast"): A cup resembling a woman's breast, with a nipple base or foot, usually with one vertical and one horizontal handle.

Mortar: A grinding bowl for food preparation (usually of stone).

Mug: A deep one-handled drinking vessel.

Nestoris (pl. *nestorides*): A wide-mouthed jar with two horizontal handles, from south Italy.

Oinochoe (pl. *oinochoai*, wine-pourer): (Greek, *oinokhoe*) A wine jug of various shapes, often with a trefoil spout and a single vertical handle.

Olpe (pl. *olpai*): A jug, usually with a circular mouth with broad lip, and a low handle.

One-handler: A shallow bowl with one horizontal handle.

Pelike (pl. *pelikai*): A type of amphora with a sagging body and wide mouth.

Peirrhanterion (pl. *peirrhanteria*, sprinkling around): A shallow ritual water basin on a stand, usually made of stone.

Phiale (pl. *phialai*): A flat handleless libation bowl, with a raised central navel (omphalos) in the center.

Phormiskos (pl. *phormiskoi*, literally "basket"): A bag-shaped flask with narrow neck, used as a sprinkler in rituals.

Pinax (pl. *pinakes*): Literally a plate, but the term is used for a flat rectangular plaque hung in tombs and sanctuaries.

Pithos (pl. *pithoi*): A very large, tall storage jar, also used for interments. Smaller examples were called *pitharia*.

Plastic vases: Vases with relief figures or in the shape of a figure, such as a face.

Psykter (pl. *psykteres*, literally a "cooler"): A vessel with a stem, a mushroom-shaped body and sometimes a lid. It was filled with snow or cold water and placed in a krater to cool wine.

Pyxis (pl. *pyxides*): A lidded cosmetic or jewelry box of various shapes and sizes, some of which were placed in tombs. They were used mainly by women. Some have handles.

Rhyton (pl. *rhyta*): A drinking horn with one handle, often in the shape of an animal's head (fig. 9.2).

Salt cellar: A small open shallow bowl with turned-in rim.

Situla (pl. *situlae*): A Latin word for a deep bowl for wine, mainly from south Italy.

Skyphos (pl. *skyphoi*): A drinking cup with two handles, deeper than a kylix.

Stamnos (pl. *stamnoi*): A wide-mouthed storage and mixing bowl with two small horizontal handles, bulbous body and short neck and lid.

Stirrup jars: Vessels with a stirrup-like handle next to a spout, used for olive oil and wine.

Strainer: Perforated bowl used in cooking or for straining wine.

Thymiaterion (pl. *thymiateria*): A small bowl, sometimes on a tall stem, with a perforated lid for censing the house, tomb or sanctuary.

EARLY BRONZE AGE

In Crete, Early Minoan I pottery has many different shapes, and is either monochrome (gray or red), white on a dark background (light-on-dark) or a dark color on a light background (dark-on-light).

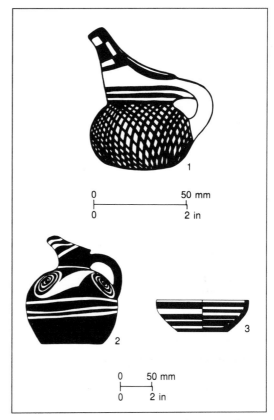

Fig. 9.3 Early and Middle Bronze Age pottery from Crete: 1. EMIIA Koumasa ware jug; 2. EMIII white-on-dark ware; 3. MMII dark-on-light style bowl.

EMI pottery includes Pyrgos and Aghios Onouphrios wares. Pyrgos ware has burnished patterns and varies from gray to black; most common are plain or footed bowls, with the chalice being a distinctive drinking vessel. Aghios Onouphrios wares were oxidized, with red linear decoration on a buff ground, and included distinctive decorated jugs.

Early Minoan II pottery includes Aghios Onouphrios ware, Koumasa ware and Vasilike ware, and Early Minoan III pottery includes Vasilike ware and white-on-dark ware (fig. 9.3). Large pithoi are also known. Koumasa ware has red to black painted linear decoration on a light background. It declined in favor of Vasilike ware, whose typical shapes are cups and long-spouted jugs (like teapots), with mottled black, red and brown decoration imitating stone vessels. In Early Minoan III, mottled decoration was replaced by geometric designs (white-on-dark ware), and vessels had less pronounced spouts.

In the Cyclades Islands, Early Cycladic I has limited pottery shapes and decoration, including lidded boxes (pyxides), probably for cosmetics, and the first frying pans. Early Cycladic II pottery copied stone vessels, with incised decoration, sometimes inlaid in white. Frying pans and cosmetic boxes continued, as well as zoomorphic forms such as hedgehogs (fig. 9.4). In Early Cycladic III the kernos appears for the first time.

On the mainland in Early Helladic II, various new shapes of pottery appeared, including the "sauceboat" (a pouring vessel), as well as spouted jugs and saucers. The pottery often has a dark glossy appearance, described by the German term "Urfirnis." In Early Helladic III there were plain burnished or painted pots and geometrically decorated ones (light-on-dark and dark-on-light). Forms include a two-handled tankard, large jars with trumpet mouths and lug handles, and small cylindrical cups. A few wheel-thrown pottery vessels occur, forerunners of the grey Minyan ware of Middle Helladic Greece.

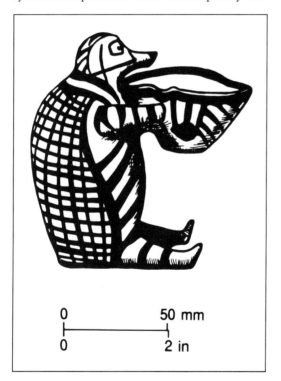

Fig. 9.4   Early Cycladic II zoomorphic pottery vessel from Syros, in the form of a bear or hedgehog drinking from a bowl.

MIDDLE BRONZE AGE

The potter's wheel became widespread in Middle Minoan IB. Kamares ware was common in Middle Minoan I and II, and had two fabrics—a coarse one for storage and pouring vessels, and a very thin wheel-made eggshell tableware. Shapes included the single-handled cup, spouted jar and beak-spouted jug, with teacups the main form of the eggshell ware. Abstract and naturalistic decoration was in light-on-dark, with added yellow, orange and red. Barbotine decoration also appears in this period. Kamares ware is also found in the eastern Mediterranean, in mainland Greece and the Cyclades. In Middle Minoan III it continued, but with more restrained decoration, including vegetation motifs, such as lilies. Middle Minoan pottery also included a dark-on-light style, used mostly for domestic vessels.

In the Cyclades, pottery originally underwent little change from Early Cycladic III, but in Middle Cycladic II the main shape was the beak-spouted jug decorated with a mat paint using dark-on-light abstract designs. In Middle Cycladic III this became especially popular on Melos, where vegetation motifs, birds, animals and fish were also introduced, and even a design of four fishermen was used on one vase.

On mainland Greece, pottery was no longer of the same artistic quality. Minyan ware pottery, which first appeared in Early Helladic III, is characteristic of the Middle Helladic period. It was named after the legendary king Minyas and should not be confused with Minoan. It has a fine hard-fired clay, always monochrome, initially gray and later yellow. There were few shapes—thick-stemmed goblets and kantharoi, made on the fast wheel. Contemporary with this pottery was handmade matte-painted pottery, decorated with geometric patterns and with coarse fabrics; the forms include huge storage jars, beak-spouted jugs and kantharoi.

LATE BRONZE AGE

Pottery styles changed from the bright polychrome designs to black-and-white (mainly dark-on-light), with occasional use of red and yellow. The many types of pottery included small cups and goblets,

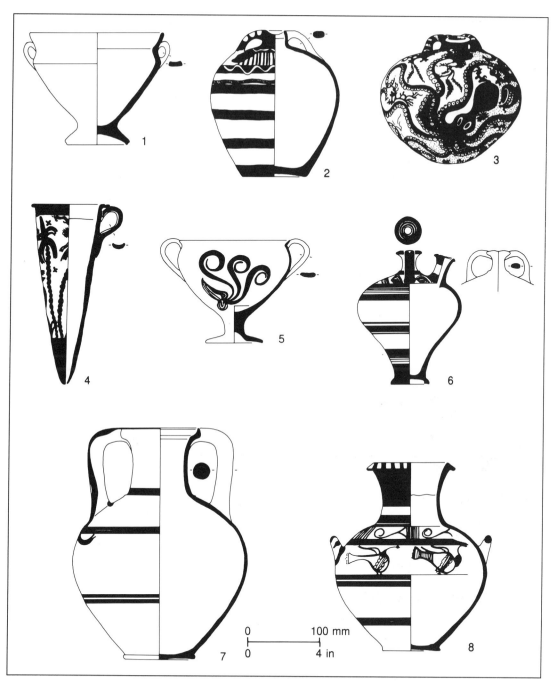

Fig. 9.5   Late Bronze Age pottery: 1. LHI Yellow Minyan; 2. LH1 Lustrous Decorated ware; 3. LMIB Marine Style stirrup jar; 4. LHIIA Pictorial Style conical rhyton depicting a palm; 5. LHIIB stylized decoration (an argonaut) on an Ephyraean goblet; 6. LHIIIA2 Pattern Style stirrup jar, with banding consisting of groups of fine lines flanked by single broad bands; 7. LHIIIC Granary Style amphora with linear decoration and a large hook painted below the handle; 8. LHIIIC Pictorial Style belly-handled amphora with a single bird painted on the back and two on the front.

ART, SCIENCE AND PHILOSOPHY

jugs with horizontal spouts, rhytons, pilgrim's flasks and large pithoi in the palace magazines (fig. 6.3). Some pottery of this period occurs only at Knossos. Late Minoan IA has a Pattern Style (abstract motifs) and a Floral Style (naturalistic designs). In Late Minoan IB the Marine Style appears, depicting various types of marine life. The designs became more stylized.

In the Cyclades, pottery was increasingly influenced by Crete, with beak-spouted jugs, the *askos*, spouted jars, rhytons and cups. Birds continued as a popular motif, joined by vegetation and marine motifs. Pottery then came under Mycenaean influence.

During the Late Helladic I and II, shapes and decoration in mainland Greece were derived from Minoan pottery, possibly made by immigrant Minoan potters. Minyan type pottery also continued in LHI, along with a Lustrous Decorated Ware (decorated in a lustrous paint). Decoration of LHIIA pottery is much more elaborate, including a Marine Style and Pictorial Style. Large decorated jars are known as Palace Style Jars (an inaccurate term). The Ephyraean goblet (named after the site at Ephyra) is an example of the more stylized decoration characteristic of Late Helladic IIB pottery.

From about 1400 BC, Late Helladic IIIA pottery of the Greek mainland was mass produced and exported all over the Mediterranean. It was made in a fine fabric, with sparse decoration and standardized shapes, particularly the kylikes, tankards, stirrup jars, kraters and alabastra. The naturalistic designs became more constrained and eventually stylized, and horizontal bands of paint became common. This style is known as the Pattern Style (different from the Pattern Style seen earlier on Crete). Some decoration included scenes of charioteers, horses and warriors, as well as various animals and mythological creatures, a style known as the Pictorial Style. Particularly important are large stirrup jars for the transport of wine and olive oil, some of which have Linear B inscriptions.

The Pictorial Style continued into Late Helladic IIIC. In this period mostly linear decoration is used, but local styles began to emerge and a variety of decoration appears, including an octopus stirrup jar (favored on Naxos and nearby islands, with one or two elaborate octopuses covering the belly of the vessel), a Close Style (in the Argolid) and a Pictorial Style on mainland Greece and the Aegean islands. A Granary Style (named after a building at Mycenae) consisted of simple horizontal dark bands and occasional wavy lines. The Close Style was used mainly on the stirrup jar and had numerous animals, such as birds and marine life, surrounded by a variety of geometric motifs, such as crosshatched lozenges, triangles, zigzags and semicircles. The designs were closely packed (hence its name). At times the style is so flamboyant that it has been termed the Wild Style. The Pictorial Style is commonly found on kraters and sometimes on other shapes, and consisted of chariot scenes, hunting scenes and scenes of warfare, animals and mythical beasts. They include the famous Warrior Vase from Mycenae. In Late Helladic IIIC, pottery styles and decoration declined, and the Granary Style prevailed. The submycenaean phase (from about 1050 BC) saw a gradual transition toward Protogeometric, with badly made pottery and a limited range of decorative motifs.

GEOMETRIC

Protogeometric pottery occurs from about 1050 BC to 900 BC, mainly in Athens. The most common shapes were the storage amphora, krater, oinochoe and various cups; the stirrup jar disappeared. A faster wheel was now used. The pots had a black gloss, with decoration limited to concentric circles and semicircles, crosshatched triangles and panels, and zigzags, drawn by compasses and multiple brushes. From about 900 BC the full Geometric style appears, the main shapes being the amphora, oinochoe, krater and cup. Various geometric designs became common, especially battlement maeanders, lozenges, squares, triangles and crosshatching. The entire pot was decorated in this way, dark-on-light. In the 8th century BC stylized animals appeared, repeated as patterns, and then human figures, again in stylized form (fig. 3.19). Many such huge vessels were used as gravemarkers, with scenes of funerals, chariot processions and warfare most popular.

ORIENTALIZING

In Corinth, Geometric pottery was produced, but from about 720 BC Oriental designs affected the pottery, and many of these pots were exported to Sicily and southern Italy (some possibly for the perfumes and oils they held, rather than for the pots themselves). This new style of pottery is termed Protocorinthian and lasted for about 100 years.

The main shapes were the aryballos, olpe, oinochoe and kotyle. Motifs included floral and vegetation designs, as well as various animals and dotted rosettes to fill spaces. Human figures were less common than animals. The drawings were originally done in outline or silhouette. Later, anatomical details were highlighted by incision—the black-figure technique, which appeared in Corinth about 100 years earlier than in Athens. Added color was also used in this black-figure technique. A new type of perfume flask (alabastron) also appeared at this time.

Around 625 BC the full (Ripe) Corinthian style emerged. Oriental-type animals and mythological beasts were still used, but less carefully drawn, along with floral motifs, including enlarged rosettes as fillers. The first phase (to c. 600 BC) was very popular and widely copied.

In Athens this period of pottery is called Proto-attic. It was not as popular as Protocorinthian (rarely found abroad) and did not use the black-figure technique. The main shapes were the amphora and krater, as well as the oinochoe and skyphos, but other shapes were imported from Corinth. There were fewer Oriental animals but more human figures and larger painted designs. The figures were drawn partly in outline, partly in silhouette, with numerous motifs derived from the Geometric style. Throughout the 7th century BC narrative mythological scenes became increasingly common. Around 625–600 BC the black-figure technique was introduced to Athens, and geometric filler motifs became less common.

Other styles of pottery are also seen elsewhere in the Greek world, such as the Wild Goat style in Rhodes, characterized by goats and other animals as well as lotus and bud friezes. In the islands pots were manufactured with figured scenes in relief decoration.

BLACK-FIGURE VASES

From the beginning of the 6th century BC Athens employed the black-figure technique, large narrative scenes and Oriental motifs, and began to compete with the Corinthian trade in tablewares. The decoration was painted on with a highly purified clay slip known as a gloss before the pots were fired. When fired in an oxidizing kiln, the pots were fired red, while the decorated figures turned black, due to the type of gloss and the firing techniques.

Black-figure pottery therefore had a light background (red or cream) and black decoration (fig. 9.6), with details incised or painted without incision (such as red for men's beards, white for women's faces). When incised, the light clay underneath showed through.

The first pots used friezes of figures and animals depicted close together, often with inscriptions naming the figures in the story. Many themes were of gods and heroes (especially Heracles), but everyday scenes were introduced in the second half of the 6th century BC, as well as symposia and athletics. On hydriai (water jars) of the late 6th century BC, women were depicted at fountain houses. In the later 6th century BC the two main painters were the Amasis Painter and Execias. At this time the main

Fig. 9.6 Black-figure vase amphora depicting a Corinthian-type helmet with a crest. The vase is 29.5 in (0.75 m) high.

body of the pot was opened up, with figures no longer confined to friezes; large areas of the vessel could also be covered in a black gloss, with one main scene of black figures on a red background.

Some of the pots were signed with painted inscriptions, and the first known painter is Sophilos. Different painters can be identified according to the styles used, but not all are known by their actual name; they are often named after the place where their works were most popular. The Amasis Painter is named after the potter who signed his name; the painter's name is actually unknown. The Taras Painter is named after Taras, because many cups made by this anonymous painter were exported to that place.

In Corinth the Animal Style continued but was obsolete by 550 BC. By the later 6th century BC figure vases here had declined in output due to the competition with Athenian vases, and exports ceased. In Laconia the outline technique had been used for decoration, but black-figure designs began to be made from about 600 BC, mainly for local use but also for export to Taras and north Africa. Apart from narrative scenes, fishes, dolphins and other marine motifs were popular. In the east the Wild Goat style and the drawing of animals declined, even though the black-figure style was introduced. In Sicily and Italy much pottery was imported, but some pottery was produced in the area of Rhegium (known as the Chalcidian school), where high-quality black-figure vases were made from 550 to 500 BC.

From the mid-6th century BC the Athenians awarded amphorae of olive oil as prizes in the Panathenaic games, which are now known as Panathenaic prize amphorae. They were decorated in black-figure, with Athena on one side and a scene from the games on the other. They continued to be made to the end of the 3rd century BC, long after the introduction of red-figure. Many of the pots can be precisely dated, because by 375 BC the name of the eponymous archon was added. In the later 4th century BC names of other officials were also added.

RED-FIGURE VASES

Around 530–520 BC a number of new techniques were tried. Red figure was the reverse of black figure. The figures remained the red color of the clay; their outlines were drawn, and the finer details were drawn with a thinner line that fired brown rather than black. The remaining pot was painted in a black gloss. The anonymous Andocides Painter (named after the potter) allegedly invented this technique. Athens continued to dominate the market, exporting as far afield as the Black Sea and Egypt. In Corinth the red-figure technique was used for a very short period only. Some pots in Athens used black-figure technique on one side and red-figure on the other (bilingual vessels). They were possibly display pieces.

Popular designs were mythological, heroic and everyday scenes, including Dionysiac and erotic themes. Red-figure vases continued throughout the 5th century BC. In the early 5th century BC the potter Sotades made several pots with modeled parts, such as a vase with a sphinx. Rather than appearing along a single groundline, figures appear all over the surface of the pot, but all at the same scale. By the mid-5th century BC heroic and mythological scenes became less popular; instead, there were scenes of daily life, especially nude young women. Drapery also appeared more transparent, following sculpture styles.

Even during the Peloponnesian War, the red-figure technique continued at Athens. In the 4th century BC the Kerch style used added color, especially yellow, white and gold and to a lesser extent blue and green. The style was named after the site at Kerch in the Ukraine, where numerous such Athenian vases have been found. Although the mid-4th century BC experienced some fine painters at Athens, production weakened in the later part of the century and ceased by around 320 BC.

In the Greek west (Italy and Sicily), painted pottery was imported, but in the mid-5th century BC south Italian red-figure pottery began to be made (fig. 9.7). Four major workshops emerged: the Apulian, Lucanian, Campanian and Paestan. At Apulia two styles developed, an early Plain Style and the Ornate Style; the latter was used for large vases, especially those used in burials, many with funerary scenes. In Paestum, scenes from the theater were depicted. Gnathian ware was produced in the second half of the 4th century BC. It was a simple black gloss ware, decorated in white, brown, yellow and red, with animal and vegetation motifs, floral motifs, wreaths and occasional female heads. Production continued to the end of the 3rd century BC, and this pottery was exported as far as Egypt and the Black Sea.

Numerous red-figure painters are known. At Athens they included the Andocides Painter, Euphronios, Euthymides, Gorgos, Berlin Painter, Kleophrades Painter, Douris, Brygos Painter, Pan Painter, Niobid Painter, Meidias Painter, Meleager Painter and the Marsyas Painter. In Italy the leading painters included the Sisyphus Painter, Ilioupersis Painter, Assteas and Python.

WHITE-GROUND

During the experimentation that led to the introduction of the red-figure technique, a white background was briefly tried. In the first half of the 5th century BC this was tried again, with the figures drawn in outline. It was used for various shapes, but as the white ground was fragile (it did not adhere closely to the clay body in firing), it was mainly used for vessels that received little use, notably lekythoi deposited in burials. Several colors were used, although often they have faded. By the end of the 5th century BC, red, black and brown were used for outlines and polychrome washes applied to areas such as drapery. Many designs are funerary in nature.

In Alexandria a series of hydriai were produced with a white ground, most of which have been found in the cemetery at Hadra (east of the city). They were used for the burial of dead foreigners, and some have modest decoration and datable inscriptions. At the end of the 3rd century BC the lagynos was often decorated with brown paint on a white slip. The decoration consisted mostly of garlands of wreaths and objects related to feasting.

HELLENISTIC

From the end of the 4th century BC the new styles and colors of painting could not be achieved on pots, unless applied after firing (which was not durable). Vase painting therefore largely ceased at this time, although pottery continued to be decorated with wreaths, festoons and abstract patterns. At the end of the 4th century BC painted pottery gave way to vessels made in molds with relief decoration. Although called Megarian bowls, they were made in many places all over the Hellenistic world from the late 3rd to 1st centuries BC. The decoration was largely floral, with some figures and mythological scenes.

Fig. 9.7 4th-century-BC red-figure squat lekythos with one handle, depicting winged Nike, from Italy;. height 4.7 in (0.12 m).   Courtesy of Somerset County Museums Service.

EVERYDAY POTS

Apart from painted pottery, Athenian potters made vast quantities of plain simple wares for everyday use. From the 5th century BC plain glossy black pots became common as everyday tablewares. By this period everyday wares were still handmade and of coarse fabrics, broadly similar to those produced for the same purpose in earlier periods. They included coarse, undecorated transport amphorae (for transport of wine and olive oil), cooking pots and portable stoves.

Amphorae all had two handles and a knoblike foot but the profiles differ, which gives an indication of their provenance. Transport amphorae developed from the 6th century BC, initially from the island of Chios. Particularly in the Hellenistic period, they were often stamped on the handle before firing, indicating the origin of the oil or wine, the name of the governing magistrate and the contents. On average they contained about 7 gallons (26.5 liters). They were placed on their sides for transport, and many have been found in this position in shipwrecks. Over time, the forms of transport amphorae became more elongated.

Sculpture

FIGURINES

Small figures (figurines or statuettes) could be made from a variety of materials, such as stone, faience, ivory and terra-cotta. There is no rigid dividing line in size between a statue and a figurine. Many were used as votive offerings and have been found in sanctuaries or in tombs, although some may have been children's toys. They were of females and males, often depicting worshipers, sometimes the deity, although the identification is generally uncertain.

Stone: Cycladic figurines date from Early Cycladic I but are mainly Early Cycladic II (fig. 9.8). They were made of local marble (especially from Naxos and Paros) and are schematic sculptures of females, males and musicians. The earliest figures are violin-shaped. A number of categories have been distinguished, such as the Plastiras type (the most naturalistic) and the Spedos type (more schematic, including folded-arms figurines). They

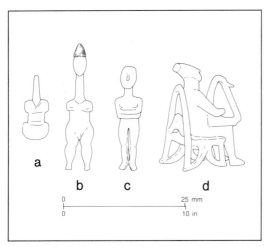

Fig. 9.8 Early Cycladic figurines: a. ECI schematic figurine, probably female; b. ECI Plastiras type, male; c. Spedos type of female with folded arms, ECIII; d. ECII cithara player.

range in height from figurines of 8 in (200 mm) to statues of 5 ft (1.5 m). Many have been found in graves. Small limestone figures in the Daedalic style (see below) date from the mid-7th century BC and were originally painted. Large feet appear from beneath their long dresses.

Terra-cotta: From Middle Minoan I there are terra-cotta figurines of humans and animals and also of human limbs. They are fairly stylized, and the females wear elaborate hats and have bared breasts. Similar female terra-cotta figures date to the Late Helladic period, ranging in size from about 27½ in (0.7 m) to almost lifesize. Figures of females of the Late Minoan period have wheel-made cylindrical bodies; their hands are held aloft. These figurines were made for over 300 years, and in the Dark Age from about 1000 BC similar ones were made, along with animals and mythical creatures such as centaurs.

The most common Mycenaean sculptures are terra-cotta figurines, dating to the 14th and 13th centuries BC. They are found from Italy to Syria and range in height from 2 in (50 mm) to 5 in (130 mm). The main types are named psi and phi figurines (fig. 9.9), after the shape of the Greek letters, and they were very stylized. Ones of animals were also made. From the 10th century BC terra-cotta figurines were one of the most common votive offerings at sanctuaries.

From the 7th century BC molds began to be used, enabling terra-cotta figurines to be inexpensively mass produced. When a mold became worn, a new one could be made from an existing figurine. These mold-produced figurines are found across the Greek world and most are of females, largely standing but often seated. The Daedalic style was introduced from the Near East, possessing a typical vertical wavy hairstyle (resembling a wig), frontal and rigid pose, triangular or U-shaped face, and flatness. This style is also found in bronze, ivory, gold and stone figurines.

In the Classical period thousands of terra-cotta figurines were made in most parts of the Greek world, to be used as votive offerings at sanctuaries; they represented either the worshiper or the deity. Some may have been children's toys. Most figurines were now made in molds and were hollow. The main centers for production were Athens and Boeotia.

In the Hellenistic period terra-cotta figurines continued to be produced, notably in Italy, Athens and Asia Minor. Ones of comic actors became popular, and at the end of the 4th century BC the finest were produced at Athens and at Tanagra in Boeotia. Hundreds of these "Tanagra" figurines (named after the site near Thebes where large quantities were first discovered) have been found, mainly in graves and tombs. They developed from about 330 BC. The most popular Tanagra figurine is of a standing draped female. Less commonly depicted were seated females, men, boys and flying Eros figures. Like Hellenistic statues figurines now have much greater realism; different parts of the figures were made in different molds. All these figurines were brightly painted and some were gilded.

Faience: A group of female faience figurines from Knossos dates to Middle Minoan I, the largest being 13.5 in (345mm) high. They have outstretched arms and bare breasts (fig. 9.10).

Ivory: Ivory figurines date from Late Minoan I on Crete; some were chryselephantine figures (of gold and ivory). The larger examples were made in several pieces. They were popular in the Late Helladic period and reappear around 730 BC.

Lead: Lead figurines are known from the Second Palace Period and also Late Helladic IIA. Hundreds of thousands of small lead figurines dating to the 7th century BC have been found at the sanctuary of Artemis Orthia at Sparta.

Bronze: Figurines of males and females and some animals began to be made in solid bronze on Crete from Late Minoan I, or possibly a little earlier. It is only from the 8th century BC that they are found on the mainland. Votive offerings in bronze are found at sanctuaries, such as Delphi, Olympia and Delos; the earliest were animal figures cut from bronze or copper sheet, but they were later cast. Of the human figurines the warrior was most popular. From the 7th century BC these warrior figures became more naturalistic. In the Classical period large numbers of bronze figurines were made as grave goods or as votive offerings in sanctuaries. By the 5th century BC many were made as mirror handles.

STATUES

From about the mid-7th century BC lifesize male statues began to be made of marble on the islands of Naxos, Samos and Paros. The style was at first Daedalic, with the typical wavy hairstyle (like a wig), frontal and rigid pose, and triangular face. The figures were naked, except for a belt, and one leg was slightly advanced. They display Egyptian influence (although Egyptian figures are clothed). They were used as gravemarkers and in sanctuaries. By the end of the 7th century BC, such sculptures were also being made on the mainland. Like architectural sculpture, these statues were painted in bright colors.

There were two main types of marble sculpture in the 6th century BC: the standing nude male (*kouros*, pl. *kouroi*) and the standing clothed or draped female (*kore*, pl. *korai*). They were dedicated in sanctuaries (mainly as votive offerings, sometimes as representations of deities), and some were gravemarkers in cemeteries. They were usually larger than lifesize and retained a frontal stance and hairstyle reminiscent of the Daedalic style, with one leg advanced (walking pose), arms by the side and large feet. The naked males no longer had a belt, and anatomy was rather abstract and rigid. During the 6th century BC the depiction of anatomy became more naturalistic. By the mid-

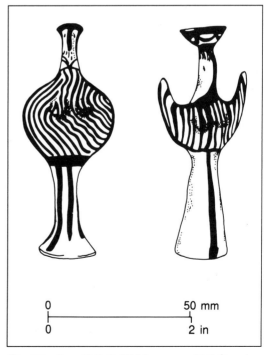

Fig. 9.9 Late Helladic III Mycenaean phi (left) and psi (right) terra-cotta figurines.

Fig. 9.10 A polychrome faience figurine (so-called snake goddess) found at Knossos, Second Palace Period.

6th century BC other male statues were being produced, such as a man carrying a calf, but still in a similar style.

The female kore figures appear slightly later than the male ones and display a variety of patterns in the clothing, often with lavish painting, abstract linear patterns, complex hairstyles and protruding large feet (not the walking pose). By the mid-6th century BC other female figures appear, including some in the form of a sphinx. Seated figures, particularly deities, were also quite common in the Archaic period.

There is evidence that bronze was widely used for kouros statues in the late 6th century BC, but little has survived, because bronze tended to be melted down and recast. While probably not painted, bronze statues in all periods would have had a brass or golden color (not the patina they have acquired today); lips and nipples were picked out in red copper, teeth with silver, eyes were inlaid with glass or stone, and patterns on clothing were inlaid with various materials.

From the 5th century BC, graves were rarely marked by statues. Statues of marble or bronze were commissioned by individuals to stand in sanctuaries or public places such as the agora. They were not portraits of the donors, but reflected the subject (such as a successful athlete commissioning an athlete statue). Simple cult statues in temples also began to be replaced by bronze or marble, and some ivory and gold ones were made.

For about 30 years from the end of the Archaic period (c. 480–450 BC), the period of sculpture is known as the Transitional or Early Classical Period, or Severe Style, with many statues having a stern or serious expression, lifelike but not totally realistic. These statues were a transitional phase between the Archaic kouroi and korai statues and those of the High Classical period. Most freestanding statues were in bronze, but very few have survived (fig. 9.11). Anatomy and drapery began to be more realistically portrayed. Some of the bronze statues have survived as Roman copies, mainly in marble (where the copying often necessitated some changes, such as the addition of a tree trunk for support). Sculptors in this period also produced lifesize statues in terra-cotta, which were painted, particularly in the Greek west where marble was unavailable.

From c. 450 BC the Severe Style was replaced by the High Classical Style, in which young men and women were carved with uniform, idealized appearance and expressions, and no individuality. Drapery is carved much deeper, and by the end of the century is more transparent (rather like clinging wet or windblown drapery), allowing the figure underneath to be apparent. Human anatomy is correctly shown. There is much more movement in the figures, particularly the drapery. The naked female appeared from the 4th century BC. Portrait statues also began to appear, although at first they were of dead people, and an ideal rather than a true likeness was made. Copies of the heads of these statues were often later set up as herms (on rectangular pillars) (fig. 2.6).

From about 400 BC to the death of Alexander the Great (323 BC), the period of sculpture is often called Late Classical. Sculptures began to appear more realistic, less austere and with emotion. The standing naked male figure continued to be a dominant subject, as well as the naked male athlete. Again, few bronze originals have survived from this period.

Cult statues placed in temples were sometimes very simple, and many were made of wood. Ones for Classical temples were of bronze or marble, with a few huge ones of gold and ivory constructed over a wooden core (such as those by Pheidias).

Sculpture in the Hellenistic period (from 323 BC) is characterized by greater realism and a greater variety of subjects and poses. There was more interest in individual people, and realistic portrait statues became extremely popular, including those of rulers of Hellenistic kingdoms, philosophers, orators, generals, politicians and poets, as well as old people, women and children (not shown realistically before). No longer were portraits confined to those of the dead. The standing naked male was also presented in a variety of poses, such as the body being twisted. A large number of naked male athletes were also produced. Many statues were presented as groups, particularly historical and mythological groups. Some of the greatest sculpture was produced at Pergamum and is termed Hellenistic baroque. Also popular were statues of Dionysus, satyrs, maenads, nymphs and centaurs.

Numerous statues were produced in this period, mainly in bronze. Cult statues of deities, however, were often of marble. Many Hellenistic and earlier statues were taken to Rome by collectors following conquest of Greek territory by the Romans. They were also copied by the Romans, although bronze statues were often copied in stone, and heads rather than the entire statue were often copied.

Fig. 9.11 Bronze sculpture of a charioteer celebrating the victory in a chariot race of the Sicilian ruler Polyzalus at the games at Delphi in 478 or 474 BC. The charioteer was originally cast in eight pieces. It has copper lips and eyelashes, a silver headband and inlaid eyes, and it is in the Severe Style of sculpture. It once formed part of a group with chariots and horses.

GRAVEMARKERS

At Mycenae, grave steles were carved with relief sculpture from the 16th century BC, with scenes such as warriors and animals, and the remaining space was filled with carved spiral designs, a decoration typical of that period (fig. 3.3). There were also plain grave steles, implying that they may have been originally plastered and painted in a manner similar to wall frescoes.

From about 600 BC grave steles (*stelai*, sing. *stele*) in Attica consisted of tall, narrow rectangular slabs. Initially they were surmounted by capitals, then scrolls with sphinxes on top; the sphinxes were later replaced by palmettes. The flat face of the stele itself was usually carved in relief with a single male figure (usually a warrior or athlete facing right—the sign of a victor in Greek art—or a cloaked older man) or sometimes a group of figures, all colorfully

Fig. 9.12   A sculptured grave relief from the Kerameikos Cemetery in Athens. The deceased (Hegeso) is seated in a chair, and in front of her stands her maid, depicted at a smaller scale. The maid holds a jewel box, which her mistress also supports with her left hand. Both are depicted with slightly transparent garments.

painted. The figures were in profile, but similar in appearance to the kouros statues. Similar sculptured reliefs were set up as votive offerings.

Grave reliefs ceased from the early 5th century BC, then began to be produced in Attica once more around 430 BC, although they had continued elsewhere in the Greek world. The tall steles with single figures were replaced by smaller, broader steles, with two or more figures in relief, one of whom was often seated (fig. 9.12). Some show companions or family members saying farewell to the deceased. The sculptured relief may represent the deceased, although it is not always possible to distinguish the deceased person amongst the group with certainty. Sculptured figures are now more lifelike, with transparent drapery and idealized features. Some

are set within an architectural setting such as a pediment (figs. 1.8, 9.12).

Throughout the 4th century BC grave reliefs were produced in quantity in Athens, until laws forbade their use around 317 BC. Many have a more pronounced architectural setting. Some figures are carved in high relief (as in fig. 1.8), with some virtually in the round. In the East, carved relief sculptures occur on sarcophagi, which were also painted. During the 3rd century BC in the Aegean and Asia Minor, a smaller type of grave stele emerged. See also chapter 10, gravemarkers.

ARCHITECTURAL SCULPTURE

The earliest example of monumental sculpture is the Lion Gate at Mycenae (fig. 3.15). From the late 7th century BC the first architectural sculpture appears in stone on temples. The earliest architectural order (see chapter 6) was the Doric, and the metopes were frequently decorated, as were the pediments, at first in low or high relief but eventually completely in the round, with the figures supported on a floor or ledge and attached to the back of the pediment or metope by rods. External metopes could be left plain, with the ones inside the temple (such as over the porch) decorated. Where marble was not available (such as in Sicily and Italy), sculptures were often in terra-cotta, or else of imported marble used just for the sculptures. In the Ionic order there was a continuous frieze (not metopes) that was sometimes decorated, both on the exterior of the temple and around the cella.

The sculptured figures on temples were brightly painted in blue, green, red and white, and there were even metal additions, such as bronze weapons and horse harnesses. Particularly favored as a theme was the triumph of Greek gods over barbaric giants. Architectural sculpture tended to follow the same styles as freestanding statues (many were virtually freestanding, particularly on the pediments), becoming more naturalistic over time. In the Hellenistic period other architectural sculptures included immense altars, such as that of Zeus at Pergamum.

STONE VESSELS

From the Neolithic period Cycladic marble workers made stone vessels (mainly in marble) of various shapes, some with zoomorphic forms. In the

Early Minoan period on Crete, small brightly colored vases were made from various stones. Many were of miniature size and were probably intended as grave goods or to hold offerings. In the Late Minoan period a number of stone ritual vessels (*rhyta*, sing. *rhyton*) were decorated with relief scenes or were zoomorphic in form (such as one of a bull's head). Some seem to have been covered in gold leaf (gilt).

SEALSTONES, GEMS AND COIN DIES

Seals were carved from a variety of materials (such as bone, soft and hard stone, ivory and wood). They were finely engraved with a wide range of topics, using the aid of a drill (see also chapter 7). They date from the Neolithic period. Gold signet rings of Bronze Age date are known, but most seals in that period were of other materials (fig. 7.7). Topics include humans, animals and abstract designs, with the emphasis on the appearance of the sealstone rather than the sealing. They reappear in the Archaic period from the 8th century BC, with carved hardstones from the 6th century BC (these may have been gems rather than sealstones, although a few have inscriptions suggesting use as sealstones). Common topics were animals, humans and mythology. Engraved gems of the Classical period tend to be larger than earlier ones. Gem engraving continued throughout the Hellenistic period, with even greater virtuosity. In the 3rd century BC the cameo technique (rather than intaglio as before) was used for carving semiprecious stones: the design was carved out of the surface.

A related art from the 6th centure BC was that of engraving coin dies. Some states hardly varied their dies, but others had very fine designs (see chapter 5).

Wall Paintings

Wall paintings in the Late Bronze Age are traditionally termed frescoes, implying paint applied while the plaster is still damp, although most Bronze Age ones were probably painted on dry plaster. From the 3rd millennium BC plastered walls were commonly painted dark red, which remained a favorite color for backgrounds, although they were sometimes painted black. By the First Palace Period other colors are known, with geometric patterns. Paintings with decorative scenes are known from the Minoan palaces on Crete by the Late Minoan IA, and naturalistic scenes were common. The most famous is the bull-vaulting scene from Knossos, with a combination of scenes from nature and religious ritual. Red was used for women and white for men. Most Cretan frescoes were done on flat surfaces, but there were some relief frescoes that combined paintings with plaster relief, which compensated for the lack of shading used. They include lifesize frescoes of figures and animals. The main fresco was on a central zone of the wall, flanked by colored or patterned bands, some imitating wood or stone.

Some paintings are known as miniature frescoes (2.4–3.9 in, 60–100 mm high), either literally miniature friezes or tiny scenes depicted on the clothing of the men and women. From Late Minoan IB painted processions appear, inspired by Egyptian painters. In the Second Palace Period, frescoes also spread to islands such as Melos and Thera, with many based on scenes of nature. Some frescoes are also known on the mainland, using a technique adopted from Crete and dating from Late Helladic I. Particularly popular were procession scenes in the Egyptian style.

Plaster floors were also decorated by painting in the Minoan and especially the Mycenaean palaces. They were divided into rectangles or squares, in imitation of gypsum slabs, with geometric designs and ones of sea creatures.

Evidence for painting in the later Greek world comes largely from pottery vases: very few large-scale paintings on flat surfaces (walls or panels) have survived. Evidence for wall paintings of the 5th and 4th centuries BC is scarce, although painters were held in high regard at this time. The only substantial wall painting of this period is from the Tomb of the Diver at Paestum. Names of painters are known from historical sources, some of whom were apparently commissioned to paint major friezes on large wooden panels that were hung on interior walls of public buildings. Toward the end of the 5th century BC there was an improvement in painting styles, with use of shading and lighting and greater realism.

Such paintings are also scarce in the Hellenistic period, although some are known from elaborately painted Macedonian tombs. There was greater depiction of landscape, as well as still lifes, erotic scenes and portraits. Scene painting in theaters became important, with various back-drops for different types of plays. This led to the development of linear perspective, and the term for perspective painting was *skenographia* (stage painting).

Some fine paintings of the 1st century BC have been found in Rome (Odyssey Landscapes) and may have been done by a Greek painter. Literary sources say that Romans often copied Greek paintings, apparently mainly 4th-century-BC paintings, and many surviving Roman wall paintings and mosaics from Pompeii and Herculaneum in Italy were reproductions or adaptations of original Greek paintings. Artists included Polygnotus, Apollodorus, Zeuxis, Parrhasius, Nicias and Apelles, the latter being the most famous.

Mosaics

The earliest floor mosaics in the Greek world are those at Olynthus, dating to 400 BC. They were made from natural pebbles and were mainly white on dark, with geometric patterns and some figured designs in a panel (*emblema*) surrounded by patterns. By the late 4th century BC the pebbles selected for use became smaller and were packed more closely, with a greater range of colors. The finest examples are from Pella (fig. 9.13), and the figures in the central panels (*emblemata*) were depicted with shading. All mosaics were of pebbles until the early or mid-3rd century BC, when they were gradually superseded by tessellated mosaics. This technique was probably developed in Sicily and involved a system of cutting stone and tile cubes to make close-fitting mosaic floors. *Tessellae* is a diminutive of the Latin word *tesserae*, meaning "cubes." Tessellated mosaics spread throughout the Greek world. Most were of abstract designs, but there were also figured central panels of fine tesserae surrounded by borders of larger tesserae. They could be in black and white or color. One of the most famous Hellenistic mosaicists was Sosus of Pergamum. Tessellated mosaics continued into the Roman period. Roman mosaics can sometimes be identified as copies of Greek paintings or mosaics, including two works of Sosus (*Unswept Room* and *Doves*).

Minor Arts

A range of materials was used for various other artifacts that can be classified as art. The materials include stone, semiprecious stones, ivory, terra-cotta, gold, silver, lead, bone, bronze, faience and wood. The range of other art forms was considerable, including furniture, jewelry, tableware, tripods, lamps, votive offerings, some weapons, model objects, altars, decorative boxes, and votive and terra-cotta relief plaques. See also chapter 5, Economy and Industry.

ARTISTS AND ARCHITECTS: BIOGRAPHIES

From the 6th century BC in particular, many rulers of city-states were patrons of the arts, including art and architecture. Most artists and architects were artisans who earned little money; they worked in family businesses, passing skills from father to son. Many works of art were unsigned, and the artists are unknown. Very few women are known as artists—their traditional pursuits were weaving and embroidery, about which little is known. In the Hellenistic period artists enjoyed royal patronage and great wealth and traveled to various cities to conduct their work. Following are the major artists and architects, with the Greek version of their name, in italics.

AGATHARCUS (*Agatharkhos*): Painter, from Samos, floruit c. 440–410 BC. He apparently worked in Athens and painted the walls of the house of Alcibiades c. 430 BC—the first record of such decoration. He painted a scene for a play by Aeschylus and wrote a treatise on scene painting, which inspired Anaxagoras and Democritus to work out the rules of perspective.

AGORACRITUS (*Agorakritos*): Sculptor, floruit c. 440–400 BC. He was a native of Paros and pupil of Pheidias. He was primarily a marble sculptor. His most famous work was the cult statue of Nemesis at Rhamnus (before 431 BC), of which fragments have been excavated. The work was also attributed to Pheidias. Agoracritus is also known to have made a colossal marble statue of the Mother of the Gods for the metroon in Athens' agora. Two bronze statues by him are also recorded.

ALCAMENES (*Alkamenes*):   Sculptor, possibly Athenian, floruit c. 440–400 BC. A pupil and rival of Pheidias. He worked at or near Athens, and about 12 of his works are known, many of which were copied by the Romans. He mostly produced statues of gods in marble, but also worked in bronze, gold and ivory. His works included a chryselephantine cult statue of Dionysus, a bronze athlete, a statue of Aphrodite of the Gardens, a marble group of Procne and Itys on the Athenian Acropolis (possibly not his work) and Hermes of the Gateway. Pausanias incorrectly attributes to him the west pediment of the temple of Zeus at Olympia.

AMASIS (*Amasis*):   Floruit c. 560–530 BC. A potter who is known from nine signed vases, all painted by the same artist known as the Amasis Painter. Over 100 black-figure vases have been attributed to this painter, who may have been the potter. He painted a variety of scenes on amphorae, oinochoai, lekythoi and cups.

ANTENOR (*Antenor*):   An Athenian sculptor, floruit c. 540–500 BC. He made the famous bronze group of Harmodius and Aristogiton (who killed Hipparchus in 514 BC). It was stolen by Xerxes in 480 BC but was later restored in the agora. It is now lost and its form is unknown. Antenor was also responsible for the Caryatids of the Erechtheum, and possibly for the east pediment of the temple of Apollo at Delphi.

ANTIGONUS OF CARYSTUS (*Antigonos*): Late-3rd-century-BC bronzeworker and writer. He worked under Attalus I at Pergamum, and created statues that celebrated Attalus I's victory over the Gauls (the "dying Gaul" triumphal monument).

APELLES (*Apelles*):   First half of 4th century BC. Painter from Colophon (or Cos) who moved to Ephesus and later worked at Corinth, Athens and

Fig. 9.13   Part of the Stag Hunt mosaic at Pella in Macedonia, constructed from colored pebbles.

ART, SCIENCE AND PHILOSOPHY

the Macedonian court at Pella (for Philip II and Alexander the Great). He was the most famous and praised of Greek painters, mainly of portraits. His most famous picture was of Aphrodite Anadyomene (Aphrodite rising from the sea), and other known works include Alexander with a Thunderbolt and a self-portrait (the first ever recorded). He wrote a treatise on painting. All his works are lost.

APOLLODORUS (*Apollodoros*): Floruit c. 430–390 BC. A painter from Athens who was known for *skiagraphos*—painting with light and shade by a gradation of color. He was evidently an important painter, but few of his works were recorded and all are lost.

ARCHERMUS (*Arkhermos*): Sixth-century-BC sculptor from Chios, probably responsible for the Nike of Delos and the first to represent her with wings.

ARISTION (*Aristion*): Floruit c. 550–520 BC. A sculptor from Paros, who later moved to Athens. He is known from signed statue bases and for an Archaic kore statue.

BRYGUS (*Brygos*): Floruit 500–480 BC. Athenian potter who is known from over 13 signatures, all on cups. The painter of several of his vessels is known as the "Brygos Painter," to whom over 200 other red-figure vases (nearly all cups) are attributed.

CALAMIS (*Kalamis*): Floruit c. 470–430 BC. Possibly from Boeotia or Athens. One of the most important bronze sculptors, who also worked in marble, gold and ivory. A few works by him are recorded, including Zeus Ammon made for Pindar, a colossal bronze statue of Apollo made for Apollonia Pontica, a chryselephantine Asclepius in Sicyon, and the Sosandra on the Acropolis at Athens.

CALLICRATES (*Kallikrates*): Fifth-century-BC architect who collaborated with Ictinus (architect) and Pheidias (sculptor) in building the Parthenon.

COLOTES (*Kolotes*): Second half of 5th century BC. A sculptor, possibly from Paros. He apparently helped Pheidias with the chryselephantine Zeus statue at Olympia, and made other chryselephantine statues and some bronze ones of philosophers.

CRESILAS (*Kresilas*): Floruit c. 450–430 BC. A sculptor from Cydonia in Crete, who worked mostly in Athens. He is known from literature, from signed statue bases and Roman copies (a portrait statue of Pericles [fig. 2.6] and a statue of a wounded Amazon).

CRITIUS (*Kritios*): Floruit c. 480–460 BC. Sculptor, probably an Athenian. He is known from six statue bases signed by him and Nesiotes; in 477 BC they were commissioned to make the group of the tyrannicides Harmodius and Aristogiton to replace those by Antenor. Numerous copies are known. Other statues have been attributed to Critius based on their style, including the "Critius Boy" of c. 480 BC found at Athens.

DAMOPHON (*Damophon*): Floruit c. 200–150 BC. Sculptor from Messene. His works were mainly cult statues and larger groups for sites within the Peloponnese. He also repaired Pheidias' statue of Zeus at Olympia.

DOURIS (*Douris*): Floruit to 470s BC. Possibly from Samos, he was a painter of red-figure cups, contemporary with the Brygos Painter. He signed 39 vases as a painter, although around 300 have been attributed to him, mainly cups.

ENDOIOS (*Endoios*): Floruit c. 530–500 BC. A sculptor who worked mainly in Athens. Four signatures are known (three from Athens). His surviving work includes remains of a marble seated Athena from the Acropolis at Athens, seen by Pausanias.

EUBULIDES THE YOUNGER (*Euboulides*): Floruit c. 140–120 BC. A sculptor from an Athenian family of sculptors. Son of the sculptor Eucheir (with whom he often collaborated) and grandson of the sculptor Eubulides the Elder. He was responsible for a colossal group of Athena, Zeus, Mnemosyne, the Muses and Apollo at Athens, fragments of which have been found; it was seen by Pausanias.

EUPHRANOR (*Euphranor*): Floruit c. 360–330 BC. A sculptor and painter who apparently worked mainly in Athens. About 12 sculptures are known, some colossal, including Philip II and Alexander the Great riding in chariots, a statue of Paris and a cult statue of Apollo Patroos (found in the Athenian agora). Three paintings on the interior of the Stoa of Zeus in the agora were a cavalry scene before the battle of Mantinea, the 12 gods, and Theseus with personified Democracy and the People. He wrote treatises on colors and symmetry.

EUPHRONIUS (*Euphronios*): Floruit c. 515–480 BC. A potter and one of the finest red-figure vase painters who worked at Athens. He is known from 16 signatures: he signed six vases as a painter and 10 as a potter (decorated by other painters, including Onesimus and the Pistoxenus painter). His finest vases were calyx kraters.

EXECIAS (*Exekias*): Floruit c. 550–530 BC. The finest Attic black-figure vase painter, and a potter who made vases for others and for himself to paint. Several signatures are known (two as both potter and painter). He invented several new vase shapes. His amphora showing Achilles and Ajax playing dice, and his painting of the death of Ajax are well known. He also painted several terra-cotta plaques.

HERMOGENES (*Hermogenes*): Second-century-BC architect, possibly from Priene. Active c. 200 BC or c. 130 BC. Attributed to him are the temple of Dionysus at Teos and the temple of Artemis Leucophryene at Magnesia ad Maeandrum, both in Ionic style (he objected to the Doric order in sacred buildings). He wrote treatises on these temples, with principles for Ionic architecture that appear in Vitruvius.

HIPPODAMUS (*Hippodamos*): Fifth century BC (born c. 500 BC). The most famous town planner, although not the inventor of the gridiron type of town plan. He was from Miletus (destroyed 494 BC); it was rebuilt with a grid layout, for which Hippodamus is unlikely to have been responsible. He planned the town of Piraeus around the old seaport in the mid-5th century BC, and in 444/443 BC he went with the group founding the colony of Thurii and probably undertook its planning. He may have been responsible for the plan of the city of Rhodes (408/407 BC), but this is possibly too late.

ICTINUS (*Iktinos*, kite): Floruit c. 450–420 BC. An architect who collaborated with Callicrates (architect) and Pheidias (sculptor) in building the Parthenon at Athens, of which he wrote an account.

He was also responsible for the temple of Apollo at Bassae (possibly begun c. 430 BC) and was one of the architects who worked on the Telesterion at Eleusis.

LYSIPPUS (*Lysippos*): Floruit c. 328 BC. Famous sculptor from Sicyon who worked exclusively in bronze; he reputedly made over 1,500 statues and created new and slender proportions. He made mainly athletic statues, ones of Zeus and Heracles, and portraits. Many of his commissions were at Olympia, but some were as far afield as Tarentum, Asia Minor and Rhodes. Works attributed to him include several statues of Alexander the Great (from 340 BC), the Apoxyomenus (athlete scraping himself clean), Olympic victors, Socrates, Chilon, Alexander's lion hunt, Zeus at Tarentum, Eros at Thespiae, Heracles (several), Satyrs in Athens and Kairos in Sicyon. Some are known from Roman copies.

MNESICLES (*Mnesikles*): An architect of the later 5th century BC who designed the Propylaea on the Acropolis at Athens, built between 437 and 432 BC. It was never completed to his original plan.

MYRON (*Myron*): Floruit c. 460–430 BC. Sculptor from Eleutherae, one of the most famous sculptors of his time. He worked largely in bronze, although some of his statues are known from later marble copies and other representations, including the "Discus thrower" (Discobolus) and a group of Athena and Marsyas. Seventeen other commissions are known from literary sources, the most famous of which is a bronze cow on the Acropolis at Athens.

NICIAS (*Nikias*): Fourth century BC. Painter from Athens. About 12 paintings are known, including Nemea, Necyomantea, Alexander, Io, Andromeda and Calypso. The latter three seem to be copied at Pompeii. Nicias also painted marble statues carved by Praxiteles. He was the first to attempt to paint women three-dimensionally with shading.

PAEONIUS (*Paionios*): Floruit 425 BC. Sculptor from Mende. In 1875 a marble statue of a winged victory (Nike) on a triangular pillar was found at Olympia. The inscription attributes it to Paeonius, and it was dedicated by the Messenians and Naupactians after defeating the Spartans at Pylos in 425 BC.

PARRHASIUS (*Parrhasios*): Floruit c. 430–390 BC. A painter from Ephesus who worked mainly in Athens, a contemporary and rival of Zeuxis. His paintings were very lifelike, and over 20 are known (all lost). They were mainly of single mythological figures, although one of his most famous pictures was the *Athenian People*, showing their various qualities. He also made drawings on wood and parchment for use by later craftsmen, and wrote about painting.

PHEIDIAS or PHIDIAS (*Pheidias*): c. 490–430 BC. A sculptor from Athens, the most famous in antiquity. He worked mainly in bronze but also in marble and chryselephantine (for cult statues). He was also an architect and painter. His works include a bronze Athena Promachos about 33 ft (10 m) high (erected on the Acropolis c. 456 BC), the Lemnian Athena, an Amazon at Ephesus and a colossal chryselephantine Athena made for the Parthenon (completed 438 BC). Pheidias probably went into exile and then made a colossal chryselephantine Zeus at Olympia (c. 430 BC), one of the Seven Wonders of the World. His workshop at Olympia has been excavated. Pheidias may also have been responsible for the sculptures on the Parthenon. In 432 BC he was charged with embezzling gold (probably by enemies of Pericles) and later with impiety. He was put into prison and was probably executed.

PHILON (*Philon*): Fourth-century-BC architect from Eleusis who designed the naval stores (arsenal) at Piraeus and added a porch to the Telesterion at Eleusis. His writings on architecture have not survived.

POLYCLEITUS or POLYCLITUS (*Polykleitos*): Second half of 5th century BC. A sculptor from Argos, the most celebrated after Pheidias. He worked largely in the Peloponnese, specializing in statues of naked athletes at Olympia and elsewhere. Most of his work was in bronze, with some marble and gold and ivory. Several inscribed bases have been found, and about 20 statues can be attributed to him. These include several Roman marble copies of the Doryphorus (youth holding a spear) and Diadumenus (youth tying a fillet round his head). He was also responsible for a chryselephantine

statue of Hera at Argos, judged to be finer than that of Pheidias. He wrote a book on rhythm and proportion.

POLYGNOTUS (*Polygnotos*): Floruit 475–447 BC. A painter from Thasos who worked mainly in Athens and became a citizen there. None of his wall paintings survive, but they were mainly mythological and included the *Iliupersis* (capture of Troy) and *Nekyia* (descent of Odysseus to the underworld) in the Cnidian Lesche (public room) at Delphi; each contained over 70 figures and was probably painted between 458 and 447 BC. At Athens he decorated part of the Stoa Poikile (painted stoa) and Theseum and Anakeion. He was one of the most famous painters and adopted a much freer style (for example, the figures were grouped across the painting, not just along a single line), although no shading was used.

PRAXITELES (*Praxiteles*): Floruit c. 370–330 BC. An Athenian sculptor, one of the most famous and influential. He worked mostly in mainland Greece but undertook some commissions elsewhere (islands and Asia Minor). He was most proficient in marble but also worked in bronze. Nicias painted many of his marble statues. Over 50 commissions (more than 75 statues) are recorded, particularly cult statues and cult groups. Some are known from later copies. They include Aphrodite (especially famous being the naked marble Aphrodite of Cnidus), Apollo, a bronze Apollo Sauroctonus (lizard slayer), Satyrs, Artemis, Eros, Dionysus, Leto and two statues of Phryne (his mistress). A famous statue of Hermes with the infant god Dionysus was found at Olympia and is probably an original version (but some say a Hellenistic copy).

PYTHIUS or PYTHEUS (*Pytheus*): Fourth-century-BC architect from Priene. The spelling of his name in ancient sources varies, but he is possibly the same person who designed the Mausoleum at Halicarnassus and the temple of Athena Polias at Priene (fig. 9.14), both of the Ionic order. He wrote books on both buildings; neither has survived.

SCOPAS (*Skopas*): Fourth century BC. A sculptor from Paros who was a contemporary of Praxiteles. He worked mainly in marble, specializing in cult statues. He was especially known for

Fig. 9.14   Pythius was the architect of the temple of Athena Polias at Priene, which was dedicated by Alexander the Great.

the expression of violent emotion. About 30 statues are attributed to him (around 20 of which are cult statues). He is also recorded as being the architect of the temple of Athena Alea at Tegea, and he undertook the east side of the Mausoleum at Halicarnassus.

SILANION (*Silanion*):   Fourth-century-BC sculptor from Athens. Ten works are known: Achilles, Theseus, Dying Jocasta (bronze with some silver) and seven portraits of Sappho, Corinna, Plato, the sculptor Apollodorus and three boxers from Olympia (one, possibly Satyrus, is in bronze). He also wrote on the rules of proportion.

SOSUS (*Sosos*):   Second-century-BC mosaicist from Pergamum, who was famous for his realistic mosaics, such as an unswept floor and doves drinking from a bowl.

TIMOTHEUS (*Timotheos*):   Floruit c. 380–340 BC. A sculptor who worked on the temple of Asclepius at Epidaurus (c. 370 BC) and the Mausoleum at Halicarnassus (c. 350 BC), the latter with Scopas, Bryaxis and Leochares. His work at both monuments cannot be specifically identified.

ZEUXIS (*Zeuxis*):   Active c. 430–390 BC. A painter from Heraclea (Italy) who went to Athens in the 430s or 420s BC where he undertook various commissions. He later went to the court of Archelaus of Macedonia (409–397 BC) to paint his palace; he also gave him a picture of Pan. Zeuxis was a famous painter and a rival of Parrhasius. His paintings were so lifelike that birds flew down to eat the grapes. His best-known pictures were of Helen of Troy and of a female centaur with her young. He also did monochrome paintings.

PHILOSOPHY

Introduction

Greek philosophy (*philosophia*, meaning "love of knowledge") covered a wider range of subjects than modern philosophy. It was the pursuit of knowledge by reasoning, and it came to include scientific inquiry, speculation about how political and social life should be conducted, morality and even some religious questions.

Greek philosophy seems to have had its origin in the Ionian cities of Asia Minor in the 6th century BC. At this time philosophers such as Thales, Anaximander and Anaximenes (all from Miletus) were mainly concerned with speculation about the universe and the search for a single substance that they believed had undergone various modifications to produce the phenomena of the world.

Pythagoras (late 6th century BC) saw the basis of the universe in numbers and the relationships between numbers. Heracleitus (c. 50 BC) rejected the idea of a single permanent substance that was modified in various ways. He thought that matter itself was constantly changing and that everything was in a state of flux. Xenophanes (late 6th to early 5th century BC) created a rationalization for theology.

In the early 5th century BC Parmenides and Zeno distinguished between what they saw as the true, eternal and unchangeable material of the universe and the unreal phenomena of change and diversity that was apparent to the senses. Empedocles was the first to propose the theory that the universe comprised only four elements (earth, air, fire and water), with different things composed of different proportions of these four elements. Anaxagoras of Clazomenae thought that the universe contained the "seeds" of every material. He also introduced the idea of an intelligence (*nous*) as something distinct from matter, an animating principle of force and order. Leucippus was credited with originating the theory that the universe was composed of a large number of atoms that were combined mechanically, a theory developed by Democritus.

The culmination of Greek philosophy came with Socrates in the second half of the 5th century BC and Plato and Aristotle in the 4th century BC. However, the context in which their ideas occurred—the independent city-state (which they had assumed would continue to exist)—was destroyed by the conquests of Alexander the Great. This changed the outlook of subsequent philosophers, such as the Stoics and the Epicureans, whose focus of interest was quite different. Instead of the nature of reality and knowledge, Hellenistic philosophers were more interested in practical problems of everyday behavior. Such philosophies tended to search for means of achieving a state of mind that allowed an individual to be happy, or at least content, irrespective of their external circumstances. Other philosophical ideas, such as those of the Sceptics and the Cynics, also reflected this change of attitude, which was to some extent a move toward philosophies of acceptance and resignation, rather than speculation and inquiry.

Individual Philosophies

THALES OF MILETUS

Thales (early 6th century BC) was traditionally regarded as the earliest Greek philosopher. Nothing written by him has survived, and it is even doubtful that he wrote anything. Aristotle attributed to him the view that the world and everything in it originate as water and eventually return to water. Thus water was regarded as both eternal and divine. This philosophy was encapsulated in his saying "all things are full of gods."

ANAXIMANDER OF MILETUS

Working at the beginning of the 6th century BC Anaximander was the first philosopher to attempt to propose a rational explanation for the origin of the world. He said that the origin of all things was "the unbounded" (*to apeiron*), which was divine, immortal and indestructible. "The unbounded" controlled and "enfolded" the *kosmos*, or even many *kosmoi*, although it is unclear whether he thought that *kosmoi* coexisted or succeeded one another. The word *kosmos* (cosmos) meant "good order," as well as the world or universe in its perfect order.

To Anaximander the most important forces at work in the world were pairs of opposites, such as heat and cold. He thought that the first living things were created by spontaneous generation from mud, which was caused by the action of the sun. This was long accepted as a standard explanation. He thought that the Earth was shaped like the drum of a column, with people living on the upper surface.

ANAXIMENES OF MILETUS

Anaximenes (mid-6th century BC) thought that air was the substance from which everything was made. It could be rarified to form fire or condensed to form water or earth, and these elements were compounded to make the world and everything on it. He regarded air as the breath of the cosmos, its divine and immortal source. He also thought that Earth was flat and shallow like a disc and was supported by air.

PYTHAGORAS

Pythagoras founded a religious community at Croton around 530 BC, open to both men and women. Pythagoras was a worshiper of Apollo and believed in reincarnation. He thought that the soul was a fallen divinity entombed within the body and destined to pass through a number of reincarnations, until it developed an Apollo-like purity that would release it. Such purity was attained especially through study. His mathematical studies led him to interpret the whole world through numbers. He initiated a systematic study of the numerical basis of the world, which was continued by his followers.

Pythagoreans thought that the universe was created by the First Unit (the Heaven) inhaling the Infinite or Void to produce groups of units or numbers. All things in the universe (even abstractions such as opinion and justice) were actually numbers and had a position in the cosmos. Pythagoreans came to believe that Earth was spherical and that the heavenly bodies (including the sun) revolved around a central fire. A similar, earlier cosmological system called "harmony of the spheres" was accommodated to the Pythagorean view.

XENOPHANES

Xenophanes (late 6th to early 5th centuries BC) was best known for his rationalization of religion. He attacked the polytheism and anthropomorphism of Greek religion and denounced the immoral stories about the gods that are found in the poetry of Homer and Hesiod. He believed in a single eternal god who did not resemble humans and caused things to happen by mind alone. This monotheism was a radical departure from traditional Greek thought and religion.

HERACLEITUS

Heracleitus (c. 500 BC) did not believe that it was possible to understand reality fully. He thought that appearances were unreliable, but that some sort of knowledge was attainable. He believed that the world had an underlying unity, which depended on a balance between opposites. This balance meant that a change in one direction resulted in a change in the opposite direction, so everything was in a state of flux. He thought that the essential material of the universe was pure fire, some of which was being extinguished to form the sea and earth, while some pure fire was always being kindled. Souls were also composed of this fire, and after death the souls of the virtuous joined the cosmic fire.

PARMENIDES, ZENO AND THE ELEATIC SCHOOL

Parmenides founded the Eleatic school of philosophy (named after Elea where he lived) in the early 5th century BC. He believed that the essential matter ("what exists") was single, unchanging and indivisible. From this the universe was created. This theory denied that there was any real motion or change in the universe. Parmenides apparently considered that a fundamental difference existed between the world as explained by reason and the world as perceived by the senses.

Zeno was a disciple of Parmenides and a member of the Eleatic school of philosophy. He produced arguments intended to reduce his opponents' arguments to absurdity by illustrating the contradictions within them. His attacks were not against specific theories but against popularly held beliefs that he thought were erroneous. The way he framed his arguments caused Aristotle to call him the "inventor of dialectic."

EMPEDOCLES

After his death (432 BC) Empedocles attracted a number of apocryphal stories, casting doubt on some of his writings, particularly since two of his poems appear contradictory. One indicates a belief in the transmigration of souls while another appears to deny the existence of a soul. Nevertheless, both works do appear to be genuine. While accepting many arguments of the Eleatic school, Empedocles did not accept the idea of a single indivisible element. He proposed four "roots" or elements—earth, air, fire and water. He thought that these elements were eternally distinct but were combined to create everything. They continually combined and separated under the influence of Love and Strife, which caused the generation and dissolution of all "mortal" things. Generation and dissolution therefore changed only the combinations of the four elements. Empedocles also proposed that Love and Strife alternately dominated the cosmos, causing a cosmic cycle of generation and dissolution. Adapted by later philosophers, Empedocles' theory of the four elements dominated natural science for nearly 2,000 years.

ANAXAGORAS OF CLAZOMENAE

The surviving evidence for the philosophy of Anaxagoras (5th century BC) is difficult to interpret, but he apparently regarded the universe as composed of "seeds" of every distinct substance, so that "everything has a share of everything." He thought that changes in something occurred as a result of the rearrangement of its constituent substances. He also regarded mind or intelligence (*nous*) as separate from other substances, omnipresent and eternal; *nous* was the animating principle of all living things and the initiator of cosmic motion. According to Anaxagoras the Earth was flat and supported by air, but the heavenly bodies rotated and the moon acquired light from the sun. He apparently understood the principle of eclipses.

LEUCIPPUS AND DEMOCRITUS

Leucippus (mid- to late 5th century BC) originated the atomic theory, believing that the universe was composed of a large number of atoms that were combined mechanically. This theory was evolved to counter the arguments of the Eleatic school, which denied all motion and change in the universe. Leucippus was overshadowed by his pupil, Democritus, and their individual work is extremely difficult to separate. Their work sought to rehabilitate the idea that the perceivable physical world was real (a concept denied by the Eleatic school). They

thought that everything was created by the chance collision of solid particles that were homogeneous and indivisible, and which continually moved through an infinite void in infinite numbers.

SOCRATES

Socrates (469–399 BC) was initially interested in natural philosophy but abandoned this in favor of ethical inquiry. He pretended to know nothing himself but relentlessly questioned those with pretensions to wisdom, in order to show that their assumptions were wrong. He attracted a diverse circle of friends and young men wishing to learn from him. It was Socrates' integrity and philosophic lifestyle that had the greatest impact on subsequent philosophers. He wrote no books, and our knowledge of him comes largely from the works of Plato, Aristophanes and Xenophon. Socrates marks such a watershed in Greek philosophy that Greek philosophers are sometimes categorized as pre-Socratic or post-Socratic. He believed that philosophers should study ethics and human relationships rather than the natural and physical world. His influence on subsequent philosophers moved philosophy away from natural science and toward logic, ethics and morals.

PLATO AND THE ACADEMY

Plato (c. 429–347 BC) was one of Socrates' disciples and was greatly influenced by him. He withdrew from Athens after Socrates' death, but on his return he established the Academy school (c. 385 BC), over which he presided for the next 40 years. Plato's writings do not provide a systematic explanation of his views; this is partly because he does not seem to have reached a final philosophical system and partly because his views are put forward as a series of dialogues, from which his philosophy has to be interpreted. The ideas in these dialogues are complex. For example, he believed that just by holding the right opinions, it was possible to be a good man, without knowing what goodness is; however, this was a precarious state, since holding the right opinion without knowing it is right leaves no method of judging whether a new idea is right or wrong.

Plato thought that objects of knowledge (including abstract things such as "beauty") were real, whereas objects of mathematical knowledge, such as "the ideal triangle," existed only in the world of

Ideas or Forms. The relationship between the latter and the real world is unclear. He thought that a duality existed between the soul and the body, and that the soul was aware of the world of Ideas before birth, so that knowledge came from the soul's recollection of the world of Ideas. He therefore advocated cultivation of the soul and suppression of the body. In some way (which he never explained), the Good was beyond all other Ideas and was the cause of all things. It was therefore the soul's ambition to attain knowledge of the Good. Plato's philosophy was most greatly influenced by Socrates, but other influences included Heracleitus, Parmenides, Empedocles and the Pythagoreans.

Plato's primary aim in founding the Academy was to give potential statesmen the necessary philosophical insight for governing. It is thought that the curriculum was similar to the one described in Plato's *Republic* and probably included political theory, mathematics and dialectic. It survived as an institution teaching philosophy and science until the Roman emperor Justinian closed the philosophy schools in Athens in AD 529, although it underwent many changes during its long history.

In the Roman period in the 3rd century AD, a philosophy of Neoplatonism was developed, based on the philosophy of Plato but incorporating aspects of other philosophers' teachings, such as Aristotle and the Stoics.

ARISTOTLE AND THE PERIPATETIC SCHOOL

Aristotle (384–322 BC) was a pupil of Plato at the Academy, remaining there for 20 years until Plato's death. He then left Athens but returned in 335 BC and founded his school, the Lyceum (also known as the Peripatetic school of philosophy). He developed a comprehensive system covering every branch of philosophy and science recognized in his day. Plato was a major influence on Aristotle's philosophy, but Aristotle rejected some aspects of Plato's work. He was the first to examine the science of reasoning. He thought that the universe must have a single unchanging cause (an "unmoved mover" engaged in eternal contemplation or thought, who has no interest in the universe). He also explored the constituent elements of natural things. He knew that the Earth was spherical, but thought it was the center of the universe. He put forward the proposition that the soul and body were two aspects of a single

being, but it is unclear whether he held that the soul survived death.

In the realm of ethics Aristotle thought happiness, achievement and success were the proper human aims in life. Because so many of his writings survived, and because they covered such a broad area of philosophy and science, Aristotle's influence on later philosophers was immense, and parts of his work were still being used in the 16th century.

CYNICS

The Cynics were a group of philosophers who followed the principles of Antisthenes and Diogenes of Sinope. Antisthenes was considered the founder of the Cynics. He was a pupil of Socrates, but his views differed from other pupils of Socrates, such as Plato. Antisthenes thought that happiness was based on virtue, and that virtue consisted of action and was a practical quality that could be taught. He thought that the mythical life of Heracles was an ideal example. He believed that because happiness was derived only from virtue, most pleasures did not bring happiness; he also believed that a wise man could not act unwisely, since once he had acquired a knowledge of virtue, it could not be lost.

Diogenes was influenced by Antisthenes and became the most famous exponent of the sect. He rejected all conventional views of what contributed to happiness and led an austere life, renouncing all possessions and relationships. He thought that happiness would come from self-sufficiency, which could be achieved by self-discipline and a loss of the conventional sense of shame. Apparently it was the latter characteristic that led to him being nicknamed *kyon* (dog), from which the name Cynic was derived. An alternative derivation was from Cynosarges outside the walls of Athens, where Antisthenes established a school. Crates, a pupil of Diogenes, was also a famous Cynic. The Cynics did not develop a philosophical system or an organized school. Their common belief was in self-sufficiency as a means of contentment, but they otherwise held a range of differing views.

STOICS

The Stoic school of philosophy was named after the Stoa Poikile in Athens. Here the founder of the school, Zeno of Citium, taught in the early 3rd century BC. This school of philosophy is sometimes known as the Stoa. Influenced by the Cynics and by Socratic philosophy, Zeno developed his own doctrines about logic, knowledge, physics and ethics. He was succeeded by Cleanthes, who completed and systematized the Stoic doctrines, and in turn was succeeded by Chrysippus. The Stoic school continued into the Roman period.

Stoicism was primarily a doctrine of detachment from and independence of the world. The universe was thought to be controlled by reason (*logos*), so that whatever happened was divinely ordained by reason. Consequently someone knowing this must accept whatever happens and live in harmony with the divine reason. The term *logos* combined the meaning of speech and reason, and later philosophers used *logos* for various divine principles or powers from which the world originated. The Stoics thought that to live in such acceptant harmony with the divine reason was the only virtue. Failure to achieve willing acceptance of whatever happened was regarded as moral weakness. Stoics also held that everyone possessed a spark of divine fire within them, which led to the concept of a universal fellowship, irrespective of race or status.

MEGARIAN SCHOOL

The Megarian school of philosophy was founded by Eucleides of Megara. It adopted the beliefs of the Eleatic school. Following the example of Zeno of Elea, its members became known for their skilled dialectical argument.

ARISTIPPUS OF CYRENE

There were two philosophers of this name, one the grandson of the other, and some confusion exists between them. The elder Aristippus was a pupil of Socrates, but it was probably the younger Aristippus who founded the Cyrenaic school of philosophy. Its fundamental belief was that knowledge is based on sensation and that the present moment is the only reality, so immediate pleasure should be a person's primary aim in life. This was a more extreme hedonistic doctrine than that of the Epicureans.

EPICUREANS

The Epicureans followed the philosophy of Epicurus (341–270 BC). He was influenced by the philosophy of Democritus and established his own philosophical groups at Mytilene and Lampsacus. Around 307 BC he settled in Athens, where he gathered a community of followers, including women and slaves. They apparently lived in austere seclusion, but their communal living attracted criticism and mockery. The basis of his doctrine was a reliance on the evidence of the senses and elimination of belief in supernatural intervention and superstition. He accepted the atomic theory of Democritus and thought that the soul perished with the body. He believed that happiness came from attaining a tranquillity of mind derived from a proper understanding of the natural world, and that pleasure was identical with good. He thought that the main aim in life was freedom from trouble, but his philosophy was often misrepresented as merely being the pursuit of pleasure, notably the pursuit of physical pleasure.

SCEPTICS

As a school of philosophy Scepticism was founded by Pyrrhon, although sceptical attitudes formed part of some philosophers' teachings at a much earlier date. Pyrrhon believed that knowledge of the true nature of things was unattainable, because the senses were unreliable and the teachings of dogmatic philosophers were contradictory. The aim of Sceptic philosophers was to achieve tranquillity by following the appearance of things, but suspending judgment and avoiding commitment and dogmatism.

SCIENCE

Introduction

The ancient Greeks made little distinction between science and philosophy, and no specialization of different disciplines existed within science, as today. Philosophers might study astronomy, and mathematicians might evolve a world view including moral codes. Many philosophers were heavily involved in some kind of scientific study, and the level of available detailed knowledge was sufficiently low that one person might master a number of different branches of learning. Although the Greeks did not divide science into a number of separate disciplines, it is convenient to consider Greek science in relation to some modern subdivisions of the subject.

Mathematics

This was the area of science that most interested the Greeks and in which they had greatest success. The Egyptians were thought to have invented geometry, and Thales was credited with introducing geometry to Greece from Egypt. The Egyptians were practical mathematicians, however, and had no conception of the deductive proof of a mathematical principle, which was invented by the Greeks. The Greeks also introduced the use of a chain of theorems to develop a mathematical subject.

Pythagorean philosophers attempted to explain the order underlying the universe in terms of numbers, which led to an emphasis on arithmetic and the theory of numbers, rather than the process of calculation and the solving of particular problems. Discovery of flaws in the theory of numbers switched attention to geometry, which developed rapidly over a period of 300 years. It culminated in the work of Euclid (who systematized previous work), Archimedes and Apollonius of Perge (who developed new areas of geometrical research). This development of pure mathematics was paralleled by the use of applied mathematics in the related disciplines of astronomy and physics.

Astronomy

Astronomy was important for navigation, timekeeping and regulating the agricultural year. The Egyptians and Babylonians already used some astronomical cycles for navigation and for maintaining a calendar, and the Greeks also used astronomy for these purposes. The pre-Socratic philosophers began to rationalize the study of astronomy, which greatly benefited from the use of mathematics. Geometrical systems were used to represent the observed motions of heavenly bodies, an idea that probably began with Anaximander. The Pythagoreans laid the foundation of

the science by greatly increasing the use of mathematics in astronomy.

In the 4th century BC Eudoxus of Cnidus was able to use mathematics to propose how the observed irregular motions of the planets could be the result of regular circular motions. His work was improved and expanded by Callippus. Difficulties in this system led to it being replaced by improved systems devised by later astronomers. All these systems put the Earth at the center of the universe, but in the 3rd century BC Aristarchus proposed a more accurate system that placed the sun at the center of the universe. Other astronomers were not prepared to accept that the stars were so far away, as would be necessary for this system, and so it was not adopted. In fact the Greek system (revised by Ptolemy in the 2nd century AD), which had the planets revolving around the Earth, was accepted as accurate for nearly 1,400 years.

Physics

Physics, as the study of all aspects of the natural world (*physeos*, nature), began with the work of the philosophers Thales, Anaximander and Anaximenes in the 6th century BC. They were convinced that there was an order that governed the diverse natural phenomena and attempted to find this order and explain the world and its origins. Their search for a unifying hypothesis rejected the supernatural agencies that were invoked by others, and relied on rational explanations. The deductive logic of Parmenides and followers of the Eleatic school brought an end to such speculation about the natural world, by apparently proving that the material from which the universe was made was single, unchanging and indivisible, leaving no room for theories about change or development.

Following this impasse, two important theories were developed. Empedocles originated the theory of four basic physical elements (earth, air, fire, water), which was later adopted by the Academy, the Peripatetic school and the Stoics. The atomic theory was developed by Leucippus and Democritus, and was later adopted in a modified form by the Epicureans. These two theories dominated natural science until the 16th century.

What was lacking in ancient Greek physics was the use of systematic experimentation and the formulation of specific laws. Rare examples of the latter are Pythagoras' laws of musical harmony and Archimedes' law of leverage.

Zoology

From earliest times ancient Greeks were interested in the origin of life, particularly human life. The belief that animals and humans sprang from the earth occurs in Greek mythology, but with the development of philosophy, rational explanations were sought. In the 6th century BC Anaximander advanced the theory that the first living beings, enclosed in prickly membranes, came from primeval liquid that was evaporated by the sun. He also realized that the first creatures would need some sort of protection, not having parents to protect them in early life. Despite claims to the contrary, he does not appear to have had any idea of the principles of evolution.

Although speculation about the origins of life are found in the works of other philosophers, the only philosophers to consider zoology in any detail were Aristotle and possibly Hippocrates. A work on zoology exists in the Hippocratic Corpus (which may not have been written by Hippocrates), while Aristotle wrote several treatises on zoology. The most important were *History of Animals*, *On the Generation of Animals*, *On the Parts of Animals*, *On the Motion of Animals* and *On the Progression of Animals*. The careful description and classification of these works laid the foundation of systematic zoology.

Botany

As a source of food, drink and medicine, plants were of interest to the Greeks from earliest times, but were often surrounded by superstition. Some early philosophers put forward rational speculations about plants, but it is not until the 4th century BC that any great interest was taken in botany. Philosophers of both the Academy and the Lyceum were interested in botany. Aristotle regarded plants as a lower order than animals, but although numerous references to botany occur in his work, he did not produce the same detailed study of plants as he did of animals. Aristotle's work influenced Theophrastus who produced two works on botany, *History of Plants* and *Causes of Plants*. Plants were the main source of medicines, and so an overlap existed between medicine and botany. Physicians such as

Diocles and Crateuas produced herbals that are also very important for the history of botany.

Anatomy

Despite the fact that wounds were described with anatomical accuracy in works such as Homer's *Iliad*, the treatises in the Hippocratic Corpus show that even in the early 4th century BC there was little anatomical knowledge, and that knowledge was probably not based on dissection of animals or humans. Greek religion prohibited human dissection, and although Diocles was said to have been the first to write a work on anatomy, he was describing animal anatomy. Human dissection was not undertaken systematically until the 3rd century BC, when Herophilus and Erasistratus carried out anatomical research at Alexandria, under the protection of the Ptolemies. Their work attained a high level of sophistication and was not surpassed for many centuries.

Medicine

RELIGION AND PHILOSOPHY

From earliest times the treatment of sickness and disease was the province of religion. Various gods were regarded as healing deities, but from the 5th century BC Asclepius became the preeminent healing god. Asclepius and other healing deities had sanctuaries where an illness could be diagnosed and various remedies prescribed. It was thought that the temple of Asclepius at Cos was the origin of Greek medicine, but this temple was not built until the late 4th century BC.

The practice of rational medicine grew out of attempts by early philosophers to examine and explain natural phenomena. Over 60 medical treatises form the Hippocratic Corpus, but their authorship is uncertain. They deal with causes and symptoms of disease in rational terms, without invoking supernatural agencies. Although initially beneficial there was potential danger in the philosophical approach to medicine—the clash between the strictly rational approach of the philosopher and the empirical approach of the physician. One work in the Hippocratic Corpus (*Nature of Man*) advanced the theory of four humors (blood, black bile, yellow bile and phlegm), which was a medical analogue of the four elements (air, earth, fire and water).

Although philosophical in origin, this theory was claimed to be empirically justified, and it came to dominate medicine for the next 2,000 years.

Probably to explain the similarities between some later practices in healing sanctuaries and those used by rational physicians, it was said that Hippocrates had studied medicine at the temple of Asclepius on Cos, but this was inaccurate. Similarities between later healing practices in temples of Asclepius (Asclepieia) and Hippocratic medicine are most likely to have arisen due to the influence of rational medicine on temple priests. Rational medicine did not supplant temple medicine; rather, religious healing shrines employed a mixture of religion, magic and rational medicine to effect cures. However, the religious taboo on human dissection held back the continued development of rational medicine until the Hellenistic period.

From the 5th century BC dietetics became an established part of medicine. Dietetics originally formed the regime adopted by those training for the games, but physicians began to prescribe certain regimes for treating some ailments. They formulated rules, based on all the factors influencing the body and designed to regulate in detail all aspects of the patient's life. In time such regimes were recommended for healthy people to prevent illness. Although physicians admitted that the poor could not afford to carry out such regimes properly, they urged the rich to do so. This resulted in the rich becoming nervous and overconscious of their health and tending to refrain from any useful activity. See also chapter 8, healing shrines and sanctuaries.

PHYSICIANS

At first the status of a physician was not much higher than that of a skilled craftsman. Physicians tended to move from town to town, setting up a workshop or surgery (*iatreion*), from which to work. A physician would have pupils, bound to him by a legal contract, who acted as assistants and nurses. Some physicians were slaves, although they may have been engaged solely in treating illnesses of other slaves. There were also some state physicians, but very little is known about them.

Hippocrates was the most famous physician of rational Greek medicine. He lived from the late 5th century into the 4th century BC, but despite his fame little is known about him. Many works on medicine were attributed to him (the Hippocratic Corpus), although there is no evidence that he wrote any of them. The status of physicians rose in the Hellenistic period, mainly because of the school of physicians in Alexandria in Egypt, where medical research was carried out unhindered by religious prohibitions and where systematic medical instruction was given to pupils.

SURGERY

Descriptions of the treatment of wounds occur in Homer's *Iliad*. Together with the evidence of early Greek surgical instruments, this suggests that surgery before Classical times was derived from medical practices in Egypt and Mesopotamia. The Hippocratic Corpus contains a number of works on various aspects of surgery, dealing mainly with wounds, fractures and dislocations. These works reflect the development of a high degree of skill and knowledge of the subject, and contain detailed directions for preparing an operating room, making a diagnosis, carrying out various operations, dressing wounds and treating fractures. Dentistry was also performed, including extractions and use of gold wire to secure loose teeth. Fillings were unknown.

In the 3rd century BC surgery benefited from an increased knowledge of anatomy that resulted from dissections carried out in the Alexandrian school. Twenty different operations were devised for the treatment of various disorders of the eye, showing a great advance in opthalmology that was not surpassed until the 18th century.

Engineering

The elements of engineering needed for agriculture and industry were discovered before the end of the Dark Age, many apparently inherited from earlier civilizations. Despite impressive architectural and artistic achievements, the Greeks were not responsible for many important engineering innovations. Inventions that can be credited to them include the gear, screw, rotary mills, screw press, bronze-casting techniques, water clock, water organ, torsion catapult and the use of steam to operate some experimental machines and toys. Many of these inventions occurred late in the Greek period, often inspired by the need to improve weapons and tactics in war.

No power sources were effectively utilized. Even the traction power of animals was limited by the lack of an efficient harness. High value does not appear to have been placed on material progress, and inventions were utilized slowly. Only in warfare were mechanical inventions developed and used to any great extent, mainly because improved defensive fortifications could be overcome only by improved siege engines (see chapter 3). Consequently gifted inventors like Archimedes were mainly employed as military engineers, and their other inventions were regarded as of secondary importance.

The failure of the Greeks to develop their technology has sometimes been attributed to the easy availability of slave labor, removing the need to develop labor-saving devices. However, slavery in Egypt apparently did not inhibit technological development. A more likely explanation was the Greek attitude to the social status of people providing labor. Manual labor was despised, and anyone attempting to apply science to it was likely to lose status in society, removing much of the incentive to seek technological innovation.

Meteorology

Initially natural phenomena, such as wind, rain, meteors, thunder and lightning, were attributed to the actions of supernatural agencies. With the growth of philosophy and the interest of philosophers in all aspects of the universe, rational explanations were provided instead. Aristotle classified many phenomena in his *Meteorologica*, and his study was continued by Theophrastus and the Epicureans.

PHILOSOPHERS AND SCIENTISTS: BIOGRAPHIES

Following is a list of the major philosophers and scientists, with the Greek version of their name, in italics. See also individual philosophies.

ANAXAGORAS OF CLAZOMENAE (*Anaxagoras*): c. 500–428 BC. A philosopher who moved to Athens at the age of 20 and was the first philoso-

pher to reside there. He was the teacher and friend of Pericles. He was indicted by enemies of Pericles on charges of impiety, but escaped to Lampsacus where he founded a school and remained until his death.

ANAXARCHUS OF ABDERA (*Anaxarkhos*): Fourth-century BC philosopher, a follower of Democritus and teacher of Pyrrhon. He accompanied Alexander the Great on his campaigns in Asia. He was put to death by the Cypriot prince Nicocreon.

ANAXIMANDER OF MILETUS (*Anaximandros*): c. 610–540 BC. A philosopher and astronomer. He was credited with writing the first philosophic treatise in prose, introducing the gnomon into Greece and drawing the first map of the Earth. He also rationalized astronomy.

ANAXIMENES OF MILETUS (*Anaximenes*): Floruit c. 546 BC. A philosopher who wrote a book on the subject.

ANTIOCHUS OF ASCALON (*Antiokhos*): Born c. 130–120 BC, died c. 68 BC. A philosopher and pupil of Philon of Larissa at Athens. He accompanied him to Rome in 88 BC and met the Roman general Lucullus. In 79–78 BC he was head of the Academy in Athens when it was attended by Cicero. He joined Lucullus during the Second Mithridatic War in 73 BC.

ANTISTHENES (*Antisthenes*): c. 445–360 BC. A philosopher and founder of what became known as the Cynic school of philosophy. He was a pupil of Socrates and later established a school at Cynosarges outside the walls of Athens.

APOLLODORUS OF ALEXANDRIA (*Apollodoros*): Early 3rd-century-BC physician and scientist, who wrote *On Poisonous Creatures* and a work on pharmacology.

APOLLONIUS OF PERGE (*Apollonios*): Second half of 3rd century BC, a mathematician who studied at Alexandria and composed *Conics*, a work in eight books (much of which survives, some in Arabic), as well as several other works. He also worked on theoretical astronomy, and as a mathematician ranked second only to Archimedes.

ARCESILAUS (*Arkesilaos*): c. 316–242 BC. A philosopher from Pitane in Aeolia who studied philosophy under Theophrastus. He became head of the Academy. He followed the Socratic practice of argument and debate, without reaching conclusions, and probably published nothing. His main moral principle was to follow what is reasonable (*to eulogon*).

ARCHIMEDES (*Arkhimedes*): 287–212 BC. Born at Syracuse, son of the astronomer Pheidias. He was one of the greatest Greek mathematicians and an inventor, physicist and astronomer. He probably studied at Alexandria and then lived at the court of Hieron II of Syracuse. He was killed in the Roman siege of Syracuse. Several of his mathematical treatises survive in Greek (and two in Arabic) on various topics such as the circle, sphere and cylinder. They include *On the Sphere and Cylinder*, *On Floating Bodies* (the science of hydrostatics, invented by him), *On Spirals*, *Method of Mechanical Theorems* and *The Sand-Reckoner* (a means of expressing huge numbers in words). He exclaimed the famous *eureka* (I have found it) on discovering how to determine the proportions of gold and silver in a crown made for Hieron.

ARCHYTAS (*Arkhytas*): Early 4th century BC. A mathematician and Pythagorean philosopher from Tarentum and a successful general. Fragments of his mathematical works survive.

ARISTAEUS OF CROTON (*Aristaios*): Son-in-law of Pythagoras. He apparently wrote works on mathematics.

ARISTARCHUS OF SAMOS (*Aristarkhos*): First half of 3rd century BC. An astronomer who is famous for the heliocentric theory that the sun and stars are fixed and the Earth moves around the sun. His only extant treatise is *On the sizes and distances of the sun and moon*.

ARISTIPPUS OF CYRENE (the elder) (*Aristippos*): Uncertain date, but a pupil of Socrates. He was apparently a teacher of rhetoric, and at one time a courtier of Dionysius I. He was sometimes thought to have founded the Cyrenaic school of philosophy, but this was probably his grandson Aristippus the younger.

ARISTIPPUS OF CYRENE (the younger) (*Aristippos*): Uncertain date. Grandson of Aristippus the elder through the latter's daughter Arete. He probably founded the Cyrenaic school of philosophy, which held a more extreme hedonistic doctrine than the Epicureans.

ARISTOTLE (*Aristoteles*): 384–322 BC. A philosopher and author of books covering every branch of philosophy and science. He was born at Stagira in Chalcidice. His father was Nicomachus, a member of the Asclepiadae medical guild. Aristotle may have spent his youth at the royal court at Pella. He entered the Academy at Athens at the age of 17. He remained there until Plato's death (347 BC), then left to join a group of Platonists at Assus in Mysia. There he married Pythias, niece of Hermias (ruler of Assus and nearby Atarneus). After the fall and death of Hermias in 345 BC, Aristotle went to Mytilene where he collaborated with Theophrastus in zoological research and taught until 343/342 BC.

Aristotle was next invited by Philip II of Macedonia to be tutor to his son Alexander, then 13 years old. In 335 BC Alexander the Great succeeded to the throne and started on his expedition to Asia, so Aristotle returned to Athens and set up his school, the Lyceum (see chapter 7, education). Here Aristotle also collected a library of manuscripts and maps and a museum of natural objects. During this period Pythias died, and afterward Aristotle lived with Herpyllis, by whom he had a son, Nicomachus. During the anti-Macedonian period in Athens, following the death of Alexander, Aristotle was charged with impiety. He left Athens and retired to Chalcis, where he died.

Aristotle wrote a large number of works, some now lost, and many others may have been attributed to him incorrectly. They fall broadly into three categories: early popular works on philosophy, large collections of historical and scientific facts and philosophical and scientific works. Most surviving material comes from the latter category. Extant works include *Prior Analytics*, *Posterior Analytics*, *Topics*, *Physics*, *On the Heavens*, *Inquiry into Animals*, *On the Soul*, *Politics*, *On Interpretation*, *Metaphysics* and *Rhetoric*.

ARISTOXENUS (*Aristoxenos*): Born between 375 and 360 BC. A philosopher and musical theorist, famous for his works on rhythm and harmonics. He was born at Tarentum and received musical training from his father, Spintharus, and from

Lamprus of Erythrae. He lived at Mantinea and Corinth and then studied at Athens, first under Xenophilus and then under Aristotle. He was passed over for the headship of the Lyceum in favor of Theophrastus. He wrote various works, parts of which survive, including *Principles and Elements of Harmonics, Elements of Rhythm, On Music, On Melody, Pythagorean Maxims, Political Laws* and *Historical Notes*.

ASCLEPIADES (*Asklepiades*): Floruit 1st century BC. A physician from Prusa in Bithynia. He studied rhetoric in Athens and was influenced by the philosophy of Epicurus and Heracleides Ponticus. He was opposed to the theory of humors and relied on diet rather than drugs for treatment. He became an influential physician in Rome.

AUTOLYCUS OF PITANE (*Autolykos*): Late 4th century BC. Astronomer and author of two astronomical works, *On the Moving Sphere* and *On Risings and Settings*—the earliest complete surviving Greek mathematical treatises.

BION THE BORYSTHENITE (*Bion*): c. 325–c. 255 BC. A philosopher. The son of a freedman and a former hetaera of Borysthenes. His family was sold into slavery after his father committed a fraud. Bion, however, received a good education and was eventually freed. He studied in various philosophical schools in Athens, but did not become a follower of any particular school. He spent much of his life wandering from city to city, earning a living by lecturing and teaching. He popularized the *diatribe* (amusement, discussion) as a written sermon so that it could reach a wider audience. His humorous but sharp attacks in these works gave the diatribe its connotation of abusiveness.

CALLIPPUS (*Kallippos*): Late-4th-century-BC astronomer from Cyzicus who worked with Aristotle in Athens. He proposed a year of 365¼ days. He improved Eudoxus of Cnidus' theory of movement of the sun, moon and stars by introducing additional spheres.

CARNEADES (*Karneades*): c. 213–129 BC. A philosopher from Cyrene, the son of Epicomus or Philocomus. He studied at the Academy in Athens and then became its head some time before 155 BC. He retired around 137 BC on the grounds of age.

CEBES OF THEBES (*Kebes*): Fourth-century-BC Pythagorean philosopher. He was a pupil of Philolaus. According to Plato, Cebes was one of those who took part in the discussion on immortality just before Socrates drank hemlock.

CHRYSIPPUS (*Khrysippos*): c. 280–207 BC. A Stoic philosopher, the son of Apollonius of Soli. He moved to Athens c. 260 BC and attended the lectures of Arcesilaus at the Academy. He was later converted to Stoicism by Cleanthes, whom he succeeded as head of the Stoic school of philosophy in 232 BC.

CLEANTHES (*Kleanthes*): c. 331–232 BC. A Stoic philosopher, the son of Phanias of Assus. He studied under Zeno of Citium at Athens, where he later became head of the Stoic school of philosophy.

CLEITOMACHUS (*Kleitomakhos*): c. 186–109 BC. A philosopher who was Carthaginian, originally named Hasdrubal. He moved to Athens and studied at the Academy under Carneades. He established his own school of philosophy, but returned to the Academy with his followers and later became its head. He was said to have written over 400 books, but none survive.

COLOTES OF LAMPSACUS (*Kolotes*): An Epicurean philosopher, 4th–3rd centuries BC. He was a pupil and fanatical admirer of Epicurus. He wrote works trying to show that adherence to the teachings of earlier philosophers would make life impossible, including *Against Plato's "Lysis"* and *Against the "Republic"*.

CONON OF SAMOS (*Konon*): Third-century-BC astronomer and mathematician, much admired by Archimedes. Little is known of his work, but he apparently discovered the constellation Coma Berenices (Lock of Berenice).

CRANTOR (*Krantor*): Late 4th to early 3rd centuries BC. A philosopher from Soli in Cilicia. He moved to Athens to study at the Academy under Xenocrates and Polemon. He wrote many works, of which only fragments survive. His most famous work, *On Grief*, was much admired by later writers.

CRATES OF THEBES (*Krates*): c. 365–285 BC. A Cynic philosopher. He was the son of

Ascondas of Thebes. At Athens he initially studied the philosophy of the Megarian school but was converted to Cynicism by Diogenes of Sinope. He decided to live a life of wandering and poverty with his wife Hipparchia, who shared his philosophical beliefs.

CRATEUAS (*Krateuas*):   Floruit early 1st century BC. A botanist and physician to Mithridates VI. He wrote at least two works—an herbal illustrated with colored drawings of plants (of which fragments survive) and a work on the pharmacological use of plants.

CRATYLUS (*Kratylos*):   Floruit late 5th century BC. A philosopher who developed Heracleitus' theory of constant change to an extreme level.

CRITOLAUS OF PHASELIS (*Kritolaos*):   Floruit 2nd century BC. A philosopher who was a head of the Peripatetic school of philosophy in Athens and revived the philosophical and scientific work of the school, which had begun to flag. Only fragments of his writings survive.

CTESIBIUS (*Ktesibios*):   Floruit c. 275–260 BC. An inventor from Alexandria, the most famous of his day, who worked under the Ptolemies. He had an interest in pneumatics and various mechanical devices. His inventions included a torsion catapult, air catapult, water organ, the first accurate water clock, a force pump with cylinder and plunger, and ingenious toys.

DEMOCEDES (*Demokedes*):   Sixth-century-BC physician of great repute, from Croton. He practiced in Aegina and Athens, then at the court of Polycrates of Samos. In 522 BC he became court physician of Darius I, later returning to Croton.

DEMOCRITUS (*Demokritos*):   Born c. 460 BC. A philosopher, born at Abdera. He traveled widely in Egypt and Asia and visited Athens. He was taught by Leucippus and possibly by Anaxagoras. Over 60 works are attributed to him, covering as broad a range of philosophy and science as that covered by Aristotle. About 300 fragments from his works survive. He was said to have lived to a great age, but the date of his death is unknown.

DIOCLES (*Diokles*):   Possibly c. 200 BC. A mathematician who wrote *On Burning-Mirrors*, important in the history of conic sections.

DIOCLES OF CARYSTUS (*Diokles*):   4th-century-BC physician who worked in Athens. After Hippocrates he was the second most famous physician and the first to write in Attic. He was especially renowned for his medical writings.

DIOGENES OF APOLLONIA (*Diogenes*):   Floruit 440/425 BC. An Eclectic philosopher (one who collects and amalgamates elements from different philosophies). He was probably from Apollonia in Phrygia. He revived the views of Anaximenes, but was also influenced by the work of Empedocles, Anaxagoras and Leucippus. He wrote a number of works, including *On Nature*, *Against the Sophists*, *Meteorology* and *Nature of Man*. His work on the arrangement of veins in the body was quoted by Aristotle.

DIOGENES OF SELEUCIA (sometimes called Diogenes of Babylon) (*Diogenes*):   c. 240–152 BC. A Stoic philosopher from Seleucia on the Tigris. He was a pupil of Chrysippus and became head of the Stoic school of philosophy.

DIOGENES OF SINOPE (*Diogenes*):   c. 400–325 BC. A philosopher, the main proponent of the Cynic school of philosophy. He moved to Athens after he and/or his father Hicesias (who was in charge of the mint at Sinope) was accused of adulterating the coinage. From his life-style he became known as "dog" (*kyon*), a possible origin of the name Cynic. He did not develop a comprehensive system of philosophy, but he was influential through his life-style and his pointed remarks.

ECHECRATES OF PHILIUS (*Ekhekrates*):   Floruit c. 367 BC. A Pythagorean philosopher, he was one of the last members of the Pythagorean school of philosophy.

EMPEDOCLES (*Empedokles*):   c. 492–432 BC. A philosopher and poet. He was the son of Meton, an aristocrat from Acragas in Sicily. He supported democracy there and allegedly refused the kingship. He was later exiled and fled to the Peloponnese. He combined the roles of philosopher, scientist, poet and statesman. Many fragments survive from his two books, written in verse, *On Nature* and *Purifications*.

EPICURUS (*Epikouros*): 341–270 BC. A philosopher, the son of Chaerestrate and Neocles (an Athenian). He was born in Samos and as a boy was taught by the Platonist Pamphilus. At the age of 18 he was required to go to Athens as an *ephebos*. He later rejoined his family, who had moved to Colophon. At some stage, he studied under Nausiphanes. At the age of 32 he moved to Mytilene and then to Lampsacus. In both places he established schools of philosophy. Around 307 BC he returned to Athens and bought a house with a garden, where he set up the Epicurean school of philosophy, which became known as "the garden." Apart from some visits to Asia, he remained in Athens until his death. He bequeathed his library and the garden to Hermarchus of Mytilene to ensure the continuation of the school. Epicurus wrote a great deal, most of which is lost.

ERASISTRATUS (*Erasistratos*): First half of 3rd century BC. A physician from Ceos. He probably studied philosophy, then practiced medicine at Alexandria or possibly Antioch. He was a younger contemporary of Herophilus and continued the latter's anatomical research, distinguishing between motor and sensory nerves. His work on blood circulation was not surpassed until the 17th century. His books were still read in the 4th century AD, but only fragments survive.

EUCLEIDES OF MEGARA (*Eukleides*): c. 450–380 BC. A philosopher. He was an associate of Socrates and founded the Megarian school of philosophy, in which logic and logical paradoxes were a central concern. Plato and other philosophers took refuge with him at Megara after Socrates' death in 399 BC.

EUCLID (*Eukleides*): Floruit c. 300 BC. A mathematician who lived and taught at Alexandria under Ptolemy I, but little else is known of him. His textbook *Stoicheia* (*Elements*) in 13 books was so famous that "Euclid" became virtually synonymous with geometry. He also wrote other works on geometry. The term QED apparently derived from Euclid—*quod erat demonstrandum*, a Latin translation of his original Greek *hoper edei deixai*. Until the 12th century his work was only known in Arabic.

EUDEMUS OF RHODES (*Eudemos*): Floruit late 4th century BC. A philosopher. He was a pupil of Aristotle and may have been in line to succeed Aristotle as head of the Lyceum, though it was Theophrastus who actually succeeded Aristotle. Little is known about his life. He wrote extensively, possibly organizing and clarifying Aristotle's work, but only fragments have survived.

EUDOXUS OF CNIDUS (*Eudoxos*): c. 400– c. 350 BC. An outstanding mathematician, and also astronomer, geographer and philosopher. He apparently spent time in Egypt and also at the court of Mausolus and at Athens. None of his works survive, but some of his work on geometry was included in Euclid's *Elements*. Eudoxus undertook research on the movement of planets and stars, and calculated the circumference of the Earth. Aratus' poem *Phaenomena* was based on Eudoxus' description of constellations.

HERACLEIDES PONTICUS (*Herakleides*): Floruit 4th century BC. Philosopher, astronomer and writer. He was born into an aristocratic family at Heraclea Pontica. He studied under Aristotle and Speusippus at the Academy. After the death of Speusippus, he was narrowly defeated in the election for leadership of the Academy. He returned to Heraclea and may have set up his own school of philosophy. He wrote on a wide range of subjects, but only fragments have survived.

HERACLEITUS or HERACLITUS (*Herakleitos*): Floruit c. 500 BC. A philosopher, and son of Bloson of Ephesus, he was probably of royal blood and was said to have given up any claim to kingship in favor of his brother. Over 100 small fragments of his work survive.

HERMARCHUS OF MYTILENE (*Hermarkhos*): Floruit 3rd century BC. An Epicurean philosopher, he studied under Epicurus at Mytilene, before the school moved to Lampsacus in 310 BC. He became head of the school after the death of Epicurus in 270 BC. Epicurus bequeathed him his library and revenues to support the school of philosophy.

HEROPHILUS (*Herophilos*): Early 3rd century BC, from Chalcedon. One of the leading physicians at Alexandria (with Erasistratus). He is known particularly for anatomical research, apparently undertaking human dissection on criminals. His work on specific organs was famous; he also discovered the rhythm of the pulse and used drugs extensively. Many of his technical terms have passed into common usage.

HIPPARCHUS OF NICAEA (*Hipparkhos*): c. 190–after 126 BC. Astronomer from Nicaea (Bithynia) who lived mainly at Rhodes. He systematically used trigonometry and old Babylonian records dating from the 8th century BC to undertake astronomical calculations. He is particularly famous for the discovery of the precession of the equinoxes and determining the sizes and distances of the sun and moon. Much is known from the 2nd-century-AD *Almagest* of Ptolemy (an astronomical textbook). His only surviving work is a commentary on *Phaenomena* by Aratus.

HIPPASUS OF METAPONTUM (*Hippasos*): Floruit 5th century BC. A Pythagorean philosopher who was apparently punished for revealing a mathematical secret of the Pythagoreans.

HIPPOCRATES OF CHIOS (*Hippokrates*): c. 470–400 BC. A mathematician who wrote the first *Elements of Geometry* (now lost), a forerunner of Euclid's *Elements*.

HIPPOCRATES OF COS (*Hippokrates*): Traditional dates c. 460–380 BC. A physician about whom very little is known. He apparently died at Larissa (Thessaly). A collection of some 60 medical works known as the *Hippocratic Corpus* is in the Ionic dialect; as the works were written between c. 430 and 330 BC (possibly later), they may represent the library associated with the Hippocratic school of medicine at the healing shrine of Asclepius on Cos. They include *On Ancient Medicine, On the Sacred Disease* (epilepsy), *On Airs, Waters, Places* and *Epidemics*. Hippocrates' own works seem to be lost, as no works in the *Hippocratic Corpus* can be definitely attributed to him. He was regarded as the ideal physician, to whom the Hippocratic Oath was attributed. He was famous from the time of Plato.

LACYDES OF CYRENE (*Lakydes*): Floruit 3rd century BC. A philosopher who became head of the Academy. He was said to have been earnest and hard working, but retired from the Academy some years before he died of excessive drinking.

LEUCIPPUS (*Leukippos*): Floruit mid- to late 5th century BC. A philosopher. He was said to have been born at Elea, Abdera or Miletus, none of which may be correct. He originated the atomic theory, which was developed by his follower Democritus.

LYCON (*Lykon*): c. 300–c. 226 BC. A philosopher, the son of Astyanax of Troas. He studied under Straton of Lampsacus, succeeding him as head of the Peripatetic school of philosophy, where he remained for 44 years.

MELISSUS OF SAMOS (*Melissos*): Floruit mid-5th century BC. A philosopher and general, he was the last important member of the Eleatic school of philosophy. He followed Parmenides' philosophy, but differed in regarding reality as infinite. He commanded the Samian fleet that defeated the Athenians in 441 BC.

MENEDEMUS OF ERETRIA (*Menedemos*): c. 339–265 BC. A philosopher. He was sent to Megara on military service and became involved in philosophy there. He studied under Stilpon and moved to Elis to join the school founded by Phaedon. He became leader of this school and transferred it to Eretria. He was actively involved in politics and attained high office, but his opponents forced him into exile. He retreated to the court of Antigonus II Gonatas in Macedonia, remaining there until his death. Little is known about his philosophy.

MENIPPUS OF GADARA (*Menippos*): Floruit first half of 3rd century BC. A Cynic philosopher, he was noted for using satire to popularize the Cynical outlook on life. His works include *Descent to the Underworld, Wills* and *Letters from Gods*, of which only small fragments survive. He was said by some to have originally been a slave who bought his freedom and became a citizen of Thebes.

METON (*Meton*): c. 432 BC. Athenian astronomer who attempted to correlate the lunar month with the solar year (Metonic cycle), later improved by Callippus and Hipparchus of Nicaea.

METRODORUS OF LAMPSACUS (*Metrodoros*): 331/330–278/277 BC. An Epicurean philosopher. He was a favorite pupil of Epicurus who dedicated *Eurylochus* and *Metrodorus* to him.

Metrodorus died before Epicurus, who provided for the care of the son and daughter of Metrodorus in his will.

NAUSIPHANES OF TEOS (*Nausiphanes*): Born c. 360 BC. A philosopher who studied under Pyrrhon, probably when they were both soldiers in Alexander the Great's campaigns. Nausiphanes established a school at Teos, where Epicurus studied under him c. 324 BC. Nausiphanes was a follower of Democritus and believed in his atomic theory.

NICOMACHUS (*Nikomakhos*): Fourth-century-BC philosopher, the son of Aristotle.

PANAETIUS (*Panaitios*): c. 185–109 BC. A Stoic philosopher and son of the Stoic philosopher Nicagoras of Rhodes. He studied under Crates of Mallus at Pergamum and then went to Athens, where he studied under Diogenes of Seleucia. He was, for a short time, a priest of Poseidon Hippios on Rhodes but went to Rome c. 144 BC. He joined the followers of the Roman general Scipio and accompanied him on his travels in the East. Afterward he lived alternately in Rome and Athens. In 129 BC Panaetius became head of the Stoic school in Athens until his death.

PARMENIDES (*Parmenides*): Born c. 515/510 BC. A philosopher who founded the Eleatic school of philosophy, named after Elea in Italy where he lived. Little is known about his life.

PHAEDON OF ELIS (*Phaidon*): Born c. 417 BC. A philosopher. An aristocrat in Elis, he was taken as a slave to Athens and was forced into prostitution. He was released by ransom and became a pupil of Socrates. He later returned to Elis, where he founded a school of philosophy.

PHAEDRUS (*Phaidros*): c. 140–70 BC. An Epicurean philosopher who may have been born in Athens. Before 88 BC he is known to have been in Rome where Cicero heard him lecture. Phaedrus was head of the Epicurean school in Rome for a short time.

PHAEDRUS OF ATHENS (*Phaidros*): c. 450–400 BC. A Socratic philosopher mentioned in Plato's dialogues.

PHILINUS (*Philinos*): Floruit c. 250 BC. A physician from Cos and a pupil of Herophilus. He apparently founded the empiric school of medicine, which relied on experience and observation of symptoms rather than scientific theory.

PHILISTION (*Philistion*): Early 4th-century-BC physician from Locri and a contemporary of Plato. He followed Empedocles in believing that health depended on the four elements of fire, air, water and earth. He wrote a book on dietetics.

PHILOLAUS (*Philolaos*): Born c. 470 BC. A Pythagorean philosopher. Born at Croton or Tarentum in Italy, he went to Thebes around 450 BC. Fragments of writing attributed to him, such as those proposing theories that the Earth was not the center of the universe, are suspected of being forgeries.

PHILON OF BYZANTIUM (*Philon*): 3rd–2nd centuries BC (date uncertain). Writer on technology. He wrote a *Mechanical Handbook*, in possibly nine books. Surviving parts include book four on siege warfare machines; book five on siphons and other devices operated by air and water; and parts of books seven and eight on siege warfare techniques. Book six (now lost) was on automata.

PHILON OF LARISSA (*Philon*): 159–c. 80 BC. A philosopher who went to Athens at the age of 24, having previously studied in his home town. At Athens he studied under Clitomachus, whom he succeeded as head of the Academy. In 88 BC during the Mithridatic Wars, he went to Rome where he lectured on philosophy and rhetoric. He wrote many books, but not even their titles have survived.

PLATO (*Platon*): c. 429–347 BC. A philosopher, the son of Ariston and Perictione, Athenians of aristocratic descent. He became a follower of Socrates, but after Socrates' death in 399 BC he took refuge with Eucleides in Megara. He then spent some years traveling, visiting Egypt, Italy and Sicily. He returned to Athens and established a school at the grove of Academus c. 385 BC that became known as the Academy (see chapter 7, education). He returned to Syracuse in 367 BC to try (unsuccessfully) to persuade Dionysius II to adopt true philosophical principles of government. He visited Syracuse again in 362 BC.

His works, which all survive, consist of about 25 dialogues (some others attributed to him are unlikely to be genuine), some letters and the *Apology*. Plato was greatly influenced by Socrates, who appears as a character in the dialogues.

POLEMON (*Polemon*): Died c. 270 BC. Philosopher who was head of the Academy at Athens from 314 BC until his death. He was allegedly a drunk who burst into a lecture by Xenocrates, but was so impressed by the lecture that he reformed and became a pupil of Xenocrates.

POLYAENUS OF LAMPSACUS (*Polyainos*): Floruit 3rd century BC. An Epicurean philosopher. He was a distinguished mathematician who was persuaded by Epicurus to turn his attention to philosophy.

PROTAGORAS OF ABDERA (*Protagoras*): c. 490–c. 420 BC. A philosopher and one of the earliest and most successful sophists. He was a friend of Pericles at Athens, which he visited several times. He was appointed to draw up the laws for the new colony at Thurii. He wrote at least two works, *Truth* and *On the Gods*.

PYRRHON (*Pyrrhon*): c. 365–c. 275 BC. A philosopher from Elis who was regarded as the first of the Sceptics. Originally a painter he studied under Anaxarchus whom he followed to India in the entourage of Alexander the Great. He returned to Elis, where he lived quietly and was elected high priest by the citizens.

PYTHAGORAS (*Pythagoras*): Floruit late 6th century BC. Philosopher and mathematician. He was the son of Mnesarchus of Samos, from where he moved to Croton c. 531 BC, probably to escape the tyranny of Polycrates. He was a worshiper of Apollo and founded a religious society in Croton, under the government of which Croton became the foremost city among Achaean colonies in Italy. An uprising later forced him to retire to Metapontum, where he remained until death. He was noted for his mathematical and musical theories. He wrote no books, and many legends grew up about him.

SOCRATES (*Sokrates*): 469–399 BC. A philosopher. He was an Athenian of the deme of Alopece, son of Sophroniscus (a sculptor or stonemason) and Phaenarete. He served in the army as a hoplite. He married Xanthippe late in life, possibly his second marriage. As president of the Assembly he refused to put to the vote the illegal motion to execute the generals after their defeat at Arginusae. He also resisted the Thirty Tyrants when they tried to involve him in their crimes. After the restoration of democracy in Athens, he was condemned to death for "introducing new gods" and "corrupting the young." He refused to escape during the 30 days allowed after sentence and died by drinking hemlock.

Socrates was initially interested in natural philosophy, which he abandoned in favor of ethical inquiry. He attracted a diverse circle of friends and young men wishing to learn from him. It was his integrity and philosophic life-style that had the greatest impact on subsequent philosophers. He wrote no books, and knowledge of him comes largely from the works of Plato, Aristophanes and Xenophon.

SPEUSIPPUS (*Speusippos*): c. 407–339 BC. A philosopher, he was an Athenian, the son of Eurymedon and Plato's sister Potone. He accompanied Plato on his last visit to Sicily and became head of the Academy after Plato's death. He wrote many books, but only fragments survive.

SPHAERUS OF BORYSTHENES (*Sphairos*): Floruit mid- to late 3rd century BC. A Stoic philosopher, he was a pupil of Zeno of Citium and then studied under Cleanthes. He visited Sparta and helped Cleomenes III with his reforms. His definitions were especially esteemed by Stoic philosophers. He wrote works on all branches of philosophy, but none have survived.

STILPON (*Stilpon*): c. 380–300 BC. A philosopher. He was the third head of the Megarian school of philosophy, and under his rule it became the most popular school in Greece. He may have studied under Diogenes the Cynic as well as under Eucleides. Stilpon wrote some 20 dialogues, but only a few titles have survived.

STRATON OF LAMPSACUS (*Straton*): Died c. 268 BC. An Aristotelian philosopher. After studying at the Lyceum he became tutor to the future Ptolemy II Philadelphus at Alexandria. He became head of the Lyceum after Theophrastus' death c. 287 BC. His main interest was natural science, and he wrote works on subjects such as logic, ethics, cosmology, physics, zoology, physiology and psychology. Only fragments of his work survive.

THALES (*Thales*):   Early 6th-century-BC scientist and philosopher from Miletus. He was one of the Seven Sages and gave advice on many issues, including politics and science. He was particularly known for geometry and astronomy.

THEAETETUS (*Theaitetos*):   c. 415/414–369 BC. Mathematician from Athens. A pupil of Theodorus of Cyrene, he developed a theory of irrational numbers and was the main source for Euclid's *Elements*, books 10 and 13. He died after fighting in a battle near Corinth.

THEODORUS OF CYRENE (*Theodoros*): Fifth-century-BC mathematician. Originally a pupil of Protagoras, he turned to mathematics (especially geometry). Plato and Theaetetus were his pupils. His research on irrational numbers was developed by Theaetetus.

THEOPHRASTUS OF ERESUS (*Theophrastos*): c. 370–288/285 BC. A philosopher. Born at Eresus, he became a pupil of Aristotle, later succeeding him as head of the Lyceum. He probably joined Aristotle at Assus, moving with him to Macedonia and then Athens. Only a small part of his works survive, including *History of Plants*, *Causes of Plants*, *Characters*, *Metaphysics* and fragments from *The Doctrines of the Natural Philosophers* and *Laws*.

TIMON OF PHILIUS (*Timon*):   c. 320–230 BC. A Sceptical philosopher. After poverty in his youth, when he earned a living as a dancer, he studied with Stilpon in Megara and then became a follower of the Sceptic Pyrrhon in Elis. He later worked as a sophist in Chalcedon; when he had enough money, he moved to Athens, remaining there until his death. Only fragments of his work survive, mostly from his lampoons of other philosophers in defense of Pyrrhon's views.

XENOCRATES OF CHALCEDON (*Xenokrates*):   c. 395–314 BC. A philosopher who spent most of his life studying at the Academy in Athens. He was head of the Academy from 399 BC until his death. More than 70 works are attributed to him, but only their titles survive.

XENOPHANES (*Xenophanes*):   c. 570–c. 478 BC. A philosopher and poet. Writing at the age of 92, he indicated that he was born c. 570 BC and he was said to have lived until the time of Hieron of Syracuse (ruled 478–467 BC). Born at Colophon in Ionia, he left around 545 BC and spent the rest of his life traveling around the Greek world. He was mainly known for his rationalization of theology, attacking the polytheism and anthropomorphism of traditional Greek religion.

ZENO OF ELEA (*Zenon*):   c. 490–after 445 BC. Philosopher of the Eleatic school. He was a disciple and friend of Parmenides. He wrote possiby just one book, in which he supports the views of Parmenides.

ZENO OF CITIUM (*Zenon*):   c. 333–262 BC. Philosopher and founder of the Stoic school of philosophy. Son of Mnaseas of Citium in Cyprus, he was considered to be a Phoenician. He moved to Athens in 313 BC and attended Plato's Academy, but was converted to Cynicism by Crates. He developed his own philosophy and taught in the Stoa Poikile, from which the Stoics got their name.

ZOILUS OF AMPHIPOLIS (*Zoilos*):   Floruit 4th century BC. A Cynic philosopher and rhetorician. He was a pupil of Polycrates and a teacher of Anaximenes of Lampsacus. He was known for his bitter attacks on Isocrates, Plato and particularly Homer.

READING

Art

Beazley 1986: black-figure vases; Betancourt 1985: Minoan pottery; Boardman 1974: black-figure vases and painters; Boardman 1989: red-figure vases; Boardman (ed.) 1993: many aspects of art (well-illustrated); Dickinson 1994: includes Bronze Age arts and crafts; Higgins 1961: jewelry; Higgins 1967: terra-cotta figurines; Higgins 1981: Minoan and Mycenaean art; Hood 1978: many aspects of prehistoric art; Mountjoy 1993: Mycenaean pottery; Pedley 1992: general well-illustrated overview from the Bronze Age onward; Pollitt 1988a: sculpture; Pollitt 1988b: painting, mosaics; Popham

1967: Late Minoan pottery; Rasmussen and Spivey (eds.) 1991: articles on vases; Robertson 1992: red-figure vases; Sakellarakis 1992: Mycenaean Pictorial pottery; Smith 1991: Hellenistic sculpture; Sparkes 1991: various aspects of pottery; Tsakirgis 1989: mosaics; Vermeule and Karageorghis 1982: Mycenaean Pictorial pottery; Trendall 1989: Italian and Sicilian red-figure vases; Webb 1978: faience objects; Whibley (ed.) 1931, 322–324: painting.

Artists and Architects

Bowder (ed.) 1982; Hammond and Scullard (eds.) 1970.

Philosophy and Science

PHILOSOPHY

Armstrong (ed.) 1967; Barnes 1987; Barnes 1988: Hellenistic; Burnet 1920; Guthrie 1962, 1965, 1969, 1975, 1978, 1981; Hammond and Scullard (eds.) 1970 passim; Kirk et al. 1983; Luce 1992.

SCIENCE

Barnes 1988: Hellenistic; Brothwell 1988, 252: medicines and drugs; Brumbaugh 1966: engineering; Clagett 1957; Demand 1994: includes medicine relating to women and children, with extensive bibliography; Dicks 1970: astronomy; Farrington 1961; Grmek 1989: diseases; Hammond and Scullard (eds.) 1970, 660–664: medicine, 752–753: opthalmology, 1,024–1,025: surgery; Harris 1973: medicine; Lloyd 1970, 1973, 1991; Phillips 1973: medicine; Ronan 1983, 62–124; Sallares 1991, 221–293: disease; Scarsborough 1988.

Philosophers and Scientists

Bowder (ed.) 1982; Dicks 1970; Hammond and Scullard (eds.) 1970.

10

EVERYDAY
LIFE

CALENDAR

Little is known about early Greek calendars. Names of months do occur in Mycenaean Linear B texts, where months seem to be lunar. In Homer the calendar is seasonal, and no names of months are mentioned. One theory was that the calendar was reformed at Delphi in the 8th century BC. Calendars were usually lunisolar, based both on the sun and the moon.

All Greek states had 12 months, with alternate months having 29 days (hollow months) or 30 days (full months), all beginning with the new moon. The lunar month (the period between one new moon and the next) measures 29½ days, but the yearly cycle of the Earth around the sun is about 365¼ days (about 11 days longer than 12 lunar months). All calendars were originally lunar, but they also had to be reconciled with the solar year, otherwise the months would slip according to the season. This was done by intercalation—inserting an extra month (in Athens usually another Poseideon) in the year or extra days within the month. Each state had a different system, but it was common for alternate years to have an extra 30 days, with alternate years of 354 and 384 days. This system still led to discrepancies, and astronomers devised astronomical cycles to control the intercalation. Magistrates were responsible for bringing the lunar months in line with the seasons (in particular so that festivals could be held at appropriate times), but there is no evidence that astronomical methods were used in civil calendars until Hellenistic times.

In the late 4th century BC Egypt and the East came under Greek control. Egypt had used a local 25-year cycle that regulated the Egyptian religious lunar calendar. In the mid-3rd century BC this was adapted to the Macedonian calendar for use in Ptolemaic Egypt. There were 12 months of 30 days each, and five additional days at the end of the year, in total, 365 days. At the end of the 3rd century BC Ptolemy III decreed that an extra day should be added at the end of every four years, although this was never done. This Egyptian calendar was used into the Roman period.

In Syria and elsewhere in the East, the Macedonian calendar was adjusted so that its months coincided with the Babylonian calendar, which was regulated by a 19-year cycle. This system continued until Roman times.

Months

A month (*men*) is a moon-period. Each city-state had its own list of months, and colonies tended to have the same system as their mother cities. The Athenians divided the year into 12 months, beginning in summer. Before 411 BC the year of the boule of 500 may have begun in Skirophorion, while the civil calendar, which was controlled by the archons, began in Hekatombaion. Archons were responsible for making adjustments to the civil calendar (inserting extra days or an extra month), and the civil calendar could be out of phase with the moon.

Festivals followed the civil calendar rather than the lunar calendar. Each Greek state had different names for the months, with many named after festivals. Some names of months may date back to Mycenaean times. Most is known about the Athenian (Attic) calendar, whose months had the following names (given with approximate modern equivalents):

Hekatombaion (July)
Metageitnion (August)
Boedromion (September)
Pyanopsion (October)
Maimakterion (November)
Poseideon (December)
Gamelion (January)
Anthesterion (February)
Elaphebolion (March)
Mounichion (April)
Thargelion (May)
Skirophorion (June)

In Macedonia the names of months were Loios, Gorpaios, Hyperberetaios, Dios, Apellaios, Audnaios, Peritios, Dustros, Xandikos, Artemisios, Daisios and Panemos. Seleucus I ordered that Babylonian months should receive Macedonian names. Not all the names of months of every state are known, and the succession of months in some city-states is not known.

Days

The days in the month were named and numbered, beginning at sunset. In Athens and other Greek cities, days within the month were divided into three periods of (mostly) 10 days (decades, *dekades*). The days within each decade were counted, those of the first decade being expressed in terms of the rising moon. The first day was the "new moon" (*noumenia*), and the following days were numbered from second to tenth. The days of the middle third were usually eleventh to twentieth, but in the last third, the days were numbered backward (tenth to the first) in terms of the dying month. There were many variations, even in Athens itself. In some calendars there was no division of the month, and days were numbered from one to 29 or 30, with no backward counting. This system was operative in the Macedonian calendar, in use all over the Greek world in Hellenistic times. Each Macedonian month ended as day 30; for months with 29 days, the number 29 was omitted. There is no evidence of the use of weeks in the Greek world before the Roman period.

Dates of Years

It can be very difficult to convert an ancient Greek event to the modern calendar, because many different systems of designating years were used, often side by side. In many places the calendar year started at different times: the Athenian one started in summer (possibly after the summer solstice), and the Olympiad year began in midsummer. Dates converted to the modern calendar from Hellenistic and Babylonian calendars are usually more accurate than those of the Greek cities.

Most commonly a year was named after an eponymous magistrate, such as the eponymous archons in Athens and senior ephors in Sparta, or after other officeholders such as the priestesses of Hera at Argos. Dates can be related to the modern calendar if lists of such officials are known. At Athens lists of archons (some of which have survived) were maintained from the 7th century BC, but they are not reliable until the 5th century BC, when dates in Greek history can be assigned with greater certainty. The Athenian year was from about July to June, so in the modern calendar there can be a discrepancy of one year when converting dates.

At Athens three calendars were used: lunar calendar, archon (civil or festival) calendar and prytany calendar. Dates could be designated according to the lunar or civil calendar, but these could differ by up to 30 days. In Athens dates could also be given according to another civil calendar, that of the prytany (or bouleutic or conciliar) calendar. There were 10 prytanies in the year in the 5th and 4th centuries BC (see chapter 1, Council). This was the period when representatives from each of the 10 tribes to the Council (boule) of 500 served as presidents (or executive committee). Prytanies varied between 34 and 39 days. Official dates at Athens were usually given as double dates, by naming the archon (the civil calendar) and the prytany (the prytany calendar). From 394 BC the prytanies were numbered, and from 346 BC the day within the prytany was also stated.

Another system of designating dates was based on the Olympic Games, held every four years. The four-year period was called an Olympiad, and the first year of the first Olympiad equates to 776 BC. By the end of the 5th century BC a list of these games and the victors had been drawn up, and the system was used by Greek historians by the 4th century BC. The Olympiads were numbered, and sometimes the particular year of an Olympiad was also noted (such as 3rd year of the 15th Olympiad). Another system of keeping track of years was based on eras, which measured a succession of time from a notable event, a system used only in the Greek world from Hellenistic times. The Seleucid Era was widely used in the Greek East; year 1 was reckoned to be that when Seleucus I became satrap at Babylon. This equates to 312 BC, or 311 BC using the Babylonian calendar. Cities that became liberated from the Seleucid Empire (such as Tyre) began to use their own era system commencing with the year of liberation.

Clocks

The day was divided into 12 equal segments of night and 12 of day, so that a daylight hour was not the same as a night hour (except at equinox) and varied in length from month to month and according to latitude. Time was generally measured according to names given to parts of the day from sunrise to sunset, such as "first light" and "midday." Time could be measured by the stars or by the passage of the sun. Hellenistic astronomers followed the Egyptian method of dividing the day into 24 equal parts; following the Babylonian system they divided these Egyptian hours into 60 equal parts.

Various mechanisms for measuring time were known to the Egyptians and Babylonians, and were adopted by the Greeks. Two basic types of clocks were used by the Greeks, the shadow clock or sundial and the water clock. The shadow clock consisted of a vertical staff (*gnomon*), whose shadow could be measured on a flat or concave surface.

A water clock or clepsydra (*klepsydra*) allowed a predetermined quantity of water to flow out at a regular rate and was used at Athens to time speeches. It could consist of a vessel from which water flowed through a small hole, or a graduated container into which water flowed. Ctesibius apparently invented a water clock in which dripping water turned wheels that gradually raised a small statue with a stick, which pointed to the time. Other complex mechanisms were also invented based upon astronomy, but these never became widespread, and clocks were never accurate.

THE FAMILY

The family or household (*oikos*) was considered a very important part of Greek life, an essential element of the city-state.

Women

The position of women depended very much on their social status, and more is known about the status of wealthier classes and of those living in Athens. In contrast to what was written about men, very little was written about women, and most ancient authors were men. Although men were part of both the polis and *oikos*, women had a role only in the *oikos*.

As depicted in Homer's poetry, female characters of the upper classes led a relatively independent life, and there is evidence that this was the case for other circles of women in later times, such as the poetess Sappho and her group in the 7th century BC. The role of women was somewhat limited in Athens in the 5th and 4th centuries BC. Although women (not slaves, freedwomen or metics) were technically of citizen status, they had no rights of citizenship. Women had no political rights and could take no part whatsoever in government; they had no more rights than slaves. They could conduct only limited business and hold limited property. All business was conducted on a woman's behalf by her husband or father.

Women rarely received inheritances, since the law of inheritance was through the male line. Indeed, written wills were allowed at Athens only if there was no son. At Sparta women were able to own and inherit property. Marriage was arranged for a woman by her father or male guardian.

In the home women were kept segregated in their own quarters (*gynaikonitis* or *gynaikeion*) and were virtually unseen. They were responsible for the total control of their household (*oikos*), including slaves, children, cooking, cleaning, caring for the sick and making clothes (from spinning wool to finishing the garments). Much would be done by female slaves under the supervision of the mistress (*despoina*). Women rarely left the house, and even then would be accompanied by female slaves. Women did go shopping and to the wells to fetch water, but this was done mainly by slaves and by poorer women without slaves. Older women and widows had more freedom, as did Spartan wives. Poorer women undertook work, including selling goods in the market, spinning, making bread, acting as wet nurses or working alongside their husbands. It was not possible in such households to segregate men from women. Poorer widows often had to work, if they had no means of financial support.

Within religion women did play an important role, such as a dominant role at funerals, weddings, and a large number of public festivals (see chapter 8, priesthoods, festivals). There were many priestesses, and women also had their own festivals.

In Hellenistic times Macedonian women wielded much power, and contemporary philosophies also encouraged greater freedom for women. Many women, such as in the Ptolemaic world, wielded great political influence.

Fig. 10.1   A bride is led to her future husband who stands by the door of his house. Scene on a red-figure vase.

HETAERAE

Foreign women, female slaves, freedwomen and abandoned (exposed) girls (rarely women of citizen status) could become prostitutes or courtesans. The term hetaerae (*hetairai*, female companions) was a euphemism for such women trading in sex; they were widely available either on the street, in brothels or as very accomplished courtesans. They enjoyed more liberated lives and may have been able to own property. They had to pay taxes and enjoyed legal safeguards in many city-states. They were unknown in Homer's heroic age or at Sparta; most is known about them in the 5th–3rd centuries BC. Prostitutes were particularly common at Piraeus.

Many hetaerae were professional dancers and musicians, hired to entertain at men's functions such as symposia, and many were highly accomplished. Hetaerae could also become mistresses of men, such as Aspasia, mistress of Pericles. Retired hetaerae could become brothel keepers. From the late 4th century BC a distinction tended to be made between the common prostitutes (*pornai*) and the hetaerae of higher class. There were also sacred slave prostitutes at temples (*hierodouloi hetairai*).

Marriage

By far the most information about marriage comes from Athens. Differences occurred in other states. Marriages were usually monogamous, and at Athens polygamy was not allowed and was considered barbaric. Nearly all women citizens were married, and marriage was very much for political and economic expediency, and for the continuance of the family by procreation of children. Women were effectively lent to their husbands and could be recalled if they had to act as *epikleros* (see below).

There was no minimum legal age for marriage. A woman at the age of about 15 was usually married to an older man (about 30), usually a relative. It was quite common to marry first cousins or uncles. Relationships between children, parents, siblings and half-siblings with the same mother (but not the same father) were considered incest.

A betrothal was arranged for a young woman by her *kyrios* (father or guardian) after the age of five. At Athens a formal betrothal (*engye*) took place, with witnesses on both sides. In early times a bride gift (or bride price) may have been given to the bride's father by the family of the bridegroom, although this is disputed and possibly represented a token exchange of gifts. In later times a dowry was universally given by the bride's father at the time of the betrothal and was part of the betrothal conditions, although not compulsory. The dowry was given to her future husband, and on his death it would pass to her children.

Inheritance was usually through the male line. At Athens a woman inherited her father's property only if she had no brothers. Even then she did not inherit the property, but it was bequeathed through her husband to her sons. She was known as an *epikleros* (heiress, but literally "attached to the estate"). The nearest male relative had the right to marry her to continue her father's *oikos*, even if both were already married. Alternatively he could arrange for her to marry someone else, such as a more distant relative, the man to whom she was betrothed or the man appointed in her father's will. This was the case even for poor people with nothing to inherit, thus ensuring marriage for fatherless daughters.

Marriage was the act of living together, although it was usually accompanied by various rituals and ceremonies (*ekdosis*, giving away). On marriage (which could take place some years after the betrothal), the bride went to the bridegroom's house and became part of his family. The favorite time for marriage at Athens was at the full moon in the month of Gamelion (from *gamos*, marriage), traditionally the time in the agricultural year when the least work was required. A sacrifice was made to appropriate deities, such as Zeus and Hera, and the bride could dedicate a lock of hair. The bride and groom then each took prenuptial ritual baths with water fetched in a loutrophoros, and a feast was held at the groom's father's house.

In the evening the bride was taken to the groom's house (fig. 10.1) in a torchlight procession, with attendants singing the hymenaeus (wedding song). The veiled bride was conducted by the groom's mother into the house. The married couple went into the bedroom (*thalamos*) to consummate the marriage, and young men and girls sung the epithalamium (wedding song) outside the bedroom door. Although religious rituals could take place at marriage ceremonies, it was in effect a civil contract. After marriage the most important role of the woman was to produce a child as soon as possible to ensure her status in her new household.

Most cities did not recognize marriage between slaves or between people of nonequal status, but marriage between metics at Athens was similar to that between citizens. A childless widow would return with her dowry to her original family, and would often be provided with a new husband.

Although married men could practice homosexuality, take mistresses and use prostitutes, in Greek law adultery (*moikheia*) was between a man and a wife, widowed mother, unmarried daughter, sister or niece, as it was an offense against the head of the household. If a man's wife was involved (or had been raped), he had to divorce her. He could deal with the adulterer as he wished (including killing or maiming him), or the adulterer could pay a financial penalty. It was also possible to take legal proceedings against an adulterer, and penalties were very harsh. Some papyri found in Egypt mention financial penalities for adultery in marriage contracts. There were fewer taboos on adultery in Sparta. Marriage could be easily dissolved by the husband or wife living apart; a man could divorce his wife by expelling her from the house, or she could leave him by leaving the household.

In time, particularly in the Hellenistic period, marriage changed. For example, the groom married at a younger age. In Macedonia polygamy was practiced. Alexander the Great allowed his soldiers to marry captive women in Persia while keeping their wives in Macedonia. Marriage between brothers and sisters was practiced among Hellenistic rulers, such as the Ptolemies. In Hellenistic states marriage was not based on the *oikos* system, and women could not, for example, become *epikleroi*. Marital law improved for women in this period.

Men

A man was the head of the household (*oikos*). Men's work was usually outdoors, away from the home. For the role of men in society, see chapter 1, population, government.

Homosexuality

From at least the 7th century BC, homosexuality became an accepted part of everyday life. Marriage was for convenience, rarely for love. Although men used prostitutes and took mistresses, the type of all-male society greatly encouraged homosexuality (technically bisexuality), particularly among the upper classes. The usual sexual relationship was between an older man (*erastes*, lover) and a submissive adolescent (*eromenos*, loved one). The older man would look after the younger one for as long as the relationship existed; a prolonged affair was not accepted. There are many references to homosexuality, such as in poetry and graffiti, and numerous inscriptions on black-figure vases and red-figure vases refer to the beauty of particular boys. The Theban Sacred Band allegedly comprised pairs of homosexual lovers (see chapter 3, p. 93), and in Sparta homosexuality was common.

Male prostitution was not acceptable and could lead to loss of citizenship at Athens. There is some evidence for female homosexuality, such as in the poetry of Sappho, although there is doubt about whether the relationships were ever physical.

Children

Contraception and abortion were probably practiced mainly by prostitutes and poorer families. There was no effective means of contraception, but several methods were used. These included pessaries soaked in materials such as vinegar and the use of cedar resin as a prophylactic. Abortion is known to have been induced by instruments and physical exercise, and was regarded as another means of contraception, as was exposure (*ekthesis*) of babies. Unwanted newborn children, undoubtedly mainly girls, were exposed to die (technically, they were not killed). Abortion and exposure were legitimate, and in Sparta exposure was required for deformed infants. Exposed children could be rescued for use as slaves or prostitutes.

Childbirth took place at home, with all the women of the household in attendance. A female midwife may have been present, and a male doctor called in if complications arose. The mortality rate for women during and after childbirth must have been high. Gynecological treatises comprise a large proportion of the Hippocratic Corpus. At birth the guardian (usually the father) had to decide whether to keep the child or expose it. If it was kept a purification ceremony (*amphidromia*) took place on the fifth or seventh day after birth.

At Athens children were swaddled, but not in Sparta. Mothers nursed their children or used wet nurses, and pottery feeding bottles are also known (several found in graves of deceased infants) (fig. 10.2). There is evidence from vase paintings for cradles of wickerwork or wood, and children's toys (*paignia*) are known. From the 4th century BC children appear much more in artistic representations. Children played a number of games, and evidence of toys comes from literature, vase paintings and surviving examples of the actual toys. Various types of games using balls (*sphairai*) were popular, as were hoops and spinning tops. Infants had rattles, clappers and bells in a variety of forms, such as a hollow animal with loose pebbles inside. Dolls made of wood, bone, clay or rag are known, as well as dolls' houses complete with furniture and utensils. Swings, seesaws and yo-yos were used, as well as miniature carts or chariots, and games of dice (*kuboi*) and knucklebones (*astragaloi*) were played.

Fig. 10.2 A pottery feeding bottle of a child, with small perforations in the top. Diameter (excluding spout and handles) 3.5 in (0.09 m). Courtesy of Somerset County Museums Service.

It was customary at various festivals to give children toys. When girls were about to marry and when boys reached adolescence, it was customary for them to dedicate their playthings to deities.

Male children were favored for many reasons. They perpetuated the family and family cult, cared for parents in old age and arranged a proper funeral for deceased parents. In addition sons could inherit the dowry. Boys were educated in schools, but girls remained under the close supervision of their mothers until they married. They rarely went out of the women's section of the house and were taught domestic skills at home, though they did attend some religious festivals. In Sparta boys were removed from their families at the age of seven to be reared by the state. See chapter 7, education.

ADOPTION

In order to continue the family it was possible for a man to adopt a son, although the adopted son did not have as many rights of inheritance as a son by birth. It was usually a method of providing a man with an heir. By the 4th century BC in Athens, adoption could be *inter vivos* (adoptive father and adopted son both alive), or a son could be adopted after a man's death through a will, or assigned to the family after his death if none was mentioned in a will and there was no heir. The adoption of a daughter's husband was commonplace.

Pets

Some animals were kept in the home from at least the time of Homer, who mentions dogs. The most popular pet was a small dog, often represented on 5th-century-BC Attic gravestones.

SLAVES

The civilization of the Greek world was enjoyed by the few at the expense of the majority. Distribution of wealth and resources was unequal, with relatively little social mobility. A large labor force of slaves existed, as well as free labor, which at times was poorly paid and was to some extent indistinguishable from the slaves. There were also serfs, who were not technically slaves but were tied to the land, and helots. See chapter 1, population.

Slavery occurred in Greece from the Bronze Age onward. Slaves and their children were the property of their owners, to be traded like any other commodity. Slaves were sold or rented out by slave dealers, or they could be bought and sold between individuals. They were virtually without rights and were often distinguished from serfs and other workers as "chattel slaves," being the property of their owners. They were regarded as "living tools" and were supplied from several sources, such as warfare and piracy (see chapter 5, p. 187). Usually slaves were foreigners. The majority of slaves in Athens, for example, were not Athenians, and generally there was a great mixture of nationalities.

Slaves were employed in every form of skilled and unskilled labor. No tasks were performed solely by slaves, but they formed the overwhelming majority of workers in mining, manual and manufacturing work, entertainment, prostitution and domestic service in private households. Everyone who was not very poor had at least one slave. Craftsmen and tradesmen aimed to have at least one slave to train in their business so that the work would be continued by the slave on their retirement. Slaves could also be leased out to industrial establishments, providing a profit for their owners. A number of slaves were also owned by towns and cities to undertake public works.

The treatment of slaves varied enormously, depending on their employment and their owner. Harsh treatment was often restrained by the fact that the slave was an investment, and impairment of the slave's performance might involve financial loss. Treatment tended to be more harsh in industrial establishments, factories, agriculture and mining. Relatively few slaves worked in the professions, although slave doctors are known, and some slaves reached high levels of management in businesses.

As property, slaves could be sold, bequeathed or given away by their owners, but not killed. Anyone injuring a slave had to pay compensation to the owner. Slaves could seek asylum at some temples and shrines, but they were often excluded from religious cults. A slave's evidence was admissible in law only if it had been obtained under torture, apparently on the premise that only fear of further torture would counteract the influence of the slave's owner. There is little evidence of slaves being used as witnesses.

Freedom

Slaves could be freed (manumitted) by their masters. In Athens a simple declaration by the owner, before witnesses, was sufficient. Such freedom was often conditional, and freed slaves might be required to continue performing certain services for the former owner. Apart from giving other slaves some incentive, an owner often freed a slave toward the end of the slave's useful life to avoid an asset becoming a liability. In some emergencies large-scale freeing of slaves took place in order for them to enlist or be conscripted into the army or navy. Apart from helot revolts there is no record of slave revolts in Greek history, although many may have attempted to escape.

Freed slaves did not become completely free but were classed as freedmen or freedwomen. In Athens they had the same status as metics and had to register with a citizen (their former owner) as their patron and legal representative. The freeing of slaves was sometimes recorded in inscriptions, and such inscriptions are known from several places, including Athens and Delphi (fig. 10.3).

Fig. 10.3 Inscriptions on a polygonal masonry wall by the temple of Apollo at Delphi relate to the manumission of slaves. Over 1,000 such inscriptions at the site date from the 5th century BC to 3rd century AD.

FOOD AND DRINK

Evidence for food and drink comes mainly from ancient authors, archaeological deposits (such as seeds and animal bones) and some artistic representations. There were various writings on cookery by ancient authors, but only fragments from the works of later writers survive. See also chapter 5, agriculture.

Food

Diet and dining customs depended on the standard of living and geographical region—Spartan food was said to be the worst in all of Greece. The diet of most people was frugal, based on cereals, olive oil and wine, but exotic foods and recipes were available for the dinner parties of the wealthy. Cereals, mainly barley and wheat, provided the staple food. Originally husked barley was predominant (ground to make a paste, bread or a gruel), but later naked species of wheat were cultivated and made into bread.

By the 5th century BC the wealthy could afford more exotic foods, and the importance of cereals in the diet of the upper classes was diminished. For those that could afford them, there was a great variety of breads, cakes and pastries. Some were sweetened by honey, while others were prepared with milk, eggs, suet or cheese. Bread was eaten at most meals, accompanied by products such as cheese, fruit, vegetables, eggs, fish, shellfish and meat.

Butter was not used except occasionally in medicine, and cheese, yogurt and milk came from goats rather than cows.

Fish was particularly popular, and all kinds of fish were eaten—fresh, dried or pickled. A range of shellfish was eaten, and meat (especially pork, mutton and goat) was available. A great variety of birds were eaten, including fowl, ducks, geese, swans, pelicans, cranes, owls, pigeons, thrushes, larks, jays, wagtails and nightingales. Wild boar, deer and hares also provided meat.

Olives and particularly olive oil formed an important part of the diet. The range of vegetables, fruits and nuts was also wide. For many people meat and even fish were luxuries, and their diet consisted largely of bread or *maza* (a paste made from grain and other products, such as lentils and beans) and olives, cheese and eggs, as well as vegetables made into soups and stews. The very poor generally had bread, paste and gruel made from barley. See also chapter 5, p. 174.

Cooking

Bread, cakes and pastries were produced both commercially and at home. Circular domed ovens, heated by a fire underneath, were used mainly for baking bread and pastries. Individual loaves could be baked in lidded earthenware pans or under upturned pots that were placed in the fire and then covered with embers. See also chapter 5, p. 174.

Most food was cooked over a brazier or open hearth, with cauldrons suspended from a chain or cooking vessels set on gridirons or trivets. Food could be grilled, fried, roasted, boiled or stewed. Cooking was done outdoors or in kitchens, where smoke from fires escaped through a vent in the roof or wall. Soups and sauces were popular with meat dishes. Sausages and black puddings were also eaten, and flavorings of herbs and spices were commonly used in food. Honey was important for sweetening. In many households the cooking was done by one or more slaves. Apart from a few famous chefs, women were generally regarded as better cooks than men, and cooking was one of their duties within the household.

The preservation of food would have been difficult. Fish and shellfish were probably transported live to their destination. Some fruits were dried to preserve them. Various other foods could be preserved by pickling, and meat and fish by drying, smoking and salting. Nevertheless, contaminated food must have been eaten, and food poisoning was probably not uncommon.

Drink

Wine was the most common drink, generally watered down. Some wine was spiced and flavored, and some was heated to make a warming drink. Drinking undiluted wine was considered barbaric. The best wines were the most expensive, and wines drunk by the poor were of the lowest quality. Drinking beer and milk was also regarded as barbaric. Milk, usually from sheep or goats, was reserved for making cheese and for medicinal purposes. There were no infused drinks like tea and coffee, nor any distilled liquors. See also chapter 5, wine production (pp. 174–175).

Meals

The times of day when meals were taken and the names of the meals themselves varied at different periods. In early Greece breakfast (*ariston*) was eaten soon after sunrise. There was a main meal (*deipnon*) in the middle of the day and a supper (*dorpon*) in the evening. In Athens in the Classical period only a light lunch (*ariston*) and a dinner (*deipnon*) in the evening appear to have been eaten, but from the 4th century BC breakfast (*akratisma*) was again added to the daily meals.

For most people meals were relatively simple, with little difference between the town and the countryside. Breakfast and lunch were light meals and may frequently have been eaten outdoors, whereas the main meal was usually eaten indoors. People ate their food with their fingers, and those that could afford it had slaves standing by to wash their hands when necessary. Men and women would have eaten separately in many households. A symposium was a drinking party that followed an evening meal (see entertainment, below).

PERSONAL APPEARANCE

Clothing

The clothing of the Minoan and Mycenaean periods is quite distinct from that of the 8th century BC onward. Mycenaean dress was similar to Minoan dress. However, artistic representations of Mycenaean dress were heavily influenced by Minoan art and may not provide an accurate record. Virtually no representations survive from the Dark Age, so the next evidence for dress comes from the 8th century BC. From then relatively little change took place in the range of garments worn by the Greeks. Fashions did not change drastically or rapidly, and both men's and women's clothes were remarkably similar.

In contrast to Minoan and Mycenaean depictions of dress, clothing from the 8th century BC onward was generally plain, sometimes with decorative borders, and highly decorated clothing was much less common. In some cases clothes were interchangeable. For example, a woman might wear her husband's outdoor cloak. Most clothes were of wool and were made by women at home. Increased contact with other cultures, particularly the Romans, began to influence Greek dress from the late 2nd century BC.

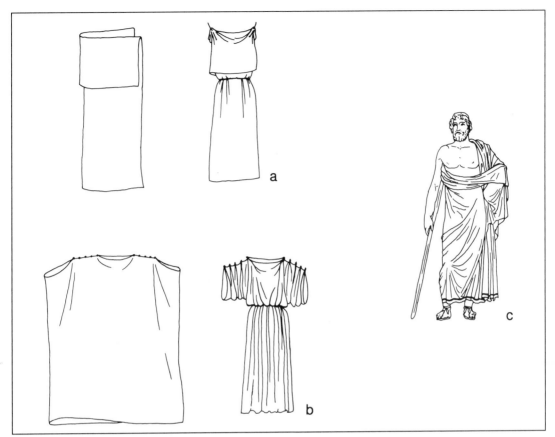

Fig. 10.4   Examples of clothing: a. peplos; b. Ionic chiton; c. himation cloak worn as the sole garment.

WOMEN'S CLOTHES

Minoan dress for women consisted of flowing floor-length dresses, some of which had flounces. Some women are portrayed naked above the waist, while others have a tight-fitting bodice leaving the breasts bare, and there was a belt at the waist. A variety of hats or headdresses seem to have been worn, often rising well above the top of the head (fig. 9.10). In Mycenaean representations women are often shown in a similar long flounced skirt, with a tight bodice apparently worn over a blouse. In both Minoan and Mycenaean representations this type of dress is highly decorated. Mycenaean women are also portrayed wearing a long, ankle-length tunic with short sleeves and a girdle at the waist. There is one portrayal of a fringed shawl, but otherwise little is known about outer garments such as cloaks.

In the Archaic period the normal female dress seems to have been the *peplos*. It was made from a rectangle of woolen cloth, taller than the woman wearing it and more than twice her width. The top of the rectangle was folded over outward, so that the cloth was of double thickness above the waist (fig. 10.4a). The cloth was then wrapped around the body, and a piece of the cloth (*epomis*) was pulled over each shoulder and fastened in front with pins. The garment was held secure and supported by a girdle at the waist. Some examples of peplos had the open side of the garment sewn up, but mostly they overlapped and were held in place by the girdle. These dresses are often depicted as richly decorated. A linen cloak or shawl could be worn over the peplos, in later times called a *himation*.

In the Classical period there was a change from the peplos to the chiton (*khiton*), which was a wide tunic worn by both men and women. The various forms of chitons included the Ionic chiton, made from a rectangle of cloth, with two edges sewn together to form a tube (fig. 10.4b). It was a sleeved garment, closed across the shoulders and upper arms by buttons or several small brooches. The excess length was pulled up and held by a girdle at the waist to form a kind of pouch called a *kolpos*. Sometimes it was also held in place by cross cords running from the shoulders to the waist (fig. 8.4).

The Archaic peplos was not immediately superseded, and was sometimes worn over the chiton. It continued to be worn in the Peloponnese into the 5th century BC. The peplos developed a large overfold at the waist, and this developed garment was now called the Doric chiton. Eventually the two styles of Ionic and Doric chiton began to be mixed, and sometimes both types were worn at once, one over the other.

Outside the house women always wore a wrap or cloak called a himation (fig. 10.1), apparently a generic term for such garments. There were variations in size, style and the way they were worn. For example, the *khlanis* was a wrap of very fine wool, the most famous of which came from Miletus (*khlanis Milesia*). The *xystis* was a long robe of fine material for special occasions, and the *ephestris* was of thicker wool.

In Hellenistic times the dress of the Classical period continued to be worn, but there was increasing variety in the combinations of the various garments and the ways in which they were worn.

MEN'S CLOTHES

The earliest Minoan depictions show men wearing only a belt and codpiece, possibly made from soft leather. Later they are shown with one of two types of dress that have been called the kilt and the apron, both supported by a decorated belt. The kilt was a skirt reaching to the thighs at the back, and to the knees in the front, often ending in a long tassel. There were two forms of apron. The double apron reached the thighs at the back and front, but was cut away at the sides. It was often worn with a codpiece. The single apron was the back half of the double apron and was worn with a codpiece. Like female Minoan dress, kilts and aprons could be lavishly decorated. In Mycenaean artistic representations men are generally shown wearing a tunic reaching to the thighs, with short sleeves and a belt or girdle at the waist. Men are also shown in a short

flared kilt or in what appears to be shorts decorated with rows of tassels or fringes.

In the Archaic period men wore the Ionic tunic (chiton), which appears to have been sewn rather than pinned. Older men, and wealthy younger men, usually wore an ankle-length chiton without a girdle, while younger men and those involved in activities wore a thigh-length chiton. The garment was often made of linen, but woolen versions were warmer and cheaper. A wrap or cloak could be worn over the chiton, and occasionally the cloak was the only garment that was worn. *Khlaina* (in later Greek, *himation*) referred to various types of cloaks or wraps. Male craftsmen and laborers (fig. 5.1) were often depicted wearing a loincloth or short kilt (*zoma*), possibly also worn as underclothes.

Men's dress in the Classical period was even more like women's dress than previously. The various types of Ionic chitons continued to be worn (fig. 9.11), and there was a male version of the Doric chiton. This was a shorter tunic without an overfold that reached only to the thighs or the knees and was pinned at the shoulders. The *exomis*, a variation on the Doric chiton, was only pinned at the left shoulder, leaving the right shoulder and breast bare.

Various cloaks and wraps were also worn over tunics or as the sole garment (figs. 1.8, 10.1). The generic term *himation* is used for these garments, although different types can be distinguished. The himation was usually a large piece of cloth wrapped around the body and over one or both shoulders (fig. 10.4c). The *tribon* was a cloak of coarse, dark-colored wool; it was worn on its own and was the traditional dress of the men of Sparta. The chlamys (*khlamys*) cloak was usually worn over the left shoulder and fastened over the right shoulder with a pin or brooch, leaving much of the right side uncovered. It could also be fastened at the throat, allowing both shoulders to be covered. The chlaina (*khlaina*) was a thick winter woolen cloak.

In the countryside peasants often wore garments made of animal skins, such as the *diphthera* and *spolas* (goatskin or leather jerkins), and a goatskin or sheepskin cloak called a *sisyra* or *baite*, which was cured with the hair or wool left on.

In Hellenistic times men's tunics were usually sewn rather than pinned, and generally had long or short sleeves rather than being sleeveless. The draped himation was often the only garment worn.

UNDERCLOTHES

There is little evidence for underclothes. Women occasionally wore a soft band of cloth beneath or around the breasts, which was sometimes called a *strophion* (fig. 8.14). A rare representation of this garment also depicts the heroine Atalanta wearing a form of loincloth similar to the *zoma* worn by men. Such a garment may therefore have been worn as underclothes by women. Male workers are often depicted wearing the loincloth known as the *zoma*, *diazoma* or *perizoma*. This was a length of cloth wrapped around as a short kilt. The evidence suggests that it was sometimes worn as underclothing by men, either beneath clothes or under armor.

SHOES

Indoors, and often outdoors, many people went barefoot much of the time, but a variety of footwear is also known, including sandals, shoes and boots. Shoes were made from cattle hides, or finer shoes from skins of sheep, goats and calves. Felt was used in the production of warm boots, and soles were sometimes made of wood. *Kroupezai* were high shoes made of wood, some worn by flute players to beat time and some worn for treading olives. Various types of sandals (called *sandalia* and *pedila*) consisted mainly of a sole strapped to the foot, sometimes with thongs carried a short way up the leg. Shoes or short boots (*hypodemata koila*) were similar to sandals but enclosed the whole foot. They ranged from light, loose-fitting shoes that were almost like slippers to heavy-duty nail-studded types.

HATS

Hats were rarely worn except when traveling or in extreme weather. They were usually made of felt. Various types of the traveler's hat (*petasos*) frequently occur in artistic representations, and could be secured by a strap under the chin or around the nape of the neck. They had a wide brim that was often cut into a decorative shape and might be turned up or down. Hats of skin or leather called *kynai* were also worn, and conical hats were popular. In Hellenistic times two other types of hats became popular, the *tholia* and *kausia*. The *tholia* was a conical hat with a flat broad brim. It was worn as a sun hat, mainly by women, and was probably made

Fig. 10.5   Silver tetradrachm of Syracuse, depicting the goddess Arethusa with her hair secured by several headbands. The obverse (fig. 5.13) shows a quadriga. Courtesy of Somerset County Museums Service.

of straw. The felt *kausia* had its origin in Macedonia and was a broad-rimmed hat for protection against the heat (*kausis*).

Hairstyles

Wigs and hairpieces were worn by both men and women. Dyes were mainly used to darken gray hair or to color the hair blond, which was a fashionable color.

WOMEN

Most women wore their hair long but cut it short when in mourning. Slaves also had short hair. In the 7th and 6th centuries BC women's hair was usually allowed to fall over the shoulders and back, fastened by a headband (*mitra*, *tainia*, *ampyx* or *anadesme*) or a decorative diadem headdress (*stephane*).

Around the beginning of the 5th century BC the hair began to be restrained. The ends of the hair could be gathered in a small bag or tucked under the hairband. By the end of the 5th century BC women's hair was worn up on the head in a variety of styles, pinned or tied into a bun or held in place

Fig. 10.6 *Part of the starting line of the foot races at the stadium at Delphi.*

with a complex arrangement of headbands or a *stephane* (fig. 10.5). Except possibly for a fringe, the hair might be almost completely wrapped in a *sakkos*, a length of cloth or scarf wound round the head and secured (fig. 9.12). Sometimes a tail of hair was left protruding from the *sakkos*. A *sphendone* (a broad headband, smaller version of the *sakkos*) did not completely cover the hair. The *stephane* could also be worn with the *sakkos*.

In Hellenistic times the *sakkos* and *sphendone* appear to have been discarded. Women still wore their hair up, but it was artificially curled and waved in a variety of styles.

MEN

In the 7th and 6th centuries BC men wore their hair long and usually held it in place with a headband (*mitra*). Slaves had short hair. In the 5th century BC an alternative was to roll up the long hair tightly and tuck it into the headband, or else twist it into two plaits that were wound around the head. Short hair became more common among free men in the 6th century BC, especially among younger men. Older men wore long hair well into the 5th century BC. Even beyond the 5th century BC boys commonly wore long hair, although in Sparta boys had short hair and men wore long hair.

Short hair remained fashionable until Alexander the Great wore his a little longer, which set a trend. He also introduced the *diadema*, a headband or fillet tied at the back with the loose ends left hanging. Until the 5th century BC it was usual for men to wear a beard—*pogon, geneion* (literally, "the chin covered by the beard") or *hypene* (technically moustache, but often used for beard). A moustache (*mys-*

tax, hypene) was at times worn with a beard, but never without a beard (figs. 2.6, 7.16). Youths and young men were frequently clean-shaven. In the 5th and 4th centuries BC beards were optional, but again Alexander's clean-shaven face set the fashion for the Hellenistic period (fig. 2.1).

Jewelry

Many types of jewelry were worn from earliest times. Particularly common were pins (*belonai*) and brooches (*peronai*), used by both men and women for fastening clothes. Jewelry was mainly worn by women, but men wore finger rings (*daktylioi*) as ornaments and sometimes as signet rings. Rings might be made entirely of a metal or have an inset gem or sealstone. Spartans, with their reputation for austerity, were said to wear only iron rings.

Women also wore earrings, necklaces and bracelets. Earrings (*ellobia* or *hermata*) were common and took the form of rings, discs, or hooks with pendants. Necklaces (*hormoi*) were usually of beads or of pendants suspended from a neck band. Bracelets (*pselia*) were worn on the wrist or above the elbow on one or both arms. An anklet (*periskelis*) was also sometimes worn. See also chapter 5, jewelry manufacture, and chapter 7, seals.

Cosmetics and Toiletries

Women and sometimes men used a variety of perfumes and cosmetics. Perfumes were generally oils scented with flowers or blossoms, used on the skin and hair. A white face was fashionable for women, achieved by painting the face with *psimythion* (white lead). It was made by soaking lead in vinegar to produce corrosion, which was scraped off, powdered and heated to form a whitener. Rouge (*phykos*) was made from various materials, including seaweed, mulberries and some plants. Eyebrows and eyelids could be emphasized with black from soot, charcoal or a preparation made from antimony.

Soap was not used for washing, but instead the body was rubbed with olive oil, which was then scraped off with a strigil. The frequency of washing is not known, but baths were used. Mirrors of burnished metal, combs, bronze razors and manicure implements are all known. Unwanted hair was removed by various preparations and with tweezers. Teeth were cleaned with a whitener, and toothpicks were used. There were also remedies for bad breath.

ENTERTAINMENT

Main public entertainments in ancient Greece were all closely connected with religious festivals, including athletics, horse and chariot racing, music and theater. Many were held as competitions, and prizes were symbolic, usually wreaths or ribbons. Participants took part for the glory rather than personal gain. Many private types of entertainment also took place; board games, possibly for gambling, were played, as well as games with dice and knucklebones. Some evidence exists for cock fighting. For children's toys, see the family (p. 411).

Singing, Dancing, Theater

Theater performances developed from the songs and dances performed in honor of Dionysus. Other religious festivals included music contests, and some festivals provided the opportunity for ordinary citizens to take part in singing and dancing, often in procession. Dancing also took place at other events such as weddings, funerals, harvests and victory celebrations. See chapter 7, literature (p. 255), music and dance (p. 263).

Athletics

At games such as the Olympic Games, various athletic and other contests took place. Generally these contests were only for male Greek citizens, and only men were allowed as spectators. Athletes competed naked but oiled their bodies for protection against the sun. The contests were usually for individuals rather than teams and included foot races, throwing the discus and javelin, long jumping, wrestling, boxing and the pancratium.

Foot races consisted of one length of the stadium (*stadion*, about 600 ft, 183 m), two lengths of the stadium (about 1,200 ft, 365 m), a long distance race that might be up to 24 lengths of the stadium (figs. 6.11, 8.29, 10.6) and a race in armor where the competitors wore a helmet and greaves and carried a shield. The length of a stadium varied between states. There was also a pentathlon, in which the two best competitors at javelin and discus throwing, running and jumping also took part in a wrestling contest.

Some contests were different from their modern equivalents. Long jumpers were aided by holding a weight (*halter*, pl. *halteres*) in each hand, which they swung forward as they jumped (fig. 10.7). Wrestling matches continued until one man had been thrown three times or until one competitor gave up. The pancratium (*pankration*) was a violent mixture of boxing, wrestling, kicking and strangling. Apart from biting and gouging, most holds and moves were allowed, but there were strict rules enforced by umpires.

Women were usually excluded from athletic contests, but while the Olympic Games were in progress, races for women took place nearby as part of a festival in honor of Hera. Women may have participated in athletic contests at some other festi-

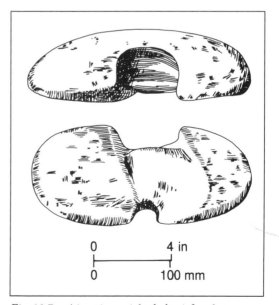

Fig. 10.7 *A jumping weight* (halter) *found at Olympia. It was slightly over 10 lb (4.5 kg) in weight.*

vals, but there is no direct evidence. Athletic contests (including those women's races that are known to have taken place) were dominated by the Spartans, because of their rigorous training of both girls and boys. See chapter 7, education.

Another form of public entertainment was the gymnasium, where male citizens could go to exercise and take part in sports. Various ball games were apparently played by adults as well as children, and there were games similar to hockey and handball or basketball. Swimming also appears to have been regarded as a recreation.

Chariot Races

Chariot races in the Panhellenic festivals took place from earliest times, initially using two-wheeled chariots. Chariot racing with four horses side by side traditionally began at the Olympic Games in 680 BC. The charioteer stood in the chariot (fig. 5.13), and wore a traditional long white chiton. He held a whip in one hand and the reins in the other (fig. 9.11). The largest recorded number of chariots entered in one race was 41, of which only one finished, and accidents at the turning posts were probably numerous. The races were held in hippodromes (see chapter 6, p. 218). At Olympia the race consisted of 12 laps of the course, a lap being about 900–1,000 yds (823–914 m). The owner of the winning chariot, not the charioteer, received the glory. In the Great Panathenaea, chariot races involved various acrobatic feats, including naked drivers (with shield and helmet) leaping from their chariots and jumping back on (fig. 8.30). They were called *apobatai* (sing. *apobates*), a term also used for the acrobatic feat that involved jumping from one moving horse to another, which was another feature of these games.

Horse racing was introduced to the Olympic Games in 648 BC and became an event at many games. The horses were unshod, and the riders rode bareback. The race was one lap of the hippodrome. Horse races were less important than chariot races.

Symposia

Symposia were a popular form of private entertainment for the wealthy. A symposium (*symposion*) was a drinking party that followed an evening meal. It was not really a dinner party, in that the food was only a preliminary to the symposium. Only men took part, although hetaerae might also be present as entertainers. The men reclined on couches for the meal, which was served by slaves. After the meal, libations to deities were poured and a hymn was sung. The participants then drank wine and conversed. They might also tell riddles and stories, sing drinking songs and play games. One popular game was called "cottabos." This involved participants keeping some wine in the bottom of their drinking cups and flicking it at a chosen target. Music was usually by a woman flute player, sometimes accompanied by other musicians, and other entertainment included dancers, jugglers and acrobats. The purpose of the symposium ranged from serious philosophical discussions to drunken revels, depending on who took part.

Apart from symposia there were other kinds of dinner parties, both formal and informal. Men might belong to dining clubs or other associations, and there were various types of public feasts and banquets.

DEATH AND AFTERLIFE

Afterlife

Views on afterlife changed over the centuries, but at all times there was belief in some form of life after death. There was no generally accepted view on afterlife, and many views were contradictory. Numerous myths concerning the underworld existed. It was usually believed that life after death was separate from the life of the gods. A common belief was that the dead lived on in their tombs or in their gravemarkers, so offerings were repeatedly made to them by their families. Another view was that all souls (good and bad alike) went to the rather grim underworld (beneath the earth), the kingdom of Hades guarded by the dog Cerberus. Here some wrongdoers suffered punishment. Instead of dying, favored heroes went to the Isles of the Blessed (*nesoi makaron*) or Elysium (*Elysion*) at the far west of the world, beyond the ocean, for a life of endless pleasure.

From the 6th century BC ideas of possible happiness after death developed, with eternal punishment taking place in the underworld or in Tartarus (a place of punishment beyond or below the underworld). This idea of happiness and punishment was encouraged by religions such as Orphism, the Eleusinian Mysteries and other mystery religions. Philosophers such as Plato put forward various views on the afterlife and the immortality of the soul, while later philosophers tended to be sceptical. See chapter 9, philosophy.

Funerals and Burials

Very little is known of funerals in the Minoan and Mycenaean periods, although there are representations of mourners. The type of funeral (*kedeia*) in later ages depended largely on the status and wealth of the deceased, and some magnificent public funerals could be given to heroes killed in battle. A funeral commenced with women washing and anointing the body with olive oil, which was followed by the dressing (usually in white garments) and laying out of the body (the *prothesis*). The body was placed on a bed, with the head on a pillow and the feet facing the door. The eyes were closed, a chin strap was tied around the head, and the body was covered by a bier cloth. The house was cleaned and hung with wreaths and other foliage. The family and other female mourners (some hired) held a vigil and sung laments, and the burial then took place at night. The body was transported to the place of burial (the *ekphora*), usually carried by pall bearers or possibly on a cart. A procession of mourners, accompanied by flute players, went with the body. A funeral speech (*epitaphios*) could be delivered.

The body was either burned on a funeral pyre (*pyra*) and the ashes placed in a vessel, or the body was placed in a coffin and buried. Throughout antiquity both cremation and inhumation were practiced, with one method sometimes being more popular. For example, inhumation was most common in Mycenaean times, but by c. 1200 BC cremation became the main method of burial and was universal in Homer's time. By the 5th century BC inhumation was again more common, possibly because of the shortage of wood for cremations.

Neither method of burial seems to have been affected by ideas of the afterlife. The most important aspect of burial was to ensure that the correct rites were carried out. In inhumation, the dead were normally placed in coffins and buried in the earth. In cremation, bodies were burned on a pyre, probably with some grave goods. In the Archaic period the pyre tended to be very large, with numerous grave goods, but this declined in later periods. The ashes were quenched with wine, and the bones were collected and placed in a container, which was then buried. The type of container varied throughout Greek history.

The most important aspect of a funeral was to cover the inhumed or cremated body with earth (even three handfuls would suffice) to prevent it from polluting the gods and their altars. This also allowed the dead to pass to the underworld. Before dawn the grave was covered, then marked later on. Those attending a funeral were considered polluted and had to be purified by washing. Priests did not attend funerals. After funerals a communal meal was served, and sometimes funeral games took place.

Young children were usually buried as inhumations (not cremated), often near houses, probably because they were not considered to cause religious pollution. Cremation for the young is virtually unknown. Other dead were buried outside city walls in order to avoid pollution, such as outside the Dipylon gate in the Kerameikos Cemetery at Athens (fig. 4.7). In Sparta people were allowed to bury their dead within the city walls, even near temples. In Bronze Age Greece, burials are found inside settlements until the Mycenaeans established extramural cemeteries. Executed criminals were left unburied, by being thrown into the sea or into open pits. One belief was that the unburied (*ataphoi*) could not enter the underworld and were condemned to haunt the Earth.

At Athens and possibly other cities, soldiers killed in warfare were only rarely buried on the battlefield. Two known examples of burial on the battlefield (an exceptional honor) were after the battles of Marathon (490 BC) and Plataea (479 BC). The war dead were usually given a state burial at Athens.

At the point of burial, some ritual sacrifice of animals (for example, horses) and possibly even humans took place in Dark Age Greece, and perhaps in Minoan and Mycenaean Greece.

GRAVES AND TOMBS

Methods of burials and types of graves and tombs were extremely varied. In the Early Bronze Age,

Fig. 10.8   Shaft grave circle A at Mycenae c. 1550 BC.

burials in cists (built of upright stone slabs) were common in the Cyclades. In Crete during the Bronze Age, the two major types of tombs are circular tombs and rectangular house tombs, with some use of cists, pits, caves, rock shelters and rock-cut chamber tombs (tombs with a chamber or room). House tombs resembled the plan of a house, with adjoining rectangular rooms. The tombs were used for collective burial, possibly by families. From Early Minoan III on Crete, inhumations were placed in clay pithoi and larnakes, some in cemeteries and some in tombs.

Outside Crete a similar diversity of tombs occurred, including some tumuli. On the mainland, Mycenaean burials were in cists and pits, some under tumuli. The shaft graves at Mycenae consist of a circular plot surrounded by a low stone wall (fig. 10.8), inside which were numerous burials (mainly of the ruling elite) within deep narrow pits ("shafts"). Grave Circle B dates to c. 1600 BC and Grave Circle A to c. 1550 BC. Various types of chamber tombs were also adopted on mainland Greece, including stone-built tholos tombs for elite

burials. These comprised an underground vaulted roofed chamber of circular shape, some with a long passageway (dromos). They are also known as beehive tombs and date to c. 1550–1300 BC (fig. 10.9). The main types of Mycenaean tombs spread throughout the Aegean during the Late Bronze Age, and the rock-cut chamber tomb became dominant. In Crete in Late Minoan III, larnax burials were frequent, although only occasionally found on the mainland. In the Postpalatial Period, chamber tombs began to be abandoned, and there was a return of cist and pit graves, with the gradual introduction of cremations.

In the Protogeometric and Geometric periods, cremations continued, often buried in pottery vessels within pits, along with other grave goods. Inhumation was also resumed. In the Geometric and Archaic periods, there were family plots or groups of related graves; the individual graves were marked by a simple mound of earth, usually circular (although some were rectangular), and were later surmounted by vases and sculptures. The mounds became increasingly larger, so that space became a

Fig. 10.9   Treasury of Atreus at Mycenae, with the long dromos approaching the vaulted chamber tomb. It dates to c. 1330 BC.

problem in cemeteries. From c. 600 BC smaller tombs were constructed with walls. Toward the end of the 5th century BC at Athens, family enclosures (*periboloi*) became popular. Many of these lined major roads leading into a town or city and were surrounded by tall walls on which the gravemarkers were placed.

Knowledge of Hellenistic burial practices is more limited, apart from some of the more monumental burials. For example, in Macedonia very rich burials have been found in vaulted chamber tombs, some with rich grave goods and painted plastered walls. Large tomb monuments also appear, such as the mausoleum of Mausolus erected at Halicarnassus. Some rock-cut tombs of this period have architectural facades, such as ones in Asia Minor. In Alexandria in Egypt and at Paphos Nea in Cyprus, underground rock-cut tombs have plans similar to Hellenistic peristyle houses. They contained rooms lined with niches (loculi), closed by a plaster or stone slab, a prototype for later catacombs (fig. 10.10).

COFFINS

The coffin (*soros* or *larnax*) was usually of wood, although pottery and stone ones are known. On Crete from Early Minoan III, inhumations were placed in clay pithoi (large storage vessels) or in clay *larnakes* (sing. *larnax*), tubs with lids, similar to coffins. Some were richly painted. In Late Minoan III, larnakes became particularly common on Crete and resembled a rectangular chest with feet. In Geometric and Archaic Athens a few adult inhumation burials were placed in large pithoi. Sculptured stone sarcophagi appeared in Asia Minor from the 5th century BC and became popular among the wealthy in Hellenistic times. In southern Russia painted wooden sarcophagi of Hellenistic date have also survived.

In the Bronze Age, infants were sometimes buried in pots or under fragments of pithoi, a trend that continues throughout Greek history. From the Classical period a pair of clay tubs was also used for infant burials, one placed over the other. Some were brightly painted.

Fig. 10.10   Sealed loculi in a rock-cut Hellenistic tomb at Paphos Nea in Cyprus.

GRAVEMARKERS

Graves were usually marked with an engraved stone slab (*stele*, pl. *stelai*) to identify the dead. They are first found above Bronze Age shaft graves at Mycenae from the 16th century BC (fig. 3.3). In Geometric and Archaic times, pottery vases, some very large, were used as gravemarkers, and wooden markers were probably used as well. From about the mid to late 7th century BC, statues (korai and kouroi) were erected as gravemarkers, and ceramic plaques also began to be used. From about 600 BC the stele began to replace ceramic gravemarkers. The earliest versions date from around 600 to 500 BC at Athens and were tall and slim. Some are crowned by a sphinx, lion or later a siren, beasts often used symbolically to guard tombs and probably borrowed from the Egyptians. By 530 BC the sphinx was replaced by a palmette finial (fig. 10.11).

From c. 500 to 430 BC very few stelai occur, except for a few publicly erected ones. From 430 to 417 BC stelai are broader, with more complex sculpture (figs. 1.8, 9.12), but the funerary legisla-tion of Demetrius of Phalerum in Athens c. 317–315 BC forbade this type of gravemarker, and subsequently simple short cylindrical slabs were used. Toward the end of the 5th century BC marble vases carved in the round (including lekythoi and loutrophoroi) came into fashion as gravemarkers. Marble loutrophoroi were used as gravemarkers for the unmarried, two-handled ones for men and three-handled ones for women (fig. 10.12). See also chapter 7, funerary inscriptions (p. 251), chap-ter 9, sculpture (p. 374).

GRAVE GOODS AND GIFTS

Grave goods were usually deposited with the dead (inhumations and cremations) for their use in the afterlife. Richer grave goods began to be provided from the Late Bronze Age, the most notable being in the shaft graves at Mycenae, where grave goods included spears, daggers, gold cups, silver vases, amber necklaces, stone vases, gold jewelry and other ornaments, and five gold death masks (fig. 10.13). From the Geometric period grave goods included food, pots, jewelry, weapons, figurines and other model objects. From the Classical period a decreasing number of such goods was deposited in the grave. Traditional objects for traveling to the underworld (such as shoes, lamps and coins for the boat fee of Charon) were not universally deposited with burials. In Sparta few if any grave goods were deposited.

Various rites continued to take place at the graveside, on the third, ninth and thirtieth days after death. It was as important to visit the tomb at subsequent festivals and various anniversaries as at the actual interment. Particularly important were visits by the son or adopted heir. The tomb was decorated with wreaths and colorful ribbons, and

offerings of food, drink and oil were left. Celery (*selinon*) was a popular offering to the dead. The lekythos appears as a grave gift from c. 600 BC, and from 470 to 410 BC it was the favorite grave gift at Athens. Lekythoi were filled with oil, but some had a small, false internal container to minimize the amount of oil that was left.

Fig. 10.11   Examples of 6th-century-BC tall Attic grave stelai, one surmounted by a sphinx and one by a palmette finial.

Fig. 10.12   Marble two-handled loutrophoros grave-marker in the Kerameikos Cemetery, Athens, set up for unmarried Olympichus, son of Diodorus. Early 4th century BC.

From the late 4th century BC it was common in Asia Minor and the Aegean islands to bequeath a sum of money for rites to be held in honor of the deceased in perpetuity.

READING

Calendar

Bickerman 1980; Samuel 1972 and 1988.

The Family

Demand 1994: women, marriage and childbirth, with extensive bibliography; Dover 1978: homosexuality and prostitution; Foley 1988: women; Garland 1990b: childbirth, children, marriage, old age; Golden 1990: children; Henderson 1988: sexual attitudes; Just 1989: women; Krenkel 1988: prostitution; Lacey 1968: many aspects of the family; Pomeroy 1988: marriage; Sallares 1991, 129–160: birth control.

Slaves

Fisher 1993; Hammond and Scullard (eds.) 1970, 994–996; Wiedemann 1988.

Food and Drink

Braum 1995: *maza* and bread; Brothwell 1988: food and cooking; Dalby 1996: many aspects of food, wine and olive oil, with extensive bibliography; Hammond and Scullard (eds.) 1970, 443–444; Mitchell 1940, 193–196: cooking; Vickery 1936: food and cooking.

Fig. 10.13   Gold death mask, dating to c. 1550 BC, as found by Heinrich Schliemann in 1876 in one of the shaft graves in Grave Circle A at Mycenae.

Personal Appearance

Hammond and Scullard (eds.) 1970, 364–365: clothing; Houston 1947, 1–82: clothing and jewelry; Johnson (ed.) 1964: clothing; Saatsoglu-Paliadeli 1993: Macedonian costume; Symons 1987: all aspects of personal appearance.

Entertainment

Fisher 1988: symposia, clubs and banquets; Gardiner 1930: athletics; Garland 1988: festivals; Harris 1972: sports; Olivova 1984, 63–153: sports; Sweet 1987: major source; Young 1988: athletics.

Death and Afterlife

Dickinson 1994: Bronze Age burial; Garland 1985: major source, with extensive bibliography; Hägg and Sieurin 1982: wooden coffins; Kurtz and Boardman 1971: major source; Morris 1992: burials as evidence for social structure; Musgrave 1990: cremation; Vermeule 1988: afterlife; Watrous 1991: larnax.

BIBLIOGRAPHY

Alderink, L.J. 1981. *Creation and Salvation in Ancient Orphism.* Chico, California: Scholars Press/The American Philological Association American Classical Studies 8.

Allen, R.E. 1981. *The Attalid Kingdom. A Constitutional History.* Oxford: Clarendon Press.

Allsopp, B. 1965. *A History of Classical Architecture.* London: Sir Isaac Pitman & Sons.

Anderson, J.K. 1970. *Military Theory and Practice in the Age of Xenophon.* Berkeley: University of California Press.

Andrewes, A. 1956. *The Greek Tyrants.* London: Hutchinson.

Antonaccio, C.M. 1994. "Contesting the Past: Hero Cult, Tomb Cult, and Epic in Early Greece." *American Journal of Archaeology* 98, 389–410.

Armstrong, A.H., ed. 1967. *The Cambridge History of Later Greek and Early Medieval Philosophy.* London and New York: Cambridge University Press.

Armstrong, P., Cavanagh, W.G. and Shipley, G. 1992. "Crossing the River: Observations on Routes and Bridges in Laconia from the Archaic to Byzantine Periods." *The Annual of the British School at Athens* 87, 293–310.

Arnott, P.D. 1988. "Drama." In M. Grant and R. Kitzinger, eds., *Civilization of the Ancient Mediterranean. Greece and Rome*, vol. 3, pp. 1,477–1,793. New York: Charles Scribner's Sons.

Bailey, D.M. 1975. *A Catalogue of the Lamps in the British Museum. I Greek, Hellenistic, and Early Roman Pottery Lamps.* London: British Museum Publications.

Balcer, J.M. 1995. *The Persian Conquests of the Greeks, 545–450 BC.* Konstanz: Universitätsverlag Konstanz.

Barber, R.L.N. 1987. *The Cyclades in the Bronze Age.* London: Duckworth.

Bar-Kochva, B. 1976. *The Seleucid Army. Organization and Tactics in the Great Campaigns.* London and New York: Cambridge University Press.

Barnes, J. 1987. *Early Greek Philosophy.* London and New York: Penguin Books.

Barnes, J. 1988. "Hellenistic Philosophy and Science." In J. Boardman et al., eds., *The Oxford History of the Classical World. Greece and the Hellenistic World*, pp. 359–379. Oxford and New York: Oxford University Press.

Bass, G.F., ed. 1972. *A History of Seafaring Based on Underwater Archaeology.* London: Thames and Hudson.

Bauman, R.A. 1990. *Political Trials in Ancient Greece.* London and New York: Routledge.

Beard, M. and North, J., eds. 1990. *Pagan Priests. Religion and Power in the Ancient World.* London: Duckworth.

Beazley, J.D. 1986. *The Development of Attic Black-Figure.* Berkeley, Los Angeles and London: University of California Press.

Beck, F.A.G. 1964. *Greek Education, 450–350 B.C.* London: Methuen.

Bell, R.E. 1989. *Place-Names in Classical Mythology: Greece.* Santa Barbara: ABC-Clio.

Best, J.G.P. 1969. *Thracian Peltasts and Their Influence on Greek Warfare.* Groningen: Wolters-Noordhoff.

Betancourt, P.P. 1985. *The History of Minoan Pottery.* Princeton, New Jersey: Princeton University Press.

Bickerman, E.J. 1980. *Chronology of the Ancient World*, 2nd ed. London: Thames and Hudson.

Biers, W.R. 1992. *Art, Artefacts and Chronology in Classical Archaeology.* London and New York: Routledge.

Billows, R.A. 1990. *Antigonos the One-Eyed and the Creation of the Hellenistic State.* Berkeley, Los Angeles and London: University of California Press.

Boardman, J. 1974. *Athenian Black Figure Vases.* London: Thames and Hudson.

Boardman, J. 1980. *The Greeks Overseas. Their Early Colonies and Trade* (rev. ed.). London: Thames and Hudson.

Boardman, J. 1989. *Athenian Red Figure Vases. The Classical Period, A Handbook.* London: Thames and Hudson.

Boardman, J., ed. 1993. *The Oxford History of Classical Art.* Oxford: Oxford University Press.

Boardman, J., Griffin, J. and Murray, O., eds. 1988. *The Oxford History of the Classical World. Greece and the Hellenistic World.* Oxford and New York: Oxford University Press.

Boersma, J.S. 1970. *Athenian Building Policy from 561/0 to 405/4 B.C.* Groningen: Wolters-Noordhoff.

Bolkestein, H. 1958. *Economic Life in Greece's Golden Age.* New edition revised and annotated by E.J. Jonkers. Leiden: E.J. Brill.

Bonfante, L. and Jaunzems, E. 1988. "Clothing and Ornament." In M. Grant and R. Kitzinger., eds., *Civilization of the Ancient Mediterranean. Greece and Rome*, vol. 3, pp. 1,385–1,413. New York: Charles Scribner's Sons.

Borthwick, E.K. 1988. "Music and Dance." In M. Grant and R. Kitzinger., eds., *Civilization of the Ancient Mediterranean. Greece and Rome*, vol. 3, pp. 1,505–1,514. New York: Charles Scribner's Sons.

Borza, E.N. 1990. *In the Shadow of Olympus. The Emergence of Macedon.* Princeton: Princeton University Press.

Bosworth, A.B. 1988. *Conquest and Empire. The Reign of Alexander the Great.* Cambridge and New York: Cambridge University Press.

Bourgeaud, P. 1988. *The Cult of Pan in Ancient Greece.* Translation of 1979 version. Chicago, London: University of Chicago Press.

Bowder, D., ed. 1982. *Who Was Who in the Greek World, 776 BC–30 BC.* Oxford: Phaidon.

Bowie, E. 1988. "Lyric and Elegiac Poetry." In J. Boardman et al., eds. *The Oxford History of the Classical World. Greece and the Hellenistic World*, pp. 93–106. Oxford and New York: Oxford University Press.

Boyd, T.D. 1988. "Urban Planning." In M. Grant and R. Kitzinger., eds., *Civilization of the Ancient Mediterranean. Greece and Rome*, vol. 3, pp. 1691–1700. New York: Charles Scribner's Sons.

Branigan, K. 1967. "The Early Bronze Age Daggers of Crete." *Annual of the British School at Athens* 62, 211–239.

Braum, T. 1995. "Barley Cakes and Emmer Bread." In J. Wilkins et al., eds., *Food in Antiquity*, pp. 25–37. Exeter: Exeter University Press.

Bremmer, J.N. 1994. *Greek Religion.* Oxford and New York: Oxford University Press/Classical Association.

Brenne, S. 1994. "Ostraka and the Process of Ostra-kophoria." In W.D.E. Coulson et al., eds., *The Archaeology of Athens and Attica Under the Democracy*, pp. 13–24. Oxford: Oxbow Monograph 37.

Brothwell, D.R. 1988. *"Foodstuffs, Cooking, and Drugs."* In M. Grant and R. Kitzinger., eds., *Civilization of the Ancient Mediterranean. Greece and Rome*, vol. 1, pp. 247–261. New York: Charles Scribner's Sons.

Bruit Zaidman, L. and Schmitt Pantel, P. 1992. *Religion in the Ancient Greek City.* Translated by Paul Cartledge. Cambridge and New York: Cambridge University Press.

Brumbaugh, R.S. 1966. *Ancient Greek Gadgets and Machines.* New York: Thomas Y. Crowell Company.

Buck, R.J. 1979. *A History of Boeotia.* Edmonton: University of Alberta Press.

Buckler, J. 1989. *Philip II and the Sacred War.* Leiden, New York: E.J. Brill.

Bugh, G.R. 1988. *The Horsemen of Athens.* Princeton, New Jersey: Princeton University Press.

Burford, A. 1993. *Land and Labor in the Greek World.* Baltimore and London: Johns Hopkins University Press.

Burkert, W. 1985. *Greek Religion. Archaic and Classical.* Translated by J. Raffan. Oxford: Basil Blackwell.

Burn, A.R. and Burn, M. 1980. *The Living Past of Greece.* London: Herbert Press.

Burnet, J. 1920. *Early Greek Philosophy*. London: A. and C. Black.

Burstein, S.M. 1988. "Greek Class Structures and Relations." In M. Grant and R. Kitzinger, eds., *Civilization of the Ancient Mediterranean. Greece and Rome*, vol. 1, pp. 529–527. New York: Charles Scribner's Sons.

Bury, J.B. and Meiggs, R. 1975. *A History of Greece to the Death of Alexander*, 4th ed. London: Macmillan.

Camp, J. McK. II and Dinsmoor, W.B. Jr. 1984. *Ancient Athenian Building Methods*. Princeton: American School of Classical Studies at Athens.

Carpenter, T.H. and Faraone, C.A., eds. 1993. *Masks of Dionysus*. Ithaca and London: Cornell University Press.

Carson, R.A.G. 1988. "Coins." In M. Grant and R. Kitzinger, eds., *Civilization of the Ancient Mediterranean. Greece and Rome*, vol. 3, pp. 1,795–1,816. New York: Charles Scribner's Sons.

Carter, J.C. 1983. *The Sculpture of the Sanctuary of Athena Polias at Priene*. London: Thames and Hudson and Society of Antiquaries.

Cartledge, P. 1987. *Agesilaos and the Crisis of Sparta*. London: Duckworth.

Cartledge, P., Millett, P. and Todd, S., eds. 1990. *Nomos. Essays in Athenian Law, Politics and Society*. Cambridge and New York: Cambridge University Press.

Casson, L. 1971. *Ships and Seamanship in the Ancient World*. Princeton, New Jersey: Princeton University Press.

Casson, L. 1988. "Piracy." In M. Grant and R. Kitzinger, eds., *Civilization of the Ancient Mediterranean. Greece and Rome*, vol. 2, pp. 837–844. New York: Charles Scribner's Sons.

Casson, L. 1994. *Ships and Seafaring in Ancient Times*. London: British Museum Press.

Caven, B. 1990. *Dionysius I. War-Lord of Sicily*. New Haven and London: Yale University Press.

Chadwick, J. 1987. *Reading the Past. Linear B and Related Scripts*. London: British Museum Publications.

Clagett, M. 1957. *Greek Science in Antiquity*. London: Abelard-Schuman Ltd.

Clayton, P.A. 1988. "The Pharos at Alexandria." In P.A. Clayton and M.J. Price, *The Seven Wonders of the Ancient World*, pp. 138–157. London and New York: Routledge.

Clayton, P.A. and Price, M.J. 1988. *The Seven Wonders of the Ancient World*. London and New York: Routledge.

Coates, J.F., Platis, S.K. and Shaw, J.T. 1990. *The Trireme Trials, 1988. Report on the Anglo-Hellenic Sea Trials of Olympias*. Oxford: Oxbow Books.

Cole, S.G. 1988. "Greek Cults." In M. Grant and R. Kitzinger, eds., *Civilization of the Ancient Mediterranean. Greece and Rome*, vol. 2, pp. 887–908. New York: Charles Scribner's Sons.

Connolly, P. 1988. *Greece and Rome at War*. London: Macdonald & Co./Black Cat.

Cook, B.F. 1987. *Reading the Past. Greek Inscriptions*. London: British Museum Publications.

Cook, R.M. 1969. "A Note on the Absolute Chronology of the Eighth and Seventh Centuries B.C." *The Annual of the British School at Athens* 64, 13–15.

Coulson, W.D.E., Palagia, O., Shear, T.L., Shapiro, H.A. and Frost, F.J., eds. 1994. *The Archaeology of Athens and Attica Under the Democracy*. Oxford: Oxbow Monograph 37.

Coulton, J.J. 1976. *The Architectural Development of the Greek Stoa*. Oxford: Clarendon Press/Oxford University Press.

Coulton, J.J. 1977. *Greek Architects at Work. Problems of Structure and Design*. London: Paul Elek.

Coulton, J.J. 1988a. "Greek Building Techniques." In M. Grant and R. Kitzinger, eds., *Civilization of the Ancient Mediterranean. Greece and Rome*, vol. 1, pp. 277–297. New York: Charles Scribner's Sons.

Coulton, J.J. 1988b. "Greek Architecture." In M. Grant and R. Kitzinger, eds., *Civilization of the Ancient Mediterranean. Greece and Rome*, vol. 3, pp. 1653–1670. New York: Charles Scribner's Sons.

Crossland, R.A. 1988. "Early Greek Migrations." In M. Grant and R. Kitzinger, eds., *Civilization of the Ancient Mediterranean. Greece and Rome*, vol. 1, pp. 155–170. New York: Charles Scribner's Sons.

Crouch, D.P 1993. *Water Management in Ancient Greek Cities*. New York and Oxford: Oxford University Press.

Crouwel, J.H. 1981. *Chariots and Other Means of Land Transport in Bronze Age Greece*. Amsterdam: Allard Pierson Museum.

Crouwel, J.H. 1992. *Chariots and Other Wheeled Vehicles in Iron Age Greece*. Amsterdam: Allard Pierson Museum.

Cunliffe, B., ed. 1987. *Origins. The Roots of European Civilisation*. London: BBC Books.

Cunliffe, B., ed. 1994. *The Oxford Illustrated Prehistory of Europe.* Oxford and New York: Oxford University Press.

Dalby, A. 1996. *Siren Feasts. A History of Food and Gastronomy in Greece.* London and New York: Routledge.

Davis, N. 1967. *Greek Coins & Cities. Illustrated from the Collection of the Seattle Art Museum.* London: Seattle Art Museum/Spink & Son.

Dawkins, R.M., ed. 1929. *The Sanctuary of Artemis Orthia at Sparta. Excavated and Described by Members of the British School at Athens, 1906–1910.* London: Society for the Promotion of Hellenic Studies.

Demand, N. 1994. *Birth, Death and Motherhood in Classical Greece.* Baltimore and London: Johns Hopkins University Press.

Dewald, C. 1988. "Greek Education and Rhetoric." In M. Grant and R. Kitzinger, eds., *Civilization of the Ancient Mediterranean. Greece and Rome,* vol. 2, pp. 1077–1107. New York: Charles Scribner's Sons.

Dickinson, O. 1994. *The Aegean Bronze Age.* New York and London: Cambridge University Press.

Dicks, D.R. 1970. *Early Greek Astronomy to Aristotle.* London: Thames and Hudson.

Dilke, O.A.W. 1985. *Greek and Roman Maps.* Ithaca: Cornell University Press.

Dover, K.J. 1978. *Greek Homosexuality.* London: Duckworth.

Drever, J. 1912. *Greek Education. Its Practice and Principles.* Cambridge: Cambridge University Press.

Drews, R. 1993. *The End of the Bronze Age. Changes in Warfare and the Catastrophe c. 1200 B.C.* Princeton: Princeton University Press.

Ellis, W.M. 1989. *Alcibiades.* London and New York: Routledge.

Ellis, W.M. 1994. *Ptolemy of Egypt.* London and New York: Routledge.

Engels, D.W. 1978. *Alexander the Great and the Logistics of the Macedonian Army.* Berkeley and London: University of California Press.

Errington, R.M. 1969. *Philopoemen.* Oxford: Clarendon Press.

Farnell, L.R. 1921. *Greek Hero Cults and Ideas of Immortality.* Oxford: Oxford University Press.

Farrington, B. 1961. *Greek Science,* rev. ed. Harmondsworth and Baltimore: Penguin.

Ferguson, J. 1988a. "Divinities." In M. Grant and R. Kitzinger, eds. *Civilization of the Ancient Mediteranean. Greece and Rome,* vol. 2, pp. 847–860. New York: Charles Scribner's Sons.

Ferguson, J. 1988b. "Magic." In M. Grant and R. Kitzinger, eds., *Civilization of the Ancient Mediterranean. Greece and Rome,* vol. 2, pp. 881–886. New York: Charles Scribner's Sons.

Ferguson, J. 1989. *Among the Gods. An Archaeological Exploration of Ancient Greek Religion.* London and New York: Routledge.

Fine, J.V.A. 1983. *The Ancient Greeks. A Critical History.* Cambridge and London: Harvard University Press/Belknap Press.

Finley, M.I., ed., 1973. *Problèmes de da Terre en Grèce ancienne.* Paris: Mouton & Co.

Finley, M.I. 1981. *Early Greece: The Bronze and Archaic Age,* 2nd ed. London: Chatto & Windus; Toronto: Clarke, Irwin & Co.

Fisher, N.R.E. 1988. "Greek Associations, Symposia, and Clubs." In M. Grant and R. Kitzinger, eds., *Civilization of the Ancient Mediterranean. Greece and Rome,* vol. 2, pp. 1167–1197. New York: Charles Scribner's Sons.

Fisher, N.R.E. 1993. *Slavery in Classical Greece.* London: Bristol Classical Press.

Fitton, J.L., ed., 1992. *Ivory in Greece and the Eastern Mediterranean from the Bronze Age to the Hellenistic Period.* London: British Museum occasional paper 85.

Foley, H.P. 1988. "Women in Greece." In M. Grant and R. Kitzinger, eds., *Civilization of the Ancient Mediterranean. Greece and Rome,* vol. 3, pp. 1,301–1,317. New York: Charles Scribner's Sons.

Forrest, G. 1988. "Greece: the History of the Archaic Period." In J. Boardman et al., eds., *The Oxford History of the Classical World. Greece and the Hellenistic World,* pp. 13–43. Oxford and New York: Oxford University Press.

Fortenberry, D. 1991. "Single Greaves in the Late Helladic Period." *American Journal of Archaeology* 95, pp. 623–628.

Foxhall, L. and Davies, J.K., eds. 1984. *The Trojan War. Its Historicity and Context. Papers of the First Greenbank Colloquium, Liverpool, 1981.* Bristol: Bristol Classical Press.

Fraser, P.M. and Matthews, E. 1987. *A Lexicon of Greek Personal Names. The Aegean Islands, Cyprus, Cyrenaica,* vol. 1. Oxford: Clarendon Press.

Gagarin, M. 1986. *Early Greek Law.* Berkeley, Los Angeles and London: University of California Press.

Gardiner, E.N. 1930. *Athletics of the Ancient World.* Oxford: Oxford University Press.

Garland, R. 1985. *The Greek Way of Death.* London: Duckworth.

Garland, R. 1988. "Greek Spectacles and Festivals." In M. Grant and R. Kitzinger, eds., *Civilization of the Ancient Mediterranean. Greece and Rome,* vol. 2, pp. 1143–1152. New York: Charles Scribner's Sons.

Garland, R. 1990a. "Priests and Power in Classical Athens." In M. Beard and J. North, eds., *Pagan Priests. Religion and Power in the Ancient World,* pp. 75–91. London: Duckworth.

Garland, R. 1990b. *The Greek Way of Life from Conception to Old Age.* London: Duckworth.

Garland, R. 1995. *Religion and the Greeks.* Reprint with corrections of 1994 version. London: Bristol Classical Press.

Garner, R. 1987. *Law & Society in Classical Athens.* London and Sydney: Croom Helm.

Garoufalias, P. 1979. *Pyrrhus, King of Epirus,* 2nd ed. London: Stacey International.

Gesell, G.C. 1985. *Town, Palace and House Cult in Minoan Crete.* Göteborg: Paul Aströms Förlag.

Golden, M. 1990. *Children and Childhood in Classical Athens.* Baltimore and London: Johns Hopkins University Press.

Graham, A.J. 1964. *Colony and Mother City in Ancient Greece.* Manchester: Manchester University Press.

Graham, J.W. 1987. *The Palaces of Crete,* rev. ed. Princeton: Princeton University Press.

Grainger, J.D. 1990. *Seleukos Nikator. Constructing a Hellenistic Kingdom.* London and New York: Routledge.

Grant, M. 1986. *A Guide to the Ancient World. A Dictionary of Classical Place Names.* New York: H.W. Wilson Company.

Grant, M. 1987. *The Rise of the Greeks.* London: Weidenfeld and Nicolson.

Grant, M. 1988. "Alternative Paths: Greek Monarchy and Federalism." In M. Grant and R. Kitzinger, eds., *Civilization of the Ancient Mediterranean. Greece and Rome,* vol. 1, pp. 487–494. New York: Charles Scribner's Sons.

Grant, M. 1989. *The Classical Greeks.* London: Weidenfeld and Nicolson.

Grant, M. 1990. *The Hellenistic Greeks. From Alexander to Cleopatra.* London: Weidenfeld and Nicolson.

Grant, M. and Hazel, J. 1973. *Who's Who in Classical Mythology.* London: Weidenfeld and Nicolson.

Grant, M. and Kitzinger, R., eds. 1988. *Civilization of the Ancient Mediterranean. Greece and Rome,* vol. 1. New York: Charles Scribner's Sons.

Grant, M. and Kitzinger, R., eds. 1988. *Civilization of the Ancient Mediterranean. Greece and Rome,* vol. 2. New York: Charles Scribner's Sons.

Grant, M. and Kitzinger, R., eds. 1988. *Civilization of the Ancient Mediterranean. Greece and Rome,* vol. 3. New York: Charles Scribner's Sons.

Green, J.R. 1994. *Theatre in Ancient Greek Society.* London and New York: Routledge.

Green, P. 1970a. *Armada from Athens.* London, Sydney, Auckland, Toronto: Hodder and Stoughton.

Green, P. 1970b. *The Year of Salamis, 480–479 B.C.* London: Weidenfeld and Nicolson.

Green, P. 1973. *A Concise History of Ancient Greece to the Close of the Classical Era.* London: Thames and Hudson.

Green, P. 1990. *Alexander to Actium. The Hellenistic Age.* London: Thames and Hudson.

Green P. 1991. *Alexander of Macedon, 356–323 B.C. A Historical Biography.* London: Pelican, 1974; reprint, Berkeley, Los Angeles and Oxford: University of California Press.

Greenhalgh, P.A.L. 1973. *Early Greek Warfare. Horsemen and Chariots in the Homeric and Archaic Ages.* London: Cambridge University Press.

Griffin, J. 1988. "Greek Myth and Hesiod." In J. Boardman et al., eds., *The Oxford History of the Classical World. Greece and the Hellenistic World,* pp. 72–92. Oxford and New York: Oxford University Press.

Griffith, G.T. 1935. *The Mercenaries of the Hellenistic World.* Cambridge: Cambridge University Press.

Griffiths, F.T. 1988. "Literary Criticism." In M. Grant and R. Kitzinger, eds., *Civilization of the Ancient Mediterranean. Greece and Rome,* vol. 3, pp. 1,515–1,523. New York: Charles Scribner's Sons.

Grmek, M.D. 1989. *Diseases in the Ancient Greek World.* Baltimore and London: Johns Hopkins University Press. First published in French in 1983.

Grose, D.F. 1984. "The Origins and Early History of Glass." In D. Klein and W. Lloyd, eds., *The History of Glass,* pp. 9–37. London: Orbis Publishing Limited.

Guthrie, W.K.C. 1962. *A History of Greek Philosophy. The Earlier Presocratics and the Pythagoreans* (vol. 1). Cambridge and New York: Cambridge University Press.

Guthrie, W.K.C. 1965. *A History of Greek Philosophy. The Presocratic Tradition from Parmenides to Democritus* (vol. 2). Cambridge and New York: Cambridge University Press.

Guthrie, W.K.C. 1969. *A History of Greek Philosophy. The Fifth-Century Enlightenment* (vol. 3). Cambridge and New York: Cambridge University Press.

Guthrie, W.K.C. 1975. *A History of Greek Philosophy. Plato the Man and His Dialogues: Earlier Period* (vol. 4). Cambridge and New York: Cambridge University Press.

Guthrie, W.K.C. 1978. *A History of Greek Philosophy. The Later Plato and the Academy* (vol. 5). Cambridge and New York: Cambridge University Press.

Guthrie, W.K.C. 1981. *A History of Greek Philosophy. Aristotle, An Encounter* (vol. 6). Cambridge and New York: Cambridge University Press.

Hägg, R. and Sierun, F. 1982. "On the Origin of the Wooden Coffin in Late Bronze Age Crete." *Annual of the British School at Athens* 77, 177–186.

Hainsworth, B. 1988. "Epic Poetry." In M. Grant and R. Kitzinger, eds., *Civilization of the Ancient Mediterranean. Greece and Rome*, vol. 3, pp. 1,417–1,435. New York: Charles Scribner's Sons.

Halperin, D.M. 1988. "Bucolic Poetry." In M. Grant and R. Kitzinger, eds., *Civilization of the Ancient Mediterranean. Greece and Rome*, vol. 3, pp. 1,467–1,495. New York: Charles Scribner's Sons.

Hamilton, C.D. 1979. *Sparta's Bitter Victories. Politics and Diplomacy in the Corinthian War.* Ithaca and London: Cornell University Press.

Hammond, N.G.L. 1992. *Atlas of the Greek and Roman World in Antiquity.* New Jersey: Noyes Press, 1981; reprint, London: Bristol Classical Press.

Hammond, N.G.L. 1983. *Three Historians of Alexander the Great. The So-Called Vulgate Authors, Diodorus, Justin and Curtius.* Cambridge, London and New York: Cambridge University Press.

Hammond, N.G.L. 1989a. *Alexander the Great, Commander and Statesman*, 2nd ed., rev. Bristol: Bristol Press.

Hammond, N.G.L. 1989b. *The Macedonian State. Origins, Institutions and History.* Oxford: Clarendon Press.

Hammond, N.G.L. 1991. *The Miracle That Was Macedonia.* London: Sidgwick & Jackson; New York: St. Martin's Press.

Hammond, N.G.L. 1994. *Philip of Macedon.* London: Duckworth.

Hammond, N.G.L. and Scullard, H.H., eds. 1970. *The Oxford Classical Dictionary*, 2nd ed. Oxford: Clarendon Press.

Hansen, E.V. 1947. *The Attalids of Pergamon.* Ithaca: Cornell University Press.

Hanson, V.D., ed. 1991. *Hoplites: The Classical Greek Battle Experience.* London and New York: Routledge.

Harden, D.B. 1968. "Ancient Glass, I: Pre-Roman." *Archaeological Journal* 75, 46–72.

Harding, A.F. 1984. *The Mycenaeans and Europe.* London and Orlando: Academic Press.

Hardy, D.A., Keller, J., Galanapoulos, V.P., Flemming, N.C. and Druitt, T.H., eds. 1990. *Thera and the Aegean World III. Earth Sciences. Proceedings of the Third International Congress Santorini, Greece 3–9 September 1989* (vol. 2). London: Thera Foundation.

Hardy, D.A. and Renfrew, A.C., eds. 1990. *Thera and the Aegean World III. Chronology. Proceedings of the Third International Congress, Santorini, Greece 3–9 September 1989* (vol. 3). London: Thera Foundation.

Harris, C.R.S. 1973. *The Heart and the Vascular System in Ancient Greek Medicine.* Oxford: Clarendon Press.

Harris, H.A. 1972. *Sport in Greece and Rome.* London: Thames and Hudson.

Harrison, A.R.W. 1968. *The Law of Athens. The Family and Property.* Oxford: Clarendon Press.

Harrison, A.R.W. 1971. *The Law of Athens. Procedure.* Oxford: Clarendon Press.

Healy, J.F. 1978. *Mining and Metallurgy in the Greek and Roman World.* London: Thames and Hudson.

Healy, J.F. 1988. "Mines and Quarries." In M. Grant and R. Kitzinger, eds., *Civilization of the Ancient Mediterranean. Greece and Rome*, vol. 2, pp. 779–793. New York: Charles Scribner's Sons.

Heckel, W. 1992. *The Marshals of Alexander's Empire.* London and New York: Routledge.

Hemelrijk, J.M. 1991. "A Closer Look at the Potter." In T. Rasmussen and N. Spivey, eds., *Looking at Greek Vases*, pp. 233–256. Cambridge and New York: Cambridge University Press.

Henderson, J. 1988. "Greek Attitudes Towards Sex." In M. Grant and R. Kitzinger, eds., *Civilization of the Ancient Mediterranean. Greece and Rome*, vol. 2, pp. 1249–1263. New York: Charles Scribner's Sons.

Higgins, R.A. 1961. *Greek and Roman Jewellery*. London: Methuen.

Higgins, R.A. 1967. *Greek Terracottas*. London: Methuen.

Higgins, R. 1981. *Minoan and Mycenaean Art* (rev. ed.). London: Thames and Hudson.

Hill, D. 1984. *A History of Engineering in Classical and Medieval Times*. Beckenham: Croom Helm.

Holloway, R.R. 1991. *The Archaeology of Ancient Sicily*. London and New York: Routledge.

Hood, S. 1978. *The Arts in Prehistoric Greece*. London and New York: Penguin Books.

Hooker, J. 1990. "Cult-Personnel in the Linear B Texts from Pylos." In M. Beard and J. North, eds., *Pagan Priests. Religion and Power in the Ancient World*, pp. 159–174. London: Duckworth.

Hooker, J.T. 1980. *The Ancient Spartans*. London, Toronto, Melbourne: J. M. Dent.

Hope Simpson, R. and Dickinson, O.T.P.K. 1979. *A Gazetteer of Aegean Civilisation in the Bronze Age: The Mainland and Islands* (vol. 1). Göteborg: Paul Astöms Förlag.

Hopper, R.J. 1979. *Trade and Industry in Classical Greece*. London: Thames and Hudson.

Hornblower, S. 1982. *Mausolus*. Oxford: Clarendon Press; New York: Oxford University Press.

Hornblower, S. 1983. *The Greek World, 479–323 BC*. London and New York: Methuen.

Hornblower, S. 1988. "Greece: The History of the Classical Period." In J. Boardman et al., eds., *The Oxford History of the Classical World. Greece and the Hellenistic World*, pp. 118–149. Oxford and New York: Oxford University Press.

Hornblower, S. and Greenstock, M.C., eds. 1984. *The Athenian Empire*, 3rd ed. London: Association of Classical Teachers 1.

Houston, M.G. 1947. *Ancient Greek, Roman and Byzantine Costume and Decoration*. London: Adam and Charles Black.

Howatson, M.C., ed. 1989. *The Oxford Companion to Classical Literature*. Oxford and New York: Oxford University Press.

Hughes, D.D. 1991. *Human Sacrifice in Ancient Greece*. London and New York: Routledge.

Immerwahr, H.R. 1990. *Attic Script. A Survey*. Oxford: Clarendon Press.

Isager, S. and Skydsgaard, J.E. 1992. *Ancient Greek Agriculture. An Introduction*. London: Routledge.

James, P. 1991. *Centuries of Darkness. A Challenge to the Conventional Chronology of Old World Archaeology*. London: Jonathan Cape.

Jameson, M.H. 1988. "Sacrifice and Ritual: Greece." In M. Grant and R. Kitzinger, eds., *Civilization of the Ancient Mediterranean. Greece and Rome*, vol. 2, pp. 959–979. New York: Charles Scribner's Sons.

Jeffery, L.H. 1976. *Archaic Greece. The City-States c. 700–500 B.C.* London and Tonbridge: Ernest Benn.

Jeffery, L.H. 1990. *The Local Scripts of Archaic Greece. A Study of the Origin of the Greek Alphabet and Its Development from the Eighth to the Fifth Centuries B.C.* Rev. ed., with supplement by A. W. Johnstone. Oxford: Clarendon Press.

Jenkins, G.K. 1990. *Ancient Greek Coins*. London: Seaby.

Johnston, M., ed. 1964. *Ancient Greek Dress*. Chicago: Argonaut.

The Joint Association of Classical Teachers' Greek Course. 1978a. *Reading Greek. Text*. Cambridge, London and New York: Cambridge University Press.

The Joint Association of Classical Teachers' Greek Course. 1978b. *Reading Greek. Grammar, Vocabulary and Exercises*. Cambridge, London and New York: Cambridge University Press.

Jones, J.E. 1975. "Town and Country Houses of Attica in Classical Times." In H. Mussche et al., eds., *Thorikus and the Laurion in Archaic and Classical Times*, pp. 63–140. Ghent: Belgian Aechaeological Mission in Greece.

Jones, J.E. 1987. "The Silver Mines of Athens." In B. Cunliffe, ed., *Origins. The Roots and European Civilisation*, pp. 108–120. London: BBC Books.

Jones, J.M. 1986. *A Dictionary of Ancient Greek Coins*. London: Seaby.

Jordan, B. 1975. *The Athenian Navy in the Classical Period. A Study of Athenian Naval Administration and Military Organization in the Fifth and Fourth Centuries B.C.* Berkeley and London: University of California Press.

Just, R. 1989. *Women in Athenian Law and Life*. London and New York: Routledge.

Kagan, D. 1982. "The Dates of the Earliest Coins." *American Journal of Archaeology* 86, 343–360.

Kerényi, C. 1951. *The Gods of the Greeks*. London: Thames and Hudson.

Kerényi, C. 1967. *Eleusis. Archetypal Image of Mother and Daughter*. Trans. by R. Manheim. London: Routledge & Kegan Paul.

Kirk, G.S., Raven, J.E, and Schofield, M. 1983. *The Presocratic Philosophers. A Critical History with a*

Selection of Texts. Cambridge and New York: Cambridge University Press.

Kitzinger, R. 1988. "Alphabets and Writing." In M. Grant and R. Kitzinger, eds., *Civilization of the Ancient Mediterranean. Greece and Rome*, vol. 1, pp. 397–419. New York: Charles Scribner's Sons.

Klein, D. and Lloyd, W., eds. 1984. *The History of Glass*. London: Orbis Publishing Limited.

Krenkel, W.A. 1988. "Prostitution." In M. Grant and R. Kitzinger, eds., *Civilization of the Ancient Mediterranean. Greece and Rome*, vol. 2, pp. 1291–1297. New York: Charles Scribner's Sons.

Krentz, P. 1982. *The Thirty at Athens*. Ithaca and London: Cornell University Press.

Kurtz, D.C. and Boardman, J. 1971. *Greek Burial Customs*. London: Thames and Hudson.

Lacey, W.K. 1968. *The Family in Classical Greece*. London: Thames and Hudson.

Landels, J.G. 1978. *Engineering in the Ancient World*. Berkeley and Los Angeles: University of California Press.

Lane Fox, R. 1973. *Alexander the Great*. London: Allen Lane.

Lane Fox, R. 1988. "Hellenistic Culture and Literature." In J. Boardman et al., eds., *The Oxford History of the Classical World. Greece and the Hellenistic World*, pp. 332–358.

Lang, M. 1968. *Waterworks in the Athenian Agora*. Princeton: American School of Classical Studies at Athens.

Lang, M. 1976. *The Athenian Agora. Results of Excavations Conducted by the American School of Classical Studies at Athens. Graffiti and Dipinti* (vol. 21). Princeton: American School of Classical Studies at Athens.

Langslow, D. 1988. "Languages and Dialects." In M. Grant and R. Kitzinger, eds., *Civilization of the Ancient Mediterranean. Greece and Rome*, vol. 1, pp. 183–207. New York: Charles Scribner's Sons.

Lawrence, A.W, 1979. *Greek Aims in Fortification*. New York: Oxford University Press.

Lawrence, A.W. 1983. *Greek Architecture*. 4th ed., revised with additions by R. A. Tomlinson. New Haven and London: Yale University Press.

Lazenby, J.F. 1985. *The Spartan Army*. Warminster: Aris & Phillips.

Lazenby, J.F. 1993. *The Defence of Greece, 490–479 B.C.* Warminster: Aris & Phillips.

Levi, P. 1971a. *Pausanias. Guide to Greece. Central Greece* (vol. 1). London and New York: Penguin.

Levi, P. 1971b. *Pausanias. Guide to Greece. Southern Greece* (vol. 2). London and New York: Penguin.

Levi, P. 1984. *Atlas of the Greek World*. Oxford: Phaidon.

Levi, P. 1985. *The Pelican History of Greek Literature*. London and New York: Viking.

Levi, P. 1988. "Greek Drama." In J. Boardman et al., eds., *The Oxford History of the Classical World. Greece and the Hellenistic World*, pp. 150–179. Oxford and New York: Oxford University Press.

Littman, R.J. 1988. "Greek Taxation." In M. Grant and R. Kitzinger, eds., *Civilization of the Ancient Mediterranean. Greece and Rome*, vol. 2, pp. 795–808. New York: Charles Scribner's Sons.

Lloyd, G.E.R. 1970. *Early Greek Science. Thales to Aristotle*. London: Chatto and Windus.

Lloyd, G.E.R. 1973. *Greek Science After Aristotle*. London: Chatto and Windus.

Lloyd, G.E.R. 1991. *Methods and Problems in Greek Science*. Cambridge and New York: Cambridge University Press.

Luce, J.V. 1992. *An Introduction to Greek Philosophy*. London: Thames and Hudson.

Luck, G. 1985. *Arcana Mundi: Magic and the Occult in the Greek and Roman Worlds*. Baltimore and London: Johns Hopkins University Press.

Lund, H.S. 1992. *Lysimachus. A Study in Early Hellenistic Kingship*. London and New York: Routledge.

MacDowell, D.M. 1978. *The Law in Classical Athens*. London: Thames and Hudson.

MacDowell, D.M. 1986. *Spartan Law*. Edinburgh: Scottish Academic Press.

MacDowell, D.M. 1988. "Greek Law." In M. Grant and R. Kitzinger, eds., *Civilization of the Ancient Mediterranean. Greece and Rome*, vol. 1, pp. 589–605. New York: Charles Scribner's Sons.

McGing, B.C. 1986. *The Foreign Policy of Mithridates VI Eupator King of Pontus*. Leiden: E.J. Brill.

McKay, A.G. 1988. "Houses." In M. Grant and R. Kitzinger, eds., *Civilization of the Ancient Mediterranean. Greece and Rome*, vol. 3, pp. 1363–1383. New York: Charles Scribner's Sons.

McKechnie, P. 1989. *Outsiders in the Greek Cities in the Fourth Century BC*. London and New York: Routledge.

McShane, R.B. 1964. *The Foreign Policy of the Attalids*. Urbana: University of Illinois Press.

Manning, S.W. 1995. *The Absolute Chronology of the Aegean Early Bronze Age. Archaeology, Radiocarbon and History*. Sheffield: Sheffield Academic Press.

Marinatos, N. and Hägg, R., eds. 1993. *Greek Sanctuaries: New Approaches*. London and New York: Routledge.

Marsden, E.W. 1969. *Greek and Roman Artillery. Historical Development*. London: Oxford University Press.

Meiggs, R. 1982. *Trees and Timber in the Ancient Mediterranean World*. Oxford: Clarendon Press.

Miller, S.G. 1978. *The Prytaneion: Its Function and Architectural Form*. Berkeley, Los Angeles and London: University of California Press.

Mitchell, H. 1940. *The Economics of Ancient Greece*. Cambridge: Cambridge University Press.

Morford, M.P.O. and Lenardon, R.J. 1971. *Classical Mythology*. New York and London: Longman.

Morris, I. 1992. *Death-Ritual and Social Structure in Classical Antiquity*. Cambridge and New York: Cambridge University Press.

Morrison, J. 1980. *The Ship. Long Ships and Round Ships. Warfare and Trade in the Mediterranean 3000 BC–500 AD*. London: Her Majesty's Stationery Office.

Morrison, J.S. and Coates, J.F. 1986. *The Athenian Trireme. The History and Reconstruction of An Ancient Greek Warship*. Cambridge and New York: Cambridge University Press.

Morrison, J.S. and Williams, R.T. 1968. *Greek Oared Ships 900–322 B.C.* Cambridge: Cambridge University Press.

Mountjoy, P.A. 1993. *Mycenaean Pottery. An Introduction*. Oxford: Oxford University Committee for Archaeology monograph 39.

Murray, O. 1988. "Greek Forms of Government." In M. Grant and R. Kitzinger, eds., *Civilization of the Ancient Mediterranean. Greece and Rome*, vol. 1, pp. 439–486. New York: Charles Scribner's Sons.

Murray, O. 1988. "Greek Historians." In J. Boardman et al., eds., *The Oxford History of the Classical World. Greece and the Hellenistic World*, pp. 180–197. Oxford and New York: Oxford University Press.

Musgrave, J. 1990. "Dust and Damn'd Oblivion: A Study of Cremation in Ancient Greece." *Annual of the British School at Athens* 85, 271–299.

Mussche, H., Spitaels, P. and Goermaere-De Poerck, F., eds. 1975. *Thorikus and the Laurion in Archaic and Classical Times*. Ghent: Belgian Archaeological Mission in Greece.

Myers, J.W., Myers, E.E. and Cadogan, G. 1992. *The Aerial Atlas of Ancient Crete*. London: Thames and Hudson.

Mylonas, G.E. 1961. *Eleusis and the Eleusinian Mysteries*. Princeton: Princeton University Press.

Ober, J. 1987. "Early Artillery Towers: Messenia, Boiotia, Attica, Megarid." *American Journal of Archaeology* 91, 569–604.

O'Brien, J.M. 1992. *Alexander the Great: the Invisible Enemy. A Biography*. London and New York: Routledge.

Olivova, V. 1984. *Sports and Games in the Ancient World*. London: Orbis Publishing Limited.

Owens, E.J. 1991. *The City in the Greek and Roman World*. London and New York: Routledge.

Parke, H.W. 1977. *Festivals of the Athenians*. London: Thames and Hudson.

Parke, H.W. 1985. *The Oracles of Apollo in Asia Minor*. London: Croom Helm.

Parke, H.W. 1988. *Sibyls and Sibylline Prophecy in Classical Antiquity*. London and New York: Routledge.

Pecírka, J. 1973. "Homestead Farms in Classical and Hellenistic Hellas." In M.I. Finley, ed., *Problèmes de la Terre en Grèce ancienne*, pp. 113–147. Paris: Mouton and Co.

Pedley, J.G. 1993. *Greek Art and Archaeology*. London: Cassell.

Perlman, S. 1988. "Interstate Relations." In M. Grant and R. Kitzinger, eds., *Civilization of the Ancient Mediterranean. Greece and Rome*, vol. 1, pp. 667–677. New York: Charles Scribner's Sons.

Phillips, E.D. 1973. *Greek Medicine*. London: Thames and Hudson.

Piggott, S. 1983. *The Earliest Wheeled Transport*. Ithaca: Cornell University Press.

Pollard, J. 1988. "Divination and Oracles: Greece." In M. Grant and R. Kitzinger, eds., *Civilization of the Ancient Mediterranean. Greece and Rome*, vol. 2, pp. 941–950. New York: Charles Scribner's Sons.

Pollitt, J.J. 1988a. "Greek Sculpture and Gems." In M. Grant and R. Kitzinger, eds., *Civilization of the Ancient Mediterranean. Greece and Rome*, vol. 3, pp. 1,701–1,725. New York: Charles Scribner's Sons.

Pollitt, J.J. 1988b. "Greek Painting and Mosaic." In M. Grant and R. Kitzinger, eds., *Civilization of the Ancient Mediterranean. Greece and Rome*, vol. 3, pp. 1,749–1,770. New York: Charles Scribner's Sons.

Pomeroy, S.B. 1988. "Greek Marriage." In M. Grant and R. Kitzinger, eds., *Civilization of the Ancient Mediterranean. Greece and Rome*, vol. 3, pp. 1,333–1,342. New York: Charles Scribner's Sons.

Popham, M. 1967. "Late Minoan Pottery. A Summary." *Annual of the British School at Athens* 62, 337–351.

Popham, M. 1994. "The Collapse of Aegean Civilization at the End of the Late Bronze Age." In B. Cunliffe, ed., *The Oxford Illustrated Prehistory of Europe*, pp. 277–303 and 492–493. Oxford and New York: Oxford University Press.

Price, S. 1988. "The History of the Hellenistic Period." In J. Boardman et al., eds., *The Oxford History of the Classical World. Greece and the Hellenistic World*, pp. 309–331. Oxford and New York: Oxford University Press.

Pritchett, W.K. 1965. *Studies in Ancient Greek Topography*, part 1. Berkeley and Los Angeles: University of California Press.

Pritchett, W.K. 1969. *Studies in Ancient Greek Topography. Battlefields*, part 2. Berkeley and Los Angeles: University of California Press.

Pritchett, W.K. 1971. *Ancient Greek Military Practices*, part 1. Berkeley and London: University of California Press.

Pritchett, W.K. 1974. *The Greek State at War*, part 2. Berkeley and London: University of California Press.

Pritchett, W.K. 1979. *The Greek State at War. Religion*, part 3. Berkeley and London: University of California Press.

Pritchett, W.K. 1980. *Studies in Ancient Greek Topography. Roads*, part 3. Berkeley, Los Angeles and London: University of California Press.

Pritchett, W.K. 1982. *Studies in Ancient Greek Topography. Passes*, part 4. Berkeley, Los Angeles and London: University of California Press.

Pritchett, W.K. 1985. *Studies in Ancient Greek Topography*, part 5. Berkeley, Los Angeles and London: University of California Press.

Pritchett, W.K. 1989. *Studies in Ancient Greek Topography*, part 6. Berkeley, Los Angeles and London: University of California Press.

Pritchett, W.K. 1991a. *The Greek State at War*, part 4. Berkeley and London: University of California Press.

Pritchett, W.K. 1991b. *The Greek State at War*, part 5. Berkeley and London: University of California Press.

Pritchett, W.K. 1991c. *Studies in Ancient Greek Topograph*, part 7. Amsterdam: J.C. Gieben.

Pritchett, W.K. 1991c. *Studies in Ancient Greek Topography*, part 8. Amsterdam: J.C. Gieben.

Pullen, D.J. 1992. "Ox and Plow in the Early Bronze Age Aegean." *American Journal of Archaeology* 96, 45–54.

Rasmussen, T. and Spivey, N., eds. 1991. *Looking at Greek Vases*. Cambridge and New York: Cambridge University Press.

Richter, G.M.A. 1926. *Ancient Furniture. A History of Greek, Etruscan and Roman Furniture*. Oxford: Clarendon Press.

Richter, G.M.A. 1966. *The Furniture of the Greeks, Etruscans and Romans*. London: Phaidon Press.

Robertson, D.S. 1943. *Greek and Roman Architecture*. London: Cambridge University Press.

Robertson, M. 1992. *The Art of Vase-Painting in Classical Athens*. Cambridge: Cambridge University Press.

Robertson, N. 1992. *Festivals and Legends: the Formation of Greek Cities in the Light of Public Ritual*. Toronto and London: University of Toronto Press.

Rodgers, W.L. 1964. *Greek and Roman Naval Warfare*. Reprint of 1937 publication. Annapolis: United States Naval Institute.

Roisman, J. 1993. *The General Demosthenes and His Use of Military Surprise*. Stuttgart: Franz Steiner Verlag.

Ronan, C.A. 1983. *The Cambridge Illustrated History of the World's Science*. Cambridge: Cambridge University Press.

Russo, J. 1988. "Greek Lyric and Elegiac Poetry." In M. Grant and R. Kitzinger, eds., *Civilization of the Ancient Mediterranean. Greece and Rome*, vol. 3, pp. 1,437–1,454. New York: Charles Scribner's Sons.

Saatsoglu-Paliadeli, C. 1993. "Aspects of Ancient Macedonian Costume." *Journal of Hellenic Studies* 113, 122–147.

Sakellarakis, J.A. 1992. *The Mycenean Pictorial Style in the National Archaeological Museum of Athens*. Athens: Kapon Editions.

Sallares, R. 1991. *The Ecology of the Ancient Greek World*. London: Duckworth.

Samuel, A.E. 1972. *Greek and Roman Chronology. Calendars and Years in Classical Antiquity*. München: C.H. Beck'sche Verlagsbuchhandlung.

Samuel, A.E. 1988. "Calendars and Time-Telling." In M. Grant and R. Kitzinger, eds., *Civilization of the Ancient Mediterranean. Greece and Rome*, vol. 1, pp. 389–395. New York: Charles Scribner's Sons.

Sanders, L.J. 1987. *Dionysius I of Syracuse and Greek Tyranny.* London, New York and Sydney: Croom Helm.

Scarsborough, J. 1988. "Medicine." In M. Grant and R. Kitzinger, eds., *Civilization of the Ancient Mediterranean. Greece and Rome*, vol. 2, pp. 1227–1248. New York: Charles Scribner's Sons.

Sealey, R. 1976. *A History of the Greek City States c. 700–338 B.C.* Berkeley, Los Angeles and London: University of California Press.

Sealey, R. 1990. *Women and Law in Classical Greece.* Chapel Hill and London: University of North Carolina Press.

Schoder, R.V. 1974. *Ancient Greece from the Air.* London: Thames and Hudson.

Schwartz, S. 1988. "Judaism." In M. Grant and R. Kitzinger, eds., *Civilization of the Ancient Mediterranean. Greece and Rome*, vol. 2, pp. 1,027–1,045. New York: Charles Scribner's Sons.

Scullard, H.H. 1974. *The Elephant in the Greek and Roman World.* London: Thames and Hudson.

Shaw, J.W. 1972. "Greek and Roman Harbourworks." In G.F. Bass, ed., *A History of Seafaring Based on Underwater Archaeology*, pp. 88-112. London: Thames and Hudson.

Shaw, J.W. 1987. "The Early Helladic II Corridor House: Development and Form." *American Journal of Archaeology* 91, 59–79.

Shaw, T., ed. 1993. *The Trireme Project. Operational Experience 1987–90. Lessons Learnt.* Oxford: Oxbow monograph 31.

Simon, E. 1983. *Festivals of Attica. An Archaeological Commentary.* Madison, Wisconsin and London: University of Wisconsin Press.

Smith, J.S. 1990. *Greece and the Persians.* Bristol: Bristol Classical Press.

Smith, R.R. 1991. *Hellenistic Sculpture: A Handbook.* London: Thames and Hudson.

Smith, T.R. 1987. *Mycenaean Trade and Interaction in the West Central Mediterranean, 1600–1000 B.C.* Oxford: British Archaeological Reports International Series 371.

Snodgrass, A.M. 1964. *Early Greek Armour and Weapons from the End of the Bronze Age to 600 B.C.* Edinburgh: Edinburgh University Press.

Snodgrass, A.M. 1967. *Arms and Armor of the Greeks.* London: Thames and Hudson.

Soren, D., ed. 1987. *The Sanctuary of Apollo Hylates at Kourion, Cyprus.* Tucson: University of Arizona Press.

Sparkes, B.A. 1991. *Greek Pottery. An Introduction.* Manchester and New York: Manchester University Press.

Spence, I.G. 1993. *The Cavalry of Classical Greece. A Social and Military History with Particular Reference to Athens.* New York: Oxford University Press.

Stanton, G.R. 1990. *Athenian Politics c. 800–500 BC. A Sourcebook.* London and New York: Routledge.

Stanton, G.R. 1994. "The Rural Demes and Athenian Politics." In W.D.E. Coulson et al., eds., *The Archaeology of Athens under the Democracy*, pp. 217–224. Oxford: Oxbow Monograph 37.

Starr, C.G. 1988. "Greek Administration." In M. Grant and R. Kitzinger, eds., *Civilization of the Ancient Mediterranean. Greece and Rome*, vol. 1, pp. 631–647. New York: Charles Scribner's Sons.

Stephens, S.A. 1988. "Book Production." In M. Grant and R. Kitzinger, eds., *Civilization of the Ancient Mediterranean. Greece and Rome*, vol. 1, pp. 421–436. New York: Charles Scribner's Sons.

Stillwell, R., ed. 1976. *The Princeton Encyclopedia of Classical Sites.* Princeton: Princeton University Press.

Sullivan, J.P. 1988. "Epigrams and Satire." In M. Grant and R. Kitzinger, eds., *Civilization of the Ancient Mediterranean. Greece and Rome*, vol. 3, pp. 1,495–1,503. New York: Charles Scribner's Sons.

Sweet, W.E. 1987. *Sport and Recreation in Ancient Greece. A Sourcebook with Translations.* Oxford and New York: Oxford University Press.

Symons, D.J. 1987. *Costume of Ancient Greece.* London: Batsford.

Talbert, J.A., ed. 1985. *Atlas of Classical History.* London and New York: Routledge.

Taplin, O. 1988. "Homer." In J. Boardman et al., eds., *The Oxford History of the Classical World. Greece and the Hellenistic World*, pp. 44–71. Oxford and New York: Oxford University Press.

Tarn, W.W. 1913. *Antigonos Gonatas.* Oxford: Clarendon Press.

Taylour, W. 1983. *The Myceneans*, rev. ed. New York: Thames and Hudson.

Thompson, D.J. 1990. "The High Priests of Memphis under Ptolemaic Rule." In M. Beard and J. North., eds., *Pagan Priests. Religion and Power in the Ancient World*, pp. 99–116. London: Duckworth.

Thompson, W.E. 1988. "Insurance and Banking." In M. Grant and R. Kitzinger, eds., *Civilization of the Ancient Mediterranean. Greece and Rome*, vol. 2, pp. 829–836. New York: Charles Scribner's Sons.

Throckmorton, P. 1972. "Romans on the Sea." In G.F. Bass, ed., *A History of Seafaring Based on Underwater Archaeology*, pp. 66–86.

Tilley, A. 1992. "Three Men to a Room—A Completely Different Trireme." *Antiquity* 66, 599–610.

Tomlinson, R. 1976. *Greek Sanctuaries*. London: Elek Books.

Tomlinson, R. 1992. *From Mycenae to Constantinople. The Evolution of the Ancient City*. London and New York: Routledge.

Trell, B.L. 1988. "The Temple of Artemis at Ephesos." In P.A. Clayton and M.J. Price, *The Seven Wonders of the Ancient World*, pp.78–99. London and New York: Routledge.

Trendall, A.D. 1989. *Red Figure Vases of South Italy and Sicily. A Handbook*. London: Thames and Hudson.

Tritle, L.A. 1988. *Phocion the Good*. London, New York and Sydney: Croom Helm.

Tsakirgis, B. 1989. "The Decorated Pavements of Morgantina I: the Mosaics." *American Journal of Archaeology* 93, 395–416.

Usher, S. 1988. "Greek Historiography and Biography." In M. Grant and R. Kitzinger, eds., *Civilization of the Ancient Mediterranean. Greece and Rome*, vol. 3, pp. 1,525–1,540. New York: Charles Scribner's Sons.

Ussher, R.G. 1988. "Letter Writing." In M. Grant and R. Kitzinger, eds., *Civilization of the Ancient Mediterranean. Greece and Rome*, vol. 3, pp. 1,573–1,582. New York: Charles Scribner's Sons.

Vermaseren, M.J. 1977. *Cybele and Attis. The Myth and the Cult*. Trans. by A.M.H. Lemmers. London: Thames and Hudson.

Vermeule, E. 1988. "The Afterlife: Greece." In M. Grant and R. Kitzinger, eds., *Civilization of the Ancient Mediterranean. Greece and Rome*, vol. 2, pp. 987–996. New York: Charles Scribner's Sons.

Vermeule, E. and Karageorghis, V. 1982. *Mycenaean Pictorial Vase Painting*. Cambridge and London: Harvard University Press.

Vickery, K.F. 1936. *Food in Early Greece*. Urbana: University of Illinois.

Walbank, F.W. 1933. *Aratos of Sicyon*. Cambridge: Cambridge University Press.

Walbank, F.W. 1940. *Philip V of Macedon*. Cambridge: Cambridge University Press.

Wardle, K.A. 1994. "The Palace Civilizations of Minoan Crete and Mycenean Greece, 2000–1200 BC." In B. Cunliffe, ed., *The Oxford Illustrated Prehistory of Europe*, pp. 202–243 and 490–491. Oxford and New York: Oxford University Press.

Warner, R. 1972. *Men of Athens. The Story of Fifth Century Athens*. London, Sydney and Toronto: Bodley Head.

Warren, P. and Hankey, V. 1989. *Aegean Bronze Age Chronology*. Bristol: Bristol Classical Press.

Warry, J. 1980. *Warfare in the Classical World*. London: Salamander Books Ltd.

Watrows, L.V. 1991. "The Origin and Iconography of the Late Minoan Painted Larnax." *Hesperia* 60, 285–307.

Webb, V. 1978. *Archaic Greek Faience. Miniature Scent Bottles and Related Objects from East Greece, 650–500 B.C.* Warminster: Aris & Phillips.

Whibley, L., ed., 1931. *A Companion to Greek Studies*, 4th ed. Cambridge: Cambridge University Press.

White, K.D. 1977. *Country Life in Classical Times*. London: Elek Books Ltd.

White, K.D. 1988. "Farming and Animal Husbandry." In M. Grant and R. Kitzinger, eds., *Civilization of the Ancient Mediterranean. Greece and Rome*, vol. 1, pp. 211–246. New York: Charles Scribner's Sons.

Whitehead, D. 1986. *The Demes of Attica 508/7–CA. 250 B.C. A Political and Social Study*. Princeton: Princeton University Press.

Whittle, A. 1994. "The First Farmers." In B. Cunliffe, ed., *The Oxford Illustrated Prehistory of Europe*, pp. 136–166. Oxford and New York: Oxford University Press.

Wiedemann, T.E.J. 1988. "Slavery." In M. Grant and R. Kitzinger, eds., *Civilization of the Ancient Mediterranean. Greece and Rome*, vol. 1, pp. 575–588. New York: Charles Scribner's Sons.

Wilkins, J., Harvey, D. and Dobson, M., eds. 1995. *Food in Antiquity*. Exeter: Exeter University Press.

Wilson, J.B. 1979. *Pylos 425 BC. A Historical and Topographical Study of Thucydides' Account of the Campaign*. Warminster: Aris & Phillips.

Winkler, J.J. 1988. "The Novel." In M. Grant and R. Kitzinger, eds., *Civilization of the Ancient Mediterranean. Greece and Rome*, vol. 3, pp. 1,563–1,572. New York: Charles Scribner's Sons.

Winter, F.E. 1971. *Greek Fortifications*. London: Routledge & Kegan Paul.

Winter, N.A., ed. 1990. "Proceedings of the First International Conference on Archaic Greek Architectural Terracottas, December 2–4, 1988." *Hesperia. Journal of the American School of Classical Studies at Athens* 59, 1–323.

Winter, N.A. 1993. *Greek Architectural Terracottas from the Prehistoric to the End of the Archaic Period*. Oxford: Clarendon Press.

Woodhead, A.G. 1992. *The Study of Greek Inscriptions*, 2nd ed. London: Bristol Classical Press.

Worley, L.J. 1994. *Hippeis: The Cavalry of Ancient Greece*. Boulder, Colo., and Oxford: Westview Press.

Yavis, C.G. 1949. *Greek Altars. Origins and Typology, Including the Minoan-Mycenaean Offertory Apparatus. An Archaeological Study in the History of Religion*. Saint Louis: Saint Louis University Press.

Young, D.C. 1988. "Athletics." In M. Grant and R. Kitzinger, eds., *Civilization of the Ancient Mediterranean. Greece and Rome*, vol. 2, pp. 1,131–1,142. New York: Charles Scribner's Sons.

INDEX

Where several page references are given, any main ones are in **boldface**. Pages in *italics* with suffix *f* denote a figure. Most information is derived from Athens, and to a lesser extent Sparta, and so it is not practicable to index those places in full.

Menelaus his brother 287, 295, 320

quarrel with Achilles 322, 324, 328

returned from Troy 323

son of Atreus 253, 287, 295

Agamemnon (by Aeschylus) 265

Agatharchides (writer) 265–66

Agatharcus (painter) 380

Agathocles (Ptolemaic minister) 51, 76–77

Agathocles (tyrant of Syracuse) 23, **40**, 60, 65, 150, 269, 271

Agathon (tragedian) 262, 266

Agathos Daimon 287, 351

Agdistis 295, 300; *see also* Cybele

agema (King's Bodyguard) 90–91

Agenor (king of Tyre) 305, 327

Agesilaus (Xenophon) 281

Agesilaus I 82

Agesilaus II 40, 63, 82

at battle of Coronea 20, 40, 281

conquered Acarnania 130

and Corinthian War 10, 40

death 21

defeated Tissaphernes 81

fought against Persians 10, 21, 40, 57, 81

Xenophon served under him 281

Agesipolis (I–III) 82

Aghia Triadha, Crete 156*f*, 159, 240*f*

Agis I 82

Agis II 20, 41, 82

Agis III 22, **41**, 48, 82

Agis IV 24, **41**, 82

Aglaurus (mother and daughter) 287, 356

agoge see education (Sparta)

Agoracritus (sculptor) 380–81

agoranomoi (market overseers) 189

agoras 31, 126, 140, **214**

assembly meetings 33

at Athens **135–36**, *212f*, 216, 338, 340, 381–82

chariot racing *353f*

first 136

location *133f*, 136

ostraka *34f*

stoas 135, *212f*, *214f*, 383

at Priene *206f*

at Sparta 144, *144f*

boundary stones *252f*

markets 189, 214

ostracisms 34

statues 214, 376, 383

theatrical performances 216, 136

agrianes 89

agriculture 172–74, 211

Demeter goddess 301

festivals 353

Hesiod wrote on 273

slaves 412

see also barley, grain, harvesting, olives, plowing, sowing, wheat

Agyrium, Sicily *155f*, 159

Agyrrius (politician) 41

Aigeis (new tribe) 27

air (element) 388, 392, 400

aisymnetes (pl. *aisymnetai*) 30, 74

Ajax (hero) 70, **287**, 307, 383

Ajax (the Locrian) 287, 297

Ajax (Sophocles) 279

Alabanda, Turkey *154f*, 159

alabastron *see* pottery

Alalia, Corsica *124f*, 159

naval battle 16

Alcaeus (mythical) 289

Alcaeus (of Lesbos, lyric poet) 74, 256–57, 261, 264, **266**, 278

Alcaeus (of Messene, epigrammatist) 266

Alcamenes (king of Sparta) 82

Alcamenes (sculptor) 381

Alcestis (Euripides) 262, 272

Alcestis (wife of Admetus) 287–88

Alcibiades (politician) 19, **41**, 80

at battle of Cyzicus 19, 41, 80

expedition to sicily 41, 61, 64–65

house painted by Agatharcus 380

mutilation of the herms 19, 41

in Peloponnesian War 9, 41

Alcidamas (rhetorician) 266

Alcinous 288, 321

Alcmaeon (mythical) 288

Alcmaeon (son of Megacles) 42

Alcmaeonids **41–42**, 52–53, 55, 63, 67

Alcman (lyric poet) 256–57, 266

Alcmene (wife of Amphitryon) 288, 309

Alcyone 288

Aleuadae 42

Alexander (tragic poet) 259

Alexander (tyrant of Pherae) 21, **44**, 67, 151

Alexander I (of Epirus) *11f*, 22, 42, 56, 71, 141

Alexander I (of Macedonia) 17, **42**, 67, 71, 82

Alexander II (of Epirus) 42

Alexander II (of Macedonia) 42, 82

Alexander II Zabinas 26, 47, 83

Alexander III (the Great) 42–44, *42f*, 81–82

Aristotle his tutor 42, 395

birth 21

coins of 192, *195f*, *311f*

consulted Siwa oracle 43, 288

death 22, 44, 140

dedicated temple *343f*, *385f*

founded cities 43–44, 128, 140, 142, 150, 204, 208

histories (written) 44, 74, 89–90, 93, 267, 269

history 11–12, 22, 42–44, *43f*, 266, 270, 278

India Expedition 22, 44, 69, 142, 276

portrayed on coins 193

priests 77

scholars on his expedition 196, 276, 394

statues 382–83

see also armies

Alexander IV 44, 82

death 23, 44, 52, 78

joint king with Philip III 44, 71

Leonnatus his guardian 62

Olympias made him king 65

Roxane his mother 44, 78

Alexander Aetolus 263, 266

Alexander Balas 25–26, **44**, 51, 56, 76, 83

Alexander of Corinth 13, 24, **44**, 46, 54, 272

Alexander Polyhistor 266

Alexander Romance 269

Alexandria (nr. Ghazni) *158f*, 159

Alexandria (nr. Multan) *158f*, 159

Alexandria (Patala) *158f*, 159

Alexandria, Egypt 140–41, 159

Adonia festival 287

Alexander the Great buried 44

anatomical research 392–93

and Apollodorus 394

and Apollonius 394

and Archimedes 395

bank 195

comedies staged 275

and Ctesibius 397

cultural center 11, 44, 75, 135, 255

Deinocrates built 208

and Erasistratus 398

Euclid taught 398

few Greeks 140

founded 22, 43, 128, 140

Hadra vases 252, 373

harbors 141, 201

and Hermippus 273

and Herophilus (physician) 398

Jews expelled 76

location *125f*, *157f*, *158f*

and Lycophron 276

museum 74–75, 140, 247

palace 140

Pharos lighthouse 75, 141, 201

population numbers 29

and Poseidippus 278

rock-cut tombs 423

Sarapis cult/temple 330, 341

scholars 261, 267, 277

fled 263, 266

school of physicians 393

and Theocritus 280

tragic poets 259

see also libraries

Alexandria ad Caucasum *158f*, 159

Alexandria ad Issum *154f*, 159

Alexandria in Arachosia *158f*, 159

Alexandria in Aria *158f*, 159

Alexandria Eschate (farthest) 44, 150, *158f*, 159

Alexandria in Margiana *158f*, 159

Alexandria of Mygdonia *158f*, 159

Alexandria Oxiana *158f*, 159

Alexandria Troas *154f*, 159

Alexandrian poetry 255

Alexandrian War 26, 77

Alexis (comic poet) 260, 263, **266**

Aliphera, Greece *152f*, 159

Al Mina, Syria 15, 128, 150

Alopece deme 401

alphabets 241–43, 246, 261

Attic *241f*, 242

blue 242

Corinthian *241f*

East Ionic 242

as inscriptions 252

Ionic *241f*, 242, *242f*

Milesian 242

red 242

Semitic 241–42

see also writing

Alpheus (river god) 291

Alpheus River 132, 141, 291, 310

altars 216, *324f*, *342*, 360, 380

in agoras 338

of Apollo *249f*

of Athena 287

in festivals 354, 356

inside temples 342

libations 346

of Lycurgus *144f*

open-air 285, 339, 342

of Pelops *326f*

portable 342

predated temples 342

sacrifices on 313, 342

stone 180, 342

terra-cotta 342

of underworld deities 342

of Zeus 342, 378

Herkeios 321, 329

Alyattes (king of Lydia) 16, 44–45, 205

Amasia, Turkey *154f*, 159

Amasis (of Egypt) 16, 45, 73

Amasis (potter) 381

Amasis Painter 371, 381

Amastris, Turkey *154f*, 160

Amathus, Cyprus *154f*, *157f*, 160, 290

Amazons 310–311, 314, 333, 382, 384

amber 180, 184, 424

Ambracia 130, 141, *153f*, 160

Ambracus, Greece *153f*, 160

amis (pl. *amides*) 364

Amisus, Turkey 149, *154f*, 160

Ammon (god) 288–89, 335

Amorgos, Greece 53, 168, 187, 278

Amphiaraus 276, **288**, 331, 348

Amphiaraus (Aristophanes) 262, 268

Amphictyonic Council (Delphic Amphictyony) 73, 127

and Aenis 130

and Aeschines 40

Anthela first center 127, 145

and Hyperbolus 61

and Philip II 71, 149

and Phocis 71, 149

took control of Delphi 127, 148

Amphion 290, 321–22

Amphipolis, Greece *153f*, 160

battle of 19

captured by Philip II 11, 21, 70

cleruchy founded by Athens 9, 18, 67–68

Philip V died 72

taken by Brasidas 19, 51, 280

Amphissa, Greece *152f*, *153f*, 160

Amphitrite 321, 328, 333

Amphitryon 288

amphoriskos (pl. *amphoriskoi*) 364

amulets 182, 360–61

Amun 288

Amyclae, Greece *152f*, 160, 314

Amynander 45

Amyntas (pretender) 79

Amyntas I–II 82

Amyntas III 45, 70, 82

Amyntor (king of Thessaly) 328

Anacreon (lyric poet) 256, 261, **266**, 278

Ananke 288–89, 305

Anarcharsis 45

Anarrhysis 354

anatomical

models 284, 345, 348

research 398

anatomy 376, 392–93

Anaxagoras (of Clazomenae) 272, 380, 386, **388**, **394**, 397

Anaxander (king) 82

Anaxandridas I 82

Anaxandridas II 53, 82

Anaxandrides (comic poet) 260, 266

Anaxarchus of Abdera 394, 401

Anaxilas (tyrant of Rhegium) 17, 45, 60

Anaxilaus (king) 82

Anaximander (of Miletus) 195, 261, **386–87**, 391–92, 394

Anaximenes (of Miletus) 386, **387**, 391, **394**, 397

Anchises 287, **289**, 290, 317

anchors 117, **118**, 181, 200

Ancyra, Turkey *154f*, 160

Andocides (orator) 45

Andocides Painter 372–73

Andriscus (pretender) 45

Andromache (Euripides) 262, 272

Andromache (wife of Hector) 289, 307–308

Andromeda 289, 383

andron (men's room) *210f*, 212, 221

Andros, Greece 128, 138, *152f*, 168

And-otion (politician/writer) 45, 267, 274

nous 386, 388
novels 261
numerals 243–44, *244f*, *245f*, 251
Nymphaeum, Ukraine 137, *158f*, 165
Nymphs 322, *324f*
  Alseides 322
  Amalthea 288
  and Apollo 291
  Arethusa 291
  Callisto 297
  Calypso 297
  chased by Satyrs 330
  Creneids 322
  Daphne 301
  Dryades 322
  Echo 303
  Hamadryades 322
  Hesperides 311–13
  Hydriads 322
  killed bees of Aristaeus 292
  Leimoniads 322
  Liriope 321
  Naiads 322
  Napaeae 322
  Nereids 321
  Oenone 324
  Oreithyia 296
  Orestiads 322
  Pan's affairs with 323
  Potameids 322
  sacrifices 292–93, 322, 353–54
  Salmacis 312
  statues 377
  Syrinx 323, 332
Nysa, Turkey *154f*, 165
Nyx (night) 305, 313–14, 322

O

oars 198–200, 303
  see also warships
oaths 304, 308, 313, 346
oath sacrifices 346
obelos/obolos (iron spit) 191, 193
obkia (ounce) 193
obol (*obolos*, coin) 107, 190, 298
Oceanids 321–22, 332
Oceanus (Titan) 286, 303, 314, **322**, 329, 332–33
octodrachm (coin) 191
octopuses 370
Ocypete 307, 322
odeion/odeum (at Athens) 217–18, 263
odeion (pl. *odeia*) 216–18
odes see epinician odes
Odessus, Bulgaria *158f*, 165
Odysseus (hero) 322–23
  Alcinous helped 288
  as an archer 92
  Argos (dog) 291
  Autolycus his grandfather 295
  beat Thersites 332
  and Calypso 297
  captured Helenus 308
  children 297, 299, 322–23, 332
  death 332
  and Elpenor 303–4
  and Eumaeus 305
  fleet sunk 317
  imprisoned by Polyphemus 300, 328
  killed Antinous 290
  and Mentor 320
  and Nausicaa 321
  Penelope his wife 322, 325
  and Philoctetes 327
  raided Trojan camp 302
  ship building 199
  shipwreck 297, 299, 321
  and Sirens 331
  subject of *Odyssey* 274, 322–23
  in the underworld 299, 303–4, 316, 332, 384
Odyssey see Homer
Odyssey Landscapes 380
oecist (*oikistes*) 127
Oeconomicus (Xenophon) 281
Oedipus (hero) 323
  Antigone his daughter 289, 305, 323
  destroyed Sphinx 323, 331
  Eteocles his son 305, 323, 331
  in exile 305, 323, 331
  Ismene his daughter 305, 323
  Jocasta his wife/mother 289, 300, 316, 323
  in *Phoenician Women* 272
  Polynices his son 287, 289, 305, 323, 331
Oedipus at Colonus (Sophocles) 262, 279
Oedipus Rex (Sophocles) 279
Oeneus (king of Calydon) 297, 319
Oeniadae, Greece 68, *152f*, *153f*, 165
Oenone (Nymph) 324
Oenophyta, battle of 18, 64, 137
offerings/votive offerings 284–85, 343, **344–47**, 360, 384
  bronze sheet 181
  to the dead 420
  figurines 345, 374–75
  food 344–45, 425
  at healing shrines 345, 348
  in kernos 366
  Philippeum 72f
  sculpture 378
  statues 344, 375
  stored in temples 338, 342
  at tombs 425
  treasuries 342
  see also anatomical models, grave goods, lekythoi, sacrifices
Ogyia (mythical island) 297
oikos 221, 408–10
oil see lamps, lekythos, olive oil, perfumed oil, pottery (flasks)
oinochoe see pottery
oinokhoos 337
Old Comedy see comedies
oligarchic revolution (Athens)
oligarchies 9, 19, 32, 36, 48, 66, 73, 80; see also Thirty Tyrants
olive mill (*trapetum*) 175, *175f*
olive oil 413
  amphorae 364, 373
  on the body 418
  function 175
  in lighting 179, 234
  markets 189
  production 175
  stored in *pithoi* *209f*
  trade 185–86
  see also stirrup jars
olive press 175
olives 137, 172–73, *173f*, 185, 413, 417
Oloosson, Greece *153f*, 165
Olus, Crete *156f*, 165
Olympia, Greece 165
  altar of Zeus 342
  in Elis 141
  foot standard 189
  halter weight *419f*
  hippodrome 219
  Horae worshipped 314
  inscriptions *248f*, *250f*
  location 140, *152f*
  offerings 375
  oracles 348
  palaestra *217f*
  Pelops sanctuary *326f*
  Pelops worshipped 325
  Pheidias' workshop 384
  Philippeum *72f*
  stadium *352f*
  statues 382–85
  temples 335, *336f*, 339, *340f*, 381
  thigh guard 103
  trophies 116
  see also Olympic Games
Olympiad 15, 304, 349–52, 407
Olympians/Olympian gods 286, 296, 306, 330, 333
  see also specific deities (eg Poseidon, Zeus)
Olympian victors (lists) 261
Olympian Zeus see Zeus
Olympias (mother of Alexander the Great) 23, 42, 52, **65**, 70–71, 74, 78
Olympic Games 349–50
  Alcibiades entered 41
  athletics 350, 419
  chariot races 51, 350, 420
  Elis in control 141
  in honor of Zeus 335, 350
  horse racing 350, 420
  stadium *352f*
  women's races nearby 420
Olympieia festival 335, 355
Olympiodorus (Athenian leader) 65
Olympus (Mount) 124, 286, 308, 310, 321, 334
Olynthiac orations 57
Olynthus, Greece 165
  Callisthenes from 269
  coins *290f*
  destroyed 11, 21, 71–72, 138, *290f*
  houses 220–21, *221f*, 223
  location *153f*
  mosaics 380
  planned town 220–21
  Potidaea given by Philip II 70
  surrendered to Sparta 20
Ombos, Egypt *157f*, 165
omphalos 195, 245
Onchestus, Greece *152f*, 165
Onescritus (historian) 276
Onesimus (painter) 383
Onomacritus (poet) 275–76
Onomarchus (general of Phocis) **65**, 70–71, 73, 140, 149
onos (pl. *onoi*) 365
ophthamology 393
opisthodomos see temples
Opuntian Locris see Locris
Opus, Greece 144. *152f*, *153f*, 165
oracles/oracular shrines 347–48
  of Apollo 291, 347–48, 350
  Branchidae 291
  Clarus 291, 348
  cleromancy 347
  Delphi(c) 291, 330, 348, *349f*
    and Cadmus 296
    consulted by Boeotians 334
    consulted by oecists 127
    forged oracle 53, 55
    and Gaia 305
    on *gerousia* 36
    given by Pythia 336, 348
    Perseus visited 68
    questioned by Oedipus 323
    response to Croesus 54
    sang by Herophile *338f*
    and Thaletas 280
  Didyma 127, 348
  of Dionysus 348
  of Gaia 348
  of Hermes 348
  lecanomancy 347
  of Musaeus 275–76
  priestesses 347–48
  priests 347
  prophets 337, 347
    at shrine of Selene Pasiphae 330
    of Trophonius at Lebadea 334, 348
    warned Pelias 316
    Zeus Ammon at Siwa 22, 43, *43f*, 288, 348
    see also prophecy
orators (*rhetores*) 36–37
  Andocides 45
  Antiphon 48, 267
  Callistratus 21, 50, 52, 81
  Deinarchus 270
  Demetrius 55, 275, 424
  Demochares 56, 65
  Hegesias 272
  Lycurgus 62–63
  metics 29
  Phocion 73
  sculpture 377
  Theodectes 280
  Theramenes 80
  see also Aeschines, Demades, Demosthenes, Isaeus, Isocrates, Lysias, rhetoric
orchestra see theaters
Orchomenus, Arcadia 131, *152f*, 165
Orchomenus, Boeotia 21, 64–65, 137, *152f*, *153f*, 165, 306, 334
orders (of architecture) see Corinthian, Doric, Ionic
Oreithyia (Nymph) 296
Oresteia (Aeschylus) 262, 265
Oresteia (Stesichorus) 279
Orestes (Euripides) 262, 272
Orestes (king of Macedonia) 82
Orestes (son of Agamemnon) 287, 299, 303, 315, **323**
Orestiads (Nymphs) 322
organ see water organ
Orgeones 351
orgia 358
Orminium, Greece *153f*, 165
Oropernes (of Cappadocia) 25, 49
Oropus, Greece 165
  given up by Thebes 71
  healing sanctuary 288, 348
  location *152f*
  seized by Thebes 21, 52
  transport 184
Orpheus (hero) 305, 316, **323**, 358
Orphic Mysteries 358
Orphism 303, 323, 358, 421
Orthrus (dog) 311
Ortygia (Syracuse) 57
Oschophoria festival 353
Osiris (god) 287, 307, 315, **323**, 330
ostracisms 17, 34
  Aristides 17, 34, *34f*, 49
  Cimon 9, 18, *34f*, 53, 67
  Hyberbolus 19, 34, 41, 61
  introduction 53
  sign of literacy 253–54
  Themistocles 7, 18, 79
  Thucydides 18, 34, 68, 80
  Xanthippus 17, 34, 81
  see also ostrakon
ostrakon (pl. *ostraka*) 34, *34f*, 79, 252; see also ostracisms
ouragos (pl.*ouragoi*, rearguard officers) 88–90
ovens 174, 364, 413
owls *127f*, 191, *191f*, 294
  coins 191, *191f*

stirrup jars *see* pottery
stoas 214, 216, 218
  Pella 145
  Priene *206f*
  South Stoa (Athens) *133f, 214f*
  Stoa of Attalus (Athens) *133f,* 136, *212f, 214f*
  Stoa Basileos (Athens) 36, 135
  Stoa of Eumenes II (Athens) *133f, 134f,* 136
  Stoa Poikile (Painted Stoa, Athens) 52, 136, 384, 389, 402
  Stoa of Zeus (Athens) 136, 383
Stoicheia (Euclid) 398
Stoics/Stoicism 386, 389–90
  Chrysippus 389, 396–97
  Cleanthes 389, 396, 401
  Diogenes 397, 399
  elements 391
  frequented stoas 216
  Panaetius 400
  Sphaerus 401
  see also Zeno (of Citium)
stoikhedon 249, *249f*
stone
  altars 180, 342
  anchors 117–18
  arrowheads *107f,* 108
  bathtubs 216
  blocks (transport) 178–79
  coffins 423
  figurines 180, 374, *374f*
  floors 233
  functions 180
  imitated by frescoes 379
  lamps 179–80, 234
  mines 178–79
  moldings 233–34
  molds 181
  painted 180
  quarries 178–79, 186
  rubble
    foundations 227
    walls 227–28
  sculpture 233–34, 378
  seals 180, 246, *247f,* 379
  sling shot 108
  trade 186
  transport 186, 230
  vessels/vases 180, 241, **378–79**, 424
  weights 190
  see also gravemarkers, limestone, marble, masonry, sarcophagi
stone-throwers (artillery) 109
stoneworking 180
storage jars 175, 182, 368; *see also* pottery (pithos)
strainers *242f,* 367
strategia 91
strategoi (sing. *strategos,* generals) 35, 96
  Alcibiades 41
  Antigonus I 46
  Anytus 48
  Callicrates 52
  Callistratus 52
  chose trierarchs 119
  Cimon 52
  Cleon 53
  Conon 54
  Craterus 54
  Craterus the Younger 54
  Demetrius of Phalerum 55
  elected by Assembly 88
  eligibility 27
  Hellenistic 90–91
  Hieron II 60
  Hyperbolus 61
  Lamachus 61

Lydiadas 62
  in military trials 37
  Nicias 64
  Olympiodorus 65
  Patrocles 65
  Pericles 33, 68–69
  Phocion 73
  Polyperchon 52, 74
  Ptolemy III 76
  Themistocles 79
  Theramenes 80
  Thrasybulus 80
  Thrasyllus 80
  Thucydides 280
  Timotheus 81
  took on role of polemarch 35
  Xanthippus 81
strategos autokrator 57, 65, 71, 73
stratokeryx (herald) 90
Straton (of Lampsacus) 399, 401–402
Stratonice (daughter of Ariarathes IV) 49, 51
Stratonice (sister of Seleucus II) 49
Stratonice (wife of Seleucus I) 46, 78
Stratonice II 56
Stratonicea, Turkey *154f,* 167
Stratus, Greece 128, *152f, 153f,* 167
streets (towns) 204–205, *205f,* 207
  Athens 136, 204
  grid system 140, 145, *205f,* 207–8, 220, 383
  Olynthus *221f*
  plateiai 207–8
  stenophoi 207
  see also roads
Strymon River 18, 52
stucco
  coating of stone 234
  painted 210, 221, 234
  waterproofing of bathtubs 216
stylobate *222f, 224f*
stylus 246
Stymphalian Birds 310
Stymphalus, Greece *152f,* 167
Stymphalus, Lake 310
Stymphalus River 132
Styx (mythical) 322
Styx, River 132, 333
Successors of Alexander the Great (*diadokhoi*) 12–13, *12f,* 46, 63, 74, 188
Suda (lexicon) 279
·Sulla (Roman general) 13, 26, 64, 77, 135
sundial 408
superstition 360, 361, 390, 392
surgery 393; *see also* medicine
surveyors (*geometrai*) 207
Susa, Iran 22, *43f,* 44, 61, 70, 148, 276
Susarion (poet) 279
swords 106–7
  of cavalry 95
  of Chiron 325
  of Damocles 301
  of hoplites 91, 97, 107
  iron 106–7, 181
  kopis *107*
  Mycenaean 106, *105f, 106f*
  of peltasts 92
  of phalangites 91
  prehistoric *106f,* 106–7
  in sheath *102f*
  of Theseus 332
Sybaris, Italy 15, 128, 130, *155f,* 167
Sybrita, Crete *156f,* 167
sycophants (*sykophantai*) 37
Syene, Egypt *157f, 158f,* 167
symmachia (*symmakhia*) 126
sympoliteia 126, 131

symposium (*symposion,* pl. *symposia*) 256, 266, 271, 371, 409, 414, **420**; *see also* banquets
Symposium (Plato) 266
Symposium (Xenophon) 281
synoecismus 204–5
syntagma (pl. *syntagmata*) 89–91
syntagmatarch (*syntagmatarkhes*) 90
Syracuse, Sicily 167
  Aeschylus visited 265
  altar 342
  Archimedes from 395
  artillery invented 108
  Callias from 269
  coins *193f, 198f, 417f*
  colony of Corinth 5, 15, 128, 139, 150
  fish trade 186
  harbor 200
  liberated by Timoleon 21, 80
  limestone quarries 178
  location *155f*
  Moschus from 275
  petalism 34
  Philemon from 276
  Philistus from 277
  Plato there 400
  siege by Athens 9, 19, 60, 115
  siege by Romans 25, 395
  Sophron from 279
  spring 291
  Theocritus from 280
  see also Agathocles, Dion, Dionysius I & II, Gelon, Hieron I & II, Sicilian expedition
Syria 150–51
  history 13–14, 150–51
  location *131f, 157f*
  Roman province 14, 26, 149, 151
  Seleucis 150
  trade 184–85
  see also Coele-Syria, Syrian Wars
Syrian Wars 13–14, 150
  First 23, 46, 75
  Second 24, 46–47, 75
  Third 24, 47, 51, 62, 76, 78
  Fourth 24, 47, 76
  Fifth 14, 25, 47
  Sixth 14, 25, 47, 53, 76
Syrinx (Nymph) 323, 332
syrinx (Pan pipes) 264, 323, 332
Syros/Syrus 169, 368
syssita 27

T

tablets
  wax 245–46
  wooden 245, 248, 261
    whitened (*leukomata*) 245, 248–49
tagos 36, 44, 151
talent (coin/weight) 190, 193
Tanagra, Greece 137, 167, 270, 374, *152f*
  battle of 18
Tanagra figurines 375
Tanais, Russia *158f,* 167
Tantalus (Aristarchus) 268
Tantalus (king of Sipylus) 322, 325, 332
Taras (Tarentum, Spartan colony) 7, 167
  Archytas from 395
  Aristoxenus born 395
  coin *143f*
  foundation 15, 128, 143
  location *155f*
  pottery exports 372
  statues 383

surrender to Rome 24
Taras Painter 372
Tarsus, Turkey *154f,* 167, 192
Tartarus (underworld) 296, 330, 332, 334, 420
Taucheira, Libya 140, *158f,* 160
Tauri (mythical) 315
taurobolium 300
Tauromenium, Sicily *155f,* 167, 281
taxation/taxes 188–89
  eisphora 28, 188
  epidosis 188
  eponia 188
  Hippias reduced 61
  in Judaea 359
  metoikion 28, 188
  prostitutes 409
  in satrapies 29
  see also customs duties, liturgy
tax farmers 189
taxiarch (*taxiarkhos*) 67, 74, 88, 90–91
Taxiles (Indian king) 79
taxis (pl. *taxeis*) 88, 89–90
teachers (schoolteachers) 188, 254, 271, 281; *see also* sophists
Tegea, Greece 66, 131, *152f,* 167, 267–68, 385
Tegean War 16
Tegyra, Greece
  battle of 20, 67
  oracle 348
Teiresias (seer) 332
Teisias (poet) 279
tekhnopaegnia 279
Telamon (king of Salamis) 287, 325
Teleclus (king of Sparta) 82
Telegonus (son of Odysseus) 299, 323, 332
Telegony 332
Telemachus (son of Odysseus) 299, 320, 322, **332**
Telesilla (poetess) 279–80
Telesterion (*telesterion*) 358, 383–84
Telestes (poet) 262, 280
Telmessus, Turkey *154f,* 167
temenos 337
temples 216, 338–41
  in agoras 214, 338–340
  in Alexandria 140
  altars 339, 342
  of Aphaea 290
  of Apollo
    Bassae 383
    Corinth 339
    Delphi 127, 334, *338f, 349f,* 381, *413f*
    Delphinios 136
    Didyma 339–41
    Hylates *291f*
    Archaic 339, *340f*
  of Ares 340
  of Artemis 194, 339, 383
  of Asclepius 279, 340, 385, 392–93
  of Atargatis 294
  of Athena
    Alea 385
    at Athens 135, 194, 294, *343f,* 361; *see also* Athena Nike, Parthenon
    Nike 135, 340, *341f, 342f*
    Parthenos 294
    Polias *206f, 223f, 251f,* 340, *343f,* 384, *385f*
    spring-cleaning 356
    at Troy 297
  as banks 194, 339
  based on house plans 339
  built in sacred areas 338